JEAN BOYER

ADVANCED ACCOUNTING

AN ORGANIZATIONAL APPROACH

New York · London · Sydney : **JOHN WILEY & SONS, INC.**

ADVANCED ACCOUNTING

AN ORGANIZATIONAL APPROACH

SECOND EDITION

NORTON M. BEDFORD, Ph.D., C.P.A.
University of Illinois

KENNETH W. PERRY, Ph.D., C.P.A.
Parsons College

ARTHUR R. WYATT, Ph.D., C.P.A.
Arthur Andersen and Company

10 9 8 7 6 5

Library of Congress Catalog Card Number: 67–17334
Printed in the United States of America

Preface to 2nd Edition

The problem of providing textbook material suitable in content, level, and method for training and education in accountancy is rather involved. Constantly changing activities in the practice of the profession, coupled with divergent and conflicting philosophies of education, must be evaluated in some manner if a textbook is to contribute to the development of accountancy education. The large number of current textbooks and their constant revision illustrate the extent of this problem. But recent rapid and widespread changes in our economy have revealed a pressing need for additional educational material to support the further development and expansion of the profession of accountancy.

We believe that a distinction must be drawn between *training* for accountancy and *education* for accountancy. To us, *training* means any process which emphasizes proficiency in the application of a set of rules to selected business situations. If time and information are available so that all possible business situations can be covered, this approach may produce a well-qualified accountant. On the other hand, by *education* for accountancy we mean the process whereby an understanding of the concepts and principles of accounting is sought. This second approach is based on the assumption that it is not possible to train a student to act expertly in all possible business situations, and that the objective of accountancy education is to provide a broad framework of concepts and principles so that a graduate is better equipped to handle any general accounting situation than to meet one specific problem.

In general, most accounting textbooks may be placed in one of these two categories. Some are concerned primarily with the methods of accounting, giving little attention to the principles underlying the mechanistic procedures. Others are directed and devoted to the concepts and underlying economic conditions that govern the procedures of accounting. However, no current textbook can be wholly assigned to one category or the other; the differences are of degree rather than of kind. Consequently, we believe that a void now exists about midway between these two categories. It is to this midway level, skewed slightly on the conceptual side, that this textbook is directed.

The justification for the development of a textbook at this level rests on both educational and professional needs. No longer is it sufficient that accountancy education confine itself to training a student to become a mechanical expert in accounting procedures. Failure to adjust an accounting curriculum to an educational level somewhat above this, wherein concepts, reasoning, and understanding are of the essence of the program of study, will lead ultimately to a decline in the quality of students interested in the field. More directly, however, the profession of accountancy is changing and expanding, and with change has come the realization on the part of practitioners of the profession that the educational process should provide a broader approach to the practice of accountancy.

On the other hand, the changed educational requirements of an accountant have not hindered development of rather complete familiarity with the procedures and the mechanism of accountancy. It is singular that personnel representatives of the larger public accounting firms speak of the need for broad training for accountancy but frequently employ the technically proficient student. It must be concluded that both attributes are desired, and this textbook has been developed to provide such an education.

However, it seems to be an accepted "law of learning" that the student retains best that which is presented within a logically consistent framework. Thus we have reorganized the materials of advanced accounting to provide a logical learning sequence in five parts:

Part   I—Formation of the business organization.
Part   II—Maintenance of the business organization.
Part III—Expansion of the business organization.
Part IV—Contraction of the business organization.
Part   V—Liquidation of the business organization.

This arrangement of materials resulted from the observation that intermediate accounting is concerned largely with the operations of a going concern, but advanced accounting is mainly the story of accounting problems arising from activities that provide an organizational unit for operations.

In addition to changing the sequence in which familiar materials are introduced, this textbook adds certain new materials to the teaching area of advanced accounting. In Part II, covering maintenance of the organizational unit, the materials concerning business risk and consideration of the adjustment for price-level fluctuations represent new developments in accounting. Likewise in Part III, concerning business expansion, the accounting procedure leading up to decision making on expansion problems is new to an advanced accounting course. The more extended treatment of reorganizations of all types in Part IV represents material which the authors believe significant in the light of current economic conditions.

Finally, this textbook was written upon the assumption that the student of advanced accounting has had sufficient mathematics to handle simple computations in the area of compound interest and annuities. Recognizing, however, that this assumption may not always be warranted, an appendix on the fundamentals of actuarial science has been included. It is our belief that an advanced accounting textbook should include some background accounting material to furnish an orderly transition to the advanced material. To this end, the opening chapters review certain fundamental accounting concepts that are necessary to establish the background for the advanced discussion.

In this second edition we have increased the discussion of conceptual material to reflect the increasing concern within the accounting profession for wider understanding of underlying concepts and principles. Chapter 1 has been rewritten completely to incorporate the advanced thinking evidenced in various current research studies. Throughout the book, the material has been adjusted to attain an improved integration of basic concepts with important practical problems. The material in Chapter 19 on expansion by combination has been completely revised so that the basic issues, both conceptual and practical, in the business combination area are clarified. The accounting aspects of mergers and combinations have been reoriented to deal more realistically with the pooling-of-interests problem.

This revised edition also incorporates a number of significant changes in accounting thinking and business practice which developed subsequent to the original edition. For example, the use of long term leases to effect a variety of transactions has increased rapidly in recent years. The principal issues in accounting for leases, both as an asset and as a liability, are discussed. The positions expressed in opinions of the Accounting Principles Board have also been incorporated in the discussion where appropriate. To meet the demand for additional problem materials the number of problems has been increased substantially.

We wish to express our thanks to the many educators and practitioners for suggestions and assistance in the preparation of this book. Special appreciation is expressed to the American Institute of Certified Public Accountants for the use of CPA problems and other material.

NORTON M. BEDFORD
KENNETH W. PERRY
ARTHUR R. WYATT

Contents

ix

PART III · EXPANSION OF THE BUSINESS ORGANIZATION

internal sources, Utilizing nonincome operational funds; Capitalizing retained earnings, Recognition by accounting entries, Recognition by stock dividend, Recorded at par value, Recorded at market value, Proper accounting treatment, Recognition by stock split-up, Summary. *External financing of expansion:* New partner as a source of funds, Bonus to old partners, Bonus to new partner, Bonus procedure summarized, Bonus procedure evaluated, Goodwill to old partners, Goodwill to new partner, Goodwill to all partners. *Expansion and financing as one activity: Methods of expansion.*

PART IV · CONTRACTION OF THE BUSINESS ORGANIZATION

earnings. *Financial reorganizations:* Securing an extension of time for payments to creditors; Refinancing of debt, Refinancing at face value, Refinancing with a call premium, Unamortized discount or premium on issue outstanding, Immediate write-off, Amortization over life of original issue, Amortization over life of new issue; Creditor committee; *Equity receivership,* Legal procedures, Accounting procedures; Reorganizations under bankruptcy act: Legal procedures, Accounting procedures, Illustration —reorganization of the F Corporation, Summary.

PART V · LIQUIDATION OF THE BUSINESS ORGANIZATION

Corporate liquidation by trustee; Statement of affairs, Significance of current values, Nature of the statement of affairs, Illustration—Assets pledged: fully secured creditors; Assets pledged: partially secured creditors; Free assets, Liabilities having priority, Unsecured liabilities, Shareholders' equity per books, Deficiency to unsecured creditors; General comments on the statement of affairs; Summary. *Receivership in equity:* Receivership accounting, General concepts, Basic procedures, Receiver's reports, Termination of receivership. Realization and liquidation statement, Illustration, Closing out the receivership, Summary.

I

FORMATION OF THE
BUSINESS ORGANIZATION

Business organizations and accounting entities

The term "business" in a broad sense is generally used to refer to all forms of economic activity directed toward the objective of making an income. The term may also be used in some circumstances to encompass other forms of economic activity. On the other hand, business seldom has as its sole objective the making of an income. Other objectives are important in varying degrees, and it is a fact of business life today that most businesses have multigoals.

The activities of business include the processes of production and distribution of economic goods and services. Normally these activities require a combination of land, labor, capital, and managerial direction for the fulfillment of business objectives. A combination of these economic resources, whether it consists of the fisherman with his crude homemade net catching fish for the market or the million-dollar corporation, is considered a business unit.

The business world is composed of innumerable business units, each differing somewhat from the other in size, in complexity, in the type of legal organization, and in the character of product that it makes or the service that it performs. In nearly every aspect of our industrial society, we find business units ranging in size from the individual worker who uses simple tools or renders a specific service to gigantic organizations with thousands of employees, machinery worth millions of dollars, and a wide range of products and services. The business unit may be of a more or less temporary nature, such as individual proprietorships or partnerships in which the existence of the unit depends entirely upon the wishes and the lives of each of those primarily concerned; or it may be more permanent, as in the case of the corporation, which usually continues in existence in spite of dissatisfaction, death, or retirement of a stockholder. Regardless of the size, complexity, or type of organization of these business units, in the aggregate they comprise the business world.

The Nature and Role of Accounting

Accounting has found its greatest field of usefulness in recording, classifying, summarizing, and interpreting the economic events of individual business units. In fact, accounting is primarily a method of analysis based on a record of the various economic activities of an enterprise. This description of accounting embodies a number of significant features: accounting includes a system of record keeping; the records contain analyzed data; these data result from economic activities —transactions in a broad sense; the economic activities are those of the enterprise for which the records are maintained; and the data from accounting, when properly interpreted, are useful in reaching forward-looking business decisions.

Accounting serves a number of roles in our economic society. Most generally, accounting's role is described as the measurement of enterprise economic activities and the accumulation of data useful for managerial decision making. These rather broadly stated roles are valid ones for accounting, but greater insight into the real impact of accounting can come only from a more precise identification of the roles that accounting plays in an economic society.

Many authorities agree that in a competitive economic society effective management of the scarce resources of land, labor, and capital available determines in large measure the success of an enterprise. Effective management involves timely and well-informed decisions concerning these scarce resources available to an enterprise. To an increasing degree in recent years, and principally as our economic society has mushroomed in complexity, management has turned to accounting data and reports as bases for reaching decisions on important matters. Some areas of managerial decisions for which accounting information has proved useful include potential avenues of expansion, either through acquisitions, new product development, or new territory development; potential avenues of capital accumulation, either through sales of stock, long-term borrowing, leasing, or retention of earned income; potential avenues of allocating the resources available among competing demands for such things as new products, new markets, new techniques, and research; and potential alternatives for minimization of the impact of taxation.

In these and other decision areas, management has come to rely heavily on accounting information to provide bases to assist in reaching the best decisions.

On the other hand, accounting serves an additional role of considerable importance in an economic society. Through accounting data and reports, we are provided with a basis for evaluation of managerial performance in guiding the actions of the business unit. Investors and credit grantors have a direct interest in the evaluation of managerial performance, since these groups provide the land and capital for management to utilize in their business unit. A further responsibility exists, however. In any economic society there is a genuine need for society to be able to evaluate the performance of those who guide the utilization of the scarce resources available for economic effort. Accounting provides the basis for evaluation of the effectiveness of use of these resources.

The significance of these roles creates a substantial responsibility for accounting to provide data and reports of maximum usefulness. The information that accounting provides must be reliable and factual; it must be relevant to the business unit being reported on; it must be presented in a form adaptable to analysis and interpretation. These responsibilities impose on accounting the necessity to develop concepts, techniques, and procedures which will provide information possessing required levels of reliability on business activity. These concepts, techniques, and procedures must additionally give recognition to the environment in which accounting activity is expected to operate. A brief look at some aspects of this environment may help to explain further the nature and role of accounting.

Environmental Conditions Affecting Accounting

Accounting is a product of its environment just as other aspects of our society are affected by, and in turn have an effect upon, the environmental conditions existing at any time. The environmental conditions which have a direct influence on accounting are too numerous to identify completely or to discuss in detail. Social attitudes, legal conditions, business practices, economic concepts, and moral and ethical standards all have an influence on shaping the direction of accounting actions. Some environmental conditions seem to have had a more direct impact on accounting development, however, and these bear specific consideration.[1]

Scarce Means. The fact that man lives in a world of scarce economic

---

[1] For a more complete discussion of some of the ideas developed here and in the following section see *A Statement of Basic Accounting Postulates and Principles*, Center for International Education and Research in Accounting, Urbana, Illinois, 1964.

means finds considerable expression in accounting. Income measurement as the indicator of success in economic activities is directly related to this fact. Assets find expression on statements of financial condition principally because they have value to the enterprise, and this value arises from the fact of scarcity. Emphasis on control, protection of property, and reduction of waste and inefficiency are all related to the scarcity of resources. We have difficulty visualizing the shape that accounting would take in an environment in which economic scarcity was not a fact of life.

Standards of Equity. The fact that man has developed certain laws and standards of conduct to control human behavior is another environmental condition affecting accounting. Current legal and ethical ideas of property and other rights provide boundaries of a sort for accounting actions. Thus, in providing data that may be used by conflicting interests, accounting accepts standards of equity and fairness, both legal and moral, which already exist in its environment. Accounting does not make its own laws or establish its own standards of equity. Rather, accounting finds within its environment the existing standards to determine equity among the varying interests in the enterprise. These standards condition to some extent the direction of accounting actions.

Rational and Prudent Conduct. As an economic society increases in complexity, certain individuals with property (capital) are moved to entrust the custodianship and control of all or a part of their property to others. In fact, this is one of the important characteristics of a complex economy—the utilization of the property of others in an economic endeavor. Those entrusted with the use of the property are assumed to act rationally and within the accepted bounds of honesty and fairness unless there is evidence to the contrary. This condition of rational and prudent conduct is important to accounting primarily because of the incomplete nature of many transactions at any given time. The fact that rational and prudent conduct is an expected pattern of behavior means that accounting can place reliance on data flowing from transactions. The need to examine each transaction as to its motivation and authenticity does not exist in the absence of evidence suggesting irrational or irresponsible conduct.

Postulates of Accounting

A thorough understanding of the nature and role of accounting in an economic society requires consideration of certain fundamental assumptions on which accounting is based. The term "accounting postulates" has been used with increasing frequency in recent years to describe the underlying assumptions of accounting which are generally accepted as valid. These postulates describe assumptions that are made in accounting at any time to provide a basis for reasoning in the development of accounting principles and other important concepts in accounting. Because accounting is utilitarian and constantly adjusts to changed economic conditions, the postulates of accounting are more in the nature of general assumptions than in the nature of fixed and unyielding axioms. Although no authoritative listing of accounting postulates has been widely accepted, most of the following postulates have fairly widespread recognition.

Usefulness. Accounting data and reports provide useful information to a wide number of users having different interests. While this may appear to be a self-evident proposition, it is important that the ideas contained in this postulate be clearly expressed and well understood. Accounting information of an enterprise is not aimed at one single user of financial and economic reports. Rather, accounting data have wide usefulness and, therefore, emphasis must be placed on validity and reliability so as not to impair the usefulness.

Entity. Economic activity is engaged in by a business unit, an entity, which is separate and distinct from the owners of the business unit. These entities constitute units of accountability around which accounting interest centers. This proposition has greatly influenced the development of accounting. It has allowed for the extension of double-entry accounting to cover transactions between the business unit and the owners. Overall, it seems appropriate to suggest that the entity concept has contributed much to the rather amazing growth of accounting as a technique for collecting and recording economic data in a systematic manner. Of central importance here is recognition that an accounting report relates to one specific business unit or entity. This postulate has considerable impact on financial reporting and also has an impact on the boundaries of accounting.

Transactions. Accounting procedures are primarily concerned with exchange transactions, and with those other activities whose results are essentially the same as exchange transactions, between the entity and other enterprises or individuals. This postulate introduces one type of boundary of accounting. Not only is accounting concerned with specific entities, but it is concerned only with certain activities of that entity. The activities that are of interest to accounting are normally evidenced by transactions—exchanges of economic values between the entity and others. Certain other activities of substance—for example, the passage of time in connection with accrued interest, fires, thefts, or the imposition of taxes—possess attributes which make them appear to be essentially the same as transactions. Accounting includes these activities within its area of interest.

Price. The money price which is stated or implied by the transactions of the enterprise provides an appropriate basis for recording accounting data. The price generated by transactions of the enterprise with other enterprises or individuals is relevant to the enterprise, is objectively determinable, and provides useful data to facilitate subsequent analysis. This postulate is sometimes phrased in such a way as to indicate that accounting assumes that the price level is stable or that the monetary unit is stable. Such an assumption is inappropriate for accounting. The postulate as stated above does not limit accounting data to the acquisition price or historical cost. Rather, it asserts that transaction-price data hold a significant place in accounting. During times of changing price levels, modifications and adjustments of price data may be desirable or even essential. When such conditions exist, disclosure of any adjustments made and their effects on the data reported is important.

Continuity or Going Concern. The enterprise will continue to operate in the future in much the same manner as it has operated in the past unless persuasive evidence exists to the contrary. Since a substantial number of the transactions of the enterprise are in a somewhat indeterminate status at any reporting date, accounting needs to make some assumption as to the future of the enterprise. For example, receivables are not collected, items in inventory have not been sold, fixed assets possess unexpired usefulness. Some anticipation of the future disposition of these assets is necessary. This postulate merely asserts that unless persuasive evidence exists that the enterprise will fail to continue to operate in about the same manner and in about the same environment, accounting assumes that such continuity will prevail.

Periodicity. The uninterrupted flow of economic activity of an enterprise can be identified with specific periods in which the enterprise operates on a basis that is meaningful. Implicit in this postulate is the need of users of accounting data for timely reporting of the results of consummated transactions. Also implicit, however, is the idea that each transaction of an enterprise has a peculiar relevance to a specified time period. Many difficult problems in accounting have their source in this idea that the uninterrupted life of an enterprise can be divided into time periods with specific transactions being identified with a given period on some reasonable basis.

At the present time these postulates appear to provide a reasonable basis from which other important ideas and concepts in accounting can be developed. Each postulate has an important place in the theory and practice of accounting. While it is true that we may learn to carry out many technical or mechanical aspects of accounting without a thorough understanding of these postulates, it is also true that the resolution of many difficult problem areas requires a sound grounding in these important accounting ideas. Reference to these postulates should be fruitful in circumstances in which two or more possible approaches to an accounting issue appear to be justifiable.

Principles of Accounting

Much controversy exists within the accounting profession regarding the nature and role of accounting principles. In theory, principles are commonly derived from certain basic precepts, axioms, or postulates. Such derivation generally relies upon logical reasoning, or deductive analysis. Thus, accounting principles should, it would seem, flow from the basic postulates of accounting with due recognition being accorded the environmental conditions within which accounting operates.

In actuality, however, accounting principles—or at least those propositions of accounting which carry the status of accounting principles—have developed out of accounting practice, very largely in an inductive manner. As business transactions take on novel or at least different aspects, accountants have developed practices, methods, procedures, and rules for their analysis and interpretation. As these practices, methods, procedures, and rules come to be more widely recognized and accepted as useful aspects of accounting, they come, in the mass, to be recognized as "generally accepted accounting principles." Thus, the main test which any proposition must meet to warrant the label "accounting principles" has been the test of general acceptance.

It is at this point that accounting theory and accounting practice diverge. Most accountants would agree that accounting principles should be derived in logical fashion from the underlying postulates of the field. Likewise, most accountants would agree that accounting principles are derived from the mass of practices, methods, procedures, and rules that gain the label of general acceptability.

A number of topics generally discussed in elementary and intermediate accounting coverage indicate the absence of fully logical analysis. For example, the existence of FIFO, LIFO, and average cost methods of inventory pricing with all having apparently equal status as to general acceptability in any situation appears somewhat illogical. Again, the absence of fully effective guidelines on the reporting of unusual and non-recurring transactions raises certain questions regarding accounting principles. Subsequent sections of this book examine additional areas of accounting in which the generally accepted principle appears to suffer from a lack of logic.

Over the years considerable effort has been aimed at clarifying accounting principles and eliminating those that appear inappropriate. At the same time, changes in business practices have introduced new accounting methods and procedures that have gained the status of generally accepted accounting principles even though they fail to result from logical derivation from more basic underlying postulates of accounting. Likewise, considerable effort will continue to be expended to reduce the areas of illogic and inappropriateness. Attempts to relate specific accounting practices, methods, procedures, and rules to the basic postulates are fruitful for the student. Such analyses will pinpoint areas of weakness in accounting theory, areas on which more effort must be expended if accounting is to serve the economic society most beneficially.

Social Significance of Accounting

From the social standpoint accounting may be conceived of as part of the mechanism which makes possible the effective utilization of enterprise data in directing economic action. This is so because business management and others take cognizance of accounting data and act according to their implications. As a result, economic resources are directed to profitable uses and are used in an efficient manner to produce the goods and services needed by all members of the society. Consumers benefit from better products at lower prices, and the entire economy is better off by having produced more goods and services than it might have produced otherwise.

As the economy becomes more complex through increases in the size of business units, through increased demand generated by larger populations, through increased advances in technology, and through greater interaction on the part of government planning, the challenge to accounting increases in like manner. Recent years have seen many of the challenges met by utilization of the computer, and increased activity in this direction by accounting is certain. Complexity and challenge, however, do not minimize the necessity for a full grasp of basic ideas in accounting. Rather, the need for fuller understanding must increase so that maximum benefit may be derived from the computer and from other sophisticated tools of analysis.

The relatively rigid boundaries of accounting which have been widely accepted in the past need reappraisal. For example, long acceptance of the significance of the entity as a central concept of accounting is being reexamined. The previously stated entity postulate remains valid today and probably will remain valid in the foreseeable future. That is, insofar as the recording function of accounting is concerned, the entity concept is likely to remain basic. The interpretive function of accounting, on the other hand, is likely to encompass concepts which extend beyond the entity. Social and economic planning contemplates broader implications than the single entity. Accounting data, generated by economic activities of the entity, but interpreted in the light of broader social, regional, and politico-economic implications will play an increasingly significant role in reaching decisions on complex issues.

The directing force in the production and distribution of goods and services to consumers is the central management of the entity. It is this management which coordinates the utilization of land, properties, and labor in an effective manner. Management provides organization to the entity and, in fact, enables the entity to take on the necessary aspects of a business organization. Because of the need for an understanding of the social features of accounting and since accounting is one of the chief tools used by management to solve enterprise problems, it is perhaps only logical that an advanced study of accounting be approached from a study of the various problems faced by a business organization from its inception to its possible termination. Business organizations fall into many types—proprietorships, partnerships, corporations, trusts, joint ventures—but the corporation is unquestionably the most significant to our economy. Accordingly, in this book primary emphasis is placed on the corporate form of organization, although peculiar problems associated with the other forms of organization are also discussed.

Accounting View of the Enterprise— Proprietary Versus Entity Theory

The accounting concept of the business organization is that it is a distinct being or entity in and of itself. The entity postulate contributes to this concept and is consistent with many facts of business activity. Transactions are entered into and consummated by the business organization as a unit separate and distinct from identifiable parts of the organization. The view of the enterprise as an entity is simply an extension of this concept. In accounting parlance this concept is frequently referred to as the "enterprise entity concept."

Recognition and general acceptance of this view of the enterprise is relatively recent. Prior to the 1930's a different view had widespread acceptance, that being the proprietary theory. In fact, much of the breakthrough in accounting thought on the nature of the accounting entity can be traced back to this time when the question of the proper accounting entity was a topic of theoretical discussion. According to the entity theory, the assets belong to the entity and the liabilities and equities represent sources of the assets, whether in the form of capital stock, a note payable, or any other type of equity. Even when equities are viewed as claims to assets rather than sources of assets, the entity theory is a valid concept.

According to the proprietary theory, the assets of the enterprise are owned effectively by the stockholders (or other owners), and the liabilities are considered as liabilities of the stockholders. In the case of the sole proprietorship and the partnership, the proprietary theory is pretty much in accordance with the legal facts of the situation. Partners and proprietors may well have to pay business liabilities out of personal assets if the business cannot pay them. Legally the debts of the business are a liability of the partners or proprietors and the assets of the business really belong to the partners or proprietors.

In the case of the corporation, however, the legal facts of the situation support the entity theory. The stockholders of the corporation assume no liability for the debts of the corporation and cannot withdraw assets from the corporation without corporate approval and action.

The law thus provides no clear-cut support for either the entity theory or the proprietary theory. It supports each theory in different situations. This is not a desirable situation from an accounting point of view. To make the basic postulates of accounting depend upon the type of legal form of the business allows an inconsistency in accounting procedures which is held to be undesirable. While accountants might contend that the corporate form of business dominates business activity to such a degree that the accounting concept of the accounting unit should be the separate entity, many accounting procedures are based on the proprietary theory. For example, the income of a business is computed as the income accruing to the stockholders rather than as the income accruing to all creditors and equity holders. Interest charges are considered to be an expense of operations, but dividends on all types of capital stock are considered to be a distribution of income under the proprietary theory. Both interest and dividends would be a distribution of income under the entity theory. Contemporary accounting practice in the reporting of income thus conforms to the proprietary theory. But in the basic accounting equation that assets equal equities, the concept of the accounting unit as a separate distinct entity prevails.

It is the opinion of the authors that the entity theory conforms more closely to the economic reality of business operations. Prior to the growth of the corporate form of business enterprise, the proprietary theory was undoubtedly the economic reality of business operations and it still dominates accounting practice in many areas. Thus it appears that accounting procedures are in a period of transition from those based on the proprietary theory to those based on the entity theory. This causes some confusion to students learning accounting procedures because it precludes consistent reasoning from one accepted base. Both the entity theory and the proprietary theory underlie different accounting procedures.

With this general background in mind, let us now turn to a description and analysis of the problems involved in accounting for the formation of the various forms of business organizations.

Proprietorship Formation

A business owned entirely by one individual is frequently referred to as a single proprietorship. In early times the manufacture of goods and the sale of goods and services were conducted on a much smaller scale than they are at present. For that reason large amounts of capital were not necessary and, as a result, the dominant type of business organization was the single proprietorship. As the small entrepreneurial system of Adam Smith's day evolved into the capitalistic enterprise system of today, more capital was needed than one person could provide or would be willing to risk. As a consequence other forms of business organization such as the partnership and corporation took on added importance. Even today, however, there are still many units of small size. In the United States the number of single proprietorships exceeds that of all other types of ownership.

Legal Aspects of Proprietorships. From the legal standpoint there is not much involved in the formation, operation, and dissolution of a proprietorship. In formation, since no contractual arrangement or charter is necessary, all the owner has to do is to obtain the necessary operating license(s), and he is ready to start operations.

In certain types of business, it may be necessary for a man to establish proof of his ability in the field of business he is entering. For example, a pharmacist, a lawyer, a doctor, or a certified public accountant generally must pass an examination before opening an office. Also, certain types of businesses, such as a barber shop, may be subjected to special regulations. In some states a certificate of doing business has to be filed if the company has a special trade name. Essentially, however, the process of forming a sole proprietorship is one of gathering together the funds, deciding what to do, and acquiring facilities to carry on the business. During operations, the only legal requirements to be met are the usual federal, state, and local regulatory agency requirements such as the filing of various tax returns. If the owner of a single proprietorship desires to discontinue his business, he may do so without consulting anyone. No other kind of business organization can be dissolved so easily.

Accounting for Proprietorship Formation. The procedure of opening the books of a proprietorship has been discussed in elementary accounting. The most important consideration in the process is the problem of valuation of the various assets and equities of the new enterprise. In general, assets are valued at their fair market value on the date they are contributed to the business. Equities are valued on the basis of their ultimate claim to assets or on the basis of the value of the assets contributed by the equity interests. In the formation of any business, sound financing requires that certain fundamental considerations be followed. Some of these considerations, on which the accountant may be called for advice, are the following ones.

(1) The best source of funds for the business.
(2) The best use to which funds should be directed.
(3) Selection of assets for effective liquidity and maximum earning capacity.

Normally, anyone forming a new business would conduct a thorough investigation of the need for the proposed business venture. This investigation might include market surveys of consumer needs, review of the availability of supplies, employees, and materials, and a study of financing methods appropriate for the undertaking. These planning procedures normally provide data which can be developed into an accounting budget or report. Usually, projected balance sheets and income statements for a number of years in the future may be used to convey to the prospective owner an articulated view of anticipated activities of the business.

Once these considerations have been evaluated and resolved by the prospective new business owner, the process of recording the actual formation of a proprietorship follows the procedures outlined in elementary accounting.

Partnership Formation

The partnership form of business organization is used for a variety of reasons. Typical of the conditions that may lead to the formation of a partnership are the following ones.

(1) The capital requirements of a business enterprise may exceed the amount of capital that may be raised by a single proprietor or the amount of capital that an individual may wish to invest in a particu-

lar venture under conditions where he would have no one to help him assume risks.

(2) A single proprietor, partnership, or business organization may wish to obtain or retain the talents or services of others.

(3) For some reason, frequently professional in nature, a group of people may wish to form a business organization where limited liability, as found in the corporate form of business organization, is undesirable.

Legal Aspects of Partnerships. The Uniform Partnership Act, which has been adopted by a majority of the states, defines a partnership as "an association of two or more persons to carry on as co-owners a business for profit." A "person," as defined by the Act, includes individuals, partnerships, corporations, and other associations.

A partnership may be "general" or "limited." In the general partnership each partner has unlimited liability, that is, he may be liable personally for all of the organization's debts. In the limited partnership, however, the liability of a certain partner or partners is limited to a particular amount. Limited partnerships cannot be formed in all states, and in those states permitting them *at least one* partner must be a general partner.

Since a partnership is based on a contract between two or more persons, it is important, although not necessarily a legal requirement, that special attention be given to the drawing up of the partnership agreement. This agreement is generally referred to as the "Articles of Copartnership." In order to avoid unnecessary and perhaps costly litigation at some later date, the Articles should contain all of the terms of the agreement relating to the formation, operation, and dissolution of the partnership. For example, these terms should include such provisions as the ones below.

(1) Amount and nature of capital to be invested by each partner, and the basis of valuation for assets other than cash.

(2) Basis of division of profits and losses.

(3) Rate and other details concerning the calculation of interest, if any, to be charged each partner on withdrawals and to be allowed on capital.

(4) Conditions under which the partnership might be terminated before the time originally designated.

Since the partnership agreement is essentially a legal matter, partners are well advised to seek legal counsel prior to forming the partnership.

Accounting for Partnership Formation. Opening the books of a partnership differs little from opening the books of a proprietorship. It may be noted, however, that the problem of valuation of assets contributed by a partner may not be as subjective as in the case of the sole proprietor. While a partner contributing assets to a partnership will want his assets valued high, and may want those assets contributed by his fellow partners valued low, some general agreement on an appropriate valuation for assets contributed must be reached by the partners. In arriving at an appropriate valuation, major emphasis would normally be placed upon the fair market value of the assets at the time of their contribution to the partnership. The problem of asset valuation in the formation of a partnership is generally solved by mutual agreement among the partners. Such agreements normally reflect fair market value of the assets contributed by the various partners. Where a suitable fair market value is not available, the partners must reach some agreement on an acceptable valuation. The role of the accountant in this process is one of disclosing fully the implications of different valuations. Equity among partners, in partnership formation, is essential for a lasting partnership. After contributed assets have been valued correctly, the entries to open the books of the partnership would be recorded as set forth in elementary accounting.

Corporate Formation

In early business ventures the conflict of interests between creditors and owners was relatively nonexistent, since the resources upon which the enterprise operated consisted almost entirely of owner contributions. There were few, if any, resources provided by either long-term or short-term creditors. Among other factors, the social and religious ideas of the time were unfavorable to lending which, in turn, tended to keep borrowing at a minimum. At the end of a venture, debts were paid and the residue divided among the joint contributors or partners. Any creditors that might have existed were protected because they generally contributed a relatively small portion of the capital, and because of the unlimited liability of each of the venturers.

After continuing partnerships began to replace ventures, it was not long before business organizations with special charters made their appearance. One important feature of some of these charters was that they limited ownership liability. With the appearance of limited ownership liability, contributions by the owners became the essential margin of protection for creditors. As a result, careful and accurate accounting became of greater importance to creditors.

The desire of security holders, particularly stockholders, to limit their liability and perhaps their responsibility appears to have been one of the most powerful forces contributing to the growth of the business unit from the owner-manager type of Adam Smith's day into the corporate form of organization as it now exists. In the modern corporation, resources are contributed and business risks are assumed usually by absentee owners. The appointment of agents, frequently referred to as "professional managers," for business purposes by absentee owners is very common. These agents may operate at a great distance from their principals, who exercise their control largely through reports rendered to them periodically. These reports in order to be of much significance must, of course, be rendered on the basis of the corporation as a separate entity.

Legal Aspects of Corporations. As defined by Chief Justice Marshall in the Dartmouth College case, a corporation is "an artificial being, invisible, intangible, and existing only in contemplation of law." Since it is a legal entity, it must be created either by specific action of a legislative body or by application of the authority provided by a statute passed by such body. The corporation, therefore, functions as a distinct entity within a legal framework. Most states have an act, typically entitled "The Business Corporation Act," which should be studied thoroughly and complied with carefully when organizing, operating, or dissolving a corporation. A corporate charter granted by the state gives the entity certain rights and privileges and at the same time imposes certain duties and responsibilities.

The corporation laws of the state together with the "Articles of Incorporation" constitute the charter of the corporation. The Articles consist of a written statement embodying specific information required by state statutes such as the name of the corporation, names and addresses of the incorporators, the purpose or purposes for which the corporation is organized, the minimum amount of capital with which the entity will start business, and details regarding the shares of capital stock authorized for issuance. Information with respect to capital stock should include, in addition to the number of shares of each class of stock, the par value, if any, as well as a statement of the preferences, qualifications, limitations, and restrictions of each class. In addition to those prescribed by statute, the Articles may include provisions for the regulation of the internal affairs of the corporation, such as specific restriction on distributions of earnings.

Accounting for Corporate Formation. Opening the books of a corporation differs little from opening the books of a proprietorship or partnership. Assuming that proper valuations of contributed assets have been determined, the books of the corporation would be opened in the manner explained in elementary accounting.

The process of forming an entirely new corporation requires (1) state authorization, (2) issuance of stock, and (3) acquisition of assets; whereas the incorporation of an existing enterprise may require only (1) state authorization and (2) the issuance of stock.

Securing state authorization normally requires three or more persons to file an application for a charter with the incorporating agency of the state in which incorporation is sought. Normally upon approval of the application by the state and the filing of a copy of the charter with the clerk of the county where the principal office of the corporation is located, the corporation comes into existence. Authorization to issue stock is often a part of the approved charter.

Selling authorized stock or a part of it may be either (1) *direct* by the incorporators of the corporation or (2) *indirect* through an investment banking syndicate or selling group. In selling very large issues, registration with the Securities and Exchange Commission may be required.

When common stock alone is issued to the corporation organizers in payment for their investment in the company, few equity problems arise. Normally, each share of stock received represents a proportionate share of the value of all assets invested. When several classes of securities are issued, however, the problem of an equitable allocation of the different types of securities is more involved. To illustrate the nature of the problem, assume A, B, and C form a corporation by contributing the following assets to the corporation.

	A	B	C	Total
Cash	$ 50,000	$ 50,000	$ 50,000	$150,000
Goodwill	—	—	40,000	40,000
Tangible Assets	50,000	100,000	10,000	160,000
Total	$100,000	$150,000	$100,000	$350,000

Assume the corporation is authorized to issue:

(a) Preferred stock ($100 par) paying 6%, noncumulative
(b) Common stock (no par)
(c) Bonds paying 5%

Assume A, B, and C agree that income shall be distributed in a 2:3:2 ratio and also want to protect the initial contribution of each investor. They decide to issue bonds for the cash contribution and preferred stock, which is preferred on liquidation up to $100, for the tangible assets. They also want to distribute common stock equally so each will have the same voting power. This plan provides no payment to C for the goodwill contribution. Another class of nonvoting second preferred stock might solve the problem. Not authorized to issue a second preferred stock, A, B, and C will have to settle for something less than an ideal solution.

In making recommendations for a solution, it may be appropriate to suggest bonds to provide security, preferred stock to provide security upon liquidation and a right in excess earnings in the form of dividend participation rights, and common stock (as much as possible) to provide appropriate voting rights. There is, of course, no one solution. The different interests and wishes of each participant must be considered. For different participants and for different situations, different suggestions are appropriate.

Trust Formation

A trust is an entity formed by depositing a sum of money or other resources in the custody of another entity, often a bank, with direction to invest these resources for the benefit of a beneficiary. It differs from a corporation principally in that the trustee is restricted in the use of the resources. The trust entity arises whenever property is held by a trustee for the benefit of another. The *trustee* holds legal title to the property but must use it for the benefit of the *beneficiary*. A trust may be created by a will—a testamentary trust—wherein assets left to a beneficiary are assigned to a trustee to use for the benefit of the beneficiary. Also, a trust may be created by a trust agreement or indenture under which a living grantor assigns specific assets to a trustee for use for the benefit of a designated beneficiary. This living trust is referred to as an "inter vivos" trust.

Powers of Trustees. A person who occupies a position of confidence toward others by holding assets to which another has a beneficial title or who receives and controls income of another is known as a "fiduciary." A trustee is a fiduciary.

The powers and duties of the trustee are derived both from the provisions of the document creating the trust (will, deed of trust, agreement, or court decree) and from the general laws on the trust relationship. The general powers and duties of the trustee are:

(1) To take and retain possession of the trust property.

(2) To invest and reinvest trust funds appropriately. Not all property is recognized as proper for trust investments, and what are proper trust investments vary. Almost universally, however, bonds of the United States government, bonds of the state in which the trust is administered, and certain first mortgages on improved real property are recognized as proper trust investments.

(3) To pay the expenses of the trust.

(4) To distribute the trust property to those who are to receive it.

As a fiduciary the trustee is *accountable* for his actions to the beneficiary. He is responsible for all contracts made for the trust, but is not responsible for loss by theft, embezzlement, or accident if he has taken the precautions a prudent businessman would take in guarding his own property.

Accounting for the Formation of a Trust. The objective of trust accounting is directed to a significant degree to the keeping of accounts in such a manner that the trustee can prove he has accounted for the assets assigned to him and has used them appropriately. This type of accounting has been referred to as fiduciary accounting.

In recording trust transactions, care must be exercised to distinguish between transactions changing the *trust principal*, which represents the resources to be turned over to a designated beneficiary at the termination of the trust, and *trust income*, which represents the earnings of the trust which are distributable to the designated income beneficiary during the existence of the trust. The distinction between the two does not rest on the need for maintaining a certain amount of monetary value as the principal. Rather the principal is looked upon as a group of assets which must be separated from the assets which represent undistributed income. This physical concept of principal rather than monetary value raises a number of problems in distinguishing between principal and income. For example, the gain on the sale of an investment of principal funds would be considered as part of principal, whereas the interest received from the investment would be income. The result of treating certain gains as principal and other gains as income calls attention to the need for different accounting concepts of income in accounting for trusts.

A trust is formed by turning over to the trustee the assets which represent the principal of the trust. For example, assume Mr. A. T. Enden died leaving in trust certain assets, the income from which is to go to his wife until the time of her death, but with a provision that the principal shall be turned over to his son and the trust terminated at the death of the wife. Normally an inventory of these resources will be filed with a court. The values accepted by the court in the inventory must be used by the trustee in accounting for the trust principal. Assume the trust resources, valued at the court-accepted inventory, in the above illustration are:

Cash	$20,000
Investments:	
Stock of Company ZTA	15,000
Bonds of the Q Company	8,000
Real estate	42,000
Total	$85,000

The entry to open the accounts of the trust would be:

Cash	$20,000	
Stock of Company ZTA	15,000	
Bonds of the Q Company	8,000	
Real estate	42,000	
Trust principal		$85,000

The bookkeeping procedure in accounting for trusts normally requires three journals and a ledger with several subsidiary ledgers. The journals—arranged in such a way as to disclose clearly principal transactions from income transactions—are the cash receipts journal, the cash disbursements journal, and the general journal.

Controlling accounts are used extensively in trust accounting. The "investment" account in the general ledger of a trust would be supported by detailed subsidiary ledgers and schedules.

Subject to these few introductory remarks, an accountant familiar with the basic bookkeeping mechanism can quickly develop a suitable bookkeeping system for a trust.

The Co-operative

Co-operatives are of a variety of types with a variety of provisions regarding their operations. Their typical feature is the banding together of a group of consumers for the objective of saving for themselves the profits which otherwise would accrue to other forms of business organizations, by buying from the co-operative rather than from another business organization.

Because of the variety of types and operations of co-operatives, accounting for such a business organization may vary. The essential requirement in accounting for the formation of the co-operative is to designate clearly the investment made by each member of the co-operative. In the case of an apartment building owned by occupants who provide the initial investment and pay as rent only the necessary management costs, the accounting records should reveal the total investment with the owner-occupants listed individually as participants in the co-operative. The entry would be:

Building	xxxx	
J. A. Adams		xxxx
T. T. Baker		xxxx
Others		xxxx

Accounting for co-operatives is similar in principle to the accounting for other types of business organizations. Because they pose no particular accounting problems, they are not treated further in this textbook.

The accounting principles for each of these business organizations, both in the formative stages and as to subsequent operations, are consistent in large measure with the postulates previously enumerated. The accounting records are maintained from the viewpoint of the entity, entries are largely based on transactions and at prices appropriate to the transaction, adjustments and analyses are based on the assumption the enterprise will continue to operate, and reports are rendered periodically for the information of all users.

The next type of business organization to be considered differs from the foregoing and, as a result, certain accounting aspects are different.

The Joint Venture

Historically, the joint venture form of business operation—and organization—has been important. In early times it meant little more than an association of individuals who united their resources, or part of them, for some specific venture—for example, sending a ship from London to the East Indies for trading purposes. As a rule the venture was one that required a larger capital than any one of the individuals possessed, or it involved risks too great for any one of them to assume in total.

The occasional associations for a specific venture remained fairly common down to the eighteenth century, and in fact were the fore-runners of the modern-day partnership. These associations, because of their contractual and impersonal character, contributed to the close relationship of the business unit as the accounting unit. After several decades of relatively little importance in our economy, the joint venture returned to considerable prominence in the late 1950's and early 1960's. The "joint venturers" of today, however, are corporations rather than individuals. The motivations remain somewhat the same—sharing of risks, accumulation of capital, merging of know-how—with the added impact of international business via partners spanning the continents. Today's joint ventures are many times called "50%-owned companies" wherein two corporations each own 50% of the venture. The venture, however, is deemed a separate accounting entity.

Accounting for Joint Ventures. In a number of instances, accounting for joint ventures virtually parallels accounting for a partnership or corporation. This would be particularly true for many of the "50%-owned companies" noted above. In other instances, however, accounting for joint ventures has definite differences from normal accrual accounting. Generally, these differences are related to the fact that some joint ventures have a stipulated or indefinite, but limited, life-span. When this characteristic of the venture exists, the postulate of continuity or going concern is not appropriate. As noted earlier in this chapter, the postulates of accounting provide a basis from which reasoning as to suitable principles and practices can proceed. The inapplicability of any postulate in a given situation can well suggest, or even necessitate, modifications in otherwise acceptable accounting practices.

Venture accounting is sometimes distinguished from accrual accounting with the principal point of distinction being the manner of recognizing income and allocating costs. However, as will become apparent in the illustration to follow, several aspects of accrual accounting may exist in venture accounting. The differences that do exist, however, are related to the absence of the continuity postulate. The limited nature of the venture's life, as well as some uncertainties that are characteristic of many venture operations, suggest that items normally subject to deferral or accrual should be recognized in the accounts on a completed transaction basis.

While we are now concerned primarily with the formation of a business entity as a going concern, it is appropriate to examine also the accounting procedures for a nongoing-concern entity over its entire life. A simple illustration of joint-venture accounting is the case of two medical doctors, practicing separately, who combine a portion of their resources to acquire and operate an x-ray laboratory jointly. There are two approaches to accounting for such a combination:

(1) Separate books may be kept for the venture with each participating organization carrying on its respective books an account reflecting the "Investment in the Joint Venture."
(2) Each participating organization may maintain a record of the venture

along with a record of the rights and equities of the other participants without setting up a separate set of books.

SEPARATE BOOKS. A joint venture may take the form of either a partnership or a corporation. The only difference in accounting as a result of the use of one form rather than the other is in the time when the earnings of the venture may be recognized by the participating organizations. If a venture is given corporate form, earnings are not recognized by the participants until a dividend has been paid. In partnership form, however, earnings of the venture may be accrued to the participants as soon as they are earned by the venture.

To illustrate accounting for a joint venture when a separate set of books is maintained, assume the Monia Company and the Sylvanto Company formed a third company to carry on a specific venture. To start the venture the following assets were contributed by each organization:

	By Monia	By Sylvanto
Cash	$10,000	
Merchandise		$20,000
Other assets	15,000	5,000
Total	$25,000	$25,000

Subsequent operations of the venture were:

(1) Miscellaneous expenses were paid by the venture, $4,000.
(2) One-half of the merchandise was sold for $18,000 cash.
(3) Additional merchandise was purchased, $9,000 on account.
(4) Wages for the venture were paid, $3,000 cash.
(5) Depreciation of $1,000 was recognized.
(6) Merchandise costing $7,000 was sold for $16,000 cash.
(7) Other expenses were paid, $3,000 cash.
(8) The venture distributed $1,000 of the earnings to each of the participating companies.

If the venture is formed as a partnership, the entries which would be made on each company's books to record the activities of the venture would be as given in Table 1-A.

NO SEPARATE BOOKS. When a separate set of books is not maintained for a joint venture, each participating company must maintain full details of the venture on its own books. Using the data from Table 1-A, the entries to record the activities of the joint venture, assuming Monia manages the venture, would be as given as in Table 1-B.

TABLE 1-A (SEPARATE BOOKS)

Venture's Books

Account	Debit	Credit
Cash	$10,000	
Merchandise	20,000	
Other assets	20,000	
Monia, Capital		$25,000
Sylvanto, Capital		25,000
(1)		
Miscellaneous Expense	$4,000	
Cash		$ 4,000
(2)		
Cash	$18,000	
Merchandise		$10,000
Gain on sale of merchandise		8,000
(3)		
Merchandise	$9,000	
Accounts payable		$ 9,000
(4)		
Wage expense	$3,000	
Cash		$ 3,000
(5)		
Depreciation	$1,000	
Allowance for depreciation		$1,000

Monia's Books

Account	Debit	Credit
Joint venture	$25,000	
Cash		$10,000
Other assets		15,000
(1)	None.	
(2)	None.	
(3)	None.	
(4)	None.	
(5)	None.	

Sylvanto's Books

Account	Debit	Credit
Joint venture	$25,000	
Merchandise		$20,000
Other assets		5,000
(1)	None.	
(2)	None.	
(3)	None.	
(4)	None.	
(5)	None.	

(6)

Cash	$16,000	
Merchandise		$7,000
Gain on sale of merchandise		9,000

(7)

Miscellaneous expense	$3,000	
Cash		$3,000

(8)

Distribution to owners	$2,000	
Cash		$2,000

(9)

Gain on sale of merchandise	$17,000	
Miscellaneous expense		$7,000
Wage expense		3,000
Depreciation		1,000
Income for period		6,000

(10)

Income for period	$2,000	
Distribution to owners		$2,000

(11)

Income for period	$4,000	
Monica, Capital		$2,000
Sylvanto Capital		2,000

(6) None.

(7) None.

(8)

Cash	$1,000	
Income from joint venture		$1,000

(9) None.

(10) None.

(11)

Joint venture	$2,000	
Income from joint venture		$2,000

(6) None.

(7) None.

(8)

Cash	$1,000	
Income from joint venture		$1,000

(9) None.

(10) None.

(11)

Joint venture	$2,000	
Income from joint venture		$2,000

TABLE I-B (NO SEPARATE BOOKS)

Monia's Books			Sylvanto's Books		
Joint venture	$40,000		Joint venture	$40,000	
Other assets		$15,000	Merchandise		$20,000
Sylvanto		25,000	Other assets		5,000
			Monia		15,000
(1)			(1)		
Joint venture	$4,000		Joint venture	$4,000	
Cash		$4,000	Monia		$4,000
(2)			(2)		
Cash	$18,000		Monia	$18,000	
Joint venture		$18,000	Joint venture		$18,000
(3)			(3)		
Joint venture	$9,000		Joint venture	$9,000	
Accounts payable		$9,000	Monia		$9,000
(4)			(4)		
Joint venture	$3,000		Joint venture	$3,000	
Cash		$3,000	Monia		$3,000

(5)   (5)

(No entry needed)   (No entry needed)

(The portion of the fixed assets to be treated as expense will be computed when a physical inventory is taken prior to recognizing gain or loss on the joint venture.)

(6)			(6)		
Cash	$16,000		Monia	$16,000	
Joint venture		$16,000	Joint venture		$16,000
(7)			(7)		
Joint venture	$3,000		Joint venture	$3,000	
Cash		$3,000	Monia		$3,000
(8)			(8)		
Sylvanto	$1,000		Cash	$1,000	
Cash		$1,000	Monia		$1,000
(9)			(9)		
Joint venture	$6,000		Joint venture	$6,000	
Sylvanto		$3,000	Monia		$3,000
Gain on venture		3,000	Gain on venture		3,000

Entry number (9) was made on the assumption that gains and losses were shared equally. The gain is computed by balancing the joint venture account on each company's books, as follows:

Joint Venture

Opening entry	$40,000	$18,000	(2)
(1)	4,000	16,000	(6)
(3)	9,000	31,000	(X)
(4)	3,000		
(7)	3,000		
(9)	6,000		
	$65,000	$65,000	

Assets not consumed:
(X) Merchandise $12,000
(X) Other assets   19,000

Uncompleted Ventures. If a venture is not completed at the date that financial statements are to be prepared, balances in venture accounts remaining after appropriate recognition of any gains or losses should be disclosed. Normally the balances in uncompleted ventures are debits representing the unconsumed assets of the venture in which each of the participating organizations has an investment.

On the books of each of the participating organizations where a separate set of books is maintained for the venture, the investment account reflects the equity of the particular participant in the venture. Where separate books are not maintained for the venture, each participant's investment account reflects the full balance of the venture which is offset by separate accounts for the equity of the other participants. On a statement of financial position, only the equity of the reporting, participant should be included as an asset of that particular participant. When separate books are not maintained, this requires that the balance of the joint venture account be offset by the equities of the other participants. In Table 1-B, the Monia Company would report the joint venture balance, assuming separate books are not kept for the venture, as follows:

Investment:
Joint venture $31,000
Less: Sylvanto's equity   27,000
Equity in joint venture $4,000

Miscellaneous Venture Combinations. Miscellaneous business combinations of a temporary nature similar to joint ventures are rather common. The combining together of a group of investment bankers for underwriting and selling a specific issue of corporate securities is one of the better known forms of a temporary business combination. Other combinations of this type include real estate development projects and similar large scale activities requiring more resources than one company might have or be willing to invest, or in some instances to combine the special resources of different companies. In general, the accounting procedures used in joint-venture accounting can be readily adapted to various types of miscellaneous venture combinations.

PROBLEMS

Problem 1-1. Mr. T. A. Hoyer owned a building, some tools, and office equipment. On January 1, 1967, he decided to go into the TV repair business. On that date his accountant prepared the following list of assets with which Mr. Hoyer started operations.

	Cost to Mr. Hoyer	Depreciated Cost on Jan. 1, 1967	Fair Market Value on Jan. 1, 1967
Building	$8,000	$6,000	$17,000
Tools	1,500	1,200	1,000
Office equipment	800	800	1,200
Cash			10,000

On January 2, 1967, Mr Hoyer obtained an operating license from the City Hall for $10, purchased 10 TV sets on account for $800, and opened the shop for business. To provide for emergency demands for cash, he discussed his project with the local bank and made arrangements to borrow money if the need should arise.

Required:
Give the journal entry or entries necessary to record the formation of the sole proprietorship.

Problem 1-2. Don Freeman has operated a small manufacturing plant for several years. His accounting records have been maintained on an accrual basis. His inventory has been priced consistently on a LIFO basis, no estimate has been made for doubtful receivables, and depreciation has been taken on an accelerated basis. On January 1, 1967, the book value of his assets is $80,000. Late in 1966 he rejected the offer of a competitor of $115,000 for his business. Subsequently Freeman decided to expand and to admit Rich Jones as a full partner. Jones contributed $70,000 in cash and newly acquired machinery of $30,000.

Required:
(1) Discuss the accounting problems the new partners would face in the formation of the partnership.
(2) Does the continuity concept find application in this situation? Discuss.

Problem 1–3. Upon the death of his father Mr. H. D. Dugan took over his father's small furniture store. At the time of death the following assets of the store were transferred to the son.

	Fair Market Value at Time of Death	Valuation on the Father's Books
Cash	$ 6,000	$ 6,000
Accounts receivable	12,000	15,000
Notes receivable	33,000	37,000
Merchandise (furniture)	32,000	32,000
Store building (one-third interest)	15,000	12,000
Store equipment	10,000	2,000

The store building was valued at $45,000. It was owned equally by the father and two widows. The widows agree to a continuous lease of their portion of the building.

Required:

(1) Should the store be valued at $45,000 with the equity of the two widows shown as liabilities? Should the store be shown at $15,000 only?

(2) Give the journal entries necessary to set up the new proprietorship for the son, Mr. H. D. Dugan.

Problem 1–4. The Securities and Exchange Commission released for publication the following announcement:

Precon Electronics Corp., 120 E. 41st St., *New York*, filed a registration statement (File 2-14951) with the SEC on April 6, 1959, seeking registration of 175,000 shares of its 75¢ par Common Stock, to be offered for public sale at $5 per share. The offering is to be made on a best efforts basis by Charles Plohn & Co., and Netherlands Securities Company, Inc., both of New York, for which a $1 per share selling commission is to be paid. The company also has agreed to pay $30,000 of the expenses of the underwriters; and the underwriters have acquired from one stockholder of the company, for $75, 75,000 shares of the company's common stock which, according to the prospectus, they intend to hold until after 15 months from the initial public offering of stock. These shares also are included in the statement.

Precon was organized under Delaware law on February 9, 1959. In exchange for all of its then outstanding stock, the company acquired from Photographic Analysis, Inc., a California company, of North Hollywood, assets consisting of certain patents and inventions in the electro-mechanical, electronic and photographic fields which that company is said to have developed. The company intends to put into production certain devices and systems based upon these assets, and to continue developmental and research work conducted by the predecessor since 1953. Among these are three devices said to be "ready to be tooled up for production," an automation controller, a TV programmer and a data recording pulse camera. Net proceeds of the sale of stock, assuming all shares are sold, are estimated at $620,000. The company proposes to subcontract the work of fabricating and assembling the three devices. Of the net proceeds, $155,000 will be supplied to the subcontractors for tools, jigs, dies and models; $244,000 will be used for working capital; $31,000 will be used to reimburse the predecessor for certain development expenses; $96,000 for inventories and work in process; $66,000 for continuing research and development; and $28,000 for advertising and sales promotion.

The issuing company now has outstanding 325,000 common shares, of which 250,000 were issued to Photographic Analysis for its assets. The latter is said to have expended $342,145 in research and development costs to December 31, 1958. The prospectus lists Theodore C. Robinson of Northridge, Calif., as president and treasurer. Photographic Analysis owns 250,000 of the issuer's outstanding shares, Charles Plohn & Co., 50,000 and Netherlands Securities 25,000. Robinson owns $53\frac{1}{3}\%$ of the Photographic Analysis stock and two other officers, the balance.

Required:

(1) Explain how the Precon Electric Corporation was formed.

(2) Why is Precon planning to issue additional shares of stock?

(3) Give the entry or entries which would be needed to record the issuance of the stock and the use of the funds assuming the plans are carried out.

Problem 1–5. A 1959 SEC release for publication announced:

Sip'n Snack Shoppes, Inc., 1420 Walnut St., *Philadelphia, Pa.*, filed a registration statement (File 2-14920) with the SEC on March 31, 1959, seeking registration of 200,000 shares of Common Stock, to be offered for public sale on a best efforts basis by Sano & Co., of New York. The offering is to be made at $2 per share, with a 30¢ selling commission to the underwriter. The company also has agreed to issue the underwriter warrants to purchase 15,000 common shares at the public offering price through 1964 and to pay up to $13,500 of its expenses. A finder's fee of 2,000 warrants containing similar provisions are to be issued to Edward F. Henderson.

The company is engaged primarily in the operation of snack counters, bars, and refreshment stands in various retail stores and sport and amusement centers, on both a concession and management basis. It was organized March 30, 1959, under Delaware law to acquire all the outstanding stock of Sip'n Snack Shoppes of Pennsylvania, Inc., Sip'n Snack Shoppes of New Jersey, Inc., and Sip'n Snack Shoppes of New York, Inc. Its principal officers and directors and sole stockholders are Sheldon Feldman and Samuel W. Alexander. All of the stock of the three subsidiaries was transferred to the issuing company by Feldman and Alexander in exchange for 150,000 shares of its common stock.

Net proceeds of the public sale of the 200,000 common shares are estimated at $315,500. They will be applied first to repay a $30,000 bank loan. Secondly, the proceeds will be applied towards the repayment of a $49,300 loan owing to A. L. Sainer with interest. Thirdly, $15,000 each is to be applied to the purchase of equipment and to install counters required in four Indiana locations (Peoria, South Bend, Fort Wayne, and Anderson). The remaining proceeds will be added to working capital to operate these additional locations and will be held in reserve for expansion into additional locations.

Required:

Assume the balance sheet of Sip'n Snack Shoppes just prior to the proposed new issue reveals current assets of $30,000 and fixed assets of $275,000. Prepare a balance sheet which will exist if the new issue is sold and invested as indicated in the announcement.

Problem 1–6. Transactions between the enterprise and other enterprises or individuals provide the raw data of accounting. Each of the following activities of an enterprise may be considered in relation to the transaction concept:

(*a*) Sale of merchandise for cash.
(*b*) Sale of merchandise on account, terms 1/20, n/60.
(*c*) Sale of merchandise on account, terms 36 months.
(*d*) Purchase of an asset with a 5-year life on January 2, 1967.
(*e*) Use of the asset in (*d*) during 1967.
(*f*) Accrual of interest on a note receivable held by the enterprise.
(*g*) A theft of merchandise.
(*h*) An increase in market vaue of long-term securities.
(*i*) Hiring a new accountant.

Required:
(1) Discuss each of the above activities in relation to the transaction concept.
(2) Would each be the basis for an accounting entry? Why?

Problem 1–7. (*a*) The Drake Company sells about one-third of its merchandise for cash, one-third on 30-day open account, and one-third on a 3-year installment plan. An entry is made at the time of each sale as each is considered a transaction of the enterprise.

Required:
Discuss similarities and differences in accounting for the three types of sales in view of the continuity and periodicity postulates of accounting.

(*b*) The Drake Company uses fixed assets in manufacturing which are sometimes superseded in usefulness by new inventions.

Required:
In view of the continuity and periodicity postulates, discuss some of the more important issues the Drake Company must consider in accounting for these assets.

Problem 1–8. The Wall Street Journal recently carried the following news item:

> Directors of the Chicago Great Western Railway have temporarily shelved a proposed plan to offer income debenture bonds in exchange for the company's outstanding preferred stock.
> E. T. Reidy, chairman and president, said that after several months of extensive investigation the road's directors at a meeting here yesterday decided the proposal was not "in the best interests of the company's security holders" at this time.
> Mr. Reidy said yesterday's decision did not mean the carrier had dropped the proposal entirely. "I'm sure it will be taken up again sometime in the future," the executive declared, "but not, at least, for the rest of this year."
> The Great Western, which has about 366,000 preferred shares outstanding, said recently that it was studying the plan because such an exchange would improve the company's tax position. Bond interest is paid before taxes whereas preferred stock dividends are taken out of after-tax income, the carrier explained.

Required:

(1) Should accountants advise management on tax considerations in the formation of a new business?

(2) In view of the company's wish to exchange the preferred stock for income bonds, why do you think preferred stock was issued originally?

Problem 1-9. Messrs. Amber, Brown, and Kreem have formed a corporation known as the ABK Company. The corporation has been authorized to issue:
(*a*) 2,000 shares of $100 par nonvoting 6% preferred stock.
(*b*) 10,000 shares of $10 stated value voting common stock.
(*c*) $100,000 of 5% bonds.

Net assets to be contributed to the corporation by the three organizers are:

	Amber	Brown	Kreem
Miscellaneous assets	$60,000	$120,000	$80,000
Current liabilities	10,000	30,000	20,000
Net assets contributed	$50,000	$ 90,000	$60,000
Average annual earnings	$ 2,790	$ 5,010	$ 3,300

The three organizers request advice on how to issue the three types of securities to each person so as to provide for each the same right in assets and income, and the same security as to risk, as existed prior to the formation of the corporation. Also, they want to share equally in voting control of the corporation.

Required:

(1) Draw up a suggested plan for issuing securities to the three organizers. Your investigation reveals that similar companies in the industry are financed (excluding current liabilities) about 30% by bonds and 70% by stock.

(2) Point out the weaknesses and advantages of your plan.

Problem 1-10. Messrs. A. J. Cromley and E. B. Martin have decided to go into business together. Assets to be contributed by each are:

	Cromley	Martin
Cash	$ 6,000	$ 8,000
Merchandise	18,000	7,000
Building	-0-	30,000
Equipment	12,000	3,000
Other assets	6,000	4,000
	$42,000	$52,000

Required:

(1) Give the journal entries to record the formation of the new company, if
   (*a*) a partnership is formed.
   (*b*) a corporation is formed and $90,000 of par value common stock is issued as payment for the assets.

(2) How many shares of stock would be given each investor if the $90,000 stock was $50 par value stock?

Problem 1-11. The Federal Power Commission recently released for publication the following announcement:

The Federal Power Commission has authorized Arizona Public Service Company, of Phoenix, Ariz., to acquire the entire electric system of Verde Electric Cooperative, Inc., of Cottonwood, Ariz.

The Verde co-op owns and operates various lines which distribute power to some 400 customers, both residential and commercial, in the Verde Valley and contiguous areas in Yavapai and Coconino Counties, Ariz. Arizona Public Service will continue to use these facilities for the same purposes following the merger.

Arizona Public Service provides electric service in 10 of the 14 Arizona Counties, including Yavapai and Coconino, and gas service in six counties. It serves for the most part, the service area of the cooperative.

In consideration for the acquisition, Arizona Public Service will assume the total of all liabilities of Verde Electric as of the closing date of the merger. Verde Electric's assets and liabilities as of October 31, 1958, were stated as being $517,200 and $610,400, respectively.

Required:

(1) Does $517,200 and $610,400 represent book value or fair market value of Verde's assets and liabilities?

(2) Why might Arizona Public Service agree to this merger?

(3) If Arizona Public Service takes up the assets and liabilities of Verde at $517,200 and $610,400, are Arizona Public Service stockholders giving a "bonus" to Verde's creditors? Explain.

Problem 1–12. Three companies, A, B, and C, combine to form a joint venture to develop a product to compete with a new industry which poses an increasing threat to the products regularly sold by A, B, and C. Company A is to manage the venture. Transactions of the venture were:

Jan. 6, 1967—Fixed assets to be used in making the product were contributed by B—$90,000. Patents and processes contributed by C—$30,000.

Jan. 10, 1967—A purchased $10,000 of materials and $1,500 of supplies for the venture.

Jan. 31, 1967—A paid monthly expenses—$6,000.

Feb. 28, March 31, April 30, May 31, and June 30—A paid monthly expenses of $5,000, $7,000, $6,000, $6,000 and $12,000 respectively.

July 15—A spent $15,000 for advertising of the new product.

July 31—Sales for cash were $5,000. Monthly expenses were $14,000.

August 15—B contributed $15,000 additional materials.

Sales and expenses, all paid for or received by A were:

	August	September	October	November	December
Sales	$ 7,000	$10,000	$20,000	$30,000	$40,000
Expenses	15,000	14,000	16,000	12,000	10,000

On December 31, the assets in the hands of the venture, other than cash, were:

Merchandise	$ 1,000
Supplies	200
Fixed assets (net after depreciation)	80,000
Patents and processes	10,000

Profits and losses are to be shared equally by the three participating companies.

Required:

(1) Give the journal entries on the books of all companies to record the venture transactions, assuming separate books are not kept for the venture.

(2) Give the entries required if separate books are kept for the venture.

(3) Compute the profit or loss accruing to each company for the year's activities.

    (*a*) Assuming that the venture is not incorporated.

    (*b*) Assuming that the venture is incorporated.

(4) If the venture is considered unsuccessful and is to be dissolved, how much of each venture resource would A turn back to companies B and C.

Problem 1–13. The firms of Jones and Company, Smith and Associates, and Black and Company, form a syndicate to purchase and sell on an equal basis $600,000 face value of bonds of the Border Company. The bonds are sold to the underwriters at 98 and are to be issued to investors at 100. The sales commission is 1% and the expenses are to be paid by the syndicate.

Operations of the syndicate were as follows:

1. The bonds were purchased for cash, each of the three participating companies putting up one-third of the money.
2. Expenses of $1,200 were paid by Jones and Company for the syndicate.
3. Bonds sold by the participants were:

Jones & Co. @ $100	$199,000
Smith and Associates @ 100	180,000
Black & Co. @ 100	197,000
Total	$576,000

4. Unsold bonds are assigned equally to the three underwriters.
5. Cash settlement after allocating commissions and profits among the three participants was made and the venture was terminated.

Required:

Assume separate books are not kept for the venture. Prepare the journal entries to account for the underwriting by joint venture accounting.

CHAPTER 2

Valuation of assets

The process by which a new business entity acquires assets preparatory to commencing operations may be described in a rather elementary fashion as:

(1) Acquiring cash from investors and creditors of the enterprise.
(2) Investing the cash in economic resources expected to be useful in the operational process.

Acquisition Cost Valuation

Not only do the newly acquired assets become a part of the operational processes of the enterprise, but they also must enter the accounting mechanism in some manner. A rather fundamental concept, covered in elementary textbooks in accounting, is that these assets should be recorded (valued) at their acquisition cost. That is, the acquired assets should enter the accounting mechanism at the dollar consideration which was exchanged or given up to acquire the assets on the acquisition date. This concept is sometimes referred to as the valuation of assets in terms of historical or original cost.

Many of the existing problems of asset valuation would be eliminated if the foregoing elementary concept were accepted completely by accountants. Actually, of course, many economic resources are acquired directly with a promise to pay cash later. This situation exists when purchases are made on account. In other situations, owners often contribute economic resources directly rather than cash. Thus investors and creditors often supply economic resources directly to the enterprise. Likewise the enterprise may acquire economic resources in exchange for other economic resources. Determination of the dollar consideration given to acquire the new assets poses a real problem in these circumstances. In addition, situations arise wherein departure from the acquisition cost valuation appears to be not only warranted, but advisable.

Problems of Asset Valuation. There are three main problems involved in the valuation of assets. In question form they are:

(1) When shall accountants recognize on the books of account that assets have been acquired?
(2) At what amounts shall assets recognized be valued?
(3) Recognizing the impossibility of keeping a separate asset account for each asset acquired, how should the various assets recognized be combined or classified?

Overriding these problems is the fundamental question of *what* is an asset. The elementary view that an asset is anything of value owned by the enterprise is not particularly useful in the more advanced problems of accounting. A somewhat broader view would be to consider assets as of two rather distinct types:

(1) Cash and direct claims to cash.
(2) Services in the form of economic resources which are to be used in the operations of the enterprise.

The second type of asset arises because the nature of business activity is to acquire economic resources at one time but not to use them completely until a later date. As a result, at any one time the bulk of the assets of the enterprise will be of service to the enterprise in its future operations.

Acquisition Cost vs. Realizable Value. As previously mentioned, general accounting procedure suggests that the assets of an enterprise be valued at the cash or cash equivalent required to acquire the assets. While this basis is generally used by accountants for the service resources of the enterprise, many accountants endeavor to value the cash and direct claims to cash portion of assets at the amount of cash which will be provided by these items. Economists and others at times suggest that all assets—service resources as well as cash and claims to cash—should be valued according to the amount of cash which will be realized ultimately by their use. Accountants have never accepted this view as proper for valuing service resources. Acquisition cost rather than realizable value has seemed more real. In the case of receivables which represent a direct claim to cash, however, accountants think in terms of realizable value. Estimated uncollectibles are deducted to arrive at the estimated cash to be realized on the receivables.

VALUATION OF CASH AND DIRECT CLAIMS TO CASH

Cash and direct claims to cash, such as notes and accounts receivable, bonds receivable, and government securities, are generally recorded at an amount representing their cash equivalent on the date acquired. However, these items are sometimes measured by the amount of cash which the acquired asset will provide at some future date.

For example, assume that a company sells merchandise, with a sale price of $950, in exchange for a $1,000 bond of the buying company. The entry to record this sale would be:

Bonds receivable	$950	
Sales		$950

But, if the same company sells merchandise, with a sales price of $950, in exchange for a noninterest-bearing note receivable in the face amount of $1,000, the entry would be:

Notes receivable	$1,000	
Sales		$950
Unearned interest income		50

The justification for this different valuation of direct claims to cash seems to lie in the length of the waiting period before cash will be realized and in the amount involved. If the waiting period is relatively short and if the amount of the variation is not especially large, there seems to be no objection to measuring the claim to cash in terms of the total cash which will be provided in the reasonably near future. When the waiting period is long, the amount involved material, or when the interest charge for waiting is not included in the face amount of the claim to cash (as with an interest-bearing note), valuation is usually made on the basis of the sale price or cash equivalent on the date the asset is acquired.

Realizable Value—Reporting Date vs. Future Date

At each reporting date the accountant generally attempts to value cash and claims to cash items at an approximation of the cash which the various assets will provide. This valuation commonly requires some adjustment of the recorded amount. The basic problem, and one which is frequently overlooked, lies in distinguishing clearly the two possible modifications of the original valuation:

(1) The amount of cash which the assets will provide as of the balance sheet or reporting date.

(2) The amount of cash which the assets will provide at some future date.

Thus, for certain types of receivables, such as accounts receivable and some short-term notes, valuation at the amount of cash which will be provided at some future date is accepted. Consequently, the recording of estimated uncollectible accounts and the deduction of this amount from accounts receivable on the balance sheet accomplishes a receivable valuation in terms of estimated cash to be provided at some future date. On the other hand, certain long-term notes and bonds receivable, which also represent direct claims to cash, are valued in terms of the amount of cash which could be provided on the reporting date. However, even this latter valuation is sometimes further modified—in a somewhat inconsistent manner—for fluctuations in market valuations. Thus, for a bond receivable (which a company expects to hold for a relatively short period) which was initially valued at the cash equivalent required to acquire the bond, a measure of its cash equivalent at the reporting date is used only when the market (selling price) price is below the original or previously modified valuation. This procedure for valuing receivables is an application of the time-honored, though logically inconsistent, "cost or market, whichever is lower" rule.

Materiality and Realizable Valuation. From the above discussion one should not conclude that the accountant expends considerable effort at each reporting date to make certain that each cash or claim-to-cash item is valued at its cash equivalent at the reporting date or at some future date. While such a valuation might be desirable from a theoretical standpoint, the implementation might involve numerous minor adjustments of an insignificant nature. Thus, for receivables it might be considered desirable to adjust normal accounts for estimated bad debts, estimated discounts still available, estimated costs of collecting the receivables, estimated administrative costs of booking and billing, and, possibly, for the interest which could have been earned if the receivables had been in the form of cash as of the reporting date. Carried to this extreme the valuation of accounts receivable at their cash equivalent on the reporting date might appear somewhat as shown at top of next page.

Certainly such an extremely detailed presentation is difficult to justify on the basis of disclosure of materially significant information. It should be recognized, however, that the bad debt allowance, which is an adjustment normally made, is similar in nature to the other items listed. The

CURRENT ASSETS:

Cash			$2,000.00
Accounts receivable		$8,000.00	
Less: Bad debt allowance	$100.00		
Sales discounts available	20.00		
Estimated collection costs	10.00		
Booking costs	5.00		
Implicit interest allowance	15.00		
Miscellaneous adjustments	8.00	158.00	
Cash equivalent of accounts receivable			7,842.00

purpose of each is, partially at least, to modify the acquisition price of the receivables toward an amount closer to their cash equivalent.

The important point to recognize here is that adjustments of the recorded cash equivalent (of cash and claims to cash) are made in the interest of reporting these items at an approximation of the cash they will provide. Numerous other possible adjustments are not regularly made, principally because the additional accuracy that would result is not particularly significant. Consistent valuation over a period of time is more to be desired than an attempt at excessive accuracy. This conclusion, of course, is subject to the standard that no material aspect of valuation may be omitted in determination of asset valuation.

Valuation of Long-Term Receivables. The concept that accountants value cash and claims to cash at the amount of cash which will be provided by these items is subject to question in the case of long-term receivables. Typical of such long-term receivables is the accounting for bonds receivable. Bonds are normally recorded at their acquisition cost and then periodically revalued upward or downward as the discount or premium on purchase is amortized in some systematic and rational manner. The following example illustrates this process:

On January 1, 1968, Company A purchases for $9,600 bonds of Company B which have a maturity value of $10,000 on December 31, 1971. At the time of acquisition of this investment receivable Company A would make this entry:

Investment in bonds of B	$9,600	
Cash		$9,600

Company A officials expect to hold these bonds until maturity. If the bonds were to be accounted for in a manner similar to the various service resources of an enterprise, such as machinery or materials, no adjustment of this initial valuation would be made until the resources were disposed of. That is, the asset would continue to be carried at cost. However, accountants generally adjust the acquisition cost of bonds receivable when such cost differs from the maturity value. At the end of each year the bonds would be "revalued" until, at maturity date, they would reveal a value of $10,000. If Company A elects to make such "revaluation," more commonly called amortization of the purchase discount, by the straight line process, the adjustment entry December 31, 1968 (and each subsequent December 31 until maturity) would be:

Investment in bonds of B	$100	
Interest income		$100

As a result of this entry Company A would report the bonds receivable from B at $9,700 on December 31, 1968. Similarly, the bonds would be reported at an additional $100 each December 31 until maturity. At maturity the bonds would be reported at their cash equivalent at that date of $10,000.

The above procedure indicates that accountants value long-term receivables on a basis different from that used in the valuation of service resources. Acquisition cost is not strictly followed. Likewise, the modification in value is not strictly governed by the cash equivalent of the bonds at the reporting date, for market values are included only parenthetically. The governing concept appears to be to modify the acquisition cost in order to get the bonds receivable to a cash equivalent value at maturity date. Thus, we might say that accountants initially value long-term receivables at acquisition cost, but that they may subsequently be revalued in order to obtain their cash equivalent value at maturity date. At reporting dates between acquisition and maturity the bonds will be reported at a "going-concern value" between the acquisition cost and the maturity value.

The Use of Current Market Value

Some evidence of accountants' support for the valuation of cash and claims to cash in terms of the amount of cash which the item will provide on the reporting date is found in the common usage of cost or market, whichever is lower, for claims to cash not expected to be held until maturity. To illustrate this practice, we can again refer to the example in the preceding section.

If Company A acquires $10,000 maturity value of Company B Bonds on January 1, 1968, for $9,600, the following entry would be made, even if Company A did not intend to hold these bonds until their December 31, 1971, maturity date:

Investment in bonds of B	$9,600	
Cash		$9,600

If Company A does not intend to hold these bonds until their maturity date, there appears to be little reason to amortize the bond discount over the period remaining until maturity. Thus, the valuation of the asset is not guided by an attempt to base the asset value on the amount of cash to be provided at some future date. For an asset of this type, at any balance sheet date the accountant has a choice of adhering to the acquisition cost, as reflected by the entry made at acquisition, or of modifying the acquisition cost in an attempt to approach the cash equivalent at the balance sheet date. If one were to follow logically the previously indicated concept of valuing claims to cash at their cash equivalent, we might expect to find the bonds reported at their market value at the reporting date. The general practice followed by accountants, however, is to use such market value only when the market price of bonds is below acquisition cost. As a result, temporary investments are commonly reported at acquisition cost or at cash (market) equivalent at the reporting date, whichever value is lower.

It might be noted at this point that the selling market price rather than the buying market price is used for this revaluation purpose. Where no market price exists, bid price by buyers is used in preference to the asked price by sellers of the security. Because bid price is used, the inference is that accountants endeavor to value these receivables in terms of their cash equivalent as of the balance sheet date.

Thus, for the bonds of Company B in the above example, at December 31, 1968, the acquisition cost would be $9,600. If the asked price by sellers were $95\frac{1}{2}$ and the bid price by buyers $94\frac{1}{2}$, the choice of values for the bonds would be: acquisition value, $9,600; selling market value, $9,550; or buying market value, $9,450. Applying the cost or market, whichever is lower, rule, and using the bid price as the market value, the bonds of Company B would be valued at $9,450 for balance sheet purposes.

Some firms go so far as to value all temporary receivables, whenever a suitable market exists, in terms of the selling market price prevailing at the reporting date. When the market revaluation procedure is carried to this point, that is, when market price is used regardless of its relation to cost, support exists for the concept that cash and claims to cash are valued by accountants at their cash equivalent at the reporting date.

Cash Surrender Value. Further evidence of acceptance by accountants of the concept that claims to cash should be valued in terms of the cash which could be realized on the reporting date is found in the valuation of insurance policies which have a cash surrender feature. Assume that Company A decided on January 1, 1968, to take out a

$100,000 life insurance policy on the life of the president with the company designated as beneficiary. Also assume that the annual premium on this policy is $3,000, and that upon payment of the third annual premium the initial cash surrender value of $600 arises. The following entries might be made:

Jan. 1, 1968	Insurance expense	$3,000	
	Cash		$3,000
Jan. 1, 1969	Insurance expense	$3,000	
	Cash		$3,000
Jan. 1, 1970	Insurance expense	$2,400	
	Cash surrender value of life insurance	600	
	Cash		$3,000

Each subsequent year the $3,000 premium would be apportioned (1) to record the increase in the cash surrender value and (2) to record the remainder as the insurance expense for that year.[1] The asset, cash surrender value of life insurance, would thereby be reported periodically in terms of the cash which could be received on the reporting date through surrender of the policy.

Summary of Valuation of Cash and Claims to Cash Items. The amount at which cash and direct claims to cash should be valued may be summarized in this manner:

(1) Cash, which may best be defined as anything which will be accepted by a commercial bank for deposit at the face amount of the negotiable instrument, should be valued at the amount of cash which could be disposed of on the reporting date. In the case of cash not readily available for disposition, such as when cash is tied up in an insolvent bank, some adjustment is required. A simple reclassification to remove the amount from disposable cash may be all that is required. At times the actual value of the "frozen" cash may have to be reduced for reporting purposes, but this action would normally require objective evidence that less than the amount carried will subsequently be realized.

(2) Direct claims to cash take several forms. They may be in the form of:
    (a) Immediate claims to cash, as in the case of surrender value of life insurance policies; savings deposits, where the funds are technically not available for immediate disbursements but in fact can be

---

[1] The above procedure may be questioned on theoretical grounds that the initial $600 cash surrender value is applicable to the entire three year period rather than entirely to the third year. Thus, we might find some support for allocating the $600 as follows: $400 to correction of prior years' income and $200 to reduction of the current year's expense. Further discussion of this subject will be found in Chapter 4.

readily obtained; and United States savings bonds. Normally, these items are to be valued at an amount equal to the cash which could be claimed on the reporting date.

(b) Claims to cash due in the near future, such as accounts and notes receivable. These items are valued at an amount equal to the cash which will be realized on the claim. Normally, adjustments are made only for bad debts and, in a few cases where the amount involved is material, for sales discounts available. Possible additional adjustments which would make the amount reported approach more closely the actual realizable cash at the reporting date (and also sharpen the determination of net income) are presently passed over because of immateriality and difficulties in computation.

(c) Claims to cash due in the distant future, such as bonds receivable. Normally these items are valued at a computed amount somewhat representative of the claim to cash on a going-concern basis as of the reporting date. It is sometimes stated that the appropriate valuation for these items is amortized cost. This is an indirect method of saying that cost is not the correct valuation, but that by amortizing cost—in order to achieve face value by maturity date—an approximation of the cash equivalent is achieved on the reporting date from a going-concern viewpoint. In those instances wherein the intent of management is to dispose of the receivable by sale prior to its maturity date, so that the ultimate cash to be realized is unknown, it is customary accounting practice to value the receivable at cost provided such cost is above the buying market price at the reporting date. When the selling market price is below cost the market valuation is generally used.

The following paragraphs illustrate some of the problems in the valuation of specific claims to cash.

Valuation of Accounts Receivable. The ABC Company sells on account merchandise at an invoice price of $1,000, terms 5/10, net 30. At the time of the sale two possible bases for valuing this receivable exist: (1) the amount of the cash claim the receivable represents at the date of the sale, or (2) the amount of the cash claim the receivable represents if the customer does not take the discount available. Theoretically, strict adherence to the view that cash and direct claims to cash should be valued at their cash equivalent would require an entry to record the sale as follows:

Accounts receivable	$950	
Sales		$950

Practically, however, many companies follow the practice of recording the receivable at the invoice amount, as follows:

Accounts receivable	$1,000	
Sales		$1,000

In the first entry, where the receivable is recorded at the net amount, if the discount available does lapse, through expiration of the discount period, an entry would be required to restate the receivable to the corrected amount, as follows:

Accounts receivable	$50	
Sales discounts not taken		$50

As far as the valuation of the receivable is concerned, the following question should be asked: Does the gross procedure result in a material misrepresentation of the valuation of the receivable? In general, accountants have decided that such a procedure is not a material departure from theoretical accuracy and that recording at the gross amount is a satisfactory representation of the valuation of the receivable. The gross procedure does lend itself to ease in recording and in verification, since the booking would involve the actual invoice amounts without adjustment for possible discounts. Many businesses are presently billing customers at net in recognition of the high frequency of discounts taken. Under these business conditions the booking of receivables at the net price would seem to be practical and would also achieve more theoretically proper asset values.

Valuation of Notes Receivable. Assume the ABC Company accepts a $1,000 note bearing interest at 3% and due in 60 days in payment for a sale of merchandise. At the sale date, the note could be sold at a discount rate of 6%. At the date of the sale the question arises as to the appropriate valuation of the note and the sale.

Three possible valuations are represented by the following entries:

(1)

Notes receivable	$1,005	
Sales		$1,000
Unearned interest income		5

This entry values the asset at its total eventual cash equivalent and reports as sales revenue the face amount of the asset received in exchange.

(2)

Notes receivable	$1,000	
Sales		$994.95
Unearned interest income		5.05

This entry values the asset at its face amount, but the sale is reported at its cash equivalent at the sale date. This amount is the discounted maturity value ($1,005 at 6% for 60 days) of the asset received in exchange.

(3)

| Notes receivable | $1,000 | |
| Sales | | $1,000 |

This entry values the asset at its face value and the sale in like terms. Any interest for waiting would be recognized when earned and/or received.

Normally, explicit interest payments, such as 3% in entry (1) above, are not included as a part of the receivable until the explicit interest has been earned by the passage of time. Even when the interest receivable is granted a valuation after the passage of time, it is generally not included as a part of the valuation of the note, but is classified separately as interest receivable. Thus, the claim to cash represented by interest receivable is not normally reported as an asset until the passage of time has produced an existing claim. This procedure is consistent with the concept of valuing cash items at their cash equivalent at the reporting date.

The face amount of the note is commonly accepted as the appropriate valuation of the note, as in entries (2) and (3) above. This valuation is justified on the ground that it does not result in any material distortion from valuation of the claim to cash in existence at the reporting date. Thus, entry (2) above, while theoretically reporting the sale at the cash equivalent of the asset received in exchange, normally is not made. Unless the refinement indicated in entry (2) is significant, entry (3) is considered satisfactory. Of course, at any subsequent reporting date accrued interest on the note would be reported as a receivable and as income.

The above example again illustrates that theoretical accuracy is sometimes sacrificed for practical ease in recording. On a consistent basis, the use of the third alternative above results in reasonably satisfactory measurement of assets (and income) and accomplishes this in a practicably justifiable manner.

Valuation of Long-Term Receivables Arising from a Sale. Assume the ABC Company accepts a noninterest-bearing note due in three years, having a face amount of $1,000, in payment for a sale of merchandise. The question then arises as to the appropriate valuation of the note. The situation is unusual, but will serve to illustrate further the proper valuation of all long-term receivables. If the market rate of interest is 5% so that on exchange the note could be sold for $863.84, there is considerable support for the view that the note or bond should be valued as follows:

(1)

| Notes receivable | $863.84 | |
| Sales | | $863.84 |

or as:

(2)

Notes receivable	$1,000	
Sales		$863.84
Unearned interest income		136.16

In practice an entry might be made at the gross amount:

(3)

| Notes receivable | $1,000 | |
| Sales | | $1,000 |

The effect of recording such a transaction at the gross amount is to anticipate revenue by including as sales the interest implicit in the face of the noninterest-bearing note. Where this amount of interest is material, it would appear that the cash equivalent valuation is more meaningful and useful. An aspect aside from proper valuation is the classification of the nature of the revenue. To treat as sales that which is properly interest revenue, if material, may cause management to overlook the important feature of interest in business decisions.

Procedures in Valuation of Receivables. To some extent the valuation of receivables in practice is dictated more by the manner in which the receivable is acquired than by adherence to the concept that receivables should be valued at their cash equivalent on the reporting date.

If the receivable arises due to a loan of money by the company, which is the essential nature of the purchase of a bond, as noted previously, there is a supposition on the part of the accountant that the valuation of the exchange is expressed in terms of the cash exchanged to acquire the receivable. Thus, the incoming asset is valued in terms of the outgoing asset. However, if the receivable arises due to a sale or by a contribution, the view of the accountant shifts decidedly to the concept that realizable cash is the proper valuation. Thus, the incoming asset is valued in terms of its cash equivalent at the acquisition date. The strong support for the view that receivables should be valued in terms of the cash equivalent claim suggests that valuation in terms of cash exchanged to acquire the receivable may be based on a supposition that cost price properly reflects realizable cash on the acquisition date.

While it is imperative that a student of accountancy understand the conceptual background of accounting procedures in order to cope with unusual situations that may arise, it is also necessary that customary procedures of accounting practice be a part of accountancy education. As far as receivables are concerned, the procedures of accounting may be generalized by stating that unless cash is exchanged to acquire the receivable, the proper valuation is the cash equivalent claim of the receivable on the reporting date. An exception is that, for convenience in recording, a receivable due to be converted into cash within a short period of time may be valued at the cash ultimately to be received. This holds true provided such a procedure does not materially depart from the valuation on the reporting date. For example, if a company made a $1,000 sale and received in exchange a $1,000 noninterest-bearing note due in 15 days, in terms of cash or cash equivalent value, if interest is 6% per year, the proper valuation of the note is $997.50 ($1,000 less 6% of $1,000 for 15 days). Because the amount involved is not material, for convenience in recording, the note may be valued at the cash ultimately to be received, $1,000. On the other hand, if the amount involved were material, the proper valuation would be the discounted amount.

VALUATION OF SERVICE RESOURCES

Contrary to the conceptual valuation of cash and direct claims to cash in terms of the cash to be *realized* by the asset, service resources such as buildings, materials, and labor are generally measured in terms of the cash or cash equivalent *invested* in them.

At the procedural level this concept is sometimes expressed: Assets, except cash and receivables, should be valued at the total of all costs required to have the asset available for use. There are, however, several departures from this procedural rule, and these departures can generally be explained in terms of materiality or in terms of difficulties of measurement. Typical of these departures is the procedure of charging to the period as expense freight-in and purchasing costs on material acquisitions, rather than deferring these items to the future as inventoriable costs. The student has been subjected to these procedures at the elementary and intermediate level of accountancy education. It now becomes necessary to establish an understanding of the concepts underlying these procedures.

The essential problem involved in implementing the concept that service resources should be valued in terms of invested cash or cash equivalent at acquisition is the determination of the amount of cash equivalent invested. When the investment is in terms of cash, the problem involved is one of classifying the acquisitions in a significant manner. The problem of classification will be discussed later. In those instances where the investment is not a cash outlay, but involves either the promise to pay cash at a later date or the exchange of other assets, determination of the amount of the investment presents a more difficult problem.

Discounts in Valuation. Assume that the ABC Company purchases a machine on account at an invoice amount of $1,000 terms 2/10, net 30. It is quite apparent that as of the date of acquisition the cash obligation is only $980. Acceptance of the view that service resources acquired should be measured in terms of the cash equivalent outlay required to obtain them indicates that the correct valuation of the machine would be $980. If the discount is not taken and an additional $20 is paid out, the additional expenditure should be charged off as an expense of the period. In practice, however, refinements such as this illustration poses may be ignored if the amount involved is not substantial enough to distort materially the valuation.

Exchange of Service Resources for Other Service Resources. When service resources on hand are exchanged for other service resources, as might be the case in trading machinery for equipment, it appears that the acquired resources should be valued at the cash equivalent of the resources given up. When this valuation cannot be determined, the cash equivalent price of the resource acquired may be used as a measure of the cash valuation of the transaction. When a cash valuation for the resources acquired or for the resources given up in exchange cannot be determined, it seems reasonable to suggest that the book valuation of the resources exchanged may be used. The procedures involved in accounting for exchange of service resources have been discussed in intermediate accounting.

Contributed Service Resources. The valuation of assets contributed by a sole proprietor or by partners in a partnership has been discussed. The term "fair market value" was used to designate a reasonable measure of the proper cash or cash equivalent valuation. In the case of a corporation more accurate measures of "fair market value" are often available than is true for proprietorships or partnerships. When service resources are contributed by stockholders or owners of the enterprise in exchange for stock, the normal rule is that the services acquired should be valued at the cash which could have been obtained if the shares of stock or other ownership equity had been issued for cash. Actually, the determination of the cash equivalent exchanged in this manner is often not possible, so that recourse to other methods of valuation is necessary. As a substitute, the cash equivalent price of the resources received may be used as a basis of valuation. In many cases neither the market price of the stock issued nor the cash equivalent of the resources acquired is readily determinable to a satisfactory degree. As a consequence, it is generally accepted accounting procedure to assume that the exchange is an exchange of equal values and that valuation should be determined by the more readily and accurately determinable *estimate* of the cash equivalent of either the stock issued or the resources acquired. The procedures involved in recording this type of transaction have been discussed in intermediate accounting.

The valuation of service resources acquired frequently requires the use of estimates. With a variety of estimates available, it is only through the exercise of sound judgment that the most appropriate value estimate may be determined. The accountant, who frequently must provide management with sound advice in this area, must exercise considerable care in preparing his recommendations and must also be cognizant of the possible long-run effects of these recommendations. For example, when capital stock is issued in exchange for a building, the accountant must recognize that the effect of the value-estimate determined to be proper will be reflected through several subsequent income statements, as the value-estimate for the building is amortized through depreciation entries. The accountant must consider carefully the various alternatives prior to presenting management with his considered recommendation on the proper value for the assets involved.

Leased Resources. A number of unusual problems arise when an enterprise uses resources leased from others. Since a lease agreement generally involves the right to use a resource in exchange for regular rental payments, and since title to the resource generally remains with the lessor, the user of leased resources commonly will not record the leased resource as an asset. In this case, no accounting problem exists for the lessee. Rental payments for the use of leased resources are a cost of operations in the period incurred.

Some lease agreements, however, are essentially the same as installment purchases of property. In such a lease, a strong case can be made for recognizing the substance of the lease rather than relying on its legal form. Here the resource leased should be recognized as an asset, the valuation of it being the discounted amount of future lease rental payments, less the portion of the payments for such things as taxes or insurance. A liability for a like amount should also be recorded. The amount capitalized for the leased resource should be allocated as a depreciation charge over the useful life of the resource, rather than over the initial period of the lease.

The lessor of leased property also faces problems in accounting for resources which it leases. Again, the nature of the lease agreement is important in determining the appropriate accounting. Generally, the investment incurred in the manufacture or acquisition of the leased resources is the accepted basis for valuation of such resources. Amortization of these costs is appropriate over the useful life of the leased resources.

Asset Classification and Recognition

Classification. There are two aspects to the problem of classification of assets. One relates to the question of how various acquisitions of resources should be classified. A typical example would be the question of whether an expenditure to add a new electric system should be classified as building, machinery, fixtures, or in some other manner. Another example is the question of how to classify expenditures of the removal of an old building. There is no one answer to these problems of classification. It has been suggested, however, that resources to be used together should be classified together. In the case of the electric system, if it were expected that it would be used over the entire life of the building, it should be classified as part of the building. If, on the other hand, the use of the system were to be restricted to a special type of machine, the cost of the system should be added to the cost of the machine. Expected use thus often dictates the proper classification of many resources.

Service resources are generally classified according to a natural usage, such as buildings, machinery, and the like, but this manner of classification is not necessarily the most useful. In some situations it may be more appropriate to classify service resources according to the function to be performed by the use of the services, such as in the case of delivery services (which might include trucks and other natural objects used in the delivery function), warehousing (which might include building, fixtures, and other natural objects used in the warehousing function), and other functional activities. In practice, the natural classification is most often used because it is more objective and does not lend itself to being changed by managerial intent.

The second aspect of asset classification relates to the question of how specific assets should be presented in financial statements. Other than for the reporting of leased resources, discussion of asset classification has been covered in elementary and intermediate courses. Disclosure of leased resources in the financial statements of the lessee generally depends on the nature of the lease. If the lease agreement is essentially an installment purchase of property, the discounted value of future lease rental payments is capitalized as an asset. This asset would normally be reported as a fixed asset, with a related reduction for estimated depreciation to date on the capitalized value. Leases that are not essentially installment purchases may be disclosed by footnotes to the financial statements. The footnote should enable the reader to assess the effect of lease commitments on the financial position and results of operations.

The lessor of resources generally will report as an asset the unamortized cost of any such assets leased. Again, the nature of the lease determines the classification of the cost involved. Some leases have characteristics indicating that the lease arrangement is primarily a financing medium for the lessee. These leases are generally reported among the receivables, with separate disclosure if amounts are material. Other leases are more in the nature of operating leases in which the lessor retains the normal risks or rewards of ownership. Costs invested in the leased resources are properly reported with or near property, plant, and equipment as a separately disclosed item, where material.

Recognition. The time at which assets should be recognized by the enterprise varies from situation to situation, but in general recognition that an asset has been acquired turns on the passage of legal title to the asset to the acquiring enterprise. Exceptions to this general rule arise when title has not legally passed, but when evidence exists that the asset is essentially or constructively owned. An example of this would be the situation under a conditional purchase, where the economic facts indicate that acquisition has taken place, even though legal title to the resource has not been acquired.

Underlying this general idea of the time for recognizing assets on the books of record is the practical point that assets may be recorded as acquired when certain types of business papers, such as invoices from sellers, are available as evidence of the acquisition. This practical procedure, which does not always represent legal passage of title, often requires adjustments at the reporting date to assure that only assets which meet the more fundamental test of being owned are reported.

APPLICATION OF PRINCIPLES

The concepts and standards set forth in this book for recording assets rest upon the concept that assets should be stated in terms of the reporting enterprise. Thus, the cash or cash equivalent should be in terms of the investment made by the company to acquire the assets and not stated at the valuation which some previous owner may have placed on them.

Illustration—Partnership Formed from Proprietorship

Assume that A is a sole proprietor having the following assets, among others, valued at cost to him:

Building	$30,000
Equipment	10,000
Inventory	18,000
Total	$58,000

If A decides to form a partnership with B and contributes the above assets to the partnership, the proper valuation of the assets would not necessarily be their cost to A, but should be their cost to the partnership. This cost would normally be determined by bargaining between A and B. If the bargain agreement does not disclose this valuation, it is customary to accept current market price as the proper valuation of the assets. In the above instance, if the fair market value of the assets were some other amounts, these amounts would be the basis for an entry on the books of the new enterprise. If the building were considered to be worth $45,000, the equipment $8,000, and the inventory $18,000, the entry on the books of the partnership to record the admission of A to the partnership would be:

Building	$45,000	
Equipment	8,000	
Inventory	18,000	
A, Capital		$71,000

This same principle applies if a corporation is formed to take over the assets of another corporation, a partnership, or a sole proprietorship. Likewise, as noted in Chapter 1, it would seem that an individual having personal assets which the individual proposes to use in his sole proprietorship business would follow the procedure of revaluing the personal assets to their market valuation as of the time the assets are turned over to the business. Actually, this refinement is often ignored on the grounds that the personal assets and the proprietorship assets both belong to the individual and should be valued at cost to the individual, rather than at cost to the business. This departure from principle seems to have considerable support in practice in order to assure a more objective basis for the valuation of proprietorship assets.

The need for valuing partnership contributed assets at fair market value rather than at cost to the individual making the contribution may be demonstrated in the following example. Assume A contributed assets which cost him $58,000 (as noted first above) and B contributed cash of $58,000. If the assets contributed by A had a market value of $71,000 (as noted later above), it is immediately apparent that A has contributed more than 50% of the total asset values. If A had sold the assets for the $71,000, he personally would have recognized a gain of $13,000. On the other hand, if A contributed the assets to the partnership at his original cost of $58,000, and if the partnership subsequently sold these assets for $71,000, the resulting gain of $13,000 would be divided between the partners in their income-sharing ratio. If such ratio were 50% to each partner, A would be given credit for only $6,500 of the gain to the partnership. To avoid this inequity, or the reverse when market price is below cost to the original owner, the accounting principle that assets should be valued at their cost to the acquiring enterprise is generally accepted in practice.

The foregoing illustration may be explained more clearly by indicating the entries which would appear on the books of the partnership if A allowed his contribution to be valued at his cost of $58,000.

(1)

Building	$30,000	
Equipment	10,000	
Inventory	18,000	
A, Capital		$58,000

(2)

Cash	$58,000	
B, Capital		$58,000

By the foregoing entries each partner has been given a capital credit of $58,000. Assume now that the partnership sells the assets contributed by A for $71,000. The entries to record the sale and to distribute the income realized would be:

(1)

Cash	$71,000	
Building		$30,000
Equipment		10,000
Inventory		18,000
Gain on sale of assets		13,000

(2)

Gain on sale of assets	$13,000	
A, Capital		$6,500
B, Capital		6,500

This clearly demonstrates that A has in fact contributed to B the sum of $6,500, or one-half the profit which had existed on A's personal assets prior to the transfer of these assets to the partnership.

Now let us assume the partnership does not resell the assets, but uses them in producing goods and services which are subsequently sold. Even under this alternative an inequity will arise, since partnership expenses will be lower than they would otherwise have been by the $13,000. That is, as the service resources contributed by A are used up by the partnership, $13,000 less cost will be charged to operations than if the assets had been recorded at their cash equivalent to the partnership of $71,000. This will result in an income greater than that actually earned by the partnership in the amount of the $13,000. If this additional income is divided on a 50–50 basis, A will have in effect contributed $6,500 of his income to B. This is one-half the unrealized profit which existed on A's assets at the date of contribution of the assets to the partnership.

Goodwill

At times it is possible that an individual may have assets at one cost which have another market valuation but which are worth more than either of these amounts to the new enterprise being formed. The new business may then agree to allow the individual contributing these assets a capital credit greater than the market value of the assets contributed. One example of a reason for the increased valuation may be the ability and "know-how" of the contributing individual to use the assets profitably. In a situation such as this, accountants are reluctant to place a valuation other than fair market value on the assets contributed. The excess contribution often is construed to be goodwill.

The typical definition of goodwill runs in terms of the excessive earning power attributable not to the individual assets of the entity but to the entity itself. It has been referred to as "going-value" because its existence depends upon the continued operations of the entity. It cannot be sold as a separate asset but attaches to the combination and use made of the tangible assets as a whole. In a more realistic sense, goodwill is also held to attach to individuals or groups of individuals within the entity. It has been referred to also as a "master valuation" account. In this sense it refers to the additional value attaching to the individual assets because they are in organized form as a business enterprise. This concept of goodwill represents an additional valuation to enterprise assets. This additional valuation would not be recorded under the normal accounting valuations of assets. For purposes of this textbook goodwill will be considered as embodying one or more or all of these various views of the nature of goodwill.

Partnership Goodwill. To illustrate this treatment, assume that A has assets which cost him $58,000, but which have a market value of $71,000 on the date they are contributed to the partnership, and that B agrees to give A credit for a $90,000 contribution. B also agrees to contribute cash of $90,000 for a 50% interest in the new partnership. The presumption, following the reasoning in the paragraph above, would be that A has contributed goodwill of $19,000, as well as the assets to be recorded at $71,000. The formation of the partnership would be recorded as follows:

(1)

Building	$45,000	
Equipment	8,000	
Inventory	18,000	
Goodwill	19,000	
A, Capital		$90,000

(2)

Cash	$90,000	
B, Capital		$90,000

The result of this recording is that each partner has a 50% equity in the partnership assets, and that these assets include $19,000 goodwill. Many businessmen desire to avoid having the intangible asset "goodwill" appear in their records and on their reports. Accordingly, in practice the procedure of allocating the goodwill to the other assets is at times followed. It is apparent, however, that any allocation of the goodwill to individual assets may be largely an arbitrary procedure. Therefore, if goodwill is not to be recorded, an equitable alternative would be for one partner to give a capital bonus to the partner bringing in the goodwill. Acceptance of the bonus concept would mean that the partner not contributing goodwill (partner B above) would allow the other partner (A) to take capital credit for some of his (B's) contribution.

The following illustration indicates the bonus procedure. A contributes the individual assets of $71,000 and goodwill of $19,000, while B contributes $90,000 cash. It is evident that both partners have made an equal contribution. Total assets are $180,000, which includes the $19,000 of goodwill. If goodwill is not to be recognized as an asset, the total assets of the partnership will be $161,000 ($180,000 − $19,000) and, if partners' capitals are to be equal, each should be credited for $80,500. If B contributes $90,000 of cash and receives credit for only $80,500, and if A contributes recognized assets of only $71,000 and receives a capital credit of $80,500, it is apparent that B has given a bonus in capital to A, and that goodwill will not be recorded on the books of the partnership. The entries to record the foregoing example would be as follows:

(1)

Building	$45,000	
Equipment	8,000	
Inventory	18,000	
A, Capital		$71,000

(2)

Cash	$90,000	
B, Capital		$80,500
A, Capital		9,500

Corporation Goodwill. While it is acceptable accounting procedure to recognize goodwill as an asset under partnership accounting,
similar situations in corporation accounting are, in effect, handled
according to the bonus procedure. Substituting in the foregoing example,
assume that 500 shares of $100 par value stock are issued to both A and B
in exchange for their asset contributions. The entries to record the formation of the corporate enterprise would be

(1)

Building	$45,000	
Equipment	8,000	
Inventory	18,000	
Capital stock (issued to A)		$50,000
Paid-in surplus		21,000

(2)

Cash	$90,000	
Capital stock (issued to B)		$50,000
Paid-in surplus		40,000

Since surplus attaches equally to each share of stock outstanding, it is
apparent that the equity of each individual at book value would be the
$50,000 of capital stock plus one-half of the surplus (or $30,500), for a
total equity of $80,500. This is the result also obtained under the partner-
ship procedure when the bonus alternative was used.

It should not be assumed that corporations never recognize goodwill as
an asset. When a corporation pays cash for goodwill, or whenever stock
is issued for assets, both tangible and intangible, and one of the assets is
specifically determined to be goodwill, the goodwill is recognized as an
asset. In addition, a special type of goodwill frequently arises through
the procedures involved in preparation of consolidated statements.
Goodwill from consolidation may appear on consolidated financial
statements if the parent corporation has acquired a controlling interest in
the stock of another (subsidiary) corporation at a cost price in excess of
the book value of the shares of stock acquired. Goodwill from consoli-

dation, as well as the entire area of preparation of consolidated statements, is discussed later, beginning with Chapter 9.

Problems in Partnership Goodwill and Bonus. Occasionally the intentions of partners in reaching an agreement on their respective interests in a partnership are not clearly discernible. The interest each partner is to have in the partnership, whether or not goodwill is to be recognized, and, if goodwill is involved, the amount to be recognized, are questions which sometimes are difficult to resolve.

Thus, for example, the agreement may indicate that A is to contribute tangible assets of $60,000, that B is to contribute tangible assets of $80,000, and that the two partners are to share equally in the partnership assets. While these points of agreement may appear clear enough at first glance, further study indicates that it is impossible to determine whether both A and B contributed goodwill which is to be recognized or whether the bonus procedure is to be used. If the bonus procedure is to be used, the entries would be:

(1)

| Assets | $60,000 | |
| A, Capital | | $60,000 |

(2)

Assets	$80,000	
A, Capital		$10,000
B, Capital		70,000

If, however, the partners agree that B contributes no goodwill, and if the partners have agreed to have equal capital in the partnership, then A must have contributed goodwill of $20,000. The entries would be:

(1)

Assets	$60,000	
Goodwill	20,000	
A, Capital		$80,000

(2)

| Assets | $80,000 | |
| B, Capital | | $80,000 |

If the partners should indicate that only $10,000 of goodwill is to be recognized, but that each partner is to have a 50% equity in the enterprise, both goodwill and bonus appear to exist. The entries would be:

(1)

Assets	$60,000	
Goodwill	10,000	
A, Capital		$70,000

(2)

Assets	$80,000	
B, Capital		$75,000
A, Capital		5,000

Economic Valuation of Enterprise Assets

Earlier in the chapter it was stated that accountants for recording purposes value service resource assets at the cash or cash equivalent invested in these assets, but tend to value cash and direct claims to cash at the amount of cash to be received from such assets. Some economists and others maintain that proper valuations of all assets should be in terms of the cash to be received from such assets. Invested cost to them has little significance, for the only significant value of an asset is the cash or cash equivalent which it can provide. Since at any date the cash potential of each asset is unknown, the cash to be received must be estimated. Because the cash equivalent requires estimation it is apparent that economic valuations will have a large amount of subjective opinion in them.

Another fundamental difference between recorded accounting and "economic" valuation lies in the different approaches to the valuation of an enterprise. Economic valuations are based on a view of the enterprise itself as a single asset and provide for the valuation of the enterprise in terms of the net receipts expressed in terms of cash or cash equivalent which the enterprise will provide over its life. Accounting, of course, considers individual assets as valuation units, and the sum of the asset values is one measure of the value of the enterprise.

The Discounting Process. In valuing an enterprise many economists accept the concept of interest as a cost. They value the enterprise at the total net receipts which the enterprise will provide over its future life, after deducting the interest involved by having funds tied up in the enterprise. To illustrate, assume an enterprise to have a life of three years with an estimate of cash receipts in excess of cash disbursements of $1,000 each year for three years. After determining the total net receipts to be $3,000, an adjustment for the interest would be made to provide a valuation for the enterprise. The adjustment would be as follows:

First year net receipts are $1,000, but because this sum is not available until the end of the year, it is not worth that sum at the start of the year. That is, it would be necessary to wait one year to get the $1,000. If the interest rate is 10%, the $1,000 at the end of the year is equal to 110% of its value at the start of the year. The valuation of the first year's net receipts, as of the start of the year, would then be $1,000 divided by the

110%, or approximately $909. Applying this procedure to the second year's net receipts a present value at the start of the first year of the second year's net receipts would be approximately $826. That is, it would be necessary to wait two years to get the second year's $1,000. The value of this $1,000 is even less than the value of the first year's $1,000, since the waiting would be twice as long to get it. Likewise, the third year's net receipts of $1,000 would have to be discounted back three years to get its present worth. The value today of $1,000 to be received three years hence is approximately $751 if the interest rate is 10%. The sum of these present values ($909 + $826 + $751, or $2,486) would be the valuation of the enterprise. Accountants need to be aware of the discounting concept in order to understand the differences between the two concepts in existence in the business world and when to use each valuation.

PROBLEMS

Problem 2–1. The following information relates to the purchase of an asset which was paid for by a trade-in of an old asset and the balance in cash:

List price of the new asset	$10,000
Cash payment	5,800
Cost of old asset	8,000
Depreciation accrued—old asset	5,000
Second hand market value—old asset	3,600

Required:

(1) You are to prepare entries to show three different methods of recording the transaction.

(2) Following each entry give an explanation of the reasoning behind that method of recording and indicate the circumstances in which it might be appropriate.   (AICPA adapted)

Problem 2–2. A commonly accepted method of inventory pricing, or costing, is last-in, first-out (LIFO). Under this method the assumption is made that goods sold come from those most recently acquired. This results in the cost of the most recently acquired goods being embodied in cost of sales. Likewise, the remaining inventory at any date will contain costs related to inventory acquired several periods earlier.

Required:

Discuss, in terms of the concepts presented in this chapter, the result of the LIFO method of inventory pricing insofar as valuation of the asset, inventory, is concerned.

Problem 2–3. (1) Present briefly the arguments for using each of the following valuation bases for reporting assets in the balance sheet:

(a) Market value or realizable value.

(b) Original cost, or original cost less estimated depreciation.

(c) Appraised value.

(2) Explain the relation of the "going concern concept" to each of the above bases of valuation. (AICPA adapted)

Problem 2–4. ABC Corporation purchased a machine in 1967, trading in an older machine of a similar type. The old machine, which was acquired in 1954, had a cost basis of $77,250 but was written up $47,750 to $125,000 in 1958 with a corresponding credit made to surplus from unrealized appreciation. In subsequent years this appreciation amount has been partially amortized. Both the old and new machines have an estimated 20-year life, and reappraisal of the old machine did not affect its estimated life. ABC Corporation takes one-half year of depreciation in years of acquisition and disposal.

The terms of purchase provided for a trade-in allowance of $25,000 and called for a cash payment of $125,000 or 12 monthly payments of $11,000 each. ABC Corporation chose to accept the latter alternative. Other expenses incurred in connection with the exchange were as follows:

Payroll charges:	
Removal of old machine	$ 800
Repairs to factory floor	700
Installation of new machine	900
Invoices received:	
Sales engineer who supervised installation	
40 hours at $10.00	400
Hotel, meals, travel, etc. for sales engineer	200
Freight in—new machine	1,100
Freight out—old machine	1,000

Required:

Prepare entries to reflect the exchange on the books of ABC on a basis acceptable for federal income tax purposes. Show all computations clearly labeled. (AICPA adapted)

Problem 2–5. Messrs. R. T. Robbins and C. A. Taylor decide to go into partnership. The two partners contribute the assets listed below and accept the values indicated:

	Robbins' Valuation	Taylor's Valuation	Accepted for Partnership
Cash	$10,000	$10,000	$ 20,000
Building	40,000	–0–	60,000
Merchandise		12,000	12,000
Equipment		10,000	28,000
Goodwill		1,000	5,000
Total	$50,000	$33,000	$125,000

Required:

(1) If Taylor were forming a sole proprietorship, should the $1,000 of goodwill Mr. Taylor believes he has be accepted as an asset?

(2) Give the entry to record the formation of the partnership.

Problem 2–6. N. M. Cleary and W. B. Bonnell operated separate proprietorships with results for 1967, considered typical, as follows:

December 31, 1967	Cleary	Bonnell
Total assets	$100,000	$120,000
Liabilities	10,000	20,000
Proprietorship	$ 90,000	$100,000
Earnings in 1967	$ 18,000	$ 15,000

As separate businesses, the two companies earned a total of $33,000 ($18,000 plus $15,000). Both men agree if the two companies were combined as a partnership, total income would increase about $6,000 to an average of $39,000. The partners agree the excess $6,000 would be contributed equally by each company.

The two men decide to form the partnership. They believe an appropriate rate of return for the partnership would be 15%. From this they conclude that if $39,000 represents 15%, 100% of the business would be $260,000. Since the combined net assets of the separate companies is only $190,000 ($90,000 + $100,000), the partners agree to recognize $70,000 of goodwill.

Required:
Give the entries to set up the partnership books.

Problem 2–7. V. N. Smith and A. K. Brown own separate businesses with operating results substantially as follows:

	Smith	Brown
Assets	$80,000	$30,000
Liabilities	none	none
Proprietorship	$80,000	$30,000
Earnings each year	$ 8,000	$ 8,000

It is agreed by both men that Mr. Brown's high earnings, $8,000 a year on a $30,000 investment, is due to the goodwill which attaches to his company.

The men agree that upon the formation of a partnership, the $50,000 of goodwill which they decide Mr. Brown has (calculated by assuming the $8,000 represents a 10% return on the investment, so 100% of the investment would be $80,000 of which $30,000 is represented by tangible assets leaving $50,000 of goodwill) should be considered but they do not want to put it on the books. They decide to have Mr. Smith give Mr. Brown a bonus of an appropriate amount when the partnership is formed and to recognize no goodwill.

Required:
(1) Give the entry to record the formation of the partnership.
(2) Discuss the appropriateness of the bonus procedure.

Problem 2–8. The Alpha Company purchased a store building for $100,000. Immediately thereafter $10,000 was spent to remodel the store front. In the opinion of competent real estate firms, the expenditure of this additional $10,000 did not add to the "resale-value" of the building—that is, this building which was purchased for $100,000 could not be resold for more than that amount, even though the additional $10,000 was spent in improving the store front.

What is your advice regarding the accounting treatment of this $10,000 expenditure? *Discuss fully.*   (AICPA adapted)

Problem 2–9. A small but growing road building contractor would like to bid on a contract to rebuild and surface 10.6 miles of road. The job is considerably larger than any he has attempted in the past and, if he wins the contract, he estimates that he will need a $100,000 line of credit for working capital.

The contractor's most recent statement of financial position shows that he has a net worth of $170,000, of which $110,000 represents the book value of road building equipment. Most of the equipment was acquired a few years ago at a bankruptcy sale. The equipment has a fair value several times as great as book value.

The contractor knows that his bank will not give him a $100,000 line of credit on the basis of a position statement (balance sheet) which shows his net worth at $170,000. He wants to adjust his accounting records to show the current fair value of the equipment and to prepare a revised position statement.

Required:
(1) List the factors that, alone or in combination, may have caused the difference between the book value and the current fair value of the equipment.
(2) The current fair value of fixed assets may be estimated by using one of the following methods:
(*a*) Reproduction cost.
(*b*) Replacement cost.
(*c*) Capitalization of earnings.
Describe each of the three methods of estimating the current fair value of fixed assets and discuss the possible limitations of each.
(3) Discuss the propriety of adjusting the accounting records to show the fair value of the equipment and of preparing a revised position statement.
                                                                (AICPA adapted)

Problem 2–10. The abbreviated balance sheet of the B. E. Ornot Company on December 31, 1967, appears as follows:

Current assets	$100,000	Liabilities	$ 80,000
Fixed assets	300,000	Stockholders' equity	320,000
	$400,000		$400,000

On this date the company signed a contract with a large company to take all of the output of the company for which the Ornot Company would be paid net receipts (receipts over cash disbursements) of $60,000 a year for an indefinite period in the future.

Required:
(1) Assuming money is worth 10%, what is the capitalized value of the assets of the Company?
(2) Account for the difference between the $400,000 valuation of the assets and the capitalized value.

Problem 2–11. Give the journal entry to record the following transactions:

(1) A sale was made in exchange for a $1,000 note receivable, bearing interest at 3% a year, due in one year. On the date of sale, the bank discount rate used for discounting notes receivable was 6%.

(2) On December 31, 1967, the Cam Company sold for $100,000 merchandise on account with terms of 2/10, n/30. The company prepares financial statements as of December 31 of each year. Annual sales of the company, if the $100,000 is included, will be $185,000.

Problem 2–12. Assume R. U. Semhi and I. C. Haff contributed the following assets to the partnership of Semhi and Haff.

	Semhi	Haff	Accepted for Partnership
Cash	$11,000	$12,000	$23,000
Building	18,000	–0–	25,000
Equipment	–0–	9,000	8,000
Goodwill	(Mr. Semhi knows a considerable number of future customers which will increase the earnings of the new partnership about $1,000 a year above what they would otherwise be. The two partners agree to value this intangible asset at an amount equal to 4 times the estimated excess earnings of $1,000.)		4,000
Total	$29,000	$21,000	$60,000

For purposes of the partnership, the assets contributed by each partner would be:

	Semhi	Haff
Cash	$11,000	$12,000
Building	25,000	–0–
Equipment	–0–	8,000
Goodwill	4,000	–0–
Total	$40,000	$20,000

The partners are reluctant to have goodwill on the books of the partnership.

Required:

Give the journal entries to record the formation of the partnership.

Problem 2–13. The Per Pet Yule Corporation was formed on July 1, 1967, by a charter from the Secretary of State, and was authorized to issue 100,000 shares of $50 par value common stock. The three incorporators, Messrs. Ace, Black, and Cash each contributed one section of land and each took 100 shares of stock in payment. On the date the land was turned over to the corporation, it had a fair-market value as follows:

	Fair-Market Value
Land contributed by Mr. Ace	$ 4,000
Land contributed by Mr. Black	3,800
Land contributed by Mr. Cash	4,100
Total	$11,900

Required:

(1) Mr. Ace suggests you value each section of land at $5,000 and issue the stock at par. As an accountant would you follow this procedure? Explain.

(2) Give the most appropriate entry to record the acquisition of the land and the issuance of the 300 shares of stock.

CHAPTER **3**

Valuation of equities

The sources of assets are normally set forth under the heading of equities. "Equities" is a broad term encompassing the investments by both creditors and owners in the enterprise, and thereby includes both the liabilities and the owners' equity in the enterprise. The term arose because of the emphasis in recent years of the similarity between creditors and owners. Numerous differences exist between liabilities and an owner's interest, but to the separate business enterprise an important overall similarity also exists in that both are essentially sources of funds needed to develop and operate the company. While we shall have to consider separately the different types of equities, it is possible to draw together certain problems of valuation common to all types of equities.

EQUITIES AS CLAIMS VS. EQUITIES AS SOURCES

Valuation of Creditorship Equities

Possibly the basic unsettled question in the valuation of equities is whether equities represent (1) a claim to the assets of an enterprise, or (2) a statement of the sources of the assets of the business. The distinction between the two points of view may be illustrated by assuming that a firm issues $100,000 of bonds at a discount of $5,000, so that the company receives only $95,000 in cash. Whether equities are considered a claim to assets or a record of the source of assets, the entry to record the issuance of the bonds is normally:

Cash	$95,000	
Discount on bonds payable	5,000	
Bonds payable		$100,000

The distinction between the two views arises when the results of this transaction are to be presented on a balance sheet. If the creditorship equity is considered to represent the source of assets, and if the sale of the bonds has provided only $95,000 in cash, it appears that the bond discount should properly be shown on the balance sheet as a deduction from bonds payable, as follows:

Assets		Equities	
Cash	$95,000	Bonds payable	$100,000
		Less:	
	x x x x	Bond discount	5,000
		Bondholders' contribution	$95,000
	x x x x		x x x x
	XXXX		XXXX

On the other hand, if the equities are to be considered as claims to the assets, bonds payable may be shown at $100,000 (the amount of assets eventually to be claimed) and the bond discount treated as a type of prepaid interest:

Assets		Equities	
Cash	$95,000	Bonds payable	$100,000
Bond discount	5,000		
	x x x x		x x x x
	XXXX		XXXX

The procedure normally used in accounting practice is to treat bond discount as an asset classified as a deferred charge. Because this procedure is followed, it may be concluded that accountants feel creditorship equities should be valued in terms of claims to assets rather than as a record of the source of assets. Before accepting this conclusion, however, a student of accountancy should be aware of two limitations involved in the concept that creditorship equities should be valued in terms of the claim to assets. These limitations are:

(1) Adoption of the view that equities are claims to assets fails to distinguish among the varying dates at which equities will have to be paid.
(2) Adoption of the view that equities are claims to assets fails to recognize that the recording of all claims against assets, whenever due, is normally not a valid position of the accountant. Perhaps the best illustration of this limitation, discussed later in this chapter, is bond interest which will have to be paid in the future. Legally and contractually, bond interest represents a claim to company assets which will normally be paid before the maturity value of the bonds is paid. Yet accepted accounting procedures do involve recording the claim of the bonds but not the claim of bond interest until the interest has accrued.

Varying Maturity Dates. Since the various equities will be paid off at many different dates, on any given financial statement the equities reported are not always claims against the assets also reported. This becomes particularly evident when we recognize the going concern assumption, which accountants normally employ in financial statement presentation, implies possible payment out of future assets.

Varying Recognition Dates. It is seldom, if ever, appropriate accounting to report all the interest which will have to be paid on a bond issue as a liability at the date the bond is issued. However, from a claim point of view the total interest liability is just as valid a claim against assets as is the face amount of the bond. In fact, most of the interest liability will have to be paid off prior to the payment of the maturity amount of the bond. There exists, however, in accounting the principle that an equity cannot exist until the activity causing the existence of the equity has been recognized. This principle results in the recognition of similar liabilities at different dates dependent upon the circumstances in a given situation.

At this point we might summarize the current accounting practice regarding creditorship equities by stating that accountants generally appear to view these equities as claims to assets rather than as sources of assets. However, since accountants do not show *all* claims to assets of an enterprise on a given balance sheet, it is apparent that all claims to assets are not included among the equities. Thus, a more accurate summary might be that, to the extent creditorship equities are recognized on a balance sheet, accountants tend to conceive of them as claims to the assets also reported.

Time of Retirement. The failure of accountants to distinguish between the amount of claim in existence at the reporting date and the amount which will have to be paid off ultimately also influences the valuation of the equities. To illustrate, assume Company X purchased merchandise on account at an invoice amount of $1,000, terms 2/10, n/30. This purchase may be recorded:

Purchases (merchandise)	$1,000	
Accounts payable		$1,000

If financial statements are to be prepared on the day following the purchase, a question arises as to the correct valuation of the accounts payable. On the reporting date the correct liability is $980, but if the company never takes discounts, or if there is no intention to take this discount, the amount which will ultimately have to be paid is $1,000. Current accounting practice would sanction the reporting of a liability of either $1,000 or of $980 on the grounds that the difference is not material. The amount reported would generally be determined by the method of recording the liability initially, gross or net.

On the other hand, assume the liability is in the form of bonds payable which are callable on the balance sheet date for $105,000, but which have an ultimate maturity amount due of $100,000. Here a question may arise as to the proper amount which should be used for valuing the liability. Normally, accountants have assumed a going concern point of view and have valued the bonds at the maturity amount. If there was a definite intention to call the bonds shortly after the balance sheet date, the call price of $105,000 would likely be used. Likewise, even though the current market price of the bonds may indicate that the bonds could, at least in part, be retired well below the maturity value of the bonds, accountants would report the liability at the maturity value in the absence of clear evidence of an intent to retire the bonds.

Valuation of Owners' Equities

As indicated above, the valuation of liabilities tends to run in terms of ultimate claims against assets which the equity commands. The reverse is true of the owners' equity. While there is not complete agreement, considerable support exists for the view that shareholders' equity should be valued in terms of the contributions made by the equity holders. Typical of this treatment is the accounting procedure of presenting preferred stock on the balance sheet at par less applicable discount on the stock. A similar example is found in the failure to include as a portion of preferred stock equity any dividend in arrears which may exist until the dividend is declared payable by the board of directors of the company. The fact that accountants do accept the source point of view in valuing ownership equities may be illustrated by assuming that a corporation issues 1,000 shares of $100 par preferred stock at $98 per share. The entry to record the sale of this stock would be:

Cash	$98,000	
Discount on preferred stock	2,000	
Preferred stock		$100,000

The point of view that ownership equities are valued to represent the source of assets is revealed by the proper balance sheet presentation of the above example, which indicates that $98,000 was contributed by stock-holders, as follows:

Assets		Equities	
Cash	$98,000	Preferred stock $100,000	
		Less:	
		Discount on sale 2,000	
		Shareholders' contribution	$98,000
	$98,000		$98,000

By way of emphasis, it may be recalled that had the foregoing transaction involved the issuance of bonds, the normal valuation of the bonds payable would have been $100,000, and the discount would have been treated as an asset in the nature of prepaid interest.

Source vs. Claim—Summarization

By what is done in the practice of accounting there is evidence that accountants value creditorship or liability equities as claims against the enterprise present or future assets. There is no implication that the claim attaches only to the assets currently recorded by the accountant. When it is apparent that liability equities will be paid from currently recorded assets, there is a tendency to value such equities at an amount equal to the claim existing at the reporting date. It is not uncommon, however, to find departures from this concept when the amount involved is not material. Thus, cash discounts available on unpaid accounts payable are usually disregarded in arriving at the financial statement valuation for accounts payable.

On the other hand, when the liability will in all probability be paid out of the future assets of the enterprise, customary accounting practice values the claim at the amount which will ultimately have to be paid, as in the case of long-term debt. Accompanying this valuation of long-term liabilities is the view that a liability should not be recognized if prior to its payment there will be a contribution of services or assets to the enterprise by action of the equity interest. Thus, wages to be paid employees for work in the near future do not become a liability until the employees render the services required. Similarly, bond interest does not become a liability until the money borrowed has been used for the period of time for which the interest accrues.

The view that ownership equities should be valued from the source of assets point of view is the general rule in accounting practice. However, a tendency still exists in the laws of the various states to consider accumulated earnings in the nature of a claim to assets.

Lease Liabilities

Commitments of a business enterprise under long-term lease agreements pose a variety of accounting problems. Traditionally, accounting for such leases involved simply an entry to record the annual rental payments. Gradually, disclosure of lease obligations in financial statement footnotes gained a measure of acceptance. Recognition has come more recently that some leases are in essence installment purchases of property and that these leases should be accounted for in relation to their substance as a purchase. A problem arises here, however, in determining the valuation to attach to the lease.

One approach to accounting for leases which are in substance installment purchases is to capitalize the discounted amount of the future lease rental payments as both an asset and a liability. This procedure, recommended in *Opinion 5* of the AICPA Accounting Principles Board, proposes inclusion of certain lease obligations as liabilities on the statement of financial position. The rationale for this accounting procedure lies in the fact that leases have increasingly come to be used as a financing vehicle for the acquisition of long-lived service resources. Recognition of the total obligation under the lease terms on a discounted basis appears to represent a better accounting procedure for certain leases than either footnote disclosure or a simple entry to record rental payments.

Estimated Liabilities

Another example of an apparent departure from general principles in accounting for liabilities lies in the area of estimated liabilities. These liabilities represent claims which are expected to fall due in the future, even though at the reporting date the exact amount of the claim may not be known. While no liability in the legal sense may exist at the reporting date—based on past transactions and experience, as well as on future expectations—recognition of the estimated liability can be justified.

A common situation indicating recognition of an estimated liability evolves from selling products under terms including a money-back guarantee. At any year end it is evident that some refund claims will be made in the future on sales agreements entered into during the past year. Based on past experience, expected sales volume, and other variables, an estimate can be determined for future refunds from the past year's sales. The amount so determined will be reported on the statement of financial position as a liability (Estimated Liability on Product Guarantee) and in the income statement as an expense (Loss on Product Guarantee).

The Estimated Liability on Product Guarantee is similar to other creditorship equities in that it more closely represents a claim on assets than a source of assets. Other estimated liabilities are sometimes reported in a similar manner on the statement of financial position. Thus, liabilities under pension plans and tax obligations are at times based upon estimates and reported as liabilities even though actual amounts due may not be known accurately.

As was noted in the discussion on lease liabilities, recognition of certain liabilities at estimated amounts appears to represent a sound accounting procedure. While not all the normal tests of liability classification are met by lease commitments or by various estimated claims, financial reporting appears to be more complete with inclusion of these items as liabilities.

CLASSIFICATION OF EQUITIES

Classification of Liabilities

There are numerous possibilities as to how liabilities might be classified. They may be classified:

(1) According to the time when due for payment.
(2) By the name of the entity to whom payment will be made.
(3) According to the nature of the document evidencing the liability.

There seems to be some agreement, as far as published reports are concerned, that liabilities should be classified according to the nature of the liability, such as accounts payable, notes payable, bonds payable, accrued items, and special items payable by a descriptive title. For balance sheet purposes these items are then grouped under the headings of current or long-term liabilities. These classifications are considered more extensively in elementary and intermediate accounting textbooks.

Classification of Ownership Equities—Proprietorship

The formation of a sole proprietorship normally involves the setting aside of assets by an individual to be used in the business enterprise. The valuation of such assets is the sum of the valuation of all the assets contributed to the enterprise, and this sum in turn measures the valuation of the proprietor's capital account. Thus, the capital account is measured by the valuation of the assets contributed to the enterprise and is a reflection of the source of certain of the assets to the firm.

To a creditor, the capital account of the proprietorship is a reflection of the investment of the proprietor which may be expected to remain in the enterprise on a rather permanent basis. A *personal* account separate from the capital account is normally used to record current withdrawals and the accumulation of earnings to be withdrawn.

The income earned by the proprietorship should be credited to the personal account if such income is to be withdrawn or has previously been withdrawn. Should it become apparent that any credit or debit balances in the personal account are permanent or intended to be permanent, such balances should be transferred to the capital account.

It is sometimes contended that the personal account should always be closed out to the capital account and the separate classification of the two elements of proprietor equity abandoned, because a sole proprietor is personally liable for all debts of the business. However, creditors are frequently not only interested in the debt-paying ability of the owner of the business, but also are interested in the debt-paying ability of the business as a separate entity. Many reasons may explain this point of view, but the fact that such a view does exist suggests that the capital account of the enterprise should reflect only the more or less permanent capital of the firm.

Classification of Ownership Equities—Partnership

Like the sole proprietor's equity accounts, each partner in a partnership should have his equity interest disclosed by using two accounts: a capital account and a drawing (or personal) account. In the balance sheet these two accounts might be presented as follows:

Assets		Equities		
Various	x x x x x x	Liabilities		x x x x x x
		Owners' equity:		
		A, Capital	x x x x x	
		A, Drawing (credit)	x x x x	x x x x x
		B, Capital	x x x x x	
		B, Drawing (debit)	x x x x	x x x x x
	XXXXXX			XXXXXX

At the time of formation of a partnership the partnership agreement sometimes provides that the partners shall share in profits and losses of the enterprise in a ratio different from their capital contributions. This type of agreement may present a problem of determining the proper valuation in the capital accounts of the partners. Other problems resulting from this situation will be discussed in later chapters dealing with the distribution of partnership income.

Assume that A and B form a partnership, with A contributing $40,000 and B contributing $20,000 with the understanding that profits and losses are to be shared equally. In recording the contribution by the partners, accountants would ignore the profit-and-loss sharing agreement and would record the capital contributions, as follows:

Assets	$60,000	
A, Capital		$40,000
B, Capital		20,000

Partners' Capital and Risk. Care should be taken, however, in interpreting the meaning of such recording. The above capital balances do not mean that A is risking $40,000 and B only $20,000. To the extent that B does have additional personal assets, which may be needed to settle partnership claims, he may be assuming a risk greater than indicated by the $20,000 investment. This may be illustrated by assuming that the partnership loses the entire $60,000. The loss would be distributed equally to the partners in accordance with the profit-and-loss ratio, as follows:

A, Capital (Drawing)	$30,000	
B, Capital (Drawing)	30,000	
Assets		$60,000

As a result of this distribution of the loss, the capital accounts of the partners appear as follows:

A, Capital		B, Capital	
$30,000	$40,000	$30,000	$20,000

Thus, B owes the partnership the sum of $10,000, while A has a capital claim of $10,000. The final result of the partnership would be that B would contribute $10,000 of his personal assets to satisfy his debt to the partnership, and A would take this $10,000 in settlement of his claim against the partnership. Thus, each partner would bear the risk of the partnership in accordance with the profit-and-loss sharing ratio.

Valuation of Partners' Capital. A well-established accounting procedure is to record partnership equities at an amount equal to the contribution made by the partners. In those situations where partners contribute assets other than cash, certain problems may arise in applying this rule. From the preceding chapter we know that assets should be valued at their fair market value at the time of their contribution to the partnership. The determination of fair market value, however, often involves an estimation and is therefore frequently subject to question. As a result, the accountant should have the partners reach an agreement on the valuation of the assets contributed by each partner before attempting to provide a valuation of the respective capital accounts of the partners. To illustrate, assume A contributes assets with a market valuation of $10,000 and B contributes assets with a fair market valuation of $15,000. A contends and B agrees, however, that to the partnership the special type of assets contributed by A are worth $12,000. The fact that the two partners agree is normally presumptive evidence that the $12,000 valuation is appropriate, and A should be given credit in his capital account for the $12,000 contribution. The following entry reflects the agreement reached:

Assets	$27,000	
A, Capital		$12,000
B, Capital		15,000

In some instances, however, the evidence may clearly indicate that the $12,000 value is not proper, that the assets contributed by A have a fair market value of only $10,000, and that the agreement between A and B is in reality an agreement that B is giving A a bonus for joining the partnership. Here, a revaluation of the assets might not be appropriate, but the capital accounts should be divided on the ratio agreed upon by the partners. Thus, in the example in the previous paragraph, the partners may agree that A is to receive 12/27 of the capital contribution and B is to receive 15/27. The fair value of the total assets contributed would be $25,000, and A would receive credit for more than his $10,000 because of the bonus received, while B would receive credit for less than his $15,000 contribution because of the bonus given. The following entry reflects this distribution:

Assets	$25,000	
A, Capital		$11,111.11
B, Capital		13,888.89

Some accountants would contend that the valuation in the previous situation can best be accomplished by recognizing as goodwill the difference between the fair market value of the assets contributed by the partners and the value agreed upon by the partners. In the above example, the goodwill would be $2,000 ($27,000 − $25,000). But, unless the income and loss sharing ratio is the same as the capital ratio, the $2,000 as it is written off will be charged against the partners in a proportion different from that used under the bonus procedure. However, the goodwill alternative is seldom used for situations of this kind. Normally, the valuation agreed upon by the partners is acceptable, but if the accountant has reason to question such a valuation, he should encourage the partners to use the bonus procedure indicated above, since it would be more satisfactory and equitable to each of the partners.

Classification of Ownership Equities—Corporation

While there is some agreement that corporation ownership equities should be valued at an amount equal to the assets contributed to the enterprise, with the ownership equities thereby being treated as a record of the source of assets, several problems arise in determining the accounts to be used and the method of presenting the accounts in the balance sheet.

The shares of stock evidencing ownership equity of a corporation are frequently assigned a par or stated value. These shares may then be issued to the shareholders for assets valued at an amount other than the par or stated value of the stock issued. In this type of situation the difference between the par or stated value of the stock issued and the value of the assets received is normally recorded by the use of an adjunct or contra account to the capital stock account.

From an accounting point of view there seems to be little reason to use adjunct and contra accounts. The asset contribution of the shareholders could be reported in the capital stock account, with this account then reflecting the owners' equity from assets contributed. However, the procedure is well established in practice, and in addition has legal backing in many states. The legal support undoubtedly lends impetus to its continuance in accounting practice. The legal implication normally associated with the procedure is that par or stated value per share represents the permanent capital of the corporation. This permanent capital serves as a buffer of protection for the creditors of the enterprise, since it cannot be distributed legally in the form of dividends and thereby weaken the security behind any loan extended by a creditor. In many states any asset contribution by the shareholders in excess of the par or stated value of the stock issued is available for certain types of dividend distribution. This excess appears to have less permanence as capital than does the par or stated value.

Financing the Enterprise

The problem of suitable financing for a business enterprise is most complex, and the role of accounting in this analysis is necessarily involved. The student of accountancy must of necessity be somewhat familiar with the overall problem. Essentially, the question involved is the source from which the business enterprise should derive its assets for operational purposes. Contributing to the complexity of the problem is the practical fact that for most corporate enterprises no one source will provide all the funds needed by the enterprise. Normally, creditors will not supply all the funds, either on policy grounds or because of the risk involved. Thus, for most enterprises some funds must be acquired from the owners of the business before creditors will make loans. But the amount to be derived from creditors versus the amount to be acquired from owners is only a small aspect of the problem, for there are various types of creditor loans with varying degrees of maturity and with varying types of security, and in addition there are varying types of ownership equities. Further, the most suitable financing arrangement for one firm is not necessarily the most appropriate for even another similar firm. Financing plans will differ among industries and among enterprises within any given industry.

Trading on the Equity. Normally, the financing plan adopted will have to be initiated by representatives of the owners of the enterprise. While the owners might desire to rely rather heavily on creditor financing, through bonds or long- or medium-term bank notes, for example, the owners must recognize that excessive financing with creditor money means assumption of heavy, and possibly excessive, risk by the owners. Most creditor financing carries with it a heavy risk of loss by the owners if interest payments are not maintained. Recognizing this risk element which is a part of creditor financing, the owners might decide to finance largely or fully with owner capital. While heavy utilization of owner financing (sometimes called equity financing) may reduce the risk element, enterprise owners must recognize that it may also reduce their rate of return on invested capital. If an enterprise is able to earn a higher rate of return on all its assets than it is necessary to pay in interest for creditor financing, there is a definite incentive to finance in part through use of creditor financing. An example may demonstrate this more clearly.

Assume that Company A acquires assets of $100,000 by issuing $80,000 of bonds and $20,000 of stock. Assume the bonds bear interest at 5%. If the company should earn exactly 5% on the $100,000, or $5,000, the bondholders and the stockholders would receive an identical return on their respective investments:

	Bonds (5%)	Stock
Amount of financing	$80,000	$20,000
Portion of $5,000 return on assets	4,000	1,000
Rate of return on investment	5%	5%

Now assume the enterprise earns $6,000 on its assets, an increase of 20% over the amount earned in the first example. The creditors (bondholders) will still receive $4,000 in interest, and the remaining $2,000 will be applicable to the owners (stockholders). This $2,000 return on the $20,000 owner investment will mean a return to the owners of 10%, or twice as much as in the above example, on invested capital:

	Bonds (5%)	Stock
Amount of financing	$80,000	$20,000
Portion of $6,000 return on assets	4,000	2,000
Rate of return on investment	5%	10%

Thus borrowing at 5% in order to earn 6% on the assets borrowed proved to be advantageous to the owners.

On the other hand, if earnings decreased 20% from those in the first example, to $4,000, the owners would earn nothing on their investment, as the entire $4,000 would be needed to pay the bondholders their interest:

	Bonds (5%)	Stock
Amount of financing	$80,000	$20,000
Portion of $4,000 return on assets	4,000	-0-
Rate of return on investment	5%	-0-

Here, borrowing at 5% in order to earn 4% on the assets borrowed does not prove to be advantageous to the owners.

This process of financing the enterprise by borrowing, whereby the owners undergo the risk of excessive loss or excessive gain, is known as trading on the equity or *leverage*. Excessive trading on the equity (excessive borrowing) can make investment in stock quite a risky undertaking.

Short-term vs. Long-term Financing. The question of whether borrowing should be on a short-term or a long-term basis largely resolves itself into the length of time required to convert the assets acquired back into a liquid form. If the assets are to be converted back into cash through sale in the near future, as in the case of merchandise, short-term financing may be appropriate. On the other hand, if the assets acquired will not be sold or used up in production within a relatively short period of time, short-term financing might be inappropriate. Thus, the acquisition of long-lived assets is commonly financed by long-term borrowing.

In summary, the decision on the most appropriate method of financing depends, in part at least, upon (1) the prospects that the firm will have funds available to repay the financing source when due, and (2) the prospects of having stable and sufficient earnings to cover the cost of carrying the obligation, in the form of interest or dividend payments. While the final decision on the financing plan rests upon the owners of the enterprise, both as to type and length of the financing, the accountant can render valuable service to the owners through preparation of analyses disclosing the effects, both short-term and long-term, of the alternative plans under consideration.

Variations in Classification of Shareholders' Equity

The presentation of the status of the equities of a business enterprise to interested parties is normally accomplished through the use of the balance sheet. On the balance sheet, however, the equities are frequently classified in a manner different from what might be expected by a strict application of accounting concepts. The classification of equities in practice results from attempts to reveal various types of information about the enterprise, not all of which are accounting oriented. As an illustration of this, there is a tendency in the law to assume that the capital stock of the corporation represents a buffer of assets which cannot be reduced until the creditors are satisfied. This means that no distribution to stockholders should be made which would result in the reduction of the capital stock below its legal amount. Implementation of this concept would require that premium and discount on capital stock, treasury stock, and other adjunct and contra items to the capital stock account should be separately disclosed, possibly in the following manner:

Shareholders' equity:

Capital stock (1,000 shares, $100 par)		$100,000
Capital surplus:		
Premium on stock sold	$ 4,000	
Less: Discount on stock sold	1,000	
	3,000	
Surplus from appraisal of assets	12,000	
Total	15,000	

Retained earnings:
Accumulated earnings	$12,000	
Less: Treasury stock (at cost)	4,000	
Unrestricted		8,000
Total surplus		23,000
Total Shareholders' equity		$123,000

This type of presentation of the shareholders' equity conveys the impression that capital stock of $100,000 is permanently invested in the business and will not be withdrawn until liquidation. As such, it serves as a buffer of protection for creditors in that losses by the firm up to $100,000 could be absorbed by the company before the creditors would be unable to get back their loaned money.

If the state law provides that dividends cannot be paid out of capital surplus, the effect is to include the capital surplus as part of the buffer protection for the creditors. Capital surplus presented under such laws would properly be included as part of permanent capital. Thus in the preceding illustration the $15,000 capital surplus could be added to the capital stock to give a permanent capital equity of $115,000.

Currently, the trend in shareholder equity presentation utilizes accounting concepts rather than to attempt to comply rigidly with the legal aspects of net worth. The result is an attempt to classify shareholder equity items either as contributed capital or as accumulated earnings. Thus, a revision of the shareholders' equity section presented above might be:

Shareholders' equity:
Capital stock (1,000 shares, $100 par)		$100,000
Less: Treasury stock (at par)		4,000
Capital stock outstanding, at par		96,000
Premium on stock sold	$4,000	
Less: Discount on stock sold	1,000	3,000
Contributed capital		99,000
Surplus from appraisal of assets		12,000
Retained earnings:		
Restricted by treasury stock	$4,000	
Unrestricted	8,000	
Total Retained earnings		12,000
Total Shareholders' equity		$123,000

Supplementary Data

Whatever the classification used in a financial statement the purpose determines the appropriate presentation. Quite recently there has developed an attempt to provide additional information to stockholders to supplement the data provided in the balance sheet. This development seems to have arisen in part because of the wide variation between book value and market value of shares of stock. There are, of course, several reasons for the variation between book value and market value. In part, the difference may arise from company policy as to the capital versus maintenance charges of the firm—some capital investments are often charged off as maintenance expense, or vice versa—and to overcome any question of this point, a statement of the capital maintenance policy of the firm is sometimes included in the reports to shareholders. Unrecognized appreciation of assets may also contribute to a variation between book value and market value per share. Indication of the unrealized appreciation of assets is sometimes made in financial statements by reporting the dates at which specific assets were purchased and also reporting specific and general index numbers to permit additional interpretation by the readers of the accounting reports. Other factors contributing to the variation between book value and market value, such as particularly promising sales market outlook for the future, are more difficult to disclose objectively.

While a definite trend in financial reporting is to disclose all material data necessary to make the statements not misleading, accountants still generally require "objective" evidence of its existence before reporting supplementary data. Informative disclosures present accountants with a real challenge in their efforts to improve financial reporting.

PROBLEMS

Problem 3–1. The Federal Land Banks issued $201,000,000, $3\frac{7}{8}\%$ Consolidated Federal Farm Loan Bonds, dated May 1, 1967, and due April 20, 1968, at $99\frac{7}{8}\%$. The bonds were the secured joint and several obligations of the twelve Federal Land Banks and were issued under the authority of the Federal Farm Loan Act as amended.

Required:
(1) Give the journal entry on the books of the Federal Land Banks to record the sale of the bonds.

Problem 3–2. An announcement carried in several newspapers in the early part of 1959 was as follows:

Black & Decker Co. announced the formation of a new subsidiary, Master Power Corp., which has acquired all the assets of Master Pneumatic Tool Co., Inc., of Bedford, Ohio, and its subsidiary, Master Pneumatic Tools (Canada), Ltd.

The acquisition, according to Robert Black, president and chairman of

Black and Decker Co., was made through the exchange of 34,004 shares of Black & Decker stock for the assets of Master Pneumatic. At recent prices, about $63 a share, the stock is valued at about $2,142,000.

Required:

(1) Journal entry on the books of the Master Power Corporation to record the acquisition. (Assume Master Power Corporation did not own the 34,004 shares of Black and Decker stock.)

Problem 3–3. Messrs. A, B, and C each went to a bank to borrow $100 cash, for 60 days. The bank charged each 6% annual interest. The three men elected to borrow as follows:

1. Mr. A decided to give the bank a $101.01 noninterest-bearing note payable which the bank discounted and gave Mr. A the $100.
2. Mr. B gave the bank a $100 note payable bearing interest at 6.06% a year which the bank discounted and gave Mr. B the $100.
3. Mr. C gave the bank a $100.50 note payable bearing interest at 3% a year which the bank discounted and gave Mr. C the $100.

Required:

(1) Give the journal entries to record the transaction on each man's books.
(2) What is the liability in each case
    (*a*) At the time the money is borrowed?
    (*b*) At the time the money is to be repaid?
(3) (*a*) What liability should be shown on each man's balance sheet immediately after borrowing the money?
    (*b*) Would your answer be different if $1,000,000 had been borrowed instead of $100? Explain.

Problem 3–4. The Horace Corporation has an opportunity to acquire a substantial amount of its raw materials at what it considers to be a favorable price. The terms of this purchase, the invoice price of which is $120,000, are 1/10, n/60. After expiration of 60 days, interest is charged by the supplier on any unpaid balance at the rate of $\frac{1}{2}$% per month. Since the Horace Corporation's operations are very seasonal in nature, the expectation is that it will be nine months from the date of this purchase before payment could be made.

The president of the Horace Corporation has arranged with his bankers to obtain a 9-month loan to cover this purchase. He would obtain this loan at 6% interest and receive the proceeds just in time to be entitled to his purchase discount. The face of the note would be equal to the amount due his supplier at that date.

Required:

(1) Is it advantageous to borrow at the bank? Support your answer.
(2) At what amount and in what manner should the liability for this purchase be reported (*a*) if the purchase is made on open account and (*b*) if the bank borrowing is utilized? Reconcile or rationalize any difference.
(3) At what amount should the purchase of materials be recorded under each alternative means of payment?
(4) Would your answer to (3) be different if the purchase involved machinery rather than raw materials? Why?

Problem 3–5. The Retail Department Store received a deposit from a customer of $300 in payment for a television set. Not having the television set on hand, the accountant made the following entry:

Cash	$300	
Customer's deposit liability		$300

Actually the $300 represents the price of the television set and a one-year service guarantee contract. It is estimated that the television set will cost $160 and the service guarantee will cost $40.

The department sales manager claims the only liability the company has is $200 ($160 and $40).

Required:
(1) Answer the sales manager's claim.
(2) Assume the television set is delivered, should the liability for the service contract be $40 or $60?

Problem 3–6. The Thursday Realty Company purchased land from Mr. R. T. Ring. The terms of the sale were that Mr. Ring would accept as payment a house owned by Thursday. On December 31, 1967, Mr. Ring had transferred the land, but the Realty Company had a liability on the date to deliver the house. The house had cost the company $20,000 three years ago and has an estimated fair market value on December 31, 1967, of $24,000. The land has an estimated fair market value of $24,500.

Required:
(1) What amount should be shown as the liability on the December 31, 1967, statement of financial position of the Thursday Company?
(2) Give the entry required when the land was transferred on December 27, 1967.
(3) Give the entry required to pay the liability on January 10, 1968, when the house is transferred to Mr. Ring.

Problem 3–7. (*a*) The Dawson Company sold a $1,000,000 par value issue of first mortgage bonds on July 1, 1967 at 98½. The bonds are due in 40 years and bear interest at an annual rate of 5%, interest payable each July 1. The Dawson Company has a June 30 fiscal year end.

Required:
(1) Prepare the journal entry to record the sale of bonds July 1, 1967.
(2) Discuss two alternative amounts to report as long-term bond liability immediately after the sale of the bonds.
(3) Determine all amounts to be reported on a balance sheet of the Dawson Company at June 30, 1968, and explain how they would be classified.
(4) How much interest will the Dawson Company pay over the life of the bonds? Since all of this interest is due and payable before the bonds themselves are due, why is the total interest to be paid not reported as a liability on each balance sheet date?

(*b*) The Pearson Company decides to create a real estate subsidiary to finance and construct a new office building for the Company. The building cost is estimated at $5,000,000. The Pearson Company signs a lease with its subsidiary for 25 years with an option to renew for a like period. The rental rate per year is $450,000, payable one year in advance on each January 2.

Required:

(1) What amount will the Pearson Company report in its income statement each year as the cost of using this building? What item or items is it likely this amount replaces in an income statement if the Pearson Company owned the building?

(2) In a balance sheet of the Pearson Company at each December 31 what liability will be reported in connection with this building and/or its lease?

(3) If this transaction were considered to be, in essence, a purchase of the building, how should the transaction be given effect in the Pearson Company financial statements?

Problem 3–8. Jones and Smith decide to form a partnership, and to share income or loss equally. Assets contributed to the partnership, valued at fair market value, were: Jones, $20,000; Smith $12,000. Partners agree the total ownership equity is to be $32,000 ($20,000 plus $12,000). Both recognize, however, that Smith is also bringing in goodwill of $6,400. They request that the "bonus" procedure be used to provide an equitable determination of partners' capital accounts.

Required:

(1) Should the $6,400 be allocated to partners in the capital ratio or the income-or-loss ratio? Demonstrate by assuming the goodwill will last two years and income before amortization of goodwill is $5,000 each year.

(2) Give the journal entry to record the formation of the partnership.

Problem 3–9. Income taxes have been 40% of income before income taxes. The ABC Company's earnings after taxes have averaged $3,000 on a $100,000 capital stock. The company is considering refinancing by issuing $50,000 of 4% bonds and reducing capital stock by $50,000 (i.e., the stockholders would exchange $50,000 of stock for $50,000 of bonds).

Required:

(1) Compute:

   (*a*) The change in company income after taxes by adopting the refinancing plan.

   (*b*) The change in the rate of return on the capital stock.

   (*c*) The change in the total dollar return accruing to the $100,000 investment in stock and bonds.

Problem 3–10. The Albert Holmes Company entered into a lease agreement according to which it would pay $20,000 a year for a 20-year lease on a building. One of the creditors contends the $400,000 ($20,000 times 20 years) is a liability. He points out that after 20 years the building will have no value. In effect, he claims the company bought the building and is paying for it at the rate of $20,000 a year and that the lease agreement is just like a bond liability and should be shown as a liability.

Required:

(1) Should the lease be shown as a liability? If so, what offsetting asset should be set up?

(2) Assuming the company could borrow or invest money for 5% annual interest and the company officials want to know how much money they would have to put up as one sum now to make the lease payments, compute the amount. (Refer to the present value of annuity tables in the appendix.)

Problem 3–11. The ownership interest in a corporation is customarily reported in the statement of financial position as stockholders' equity.

Required:

(1) List the principal transactions or items that reduce the amount of retained earnings. (Do not include appropriations of retained earnings.)

(2) In the stockholders' equity section of the balance sheet, a distinction is made between contributed capital and earned capital. Why is this distinction made? Discuss.

(3) There is frequently a difference between the purchase price and sale price of treasury stock, but accounting authorities agree that the purchase or sale of its own stock by a corporation cannot result in a profit or loss to the corporation. Why isn't the difference recognized as a profit or loss to the corporation? Discuss.   (AICPA adapted)

Problem 3–12. From the following information prepare the shareholders' equity section of the Roy Ann Company on December 31, 1967, according to (*A*) the legal aspects of the shareholders' equity and (*B*) contributed and earned equity.

Capital stock issued—1000 shares ($100 par)		$100,000
Premium on above issue		5,000
Retained earnings to 12/31/67	$80,000	
Less stock dividend issued (200 shares)	20,000	20,000
	60,000	
Balance, 12/31/67		60,000
Treasury stock (at cost) 200 shares		(19,000)
Total		$166,000

Problem 3–13. The Mulliken Co. operated in 1967 with assets having a book value of $5,000,000. These assets had been obtained as follows: initial contribution by shareholders, $2,000,000; earnings retained in prior years, $1,500,000; debts to trade creditors, including accruals, $700,000; an intermediate term bank loan at 5% for $800,000, dated January 15, 1966 and due December 31, 1970. Interest is paid annually.

In 1967 the Mulliken Co. reported net income after taxes of $245,000 on sales of $4,900,000. Its board of directors is contemplating a major productive expansion estimated to cost $1,500,000. If the decision is made to proceed with these plans, the facility will enter production at the end of 1968. It is expected to generate additional sales of $2,000,000 annually on which the return after depreciation—an interest element of 5% of the facility's cost—and taxes is expected to be 20% greater than on present sales.

Required:

(1) Calculate expected net income for 1969, assuming existing facilities are as profitable in 1969 as in 1967.

(2) Determine the advantage to shareholders of trading on the equity in 1967 if the Mulliken Company traded on the equity in that year.

(3) Determine the advantage to the shareholders of trading on the equity in 1969 assuming the expansion capital was borrowed at 5% and that in 1968 and 1969 the Mulliken Co. distributed net income of the prior year as dividends.

Problem 3–14. The Claire Company has the following financial plan:

Current liabilities (average interest cost, 1%)	$2,000,000
Long-term debt ($5\frac{1}{2}$%)	4,000,000
Common stock—contributed equity	4,000,000
Retained earnings	2,000,000

The Company's gross margin averages 30% of sales, and its operating expenses, including taxes but exclusive of interest, are 25% of sales. Dividends of $400,000 have been paid each of the past 6 years, being $4 per share. Sales average $15,000,000 per year.

The long-term debt is callable at par and is due in 12 years. The board of directors of the Claire Company is contemplating issuing additional stock to get the dollars to call the debt. It is expected that 40,000 shares would be needed.

Required:

(1) Prepare a proforma income statement prior to consideration of the additional stock issue.

(2) Determine the benefit, if any, to the shareholders from trading on the equity.

(3) Prepare a proforma income statement assuming the stock issue is made. Assume a 50% income tax rate is applicable.

(4) Determine the benefit, if any, to the shareholders from trading on the equity after the stock issue. Also determine the effect of the issue on return on shareholders' equity.

(5) Assuming the existing dividend rate is to be maintained, discuss the contemplated stock issue considering trading on the equity and cost of capital.

Note:

For additional problems see the Appendix—particularly Problems AP–12, 14, 15, 28, 30.

II

MAINTENANCE OF THE BUSINESS ORGANIZATION

CHAPTER 4

Accounting for insurable business risks

The formation of an organization is the first step in the successful operations of a business. Once the business organization has been successfully formed, management must then direct its efforts to maintaining that organization if the business is to continue operations. Maintenance of a business involves not only profitable operations on a current basis but also providing for business risks, effectively administering income, and maintaining the business as a unified operating unit.

The first three chapters of this textbook have been directed to the problems arising from the formation of a business organization. Some of the accounting problems involved in recording the operations of a business are covered in intermediate accounting. The accounting aspects of other features that accompany the maintaining of the business organization are covered in the next three chapters of this text.

Possibly the most involved feature encountered by management in maintaining a business is the element of risk. Business organizations constantly face the risk of loss—loss of assets by fire, storm, theft, accident, or other casualties; loss of employees by sickness, accident, or death; and loss of earning power by changes in product demand or technological change. Any single loss may be ruinous if the resulting financial burden falls entirely upon the individual firm concerned. In modern society, however, many of these risks may be shifted, for a fee, to a burden-assuming organization. These risks are usually referred to as insurable risks.

The problem of risk management is most involved. To place the accounting features of the problem in proper perspective, a distinction should be made between losses due to uncertainty—i.e. losses of such an unusual nature that they cannot be anticipated, and losses due to risk —i.e. losses which past experience indicates can be predicted within a long period of time.

This chapter is confined to the accounting problems involved in handling *risk*. That is, it is confined to a discussion of the usual risks that a business enterprise entertains because of its existence and continuation. For discussion purposes these risks are classified as:

(1) Insurable asset risks.
(2) Insurable employee risks.
(3) Miscellaneous insurable risks.

INSURABLE ASSET RISKS

It is more or less general practice for business concerns to insure their destructible assets against loss by fire, storm, theft, accident, and other casualties with an insurance company. However, there are exceptions where business organizations for one reason or another assume their own insurable risks rather than pay someone else to assume them. The accounting aspect of self-insurance is covered in a separate section of this chapter.

When an insured asset is damaged, destroyed, or lost—as, for example, when an insured building burns—the relevant accounts must be adjusted and settlement with the insurance company must be effected. The maximum amount recoverable, according to the standard insurance policy, is the cash value of the asset involved, or what it would cost to repair or replace it, with due allowance for the condition of the asset on the date of destruction, damage, or loss. This maximum recoverable amount is frequently referred to as the replacement value of the property, and is, for insurance purposes, termed "insurable value." Regardless of the face amount of the policy, therefore, the insured cannot legally expect to recover more from the insurance company than the insurable value. In the event that the insured and insurer cannot agree as to the insurable value, such value is determined by appraisers as provided for in the policy. In some instances the amount recoverable is also limited by some special feature such as a "deductible clause" in the case of automobile insurance or a "co-insurance clause" in the case of fire insurance.

Fire Insurance

The purpose of fire insurance, of course, is to protect the insured against loss resulting from a fire. A particular fire loss is predicated on the sound value of the property involved at the time the loss is sustained and not at the time of issuance of the insurance policy. The insurance company, in most instances, is liable for any loss caused directly or indirectly by the fire. Thus, a loss sustained by the insured from smoke, water, removal damage, or falling walls is usually covered, as well as any direct loss from the fire. However, only property which is specifically included in the policy is protected. Fire insurance coverage may be obtained for buildings, building contents (such as machinery, equipment, and inventories), and other miscellaneous property. The accounting treatment necessary when insurance premiums are purchased and amortized is normally considered in elementary textbooks.

Fire Loss Account

In the event of fire, as previously indicated, all relevant accounts must be adjusted and settlement with the insurance company effected. In order to centralize the accounting involved when a fire occurs a "Fire Loss" account is generally used. This account, which is a special profit and loss account, is charged with all costs and expenses and credited with all revenues resulting from the fire in order to measure the net effect of the fire. Thus, the essential features of this account are similar to the usual profit and loss summary account. A typical Fire Loss account is:

Debited for:
  (1) Book value of fixed assets destroyed or damaged.
  (2) Book value or estimated cost of inventories destroyed or damaged.
  (3) Expense related to the fire.
Credited for:
  (1) Salvage.
  (2) Insurance settlement.

Book Value of Fixed Assets Destroyed or Damaged. Since the Fire Loss account is charged with all costs and expenses related to a particular fire loss, the undepreciated cost of any fixed asset involved should be closed to this account. The undepreciated cost, frequently termed "book" or "carrying" value, is, of course, the difference between the cost of the asset and the accumulated depreciation, which is the balance in the accrued depreciation account if this account is up to date. Consequently, the asset and the related accumulated depreciation must both be transferred to the Fire Loss account. This is usually accomplished by using a compound entry such as the following (assuming that a building which originally cost $100,000, with an estimated useful life of 20 years and no anticipated scrap value, is destroyed by fire at the end of the 15th year):

Fire loss	$25,000	
Accrued depreciation of building	75,000	
Building		$100,000

Book Value or Estimated Cost of Inventories Destroyed or Damaged.

If the Fire Loss account is to be debited for all costs and expenses of a particular fire, the cost of any inventory destroyed should be closed to this account. The determination of the cost to be transferred to the Fire Loss account depends upon the system of inventory accounting in use. If a good perpetual system is in use, the determination of book value is relatively simple since the stock ledger cards and other records provide the necessary information. However, in instances where inventories are accounted for on a periodical basis only, the problem may be more difficult since it may be neither feasible nor possible to take a physical count.

When the only inventory system in use is a periodical one, there is at least one method which permits the computation of an estimated inventory valuation without a physical count. It is frequently referred to as the "gross profit method" or gross profit test. The gross profit method is based on the supposition that under like conditions a business will make approximately the same per cent of gross profit in any one period of time as in any other similar period of time. Its use is based on the assumption that the cost of goods available for sale, minus the cost of goods sold, is equal to the cost of goods on hand. Therefore, if sales reduced to cost are deducted from the cost of goods available for sale, the result will be the inventory that should be on hand. To illustrate the computation, assume that a business, which normally makes 30% gross profit based on selling price, had a beginning inventory of $100,000 and purchases of $500,000, both at cost, and sales of $400,000 up to the date of fire:

Beginning inventory (at cost)		$100,000
Purchases (at cost)		500,000
Goods available (at cost)		600,000
Less: Cost of sales (estimated cost):		
Sales	$400,000	
Less gross profit (30%)	120,000	280,000
Approximate cost of goods on hand		$320,000

If the inventory were completely destroyed by the fire, the amount calculated, $320,000, would be closed to the Fire Loss account. Likewise, if the inventory were estimated to have been 40% destroyed in the fire, $128,000 (40% of $320,000) would be charged to the Fire Loss account.

Salvage. Since the Fire Loss account is credited for all revenues related to a particular fire, any proceeds from salvage should be credited to this account. If the salvaged assets are to be repaired or rebuilt and put back into use, the particular asset account should be debited and the Fire Loss account credited with the estimated value. Occasionally the insurance company personally takes care of small repairs. In this case no entry is necessary on the insured's books.

Insurance Settlement. The Fire Loss account is credited for the proceeds of the settlement received from the insurance company. It is obvious, of course, that the insurance company will not pay more than the face of the policy, and as was emphasized earlier, the maximum recoverable amount is limited to the insurable value of the asset at the date of fire. Many fire insurance policies, however, also have an additional limiting feature called the co-insurance clause.

CO-INSURANCE CLAUSE. Since most assets when burned are only partially destroyed, many businesses would take out only enough insurance to cover the usual or average loss if they were not encouraged by the insurance company to do otherwise. The object of the co-insurance clause, therefore, is to encourage the insured to take out and to maintain a certain amount of coverage or else be a co-insurer with the insurance company. Consequently, many policies on business property provide that, unless the insured carries insurance which totals a certain per cent (frequently 80%) of the insurable value, the insurance company shall be liable for only a portion of any loss sustained by the insured.

In the case of a co-insurance clause, the insured may recover from the insurance company that portion of the loss which the amount of insurance carried bears to the amount of insurance that should be carried according to the co-insurance clause. The amount recoverable from the insurance company may be stated proportionately or as a formula, as follows:

(1) *Stated as a proportion:*
   The amount recoverable is to the loss as the amount of insurance carried is to the amount of insurance that should be carried.
(2) *Stated as a formula:*

$$\frac{\text{Amount of insurance carried}}{\text{Amount of insurance that should be carried}} \times \text{Loss} = \text{Amount Recoverable}$$

The following examples illustrate the use of the formula in determining the amount recoverable, assuming an 80% co-insurance clause. In examples *E* and *F* it should be noted that the amount recoverable will never exceed the amount of the loss or the face of the policy.

A. Insurable value $100,000

Insurance carried   80,000

Amount that should be carried (80% × $100,000)   80,000

Amount of loss   60,000

Amount recoverable $\left(\dfrac{80,000}{80,000} \times \$60,000\right)$ $ 60,000

B. Insurable value $100,000

Insurance carried   70,000

Amount that should be carried (80% × $100,000)   80,000

Amount of loss   60,000

Amount recoverable $\left(\dfrac{70,000}{80,000} \times \$60,000\right)$ $ 52,500

C. Insurable value $100,000

Insurance carried   60,000

Amount that should be carried (80% × $100,000)   80,000

Amount of loss   60,000

Amount recoverable $\left(\dfrac{60,000}{80,000} \times \$60,000\right)$ $ 45,000

D. Insurable value $100,000

Insurance carried   50,000

Amount that should be carried (80% × $100,000)   80,000

Amount of loss   60,000

Amount recoverable $\left(\dfrac{50,000}{80,000} \times \$60,000\right)$ $ 37,500

E. Insurable value $100,000

Insurance carried   90,000

Amount that should be carried (80% × $100,000)   80,000

Amount of loss   60,000

Amount recoverable $\left(\dfrac{90,000}{80,000} \times \$60,000 = \$67,500\right)$ $ 60,000*

F. Insurable value $100,000

Insurance carried   80,000

Amount that should be carried (80% × $100,000)   80,000

Amount of loss   90,000

Amount recoverable $\left(\dfrac{80,000}{80,000} \times \$90,000 = \$90,000\right)$ $ 80,000†

*Amount recoverable limited to the amount of loss.

†Amount recoverable limited to the amount of insurance carried.

CONTRIBUTION CLAUSE. When a particular asset is insured with several different insurance companies, each company whose policy contains a contribution clause is liable for only a pro-rata share of a loss. If all of the policies have the same co-insurance clause, recovery is obtained from the different companies in proportion to the face of each policy. However, if the policies have different co-insurance clauses, the amount of recovery from the different companies is obtained by multiplying the loss by a fraction, the numerator of which is the face of the individual policy, and the denominator of which is the higher of (1) the face of all policies, or (2) the amount required under the co-insurance clause of the particular policy. To illustrate, assume that an asset having an insurable value of $200,000 is insured under the policies described below, and that a loss of $100,000 is incurred. If the policies contain the same co-insurance clauses, recovery would be made as follows:

| Policy | Insurance | | Fraction | Loss | Amount Collectible |
	Carried	C. I. Clause			
No. 1	$ 60,000	$180,000	60/180	$100,000	$33,333.33
No. 2	75,000	180,000	75/180	100,000	41,666.67
No. 3	30,000	180,000	30/180	100,000	16,666.67
	$165,000				$91,666.67

If the policies contain different co-insurance clauses, the recoverable portion of the loss would be allocated as follows:

| Policy | Insurance | | Fraction | Loss | Amount Collectible |
	Carried	C. I. Clause			
No. 1	$ 60,000	$180,000	60/180	$100,000	$33,333.33
No. 2	75,000	175,000	75/175	100,000	42,857.14
No. 3	30,000	160,000	30/165	100,000	18,181.82
	$165,000				$94,372.29

MORTGAGE CLAUSE. Most mortgaged property is required by the mortgagee to be insured. Consequently, fire insurance companies have formulated a standard mortgage clause which is included in the policy when appropriate. When included in the policy, it provides that the settlement of a fire loss be paid to the mortgagee to the extent of his interest and any remaining balance be paid to the mortgagor. For example, if property mortgaged for $20,000 is fully insured and a $24,000 fire loss settlement is made, $20,000 is payable to the mortgagee and $4,000 to the mortgagor. Since the amount paid to the mortgagee reduces the amount owed by the mortgagor, both parties are protected by a single policy. The following entry illustrates how this settlement would be recorded on the mortgagor's books:

Cash	$ 4,000	
Mortgage payable	20,000	
Fire loss		$24,000

Business Interruption Insurance

In addition to protection from losses arising as the result of fire, an insured may protect his assets against other losses or damages arising from various occurrences. Some of the risks that are commonly insured against are sprinkler leakage, boiler explosion, and business interruption. Insurance policies on risks such as these vary. Except for business interruption, however, most provide protection only against loss directly connected with the risk or hazard covered in the policy. Thus, a fire insurance policy will provide protection for assets covered against loss by fire. A business enterprise, however, could well suffer a greater loss from indirect effects of the fire than from the direct fire damage. For example, the loss resulting from the interruption of profitable operations could easily be greater than the value of the property destroyed by the fire.

To cover these indirect losses, fire loss policies, as well as policies covering other types of property damage, are commonly drawn to contain a provision known as business interruption insurance. Inclusion of a business interruption provision in property damage policies will indemnify the insured for indirect losses resulting from damage to the insured business property. Policy provisions may differ widely in this area, but a business interruption provision might compensate the insured for loss of profits caused by the interruption of business activity, outlays for various expenses such as salaries, payroll, and other contractual-type expenses such as rent, interest, and utility charges which necessarily continue while a business is shut down during the replacement period following the property destruction. The policy is normally explicit on the extent of coverage and on the manner in which the loss of profits is to be determined. Past history and projections of the future usually form the basis for this determination.

Business interruption insurance, often referred to as use and occupancy insurance, is concerned not with the material loss of property but with the loss of the ability to use the property. Proceeds from such insurance are used to pay dividends to stockholders and interest to creditors, and to retain essential employees on the payroll. Essentially it does that which the company would have done had there been no interruption of business operations. To have a business interruption insurable interest, there must be more than a mere loss of use of destroyed property; there must be an expectation of business revenues to cover net income, fixed charges, and operating expenses had the property damage not occurred. Unless this revenue prospect exists, business interruption insurance is not applicable.

Various types of business interruption insurance policies may be written. Policies related to special situations are not uncommon. For example, a manufacturer may be largely dependent upon one source of supply for raw materials or component parts. The manufacturer may insure himself against the possible loss from interruption to his business arising from an interruption in the flow of materials or parts for any one of a number of causes.

INSURABLE EMPLOYEE RISKS

A business organization entertains certain employee risks merely because of its existence. It faces still others if it is to continue as a going concern. As in the case of asset risks, however, most employee risks are insurable. The lives of employees may be insured, the health of employees may be insured, and their capacity to work and earn a living is also insurable.

Life Insurance

Life insurance provides for the payment of a definite sum of money at the insured's death or, in the case of an endowment policy, at some determinable future date if the insured is still living. This provision for payment is made by the insurance company in return for the policyholder's agreement to pay periodically a sum of money (the premium) to the insurance company. Life insurance premiums are payable in advance and may be payable on an annual, semi-annual, quarterly, or monthly basis. The shorter rates are proportionately greater, since they include an element of interest and administrative costs, and most companies buy life insurance on an annual basis.

Participating. A particular life insurance policy may be participating or nonparticipating. If the policy is a participating one, the premium rate is fixed at an amount somewhat greater than is needed under normal conditions to pay for the cost of providing the insurance, and as a result of the participating feature the policyholder gets a refund or dividend. The dividend is based on actual operating experience together with an estimate of future needs. The dividend, which is usually available after premiums for the first two or three years have been paid, represents that portion of the premium not needed by the insurance company for (1) benefit payments, (2) possible contingencies, and (3) operating expenses. Deducting the yearly dividend from the regular annual premium gives the policyholder his yearly net cost. Premiums paid should be *charged* to the insurance account and dividends received should be *credited* thereto. Frequently dividends are used to reduce future premiums. In this case the net cost is the amount of the premium, and no entry is required for the dividend.

Nonparticipating. In a nonparticipating policy, the premium rate is fixed at an amount which approximates as closely as possible the amount needed to pay for the cost of providing the insurance. No dividend or refund is received by the policyholder. Thus, the periodic premium is the actual cost to the policyholder for the period.

Ordinary Life Insurance

Although individual life insurance policies may be classified in many different ways, from the standpoint of the business organization purchasing life insurance there are basically two methods of providing this type of employee insurance, namely:

(1) Ordinary life insurance.
(2) Group life insurance.

Ordinary life insurance can be used to meet almost every conceivable type of business need in which protection of human life values and loss of earning power are at stake. It is frequently used in the business world to insure the lives of business executives and other key employees for the benefit of the particular business. This makes it possible to compensate to some degree for the loss which might be sustained from the death of one of the key members of the organization. In partnerships and in small or closely held corporations the lives of all part-owners are frequently insured. This makes it possible, when a partner or stockholder dies, to pay, with a minimum amount of delay, his beneficiary or beneficiaries a prearranged or determinable price for his interest in the business. It enables the surviving partners or stockholders to continue the business without undue interruption, and it avoids unnecessary delay in settlement or liquidation.

When a business takes out an ordinary life insurance policy on its key personnel, it usually retains the right to name the beneficiary. In case the business is named as beneficiary, the premiums are not a deductible item for income tax purposes, although from a going concern viewpoint they are operating expenses. Occasionally the insured is given the right to name the beneficiary, in which case the premiums are generally considered to be additional salary.

Cash Surrender Value. The value of a life insurance policy is measured primarily on its ability to meet the basic objective for which it is purchased. In addition, however, most policies (other than the usual term policy) have additional values, one of which is the cash value or, as it is frequently termed, "cash surrender value." The cash value of a life insurance policy is the sum of money which the insurance company will owe to a policyholder who purchases insurance on a particular type of premium plan, if and when he stops paying premiums. It is a value that is guaranteed in the insurance contract. When premium payments are stopped, the policyholder has various options available as to the cash surrender value. For example, he may request that the amount be used to cover, or insure, his life on a term basis for as long as the cash surrender value will last. Or, he may request that the insurance company pay him the cash surrender value in cash. A policy usually has no cash value until it has been in force two or three years.

A cash loan is available from the insurance company on ordinary lifetime or endowment policies after the policy has been in effect one, two, or three years, depending upon the particular policy. This is known as the policy loan provision and permits the policyholder to borrow any amount up to the cash surrender value of the policy. Policies contain a table which shows the contractual loan and surrender values at various anniversary dates, for example:

TABLE 4-A
Cash Values

End of Policy Year	Cash Value	End of Policy Year	Cash Value
1	$ 0	6	$3,600
2	–0–	7	4,500
3	1,500	8	5,500
4	2,100	9	6,600
5	2,800	etc.	

ACCOUNTING FOR CASH SURRENDER VALUE. Since after a certain period of time most life insurance policies have a determinable cash value, many business organizations like to reflect this value on their books and in their financial statements. When recording these values, the accounting problems revolve around (1) the proper distinction between capital and revenue expenditures, and (2) the proper determination and allocation of insurance expense to the period benefiting therefrom.

When accounting for the cash value of a policy, part of the annual premium is a capital charge (debited to an asset account) and part of it is a revenue charge (debited to an expense account). As indicated earlier in the case of a participating policy, the insurance expense for a particular year is the annual premium minus the dividend received. However, when recording cash surrender values, the yearly expense is the annual premium minus the dividend received minus the increase in cash surrender value. The following entries illustrate the accounting involved, assuming a life insurance policy of $100,000, annual premium of $3,000, and assuming Table 4-A to be the applicable table of cash values:

FIRST YEAR
    Life insurance $3,000
      Cash $3,000
    (to record annual premium payment)

    Profit and loss $3,000
      Life insurance $3,000
    (to close life insurance expense for year to P & L)

SECOND YEAR
    Life insurance $3,000
      Cash $3,000
    (to record annual premium payment)

    Cash $ 100
      Life insurance $ 100
    (received $100 life insurance dividend)

    Profit and loss $2,900
      Life insurance $2,900
    (to close life insurance expense for year to P & L)

THIRD YEAR
    Life insurance $3,000
      Cash $3,000
    (to record annual premium payment)

    Cash $ 100
      Life insurance $ 100
    (received $100 life insurance dividend)

Cash surrender value of life insurance	$1,500	
Life insurance		$ 500
Correction of prior years' profits*		1,000
(to record cash surrender value at the end of the third year)		
Profit and loss	$2,400	
Life insurance		$2,400
(to close life insurance expense to P & L)		

FOURTH YEAR

Life insurance	$3,000	
Cash		$3,000
(to record annual premium payment)		
Cash	$ 100	
Life insurance		$ 100
(received $100 life insurance dividend)		
Cash surrender value of life insurance	$ 600	
Life insurance		$ 600
(to record the increase in cash surrender value)		
Profit and loss	$2,300	
Life insurance		$2,300
(to close life insurance expense to P & L)		

Insurance Settlements. The accounting treatment necessary when recording a life insurance settlement by the insurance company depends upon whether or not the company has properly recorded the cash surrender value as an asset. While the cash surrender value should be recorded as it arises, if the value has not been entered on the books, the proper accounting treatment upon receipt of the cash would be to debit cash and credit a nonrecurring income account or retained earnings, depending upon whether the "clean surplus" or the "current operating" concept is used. When the cash surrender value has been recorded on the books, however, settlement requires the removal of the Cash Surrender Value account from the books. To illustrate, assume $100,000 settlement and $60,000 balance in the related Cash Surrender Value account:

Cash	$100,000	
Cash surrender value of life insurance		$60,000
Proceeds from life insurance, less cash		
surrender value (or Retained earnings)		40,000

* While the division of the credit of $1,500 into two parts, one to reduce the current year's expense account and the balance to record the portion relating to the over-statement of prior years' expenses, may be theoretically proper, general practice would normally involve a credit to the current year's expense account for the entire amount. This procedure may be supported on the grounds of materiality, since the initial cash value would normally not be large enough to create a distortion of the income for a given year.

Financial Statement Presentation. Cash surrender value is usually classified on the balance sheet as a noncurrent asset and is frequently placed in the long-term investment section. It should not be classified as a current asset unless there are definite plans to cancel the policy, thereby collecting the proceeds within the next operating cycle.

Group Life Insurance

Group life insurance, as the name implies, is a form of insurance whereby a group of people are insured under one policy. The usual group life insurance policy permits a number of people, usually the employees of a business organization, to be insured without medical examination. The amount of insurance available to each employee is generally about one year's salary or earnings. A master contract is issued to the employer with each employee receiving a certificate giving the amount of his insurance, the name of his beneficiary, and a summarization of his rights and benefits.

Group life insurance is usually issued on the term basis. That is, the premium buys current protection only and does not buy permanent protection. However, in recent years various types of group permanent life insurance plans have been developed whereby an employee leaving his employer retains some part of his group protection as fully paid permanent insurance. The employee also usually has the right to buy an individual policy equal to the balance of his group protection without evidence of insurability.

Group Plans. Some group life insurance plans are contributory and others are noncontributory. In the case of contributory plans the employer and employee share the cost of the insurance, the employee's portion being deducted from his earnings and the balance of the premium being paid by the employer. When the plan is a noncontributory one, the employer pays the entire cost. The accounting treatment of both plans is illustrated in the following entries, assuming $100,000 payroll before insurance deductions, total insurance cost of $2,000, and in the case of the contributory plan the cost is divided equally between the employee and employer:

(1) *Contributory plan:*

Salaries and wages	$100,000		
Group insurance withholdings			$ 1,000
Accrued payroll			99,000
Group insurance withholdings		$ 1,000	
Insurance expense		1,000	
Cash			$ 2,000

(2) *Noncontributory plan:*

Salaries and wages	$100,000	
Accrued payroll		$100,000
Insurance expense	$ 2,000	
Cash		$ 2,000

MISCELLANEOUS INSURABLE EMPLOYEE RISKS

Health Insurance

One of the numerous employee fringe benefits which has become rather common in recent years deals with health insurance coverage. Employers may purchase health and hospitalization coverage on a group basis for their employees at a premium rate per employee somewhat lower than the employee would pay for similar coverage on an individual basis. The employer may pay the entire premium cost, or the employees may assume part of the premium cost through periodic payroll deductions. The policy coverage normally includes reimbursement to the employee for all or part of the costs incurred in connection with diseases or illnesses requiring individual attention or hospitalization. Normally, the fact of employment need bear no relationship to the disease or illness for coverage to exist. Insurance coverage on employment-connected accidents or injuries is discussed in the following section on workmen's compensation insurance.

Accounting for Health Insurance. The accounting problems of health insurance are not very involved. Premium payments may be monthly, quarterly, or annually, depending upon the policy terms, and the premiums may be charged either to an expense or to a prepaid expense account when paid. If the employees contribute to the premium cost through payroll deductions, the payroll accounting procedure must provide for the employee withholding according to the terms of the plan. Amounts withheld should be credited either to the account charged when the employer pays the premiums, or to an accrued liability account which will subsequently be closed to the insurance expense account. The difference between the premiums paid and the employee withholdings represents the cost of the health insurance plan to the employer.

Workmen's Compensation and Employers' Liability Insurance

In general, workmen's compensation insurance protects employers from liabilities which might arise under various state workmen's compensation laws. Prior to the enactment of the various state laws dealing with work-men's compensation, employees encountered considerable difficulty in recovering from employers for injuries or loss of wages occasioned by accidents arising in connection with their employment. Now most states have workmen's compensation laws which provide for the receipt of fixed sums, partial wages, or other compensations for various accidents arising during the course of employment. While the laws vary from state to state, in general they provide for compensation to employees for accidents, occupational diseases, and loss of employment arising therefrom during the course of employment. Thus, employers are subject to heavy potential liability under these laws. It is only natural that some form of workmen's compensation insurance would be developed to share the business risks arising under the state laws.

Workmen's compensation insurance policies generally provide that the insurance company will assume the risks that the employer is subject to under the specific state law on workmen's compensation. In addition, workmen's compensation insurance also generally provides protection to the employer for legal action brought by employees to recover damages for personal injuries. Because state laws vary considerably and because the terms of specific insurance policies may also be rather diverse, the accountant must become familiar with both the risks to which the business enterprise is subject and the provisions which various policies may include for insuring adequately against these risks.

Cost of Workmen's Compensation Insurance. The cost of work-men's compensation policies varies directly with the degree of risk involved in the jobs of the employees covered by the policies. The insurance company will evaluate the risk by reference to past accident experience of the occupation involved, with some modification in a standard rate for an occupation classification being made based upon the particular insured's accident experience and safety devices in operation. Thus, a company which emphasizes employee safety and which develops a good safety record over the years will effect a saving in insurance costs.

Even though the insured may have employees engaging in various kinds of occupations, all employees may be covered by the same policy. Thus, the P Corporation, a roofing contractor, may have employees who are roofers, a rather hazardous occupation, sheet metal workers, concrete finishers, and some clerical staff. The insurance company will establish a rate per $100 of payroll which is applicable to each employee group. As with most insurance, premiums on workmen's compensation policies are established in advance of the period of coverage. Since workmen's compensation rates are stated at so much per $100 of payroll, an estimate of the premium on a policy requires an estimate of the payroll for the policy period by employee classes. In general the payroll estimates are made by the insured based upon his past experience and the outlook for the future.

Accounting for Workmen's Compensation. Assume that the P Corporation takes out a new workmen's compensation policy on May 1, 1967, and that the total premium is based upon the following schedule:

Classification	Estimated Annual Payroll	Rate per $100	Estimated Premium
Roofers	$60,000	$6.36	$3,816.00
Sheet metal workers	60,000	2.21	1,326.00
Concrete finishers	15,000	3.44	516.00
Clerical office employees	20,000	.10	20.00
Total			$5,678.00

This table shows that the standard premium estimate is $5,678.00 for the policy year, and this is the basis upon which the P Corporation will pay its premium. Under some policies this premium would be payable in full at the start of the policy year. In other policies a deposit would be made on May 1, with the remaining balance being paid periodically over the policy life. For example, the P Corporation may pay an initial installment deposit of $1,419.50 (1/4 of annual estimated premium) on May 1, and nine subsequent payments of $473.17 each, beginning June 1. The entry for the advance premium payment would be:

Unexpired insurance—workmen's compensation $1,419.50
    Cash $1,419.50

Since the premium payments are based upon the payroll of the different employee classifications, the P Corporation must organize its payroll records in such a manner as to provide the data necessary to determine the expense (premium earned by insurance company) applicable to each fiscal period. Payroll records must show wages earned separately for each class of employees so that the computations of earned premiums can be made.

Assume that at the end of May the payroll records show the following data for wages earned in May. The earned premium may be calculated in the manner indicated:

Classification	May Payroll	Rate Per $100	Premium Earned
Roofers	$8,000	$6.36	$508.80
Sheet Metal Workers	5,400	2.21	119.34
Concrete Finishers	1,800	3.44	61.92
Clerical Office Employees	1,700	.10	1.70
Total Earned Premium			$691.76

If monthly financial statements are prepared, the following entry (or working paper adjusting entry) would record the expense for May:

Insurance expense—workmen's compensation $691.76
   Unexpired insurance—workmen's compensation $691.76

If the P Corporation accounting system provides for accumulation of costs by departments, or by functions, the expense charge above could be recorded as four separate charges to appropriately named expense accounts. A similar entry would be made at the end of each period based upon the wages earned in that period as reflected in the payroll records.

UNEXPIRED WORKMEN'S COMPENSATION INSURANCE ACCOUNT. Because the terms of the policy normally provide for payment of the premium at a more rapid rate than the premium is earned by the insurance company, the Unexpired Insurance—Workmen's Compensation account will normally contain a debit balance at the end of each accounting period. A debit balance is commonly reported as a prepaid expense, although there is some justification for reporting the item as a receivable from the insurance company. Toward the end of the policy year the Unexpired Insurance account may show a credit balance. This would arise when the wages earned during the policy year exceeded the estimates upon which the premium was based. A credit balance should be reported as a current payable item.

Final settlement of the premium on a workmen's compensation policy is made subsequent to the end of the policy year and is based upon an audit of the insured's payroll records conducted by representatives of the insurance company. Based upon this audit, the insurance company will refund any unearned premium arising when actual wages have been less than the estimate upon which the premium was based. Likewise, if the actual wages have exceeded the original estimate, and if the insured has not modified his original payment plan, the insured will be billed for the premium due.

Miscellaneous Policy Provisions. Workmen's compensation policies may contain various provisions that create problems in determining the expense properly applicable to a given accounting period. For example, the rates per $100 upon which the premium is based may be set high enough to provide for a periodic dividend to the insured based upon the amount of earned premium. Frequently the extent of this dividend is not known at the end of the insured's accounting period. Another provision may deal with the retrospective review of the premium. For example, a policy may provide that the insurance company reserves the right to review in retrospect the insured's accident experience during the policy year and, based upon this review, to revise upward or downward the previously established premium rate. Again, at the end of an accounting period it is difficult for the insured to determine the proper expense, since the effectiveness of this retrospective provision may not be known until after the policy year ends a few months later.

Fidelity Bonds

Employers may protect themselves to some degree from the risk of loss resulting from the dishonesty of their employees. Such protection takes the form of fidelity bonds under which a surety company agrees to reimburse the insured for losses from theft, embezzlement, etc., perpetrated by dishonest employees. Fidelity bonds may be issued in various forms to cover a variety of insurable risks. Thus, an employer may purchase a bond on a specific employee, on a specific position without reference to a specific individual, or on several specific employees or specific positions detailed in the bond schedule.

Prompt notice must be made by the insured of losses falling within the coverage of the bond. Likewise, specific time limits are commonly imposed by the bonds on the period within which claims must be filed or suits instituted for recovery of losses. When a loss becomes known by the employer he should meet the provisions of the policy for filing the claim, determine the amount of loss if possible, and adjust his accounts so that the loss is carried in a suspense-type account until final disposition of the claim is made.

SELF-INSURANCE

Business insurance provides a method whereby certain types of business losses may be borne by a large number of firms, rather than by the particular firm upon which a loss chances to fall in the first instance. As indicated earlier, the insurance company acts as a clearing house and effects the distribution of the losses for a fee. There are instances, however, where a business organization may be justified in assuming its own insurable risks. When a firm is in a position so that it can effect a distribution of risks and the clearing of losses, it may save the operating cost of the insurance company, which frequently amounts to as much as one-half of the ordinary premium.

Accrual Basis

When a company carries its own insurance, income may be charged periodically with the ordinary premiums and a "reserve" or "provision" account credited. The following entries illustrate the accounting involved, assuming $1,000 ordinary yearly premiums and a $40,000 fire loss:

Insurance expense	$ 1,000	
Provision (reserve) for self-insurance		$ 1,000
Insurance fund	$ 1,000	
Cash (or equivalent)		$ 1,000
Provision for self-insurance	$40,000	
Fire loss		$40,000
Fixed asset	$40,000	
Insurance fund		$40,000

Reporting of Provision (Reserve) for Self-Insurance. The financial statement treatment of the Provision for Self-Insurance account poses some problems. In the above example, the charge offsetting the account was closed to income at year-end. Thus, the credit should properly go to an account called "Provision for Self-Insurance," the balance of which represents insurance charges of past years expected to be absorbed by future operations as losses occur. While the nature of the account does not meet all the tests of a liability, it would appear that the account is more like an estimated liability (similar to Estimated Liability on Product Guarantee, discussed in Chapter 3) than any other type of account. Past operating periods have been charged for amounts estimated to be necessary to meet future charges, and the unabsorbed balance of the Provision for Self-Insurance may be classified on the financial statements as a liability reported between the long-term liabilities and the shareholders' (partners') equity.

If the charge offsetting the account is closed directly to Retained Earnings, the credit might well go to an account called "Reserve for Self-Insurance," the balance of which could be reported as a restriction of Retained Earnings in the shareholders' equity section of a balance sheet. It should be recognized, however, that actual losses would not be charged against the Reserve account, but would be charged either to a separate loss account or directly to Retained Earnings. In determining the classification of the account offsetting the estimate for self-insurance, the basic issue is the manner in which the account is established and not necessarily the particular wording of the account credited.

Nonaccrual Basis

Some companies are so large that losses normally insured against by a smaller company may be absorbed regularly as losses in lieu of either the payment of an insurance premium or by the accrual of a provision for self-insurance. In effect the losses occur regularly so that they are an effective substitute for the accrual of a self-insurance charge or a premium payment and amortization.

All businesses absorb some losses as they are incurred, such as wastes of all types, rather than attempting to account for these on an accrual self-insurance basis. Judgment plays an important part in managerial decisions regarding which of the three procedures (insurance with outside insurance company, self-insurance on an accrual basis, and self-insurance on an absorption of loss basis) shall be used in providing for business risk.

ACCOUNTING FOR PENSION COSTS

In recent years increased emphasis has been placed on employee pension plans. This has been a result not only of social security legislation but also of the increased recognition that pension plans fall within the scope of collective bargaining. In addition to the economic and social ramifications, this trend has created additional problems for the accountant. Since there is usually a certain amount of insurable risk associated with a pension plan, the accounting treatment involved is included at this time.

Cost of Pension Plans. As indicated in *Accounting Research Bulletin* 47, published by the American Institute of Certified Public Accountants, in addition to the basic features of a pension plan relating to employee eligibility and the level of pension payments, other factors enter into the determination of the ultimate cost, such as:

(1) Employee turnover.
(2) Future compensation levels.
(3) Length of life of employees both before and after retirement.
(4) Other benefits (such as social security) with which pension payments are integrated.
(5) In a funded plan, future rates of earnings in the fund and the status of fund investments.

Because of factors such as these, the ultimate cost of a given plan cannot be determined precisely in advance. However, by the use of actuarial techniques (see Appendix), reasonably accurate estimates can be made.

Funded vs. Unfunded Plans. Pension plans may be funded or unfunded. The funding procedure to be used in any given situation is

dependent upon the size of the company, its objectives, its desire to eliminate or minimize administrative and actuarial work, its expectancy of
turnover, etc.

In the case of a funded plan the funding transaction is recorded by
charging a prepaid or deferred account such as "Unamortized Pension
Payments." This is then systematically amortized and charged to income.
In the case of an unfunded plan, costs should be accrued. The estimated
accrual is recorded by charging an expense account and crediting a
"provision" account. When pension payments are made to the employees,
the "provision" account is charged.

According to *Bulletin* 47, accounts and financial statements should
reflect, as a minimum, accruals which equal the present worth, actuarially
determined, of pension commitments to employees to the extent that
pension rights have vested in the employees, reduced, in the case of the
statement of financial position, by any accumulated trusteed fund or
annuity contracts purchased.

Past Service Costs. As emphasized in *Bulletin* 47, one of the major
accounting problems as related to pension plans is concerned with past
service costs. The Institute recommends that pension costs based on
past service be allocated to current and future periods rather than to past
periods. This approach stresses the fact that even though the costs are
based on past services, they are nevertheless incurred in contemplation of
present and future services, not necessarily of the individual affected but of
the organization as a whole and therefore should be charged to the present
and future periods benefited.

PROBLEMS

Problem 4–1. During your audit of the XYZ Company, which closes its
books on December 31, you examine the life insurance policies, premium receipts,
and confirmations returned by the insurance companies in response to your
request for information. You find that the company paid premiums during the
year on the following policies insuring the life of Wilson Jones, president of
the company:

Sole Owner and Beneficiary	Face Amount of Policy	Premium Paid in 1967	Date of Annual Premium Payment	Cash Surrender Value Dec. 31 1967	1966
1. XYZ Company	$100,000	$2,500	June 30	$32,000	$30,000
2. Hattie T. Jones, wife of Wilson Jones	50,000	1,600	Sept. 30	15,000	14,000
3. XYZ Company	100,000	3,600	Dec. 31	22,000	19,000

Required:
Indicate how you would present the facts regarding these policies on the balance sheet of the XYZ Company at December 31, 1967, including supporting computations as part of your answer. Give the justification for the treatment which you propose, including an explanation of the disposition of the premiums paid. (AICPA adapted)

Problem 4–2. A fire at the Spillville plant of Domby Distilleries, Inc., completely destroyed a building on July 1, 1967. The company had insured the building against fire with two companies under the following three-year policies:

Company	Face	Co-insurance Clause	Unexpired Premium 1/1/67	Date of Expiration
X	$ 80,000	80%	$ 800	8/31/67
Y	120,000	80%	1,200	8/31/67

An umpire set the insurable value at the date of the fire at $260,000 and the loss at $255,000. In spite of this ruling, there proved to be no net salvage value recoverable from the building. The building was carried on the books of the corporation at a cost of $200,000 less accumulated depreciation charged to operations to date of fire of $40,000.

Required:
(1) Compute the amount recoverable under each insurance policy and the total amount recoverable. You must set forth the formula which you use in making your computation.
(2) Compute the balance of the "Fire Loss" account after such of the above data as affect it have been recorded. Label clearly the various elements entering into your computation. (AICPA adapted)

Problem 4–3. On January 1, 1966, Mort paid $3,000 for a three-year fire insurance policy. As of December 31, 1967, a question arose as to the amount of prepaid insurance that should be shown on Mort's balance sheet.
One proposal was to show prepaid insurance at $600, which was the short-rate cancellation value of the policy on December 31, 1967.
A second proposal was to show prepaid insurance at $1,000, representing one-third of the original premium cost.
A third proposal was to show prepaid insurance at $1,200 which is the one-year premium cost for a policy for the same amount as the policy in force.

Required:
Discuss each of the proposals as to acceptability, as to the general principle underlying it, and as to its effect on reported income. (AICPA adapted)

Problem 4–4. Adams, Baker, Charles, and Day are partners. Their interest in the capital and their profit and loss ratios are as follows:

Adams	40%
Baker	30%
Charles	20%
Day	10%

To provide a means whereby the remaining partners might purchase a deceased partner's interest from his estate, a life insurance program was inaugurated whereby life insurance proceeds would be paid to the remaining partners in proportion to their percentage ownership in the partnership. Since each partner was in effect insuring the life of each of the other partners, it was agreed that no partner would pay any part of the premiums on policies covering his own life.

In 1966 the premium on all policies amounted to $9,000, which was charged as an expense on the books and thereby deducted from the year's profits. The profit was then credited to each partner in proportion to his ownership percentage.

Investigation of the insurance premiums revealed the following:

Premium on the life of Adams	$3,500
Premium on the life of Baker	1,400
Premium on the life of Charles	2,300
Premium on the life of Day	1,800

Required:

You are to prepare the correcting entry that should be made to the partners' capital accounts in order to reflect properly the agreement as to the insurance. Present supporting computations in good form.   (AICPA adapted)

Problem 4–5. The Delta Tire Company suffered rather heavy fire damage on April 1, 1967. To support a claim for recovery for loss of inventory in the fire, the following data were available:

Inventory on January 1, 1967	$115,000
Sales delivered to date of fire	225,000
Purchases received to date of fire	126,000
Goods in transit at date of fire	24,000
Freight on goods received to date of fire	4,000
Inventory of salable merchandise immediately after fire	40,000
Face of policy (80% co-insurance clause)	80,000
Annual premium, paid October 1, 1966	1,680
Average rate of gross profit in 1964–66 was 40%	

The company adjusts and closes its books annually at December 31.

Required:

(1) Determine the inventory destroyed at April 1, 1967.

(2) Providing the insurance company agreed to settle on the valuation in (1), determine the amount of settlement.

Problem 4–6. The Richter Manufacturing Company had a fire January 2, 1968, that severely damaged the building it rented for its manufacturing operations; 80% of the fixed assets and all of the inventories were destroyed. The Company office was located in another building and was not damaged. On April 1, 1968, when the Company resumed operations, you were asked to assist in filing a loss claim under the Company's business interruption insurance policy.

The following information is available:

(1) The profit and loss portion of the Company's trial balance prior to closing at December 31, 1967, is as follows:

Sales		$600,000
Sales returns and allowances	$ 4,900	
Raw materials inventory, 1–1–67	44,000	
Raw materials inventory, 12–31–67		30,000
Finished goods inventory, 1–1–67	10,000	
Finished goods inventory, 12–31–67		10,000
Purchases of raw materials	340,000	
Freight in	5,000	
Direct labor	55,000	
Factory heat, light, and power	24,100	
Manufacturing supplies	8,000	
Rent—factory	12,000	
Office salaries	34,000	
Manufacturer sales representatives' commissions	28,600	
Administrative and general expense	51,000	
Depreciation:		
Machinery and equipment	24,000	
Office furniture and fixtures	5,900	
Bad debts	6,000	
Purchase discounts		6,500
Interest income—U. S. Treasury bonds		2,300
Net loss		3,700
	$652,500	$652,500

(2) The Company has business interruption insurance under a gross carnings policy with the following features:

(a) Recovery under the policy is limited to the reduction in "Insured Gross Earnings" directly resulting from such interruption of business less charges and expenses that do not necessarily continue during interruption of business.

(b) "Insured Gross Earnings" are defined as the sum of
1. Total net sales value of production, and
2. Total net sales of merchandise purchased for resale,
Less the direct cost of
1. Raw stock from which such production is derived,
2. Materials and supplies consumed directly in the manufacturing operations, and
3. Merchandise sold and services purchased from outsiders for resale which do not continue under contract.

(c) In determining "Insured Gross Earnings" due consideration shall be given to the experience of the business before the date of damage or destruction and the probable experience thereafter had no loss occurred.

(d) By additional investigations you determine that "total net sales value of production" may be interpreted as the net proceeds from the sales of goods manufactured by the Company.

(e) The policy is in the amount of $125,000 with a 70% coinsurance clause.

(3) Company policy on pricing finished goods inventory results in a reasonably consistent valuation at 80% of selling price.

(4) Neither sales nor production is seasonal in nature.

(5) The terms of the building lease provide no rental payments need be made for periods during which the premises are not fit for occupancy.

(6) The Company paid all employees their base salaries and wages from January 1 to April 1, 1968.

(7) Depreciation was recorded on the straight line method, and no assets were fully depreciated.

Required:

(1) Prepare a schedule computing the amount of the Richter Manufacturing Company's "Insured Gross Earnings" based on the year ended December 31, 1967. Compute the limitation, if any, on the insurance company's liability imposed by the coinsurance clause.

(2) Prepare a schedule computing the amount of fire loss due to lost gross earnings. Determine the amount of the fire loss, if any, to be absorbed by the Richter Manufacturing Company.   (AICPA adapted)

Problem 4–7. The Mulligan Corporation is a small manufacturing company producing a highly flammable cleaning fluid. On May 31, 1967 the Company had a fire which completely destroyed the processing building and the in-process inventory; some of the equipment was saved.

The cost of the fixed assets destroyed and their related allowances for depreciation at May 31, 1967 were:

     Building, cost $40,000; allowance $24,667.

     Machinery and equipment, cost $15,000; allowance $4,375.

At present prices the cost to replace the destroyed property would be: building, $80,000; machinery and equipment, $37,500. At the time of the fire it was determined that the destroyed building was 62.5% depreciated, and the destroyed machinery and equipment was 33.3% depreciated. The insurable value of all the building, machinery, and equipment was determined to be $75,000.

After the fire a physical inventory was taken. The raw materials were valued at $30,000, the finished goods at $60,000, and supplies at $5,000.

The inventories on January 1, 1967 consisted of:

Raw materials	$ 15,000
Work in process	50,000
Finished goods	70,000
Supplies	2,000
Total	$137,000

A review of the accounts showed that sales and gross profit for the last five years were:

	Sales	Gross Profit
1962	$300,000	$ 86,200
1963	320,000	102,400
1964	330,000	108,900
1965	250,000	62,500
1966	280,000	84,000

The sales for the first 5 months of 1967 were $150,000. Raw material purchases were $50,000. Freight on purchases was $5,000. Direct labor for the first 5 months was $40,000; for the past 5 years manufacturing overhead was 50% of direct labor.

Insurance on the property and inventory was carried with three companies. Each policy included an 80% coinsurance clause. The amount of insurance carried with the various companies was:

	Buildings, Machinery, and Equipment	Inventories
Company A	$30,000	$38,000
Company B	20,000	35,000
Company C	15,000	15,000

The cost of cleaning up the debris was $7,000. The value of the scrap salvaged from the fire was $600.

Required:
(1) Compute the value of inventory lost.
(2) Compute the expected recovery from each insurance company.

(AICPA adapted)

Problem 4-8. The City Wholesale Company lost its entire inventory of merchandise and its furniture and fixtures by fire early in January, 1968, before completing the physical inventory which was being taken as of December 31, 1967. The following information was taken from the books of the company as of December 31, 1965, 1966, and 1967:

	Dec. 31, 1965	Dec. 31, 1966	Dec. 31, 1967
Inventory, January 1	$ 35,304	$ 42,380	$ 45,755
Purchases	160,842	164,426	174,433
Purchase returns and allowances	9,163	8,021	10,015
Sales	185,904	196,603	203,317
Sales returns and allowances	3,325	2,402	2,212
Wages	15,271	17,743	18,356
Salaries	7,500	8,000	9,000
Taxes, other than income	2,647	3,732	3,648
Rent	4,800	5,400	5,400
Insurance	915	967	982
Light, heat, water	1,012	1,134	1,271
Advertising	2,875	4,250	2,680
Interest expense	3,365	2,755	3,020
Depreciation expense	1,125	1,255	1,280
Furniture and fixtures, net of depreciation	9,150	10,065	10,570
Miscellaneous expenses	6,327	6,634	6,897

Required:

(1) From the above information estimate the book amount of inventory destroyed by the fire, assuming that there were no transactions after December 31, 1967.

(2) Based on such estimate and the book value of the furniture and fixtures, determine the amount due from each insurance company in settlement of the total loss of the assets under the following concurrent policies, each containing an 80% co-insurance clause:

	Policy on	
	Inventory	Furniture
A Company	$20,000	$2,000
B Company	15,000	3,000
L and D Company	10,000	3,000

(3) Assuming that the fire loss was 50% of the amounts used in (2), determine the amount due from each company under the same three policies.

(AICPA adapted)

Problem 4–9. The Fletcher Manufacturing Company had a fire on October 1, 1967, at one of its warehouses. A survey after the fire disclosed that the building was a 60% loss and the inventory stored in the building was also a 60% loss. Records disclosed that sales since the first of the year, at an average markup of 50% on cost, were $450,000. Purchases during the same period totalled $313,000, while the inventory at the start of the year had been $75,000. Expenses per the records were: transportation-in, $8,000; storage costs, $4,000; transportation-out, $6,000. The building had a cost of $720,000, had an estimated life of 30 years, and was 40% depreciated at January 1, 1967. The company adjusts for depreciation, insurance, and other deferred and accrued items on a semi-annual basis at June 30 and December 31 each year.

The insurance adjusters and company officials agree to estimate the value of the inventory by employing the average rate of gross profit. They also agree that the building was worth $600,000 at the date of the fire.

Insurance coverage on the building and contents was as follows:

Company	Policy Face	Co-insurance Clause	Annual Premium	
			Date Paid	Amount
X	$200,000	None	3/1/67	$600
Y	150,000	90%	7/1/67	480
Z	250,000	85%	11/1/66	780

Required:

(1) Determine the settlement to be made by each insurance company.

(2) Prepare journal entries to record the events connected with the fire and the recoveries from the insurance companies.

Problem 4–10. At December 31, 1967, the Vaughn Production Company had the following account in its general ledger:

Unexpired Insurance—Workmen's Compensation

1967			1967						
Jan.	1 Balance	$ 900	Jan.	31 Est. expense for month				$300
Mar.	1 Deposit	1,000	Feb.	28	,,	,,	,,	,,	300
Apr.	1 Monthly payment	375	Mar.	31	,,	,,	,,	,,	300
Apr.	16 Final for 1966	280	Apr.	30	,,	,,	,,	,,	300
May	1 Monthly payment	375	May	31	,,	,,	,,	,,	300
June	1 Monthly payment	375	June	30	,,	,,	,,	,,	300
July	1 Monthly payment	375	July	31	,,	,,	,,	,,	300
Aug.	1 Monthly payment	375	Aug.	31	,,	,,	,,	,,	300
Sep.	1 Monthly payment	375	Sep.	30	,,	,,	,,	,,	300
Oct.	1 Monthly payment	375	Oct.	31	,,	,,	,,	,,	300
Nov.	1 Monthly payment	375	Nov.	30	,,	,,	,,	,,	300
	Bal. $1,580		Dec.	31	,,	,,	,,	,,	300

The workmen's compensation policy runs from March 1 to February 28, and the premium is payable 1/4 at March 1, the balance in eight equal monthly instalments. A final audit and billing is made each March for the past year. At December 31, 1967, the following data are taken from the Vaughn Co. policy and payroll records:

Classifi-cation	Rate per $100	Payroll Estimate 3/1/67 to 3/1/68	Estimated Premium	Actual Payroll of Company Year-1967	3/1/67 to 12/31/67
AB	$3.20	$80,000	$2,560	$82,000	$70,000
CD	2.10	40,000	840	35,600	30,400
EF	1.20	50,000	600	54,400	47,600
			$4,000		

Required:

(1) Determine the proper balance in the above account at December 31, 1967.

(2) Prepare a journal entry to adjust account to correct balance and to adjust the expense account.

(3) On what basis could the expense account as adjusted in the above entry be criticized for being inaccurate?

Problem 4–11. The partnership of Banks, Baker, and Long carried a joint policy insuring the lives of each partner for $50,000. The partnership was the beneficiary, with proceeds from any settlement being credited to the surviving partners. On August 1, 1967, the annual premium of $3,600 was paid. On that date the cash surrender value of the policy was $12,000, with the similar value having been $10,800 on August 1, 1966, and becoming $13,500 on August 1, 1968. On September 15, 1967, a check for $120 is received as a dividend for the policy year ended August 1, 1967. On March 1, 1968, Mr. Baker died.

Required:

Prepare journal entries necessary on August 1, 1967, September 15, 1967, December 31, 1967, and March 1, 1968.

Problem 4–12. The Sloan Manufacturing Company has a workmen's compensation policy which has a policy year ending each December 31, the same date as the end of the company's fiscal year. At December 31, 1966, the Unexpired Workmen's Compensation Insurance account had a credit balance of $624.60. On January 15, 1967, the initial premium payment was made on the policy covering the year 1967. The policy calls for four quarterly payments based on the annual payroll estimate. Final settlement is made by adjustment after an annual audit. The final audit for the year 1966 resulted in a receipt by the company of a debit memo from the insurance company of $620.10. The following table presents the information regarding the 1967 policy:

Classification	Rate per $100	Estimated Annual Payroll	Premium
Machinists	$1.66	$150,000	$2,490
Helpers	1.28	100,000	1,280
Storeroom	.48	70,000	336
Clerical	.09	80,000	72
Total			$4,178

During the first quarter of 1967 wages earned by the various wage classifications were:

Classification	January	February	March
Machinists	$10,000	$10,600	$12,400
Helpers	7,600	7,800	8,400
Storeroom	5,000	5,000	5,400
Clerical	6,500	6,500	6,600

At the end of each month the premium earned by the insurance company is recorded prior to the preparation of the monthly statements.

Required:

(1) Prepare journal entries to record the payment made to the insurance company on January 15 and to record the monthly adjusting entries.

(2) What is the balance of the Unexpired Insurance account on March 31? What does it represent?

Problem 4–13. The C Company is planning a pension system for certain of its employees. It wishes to provide funds for meeting the payments under the pension plan and asks you for assistance.

The company does not contemplate making any pension payments under the plan until January 1, 1973. Payments in 1973 and thereafter to the present group of covered employees are expected as follows:

January 1, 1973	$ 5,000	January 1, 1980	$22,000
1974	7,000	1981	17,000
1975	10,000	1982	12,000
1976	14,000	1983	8,000
1977	16,000	1984	5,000
1978	20,000	1985	2,000
1979	25,000	1986	2,000

Starting on January 1, 1973, and continuing for ten years, the company will deposit $10,000 a year in a special fund. On January 1, 1972, the company wishes to make a lump sum deposit of an amount sufficient to provide the remaining funds needed for meeting the pensions. It is expected that all of the above funds will earn $3\frac{1}{2}\%$ interest compounded annually during the entire life of the fund.

Required:

You are to compute the amount of payment which should be made on January 1, 1972. Show all supporting computations. Use the tables in the appendix.

(AICPA adapted)

Note:

For additional problems see the Appendix—particularly Problems AP–26 and 29.

CHAPTER **5**

Administration
of income

In this chapter some of the accounting problems involved in the administration of income will be examined. While accountants probably give more emphasis to problems involving income determination, the area of administration of income also poses some unresolved problems. The administration of income is closely related to income determination, since certain deductions sometimes made in arriving at a "net income" figure may actually involve distribution of income, which is one phase of the administration of income. For example, the interest payment for borrowed funds is usually reported as a deduction in the determination of net income, yet it also may be considered from the standpoint of the enterprise to represent a distribution of the income accruing to creditors.

The area of administration of income is considerably broader than the problem of distribution of income. Administration of income encompasses all questions on how income shall be used by the enterprise.

It has previously been noted that accountants view the enterprise for which they are accounting as an entity distinct and separate from the owners. From this viewpoint it follows that the income of an enterprise represents the increase in net assets which the enterprise has been able to accomplish. This increase in assets, or income, would then be available for allocation to the various equity interests which contributed assets for the enterprise use.

Interest Charges as a Distribution of Income. While the concept of the enterprise as an entity distinct from any particular equity interest is generally recognized by accountants, the concept is not always followed consistently in practice. For example, if income is conceived to be the increase in assets which the enterprise has realized, interest payments, like dividend payments, represent a distribution of assets for the use of funds. Although the idea that interest payments are distributions of income seems to be a logical conclusion, in practice interest expense is normally reported as a deduction in the income statement in the determination of net income.

To illustrate the point, assume Company A is formed by securing $10,000 from bondholders and $10,000 from stockholders. To Company A, as a separate accounting entity, both the bondholders and the stockholders represent a source of funds for operating the business. If income is conceived as a measure of the success with which management has been able to use the contributed funds, it would appear that all costs of acquiring the funds should be in the nature of distributions of income. In more specific terms, if Company A used the $20,000 to buy merchandise, fixtures, and similar operating assets, and then used up one-half of the acquired facilities to provide a revenue of $12,000, it may be contended that the income of the company would be $2,000 as follows:

Increase in assets (cash or cash equivalent)	$12,000
Decrease in assets (merchandise, fixtures, and similar items)	10,000
Excess of increase over decrease in assets (accruing to all investors)	$2,000

The $2,000 represents the increase in assets accomplished through the use of assets originally contributed by all investors, an increase commonly recognized as operating income. The company would then have to pay out $400 of this increase in the form of interest (assuming the $10,000 bonds bore interest at 4%), just as it would likely pay out some amount to the stockholders as dividends. To corporate management both the interest and the dividends would be considered distributions of the income as payment for the use of funds contributed for business use.

If the $400 interest charge is considered to be an expense of the enterprise, the income of the company would be $1,600 ($2,000 minus $400). The $1,600 would represent the income accruing to the stockholders. Those who contend that interest should not be considered an expense reason that the income created by the company is measured by the increase in assets before interest payments, and that interest payments represent merely a distribution of the increase in assets to the creditor investors. In addition, inclusion of interest as an expense may prevent sound comparisons of different companies, because one company may be financed entirely by owner funds while another company may have relied heavily on borrowed funds. Since the source of assets used does not seem to have any necessary effect on how well the assets are used, it may be concluded that the method of financing a business should not influence the amount of income determined. Following this reasoning, interest should not be a deduction in determining income.

Interest Charges as an Expense. Contrary to the position that interest is a distribution of income is the view that the income of a business entity is the amount earned for the owners of the business. Because interest does represent a payment which must be paid before the owners have a claim to any of the earnings of the company, it is contended that interest—at least to the owners—is as much an expense as any other payment the company might have to make to provide an income for the owners. By this line of reasoning, interest payments are properly a deduction in determining the net income of the owners.

There is, of course, considerable merit to the position that interest payments represent a distribution of income and not an expense. However, this position has not been adopted extensively in accounting practice. Most enterprises include interest as an expense, and even the income tax regulations support this practice. A noticeable trend exists, however, toward the objective of treating interest charges as a distribution of income. Many company reports now determine "income before interest charges" and "income after interest charges." The separate disclosure of interest as an expense appears to reflect a feeling that if interest is an expense, it is of a rather special nature.

NATURE OF ADMINISTRATION OF INCOME

There are two major problems in administration regardless of how the income is measured. These problems may be described as:

(1) The problem of allocating the income to the proper accounts on the books. In the case of a partnership this would involve the problem of dividing the determined income among the partners and recognizing each partner's claim for his share of the income.

(2) The problem of distributing the assets to the appropriate income recipients. This problem involves questions as to when a distribution of the income has been made. The key to this problem lies in determining whether there has been a severance of assets to the benefit of the investors.

Allocation of Income—Partnerships

The allocation of partnership income should be made in accordance with the partnership agreement as to how profits and losses shall be divided. If the partnership agreement is silent on this point, the assumption supported by legal decisions is that income and losses shall be allocated equally to each partner. This rule holds regardless of the amount of time devoted by each partner to the operation of the business or of the amount of capital invested by each partner. For example, one partner with no invested capital may be entitled to a share of the profit or loss equal to that of partners with invested capital.

For illustrative purposes, assume A, B, and C are in partnership with capital invested of $20,000, $30,000, and $40,000 respectively. Income for the year, after interest charges, amounts to $15,000. In T-account form the books of the partnership might appear as follows:

Assets	Liabilities	A, Capital
$125,000	$20,000	$20,000

B, Capital	C, Capital	Profit and Loss
$30,000	$40,000	$15,000

If the partnership agreement is silent on the matter of profit allocation, or if the agreement specifies equal allocation to each partner, profits and losses should be allocated equally to each partner. The appropriate entry to close the Profit and Loss account would be:

Profit and loss	$15,000	
A, Drawing		$5,000
B, Drawing		5,000
C, Drawing		5,000

Allocation According to Capital Ratio. On the other hand, if the partnership agreement provides that profits and losses shall be allocated in accordance with the capital ratio, the $15,000 would be allocated 2/9 to A (A's capital of $20,000 over the total partnership capital of $90,000, 3/9 to B, and 4/9 to C, so that the entry to allocate the $15,000 balance in the Profit and Loss account would be:

Profit and loss	$15,000	
A, Drawing		$3,333.33
B, Drawing		5,000.00
C, Drawing		6,666.67

When the partnership agreement provides that profits and losses shall be allocated in accordance with the capital ratio, the agreement must also state which capital ratio shall be used, since capital balances may change from time to time. For example, the capital balances to be used in determining the capital ratio might be one of the following:

(1) The capital balances at the time of the start of the partnership.
(2) The capital balances as of any arbitrary date set forth in the partnership agreement.
(3) The capital balances in the partnership accounts as of the start of the period when the profit or loss is incurred.
(4) The average capital balances maintained by each partner during the period. If this is the method to be used, the partnership agreement should also indicate the manner in which the average capital is to be computed. One satisfactory way to determine the average capital is to compute the average daily capital balances in the following manner:

Assume A had a capital balance of $40,000 on January 1 of the operational year, withdrew $30,000 on June 30, and invested an additional $10,000 on December 1. His average capital for the year could be computed by multiplying the various balances in his capital account by the number of days he carried each balance and then dividing the sum of the total by 365 days, as follows:

Balance	Number of Days Carried	Sum
$40,000	181	$7,240,000
10,000	154	1,540,000
20,000	30	600,000
Total	365	$9,380,000

Daily Average = $25,700 ($9,380,000 divided by 365)

Average capitals for the other two partners might be computed in a similar manner and the appropriate ratio be computed from such averages. Other methods of computing average capitals might involve the monthly balances, or a simple division of the sum of the beginning capital balance plus the ending capital balance by 2. In the case of A, the latter computation would be $40,000 + $20,000 divided by 2, to give an average capital of $30,000.

(5) The capital balances in the partnership accounts as of the end of the period. When this method is used, the partnership agreement should state whether or not drawing accounts are to be closed to the capital accounts before or after computing the capital balances. If B has a credit balance in his capital account of $30,000, but has a debit

balance in his drawing account of $10,000, it is obvious that a decision on the disposition of the drawing account should be made before the capital balance can be computed.

Allocation According to Specified Ratio. At times the partnership agreement may set forth a definite ratio according to which profits and losses are to be allocated among the partners. In the above illustration, there is no reason why the partnership agreement could not state that profits and losses are to be allocated to A, B, and C in a 50%, 30%, and 20% ratio, respectively. In such a situation the entry to close the Profit and Loss account would be:

Profit and loss	$15,000	
A, Drawing		$7,500
B, Drawing		4,500
C, Drawing		3,000

ALLOCATION OF PARTNERSHIP LOSSES. It should be noted that the agreement regarding the manner in which income is to be allocated to partners applies also if the partnership has a loss. For example, if A, B, and C have agreed to share profits and losses on a 5:3:2 ratio, respectively, and if the partnership reported a $12,000 loss, resulting in a debit balance in the Profit and Loss account of this amount, the entry to allocate the loss would be:

A, Drawing	$6,000	
B, Drawing	3,600	
C, Drawing	2,400	
Profit and loss		$12,000

SALARY ALLOWANCE. In those instances where one of the partners assumes administrative operation of the partnership, it is not uncommon for the partnership agreement to provide the operating partner a salary for his work. Such a salary is normally not considered to be a partnership expense, but is considered to be a method of allocating income. For example, assume the ABC partnership reports an income of $15,000, but the partnership agreement calls for a salary allowance of $6,000 to A, after which any balance is to be allocated equally to the partners. The entry to close the balance of the Profit and Loss account would be:

Profit and loss	$15,000	
A, Drawing		$9,000
B, Drawing		3,000
C, Drawing		3,000

(A's $9,000 reflects his $6,000 salary plus his 1/3 of the remaining profit of $9,000, or $3,000)

Once a partnership agreement provides that a salary is to be allowed one partner, the salary portion of the income must be allocated to the partner even if the income of the partnership is less than the salary allowance. The debit balance in the Profit and Loss account after such a salary allowance would then be allocated as a loss to the partners in the appropriate profit and loss sharing ratio. In the above illustration, if the partnership had reported an income of only $3,000, instead of $15,000, the entry to close the Profit and Loss account would be:

Profit and loss	$3,000	
B, Drawing	1,000	
C, Drawing	1,000	
A, Drawing		$5,000

(A's $5,000 credit reflects his $6,000 salary less his 1/3 of the remaining loss of $3,000, or $1,000)

At times the partnership agreement will not stipulate a specific dollar salary allowance, but will express the salary as a percentage of the net income. For example, the partnership agreement may provide that A be allowed a salary of 30% of net income (but not of a loss). A question then arises as to whether or not the 30% figure is to be applied to the net income before the salary allowance or to the net income after the salary allowance. The question is: Is the salary allowance to be deductible in arriving at the income figure on which the salary will be based? Although it is generally agreed that partnership income is that existing before the salary allowance, the partnership agreement may indicate an intent that the salary allowance be based on the amount existing after the salary allowance. To illustrate, assume the ABC partnership reports an income of $12,000 and the partnership agreement provides that A is to be allowed a salary of 20% of the income. If the 20% is to be applied to the income before the salary allowance, the entry to close the Profit and Loss account would be:

Profit and loss	$12,000	
A, Drawing		$5,600
B, Drawing		3,200
C, Drawing		3,200

(A's $5,600 reflects his $2,400 salary plus his 1/3 of the remaining profit of $9,600, or $3,200)

On the other hand, if the partnership agreement stipulates that the salary allowance shall be 20% of the income after the salary, the computation of the salary allowance becomes more involved. The $12,000 is no longer the income on which the salary is based. The $12,000 now is equal to the net income plus the salary. Thus, it could be said that the $12,000 is equal to net income plus 20% of net income, or is equal to 120% of net income. On this basis, the following computation may be made to determine the salary allowance:

$$\$12,000 = 120\% \text{ of net income}$$
$$\$100 = 1\% \text{ of net income } (\$12,000 \div 120)$$
$$\$10,000 = 100\% \text{ of net income } (100 \times \$100)$$

The salary allowance would then be 20% of the net income ($10,000), or $2,000. In this case the entry to allocate the $12,000 credit balance in the Profit and Loss account would be:

Profit and loss	$12,000	
A, Drawing		$5,334
B, Drawing		3,333
C, Drawing		3,333

(A's $5,334 reflects his $2,000 salary plus his 1/3 of the remaining profit of $10,000, or $3,334)

INTEREST ALLOWANCE. In order to compensate a partner for providing more capital to the partnership than provided by other partners, partnership agreements often provide that in the process of allocating partnership income an allowance shall first be made for interest on the invested capital. As in the case of allocation of income according to the ratio of capital balances, the agreement should indicate which capital balance is to be used as a basis for computing the interest allowance. Once the agreement has been reached to allow interest on capital in allocating income, the allowance must be made even if it reduces the balance in the Profit and Loss account to a debit balance to be allocated to the partners in the regular profit and loss sharing ratio.

As an illustration, assume the ABC partnership agreement provides that interest of 10% shall be allowed on the balance in the capital accounts at the end of the year. Assume capital balances at the end of the year were: A, $20,000; B, $40,000; and C, $50,000; and that income was $10,000. If the allocation of the income other than the interest allowance is unspecified in the partnership agreement, the balance after the interest allowance should be divided equally among the partners. As a result the allocation of the $10,000 of income would be:

```
Profit and loss                  $11,000
    A, Drawing                              $2,000
    B, Drawing                               4,000
    C, Drawing                               5,000
(to allocate interest on the basis
of ending capital balances)
    A, Drawing                      $333
    B, Drawing                       333
    C, Drawing                       334
        Profit and loss                     $1,000
(to allocate debit balance re-
sulting in Profit and Loss after
allocation of interest, 1/3 to
each partner)
```

SALARY, INTEREST, AND RATIO. The ABC Partnership books on December 31, 1967, in T-account form appear as follows:

Assets	Liabilities	Profit & Loss
$205,000 |	| $20,000	| $60,000

A, Capital	B, Capital	C, Capital
| $50,000	| $60,000	| $70,000

A, Drawing	B, Drawing	C, Drawing
$20,000 |	$30,000 |	$5,000 |

Reference to the partnership agreement indicates that A is to be allowed a salary of 20% of the income after salary; that interest is to be allowed on partners' capital at a rate of 20% on the capital balances at the end of the year; that partners are to be allowed a drawing of $10,000 a year with the understanding that any withdrawal by a partner in excess of the $10,000 shall represent a capital withdrawal; and that any income or loss balance shall be divided equally among the partners.

In more involved computations to determine the allocation of income among partners, it is sometimes helpful to set up a schedule somewhat as follows:

ABC PARTNERSHIP
Computations for Allocation of 1967 Income

Allocation Bases	Partner A	B	C	Total Allocated
Salary (1)	$10,000			$10,000
Interest (2)	8,000	$8,000	$14,000	30,000
Ratio (3)	6,666	6,667	6,667	20,000
Total	$24,666	$14,667	$20,667	$60,000

(1) The salary allowance is computed as follows:

Income before salary = net income + salary
$60,000 = net income + 20% of net income
$60,000 = 120% of net income
$50,000 = net income
$10,000 = salary (20% of net income)

(2) The interest computations would be:

For A: 20% of $40,000 ($50,000 capital less $10,000 excess drawing).
For B: 20% of $40,000 ($60,000 capital less $20,000 excess drawing).
For C: 20% of $70,000 ($70,000 capital. C had no excess drawing and receives no credit for drawings less than allowed amount).

(3) The profit remaining after allocation of the salary and the interest on capital account would be $20,000 ($60,000 − $40,000). This $20,000 will be apportioned equally among the partners.

From such a schedule it is then possible to formulate quite easily the entries to allocate the balance in the Profit and Loss account to the drawing accounts and to close the drawing accounts to the capital accounts, if such is desired:

Profit and loss	$60,000	
A, Drawing		$24,666
B, Drawing		14,667
C, Drawing		20,667
A, Drawing	$ 4,666	
B, Capital	15,333	
C, Drawing	15,667	
A, Capital		$ 4,666
B, Drawing		15,333
C, Capital		15,667

Allocation of Income—Corporations

As noted previously, interest paid on borrowed capital by an enterprise normally is reported in the income statement as a deduction prior to the determination of net income. Thus, the process of accruing interest charges and establishing the liability for interest charges results in an automatic provision in the accounting records of the amount earned by creditor investors. The income then reported is the net income to stockholders, and the problem becomes one of allocating corporate income to the various groups of stockholders. If a corporation has only common stock outstanding, there is no need to allocate income, since each share of common stock has an equal right to its proportionate share of the income of the corporation.

In those cases, however, where the corporation has both preferred and common stock outstanding, it may be suggested that an allocation of income between the two classes of stock might be appropriate. This suggestion seems especially reasonable when the preferred stock is cumulative. In the absence of any allocation of retained income, no indication exists as to which stockholders the retained income pertains. Nevertheless, current accounting practice does not provide for the allocation of stockholder income among the different classes of stock. As a result the typical Retained Earnings account of a corporation represents the income allocated to all classes of stock outstanding. Footnote disclosure is sometimes used, however, to call attention to the interest of preferred stockholders in the retained earnings of the company.

Appropriated Income. In recent years some modifications have been noted in the unsegregated nature of corporate income. The annual reports of some companies indicate the establishment of appropriate surplus reserves to report preferred dividends in arrears. Others use footnotes to disclose the arrearage. It is the opinion of the authors that accounting practice would be improved by allocating corporate retained income, through reserves or otherwise, among the different classes of stock outstanding.

Although general practice presently does not reflect any widespread efforts to allocate corporate income among various stockholder interests, the practice of making appropriations of surplus for various purposes may be considered in the nature of an allocation of retained income. This may best be explained by an illustration. Assume Corporation X has an accumulated income of $50,000. If this is reported in one amount as retained earnings, readers of the financial statements may not be informed about any intended utilization by the corporate management of the assets generated by this income. Statement readers may conclude that a distribution to stockholders is imminent, when in reality the assets may have been used in the expansion of productive facilities. In recognition of this situation many corporations have attempted to reveal the extent to which the earnings are to be used for purposes other than for distribution to the stockholders. Typical of segregations along this line are provisions for specific contingencies. Assume Corporation X decides to retain $20,000 of the $50,000 accumulated earnings for future law suit contingency. It might advise the stockholders and other readers of the company's statements of this action by reducing the amount in the Retained Earnings account and setting up another account under the title of Reserve for Pending Law Suit. The entry to record such an allocation of retained earnings would be:

Retained earnings	$20,000	
Reserve for pending law suit		$20,000

The new account would be reported in the balance sheet as a part of retained earnings, as follows:

CORPORATION X BALANCE SHEET

Assets		Equities	
·Various	xxxxxx	Liabilities	xxxxxx
		Shareholders' equity:	
		Capital stock xxxxxx	
		Retained	
		earnings:	
		Reserve for	
		pending	
		law suit 20,000	
		Unappro-	
		priated 30,000	

Whether or not the process of setting up surplus reserves represents an attempt to allocate income, it is evident that the ultimate effect of the procedure is similar to the process of allocating income.

Allocation of Income—Estates and Trusts

The distinction between the determination of income and the allocation of income normally is not made in the typical reports of executors and administrators of estates and trusts. Rather, both the reporting of income and the allocation of it which has been made may be disclosed in a Charge and Discharge Statement—As to Income. In effect the allocation of income between beneficiary and remainderman, who gets the principal, is accomplished by legal ruling or court order specifying the expense and revenue items which accrue to principal and which to income. Further details of the distinction between principal and income in the area of estates and trusts are considered in Chapter 22. The expense and revenue items allocated to the income beneficiary may be reflected in a Charge and Discharge Statement—As to Income. While this statement is not used extensively in practice, it suffices as an educational technique to indicate the accounting problem involved in determining and allocating trust or estate income accruing to the income beneficiary.

Essentially, a Charge and Discharge Statement—As to Income is a statement presented by the executor or administrator of the income of a trust or estate. The income accrues to the income beneficiary, and all expenses of providing this income are deductible in determining distributable income to the beneficiary. The typical form is:

ESTATE OF JOHN JONES

DAVID JONES, EXECUTOR

Charge and Discharge Statement—As to Income

From (Date of Death) to (Date of Report)

I Charge Myself:		
Income (Detail by sources)		$ x x x x x x
I Credit Myself:		
Expense (Detail by types)	$ x x x x x x	
Distributions of income (Detail)	x x x x x	x x x x x
Balance of Undistributed Income		$XXXXX
Balance composed of:		
Cash—income	$ x x x	
Other	x x	$XXXXX

There is an implication inherent in this statement that the undistributed income is income allocated to the beneficiary. No further allocation of income is considered appropriate unless there are several income beneficiaries and the undistributed income assets are being held for specific beneficiaries. In this latter case, an allocation of the income among these beneficiaries is appropriate.

It must be reiterated that the foregoing charge and discharge statement is not used extensively in the specific form illustrated. Reports rendered by executors and trustees will conform to the requirements of the court or trust agreement under which they operate. Further, it must be emphasized that the courts and trust agreements have defined income differently from that used by accountants in reporting business income. As noted, courts will often hold that gain or loss on the sale of stocks and bonds, property, and other items which constitute the principal of the estate or trust are not income but a revaluation of principal. Also, court rules are not uniform on whether or not accrued items are includible as expense or income. This area will be covered more completely in subsequent chapters.

Illustration: Charge and Discharge Statement—As to Income. To illustrate the preparation of the Charge and Discharge Statement—As to Income, assume X dies on January 18, 1968, and Mr. Q is appointed to administer his estate. Assume further that the transactions undertaken by Mr. Q are as follows:

(1) Collected interest on estate bonds—$2,000. (One-half of this interest had accrued prior to the death of X.)
(2) Sold estate bonds at a gain of $900.
(3) Collected dividends on stock, declared payable January 20, 1968, and actually paid on February 3, 1968—$4,000.
(4) Rent earned since January 18, 1968, on estate property rented to a wholesale firm—$19,000.
(5) Depreciation on building rented—$2,000.
(6) Miscellaneous expenses paid—$1,200.
(7) Administrator's salary—$3,000.
(8) Payments made to income beneficiary—$8,000.

The Charge and Discharge Statement reflecting the above events might appear as follows:

ESTATE OF X

MR. Q ADMINISTRATOR

Charge and Discharge Statement—Income

January 18, 1968 to July 17, 1968

I Charge Myself:		
Interest income (1)	$1,000	
Dividends on stock (3)	4,000	
Rental income (4)	19,000	$24,000
I Credit Myself:		
Depreciation expense (5)	$2,000	
Miscellaneous expense (6)	1,200	
Administrator's salary (7)	3,000	
Distribution to income beneficiary (8)	8,000	14,200
Balance of Undistributed Income		$ 9,800
Balance composed of:		
Cash	$11,800	
Less: Due to estate principal for depreciation on building rented	2,000	$ 9,800

Mr. Q (Signed)

Administrator

The numbers in parentheses in the above report identify the item with the event listed previously. One-half the interest received in item (1) pertains to the principal of the estate and would not be reflected on this report as to income. Likewise, the gain in item (2) would normally accrue to the estate principal and not to income.

DISTRIBUTION OF INCOME—SEVERANCE OF ASSETS

Allocation of income is the process of assigning to the various equity interests their claims to the assets generated by the income. As has been indicated, the process of assigning the income to an investor claimant may be somewhat involved. It should be recognized, however, that the allocation process is not the only problem involved in distributing income. Possibly more important is the problem of determining when and in what amount there has been a distribution of assets to the investors entitled to the income. The problems encountered may be described as:

(1) What accounting is necessary to disclose the intent of management not to distribute the allocated income?
(2) What is a distribution of income?
(3) When does a distribution of income take place?
(4) What is the amount or valuation to be assigned to any distribution of income?

Accounting for Undistributed Income

There are several reasons why a firm may choose not to distribute all of the income which has been generated in a given operating period. The more distinctly different reasons include the following:

Legal restrictions—such as a state law prohibiting a corporation from paying dividends when a sum equal to the retained earnings is invested in treasury stock. The amount invested in treasury stock measures the restriction on distributable retained earnings.

Contractual agreements—such as an agreement with the trustee for outstanding bonds to accumulate retained earnings up to the amount of the bonds payable, or to restrict income distribution in such a manner that an amount equal to the bond liability will be built up by the maturity date of the bonds.

Business decisions—such as expansion of productive facilities, maintenance of same level of operations in periods of rising prices, and various types of contingencies.

Whatever the reason for the nondistribution of the income, the problem of revealing that the income is not to be distributed must be faced by the accountant. In the case of partnership accounting, the decision to leave the allocated income in the firm on a more or less permanent basis normally is reflected in the accounts by closing out the drawing account to the capital account. Amounts carried forward in drawing accounts would normally be assumed to reflect temporary investments. In the case of corporations, a decision to retain the earnings in the firm may involve (1) taking no accounting action, (2) the issuance of a stock dividend, or (3) the appropriation of surplus.

Nondisclosure of Undistributed Income. Some authorities have suggested that accountants avoid the problem of disclosure of the intent not to distribute income by doing nothing. Avoiding the problem may contribute to consistency in reporting, and thus be considered desirable, but such avoidance actually contributes nothing to the solution of a legitimate desire on the part of report readers. Investors and others want to be informed if the income is not to be distributed and, further, they would like to know why no distribution will occur. The desire for such information seems to be reasonable.

Stock Dividends as a Means of Disclosure. If it is the intent of management to postpone distribution of income indefinitely, the management may consider it desirable to capitalize all or part of the income retained in the enterprise. In the case of a corporation this is generally accomplished through the issuance of a stock dividend. To illustrate this procedure, assume the X Corporation has 1,000 shares of common stock outstanding (par $100) and has retained earnings of $60,000. The management of the X Corporation may recognize that a good portion of the assets generated by these earnings are committed to the operations of the enterprise on a more or less permanent basis. For example, it may recognize that $20,000 of the retained earnings has been invested in fixed assets and that the business operations have expanded to such a degree that the $20,000 is permanent capital. In order to disclose this condition more clearly the management may declare a stock dividend of 20%. The dividend represents 20% of the capital stock outstanding and would amount to 200 shares, each share having an assumed market value of

$100, or $20,000 to be capitalized. The entries to record this process of capitalizing retained earnings are:

Retained earnings	$20,000	
Stock dividend payable		$20,000
(to record declaration of the stock dividend)		
Stock dividend payable	$20,000	
Capital stock		$20,000
(to record issuance of stock in connection with stock dividend)		

The effect of this process is to reduce the retained earnings by $20,000 and to increase capital stock by $20,000. Essentially, this is similar to the process used when the drawing accounts of a partnership are closed to the capital accounts. In either instance the end result is equivalent to the enterprise having acquired additional long-term capital from the owner interests.

Reserves as a Means of Disclosure. In many instances the failure to distribute income is attributable to less permanent decisions. When the absence of the distribution of income is temporary, corporations—but not partnerships—may employ the process known as appropriation of retained earnings to disclose the temporary retention of assets generated by earnings. For example, continuing the above illustration, assume that X Corporation, which will have a $40,000 balance of retained earnings after declaration of the stock dividend, plans to invest $6,000 in treasury stock; has an agreement with the trustee for the bonds outstanding to set aside $10,000 to protect the security of the bonds; and plans to expand facilities to take advantage of a temporary shutdown of competing firms, estimating that $15,000 should be retained in the firm for this purpose. These decisions may be reflected accountingwise by reducing the balance in the Retained Earnings account and setting up appropriations for each of the needs through appropriation of retained earnings, in the following manner:

Retained earnings	$31,000	
Reserve for investment in treasury stock		$ 6,000
Reserve for bond protection		10,000
Reserve for expansion of facilities		15,000

The above entry has no immediate effect on the assets of the enterprise, but it does disclose the intent of management as to the use of portions of the assets generated by past earnings. Thus, the management of the X Corporation is disclosing its intention to use $31,000 of the assets generated by past earnings for three purposes. To the extent of the $31,000 management is also indicating that cash dividends will not be paid presently. Investors and others are thus able to understand, to some extent at least, what the management of the X Corporation intends to do, or has done, with the past income. Properly employed, it would appear that the procedure of appropriating retained income enhances disclosure of certain management decisions.

Nature of a Distribution of Income

The essential characteristic of a distribution of income is that there is a severance of assets from the control of the enterprise to the control of the investors. The major question from an accounting viewpoint lies in the determination of the time that the shift in control takes place.

When a physical transfer of some of the assets of the enterprise to the investor has been made, there seems to be little question that a severance of assets has taken place and that some of the income has been distributed. In the case of partnerships, estates and trusts, and certain other forms of business, distributions of income are not recognized until the physical severance of assets has taken place. In the case of corporations, however, the physical severance of assets does not appear to be as important in determination of the timing of a distribution of income. For corporations the distribution of income is commonly recognized as a fact as soon as the obligation to make the severance is legally in existence.

Determination of Time of Distribution

Legal Aspects of Asset Severance. The legal obligation to make a severance of assets in connection with the distribution of income arises as soon as a board of directors of a corporation formally declares an intent to pay the dividend. Thus it becomes appropriate for accountants to recognize the distribution of income on the date that the dividends are declared by the directors. To illustrate, assume the X Corporation on February 16, 1968, declared a cash dividend payable to stockholders of record (those who have their names recorded as owners of the stock) on March 2, 1968, with payment to be made on March 18, 1968. The distribution of income would be recognized on February 16 by the following entry:

>   Dividends declared (Retained earnings) $5,000
>   Dividends payable $5,000

Scrip Dividend. The legal test for recognition of the distribution of income is also commonly applied when it is the intention of the corporate board of directors to declare a scrip dividend, a note dividend, or even a bond dividend. Thus, the distribution of income may precede the severance of assets to the extent that the intent of the board of directors is formalized in advance of the actual date of severance of the assets. For example, assume the X Corporation does not have sufficient cash currently available to distribute a cash dividend, but wishes to distribute some of the income to the investors. The corporation may decide to issue a scrip dividend (a promise to pay a certain sum at some future date). Scrip dividends normally may be negotiated by the investor-recipients in much the same manner as any negotiable instrument. The severance of assets would be recognized on the date the board of directors declared the dividend. If the scrip dividend were declared on February 16, 1968, payable to stockholders of record on March 5, 1968, to be issued on March 26, 1968, but to be redeemed in cash on June 23, 1968, the dividend would be recorded on February 16, 1968, as follows:

Dividends declared (Retained earnings)	$5,000	
Scrip dividend payable		$5,000

Bonds as a Distribution of Income. Presumably, if a corporation were to issue as a dividend distribution its own bonds not due until many years in the future, accountants would recognize the distribution of income on the date the board of directors declared the dividend. Some accountants would question recognition of the income distribution at this date in view of the fact that physical severance of assets from the control of the corporation will not take place until the distant future. These accountants would emphasize that recognition of the income distribution at the date of legal declaration is merely a convenience and that the distribution actually arises coincident with the physical severance of assets. When the time lag between legal declaration and physical severance is minor, use of the legal date is satisfactory. When the time lag becomes material, however, recognition of the income distribution should await the physical severance of assets. This line of reasoning appears to have merit. It is the opinion of the authors, however, that bonds issued as a dividend represent a distribution of income in that the owners of the bonds have received a senior claim to assets of the company. Severance of assets is considered to have proceeded to the point where recognition of the fact may be appropriate.

Stock Dividend. In many respects the payment of an ordinary stock dividend (a dividend declared payable in shares identical to those on which the dividend is based) appears to be similar to a bond dividend. However, conventional accounting does not recognize a stock dividend to be a distribution of income, but to be merely a restriction of earnings available for distribution. This treatment is supported by the arguments that no distribution of assets has, in fact, occurred nor is such a distribution intended upon declaration of a stock dividend. In fact, declaration of a stock dividend is frequently notice to the owner interests that management feels assets generated by past operations are permanently necessary to the future business operations and thus will not be available for distribution directly to the shareholders.

Valuation of Distribution of Income

The physical characteristics of distributions of income may be:

(1) Cash.
(2) Promises to pay cash in the near future.
(3) Promises to pay cash in the distant future.
(4) Securities of other corporations.
(5) Productive assets, other than cash, owned by the company.
(6) Merchandise.

In the case of a cash dividend, the proper valuation of the distribution is the amount of cash paid out. In the case of the promises to pay cash at some future date, the amount of the distribution is measured at the amount of cash which will have to be paid out, excluding any interest to be paid on such obligations. In cases where the interest to be paid on such obligations is in the face amount of the promise to pay cash later, as would be the case if a 20-year noninterest-bearing bond were issued as a dividend, it is appropriate to value the dividend at the current cash value of the promise to pay cash later. When the distribution is to be in the form of assets other than cash, problems arise as to the amount of the distribution which has taken place. Theoretically, the proper rule would be to value the distribution at the cash or cash equivalent distribution. However, this amount is not always readily determinable, in which case approximations must be used. Even when the amount is determinable, values arrived at in other ways are commonly used.

Illustration—Dividend in Kind. To illustrate the difficulty of valuing the distribution of income in noncash form, assume the X Corporation declares a dividend payable in merchandise and in securities of other corporations which the company owns. The merchandise is carried on the books of the X Corporation at a cost valuation of $6,000, but it has a market valuation ranging from $8,000 to $10,000, depending upon whether it is sold to a wholesaler or to a retailer. The securities are carried on the books at a cost valuation of $11,000, but they have a market valuation of $20,000. It is estimated, however, that it will cost $1,000 to sell them. It is evident that the valuation finally decided upon will be an approximation of the cash equivalent of the assets being distributed. While there is a considerable body of thought that the most practical procedure is to value the distribution at cost or at the value at which it is carried on the company's records, it is evident that such a procedure may represent an undesirable valuation. The board of directors may intend to distribute a greater portion of earnings than is represented by the cost of the assets to be distributed. The accounting procedures under valuation at cost and valuation at realizable value are illustrated below:

Distribution valued at cost

Dividends declared (retained earnings)	$17,000	
Dividends payable in merchandise		$ 6,000
Dividends payable in securities		11,000

Distribution valued at realizable value

Merchandise	$ 4,000	
Securities	8,000	
Gain on revaluation of merchandise and securities		
(retained earnings)		$12,000
(to revalue merchandise and securities to their		
realizable value for dividend payment purposes.)		
Dividends declared (retained earnings)	$29,000	
Dividends payable in merchandise		$10,000
Dividends payable in securities		19,000

The Gain on Revaluation account would eventually be closed to the Retained Earnings account. It should be pointed out that valuation at cost is consistent with the partnership procedure of allowing partners to withdraw merchandise at cost and not at sales price. While of questionable theoretical accuracy, the consistency and objectivity provided by valuation at cost supports such valuation in practical situations.[1]

---

[1] For several years during the 1950's Standard Oil Co. (Indiana) paid dividends in cash and in securities, the securities being shares of Standard Oil Co. (New Jersey). Retained earnings were regularly charged for the carrying value by Standard of Indiana of the securities distributed. Shareholders receiving the dividends, however, were notified that their dividend receipt was based on market value of the Jersey shares at the date of payment. While this was a practical treatment, the theoretical appropriateness may be questioned. Shareholders of Standard of Indiana who were not entitled to a full share of Jersey stock (the 1957 distribution, for example, was on the basis of 1 share of Jersey stock for each 70 shares of Indiana held) were paid in cash for fractional shares. The cash price was determined by an average of the high and low prices for the Jersey stock on the market on the stock of record date. Thus, in 1957, for each share of Jersey stock actually distributed, the retained earnings of Standard Oil of Indiana were charged for $15.82, the carrying basis per share on Indiana's books. However, in 1957, cash distributions in lieu of fractional shares were equal to $48.30 on a per share of Jersey basis. For the cash distributed, on a full share basis, $48.30 was charged to retained earnings by Standard of Indiana.

PROBLEMS

Problem 5–1. Company A and Company B each have total assets of $100,000. Reported incomes for each company were $10,000 and $8,000, respectively. Although Company B's earnings were $2,000 less than those of Company A, one of Company B's expenses was a $3,000 interest expense charge for payment on B's 5% bonds outstanding. Company A has $15,000 of current liabilities while B has $10,000 of such items.

Required:

(1) What rate of return was earned on the shareholders' equity of each company?

(2) What rate of return was earned on the total assets?

(3) Under what conditions would you feel that a better figure of B's earnings should be something other than $8,000?

Problem 5–2. C, D, and E are partners. In 1968, earnings of the partnership were $30,000. For each case below indicate how much of the income would be allocated to each partner.

Case A—The partnership agreement is silent on how profit or loss is to be shared.

Case B—The partnership agreement specifies profits or losses are to be shared according to the capital ratio existing at the start of the year. Capital accounts of C, D, and E on January 1, 1968, were $50,000, $70,000, and $30,000.

Case C—E is allowed a salary of $10,000 for running the business. Any balance is to be divided among the partners in the ratio of 2 : 2 : 1 to C, D, and E, respectively.

Case D—C is to be allowed a salary of 50% of partnership income after the salary allowance. The balance of any gain or loss is to be shared equally.

Case E—D is allowed a salary of $10,000 and all partners are to be allowed a 10% return on their capital on January 1, 1968 (see Case B above). Any balance is to be shared 50% to C, 20% to D, and 30% to E.

Problem 5–3. In T-account form, selected accounts for the G and H partnership as they appear on December 31, 1967, are as follows:

G, Capital		H, Capital	
	1/1/67 $50,000		1/1/67 $30,000
	6/30/67 10,000		

G, Drawing		H, Drawing	
3/31/67 $8,000	$10,000	6/30/67 $6,000	$10,000
		7/31/67 6,000	

Partners' Salaries		Profit and Loss	
$20,000			$30,000

The partnership agreement provides that withdrawals in excess of the salary allowance shall be treated as withdrawals of capital. It further provides that profit or loss after salary allowances shall be divided in accordance with the twelve-months average capital ratios.

Required:
(1) Compute the amount of income allocated to each partner.
(2) Give the entry or entries to close the books of the partnership.

Problem 5–4. The partnership agreement of Adams and Larrson provides that profits and losses shall be shared according to the capital ratio at the beginning of each year. It further provides that each partner may draw up to $10,000 a year. Withdrawals in excess of $10,000 are subject to a 10% penalty payable to the partnership but settled in the allocation of income at the end of the year. Selected accounts for the partnership on December 31, 1967, are:

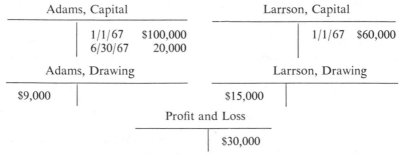

Adams, Capital			Larrson, Capital	
	1/1/67	$100,000		1/1/67 $60,000
	6/30/67	20,000		

Adams, Drawing		Larrson, Drawing	
$9,000		$15,000	

Profit and Loss	
	$30,000

Required:
(1) Compute the allocation of the $30,000 of income to the partners.
(2) Prepare a statement of changes in capital for 1967.

Problem 5–5. Partnership contracts usually specify a profit and loss ratio. They may also provide for such additional profit and loss sharing features as salaries, bonuses, and interest allowances on invested capital.

Required:
(1) What is the objective of profit and loss sharing arrangements? Why may there be a need for features in addition to the profit and loss ratio? Discuss.
(2) Discuss the arguments for recording salary and bonus allowances to partners as charges to operations.
(3) What are the arguments against treating partnership salary and bonus allowances as expenses? Discuss.
(4) In addition to its other profit and loss sharing features, a partnership agreement may state that "interest is to be allowed on invested capital." List the additional provision that should be included in the partnership agreement so that "interest to be allowed on invested capital" can be computed.

(AICPA adapted)

Problem 5–6. Hook and Fill formed a partnership on January 1, 1968, and agreed to share profits and losses, as follows:

	Hook	Fill	Profit (Loss)
1968	60%	40%	30,000
1969	50%	50%	(10,000)
1970	40%	60%	20,000

On January 1, 1971, it was discovered:

A. The ending inventory on December 31, 1968, should have been $10,000 instead of $1,000.

B. Excessive depreciation of $2,000 a year has been charged on a machine acquired January 1, 1969.

Required:

Give the journal entry to correct the books on January 1, 1971.

Problem 5–7. The pre-closing trial balance of the Jow Dones Company on December 31, 1967, contains the following accounts:

Cash	$ 10,000
Accounts receivable	62,000
Stock of the XYZ Company—500 shares	40,000
Merchandise 12/31/67	78,000
Treasury stock, common—200 shares (at cost)	18,000
Prepaid insurance	2,200
Land	17,800
Building, less accumulated depreciation	130,000
Machinery, less accumulated depreciation	100,000
Equipment, less accumulated depreciation	40,000
Accounts payable	35,000
Notes payable—due 3/1/74	20,000
Sales	300,000
Cost of goods sold	200,000
Selling expenses	50,000
Administrative expenses	20,000
Interest charges	1,000
Common stock—issued (par $100)	400,000
Retained earnings	14,000

The Company has decided tentatively to pay a 10% dividend. They are somewhat concerned, however, regarding (1) whether or not they have sufficient cash on hand to pay the dividend, (2) the legal restriction that dividends shall not reduce retained earnings below the amount invested in treasury stock, and (3) the possibility of issuing the stock of the XYZ Company as the dividend in view of the $60 per share at which the stock is currently selling.

Required:

(1) Compute the maximum amount of dividend which might be paid legally.

(2) Compute the amount of dividend which might be paid in view of the cash position of the company.

(3) Compute the maximum dividend which might be paid of XYZ stock, if the stock is valued at $60 per share for dividend purposes.

(4) Assume the company declared a 5% dividend, but before the dividend was paid another 10 shares of their own stock were purchased as treasury stock

at $92 per share. Give the journal entry to set up the dividend declaration and the subsequent acquisition of the additional 10 shares.

Problem 5–8. Evan W. Moore died on March 1, 1967, leaving the following estate:

Bonds (market value)	$20,000
Stock (market value)	32,000
Real estate (market value)	26,000
Bank account	18,000
Total	$96,000

Additional Information:
1. The bonds (face amount, $25,000) bear interest at the rate of 4% payable semi-annually on February 1, August 1.
2. Debts of the decedent at time of death were $300.
3. $2,500 was spent for the funeral.
4. Death taxes and fees came to $8,200.
5. The stock was sold on July 2, after receiving a dividend of $1,200 on July 1, for $36,000.

Required:
Prepare a Charge and Discharge Statement—As to Income for the period March 1, 1967, to July 15, 1967.

Problem 5–9. Michael Dunlap, a retired partner of a public accounting partnership, died on July 3, 1967. At the time of his death his estate included the following assets:

Bank checking account	$ 2,400
Bank savings account	8,600
Equity in partnership ($\frac{2}{5}$ of equity at retirement)	36,000
Common stocks (market value)	42,000
Apartment building (fully rented) (insurance value)	124,000
	$213,000

Between July 3 and October 31, 1967, the following events took place in connection with Mr. Dunlap's estate:
(*a*) Dividends received on common stock were $410.
(*b*) Rentals received on apartment building totaled $5,600.
(*c*) Funeral costs paid were $2,800.
(*d*) $12,000 was received from Mr. Dunlap's former partnership, representing $\frac{1}{5}$ of his equity at his retirement date.
(*e*) Operating expenses on the apartment building were $1,400.
(*f*) Debts due at death (unrelated to the above assets) and paid, $800.
(*g*) Administrator's fees paid were $1,200.
(*h*) Interest earned on savings account, $810.
(*i*) Depreciation on apartment building, $1,800.
(*j*) Property taxes on the apartment building run about $2,400 per year.

Required:
Prepare a Charge and Discharge Statement—as to income for the period July 3, 1967 to October 31, 1967.

Problem 5–10. The Carson-Allyn Company has been pressed for dividends by its common stockholders. The company's stockholders' equity account on December 31, 1967, appears as follows:

Common stock	
10,000 shares (no par)	$980,000
Retained earnings	630,000
Total	$1,610,000

Stockholders have agreed to accept a dividend in kind, composed of stock of the Abbet-Lincoln Company and merchandise regularly sold by the Carson-Allyn Company, and a 10% stock dividend. The assets and stock to be issued are valued as follows:

	On Books Of Carson-Allyn	Market Value Date Dividend Declared
Abbet-Lincoln stock	$33,000	$ 49,000
Merchandise	18,000	8,000
Stock dividend	(Book value)	210,000

Required:
(1) Give the journal entry to record the declaration and payment of the dividend.
(2) One of the auditors objects to the valuation given the dividend in merchandise. He maintains it allows the company to avoid a $10,000 loss which they would otherwise have to report. Do you agree with the auditor?

Problem 5–11. The AUDP Company paid a dividend in their own bonds. The bonds have a face amount of $10,000 but the current market price at the time the dividend was declared was $8,900. At the time the dividend was paid the market value of the bonds was $8,700.

Required:
Give the journal entries to record the declaration and payment of the dividend.

Problem 5–12. At the regular meeting of the Board of Directors of the May Corporation a dividend payable in the stock of the June Corporation is to be declared. The stock of the June Corporation is recorded on the books at cost, $87,000; market value of the stock is $100,000.

Required:
(1) Discuss the propriety of the two methods of recording the dividend liability, including in your discussion an analysis of the circumstances under which each might be acceptable.
(2) The property dividend declaration might state that "corporate property is being distributed as a dividend," or it might state that "corporate property is being distributed in payment of the dividend liability." Discuss briefly the significance of the wording of the property dividend declaration and its effect upon the stockholder receiving the dividend.   (AICPA adapted)

Problem 5–13. In the suburbs of New Orleans a few years ago a group of immigrants from Central Europe formed a corporation. Having invested the sum of $30,000, which represented the life savings of a number of the group, they were most interested in getting back their investment. During its first year of operations, the corporation made an income of $5,000 and distributed cash of $3,000 to the stockholders. Not one of the investors considered the $3,000 as income. All looked upon it as a partial return of their investment. To the internal revenue agent seeking to collect an income tax on the $3,000, they raised the question of how could they have any income until they recovered their investment.

Required:

How did the internal revenue agent know the $3,000 was a dividend? Upon what assumption was the distribution a distribution of income?

CHAPTER 6

Valuation of the enterprise

The discussion in this and succeeding chapters draws heavily upon an understanding of the fundamental aspects of actuarial science. Students not familiar with the techniques of actuarial science are advised to study the Appendix at this time.

The problem of maintaining an existing organizational unit and assuring its continuation has various aspects. The two preceding chapters have been concerned with the problems of providing for business risk and the problems of income administration. Another problem of maintaining the enterprise relates to the maintenance of the "values" entrusted to the enterprise. It is to this aspect of enterprise maintenance that this chapter is directed.

METHODS OF VALUATION

The valuation problem of a business entity may be approached from various methods of valuation. Better known business methods of valuation, all used to some extent in practice, include:

(1) Valuation of assets at acquisition costs less allocation for portions used.
(2) Valuation of assets by capitalization of the earning power of the enterprise.
(3) Valuation of assets by appraisal.
(4) Valuation of assets at acquisition costs adjusted to common dollar amounts.

Valuation at Acquisition Cost Less Allocation for Usage

The attempt to value an enterprise by valuing the individual assets and liabilities in terms of their acquisition cost has several limitations. Uninitiated readers of financial statements frequently conclude, erroneously, that a summation of the asset dollar amounts reported on the statements represents the value of the enterprise. This misunderstanding exists in spite of the fact that accountants have been most insistent that such a list of assets is not a statement of value, but is rather a statement of costs deferred to subsequent operational periods.

The use of this method of valuation involves several questions, including the following:

(1) What is the correct amount of the cost of acquiring a particular asset?
(2) When should an asset acquired be recorded?
(3) How much of an asset is used up in an accounting period?

The problem of valuation of individual assets and liabilities is the typical approach to valuation used in beginning and intermediate accounting textbooks. In addition, Chapters 2 and 3 of this text deal with various problems in valuation of individual assets and equity items.

Valuation by Earning Power

One method of valuing enterprise total assets which seems to have considerable support both in theory and in practical financial analysis is the so-called capitalization of earning-power approach. In its theoretical framework the term means that an enterprise is worth the amount of income it can create. For example, if a firm can earn regularly $10,000 a year indefinitely, and if the risk of putting money in a venture such as this is about 5% a year, it must be concluded that the $10,000 is the payment for the 5% risk factor. From this it follows:

If 10,000 is equal to 5% of the worth of the enterprise, then 1% of the worth of the enterprise is $2,000 ($10,000 divided by 5), and

If 1% of the worth of the enterprise is $2,000, then 100%, or the total worth of the enterprise is $200,000.

This method of determining the value of an enterprise is based upon the assumption that the $10,000 annual income will continue indefinitely and that the rate of risk appropriate for the enterprise will likewise remain at 5%.

Theoretical Approach. Actually, the preceding process of determining the valuation of the enterprise is a short-cut process of determining each year's annual income at its present value at the date of valuation. Present value refers to the worth now of the $10,000 to be received at a future date. If the $10,000 is to be received one year from now, and if the rate of interest involved is 5%, the present value of the $10,000 would be $9,523.81. (See Present Value of 1 table in Appendix.) If the $9,523.81 were invested at 5% a year, it would amount to $10,000 at the end of a year. In a similar manner the present value of $10,000 not to be received for two years can be computed as $9,070.29. If the present value of $10,000 a year forever is computed and the summation made of the resulting present values, the result would be the total present value of the enterprise. This approach to approximating the valuation of the business entity has considerable theoretical merit, and likewise has frequent application in practical situations, such as in the determination of a price to be paid at the time of sale of an enterprise to new owners.

To illustrate that enterprise value is the present value of the future income to be received, assume that the firm will receive an income of $10,000 a year indefinitely and that the rate of risk is 5%. The computations would be as in Table 6-A.

As the time period over which the $10,000 a year is to be received increases, the present value of such an annuity increases toward the maximum of $200,000, which is the present value of $10,000 a year at 5% forever, or in perpetuity.

Practical Approach. A general practical application of this concept of valuing an enterprise substitutes an average of annual earnings over a relatively short period for the concept of indefinite continuation of the earnings at the amount of assumed earning power. Typically, the assumed earning power to be capitalized is the average of annual earnings over the past 3 to 5 years of operations. For example, the worth of Company A could be computed as follows, using the earnings of the past four years as a base:

First year	$20,000
Second year	22,000
Third year	17,000
Fourth year	21,000
	$80,000

By dividing the total of the past four years' earnings, $80,000, by 4 an average annual earnings of $20,000 results. If the normal rate of return (risk element) in this type of industry is 20%, the worth of Company A

TABLE 6-A

No. of Years Income is Deferred	Annual Income to be Received	Rate of Capitalization	Present Value of Income
1	$10,000	5%	$9,523.81
2	10,000	5%	9,070.29
3	10,000	5%	8,638.38
4	10,000	5%	8,227.02
5	10,000	5%	7,835.26
6	10,000	5%	7,462.15
7	10,000	5%	7,106.81
8	10,000	5%	6,768.39
9	10,000	5%	6,446.09
10	10,000	5%	6,139.13

Present value of $10,000 a year for 10 years at interest of 5% $ 77,217.33

11	$10,000	5%	$5,846.79
12	10,000	5%	5,568.37
13	10,000	5%	5,303.21
14	10,000	5%	5,050.68
15	10,000	5%	4,810.17
16	10,000	5%	4,581.12
17	10,000	5%	4,362.97
18	10,000	5%	4,155.21
19	10,000	5%	3,957.34
20	10,000	5%	3,768.89

Present value of $10,000 a year for a second 10-year period at interest of 5% $ 47,404.75

21	$10,000	5%	$3,589.42
22	10,000	5%	3,418.50
23	10,000	5%	3,255.71
24	10,000	5%	3,100.68
25	10,000	5%	2,953.02
26	10,000	5%	2,812.41
27	10,000	5%	2,678.48
28	10,000	5%	2,550.93
29	10,000	5%	2,429.46
30	10,000	5%	2,313.77

Present value of $10,000 a year for a third 10-year period at interest of 5% $ 29,102.38

Present value of $10,000 a year for 30 years at 5% $153,724.46

Present value of $10,000 a year for 40 years at 5% $171,590.86

Present value of $10,000 a year for 50 years at 5% $182,559.26

Present value of $10,000 a year for 90 years at 5% $197,522.62

Present value of $10,000 a year for 100 years at 5% $198,479.10

would be computed as $100,000 ($20,000 = 20%, so $100,000 = 100%). In effect, the valuation of $100,000 is based upon an assumption that the company will continue to earn $20,000 a year indefinitely.

Some authorities contend that earnings after taxes and interest should be capitalized to determine the proper valuation of the shareholders' equity. Others contend the proper valuation should be based upon earnings after taxes but before interest to determine the appropriate valuation of the total assets of the company. A few authorities suggest that the proper valuation results from capitalizing earnings before taxes and interest.

Valuation by Appraisal

The process of appraisal has not been and probably never can be reduced to formulae to a sufficient degree to provide objective valuations. When it is considered desirable to use subjective valuations in valuing an enterprise, the use of independent appraisals undoubtedly has much merit. Various factors and exceedingly fine judgments are required in the making of an appraisal. To a large degree appraisals run in terms of current market value or reproduction cost new less depreciation, but these are not the sole means of valuation of the enterprise by appraisal.

Normally, the valuation of an enterprise by appraisal implies an appraisal of assets. Such appraisal would generally have two characteristics: (1) the dollar value attached to the assets would be determined by human estimate; and (2) the valuation of the enterprise would be determined by a summation of the various asset values after appraisal. Thus, valuation of an enterprise by appraisal is somewhat related to the first method of valuation discussed above, a valuation arrived at by summation of acquisition costs less portions allocated to past operations; "current values," or more accurately, "appraised values" are substituted for acquisition costs.

While valuation of an enterprise by appraisal has practical usefulness in a variety of business situations, accountants generally are reluctant to incorporate the results of appraisals into the accounting records of an enterprise. Probably the reluctance is attributable to the lack of objectivity existing in the appraisal procedure. Accountants normally require objective evidence as a condition precedent to the recording of a business event. The appraised values have been unilaterally determined and have not met the give-and-take of the market place which commonly validates the dollar valuation of a business transaction. It should be noted, however, that competent and experienced appraisers may well determine values for given assets which could be as acceptable as those determined in the market place.

Accounting for Appraisals. The accounting treatment for appraisals is generally considered in intermediate accounting textbooks and will not be illustrated here. *Opinion 6* of the Accounting Principles Board of the American Institute of Certified Public Accountants recommends that accounting records be maintained on a cost basis and that appraisal values not be injected into the accounts. If appraised values are recorded, however, the *Opinion* provides that depreciation charges in income statements for years subsequent to the appraisal be based upon the appraised values and not upon acquisition costs.

Although accountants are reluctant to record appraisal values in accounting records, one should not conclude that accountants object to appraisals generally for business purposes. On many occasions when the valuation of an enterprise is desired, appraisals are most helpful. For example, in determining the adequacy of insurance coverage the management of an enterprise must be aware constantly of changing asset values. Periodic appraisals are most helpful to give an indication of the adequacy of existing coverage. Likewise, in pledging collateral in a borrowing agreement an enterprise may well desire to have its collateral-assets appraised, or, more properly, the lending agency may well desire such an appraisal. The accountant must recognize the numerous valid uses of appraisals, both in valuation of an enterprise as a unit and in valuation of specific elements thereof. He should not, however, feel obligated to reflect such appraisals in the accounting records of the enterprise.

Valuation in Terms of Common Dollars

In recognition of the fluctuations in the value of the monetary unit some accountants, economists, and businessmen have suggested that the proper valuation of the enterprise may be achieved only by adjusting the original cost valuations incurred at various times to some uniform-dollar amount. The procedure in this process may be likened to the conversion of foreign currency into a domestic currency. The process of uniform-dollar accounting converts all dollar valuations to a common or uniform dollar.

Normally, the conversion of acquisition cost dollars is accomplished by means of index numbers. For example, assume that for each of four years the appropriate index numbers to be used for conversion are as follows:

1961	90	1963	115
1962	110	1964	110

Acquisition costs and the year of acquisition of assets to be converted are as follows:

1961	$10,000	1963	$10,000
1962	10,000	1964	10,000

If it were desired to get all acquisition costs expressed in terms of one year's prices, say year 1964, the conversion process to convert all dollars to the dollar in existence in 1964 would be:

1961	$10,000 times 110/90, or	$12,222
1962	10,000 times 110/110, or	10,000
1963	10,000 times 110/115, or	9,565
1964	10,000 times 110/110, or	10,000
	Total, in terms of 1964 dollars	$41,787

Thus, the total acquisition cost of the assets, $40,000, would be modified on a common dollar basis to $41,787 in terms of year 1964 dollars.

The valuation of assets in terms of common dollars has the advantage of eliminating the change in the value of money from the amount at which the asset is reported. The main limitation to this process of valuation is the inadequacy of any one set of index numbers to make an adjustment appropriate for all situations. For example, if it is the intent of the adjustment to indicate replacement cost of the assets, an index number reflecting the specific price level changes of similar assets is needed. On the other hand, if the objective is to adjust for general changes in the purchasing power of money, a more general index number would be appropriate.

Common-Dollar Valuation Illustrated. Comparative balance sheets and an income statement for the Coft Landy Corporation are presented below:

BALANCE SHEET
As of DECEMBER 31

Assets	1962	1961	Increase or Decrease*
Cash	$11,000	$10,000	$1,000
Receivables	16,000	18,000	2,000*
Merchandise	19,000	16,000	3,000
Land	20,000	20,000	—
Building	30,000	30,000	—
Allowance for depr., Building	(12,000)	(11,000)	(1,000)
Equipment	25,000	25,000	—
Allowance for depr., Equipment	(10,000)	(7,500)	(2,500)
Total assets	$99,000	$100,500	$1,500*
Equities			
Accounts payable	$ 9,000	$12,000	$3,000*
Bonds payable	20,000	20,000	—
Capital stock	50,000	50,000	—
Retained earnings	20,000	18,500	1,500
Total equities	$99,000	$100,500	$1,500*

Income Statement for 1962

Sales		$125,000
Cost of goods sold:		
Inventory, January 1	$ 16,000	
Purchases	93,000	
	$109,000	
Inventory, December 31	19,000	
	$ 90,000	
Operating expenses, excluding depreciation	17,000	
Depreciation	3,500	
Interest charges	1,000	
Income taxes	7,000	
Total expenses		$118,500
Income		$ 6,500
Dividends paid		5,000
Increase in retained earnings		$ 1,500

Price Index Numbers Prevailing at Date Various Assets and Equities Arose

Date	Item Acquired	Index No.
12/31/49	Building	80
12/31/47	Land	70
12/31/57	Equipment	90
12/31/46	Capital stock issued	60
Nov. & Dec. 1961	12/31/61, Merchandise	104
Nov. & Dec. 1962	12/31/62, Merchandise	106
Average, 1962	Appropriate 1962 operating items	105
12/31/61	December 31, 1961 Balance sheet	107
12/31/62	December 31, 1962 Balance sheet	108
12/15/62	Dividends and interest paid	109

The procedures below would be followed to prepare statements adjusted to the price level existing as of December 31, 1962:

A. The dollar amounts of dates other than December 31, 1962, may be converted to their equivalent amount of December 31, 1962, dollars by multiplying them by the ratio of the 12/31/62 index to the index prevailing at the other dates.

B. Converting the Income Statement (nearest $100):
   (1) Sales are assumed to have been sold throughout the year, when the average index was 105. This amount may be converted to 12/31/62 dollars, as follows:
   108/105 times $125,000 = $128,600

(2) Cost of goods sold:

Merchandise 12/31/61 = 108/104 × $16,000 =	$ 16,600
Purchases 108/105 × $93,000 =	95,700
Total	$112,300
Merchandise 12/31/62 = 108/106 × $19,000 =	19,400
Adjusted cost	$ 92,900

(3) Operating expenses, excluding depreciation:

$17,000 × 108/105 =	$ 17,500

(4) Depreciation:

Building $1,000 × 108/80 = 1,350 or	$ 1,400
Equipment—$2,500 × 108/90 =	3,000
	$ 4,400

(5) Interest charges (paid once a year):

$1,000 × 108/109 = $991 or	$ 1,000

(6) Income taxes (assuming this item is accrued throughout the year):

$7,000 × 108/105 =	$ 7,200

(7) Dividends paid:

$5,000 × 108/109 = $4,953 or	$ 5,000

Comparative income statements adjusted and unadjusted, might be presented as follows:

Income Statement for 1962

	Unadjusted for Price Level Changes	Adjusted to 12/31/62 Price Level	Price Level Increase Decrease*
Sales	$125,000	$128,600	$3,600
Cost of goods sold:			
Inventory 1/1/62	$ 16,000	$ 16,600	
Purchases	93,000	95,700	
	$109,000	$112,300	
Inventory 12/31/62	19,000	19,400	
	$ 90,000	$ 92,900	2,900
Operating expenses	17,000	17,500	500
Depreciation	3,500	4,400	900
Interest charges	1,000	1,000	—
Income taxes	7,000	7,200	200
Total expenses	$118,500	$123,000	$4,500
Income	$ 6,500	$ 5,600	$ 900*
Dividends paid	5,000	5,000	—
Increase in retained earnings	$ 1,500	$ 600	$ 900*

C. Converting the balan' e sheets (nearest $100):

(1) Cash on 12/31/62 is stated in terms of the price level prevailing
on 12/31/62 and would remain $11,000
Cash on 12/31/61 had a greater purchasing power on 12/31/61
than it would have had on 12/31/62. Adjustment for equivalent
purchasing power would be:
$10,000 × 108/107 =   10,100

(2) Receivables would be converted similar to cash:
12/31/62 Receivable = $16,000 × 108/108 = $16,000
12/31/61 Receivable =   18,000 × 108/107 =   18,200

(3) Inventories would be converted as shown in the cost of goods
sold:
12/31/61 Inventory = $16,000 × 108/104 = $16,600
12/31/62 Inventory = $19,000 × 108/106 =   19,400

(4) Land as converted, would appear in both balance sheets as:
$20,000 × 108/70 = $30,900

(5) Building and building depreciation would be:
Building (both years) = $30,000 × 108/80 = $40,500

Accumulated depreciation:
12/31/61—$11,000 × 108/80 =   14,900
12/31/62—$12,000 × 108/80 =   16,200

(6) Equipment and equipment depreciation:
Equipment (both years)—$25,000 × 108/90 = $30,000
Accumulated depreciation:
12/31/61—$ 7,500 × 108/90 =   9,000
12/31/62—$10,000 × 108/90 =   12,000

(7) Accounts payable would be converted on the same basis as
current receivables and cash:
12/31/62 a/c payable = $ 9,000 × 108/108 = $ 9,000
12/31/61 a/c payable = $12,000 × 108/107 =   12,100

(8) Bonds payable:
12/31/62 payable = $20,000 × 108/108 = $20,000
12/31/61 payable = $20,000 × 108/107 =   20,200

(9) Capital stock would be the converted purchasing power contributed to the Company, for both years:
$50,000 × 108/60 = $90,000

(10) Retained earnings may be computed as the amount needed
to balance the balance sheet. Since this procedure may
include unrealized gains or losses, it might better be labeled
"Additional shareholder equity."

Comparative adjusted balance sheets would be as follows:

BALANCE SHEET
As of December 31
Adjusted to 12/31/62 Price Level

Assets	1962	1961	Increase or Decrease*
Cash	$11,000	$10,100	$ 900
Receivables	16,000	18,200	2,200*
Merchandise	19,400	16,600	2,800
Land	30,900	30,900	—
Building	40,500	40,500	—
Allowance for depr., Building	(16,200)	(14,900)	(1,300)
Equipment	30,000	30,000	—
Allowance for depr., Equipment	(12,000)	(9,000)	(3,000)
Total assets	$119,600	$122,400	$2,800*
Equities			
Accounts payable	$ 9,000	$12,100	$3,100*
Bonds payable	20,000	20,200	200*
Capital stock	90,000	90,000	—
Additional shareholder equity	600	100	500
Total equities	$119,600	$122,400	$2,800*

D. Reconciliation of changes in adjusted "Additional shareholder equity" in 1962:

Balance, 12/31/61 (See adjusted balance sheet)	$100
Increase in retained earning—1962 (See adjusted total income report)	$600
Total	$700

Purchasing power loss during 1962:
(1) Loss on current monetary assets:

	1961	1962	Increase (Decrease)
Cash	$10,100	$11,000	$ 900
Receivables	18,200	16,000	(2,200)
Total	$28,300	$27,000	$(1,300)

Loss if $28,300 were held for entire year:
$28,300 × (108/108 − 107/108) or 1/108 = $ 300
Less: Saving by disposing of $1,300 ($28,300 −
     $27,000) during the year:
     $1,300 × (108/105 − 105/105) or 3/105 =   —

Net loss on current monetary assets $300

(2) Less: Gain on monetary equities:
     Accounts payable 12/31/61 = $12,100
     Bonds payable 12/31/61 =   20,200
                                ─────────
                                  $32,300

     Gain if unchanged for year $32,300 × 1/108 = $300
     Less: Loss by liquidating $3,300 (32,300 − 29,000)
           during the year: 3,300 × 3/105 =   100
                                                        ────
           Net gain on monetary equities $200
     Net purchasing power loss—1962 $100
                                                                     ────
Balance, December 31, 1962 (see adjusted balance
     sheet) $600
                                                                     ════

While there is considerable support for the use of uniform-dollar accounting, it has not had extended use in practice. More widespread application in practice must await, among other things, development of price indexes of wider applicability and greater reliability than presently exist.

VALUATION OF PARTNERSHIPS

As indicated earlier, a partnership is a group of individuals banded together as one business enterprise. When a partner withdraws from a partnership or when a partner is admitted to partnership, a new partnership is created and the old partnership is dissolved. The problem of valuing the enterprise arises every time there is an admission or withdrawal of a partner. Valuation is necessary at each of these times to determine how much must be paid out to the withdrawing partner or how much the new partner should pay in for a share of the partnership. When one or more members of an existing partnership sells all or a portion of his interest(s) in the partnership to a new partner, two alternatives exist for adjustment of the valuation of the partnership:

(1) No adjustment of asset values recorded.
(2) Adjustment of asset values is recorded based upon the sale price of the partnership interest sold.

No Valuation Adjustment Recorded

Purchase of an Interest from One Partner. In some instances one partner will sell out his interest to a new partner. In these instances there are no assets flowing in and out of the partnership, since the only change from the point of view of the partnership is a change in the composition of the partners. For example, assume C, with a partnership capital of $8,000, sells out his interest in the partnership to D for $10,000. C must have the consent of the other partners to sell out to D, but assuming such approval is obtained, the only entry on the books of the partnership would be:

C, Capital	$8,000	
D, Capital		$8,000

The price at which C sold to D is not recorded on the books of the partnership. The partnership continues as before except for the change in owners. As far as the valuation of the enterprise is concerned, if no adjustment of individual asset values is made, there is an implication that the original acquisition price of the assets continues to represent the appropriate valuation of the enterprise.

Purchase of an Interest from Several Partners. ADJUSTMENT OF CAPITAL ACCOUNTS. Another common change in partnership ownership arises when several of the partners sell a partial interest to a new incoming partner. Again, the distinction between an investment of assets into the partnership and the buying out of a former partner's interest must be maintained. In this instance the sale involves a transfer of part of several partners' interests directly to the incoming partner. The asset transfer will be between the old partners and the incoming partner, and the partnership as an enterprise will have no change in assets.

For illustrative purposes, assume the new partner D is buying a one-third interest from the original partners. The one-third interest here means one-third of the capital and one-third of the income or loss. Because partners may share profits and losses in a ratio other than the capital ratio, it is important that the incoming partner make certain that he is buying both capital interest and profit and loss interest. The transfer of each former partner's capital to the incoming partner will depend upon the agreement reached by the old partners regarding the amount of capital and profit and loss interest to be transferred by each partner. Since the new partner is to receive a one-third interest, it is apparent that in total the old partners will have to transfer one-third of their capital to the capital credit of the incoming partner. But the amount of the one-third which each old partner is to sell depends upon agreement among the old partners.

In the illustration below, assume that each old partner is to transfer one-third of his individual interest in the partnership, both capital and profit and loss sharing interests, to D. The capital accounts and the profit and loss sharing ratio of the old partners prior to selling an interest to the new partner were as follows:

Partner	Capital	Profit and Loss Ratio
A	$50,000	50%
B	40,000	30%
C	30,000	20%
Total	$120,000	100%

Assume D is to join the partnership and is to pay $40,000 to the old partners for a one-third interest in the capital of the partnership and a one-third interest in profits and losses. The portion of each old partner's capital account to be transferred to D would be computed as follows:

Partner	Capital	$\frac{1}{3}$ to D	P & L Ratio	$\frac{1}{3}$ to D
A	$50,000	$16,667	50%	$16\frac{2}{3}$%
B	40,000	13,333	30%	10%
C	30,000	10,000	20%	$6\frac{2}{3}$%
Total	$120,000	$40,000	100%	$33\frac{1}{3}$%

The entry to record the sale of the old partners' interests to the new partner would be:

A, Capital	$16,667	
B, Capital	13,333	
C, Capital	10,000	
D, Capital		$40,000

After recording the admission of the new partner the capital accounts and profit and loss sharing ratio would be:

Partner	Capital	Profit and Loss Ratio
A	$33,333	$33\frac{1}{3}$%
B	26,667	20%
C	20,000	$13\frac{1}{3}$%
D	40,000	$33\frac{1}{3}$%
Total	$120,000	100%

It should be noted that had D purchased one-third of the capital only, and had the agreement remained silent as to the sharing of profit and loss, D would have received a profit and loss sharing interest of 25% rather than $33\frac{1}{3}$%. Partnership law provides that when the partnership agreement is silent as to the profit and loss sharing ratio, profits and losses are to be divided equally. Normally, the partnership agreement provides that a sale of capital includes the sale of partners' interests in undistributed profits or withdrawals. Thus, had A, B, and C in the above illustration had credits or debits in their Drawing accounts, such would also be transferred by a sale of one-third of the capital. In those instances where the partnership agreement specifies that withdrawals in excess of profits or profits in excess of withdrawals shall not become part of capital, balances in the Drawing account are not closed to capital. Normally the total capital of a partnership can be changed only by consent of all of the old partners.

DISTRIBUTION OF CASH. While the foregoing illustration indicates the essential accounting procedures of recording the continuation of the enterprise when partners are changed, there remains a problem of dividing the cash paid by the new partner among the old partners. Three possibilities may arise:

(1) New partner pays book value for his interest ($40,000).
(2) New partner pays less than book value ($35,000).
(3) New partner pays more than book value ($42,000).

Purchase Price Equals Book Value. If the payment equals book value, the cash is distributed among the old partners at the amount of capital transferred by each old partner. In the illustration, this would be computed, assuming a purchase price of $40,000, as follows:

Partner	Capital Transferred	Cash to be Received
A	$16,667	$16,667
B	13,333	13,333
C	10,000	10,000
Total	$40,000	$40,000

Purchase Price Less than Book Value. If the payment to the old partners is less than the book value transferred, it is apparent that cash cannot be distributed in accordance with the capital transfers. The loss (difference between book value and cash paid) must be deducted in the old partnership profit and loss sharing ratio from the book value of the capital transferred in order to determine the cash distribution, as follows:

Partner	Capital Transfer	Less Loss	Cash to be Received
A	$16,667	$2,500	$14,167
B	13,333	1,500	11,833
C	10,000	1,000	9,000
Total	$40,000	$5,000	$35,000

The loss of $5,000, which is the difference between the book value acquired by the incoming partner ($40,000) and the cash paid ($35,000), is allocated to the old partners in the profit and loss sharing ratio existing prior to the admission of the new partner. The reasoning supporting this allocation is that the old partners have sustained a loss which has not been recorded on the books. Had it been recorded, it would have been allocated in the profit and loss sharing ratio prevailing in the past when the old partnership existed. Since profit and loss sharing ratios apply whether or not a gain or loss is recorded, it is equitable to allocate the loss to the old partners in the profit and loss sharing ratio existing during the period when the loss arose.

Purchase Price More than Book Value. If the payment to the old partners is more than the book value of the capital transferred, an unrecorded gain exists. While it is not necessary to record this gain on the books of the partnership, the gain must be allocated to the old partners in order to distribute the cash received from the incoming partner. Assuming that the incoming partner D paid $42,000 to acquire a one-third interest in the partnership capital of $120,000, a $2,000 gain accrues to the old partners. This gain would be allocated in the old partnership profit and loss sharing ratio, in order to determine the distribution of the cash, as follows:

Partner	Capital Transfer	Plus Gain	Cash to be Received
A	$16,667	$1,000	$17,667
B	13,333	600	13,933
C	10,000	400	10,400
Total	$40,000	$2,000	$42,000

Valuation Adjustment Recorded

The foregoing was based on the assumption that the proper valuation of enterprise assets was in terms of acquisition cost. That is, no adjustments were made to the asset values on the books of the partnership, even though the price paid for an interest by an incoming partner was not necessarily equal to the book value of the capital interest acquired. Some authorities suggest that the proper valuation of the enterprise should reflect the value of the assets indicated by the price paid by the new partner in buying a portion of the old partners' interests. This suggestion may be supported by pointing out that the purchase price arrived at for the sale would be based on an appraisal, an approximation of the earning power of the enterprise, or on some other approach to the valuation of the enterprise. The purchase price is considered to be an appropriate valuation of the partnership interest being transferred. If such purchase price exceeds book value, the assumption is that the assets and the capital of the partnership are undervalued and should be revalued upward, or that the partnership has a goodwill element existing which is not reflected on the books. On the other hand, if the purchase price is below book value, the assumption is that the partnership assets are overstated and should be revalued downward.

Using the same facts as in the previous illustration, assume the price paid by the incoming partner is used as a basis for departure from the acquisition cost valuation of the assets.

Purchase Price Less than Book Value. If the new partner pays only $35,000 for a capital interest with a $40,000 book value, it appears that $40,000 of assets are overstated by $5,000, if the purchase price is an accepted valuation. For the $120,000 of assets, the overstatement would be three times as large ($120,000 divided by $40,000), or $15,000. Thus, the book value of the net assets exceeds the accepted valuation, as evidenced by the purchase price, by $15,000. This $15,000 overvaluation should be recorded as a loss and allocated to the old partners' accounts in the old profit and loss sharing ratio, as follows:

A, Capital	$7,500	
B, Capital	4,500	
C, Capital	3,000	
Assets		$15,000

The particular asset accounts to be written down from their acquisition cost basis would depend upon a review, or appraisal, of all asset valuations to determine which should be revalued. After recognizing this as a loss, the capital accounts of the old partners and the one-third portion of the capital account which each contributes to the incoming partner would be as follows:

Partner	Capital	$\frac{1}{3}$ to New Partner	Capital Balance After Transfer
A	$42,500	$14,167	$28,333
B	35,500	11,833	23,667
C	27,000	9,000	18,000
Total	$105,000	$35,000	$70,000

The entry to record the transfer of capital to the new partner would be:

A, Capital	$14,167	
B, Capital	11,833	
C, Capital	9,000	
D, Capital		$35,000

The cash distribution would be identical to the capital transferred. It should be noted that this cash distribution is identical to the distribution which resulted when no valuation adjustment was used in determining the distribution of the cash (see p. 161).

Purchase Price More than Book Value. If the new partner pays $42,000 for a capital interest with a book value of $40,000, it appears that the book value of the assets is understated by $2,000 on $40,000 of the partnership assets. The total undervaluation would be three times this amount, or $6,000, on assets of $120,000 represented by partnership capital. Following the concept that the purchase price establishes a sound basis for valuing the enterprise, the unrecorded valuation of $6,000 should be recorded and allocated to the old partners in their profit and loss sharing ratio. The entry to record this valuation would be:

Goodwill (or Assets)	$6,000	
A, Capital		$3,000
B, Capital		1,800
C, Capital		1,200

While it would be more desirable theoretically to adjust the appropriate asset accounts upward, frequently a "goodwill" account is debited for the undervaluation. This debit is supported by the argument that it is not possible to designate specifically which of the individual assets are under-valued. After recording this gain, the capital accounts of the old partners, and the one-third each contributes to the incoming partner, would be:

Partner	Capital	$\frac{1}{3}$ to New Partner	Capital Balance After Transfer
A	$53,000	$17,667	$35,333
B	41,800	13,933	27,867
C	31,200	10,400	20,800
Total	$126,000	$42,000	$84,000

The entry to record the transfer of capital to the new partner would be:

A, Capital	$17,667	
B, Capital	13,933	
C, Capital	10,400	
D, Capital		$42,000

The distribution of cash among the old partners would be equal to the capital transferred. This is the same distribution that resulted when the acquisition cost valuation of the enterprise was used in determining the distribution of cash (see p. 162).

Special Problems if Valuation Adjustments not Recorded

From the above adjustment it should not be concluded that the decision on whether to record the valuation adjustment has no effect on any partner's respective interest in the partnership. The partners' respective interests will be affected by the decision to record or not to record the revaluation if either of the following conditions exist:

(1) The new profit and loss sharing ratio of the old partners among themselves is different from the ratio existing prior to the admission of the new partner.
(2) The new partner acquires a profit and loss ratio different from his capital ratio.

When the revaluation is not recorded and either of the above conditions exists, and there is actual realization in a subsequent period of the gain or loss evidenced by the purchase price of the new partner, a different allocation to the partners will result than if the revaluation had been recorded on the partnership books at the date of admission of the new partner.

Illustration. Assume D acquires a one-third interest in the profits and losses of the enterprise and one-third of the existing partners' capital for $35,000, that the total capital is $120,000, and that no adjustment is made for the overvaluation of the assets and capital interests of the partnership. Also, assume that A, B, and C agree to share their remaining $66\frac{2}{3}\%$ of the profits and losses as follows:

$$A = 25\%$$
$$B = 25\%$$
$$C = 16\frac{2}{3}\%$$

If, immediately after formation of the new partnership, certain assets were sold at a loss of $15,000, the following balances would result in the various partners' capital accounts:

Partner	Capital Balance	D Acquires $\frac{1}{3}$	Capital Balance	Share of Loss	Balance
A	$50,000	($16,667)	$33,333	($3,750)	$29,583
B	40,000	(13,333)	26,667	(3,750)	22,917
C	30,000	(10,000)	20,000	(2,500)	17,500
D	—	40,000	40,000	(5,000)	35,000
Total	$120,000	—	$120,000	($15,000)	$105,000

A comparison of the final balances above with those resulting in the example on page 163, in which the loss evidenced by D's acquisition price was recorded, reveals the following:

Partner	Ending Balance, Above	Ending Balance if Revaluation Recorded, page 163	Difference Increase (Decrease)
A	$29,583	$28,333	$1,250
B	22,917	23,667	(750)
C	17,500	18,000	(500)
D	35,000	35,000	—
Total	$105,000	$105,000	—

The comparison indicates that by recording no valuation adjustment at the time of D's admission to the partnership, A benefited by $1,250 at the expense of B ($750) and C ($500), when the loss was actually realized. This benefit to A arose because A's share of the loss in the new partnership was less, proportionately, than under the old agreement. The reverse of the above would have resulted from a gain situation. A similar inequity would arise if D's profit and loss ratio differed from his capital ratio.

Thus, in addition to reflecting more current asset values, recording a valuation adjustment at the date a new partner acquires an interest in a partnership may also be supported on the grounds of equity to all parties. If the price paid for the partnership interest is not representative of the current value of the assets, such a conclusion is not valid.

SPECIAL ENTERPRISE VALUATION PROBLEMS

Accountants are frequently called upon to provide guidance in business problems which may not directly bear upon accounting entries. Some of these problem areas involve the process of valuation of specific asset or equity elements of the enterprise. The process of valuation at acquisition cost for individual items within the firm is one approach used in valuing specific items. Another approach involves appraisals. In connection with certain items normally appearing as equities on financial statements, accountants may find it appropriate to employ approaches to valuation other than acquisition cost or appraisal.

Refunding Bonds Outstanding

In the case of long-term bonds outstanding, several valuations of this equity are possible, each suitable for different purposes. Possible valuations include (1) face amount of the bonds, (2) callable amount of the bonds, and (3) a discounted amount. The discounted amount is useful for several purposes. It may be particularly appropriate if an enterprise is considering refunding existing bonds prior to their maturity date. For example, assume the Lynn Company has outstanding bonds in a maturity amount of $200,000. The bonds are due in 10 years, bear interest at a rate of 4%, and are callable at any time by the Lynn Company at 108. The current market rate of interest is such that the Lynn Company believes refunding bonds can be issued at a rate of 3%. The question involved is whether the company should refund the outstanding bond issue. The cost of refunding, aside from interest charges, will amount to about $10,000, for such items as printing the new bonds, calling the old bonds, and issuing the new bonds.

Alternative Plans Available. The simplest approach to this problem is to determine the amount which would have to be deposited in the hands of a trustee at a present date in order (1) to call the old bonds, (2) to provide for their interest payments and settlement at maturity, or (3) to provide for the issuance, interest payments, and settlement of the new bonds at maturity if they were issued. The method resulting in the smallest lump-sum payment might indicate the more advantageous procedure. The computation for the foregoing illustration would be along the following lines:

	Deposit with Trustee to Call Old Bonds	Deposit with Trustee to Pay Old Bonds	Deposit with Trustee to Pay New Bonds
Deposit to pay interest for 10 years: (Present value of future interest payments)		$ 68,241.62	$ 51,181.22
Deposit to pay principal at the end of 10 years: (Present value of maturity value)		148,818.78	148,818.78
Cost of refunding— Assumed			10,000.00
Call price of old bonds	$216,000.00		
Total	$216,000.00	$217,060.40	$210,000.00

In deciding what action to take, the management of the Lynn Company has several alternatives to consider. First, if the company has available idle cash to retire the existing 4% bonds immediately, it is evidently cheaper to retire them through exercising the call option than it is to pay off the interest and maturity amount. A saving of $1,060.40 would result from immediate call. If the company does not have idle cash available to retire the old bonds, such retirement could take place through sale of the new 3% bonds. At first glance it might appear that such a sale would be advantageous. If the Lynn Company were to do this, however, the outlay to retire the old bonds would be $226,000 ($216,000 for call price plus $10,000 to sell the new bonds). Since this amount exceeds the amount of deposit required to pay off the old bonds, such action would not be advisable, disregarding all other considerations. The $1,060.40 saving would be more than offset by the $10,000 cost of issuing the new bonds.

Thus, the conclusions on the above illustration appear to be:

(1) If the company has idle cash on hand, sufficient to retire bonds, which can be invested nowhere else to earn more than 3%, it appears the most economical manner of retirement would be to call the bonds for $216,000.

(2) If the company would have to issue new bonds to obtain funds to retire the old bonds, the cost of the new issue plus the call price for the old bonds would be greater than that involved in permitting the old bonds to remain outstanding. Refunding the bonds would not be the most economical manner of retirement.

It should be noted that total present value of the issue cost, interest payments, and maturity value of the new issue of bonds normally has no bearing upon the decision. The company would refund *only* if it would be cheaper to retire the existing bonds than it would be to deposit an amount necessary to pay remaining interest and the maturity value of the bonds. The deposit to retire the old bonds could be expected to earn interest at approximately the prevailing market rate of interest, and for this reason this rate (3%) is used to discount the future payments under the old bond issue. The cost of issuing the new bonds ($10,000) may be considered as one of the costs of calling the old bonds if issuance of new bonds is the only manner of obtaining funds to call the old bonds. For comparative purposes, this cost may be considered as part of the outlay necessary to retire the old bonds immediately.

The Discounting Process. At this point further explanation of the discounting process may be in order. This process, which involves the discounting of future known amounts, is explained more fully in the Appendix. The method used in the above illustration is similar to the procedure used earlier (pp. 149–150) in arriving at a value for an enterprise in terms of its capitalized earning power. In effect, the annual interest payments of $8,000 represent an annuity of $8,000 a year payable by the company to the bondholders for 10 years, while the $200,000 maturity amount represents a future sum which the company will pay the bondholders. Using the tables of present value in the Appendix, and discounting at 3% the rate at which it is assumed funds can presently be invested, the following computations may be made:

The present value of an annuity of $1.00 a year for 10 years at 3% equals $8.53020284. Since the annuity is $8,000 a year rather than $1.00, it is necessary to multiply the $8.53020284 by $8,000 to determine the present value of an annuity of $8,000 a year for 10 years. When the multiplication is performed, the result indicates that the sum of $68,241.62 would have to be deposited today (present value) at 3% interest per year in order to pay out $8,000 a year for the next 10 years.

To determine the amount which would have to be deposited now in order to have $200,000 at the end of the 10 years, the amount necessary to pay off the maturity amount of the bonds, it is necessary to refer to the table of Present Value of 1 in the Appendix. Referring to this table, the present value of $1.00 to be received in 10 years if the interest rate is 3% is $.74409391. Since it is $200,000 rather than $1.00 to be received in 10 years, it is necessary to multiply the $.74409391 by $200,000 to determine the present value of the maturity amount of the bonds. Multiplication indicates that this valuation is $148,818.78. This means that $148,818.78 would have to be deposited so that in 10 years $200,000 would be available, assuming a 3% interest rate. Since the present value of the interest payments is $68,241.62, the present value of all the money to be deposited with a trustee would be the sum of these two amounts, or $217,060.40.

Accounting for Refunding of Bonds. To illustrate the recording process when bonds are refunded, assume that the bonds in the foregoing illustration were callable at 101, or at a cost of $202,000. When the $10,000 cost of issuing new bonds is added to this amount, the total cash outlay to refund would be $212,000. Since the cost of refunding $212,000 is now less than the cost of not refunding $217,060.40, the company might refund, providing other considerations would not make such a decision inadvisable. It should be recognized that numerous considerations other than comparative costs influence the decision on refunding. These considerations include the income tax impact from refunding as opposed to leaving the old bonds outstanding.

Assuming the decision to refund is made, the entry to record the issuance of the new bonds would be:

Cash	$190,000	
Bond issue cost	10,000	
Bonds payable		$200,000

This assumes that at 3% interest the new bonds can be sold at par.

The entry to record the retirement of the old bonds will depend upon the value at which they are being carried on the books. For illustrative purposes, assume the old bonds were carried in the accounts at a maturity amount of $200,000 but with a related unamortized bond discount and expense account of $19,000. The entry to record the call of the old bonds would be:

Bonds payable	$200,000	
Loss on retirement of bonds	21,000	
Bond discount		$ 19,000
Cash		202,000

The net effect of the transaction is that the company spends $12,000 in cash ($202,000 outlay less $190,000 receipt) and recognizes a $21,000 loss. In addition, the refunding results in a reduction in the annual cash interest payment of $2,000 ($6,000 annual payment now rather than the $8,000 previously paid).

Valuation of Bonds Payable

Two other valuations of bonds payable are book value and market price. At the time bonds are issued, these two valuations may be the same but at any time subsequent to that date different valuations would be the normal situation. The market price valuation will change because of a number of factors. Book value will change as the premium or discount on the bonds is amortized.

Bond Premium or Bond Discount. The price at which bonds can be issued depends upon two factors: (1) the interest rate which the company agrees to pay, generally referred to as the *nominal* rate of interest, and (2) the interest rate which investors will demand before investing in the bonds, generally referred to as the *effective* rate of interest. The relationship between the two rates will indicate whether the bonds will be issued at a discount or at a premium. For example, assume the Jean Brown Company decides to issue $100,000 face amount of bonds at 4%, payable 2% twice a year, due in 10 years. These bonds are being issued at a nominal rate of 2% every six months. If investors who might buy the bonds have opportunity to make a similar investment elsewhere and earn 3% every six months, it is obvious that the prospect of selling the 2% bonds at par is rather remote, and it may be expected that the bonds would sell at a discount. On the other hand, if the market rate of interest for ventures of a similar risk were 1% every six months, it is apparent that investors would want very much to acquire the bonds paying 2% every six months and would bid up the price of such bonds until they would be sold at a premium.

Determination of Issuance Price. The determination of the price at which bonds could be issued may be computed through the use of compound interest tables. To illustrate the process of estimating the price at which bonds may be issued, assume the BT Company decides to issue bonds in the face amount of $100,000, such bonds to bear annual interest of 6%, interest payable twice a year, and that the bonds are to mature in 20 years. An examination of the security markets indicates that bonds bearing a risk somewhat similar to that involved in the current issue of bonds are selling at a price to yield an effective rate of interest of 2% every six months. As a result, it may be assumed that the bonds of the BT Company can be sold at an effective rate of 2% every six months—that is, at a price to yield the purchaser a 2% return every six months. The computation of the price at which the bonds would sell requires recognition that the bond involves two types of money payments: (1) an annuity of $3,000 every six months for 20 years, and (2) a promise to pay $100,000 at the end of a 20-year period. The determination of the price of the bonds resolves itself into the question of how much should be paid now to receive the annuity of $3,000 each six months and the future $100,000 if money invested in this type of risk earns 2% every six months.

Referring to the compound interest tables in the Appendix, the price to be paid for an annuity of $1.00 a period for 40 periods, if the interest rate is 2% a period, is $27.35547924. For an annuity of $3,000 every six months for 20 years (40 "periods"), the price would be 3,000 times larger, or $82,066.44. For the second phase of the problem, the compound interest tables indicate that to have $1.00 at the end of 40 six-month periods, if the interest rate is 2% every six months, it would be necessary to deposit $.45289042. To have $100,000, the sum of $45,289.04 should be deposited. Since the bonds will provide both the annuity of $3,000 and the future $100,000, the price of the bonds would then be:

Present value of an annuity of $3,000 every six months for 20 years, if interest is assumed to be 2% every six months . .	$ 82,066.44
Present value of $100,000 at the end of a 20 year period, if interest is assumed to be 2% every six months	45,289.04
Total (Price of the bonds)	$127,355.48

For each $1,000 bond the price would be $1,273.5548, and the bonds would probably be quoted at 127.35548. The entry to record the issuance of the bonds, assuming no issue cost, would be:

Cash	$127,355.48	
Bonds payable		$100,000.00
Premium on bonds		27,355.48

Determination of Effective Interest Cost. After the bonds have been issued, $3,000 of interest will be paid each six months, but all of the $3,000 should not be considered an expense. Part of the $3,000, in effect, represents a return of part of the premium of $27,355.48. The proper interest charge for a period would be computed by taking 2% of the carrying value of the bonds (maturity amount plus unamortized premium or minus unamortized discount). For the first interest period in the above illustration the interest expense would be $2,547.11 (2% of $127,355.48). The difference between this expense and the $3,000 payment or $452.89, would be applied to reduce the amount of the premium on the bonds. For the second six-month period the carrying value of the bonds would be smaller by $452.89, and the effective interest on this smaller balance at 2% would be $2,538.05 (2% of $126,902.59). The amortization of the premium in this period would be $461.95 ($3,000 less $2,538.05). Table 6-B indicates the proper interest expense and the valuation of the bonds resulting from the use of the effective rate to amortize the premium on the bonds:

TABLE 6-B

End of Period	Interest Paid	Effective Interest	Carrying Valuation of Bonds Payable
0	0	0	$127,355.48
1	$3,000.00	$2,547.11	126,902.59
2	3,000.00	2,538.05	126,440.64
3	3,000.00	2,528.81	125,969.45
4	3,000.00	2,519.39	125,488.84
—	—	—	—
39	3,000.00	2,038.83	100,980.39
40	3,000.00	2,019.61	100,000.00

Accounting for Interest Costs. The entries each six months to record the proper interest charges and the appropriate amortization of the premium are illustrated below for the first two six-month periods:

End of first six months:		
Premium on bonds	$ 452.89	
Bond interest expense	2,547.11	
Cash		$3,000.00
End of second six months:		
Premium on bonds	$ 461.95	
Bond interest expense	2,538.05	
Cash		$3,000.00

Contrary to the straight-line method of amortizing bond discount or premium, the effective rate method of amortization results in a different amount to be amortized each period. Under straight-line amortization, each of the 40 six-month entries would be:

Premium on bonds ($27,355.48 ÷ 40)	$ 683.89	
Bond interest expense	2,316.11	
Cash		$3,000.00

Although the straight-line method of amortization of bond premium or discount is often used, the effective rate method of amortization appears to provide a more realistic valuation of the bonds outstanding.

Valuation of Fixed Assets

The valuation of fixed assets acquired was discussed in Chapter 2. But as it has been observed, "All fixed assets are on an irresistible march to the junk heap." So it becomes necessary to depreciate the fixed assets of an enterprise if management is to be advised regarding whether or not the business is being maintained. The process of straight-line and other depreciation methods has been considered in elementary accounting text-books.

Once the discounting process for valuation is understood, it becomes possible to use the process in the valuation of almost any phase of the enterprise. While its use in the area of depreciation is not extensive, it is sufficient to warrant the attention of the student of advanced accounting.

Discounting Process Applied to Depreciation. Essentially, the concept underlying the discounting process as applied to depreciating assets involves the recognition that assets are composed of services, some of which are extracted for use by the enterprise during each period of operation. From this point of view the purchase of a depreciable asset involves the purchase of a series of services to be used over a period of time. Since the services embodied in the assets are acquired in advance of their use, an enterprise may suffer a loss of interest by having funds tied up in such services in advance of their utilization. The loss of interest may be compensated for if the price of the services to be used in the future is lower than that for the services to be used immediately.

To illustrate, assume the CUP Company purchases a machine which will last three years, and will be utilized at the same rate in each of the three years, and pays the sum of $2,775.09 for the machine. Assuming no scrap value, the $2,775.09 represents the cost of three years' services from the machine. At 4% interest, this sum is the present value of $1,000 of services each year, determined as follows:

Present value of $1,000 to be received at the end of one period,
if the interest rate is 4% . . . . $ 961.54
Present value of $1,000 to be received at the end of two periods,
if the interest rate is 4% 924.56
Present value of $1,000 to be received at the end of three periods,
if the interest rate is 4% 888.99

     Total $2,775.09

Since different prices have been paid for the services to be received in different years, it might be concluded that the depreciation each year on the basis of cost should be $961.54, $924.56, and $888.99, respectively. Straight-line depreciation would, of course, result in an annual depreciation charge of $925.03.

Application of the discounting process to depreciation accounting gives rise to the need for considering imputed interest, the interest which could have been earned if the dollars invested in the long-lived asset had been invested directly in an interest-generating asset. Determination of the annual depreciation charge and the credit to the allowance account would include imputed interest when the discounting method is used.

Annuity Method. Two main procedures, known as the sinking fund method and the annuity method, might find application in this concept of depreciation accounting. Under the annuity method the objective is to charge off as depreciation expense not only the original cost of the asset (less scrap), but also the interest which would have been earned if the funds had not been tied up in the asset. Referring to the facts in the previous paragraph, in the first year the interest which would have otherwise been earned on the $2,775.09 investment at 4% would be about $111.01. This amount was earned as follows:

On the $961.54, the sum of	$38.46
On the $924.56, the sum of	36.98
On the $888.99, the sum of	35.57
Total	$111.01

If the imputed interest earnings above are added to the original cost of the annual services acquired, after one year when depreciation is to be recorded the valuation of each year's services becomes:

	Original Cost	Imputed Interest	Year End Balance
First year	$961.54	$38.46	$1,000.00
Second year	924.56	36.98	961.54
Third year	888.99	35.57	924.56
Total	$2,775.09	$111.01	$2,886.10

This total cost is $111.01 higher than original cost because of the imputed interest element. For the first year depreciation should be charged for $1,000. The allowance account, however, should be credited only for the year's service which is no longer available in the asset. The amount no longer available would be the acquisition cost of the third year's services, since that year has moved up to be the services but two years away. The entry would be:

Depreciation expense	$1,000.00	
Interest revenue		$111.01
Allowance for depreciation		888.99

Continuing the illustration, the entries for the second and third years would be:

Depreciation expense	$1,000.00	
Interest revenue		$ 75.44
Allowance for depreciation		924.56
Depreciation expense	$1,000.00	
Interest revenue		$ 38.46
Allowance for depreciation		961.54

At the end of three years the allowance for depreciation account will be equal to the original cost of the fully depreciated machine. The interest which would have been earned if the funds had not been invested in the asset will have been recorded as revenue. Depreciation will have been charged on a more or less current cost basis. If the services had not been paid for before being used, the current price of the services on a rental basis would have included an interest element.

Sinking Fund Method. Under the sinking fund method of depreciation the objective is to provide by way of depreciation a sum, which when allowed to accumulate interest, will equal the original cost of the asset at the completion of the asset's estimated useful life. Often an actual fund (of cash or cash and securities) is established equal to the depreciation charge. In the previous illustration the portion of the entry for the first year which is considered to be solely depreciation is $888.99. If this amount is set aside in a fund it is assumed that it will be able to earn 4% interest for the two remaining years. Each year $888.99 will be deposited into the fund, and these three deposits of $888.99 plus the interest earned on the fund will accumulate to $2,775.09, the original cost of the machine, at the end of the third year. The entry to record the depreciation and to set up the fund, if a fund is to be used, would be:

Depreciation expense	$888.99	
Allowance for depreciation		$888.99
Fund	$888.99	
Cash		$888.99

A direct approach to finding the amount of the deposit to be made to the fund each year would proceed in the following manner:

$1.00 invested at the end of year 1 at 4% will be worth, at the end of year 3	$1.0816
$1.00 invested at the end of year 2 at 4% will be worth, at the end of year 3	1.0400
$1.00 invested at the end of year 3 at 4% will be worth, at the end of year 3	1.0000
Total	$3.1216

Thus, $1.00 deposited at the end of each year for three years will accumulate to $3.1216 by the end of the third year. This can also be found in an Annuity of 1 table in the Appendix. The amount of an annuity of three deposits of $1.00 invested at 4% is worth $3.1216 after the third deposit is made. But, in the example, $2,775.09 is wanted, the cost of the asset after the third deposit is made. To find the amount of each deposit $2,775.09 is divided by 3.1216. The result, $888.99 is the amount of each of the three deposits.

The second year the fund will earn interest of $35.57 ($888.99 times 4%). Since the depreciation charge under the sinking fund method is equal to the increase made in the fund, the second year's depreciation charge would be $924.56 ($888.99 + $35.57). Only by increasing the depreciation charge by the interest earned on the fund during the year can the amount of depreciation charged off over the asset's life be equal to its original cost. The entries for the second year would be:

Depreciation expense	$924.56	
Allowance for depreciation		$924.56
Fund	$924.56	
Interest revenue		$ 35.57
Cash		888.99

The third year the fund ($888.99 + $888.99 + $35.57, or $1,813.55) will earn interest of $72.55, so that the depreciation for the third year would be larger by this amount. The entries would be:

Depreciation expense	$961.54	
Allowance for depreciation		$961.54
Fund	$961.54	
Interest revenue		$ 72.55
Cash		888.99

Under this method at the end of the third year the allowance for depreciation account will be equal to the original cost of the fully depreciated machine. It should be noted that the depreciation charges increase each year under this procedure. It should also be recognized that the establishment of the supporting fund is optional, and if it is not used the depreciation charges would be determined in the same manner as if the fund did exist. In practice the fund would seem to serve little useful purpose, since the cash so segregated might well be invested in productive resources, rather than in securities earning 4%.

Relationship of Annuity and Sinking Fund Method. In addition to these specific methods of depreciation and valuation of specific assets of the enterprise, there are adaptations of them which might be applied. For example, one common method involves an adaptation of the annuity method to offset the interest revenue against the depreciation charge. Under this method no credit would be made to "Interest Revenue," but a reduction of the depreciation charge by the amount of the interest would be made. Thus, the annual debits and credits to the depreciation account increase with the passage of time, since the interest revenue decreases under the annuity method. In effect this procedure converts the annuity method to the sinking fund method since the depreciation charges resulting from this adaptation are the same as those that would arise under the sinking fund method.

PROBLEMS

Problem 6–1. The Bass Company statement of financial position as of December 31, 1967, shows total assets having a book value of $6,000,000 and total liabilities of $2,500,000. Recent feelers have been received by the board of directors concerning a possible sale of the business. The board is of the opinion that the business as a going enterprise is worth considerably more than reported on the statement of financial position. As evidence they cite the past five years' earnings, which have been reported as follows:

1963	$500,000
1964	120,000
1965	580,000
1966	595,000
1967	605,000

In 1964 the Company wrote off completely $400,000 of goodwill when it was determined this "goodwill" had in fact never existed even though it had been paid for. Interest costs average $60,000 per year.

Required:

Prepare a brief report for the board of directors of the Bass Company discussing several possible values for their business. Include estimates for both the total assets and the shareholders' equity. Assume that the risk element, or normal rate of return, is about 8% in the industry.

Problem 6–2. A somewhat condensed statement of financial position of the Fisher Corporation is presented below:

FISHER CORPORATION

STATEMENT OF FINANCIAL POSITION

DECEMBER 31, 1967

Assets

Cash in bank and on hand	$ 300,000
Receivables (less estimated uncollectibles)	2,600,000
Inventories (at LIFO cost; replacement market $6,600,000)	4,000,000
Investment in Rayburn Company (at cost)	1,200,000
Plant, machinery, and equipment (at depreciated cost)	8,000,000
Total	$16,100,000

Liabilities and Equities

Current liabilities	$ 2,900,000
Long-term debt, 5%, due 7–1–1986	4,000,000
Shareholders' contributed equity	2,000,000
Earnings reinvested in the business	7,200,000
Total	$16,100,000

Additional information of interest includes: (1) the Investment in Rayburn Company was made several years ago and represents 70% of Rayburn's outstanding common stock. Net book value of Rayburn's assets on its balance sheet is $10,000,000 at December 31, 1967. (2) During 1967 an appraisal of plant, machinery, and equipment for insurance purposes indicated a replacement cost new of $21,000,000 and an insurable value of $12,500,000. (3) Receivables appear fairly valued. (4) Average net income, after interest and taxes, for the past five years has been $2,430,000. (5) The long-term debt was incurred in 1961. (6) Rayburn Company has paid no dividends since Fisher Corporation acquired its interest.

Required:

(1) Assuming that a normal rate of return is 9%, approximate the value of the Fisher Corporation.

(2) Construct a pro forma statement of financial position to give effect to the value of the enterprise determined in (1).

(3) Discuss some unknown factors in the situation which make justification of *any* value estimate for the Fisher Corporation a difficult task.

Problem 6–3. Comparative balance sheets of the Hardeen Company on December 31, 1967 and 1968, are presented below:

	December 31		Increase
Assets	1967	1968	(Decrease)
Cash	$ 160,000	$ 150,000	$(10,000)
Receivables	400,000	500,000	100,000
Merchandise	600,000	700,000	100,000
Fixed assets	3,600,000	3,800,000	200,000
Less: Allowance for depreciation	(900,000)	(1,000,000)	(100,000)
Total assets	$3,860,000	$4,150,000	$290,000
Equities			
Accounts payable	$ 200,000	$ 100,000	$(100,000)
Bonds payable	500,000	400,000	(100,000)
Common stock	3,000,000	3,000,000	—
Retained earnings	160,000	650,000	490,000
Total equities	$3,860,000	$4,150,000	$290,000

An analysis of the physical facts underlying the accounts and the changes therein during the year reveals the following:

1. The general price level remained substantially unchanged during the year.
2. The physical number of items of merchandise (a one-product company) decreased from 100,000 to 80,000.
3. Replacement cost new of the $3,600,000 of fixed assets on December 31, 1968, ($200,000 additional were acquired on December 30, 1968) was conservatively placed at $1,800,000.
4. A cash dividend of $270,000 was paid on December 15, 1968.

On January 15, 1968, the management of the company was sued by one of its stockholders. The stockholder contends that management has paid out as dividends a substantial sum of the company's capital. Because he has to pay an income tax on the dividend received, the stockholder is suing the management of the company for recovery of the income tax.

Required:
   You are engaged by the stockholder to prepare a report which he can use to prove that most of the $18,000 he received in dividends and on which he has to pay a 60% income tax represents a distribution of capital. He reports to you confidentially that had the fixed assets been replaced new on December 31, 1967, they would have cost $2,400,000.
   Prepare the requested report indicating the amount for which he should sue.

Problem 6–4. Abbreviated information on the activities of the Kart Company are presented below:

December 31

	1965	1966	1967	1968
Total assets	$600,000	$620,000	$700,000	$650,000
Bonds payable	100,000	100,000	50,000	50,000
Stockholders' equity:				
Capital stock	400,000	400,000	400,000	400,000
Retained earnings	–0–	30,000	50,000	40,000

For the Year

	1965	1966	1967	1968
Net income to stockholders	–0–	$50,000	$50,000	$30,000
Bond interest charges	3,000	6,000	3,000	3,000
Dividends paid	–0–	20,000	30,000	40,000

Mr. A. R. Kart owns all of the stock of the company and plans to sell it to Mr. C. A. Norse. The two men agree that the price of the stock will be based on the value of the assets. It is agreed further that the value of the assets shall be determined by capitalizing the earning power at 8%. Earnings for this purpose shall be the average earnings of the years 1966 and 1967. Each man computes the price to be paid for the stock, as follows:

Mr. A. R. Kart	$625,000
Mr. C. A. Norse	461,250

Required:

(1) Compute the amount to be paid for the stock according to the agreement. Present your computation in an explanatory report.

(2) Assuming the sale is to take place on December 31, 1968, and that it is further agreed between the two men that any "goodwill" arising as a result of the calculated sale price shall be valued at 50% of the computed amount, compute the sales price of the stock.

Problem 6–5. Balance sheets for the Zanadir Company for 1967 and 1968 and an income statement for 1968 are presented below:

Balance Sheet as of December 31

Assets	1967	1968
Cash	$ 20,000	$ 21,000
Receivables	30,000	35,000
Merchandise	15,000	20,000
Fixed assets	320,000	320,000
Allowance for depreciation	(80,000)	(96,000)
Total assets	$305,000	$300,000
Equities		
Current liabilities	$ 55,000	$ 30,000
Capital stock	200,000	200,000
Retained earnings	50,000	70,000
Total equities	$305,000	$300,000

Income Statement, 1968

Sales		$400,000
Cost of Goods Sold:		
Inventory; January 1	$ 15,000	
Purchases	205,000	
Available	$220,000	
Inventory; December 31	20,000	
Cost of goods sold	$200,000	
Operating expenses, excl. depreciation	109,000	
Depreciation	16,000	
Income taxes	35,000	
Total expenses		$360,000
Income		40,000
Dividends paid, June 15 and December 15		20,000
Increase in retained earnings		$20,000

Additional data:

1. The fixed assets were acquired, as follows:

Asset	Date Acquired	Accumulated Depreciation	Annual Depreciation	Cost
Land	Jan. 1, 1942	$ –0–	$ –0–	$ 40,000
Building	Jan. 1, 1953	40,000	2,500	100,000
Equipment	July 1, 1965	35,000	10,000	100,000
Fixtures	Jan. 1, 1963	21,000	3,500	80,000
Total		$96,000	$16,000	$320,000

2. Price Index Numbers, presumed to reflect the increase in the general price level, are:

Date	Index No.
1/1/42	40
1/1/53	70
1/1/54	70
1/1/63	100
7/1/65	110
Average, December, 1967	112
Average, December, 1968	113
December 31, 1967	110
December 31, 1968	112
Average, 1967	111
Average, 1968	113
June 15, 1968	110
December 15, 1968	113

3. The capital stock was issued as follows:

January 1, 1942	$ 40,000
January 1, 1954	160,000
Total	$200,000

4. Inventories, receivables, and current liabilities on the year-end balance sheets were all acquired or incurred in December.

Required:
(In all parts, round each conversion to the nearest $100.)
(1) Prepare an income statement for 1968 adjusted to the December 31, 1968, price level.
(2) Prepare comparative balance sheets, adjusted to the December 31, 1968, price level.
(3) Prepare comparative balance sheets, adjusted to the December 31, 1967, price level.

Problem 6–6. To obtain a more realistic appraisal of his investment Martin Arnett, your client, has asked you to adjust certain financial data of The Glo-Bright Company for price level changes. On January 1, 1965 he invested $50,000 in the Glo-Bright Company in return for 10,000 shares of common stock. Immediately after his investment the trial balance appeared as follows:

	Dr.	Cr.
Cash and receivables	$ 65,200	$
Merchandise inventory	4,000	
Building	50,000	
Accumulated depreciation—building		8,000
Equipment	36,000	
Accumulated depreciation—equipment		7,200
Land	10,000	
Current liabilities		50,000
Capital stock, $5 par		100,000
	$165,200	$165,200

Balances in certain selected accounts as of December 31 of each of the next three years were as follows:

	1965	1966	1967
Sales	$39,650	$39,000	$42,350
Inventory	4,500	5,600	5,347
Purchases	14,475	16,350	18,150
Operating expenses (excluding depr.)	10,050	9,050	9,075

Assume the 1965 price level as the base year and that all changes in the price level take place at the beginning of each year. Further assume that the 1966 price level is 10% above the 1965 price level and that the 1967 price level is 10% above the 1966 level.

The building was constructed in 1961 at a cost of $50,000 with an estimated life of 15 years. The price level at that time was 80% of the 1965 price level. The equipment was purchased in 1963 at a cost of $36,000 with an estimated life of 10 years. The price level at that times was 90% of the 1965 price level.

The LIFO method of inventory valuation is used. The original inventory was acquired in the same year as the building was constructed and was maintained at a constant $4,000 until 1965. In 1965 a gradual buildup of the inventory was begun in anticipation of an increase in the volume of business.

Arnett considers the return on his investment as the dividend he actually receives. In 1967 Glo-Bright paid cash dividends in the amount of $8,000.

On July 1, 1966 there was a reverse stock split-up of the Company's stock in the ratio of one-for-ten.

Required:

(1) Compute the 1967 earnings per share of common stock in terms of 1965 dollars.

(2) Compute the percentage return on investment for 1965 and 1967 in terms of 1965 dollars.   (AICPA adapted)

Problem 6–7. A and B are in partnership with capital accounts on the books of $16,000 and $20,000, respectively. The partners share profit and loss equally.

Required:

For each case described below give the journal entry to record the change in partnership interest in the partnership.

Case 1. A sold his interest in the partnership to C for $24,000.

Case 2. A sold his interest in the partnership to C for $15,000.

Case 3. A sold one-half of his interest in the partnership to C for $9,000.

Case 4. A and B equally sell C a one-third interest in the partnership for $15,000.

Case 5. A sells B one-half of his profit and loss sharing ratio for $5,000 cash.

Problem 6–8. Selected accounts of the partnership of A, B, and C on December 31, 1967, before final closing of the books are presented below:

A, Capital	B, Capital	C, Capital
$50,000	$30,000	$40,000

A, Drawing	B, Drawing	C, Drawing

Drawing	P & L	Drawing	P & L	Drawing	P & L
$1,000	$7,200	$2,000	$2,400	$2,400	$2,400

On December 31, 1967, the partners agree to sell D a one-fourth interest for $50,000 cash.

Required:

(1) Give the journal entry necessary to record the sale of the old partners' interest to the new partner.

(*a*) Assuming no goodwill is to be recognized on the books.

(*b*) Assuming goodwill should be recognized on the books.

(2) Prepare a schedule showing how the $50,000 cash should be distributed to the old partners.

(3) Assume the partners agree to share profits equally (25% to each partner) after D is admitted. By how much might A, B, and C question the distribution of any gain or loss if the business were then sold to Mr. X for $230,000 cash—if goodwill were not recognized when D was admitted to partnership.

Problem 6–9. A and B are in partnership with capitals of $10,000 and $83,000 respectively. Income or loss is shared equally. The partners sell C a one-third interest in the partnership for $10,000 cash.

Required:

(1) Give the journal entry to record the admission of C to the partnership.

(2) Prepare a schedule for distributing the $10,000 in cash to the old partners.

Problem 6–10. R. J. Adams owns a small manufacturing company in the Middle West. On December 31, 1966, his capital account was $120,000. On this date he sold a one-third interest (both capital and income and loss ratio) to C. A. Baker for $50,000. The two partners accept the valuation of $50,000 for a one-third interest for purposes of the partnership and value the combined capital accounts at $150,000. On December 31, 1967, when the capital accounts have increased to $55,000 for Baker and $110,000 for Adams, Adams sold R. W. Calvin a one-fourth interest (both capital and income and loss ratio) for $45,000. Because the relative income and loss ratio was not changed, no revaluation of the accounts was made when Calvin entered the partnership. On December 31, 1968, when the capital accounts had increased to $59,000 for Baker, $43,000 for Calvin and $75,000 for Adams, the company was changed to a corporation. Because the income and loss sharing ratio was in effect changed when common stock was issued for the respective capital accounts, it was agreed that the business should be revalued, and an amount of $201,000 was the resulting valuation of the owners' equity in the corporation.

Required:

Give the journal entries to record each change in owners' interest over the period, and indicate the number of shares of common stock each owner would receive if the stock were issued at $100 a share.

Problem 6-11. The H. W. Barker Company has bonds payable outstanding of $100,000 on which an unamortized bond discount exists on January 1, 1967, of $4,000. The bonds are selling in the market at 95 and are callable at 103 at any time.

Required:

At what valuation should the bonds be shown on the balance sheet of this date? Discuss.

Problem 6-12. The JWM Corporation has outstanding a $2,000,000 debenture bond issue on which the interest rate is $5\frac{1}{2}\%$. The bonds were sold 6 years ago at $101\frac{1}{2}$ and are due 14 years from the present date. The bonds are listed on the New York Bond Exchange and were recently quoted at 104. They are widely held. The bonds are callable at 106 for one more year, at 105 for the subsequent three years, at 104 for three additional years, and at $102\frac{1}{2}$ thereafter to maturity.

Required:

(1) Indicate the probable amount at which the bonds are carried on the statement of financial position of the JWM Corporation.

(2) Discuss possible alternative valuations for these bonds, indicating circumstances under which any alternative valuation might have significance for management.

Note:

For additional problems see the Appendix—particularly Problems AP–16 through AP–22.

III

EXPANSION OF THE BUSINESS ORGANIZATION

CHAPTER 7

Investment for expansion

Business growth has been one of the well-recognized characteristics of American industry. Small companies have grown large and other companies have merged into one company to be a part of a larger enterprise. A review of this growth reveals that the expansion has been accomplished in a variety of ways. The next several chapters of this text are directed to the accounting aspects of such expansion. This chapter covers the accounting involved when an enterprise expands by buying additional operating assets. In general the process involves two rather distinct phases:

(1) Selecting desirable areas for investment.
(2) Selecting desirable methods of financing.

At times the two phases are combined into one. For example, when a firm issues some of its own stock in exchange for the assets of a going business, both of the above phases are accomplished by the one transaction. But the fact that one transaction covers both the financing and investing of the funds does not basically alter or minimize the accounting involved.

The function of accounting in the area of business expansion is to provide (1) information useful in reaching a decision on the most appropriate investment of funds, and (2) information useful in selecting an appropriate method of financing the investment. Information of this nature is needed regardless of whether the expansion is to be accomplished in a single- or multi-step transaction.

The accounting process of providing data for making decisions on future activities of the enterprise will be the same regardless of the type of business organization. The process of financing the investment, however, raises different types of accounting problems depending upon the type of business organization involved in the expansion plans. Some of these problems are examined in the following sections.

ACCOUNTING DATA FOR INVESTMENT DECISIONS

The process by which management makes decisions on such questions as adding a new product, changing territories, and selecting new production or marketing methods may be divided into three rather distinct steps, as follows:

(1) Recognition of the various possible courses of action.
(2) Evaluation of each course of action.
(3) Determination of the best course of action.

Role of Accounting

Normally the role of accounting in this process lies in the second step, wherein the cost and revenue aspects of specific possibilities are considered. The function of accounting in this area is one of collecting appropriate financial information on the various possibilities under consideration and presenting comparative reports on all of them. The collecting of the data includes gathering estimates from a variety of sources and using available data on past experiences. Normally the comparative reports on the possibilities are in terms of the costs which are expected to be incurred and the revenues which it is anticipated will be realized adjusted for the time element. Reports prepared on such bases are sometimes referred to as pro forma reports.

The function of providing information for evaluating possible courses of action may be most involved, depending as it does on estimates of future events of varying degrees of reliability and certainty. In providing information in this area, the accountant employs certain analytical techniques. Some of the more common are:

(1) Total cost and revenue comparisons.
(2) Differential cost and revenue comparisons.
(3) Utilization cost comparisons.
(4) Rate of return comparisons.

The techniques are employed by the accountant in varying degrees of preciseness. The discussion to follow is an introduction to some basic features of these techniques.

Total Annual Cost and Revenue. The technique of comparing total average annual operating revenues and expenses is simple and widely used. It does not include as a cost the imputed interest element of investments, but serves as a general guide for investment decisions. To illustrate this form of presentation, assume two proposals for action for the coming year are under consideration. Average annual costs and revenue of each plan are estimated and presented as follows:

COMPARATIVE COST AND REVENUE REPORT
FOR 19XX OPERATIONS
UNDER PLANS A AND B

	Plan A	Plan B
Revenues obtainable under both Plan A and Plan B	$320,000	$320,000
Additional revenue of Plan A	80,000	—
Additional revenue of Plan B	—	120,000
Total revenue	$400,000	$440,000
	Plan A	Plan B
Fixed costs under both plans	$100,000	$100,000
Variable costs common to both plans	150,000	150,000
Additional cost of Plan A	20,000	—
Additional cost of Plan B	—	70,000
Total costs	$270,000	$320,000
Estimated annual income	$130,000	$120,000

On the basis of estimated revenues and costs, it appears that Plan A is the preferable plan, since it will result in $10,000 more net income than Plan B. This conclusion utilizes a total cost comparison and is based upon the difference in net income resulting from the comparative figures.

Differential Costing. At times the total cost and revenue techniques may be modified or simplified. Since it is the *difference* in income or cost which is of significance in problems of determining the most appropriate expansion program, a comparison which emphasizes the differences may be more useful in making the final decision. This difference is normally referred to as *differential* cost. Thus the costs and revenues in the foregoing illustration could have been measured in terms of the differential costs and revenues.

In analyses utilizing the differential cost approach, the plan which is used as a basis for comparison frequently involves the assumption that the plant would be left idle. The alternative plans involve the assumption that the plant would be utilized in production. Modifying the above illustration to measure the results of the alternative plans in terms of differential costs and revenues, the calculation would be as follows:

	Plan A	Plan B
Revenue obtainable if plant is not left idle	$400,000	$440,000
Cost if plant is used in accordance with plan	170,000	220,000
Differential income (measured as the increase in income resulting if the plant is not left idle)	$230,000	$220,000

The results should be read in the following manner: Plan A will provide $10,000 more income than Plan B and will provide $230,000 more income than if the plant were left idle. Plan B will provide $10,000 less income than Plan A and will provide $220,000 more income than if the plant were left idle. If the plant had been left idle, the company would have lost its fixed costs of $100,000, so that if Plan A provides a net income of $130,000, Plan A in reality provides $230,000 more income than would result from leaving the plant idle.

The use of differential costs and revenues in selecting among various possible plans is advantageous in that the computation problem is somewhat less involved than under the total cost and revenue approach. Likewise, the resulting differentials may provide a more useful basis for making comparisons.

Utilization Costing. The use of past acquisition costs in developing comparative costs for possible expansion plans under examination may not provide an adequate basis for reaching a decision. At times the unused acquisition cost of an asset does not measure appropriately the sacrifice involved in carrying out the plan. To illustrate, assume Company A purchased some machines for $40,000 a few years ago. Once the machines have been purchased their value to the enterprise lies either in the value of their production or in their net disposal price. In this case, assume the machines presently have a book value of $30,000 (one-fourth of their original estimated life having expired), and a net disposal value of $10,000. The $10,000 may be described as the utilization cost[1] of the machines

[1] Utilization cost is a concept which is more commonly used in economics than in accounting. In general, this concept refers to the economic value involved in the use or utilization of a given asset or property. This value is referred to as the utilization cost of the asset.

used to carry out the plan, if the machines are used up fully in carrying out the plan. If only a part of the machines is used on the plan, utilization cost of the plan would be measured as the difference between the net estimated disposal value of the machines before and after the plan is carried out. Assuming the machines are to be used up in carrying out the plan under consideration, the $10,000 disposal value (rather than the $30,000 of unexpired acquisition cost) would be included in the estimated costs of carrying out the plan.

That is, $10,000 is the dollar value foregone by the continued use of the machines. Utilization cost is represented by the dollars foregone by continued utilization of an asset already owned by an enterprise. In this example, utilization cost is equal to the net disposal price of the asset used.

To illustrate the significance of the difference between the $30,000 of unexpired acquisition cost and the $10,000 of utilization cost, assume the total differential costs of two plans *before* considering the use of the machines are:

Plan X	$180,000
Plan Y	200,000

Plan X requires the use of the machines, while Plan Y does not require them. If the machines are included at their unamortized acquisition cost, or $30,000, the total cost of Plan X becomes $210,000, and the implication is that Plan Y has a favorable cost differential of $10,000. Actually, this conclusion is not proper because the machines are worth only $10,000, and this amount, their utilization cost, should be used for comparative purposes in determining the most appropriate plan. If the $10,000 utilization cost is used in the above example, the result would be a total differential cost of Plan X of $190,000, leaving a favorable cost differential for Plan X of $10,000.

When utilization cost data (which differ from acquisition cost only when the machines or other resources are already on hand and do not have to be acquired) are used, it should be noted that the only sacrifice involved in adopting Plan X is the $180,000 of cash to be expended and the $10,000 of cash foregone by using the machines rather than by selling them, whereas Plan Y requires a total outlay of $200,000 in cash. The difference between the $30,000 of unexpired acquisition cost and the $10,000 of utilization cost is considered to be a loss previously sustained but not recognized on the books.

This "loss" arises because of the difference between the normal accounting concept of depreciation, which allocates the cost of an asset over its period of useful life, and an alternative concept of depreciation, which is aimed more at valuing the assets in use at various reporting dates. Depreciation charges under the normal accounting concept do not purport to measure the declining value of assets through use nor the declining value arising from technological changes. However, in evaluating alternative *future* uses for assets on hand, the disposal value, or utilization cost, may be of greater significance than book value arising from the accounting concept of depreciation. Any difference between book value and disposal value may be considered as a loss (or gain) without, however, implying that the past depreciation charges have been inappropriate in view of the facts known at the time such charges were made. It should also be recognized that utilization cost may at times be greater than undepreciated cost, but nevertheless it would be the more appropriate cost to use in analyses of this type.

MEASURING UTILIZATION COST. In the preceding illustration utilization cost was measured in terms of net disposal price. Disposal price refers to the highest of immediate sales price, future sales price discounted back to the present, or the net sales prices of the items of output discounted back to the present which the resources would provide if not used in the plan under review. In many cases, however, utilization cost should be measured in terms of replacement cost. The use of replacement cost is appropriate whenever evidence exists to indicate that if the resources on hand are used in the plan in question it will be necessary to replace these resources at some future date. In this situation utilization cost reflects the present value of the cash sacrificed by having used the resource on the plan under review. The cash is considered as sacrificed, since it will have to be paid out to make the replacement for future operations.

To illustrate this situation, assume that a company has under consideration two plans, one of which will require the use and consumption of certain properties, while the other plan will not involve the utilization of these properties. In addition, if the properties are used up completely, as the illustration assumes, in carrying out the first plan, replacement of the properties will be necessary in coming months. Exclusive of the properties in question, the alternative plans have differential costs of:

Plan A	$1,600,000
Plan B	1,900,000

The properties which would be utilized on Plan A have a book value to the company of $250,000, but would realize only $150,000 cash (after selling expenses) if sold. If the properties were used, or sold, an outlay of $400,000 would be necessary in a few months to replace them for subsequent operations.

An analysis of the above facts would indicate the following:

(1) If unamortized acquisition cost of the properties is used to arrive at Plan A's total cost, Plan A would be preferable. Its total differential cost, $1,850,000 ($1,600,000 plus $250,000), would be less than the cost of Plan B. However, as noted above, the use of past acquisition costs is usually not appropriate in making decisions involving alternatives for the future.

(2) If the present cash value of the properties is used in the comparison, Plan A again emerges as the best plan. The total cost of Plan A would be $1,750,000 ($1,600,000 plus the $150,000 foregone by using the existing properties). This cost is $150,000 less than the differential cost of plan B.

(3) However, if replacement cost of the properties is used as the proper measure of the cost for comparative purposes neither the $250,000 nor the $150,000 accurately reflects the sacrifice involved in using up the properties. The sacrifice involved in using up the properties is $400,000 and the total cost of Plan A becomes $2,000,000 ($1,600,000 plus $400,000). Now Plan B appears to be preferable, since an outlay of $1,900,000 is more economical than an outlay of $1,600,000 today, plus an additional $400,000 to replace properties used in addition to the $1,600,000.

In this example, replacement cost appears to be the most suitable measure of the utilization cost of the properties. The decision on the appropriate plan to select may well hinge on the value attached to properties, or assets, presently in use which may be utilized for one plan but not for an alternative and which, if used, will require replacement for subsequent operations.

In general, utilization cost is measured in terms of net disposal price (selling price less cost to sell), unless it is necessary to replace the resources so used. When replacement is necessary, replacement cost may be the appropriate measure of utilization cost.

Rate of Return. While analysis of expansion or investment alternatives in terms of differential costs or utilization costs may provide the basis for an eventual decision, neither of these approaches to the problem should be considered to be the only, or in some situations, the most appropriate approach possible. Each of these analytical tools results in an evaluation of the alternatives in terms of the quantity of income arising from each alternative. Quantity of income is not necessarily the only criterion to use in the evaluation of alternative plans of action.

One of the basic investment criteria often not revealed by comparisons which merely indicate the quantity of income is the rate of income earned on the investment in the project. At times rate of income earned, or rate of return on investment, provides a better measure of the various alternatives than does comparative quantities of income. Analyses relying solely on comparisons of total income may lead to unwise decisions, particularly if the plan leading to the larger total income requires a disproportionately larger investment.

For example, assume Plan P will provide an income of $10,000, but will require an investment of $100,000, while Plan Q is expected to provide an income of $8,000, but requires only a $50,000 investment. On the basis of the data available, it appears that Plan P would provide a return of 10% on investment, whereas plan Q would provide a return of 16%. Plan Q, since it yields a larger rate of return, may be the more profitable plan, assuming the company has at least $100,000 to invest. Under this plan the company could earn $8,000 on a $50,000 investment. If the additional $50,000 could be invested at a rate of return in excess of 4%, the total return on the $100,000 would be greater than if Plan P were adopted. If the second $50,000 could be invested at 5%, for example, an income of $2,500 would result from this investment. When the $2,500 is added to the $8,000 return on the first $50,000 investment, a total income of $10,500 is provided under Plan Q, as opposed to $10,000 under Plan P.

The following table indicates the desirability of Plan Q, assuming $100,000 is available for investment:

	Investment	Return	Rate of Return
Plan P	$100,000	$10,000	10%
Plan Q—Basic Plan	$ 50,000	$ 8,000	16%
Investment of balance of the $100,000	50,000	2,500	5%
Total	$100,000	$10,500	10.5%

The rate of return on investment is one of the more important criteria used to evaluate alternative expansion or investment opportunities. Rate of return comparisons rely heavily on accurate revenue and cost estimates and commonly involve considered judgments on application of overhead, administrative, and other fixed and variable costs to the plans under consideration.

Nonaccounting Considerations

One important point which has not been mentioned in the preceding sections concerns the degree of certainty of any estimated return and/or estimated costs used as the basis for management decision. Although estimates for one plan may provide both a greater income and a greater rate of return than some alternative plan, the apparently more profitable plan may also involve greater risk or uncertainty. The degree of risk may be such as to cause management to select the plan with the smaller income as being preferable to the more risky plan. The accountant can, in part, provide for some of the risks by making allowances for them as costs, but the more practical procedure is to leave these subjective evaluations to management, or disclose them in terms of statistical probabilities.

Illustration Using Accounting Data for Expansion Planning

The Zerat Company is engaged in the manufacture and sale of lighting equipment. The company is considering two expansion plans. One plan would increase the volume of present operations, while the other plan would involve expansion through adding a new product. Differential costs and revenues, measured from current operational levels, for the two possibilities are:

	Volume Expansion	New Product Expansion
Incremental (additional) revenue	$50,000	$80,000
Differential costs (includes both variable costs which require cash outlays and fixed costs with a utilization cost)	30,000	50,000
Differential Income	$20,000	$30,000

Assuming revenue is not realized until the end of the year in each case, and assuming that the outlays for the differential costs must be invested at the beginning of the year, it appears the company will need an added investment of $30,000 if volume is expanded and will realize an income of $20,000 on this investment, or a return of $66\frac{2}{3}\%$. If the new product is added, the additional investment of $50,000 will yield a return of $30,000, or a rate of return of 60%. While expansion by addition of the new product will produce the greater differential income, this expansion alternative does not provide as great a rate of return as does expansion through additional volume. Likewise, since expansion by addition of a new product will involve a greater additional cost outlay than will volume expansion, the new product plan entails a greater degree of risk to the Zerat Company. The lower rate of return and the greater risk element could cause the management to decide to expand through a volume increase, even though this alternative does not hold promise of providing the greater differential income.

Limitations and Qualifications

The exact procedure by which management reaches a decision among various expansion alternatives varies widely in practice. Some managements refuse to use estimated cost and revenue data unless they are based on past historical costs of the company. Other managements plan without formally estimating the costs and revenues of different plans. In addition, many techniques not presented at this point may be utilized by management, techniques with which the accountant should become familiar before entering into this highly specialized area of accounting. Advanced textbooks in cost and management accounting should be consulted by those interested in the more specific techniques and procedures useful as aids to management in the process of making decisions on the future activities of the company.

FINANCING PLANS—GENERAL

Funds for carrying out plans for expansion may be generated internally through operations of the enterprise or externally through borrowing or additional owner equity contributions. Profitable operations produce funds as the result of revenues being in excess of the costs and expenses chargeable against those revenues. However, funds generated internally by operations are not necessarily limited to the amount which is reported as net income. As a general rule the funds generated by operations exceed net income, since some costs and expenses chargeable against revenues in a period commonly do not require outlays of funds in the period. Thus, depreciation charges act to reduce net income reported in a period, and properly so. However, no current payout is required as a consequence of the depreciation charge. The result insofar as generation of funds is concerned is that operations produce funds in excess of reported net income. The conclusion is valid, then, that operations will generate more funds than indicated by the net income reported to the extent of any noncash charges, such as depreciation.

While profitable operations generate funds internally, the availability of these funds for expansion purposes is affected by numerous managerial decisions. These funds are available to management for whatever needs seem most pressing. Dividend payments, asset replacement, and reductions in indebtedness, for example, may absorb portions of the internally generated funds. To the extent these funds are not used for such purposes management may decide to use them to effect expansion plans. It should be evident that the balance of the Retained Earnings account is not a very good indication of the amount of funds available for expansion. The balance of this account merely represents past net income less dividend distributions. We must look to the left-hand side of the statement of financial position to determine even in a general way the availability of internally generated funds at any given date.

Accountants assist management in many ways in reaching decisions among alternative investments for expansion, whether financed by internally or externally generated funds. Statements reporting the source and application of funds in any period may be useful in providing a record of past decisions. Cash budgets or forecasts of cash receipts and expenditures assist management by indicating the extent to which funds will be available for various purposes in coming periods. Supplementary schedules, reports, and evaluations may help management to isolate the relevant differences among alternative plans. Once expansion decisions are made, accountants devise appropriate means of reporting the results of these decisions, through footnotes, reserves established out of retained earnings, or other disclosure avenues.

The following portions of this section discuss several aspects of financial expansion from internally generated funds.

Estimating Funds from Internal Sources

The process of estimating, or forecasting, the funds which will be available for expansion purposes from internal operations involves estimating period income, deductions from it for any revenue not in cash form, and additions to it for any expenses not requiring a current outlay of cash. The result will be the amount of funds provided by operations. Dividends and other claims to such operational funds should then be deducted to arrive at the funds available for expansion. The activities of accountants in the area of budgeting and cash forecasting are treated more fully in textbooks specializing in those areas.

Utilizing Nonincome Operational Funds. In a very real sense funds acquired from operations in addition to those evidenced by net income represent only a temporary source of funds. While depreciation and similar noncash expenses do, in effect, augment cash resources from operations in excess of net income, such cash resources may have to be used to replace depreciable assets as they wear out or become obsolete. If these funds are used for expansion purposes, additional funds will have to be obtained from other sources to replace assets now in use if operations are to continue at the present level. For this reason, it seems desirable to consider the financing of expansion from operating funds provided in excess of income as being in the nature of temporary financing.

In one aspect, however, nonincome funds provided by operations do represent a permanent source of funds. This situation exists when a new business is started. New buildings and other new assets will not have to be replaced for a relatively long period of time, and any new assets purchased with the funds generated by operations in excess of the net income (depreciation charges) will in turn provide operating funds through additional depreciation charges. The ultimate result of this method of expansion is that with a given investment a firm may acquire and operate a substantially greater investment in assets.

To illustrate, assume Company A invests $100,000 in a new plant. Also assume that each year the plant revenues and costs, including depreciation, are exactly equal. Thus, the funds generated by operations are equal to the depreciation charges, assuming no other noncash revenues or costs. Also assume the plant has a life of 10 years, so that in the first year the depreciation will be $10,000, which is equal to the total revenue less all other costs. Income is zero. Company A is in a position to expand facilities by using the $10,000 nonincome operational funds. Plant assets to start the second year would then be $110,000. Table 7-A indicates the expansion possibilities through application of nonincome operational funds.

The illustration indicates that with a $100,000 original investment a company can expand from nonincome operational sources of funds to an investment of $182,000 of plant assets, if all assets have a life of 10 years. It should be noted that the rate of growth is not uniform, since funds provided by this source are not uniform until the company is rather mature and until additions are equal to withdrawals of assets from the company.

TABLE 7-A

Year	Plant Investment	Accumulated Depreciation	Annual Depreciation	Replacement	Removed From Use
1	$100,000	–0–	$10,000	–0–	–0–
2	110,000	$ 10,000	11,000	–0–	–0–
3	121,000	21,000	12,100	–0–	–0–
4	133,100	33,100	13,310	–0–	–0–
5	146,410	46,410	14,641	–0–	–0–
...	...	...	...	...	...
9	214,358	114,358	21,436	–0–	–0–
10	235,794	135,794	23,579	$23,579	$100,000
...	...	...	...	...	...
20	182,871	82,871	18,287	18,287	23,579
...	...	...	...	...	...
30	181,408	81,408	18,141	18,141	18,287
...	...	...	...	...	...
40	181,741	81,741	18,174	18,174	18,141
...	...	...	...	...	...
50	181,807	81,807	18,181	18,181	18,174

Capitalizing Retained Earnings

Retained earnings represent another source of funds for expansion. When dividend payments or withdrawals by partners or proprietors are less than income after taxes, the excess of the income over these distributions becomes additional retained income. Likewise, the enterprise will have available for various uses the assets generated by the profitable operations. Retained earnings, therefore, indicate the extent to which operations have generated assets in excess of distributions to owners, disregarding for the moment noncash income charges, such as depreciation.

The assets generated by profitable operations may be used for numerous business purposes—to increase inventories, to finance sales through lengthening credit terms, to augment cash resources, to expand plant facilities, and to meet many other business needs. Regardless of the use of the assets, the account reflecting the retained income (proprietor, personal; partner, drawing; retained earnings) continues to suggest, to many people at least, the extent of past earnings which are available for distribution to owners. Obviously, however, if the assets resulting from past earnings have been utilized for other business purposes they are not available for distribution. This is particularly true, of course, if the assets have been employed to expand plant facilities.

Recognition by Accounting Entries. Thus the owners or management of the enterprise may desire to have their accounting records and reports reflect a decision to use assets from past income to expand productive facilities, to increase inventories permanently, etc. When it is decided to capitalize earnings permanently, the accountant should record this decision as follows:

For the single proprietor:

Owner, personal	$xxxxx	
Owner, capital		$xxxxx

For the partnership:

Partner A, drawing	$xxxxx	
Partner B, drawing	xxxxx	
Partner A, capital		$xxxxx
Partner B, capital		xxxxx

For the corporation formal action by management is normally required before any entry should be made. If the board of directors desires, and so authorizes, the capitalization process may be nothing more than a segregation of a portion of the retained earnings, as follows:

Retained earnings $xxxxx
    Reserve for plant expansion $xxxxx

Recognition by Stock Dividend. In some instances the board will take more formal action and will issue additional shares of stock to indicate that the retained earnings are now a part of the permanent capital of the enterprise. The issuance of additional shares may be described in various ways, and likewise, the accounting for the issuance of the additional shares may take various forms.

For example, a corporation which in the past has had earnings in excess of cash dividend payments, or which is presently earning a higher income than the board of directors desires to distribute, may declare a stock dividend. The declaration of a stock dividend is commonly prompted by a desire on the part of the board of directors to give the stockholders some evidence of their part of the accumulated past earnings without actually distributing cash or other property considered necessary to future business operations. A stock dividend is normally declared as a percentage of the total shares then outstanding. Generally, the stock dividend distribution is of a relatively small portion of additional stock, e.g., 2%, 5%, or 10%. Distributions of additional stock representing a substantial percentage of outstanding shares are sometimes erroneously referred to as stock dividends. Such distributions will be discussed at a later point.

RECORDED AT PAR VALUE. Assume that the following information is pertinent to the operations of the Bangor Corporation at December 31, 1967:

Capital stock, 1,000,000 shares authorized, 300,000
    shares outstanding, par value $10 $ 3,000,000
Retained earnings   3,240,000
Net income for 1967   450,000
Cash dividend payments for 1967 $.60 per share

Also, assume that the outlook for the Bangor Corporation is favorable, but that the cash requirements will be relatively heavy in coming months. The board of directors might decide through the medium of a stock dividend to give the stockholders greater evidence of the past year's profits than the $.60 per share cash dividend. The stock dividend percentage is dependent upon many factors, such as the amount of earnings the board desires to capitalize, the market price of the stock, and long range plans for future distributions.

From an accounting viewpoint, the basic problem lies in the determination of the valuation to be placed upon the shares of stock to be distributed. If the Bangor Corporation board of directors decides to issue a 4% stock dividend, 12,000 additional shares of stock will be issued (4% of 300,000 shares outstanding). The par value of the shares issued will be $120,000, and the following entry would be made to record the issuance of these shares, if the shares are to be valued at par.

Retained earnings	$120,000	
Capital stock		$120,000

RECORDED AT MARKET VALUE. The above entry uses par value as the valuation for the stock issued, even though the market value of the shares issued would likely be different from the par value of $10. The board of directors may intend, however, that these additional shares be considered as a distribution of earnings to the extent of the market value of the shares received. Likewise the recipient stockholders might tend to view the value of these shares at the same amount. Thus, if the market value of the Bangor Corporation stock is, for example, $22 per share at the date of payment of the dividend, the following entry would be made if the shares are to be valued at market:

Retained earnings (12,000 × $22)	$264,000	
Capital stock (12,000 × $10)		$120,000
Paid-in surplus		144,000

This entry transfers to a "paid-in capital" basis the market value of the shares issued and reduces the retained earnings by the same amount.

The significance of the different valuation illustrated in the entries is evident. If the par value per share is capitalized, $120,000 of earnings is capitalized; if the market value is capitalized, $264,000 of earnings is capitalized. If the par value basis is used, the difference of $144,000 remains in retained earnings and is presumably available for a subsequent distribution.

PROPER ACCOUNTING TREATMENT. If the board of directors looks upon the stock dividend as tangible evidence of past earnings to the extent of the market value of the shares distributed, it would seem that the board should determine the number of shares to be issued by dividing the projected market price per share of stock at the date of the distribution into the amount of earnings it desires to capitalize. If this is done, the entry to record the distribution should be made at the fair market value of the shares distributed, as in the above entry.

Recognition by Stock Split-up. It was mentioned above that the stock dividend distribution was generally of a relatively small portion of additional stock. At times a corporation may decide to increase substantially the number of shares outstanding. In most instances such a decision would be motivated largely by a desire to reduce the market price of the shares and thereby achieve a wider interest in and market for the shares. Stock distributions of an amount large enough to affect materially the market price of the stock are normally described as a stock split or stock split-up. A stock split-up, therefore, should have at least two essential characteristics:

(1) The number of shares distributed should be substantial in relation to the shares outstanding.
(2) The market value per share of the corporation's stock should be markedly affected by the split-up.

Thus, in a two-for-one split-up it would be expected that the market price after the split-up would be roughly one-half the market price prior to the split-up.

Another characteristic of a split-up which prevailed until recent years was that the split-up involved a reduction in the par or stated value of the shares. For example, the Bangor Corporation might have decided to have a two-for-one stock split-up to be effected by reducing the par value per share from $10 to $5. After the split-up was effected the corporation would have had 600,000 shares of $5 par value stock outstanding. The total par value outstanding would have been $3,000,000, the same as before the split-up. However, the shareholders' equity would have been spread over twice as many shares, and presumably the market price of the shares would have reflected this halving of the value of each share. No accounting entry would have been required to record such a split-up, since the only changes made were to reduce the par value per share and to increase the number of shares outstanding. It is obvious that a stock split-up effected in this manner does not result in a capitalization of any retained earnings.

In recent years the term "stock split-up" has been used to describe an issuance by a corporation of its own stock to its stockholders without consideration to the corporation. Such action has been prompted mainly by a desire to increase the number of outstanding shares to effect a reduction in the market price of the stock and, thereby, obtain wider distribution and improved marketability of the stock. If the split is effected as a dividend instead of a "pure split," such as a two-for-one or four-for-one, an entry is required to record the transaction to the extent occasioned by legal requirements. For example, had the Bangor Corporation issued a 100% stock dividend instead of reducing par value from $10 to $5, the following entry would have been required:

> Retained earnings $3,000,000
>   Capital stock (300,000 × $10) $3,000,000

Occasionally the situation is encountered where a stock split has some of the characteristics of a "pure split" and some of the characteristics of a stock dividend. For example, the Bangor Corporation might have effected their split by distributing two shares for every one outstanding while reducing the par value from $10 to $7.50. In order to fulfill the legal requirement of having par value in the Capital Stock account the following entry would have been required:

Retained earnings	$1,500,000	
Capital stock		$1,500,000

With 600,000 shares outstanding with a par value of $7.50 per share, $4,500,000 would have been required in the Capital Stock account. Since only $3,000,000 was in the account prior to the split, an additional $1,500,000 would have been needed to meet the legal requirement.

Summary. The development of the current concept distinguishing a stock split-up from a stock dividend is based on the *intent* of management. If the primary intent of management is to give the stockholders additional evidence of their equity in past earnings, the distribution is considered to be a dividend. If the primary intent of management is to increase the marketability of the stock, the distribution is considered to be a stock split-up. The American Institute of Certified Public Accountants and the New York Stock Exchange have established a somewhat objective standard as a guide to the determination of the intent of management. This standard indicates that, in order to increase the marketability of stock appreciably, a distribution must be greater than 20% to 25% of the stock outstanding prior to the distribution.[2]

---

[2] The following quotation indicates the care taken in attempting to overcome the apparent confusion in the use of terms in this area of capitalization of retained earnings:

"Directors of Eastman Kodak Co. declared a one-for-one stock distribution on the outstanding common shares . . . .

"Company spokesmen said the common-share distribution is not a stock split because the new Eastman common will have the same par value of $10 a share that the existing common has. A two-for-one stock split would entail cutting the par value to $5. He also said it is not a 100% stock dividend, although the full par value of the 19 million or so additional shares will be added to the company's capital in its balance sheet. He explained it is being called a distribution, rather than a stock dividend, because a stock dividend might imply that the capital would have to be increased by an amount equal to about the market value of the stock being distributed. Kodak closed at 143½, up 2½ on the New York Stock Exchange yesterday." *Wall Street Journal,* February 18, 1959, p.17.

It appears likely that clear descriptions of the intentions of the company, similar to that above, will have to be forthcoming for many years in similar situations to provide stockholders and other interested parties with sufficient information to interpret properly the action taken.

EXTERNAL FINANCING OF EXPANSION

Obtaining funds from external sources for expansion of an enterprise requires consideration of many of the same factors involved in formation of an enterprise. Since this problem area was discussed in Chapter 3, the student is referred to that chapter for the overall considerations involved. There are, however, a few accounting problems peculiar to expansion of an enterprise, particularly in the partnership form of organization, which are not faced at the time of formation.

New Partner as a Source of Funds

The preceding chapter contained a discussion of the problems involved in the valuation of a partnership at those times when a new partner was admitted to the partnership by purchasing an interest from one or more of the partners of the existing partnership. In that discussion it was assumed that no new assets were invested in the partnership, but that the amount paid in by the incoming partner was distributed among those partners who had sold all or part of their partnership interests. The discussion involved what is commonly called the purchase of a partnership interest.

At times an existing proprietorship or partnership may desire to add to its operating assets either through the investment of additional assets by the existing proprietor or partners or by a new individual or individuals who would become a partner or partners in the new partnership. Certain problems exist in determining the accounting treatment of the additional investment. The following paragraphs discuss the accounting problems for what is commonly called the investment in a partnership.

In those cases where the incoming partner invests an amount equal to the book value of the capital account credit received by making the investment, the problem is quite simple. The entry to record the investment requires a debit to the assets contributed and a credit to the new partner's capital account for the amount contributed. For example, assume A and B are in partnership with capital accounts of $30,000 each. C is admitted to the partnership with a one-third capital interest by investing $30,000 into the partnership. In this instance C will contribute $30,000 and will receive a credit to his capital account for one-third of the resulting total partnership capital ($90,000), or $30,000. The entry to record this acquisition of funds by the partnership would be:

Cash	$30,000	
C, Capital		$30,000

On the other hand, if C were to invest the $30,000 for a one-fourth or a one-half capital interest, he would receive a credit in his capital account in an amount different from the $30,000 he contributes. The total capital equity of the new partnership would amount to $90,000, and if C were to receive a capital credit for one-fourth, he would have credited to his capital account $22,500, even though he contributed $30,000. Similarly, if he acquires a one-half interest in the new partnership, he would have a capital credit of $45,000 for his $30,000 investment.

There are two approaches to the accounting treatment of this type of problem. One approach assumes the old partners either give or receive a bonus when the new partner is admitted. The other approach assumes that either the new partner or the old partners have an additional asset in the form of goodwill which should be recognized.

Bonus to Old Partners. If a new partner invests an amount different from the amount of capital credit he receives, and if the new partnership decides that goodwill is not to be recognized as an asset of the company, the new investment must involve a bonus to one or more of the partners. In the foregoing illustration, if C were admitted to a one-fourth interest in the new partnership by making an investment of $30,000 in cash, but receiving in return a capital credit of $22,500 (1/4 of $90,000), the conclusion is drawn that C gave a bonus of $7,500 to the old partners. This conclusion appears valid since the partnership received $7,500 in excess of the equity to be shown in the new partner's capital account. This bonus is divided between the two old partners in their profit and loss sharing ratio. If A and B had been sharing profits 2/3 and 1/3, respectively, the $7,500 credit would be allocated to their capital accounts in that proportion. The entry to admit C to partnership under this situation would be:

Cash	$30,000	
A, Capital		$ 5,000
B, Capital		2,500
C, Capital		22,500

Bonus to New Partner. On the other hand, if C were admitted to the partnership with a one-half capital interest by contributing $30,000, his capital account credit would be $45,000 (1/2 of the $90,000 partners' capital equity). The inference is that the old partners gave the new partner a bonus for joining the partnership. The bonus contribution made by the old partners will require a transfer of a portion of the credit in their capital accounts to the capital account of the new partner. The bonus given by the old partners, like the bonus received, is assumed to be contributed in the profit and loss sharing ratio of the old partners, unless there is an agreement to share the bonus otherwise. Assuming the old partners share profits on a 2/3 and 1/3 ratio, respectively, the bonus of $15,000 ($45,000 capital credit of C less cash contributed by C of $30,000) would be divided $10,000 to A and $5,000 to B. The entry to record the admission of C under these circumstances would be:

Cash	$30,000	
A, Capital	10,000	
B, Capital	5,000	
C, Capital		$45,000

Bonus Procedure Summarized. The procedure for recording the admission of a new partner when goodwill is not to be recognized may be summarized as follows:

(1) Determine the total capital by adding to the capital accounts of the old partners the contribution made by the new partner.

(2) Determine the new partner's share of the total capital of the new partnership by multiplying his per cent or fraction of capital interest of the partnership by the total partnership capital equity. The resulting amount is the credit which will be made to the capital account of the incoming partner.

(3) If the credit to the capital account of the new partner is *less* than the contribution made by him, it is assumed that the new partner gave a bonus to the old partners in the amount of the difference between the contribution made and the capital credit received. The bonus is allocated to the old partners in their profit and loss sharing ratio.

(4) If the credit to the capital account of the new partner is *more* than the contribution made by him, it is assumed that the old partners gave a bonus to the new partner in the amount of the difference between the contribution made and the capital credit received. The bonus is charged against the old partners in their profit and loss sharing ratio.

Bonus Procedure Evaluated. In theory it would seem that the profit and loss sharing ratio upon which the bonus to a new partner is allocated should be that which will prevail in the future activities of the partnership, rather than the profit and loss ratio existing in the previous partnership. Such a conclusion appears warranted if it is recognized that the apparent reason the old partners gave the bonus was in recognition of the excessive earnings which will prevail in the future through the admission of the new partner. As the higher income is earned in the future, the old partners should recover their bonus contribution in the form of the higher earnings, and these earnings will be allocated to capital accounts in the future profit and loss sharing ratio. If the future "excess" earnings are allocated in some ratio different from the allocation for the bonus given at the time of admission of the new partner, an apparent inequity may result. That is, a partner may receive credit for a smaller (or greater) share of excess profits than he, in effect, paid for through the bonus to the new partner.

On the other hand, it is contended that if the old partners receive a bonus, this bonus should be allocated in the past profit and loss sharing ratio of the old partners. The reasoning supporting this conclusion suggests that the bonus which is being paid to the old partners has been earned by them in the past. However, this reasoning does not appear especially valid, since the incoming partner undoubtedly feels that it is a portion of the future higher earnings which he is buying when he enters the business. Thus, it would seem to follow that it is the future earning power which the old partners are selling for the bonus. If future earning power is the basis for the bonus to the old partners, it would seem that this type of bonus should be divided in the future profit and loss ratio of the old partners.

It should be noted, however, that, in spite of the apparent soundness of allocating the bonus resulting from an investment in a partnership in the profit and loss ratio which will exist in the new partnership, such procedure is not commonly followed. In general, such bonuses are allocated on the basis of the profit and loss ratio existing in the predecessor partnership.

Goodwill to Old Partners. Instead of using the bonus procedure, which gives the incoming partner a capital credit in an amount different from his contribution to the partnership, a goodwill account is sometimes used to account for the difference between the asset contribution and the share of total capital equity acquired. In the preceding illustration where A and B each had a capital of $30,000 and C was admitted to a one-fourth capital interest by paying in an additional $30,000, it is possible to reason that if C paid $30,000 for a one-fourth interest, the total partnership capital should be four times $30,000, or $120,000. Since the tangible net assets (total tangible assets less creditorship equities) after C's contribution are only $90,000, the assumption is made that the other $30,000 is goodwill. Since C will receive a capital credit of $30,000 if the total partnership capital equity is $120,000, it appears that the $30,000 of goodwill is something which the old partners have created. The capital credit resulting from the recognition of the $30,000 of goodwill should be allocated to the old partners in proportion to their profit and loss sharing ratio in the old partnership. If the profit and loss ratio was 2/3 and 1/3 to A and B, respectively, the $30,000 goodwill would be recorded as follows:

Goodwill	$30,000	
A, Capital		$20,000
B, Capital		10,000

(to recognize goodwill created by the old partners prior to admission of the new partner)

The admission of the new partner would be recorded as follows:

Cash	$30,000	
C, Capital		$30,000

After this information has been recorded the capital accounts of the three partners would be as follows:

A	$ 50,000
B	40,000
C	30,000
Total	$120,000

The capital ratio of the three partners would be: A, 5/12; B, 4/12; and C, 3/12. Unless the partnership agreement specifically states that this ratio shall be used for the division of profits and losses, care must be taken not to use it for this purpose. The principles of allocating income have been discussed in Chapter 5.

Goodwill to New Partner. Not only may the old partners have goodwill to be recognized, but the new partner may bring goodwill into the partnership. The new partner is assumed to have brought in goodwill whenever, under the bonus procedure, he would receive a capital credit in excess of his contribution. For example, in the foregoing illustration, if C is to receive a 50% interest in the total capital equity of $120,000 by paying in only $30,000, it is apparent C is to receive a capital credit in excess of his contribution. From this, it is concluded that C brought in goodwill which should be recognized in the accounts. The computation of the amount of goodwill is based on the assumption that the two old partners have no goodwill, and, since their 50% of the new partnership is $60,000 (their capital equity), the 50% C will own must be carried at the same equity valuation. Since C contributed $30,000 of this in cash, it is concluded that the other $30,000 is goodwill contributed along with the cash. The entry to admit C under this situation would be:

Cash	$30,000	
Goodwill	30,000	
C, Capital		$60,000

After this information has been recorded the capital accounts of the new partnership would be:

Partner	Capital	Capital Ratio
A	$30,000	25%
B	30,000	25%
C	60,000	50%
Total	$120,000	100%

It should be noted that the foregoing conclusion that the old partners should have a capital credit of 25% each was based solely on the fact that this represents the ratio of capitals maintained by the old partners in their former partnership. Actually, of course, the withdrawal or admission of a partner automatically dissolves an old partnership, and a completely new agreement has to be drawn up for the new partnership. Unless there are unusual circumstances, it may be assumed that the relationship which existed between the old partners will, as far as they are concerned, continue in the same proportion in the new partnership.

Goodwill to All Partners. At times a new partner may be admitted without the agreement affording any clear indication as to whether a bonus is being given or goodwill is presumed to exist. When the agreement is silent on this matter, it is impossible to conclude that the inclusion of either is proper to the exclusion of the other. Either approach may be justified. For purposes of consistency with corporate accounting, however, it would appear that the bonus procedure is more appropriate, since corporate accounting does not recognize goodwill when a new stockholder acquires stock. For example, assume the stock of the X Corporation has a par value of $100 per share and a book value of $130 per share. Should an additional share be issued at $150, the entry would be:

Cash	$150	
Capital stock		$100
Premium on stock		50

Since the premium is divided equally among all stockholders, the new stockholder in effect contributes a bonus to the old stockholders, the bonus being the $20 in excess of book value.

Another apparently ambiguous situation arises when a new partner is admitted to a specified interest in a specified total capital equity by contributing a given sum, but without any indication whether the goodwill or bonus procedure is to be used. However, in this case, it may be possible to determine which of these is to be recognized. For example, assume

C is admitted to a one-fourth capital interest in a partnership by paying in $30,000 in cash. The old partners have capital accounts of $40,000 each. It is agreed that the total capital equity of the new partnership shall be $160,000. In this case, if C is to have a one-fourth interest, he should have a capital credit of $40,000. Since he has contributed only $30,000, he should have an additional credit of $10,000. The two old partners will have a capital equity of 75% in the new partnership, or an equity of $120,000. Since their present capital accounts amount to only $80,000, it is apparent that they need an additional credit of $40,000. Since both the old partners and the new partner are to receive additional credits to their capital accounts, it is apparent that the bonus procedure cannot be used and goodwill must be recognized, as follows:

Cash	$30,000	
Goodwill	10,000	
C, Capital		$40,000
Goodwill	$40,000	
A, Capital		$30,000
B, Capital		10,000

(assumes A and B share profit and loss in a 3/4, 1/4 ratio.)

EXPANSION AND FINANCING AS ONE ACTIVITY

While the decision to expand and the financing of such expansion are best viewed as separate problems, much of business practice combines the two into one activity. Thus, for example, an enterprise may purchase on account additional facilities for expansion, or it may issue capital stock in exchange for expansion facilities. At times, the method of financing affects the cost comparisons used in reaching a decision on whether or not to expand. The following example indicates the close relationship which frequently exists between the decision to expand and the financing alternatives available.

Assume that Company A, which presently has operating assets totaling $2,000,000, is considering expansion of facilities and has two financing plans under consideration: (1) long-term borrowing of $1,500,000 at an annual interest cost of 5%; (2) sale of additional stock for $1,500,000. The cost and revenue estimates are presented as follows:

	Present Operations	Under Expansion	
		Long-Term Borrowing	Sale of Stock
Revenues	$1,000,000	$1,800,000	$1,800,000
Fixed costs	$ 400,000	600,000	600,000
Variable costs	500,000	1,000,000	1,000,000
Interest costs		75,000	
Total costs	$ 900,000	$1,675,000	$1,600,000
Estimated net income	$ 100,000	$ 125,000	$ 200,000

While various factors influence a final decision on whether or not to expand, management should recognize the following relationships in the above illustration. Present operations are returning 5% net income on assets in use ($100,000 net income divided by $2,000,000 total assets). Expansion via the long-term borrowing route will produce $25,000 additional income after interest charges, but return on total assets will fall to 3.57% ($125,000 net income divided by $3,500,000 total assets). The rate of return to stockholders, however, would increase because of the higher income accruing to them without any increase in stockholders' equity. Expansion via the sale-of-stock route will produce $100,000 additional income and increase return on total assets to 5.71% ($200,000 divided by $3,500,000). Whether or not the average rate of return to stockholders will increase, however, depends upon the manner in which the initial $2,000,000 of assets was financed. If $1,000,000 were provided by liabilities, the former rate of return to stockholders would have been 10% ($100,000 divided by $1,000,000). If the initial $2,000,000 of assets were provided by stockholders the former rate of return to stockholders would have been 5% ($100,000 divided by $2,000,000). By computing the rate of return to stockholders from the additional $1,500,000, one can determine whether the average rate of return to stockholders will increase or decrease if expansion via sale of stock is undertaken.

Regardless of the accounting analysis, management may make a decision based on other considerations. For example, management may discard the idea of financing the possible expansion by borrowing, deciding that the additional risk involved to stockholders will not be compensated for by the additional income generated. They may decide that expansion through a stock sale looks favorable.

Continuing with this illustration, however, a different conclusion might be reached. Assume that Company A presently has $750,000 of stock outstanding and also has $250,000 of retained earnings. The company is therefore earning a 10% return on the shareholders' equity ($100,000 net income divided by $1,000,000 shareholders' equity). If expansion proceeds by sale of stock, the shareholders' equity will increase to $2,500,000, and earnings to stockholders will increase to $200,000. However, return on shareholders' equity will fall to 8% ($200,000 divided by $2,500,000). In view of this decline in rate of return on investment, management may decide to forego any expansion at this time in the hope that more favorable situations will develop in the future.

This illustration may give some small indication of the complexities of a decision regarding possible expansion. While it is frequently advisable for management to separate the analysis of the expansion activity and the financing activity into two parts, at times the two phases of the overall problem must be merged for proper consideration.

METHODS OF EXPANSION

Expansion of an enterprise may follow several routes. For example, a company may expand by using existing facilities at a more rapid rate, thus increasing the turnover of resources. This method may require no additional financing. On the other hand, it may require an additional investment if additional assets are required for the increased rate of operations. Thus if a substantial increase in inventories is necessary to the increased volume, additional short-term borrowing may be necessary.

Expansion may involve the outright purchase or construction of additional facilities for additional volume, either of the existing product or of new products. Expansion may be accomplished by forming a separate branch to facilitate the expansion process, or by purchasing the assets of a going concern. Another expansion approach might find a company merging its assets with another company, either creating a new company or retaining one of the merging companies as the surviving company. Another expansion device involves the purchase of a substantial portion of the voting stock of another company, and through this transaction, the purchaser gains control of additional productive facilities. This latter area represents the area wherein consolidated statements, as accountants use the term, are commonly prepared. The area is discussed in detail in subsequent chapters.

PROBLEMS

Problem 7-1. The M. Co., manager of an office building, is considering putting in certain concessions in the main lobby. An accounting study produces the following estimates, on an average annual basis:

Salaries		$ 7,000
Licenses and payroll taxes		200
Cost of merchandise sold:		
Beginning inventory	$ 2,000	
Purchases	40,000	
Available	$42,000	
Ending inventory	2,000	40,000
Share of heat, light, etc.		500
Pro rata building depreciation		1,000
Concession advertising		100
Share of company administrative expense		400
Sales of merchandise		49,000

The investment in equipment, which would last 10 years, would be $2,000.

As an alternative, a catering company has offered to lease the space for $750 per year, for 10 years, and to put in and operate the same concessions at no cost to the M. Co. Heat and light are to be furnished by the office building at no additional charges.

What is your advice to the M. Co.? Explain fully.

(AICPA adapted)

Problem 7-2. The Walter Company management is considering various alternative plans for improving its profit picture. Below is a condensed income statement of the company for 1967:

Sales		$2,000,000
Cost of sales		1,400,000
Gross profit		600,000
Selling expenses	$180,000	
Administrative expenses	220,000	400,000
Income from operations		$ 200,000

During 1967 the entire productive facilities were not used, and it is estimated that a cost of $15,000 applicable to the unused facilities is included in the above statement. The following data are developed with respect to a possible plan for the coming year, involving substantially full utilization of the plant facilities:

		Plan 1
Total sales expected		$2,400,000
Cost of sales		1,670,000
Gross profit		730,000
Selling expenses	$230,000	
Administrative expenses	240,000	470,000
Income from operations		$ 260,000

The company anticipates it can sell whatever volume is produced, within the above range of production. In 1967 total fixed costs were $600,000.

It is determined that the book value of the idle facilities at December 31, 1967, was $135,000, that these facilities are worth $40,000 if sold, and that if they are utilized they will have their useful life shortened by one-third over that anticipated during 1967's idleness. The costs stated above for the alternative plan do not include recognition of this accelerated depreciation through utilization of the idle facilities.

Required:

On the basis of these facts only, determine whether the company should move to "Plan 1" or should produce in 1968 on a basis comparable to that of 1967. Support your conclusions.

Problem 7–3. Paul and Taylor, operating as a partnership, desire to expand their operations by securing additional capital from new sources. Ridley accepts an offer to become an equal partner with Paul and Taylor. Ridley will invest $50,000 in the partnership and will have a one-third interest in the profits and in the capital of the partnership. At the date of investment the capital balances of Paul and Taylor are $38,000 and $42,000 respectively. The partners are undecided as to how they should reflect the investment of Ridley in their accounts. Ridley insists that his capital credit be $50,000; Paul insists that the total capital shall not exceed the net assets on the books prior to the admission of Ridley plus Ridley's investment; Taylor insists that the present balance in his capital account equals one-third of the net assets of the partnership after Ridley's investment.

Required:

Prepare a journal entry, or entries, to reflect the desires of the three partners. Describe the result, as to whether the entry involves goodwill or bonus, and whether the goodwill or bonus applies to the old or new partners. If your recommendation were requested as to the most advisable entry, which would you recommend? Why?

Problem 7–4. The board of directors of the Mortsaw Corp. has been considering an expansion of existing facilities to take advantage of favorable market conditions for its products. During 1967 the company earned a net income after taxes of $200,000 on sales of $4,000,000. Depreciation on facilities used in 1967 totaled $150,000 and was the only noncash charge against 1967 income. For each of the first five years after completion of the expansion program sales are expected to average $5,600,000 and produce a net income after taxes, but without regard to finance costs, of $305,000. The new facilities are expected to take one year to construct, will cost $1,125,000, and will have an estimated useful life of 25 years. Once the new facilities are operating, the company expects to have to carry increased inventories of $300,000, build-up of which would occur during the latter part of the construction period and in the six months following completion of the facilities. At January 1, 1968, the only available cash not required for the existing level of operations is about equal to that generated by 1967 operations. Existing facilities, which are being depreciated on a 25-year life, will not begin to require replacement until January 1, 1971, at which date it is estimated replacement will total $100,000 per year for five years and $200,000 per year thereafter, on an average basis.

Three board members with divergent views on the expansion plans present you with their ideas:

Mr. M. does not want to begin expansion until such time as sufficient cash is on hand, or will be on hand by completion of the facilities, to pay for the costs of expansion. All three board members agree that about 80% of cash generated by operations in 1968 and subsequent years will be available for expansion.

Mr. S. wants to build immediately by obtaining an intermediate-term bank loan for $1,200,000, which is available at 5% interest, to be liquidated by funds obtained from operations.

Mr. W. wants to wait until January 1, 1970, to begin construction, borrowing at that date at 5% the amount necessary after utilizing cash estimated to be available from operations at that date. Liquidation of the loan would proceed as indicated by Mr. S.

Required:

You are to summarize the effects on the company of each of these views, including time delay for construction, comparable costs, etc.

Problem 7–5. The Savoy Company was contemplating expansion, and the management was determined to explore fully the possibilities of utilizing internally generated funds for the expansion costs. Company officials listed the following items in considering possible sources of expansion funds:

Average annual net income (after dividends)	$100,000
Average annual depreciation charges	80,000
Depreciation reserves	450,000
Earned surplus	900,000
Average annual mortgage reduction	60,000
Average annual interest charges	20,000

Required:

Draft a brief report to explain to the Savoy management how each of the above would affect their cash needs, and determine how much cash the company might expect to have available on an annual basis to use for expansion.

Problem 7–6. The directors of the Weygandt Corporation are considering the issuance of a stock dividend. They have asked you to discuss the proposed action by answering the questions below.

Required:

(1) What is a stock dividend? How is a stock dividend distinguished from a stock split-up
  (a) from a legal standpoint?
  (b) from an accounting standpoint?

(2) For what reasons does a corporation usually declare a stock dividend? A stock split-up?

(3) Discuss the amount, if any, of retained earnings to be capitalized in connection with a stock dividend.   (AICPA adapted)

Problem 7–7. Austin and Bradford are partners. They share profits equally and have equal investments. The partnership's net assets are carried on the books at $20,000. Crane is admitted to the partnership with a one-third interest in profits and net assets. Crane pays $9,000 cash into the partnership for his interest.

Prepare journal entries to show three possible methods of recording on the partnership books the admission of Crane. State the conditions under which each method would be appropriate.

Problem 7–8. The Capital Budget Committee of the Walton Corporation was established to appraise and screen departmental requests for plant expansions and improvements at a time when these requests totaled $10 million. The Committee thereupon sought your professional advice and help in establishing minimum performance standards which it would demand of these projects in the way of anticipated rates of return before interest and taxes.

The Walton Corporation is a closely held family corporation in which the stockholders exert an active and unified influence on the management. At this date, the company has no long-term debt and has 1,000,000 shares of common stock outstanding. It is currently earning $5 million (net income before interest and taxes) per year. The applicable tax rate is 50%.

Should the projects under consideration be approved, management is confident the $10 million of required funds can be obtained either:

1. By borrowing—via the medium of an issue of $10 million, 4% 20-year bonds.
2. By equity financing—via the medium of an issue of 500,000 shares of common stock to the general public. It is anticipated that the ownership of these 500,000 shares would be widely dispersed and scattered.

The company has been earning $12\frac{1}{2}\%$ return after taxes. The management and the dominant stockholders consider this rate of earnings to be a fair capitalization rate (8 times earnings) as long as the company remains free of long-term debt. An increase to 15%, or $6\frac{2}{3}$ times earnings, would constitute an adequate adjustment to compensate for the risk of carrying $10 million of long-term debt. They believe that this reflects, and is consistent with, current market appraisals.

Required:

(1) Prepare columnar schedules comparing minimum returns, considering interest, taxes, and earnings ratio, which should be produced by each alternative to maintain the present capitalized value per share.

(2) What minimum rate of return on new investment is necessary for each alternative to maintain the present capitalized value per share?

(AICPA—adapted)

Problem 7–9. Ace Publishing Company is in the business of publishing and printing guide books and directories. The board of directors has engaged you to make a cost study to determine whether the Company is economically justified in continuing to print, as well as publish, its books and directories. You obtain the following information from the company's cost accounting records for the preceding fiscal year:

	Departments			
	Publishing	Printing	Shipping	Total
Salaries and wages	$275,000	$150,000	$25,000	$450,000
Telephone and telegraph	12,000	3,700	300	16,000
Materials and supplies	50,000	250,000	10,000	310,000
Occupancy costs	75,000	80,000	10,000	165,000
General and administrative	40,000	30,000	4,000	74,000
Depreciation	5,000	40,000	5,000	50,000
	$457,000	$553,700	$54,300	$1,065,000

Additional data:

(*a*) A review of personnel requirements indicates that, if printing is discontinued, the publishing department will need one additional clerk at $4,000 per year to handle correspondence with the printer. Two layout men and a proofreader will be required at an aggregate annual cost of $17,000; other personnel in the printing department can be released. One mailing clerk, at $3,000, will be retained; others in the shipping department can be released. Employees whose employment was being terminated would immediately receive, on the average, three months' termination pay. The termination pay would be amortized over a five-year period.

(*b*) Long-distance telephone and telegraph charges are identified and distributed to the responsible department. The remainder of the telephone bill, representing basic service at a cost of $4,000, was allocated in the ratio of 10 to publishing, 5 to printing, and 1 to shipping. The discontinuance of printing is not expected to have a material effect on the basic service cost.

(*c*) Shipping supplies consist of cartons, envelopes, and stamps. It is estimated that the cost of envelopes and stamps for mailing material to an outside printer would be $5,000 per year.

(*d*) If printing is discontinued, the Company would retain its present building but would sublet a portion of the space at an annual rental of $50,000. Taxes, insurance, heat, light, and other occupancy costs would not be significantly affected.

(*e*) One cost clerk would not be required ($5,000 per year) if printing is discontinued. Other general and administrative personnel would be retained.

(*f*) Included in administrative expenses is interest expense on a 5% mortgage loan of $500,000.

(*g*) Printing and shipping room machinery and equipment having a net book value of $300,000 can be sold without gain or loss. These funds in excess of termination pay would be invested in marketable securities earning 5%.

(*h*) The Company has received a proposal for a five-year contract from an outside printing concern, under which the volume of work done last year would be printed at a cost of $550,000 per year.

(*i*) Assume continued volume and prices at last year's level.

Required:

Prepare a statement setting forth in comparative form the costs of operation of the printing and shipping departments under the present arrangement and under an arrangement in which inside printing is discontinued. Summarize the net saving or extra cost in case printing is discontinued.   (AICPA adapted)

Problem 7–10. A manufacturing company, in order to improve its relationship with its principal supplier of raw materials, decides to acquire some of its common stock. The following terms are finally agreed upon: The supply company is to be issued 5,000 shares of the manufacturing company's no-par common stock. This stock has a stated value of $25 per share and is currently selling in small lots at approximately $45 per share. In return for these 5,000 shares, the supply company will give the manufacturing company 2,000 of its $100 par value common stock now held in its treasury. The supply company's stock is currently quoted at about $90 per share. The supply company has 25,000 shares of common issued and it will all be outstanding after completion of the exchange.

Discuss fully the reasons for and against at least three bases of valuation which might be considered by the manufacturing company for recording the 2,000 shares of supply company stock it will receive. Exclude income tax considerations.

Problem 7–11. A variety of alternative plans, each requiring additional capital investment, is under consideration by officials of the Sheehan Company. The details of four plans are presented below:

	Plan 1	Plan 2	Plan 3	Plan 4
Capital investment required	$100,000	$200,000	$250,000	$50,000
Additional cost, not including interest	2,000	4,000	5,000	1,000
Additional income	10,000	20,000	25,000	5,000

The company has $100,000 available for investment. Any additional amounts are estimated to be available at 5% interest. Any amounts not utilized for expansion will be invested at an expected return of 4%.

The officials are interested in which plan appears to be the most appropriate, in terms of differential income, return on investment, risk, etc.

Required:

Prepare an analysis to provide the management with the basis for deciding among the alternative plans.

Problem 7–12. The balance sheet below pertains to the Kolar and Green partnership at April 30, 1967:

Cash	$ 50,000	Liabilities		$ 60,000
Other assets	170,000	Kolar, capital	$100,000	
Goodwill	20,000	Green, capital	80,000	180,000
	$240,000			$240,000

Kolar and Green share profits and losses equally. To obtain additional working capital the partners have offered a share of the business to Burnside in return for his cash investment. The following alternative possibilities have been worked out by Burnside:

1. Burnside invests $56,000 for a one-fourth interest in the total capital of $240,000.
2. Burnside invests $56,000 for a $\frac{1}{3}$ interest in a total capital of $236,000.
3. Burnside invests $56,000 for a one-fourth interest in the total capital of $260,000.
4. Burnside invests $56,000 for a one-fourth interest in the partnership, receiving a capital credit of $56,000.

Required:

Prepare journal entries to express each of the above alternatives on the books of the partnership.

Problem 7–13. The Mosher Company has certain idle facilities which it is contemplating using for production under one alternative plan (Plan 1) being considered for the coming year. The facilities have a book value of $100,000. A recent offer to buy the facilities has been received by the Mosher Company in the amount of $40,000. Another alternative plan (Plan 2) under consideration would not use these facilities. If the facilities are used in Plan 1, it is anticipated they will have no further use to the company. While the date of their replacement is uncertain at the present time, the company officials anticipate that replacement of the facilities would require an outlay of $160,000. A recent appraisal of the value of all properties of the Mosher Company indicates a value of $60,000 for these facilities.

Company officials have determined that the differential cost of the two plans, excluding any consideration of the facilities discussed above, would be:

Plan 1	$700,000
Plan 2	820,000

Required:

Based upon the above data only, which plan would you recommend? Why?

Problem 7–14. Leddy and Giller had operated as a partnership for a number of years. At June 30, 1967, their balance sheet appeared as below:

LEDDY & GILLER
Balance Sheet, June 30, 1967

Assets		Liabilities	
Cash	$ 5,000	Accounts payable	$ 34,000
Receivables	30,000	Accrued liabilities	6,000
Inventories	60,000	Mortgage payable	80,000
Equipment (net)	80,000	Leddy, capital	75,000
Building (net)	90,000	Giller, capital	70,000
	$265,000		$265,000

Peters is interested in becoming a partner on equal terms with Leddy and Giller. The partners do not wish to have any goodwill exist on their books, and they have carefully studied their various asset values to determine the basis for Peters' investment. It is agreed that prior to admission of Peters the receivables should be reduced to $27,000, the equipment to $70,000, and the inventory should be written up to $66,000. Peters agrees to invest $75,000 for a one-third interest in the partnership. The partners agree that all capital accounts shall be equal after this investment.

Required:

Prepare journal entries necessary to reflect the above. How much cash should Giller pay Leddy on a personal basis?

Problem 7–15. The Keyser Corporation sells computer services to its clients. The Company completed a feasibility study and decided to obtain an additional computer on January 1, 1968. Information regarding the new computer follows:

(*a*) The purchase price of the computer is $230,000. Maintenance, property taxes, and insurance will be $20,000 per year. If the computer is rented, the annual rate will be $85,000 plus 5% of annual billings. The rental price includes maintenance.

(*b*) Due to competitive conditions the Company believes it will be necessary to replace the computer at the end of 3 years with one which is larger and more advanced. It is estimated that the computer will have a resale value of $110,000 at the end of 3 years. The computer will be depreciated on a straight line basis for both financial reporting and income tax purposes.

(*c*) The income tax rate is 50%.

(*d*) The estimated annual billing for the services of the new computer will be $220,000 during the first year and $260,000 during each of the second and third years. The estimated annual expense of operating the computer is $80,000 in addition to the expense mentioned above. An additional $10,000 of start-up expenses will be incurred during the first year.

(*e*) If it decides to purchase the computer, the Company will pay cash. If the computer is rented, the $230,000 can be otherwise invested at a 15% rate of return.

(*f*) If the computer is purchased, the amount of investment recovered during each of the three years can be reinvested immediately at a 15% rate of return. Each year's recovery of investment in the computer will have been reinvested for an average of six months by the end of the year.

(*g*) The present value of $1.00 due at a constant rate during each year and discounted at 15% is:

Year	Present Value
0–1	$.93
1–2	.80
2- 3	.69

The present value of $1.00 due at the end of each year and discounted at 15% is:

End of Year	Present Value
1	$.87
2	.76
3	.66

Required:

(1) Prepare a schedule comparing the estimated annual income from the new computer under the purchase plan and under the rental plan. The comparison should include a provision for the opportunity cost of the average investment in the computer during each year.

(2) Prepare a schedule showing the annual cash flows under the purchase plan and under the rental plan.

(3) Prepare a schedule comparing the present values of the cash flows under the purchase plan and under the rental plan.

(4) Comment on the results obtained in parts (1) and (3). How should the computer be financed? Why?   (AICPA adapted)

CHAPTER 8

Expansion by branch operations

Previous chapters of this book have been directed primarily to the accounting problems involved in organizing and developing a company at one central location. But, it is commonplace in business to find a company spread over a large geographic area with several plants and offices located at various points in the area. Such decentralization may be stimulated by several factors, such as a need to be near a source of supply for raw materials which are available in diverse areas, or by a belief that the impact of depressions, wars, and other contingencies may be lessened by such decentralization. One compelling reason for decentralization is to be near the customers or markets that the company products are attempting to attract.

Company expansion to provide more effective contact with customers has resulted from the development and growth of the marketing process. This has stimulated the development of large business organizations with a national market for their products. For a typical enterprise this expansion may have taken place somewhat as follows. First, salesmen are assigned a wider and wider area as the market for the company's products expands. This process of expansion has several limitations. As a result, the next step might be the establishment of various sales agencies from which salesmen might operate and through which local customers could be provided with a permanent contact point in dealing with the company. The typical sales agency may carry samples of company products and be financed by a working fund from the home office.

The next step in the expansion process might be the establishment of an almost autonomous branch. The functions and responsibilities of a branch vary considerably, but normally the branch carries for sale merchandise which may be sold for cash or on account. Responsibility for cash receipts and expenses of various kinds may be assigned to the branch. The functions of the head office may include centralized purchasing or production, shipments to the branch of goods purchased or produced, and general direction, as opposed to specific direction, of branch activities.

Separate Ledgers

As a company spreads itself geographically, it is not uncommon for its accounting system to become decentralized also. One common device to decentralize accounting activities is to separate from the general ledger those accounts that deal with the decentralized or separated activities. In a sense, the separate ledger so established is similar to a subsidiary ledger, since one impetus to establishment of subsidiary ledgers is a subdivision or decentralization of accounting activities. Both a separate ledger and a subsidiary ledger represent the withdrawal from the general ledger of selected accounts and the *substitution* for them of one account into which are summarized all the balances of the withdrawn accounts.

A distinction between these two accounting decentralizations may be drawn based on the nature of the separated accounts. Where the separated accounts are similar in nature, such as accounts receivable or accounts payable, they normally are assumed to represent a subsidiary or detailed record of the control account in the general ledger. Where the accounts withdrawn from the general ledger are not similar in nature, that is, where some of the accounts may be assets, some liabilities, expenses or incomes, the accounts are assumed to represent a separate ledger. Typical illustrations of separate ledgers are:

(1) Factory ledger.
(2) Private ledger.
(3) Branch office ledger.

Factory Ledger. The factory ledger is used most frequently in manufacturing enterprises in which the production plant is located physically some distance from the central office. Thus, the impetus to establish the factory ledger may have arisen from a decentralization of enterprise activities. The factory ledger comprises those accounts containing a detailed record of the factory operations. These accounts, and subsequent analyses of them, are necessary for efficient operation of the plant, but the accounts are of little or no concern to the central office on a day-to-day operating basis. On the books of the central office, the account "Factory Ledger" is used as a substitute for the various factory ledger accounts which would otherwise appear in the general ledger. This account is a summary account for all of the activities of the factory.

Private Ledger. Another example of a separate ledger is the so-called "private ledger." Although little used now, the private ledger is a means whereby confidential information, such as executive salaries, dividend payments, and bonuses might be removed from the general ledger and accounted for in greater privacy. A summary account, "Private Ledger," is substituted for the various accounts removed from the general ledger. The confidential information is then placed in the private ledger.

BRANCH ACCOUNTING CONCEPTS
AND PROCEDURES

According to sound principles of management, the division of responsibility within an enterprise should be clearly delineated along organizational lines. This principle applies equally well to accounting procedures. One might expect that the accounting procedures of a branch office should provide sufficiently detailed information to permit centralized management to hold branch management responsible for branch activities. Practically, this concept cannot always be applied fully to branch activities because of the difficulty of assigning responsibility to an organizational unit of this nature. While branch accounting procedures in practice may not be in full accord with the principle of organizational responsibility noted above, to the extent possible they should be consistent with this principle.

Essentially, branch accounting endeavors to account for certain of the assets, revenues, expenditures, and liabilities of the company. It attempts to account for all such items for which the branch may be responsible. The concept of controllable expenditures seems to represent the substance of the underlying objective of branch accounting procedures.

In some branch organizations almost all assets and expenditures are held to be the responsibility of the branch manager. Thus, in this type of organization, branch accounting would include accounting for depreciation of branch equipment, and the accountable assets of the branch would include those assets used in the branch operations. More often branch managers are held responsible for only a portion of the total branch expenditures with the home office assuming the responsibility for the uncontrollable (fixed) expenses. In this type of branch-home office organization depreciation on branch fixed assets, as well as other expenses not controllable by the branch manager, would not be accounted for by the branch, but would be included in the home office or central accounting system.

In summary, the transactions encompassed by branch accounting procedures depend in part upon the responsibility of the branch manager and in part upon the ability of the branch accounting system to provide information on those activities which are subject to the control of the branch manager.

Establishing the Branch

When a business enterprise decides to establish a branch outlet, a decision must also be made regarding the accounting system which the branch outlet is to maintain. As noted above, the branch manager may be given relatively little responsibility, in which case he may be provided with a working fund of cash and be expected to establish records which will account for this fund of cash. On the other hand, the branch manager may be given relatively great responsibility, in which case he may establish a separate ledger to account for the transactions in which his branch engages.

Working Fund. If the home office is to maintain the detailed records pertaining to the operations of the branch, and if it provides the branch with a working fund of cash, the accounting problems of establishing the branch are relatively simple. Under this system the home office transactions with the branch will involve transmission of merchandise for resale to the branch and the remittance to the home office by the branch of the branch receipts. These transactions would not pass through the branch records. Likewise major expenditures of the branch will be paid directly by the home office upon receipt of an invoice approved by the branch manager. All branch revenues are deposited intact in a bank by the branch to the credit of the home office. Thus, effective control of the cash rests with the home office. The working fund of cash is used by the branch to meet small branch expenditures. This manner of branch operations provides the home office with rather complete control over expenditures and receipts of the branch, yet it permits the branch to incur such costs as it deems advisable.

In practice the foregoing procedure is more often used when a sales agency is in operation than it is with a separate branch operation. Accounting for home office-branch transactions under the above procedure would be similar to the procedure of establishing a working fund for a salesman. For example, if the home office were to send the branch $1,000 as a working fund, and if such represented the only asset transferred to the branch (salesman or sales agency), appropriate accounting on the books of the home office would be:

Branch working fund	$1,000	
Cash		$1,000

The account, Branch Office, need not be used when the branch is provided only with cash by the home office.

If the branch or agency should decide to maintain a ledger, even though the limited nature of their accounting needs may indicate that such is not appropriate, the entry should be:

Cash	$1,000	
Due to home office		$1,000

As expenses are paid, the branch or agency would debit the expense accounts and credit cash appropriately. For example, if the agency purchases $50 of supplies, the entry should be:

Supplies	$50	
Cash		$50

The home or central office would make no record of this transaction until such is reported by the agency. At that time the entry on the books of the home office would be:

Supplies	$50	
Branch working fund (or cash if working fund is replenished)		$50

Revenues of the branch or agency need not be recorded by the branch. The central office could record such sales directly, as follows:

Cash (receipt acknowledged by bank)	$500	
Sales (branch or agency)		$500

Separate Ledger. If the branch is to maintain a separate ledger to account for its transactions, a few modifications in the normal accounting procedures arise because of the home office-branch relationship. Normally, both the branch and the home office will maintain some record of the assets of the branch. The home office typically uses one account, "Branch Office," into which are charged all asset resources for which the branch has accounting responsibility. This account also receives credits as the branch is relieved of accounting responsibility by making remittances to the home office. The "Branch Office" account represents a control account on the books of the home office. This account controls the branch ledger, a separate ledger generally maintained at the branch. The separate ledger provides a detailed record of the information summarized in the controlling account, "Branch Office."

The branch, in order to maintain double-entry accounting, sets up a "Home Office" account, the balance of which represents the home office equity (residual equity) of the branch. The "Home Office" account is credited with all assets contributed by or accruing to the home office, the offsetting debit going to a specific asset or expense account. The account is charged when the branch is relieved of an amount due to the home office, generally through a direct remittance to the home office.

ESTABLISHING THE BRANCH. Assume the Pier Corporation of Chicago desires to establish a branch in the city of Urbana, Illinois, by transferring to the branch certain of the activities formerly performed at the Chicago office. The home office desires that the branch shall be responsible for all assets used by the branch in performing its function. Assuming the branch uses a building valued at $10,000, equipment valued at $22,000, and inventory with a $31,000 book value, the appropriate entries to record this information would be as follows:

ON THE BOOKS OF THE HOME OFFICE

Branch Office	$63,000	
Building		$10,000
Equipment		22,000
Inventory		31,000

ON THE BOOKS OF THE BRANCH OFFICE

Building	$10,000	
Equipment	22,000	
Inventory	31,000	
Home Office		$63,000

It will be observed that from a combined, or consolidated, point of view the Home Office account and the Branch Office account are reciprocal. Both should be eliminated when the accounts of the branch are to be merged with those of the home office in the preparation of combined financial reports. Stated another way, the Branch Office account on the books of the home office is eliminated, and the details supporting this account, as reflected in the separate branch ledger, are substituted.

OPERATIONS OF THE BRANCH. Where the branch maintains a separate double entry ledger the recording procedure for home office-branch transactions requires entries on the books of both the home office and the branch. Branch transactions which do not directly involve the home office require entries only on the books of the branch. Continuing the illustration of the Pier Corporation, entries are presented below to record the more common branch operating transactions. For comparative purposes the entries on both sets of books are presented.

(a) *Transaction.* The home office ships $2,000 of merchandise to the branch.

ON HOME OFFICE BOOKS:

Branch Office	$2,000	
Merchandise		$2,000

ON BRANCH BOOKS:

Merchandise	$2,000	
Home Office		$2,000

(b) *Transaction.* The branch purchases $500 of merchandise and $100 of supplies for cash.

ON HOME OFFICE BOOKS:

No entry.

ON BRANCH BOOKS:

Merchandise	$500	
Supplies	100	
Cash		$600

(c) *Transaction.* The branch sells merchandise on account, $1,500.

ON HOME OFFICE BOOKS:

No entry.

ON BRANCH BOOKS:

Accounts receivable	$1,500	
Sales		$1,500

(d) *Transaction.* The branch pays salaries of $300, records depreciation of $100, and determines the cost of merchandise sold for the period to be $700.

ON HOME OFFICE BOOKS:

No entry.

ON BRANCH BOOKS:

Salaries	$300	
Depreciation	100	
Cost of merchandise sold	700	
Cash		$300
Allowance for depreciation		100
Merchandise		700

(e) *Transaction.* The branch closes its books and reports profit or loss to the home office.

ON BRANCH BOOKS:

Sales	$1,500	
Profit and loss		$1,500
Profit and loss	$1,200	
Supplies		$100
Salaries		300
Depreciation		100
Cost of merchandise sold		700
Profit and loss	$300	
Home Office		$300

ON HOME OFFICE BOOKS:

Branch office	$300	
Branch profit and loss		$300

(f) *Transaction.* The branch sends the home office $200 cash.

ON HOME OFFICE BOOKS:

Cash	$200	
Branch office		$200

ON BRANCH BOOKS:

Home office	$200	
Cash		$200

A study of the above transactions and entries discloses the entries on the books of the branch are very similar to those which any enterprise might have. Instead of a "capital" or similar owners' account, the residual equity of the branch is recorded in the "Home Office" account. Branch profit and loss is determined in the normal manner, and the resulting profit or loss is closed to the Home Office account. Distributions by the branch to the home office reduce the equity of the home office in the branch and are so recorded through a charge to Home Office.

The "Branch Office" account in the home office ledger may be considered as a type of investment account. The balance at any closing date indicates the amount due from the branch or the amount the home office has invested in the branch. At any date the "Branch Office" account and the "Home Office" account should contain *reciprocal* balances. The procedure to follow when these accounts do not contain reciprocal balances at a closing date is discussed in a subsequent section.

Merchandise Billed above Cost. While the home office may charge the branch at cost for merchandise shipped to the branch, frequently the home office will buy merchandise for the branch and will bill such merchandise to the branch at a price other than cost. Under this procedure the branch manager will not know the cost of the merchandise he sells, and thus will not be aware of the profit which the branch is earning. An additional advantage from this procedure may accrue to the home office if the branch is billed at selling price for merchandise shipped by the home office. Billing the branch at selling price provides the home office with continuous information on the inventory of the branch. Branch sales reported to the home office will be deducted from shipments to the branch, both being valued at selling price, and the resulting balance should be the branch inventory in terms of selling price. Periodic comparisons of the inventory so determined with a physical inventory taken at the branch provide a measure of control of branch inventories.

Shipments to Branch. The accounting procedure for recording shipments to the branch by the home office depends upon whether the home office maintains perpetual inventory records. Assume the home office sends merchandise which had cost $1,000 to a branch, but transfers it to the branch at a selling price of $1,500. The appropriate entry on the books of the home office to record the shipment would be:

If the home office maintains perpetual inventory records:

Branch office	$1,500	
Merchandise		$1,000
Unrealized margin in		
branch inventory		500

Since the Merchandise account is carried at cost, any entries to it for shipments to the branch should be made at cost. The credit to "Unrealized Margin in Branch Inventory" represents the difference between the billed price and the cost price of the merchandise. As the merchandise is sold by the branch the unrealized margin becomes "realized," and the account is adjusted to recognize the realized margin when the branch reports its sales to the home office.

If the home office does not maintain perpetual inventory records:

Branch office	$1,500	
Shipments to branch		$1,500

The "Shipments to Branch" account is used to record at selling price all shipments of merchandise to the branch. The disposition of this account will be discussed in the following section.

Regardless of the recording on the books of the home office, the entry on the branch books would be:

Merchandise from home office	$1,500	
Home office		$1,500

Branch Sales. Branch accounting for sales of merchandise billed from the home office at a price above cost is identical with the recording procedure for sales of any other type of merchandise. For example, if the branch sold for cash 40% of the $1,500 merchandise received from the home office (cost $1,000) the entry appropriate for the branch books would be:

Cash	$600	
Sales		$600

The home office would not be advised of this sale until it was reported by the branch, normally at the close of an accounting period. When the home office receives the report of the branch sale, an entry must be made to record the profit realized by the branch through the sale. If the home office follows a perpetual inventory system, the entry will recognize that portion of the previously entered "Unrealized Margin in Branch Inventory" which is no longer unrealized. Thus if 40% of the merchandise shipped to the branch in the above example is sold, the entry on the home office books to record the profit realized through the sale would be:

Unrealized margin in branch		
inventory	$200	
Branch profit and loss		$200

If the home office inventories are adjusted only periodically, an entry must be made to record the realized profit and also to record the unrealized profit applicable to the merchandise still unsold at the branch. A suitable procedure to record these facts on the home office books would be:

Shipments to branch	$1,500	
Purchases		$1,000
Branch profit and loss		200
Unrealized margin in		
branch inventory		300

The "Unrealized Margin in Branch Inventory" account is a valuation account, and it would be deducted from the merchandise inventory on a combined balance sheet of the branch and the home office in order to reduce the inventory to cost.

Determination of the income or loss of the branch requires that the income or loss reported by the branch be added to the realized margin recorded by the home office in the "Branch Profit and Loss" account.

Illustration—Branch Accounting. The Brown Company establishes a branch in the town of Deerville on February 2, 1967. On this date the home office transfers to the branch the following assets:

Cash	$ 5,000
Equipment	12,000

On February 15 the home office sends $8,000 of merchandise to the branch, but bills it to the branch at $12,000.

On February 28 the branch pays for the following items:

Merchandise	$500
Supplies	200
Salaries	800

During March the branch activities are:

Sales—on account	$5,000
Sales—cash	4,500
Salaries	1,000
Cash transferred to home office	3,000

On March 31 branch inventories are:

Merchandise from home office	$3,000
Merchandise purchased	200
Supplies	100

Depreciation on branch equipment for the two month period is $200.

On March 31 the branch reports its profit and loss to the home office and closes its books. The home office also closes its books on March 31. The above facts would be recorded on the books of the branch and home office in the following manner:

BRANCH BOOKS			HOME OFFICE BOOKS		
		Feb. 2, 1967			
Cash	$ 5,000		Branch office	$17,000	
Equipment	12,000		Cash		$ 5,000
Home office		$17,000	Equipment		12,000
		Feb. 15, 1967			
Merchandise from home			Branch office	$12,000	
office	$12,000		Shipments to		
Home office		$12,000	branch		$12,000
		Feb. 28, 1967			
Merchandise	$500		No entry.		
Supplies	200				
Salaries	800				
Cash		$1,500			
		March, 1967			
Accounts receivable	$5,000		No entry.		
Cash	4,500				
Sales		$9,500			

BRANCH BOOKS		HOME OFFICE BOOKS	
March, 1967			
Home office	$3,000	Cash	$3,000
Salaries	1,000	Branch office	$3,000
Cash	$4,000		

March 31, 1967

Cost of goods sold	$9,300	No entry.	
Merchandise from			
home office	$9,000		
Merchandise	300		

March 31, 1967

Supplies expense	$100	No entry.	
Supplies	$100		
Depreciation expense	$200	No entry.	
Allow. for Depreciation	$200		
Sales	$9,500	No entry.	
Profit and loss	$9,500		
Profit and loss	$11,400	No entry.	
Salaries	$1,800		
Cost of goods sold	9,300		
Supplies expense	100		
Depreciation expense	200		
Home office	$1,900	Branch profit and loss	$1,900	
Profit and loss	$1,900	Branch office		$1,900
No entry.		Shipments to branch	$12,000	
		Branch profit and		
		loss		$3,000
		Unrealized margin		
		in branch		
		inventory		1,000
		Purchases		8,000
No entry.		Branch profit and loss	$1,100	
		Profit and loss		$1,100

From the March 31 entries above, it can be seen that as far as the branch manager is concerned, the branch suffered an operating loss of $1,900 during the period. However, $1,900 is not the actual loss, since the merchandise shipped to the branch by the home office was billed at an amount in excess of cost. The difference between cost price and billed price could be analyzed as follows:

$8,000 merchandise cost billed to branch at $12,000 = $4,000 markup
$3,000 of merchandise billed remains in inventory
at end of period. $3,000 ÷ $12,000 (total shipped) = 1/4
Thus 1/4 of markup is unrealized at period end = $1,000
   3/4 of markup is realized at period end = $3,000

Since the $3,000 portion of the markup has been earned by the branch through its sales, the actual branch profit is $1,100 ($3,000 less $1,900 loss). This is the amount closed to the Profit and Loss account in the final entry on the home office books above.

Interbranch Transfers. Occasionally the home office may order one branch to transfer merchandise, received from a different branch or from the home office, to another branch. While generally accepted accounting procedure includes as a cost of merchandise the freight charges of acquiring merchandise held for resale, this procedure is subject to modification when the freight charges are excessive due to an indirect method of shipping, such as from the home office to Branch A and then on to Branch B. When interbranch transfers are made, the excessive freight should be charged off as a loss.

To illustrate, assume the home office sent to Branch A $1,000 merchandise on which the home office paid freight charges of $120. Later the home office directed Branch A to send the merchandise to Branch B. To accomplish this shipment A was required to pay $100 of freight charges. Had the merchandise been shipped directly to Branch B from the home office, the freight charges would have been $150. The foregoing activities would have been recorded on the three sets of books as follows:

BRANCH A BOOKS

Merchandise from home office	$1,000	
Merchandise from home office	120	
Home office		$1,120
(to record receipt of merchandise from home office and to include freight charges as a part of merchandise cost)		
Home office	$1,220	
Merchandise from home office		$1,120
Cash		100
(to record transfer of merchandise to Branch B and to charge home office for merchandise and cash given up to make transfer)		

BRANCH B BOOKS

Merchandise from home office	$1,000	
Merchandise from home office	150	
Home office		$1,150
(to record receipt of merchandise from Branch A as directed by home office and to include as cost appropriate freight charges)		

HOME OFFICE BOOKS

Branch "A"	$1,120	
Shipments to branches		$1,000
Cash		120
(to record shipment of merchandise to Branch A and to charge the branch for freight charges)		
Branch "B"	$1,150	
Interbranch transfer loss	70	
Branch "A"		$1,220
(to record transfer of merchandise to Branch B by charging B for the merchandise cost plus freight of $150. To give Branch A credit for the merchandise transfer and freight charges from home office to A of $120 and from A to B of $100. Total freight charges were $220, but only $150 is inventoriable, and $70 loss must be recognized by the home office)		

Combined Financial Statements

When the branch and the home office maintain separate ledgers, the preparation of financial statements for the combined operations requires a combination of the trial balances or the respective statements, as the case may be, of the separate entities. The process of combining financial statements is a rather simple one in most instances. The purpose of the combined report is to show the assets, equities, income, and expenses as if they pertained to a single entity. Thus, it would seem logical to combine like asset, equity, income, and expense accounts to get a combined statement. In addition to combining like accounts, the combination process must deal with the Home Office account on the books of the branch and the Branch Office account on the books of the home office. Normally, these accounts are reciprocal to each other, i.e., they contain balances of like dollar amounts, but one has a credit balance and the other a debit balance. When the accounts are in reciprocal balance one may be eliminated against the other without upsetting the combined trial balance or financial statements. At times, however, these accounts will not be reciprocal, generally because various in transit items have not been recorded properly on each set of books. If the Branch Office and the Home Office are not in reciprocal balance, it is necessary to adjust one or both accounts for the items in transit so that the reciprocal relationship will be achieved.

The illustration on the following page indicates the combining procedure.

TRIAL BALANCE
DECEMBER 31, 1967

	Branch Dr.	Branch Cr.	Home Office Dr.	Home Office Cr.	Adjustments & Eliminations Dr.	Adjustments & Eliminations Cr.	Combined Trial Balance Dr.	Combined Trial Balance Cr.
Cash	$ 3,000		$ 12,000		$ 2,000 (1)		$ 17,000	
Receivables	4,000		17,000				21,000	
Inventory	5,000		15,000				20,000	
Fixed assets	10,000		95,000				105,000	
Allowance for depreciation		$ 2,000		$ 20,000				$ 22,000
Accounts payable		1,000		8,000				9,000
Branch office			24,000			$22,000A 2,000 (1)		
Home office		22,000			22,000A			
Sales		18,000		105,000				123,000
Unrealized margin in branch inventory				10,000	7,500B			2,500
Cost of goods sold	15,000		50,000				65,000	
Expenses	6,000		25,000				31,000	
Capital stock				50,000				50,000
Retained earnings				45,000				45,000
Branch profit and loss						7,500B		7,500
Totals	$43,000	$43,000	$238,000	$238,000	$31,500	$31,500	$259,000	$259,000

(1): The $2,000 adjustment was necessary because the branch had recorded a transfer of $2,000 cash to the home office. The home office had not recorded this in transit cash.

A: This entry eliminates the reciprocal accounts.

B: This entry eliminates the intra-company profit in the branch inventory. The home office had shipped merchandise costing $10,000 to the branch at a price 100% above cost. Since $5,000 of the $20,000 billed price remains in the branch inventory, the Unrealized Margin in Branch Inventory should be reduced to $2,500.

Foreign Branches

It is not uncommon for a company to establish a branch in a foreign country. The procedures in accounting for such a branch are similar to those for a domestic branch, except that in the preparation of combined statements and the recording of the branch income it is necessary to convert the foreign currency into dollars. This conversion process becomes somewhat involved when the foreign exchange rate changes quite often. Under a constant exchange rate the process is quite simple.

Possibly the ideal basis for conversion would be to convert foreign currency valuations at the rate which will apply when the assets are to be transferred back to the home office. Since this rate is obviously unknown at any date prior to transfer, accountants must use existing rates or rates which have existed in the past. For example, to convert the fixed assets and long-term obligations, accountants normally use the rate existing at the time such items were acquired or assumed by the branch. Use of this rate is in accord with the cost principle which holds that assets should be valued at their acquisition value and not at their realizable value. Short-term assets and liabilities, which are readily transferable to or from the home office, should be converted at the current rate of exchange. Use of this rate is based on the belief that items shortly to be realized in cash and transferable should be valued at an approximation of cash equivalent at the reporting date. Operational activities, such as sales and expenses, which occur throughout the operational period are converted at the average exchange rate for the period on the grounds that they were transferable at different rates during the period and the average rate is most appropriate.

Since various exchange rates may be used to convert a trial balance in a foreign currency into dollars, it would be unlikely that the trial balance in dollars would have equal debits and credits following conversion. The amount necessary to make the trial balance in dollars balance is considered to be a gain or loss from exchange. This gain or loss may be closed out each period, or it may be carried forward in the financial statements to be offset in future periods. Foreign operations are covered in detail in Chapter 18.

PROBLEMS

Problem 8–1. The Pacific Import Company, which operates a branch in a nearby city, has had a change in its accounting department. The new chief accountant found the trial balance as of December 31, 1966, which is presented below, as well as the other information which follows:

Debits	Home Office	Branch
Cash	$ 15,000	$ 2,000
Accounts receivable	20,000	17,000
Inventory, December 31, 1966	30,000	8,000
Fixed Assets, net	150,000	
Branch office current account	44,000	
Cost of sales	220,000	93,000
Expenses	70,000	41,000
	$549,000	$161,000

Credits		
Accounts payable	$ 23,000	
Mortgage payable	50,000	
Capital Stock	100,000	
Retained earnings, January 1, 1966	26,000	
Sales	350,000	$150,000
Accrued expenses		2,000
Home office current account		9,000
	$549,000	$161,000

Additional information:

1. The branch receives all of its merchandise from the home office. The home office bills goods to the branch at 125% of cost. During 1966 the branch was billed for $105,000 on shipments from the home office.
2. The home office credits sales for the invoice price of goods shipped to the branch.
3. On January 1, 1966, the inventory of the home office was $25,000. The branch books showed a $6,000 inventory.
4. The home office billed the branch for $12,000 on December 31, 1966, representing the branch's share of expenses paid at the home office. The branch has not recorded this billing.
5. All cash collections made by the branch are deposited in a local bank to the account of the home office. Deposits of this nature included the following:

Amount	Date Deposited by Branch	Date Recorded by Home Office
$5,000	December 28, 1966	December 31, 1966
3,000	December 30, 1966	January 2, 1967
7,000	December 31, 1966	January 3, 1967
2,000	January 2, 1967	January 5, 1967

6. Expenses incurred locally by the branch are paid from an imprest bank account which is reimbursed periodically by the home office. Just prior to the end of the year the home office forwarded a reimbursement check in the amount of $3,000 which was not received by the branch office until January 1967.
7. It is not necessary to make provisions for federal income taxes.

Required:

(1) Prepare a columnar work sheet for the company and its branch with columns for "Trial balance," "Adjustments and eliminations," "Branch income

statement," "Home office income statement," and "Balance Sheet." Complete the work sheet and explain all adjustments and explanations. The Company desires to follow generally accepted accounting principles.

(2) Prepare a reconciliation of branch office and home office current accounts, showing the corrected book balances. (AICPA—adapted)

Problem 8–2. The Swain Company of Madison established a branch store in Neenah on February 1, 1967. The branch was to receive substantially all merchandise for resale from the home office, maintain its own cash account, make sales and collections, and periodically remit cash to the home office. During the remainder of 1967 the home office sent the branch $4,000 in cash and $60,000 in merchandise at cost. The branch made cash sales of $26,000; sales on account of $44,000, of which 3/4 was collected with a 2% discount allowed, and 1/2 the remainder was uncollected at December 31, 1967. Unsold merchandise was costed at $8,000 at year end. The branch purchased $3,200 additional merchandise for cash, had expenses of $8,200, all of which was paid except $400, and sent the home office sums totaling $52,000.

Required:

(1) Prepare summary entries for the above facts on the books of both the branch and the home office.

(2) Prepare branch closing entries at December 31, 1967.

(3) Prepare a branch profit and loss statement for the period ended December 31, 1967.

Problem 8–3. The Kibler Corporation decided to set up a branch operation in Central City. Shipments of merchandise to the branch totaled $72,000, which included a 20% markup on cost. The company regularly uses a periodical method of inventory determination.

The branch operations for the period are summarized below:

Sales on account	$62,000
Sales for cash	10,000
Collections on account (at 99%)	59,400
Expenses paid	9,000
Purchases of merchandise for cash	4,000
Expenses unpaid	800
Inventory on hand, year end; 90% from home office	8,000
Remittances to home office	54,000

Required:

(1) Prepare entries for the above data on the books of both the branch and the home office.

(2) Prepare closing entries for the branch at year end.

(3) Prepare entries to take up branch profit and loss on home office books and to reflect the correct profit for the period.

Problem 8–4. The Nussbaum Company has a branch in Aurora. Prior to the current year operations at the branch were not voluminous and the home office and current accounts had never been reconciled. At year end the accounts appear as follows:

HOME OFFICE CURRENT

4–1	Expenses paid by branch, allocated to home office	$ 4,200	1–1	Balance	$ 5,900
			1–10	Merchandise received	12,600
11–1	Equipment repairs— to home office	300	4–15	Merchandise received	18,400
12–1	Cash remitted to Home Office	36,600	8–20	Merchandise received	20,600
			12–31	Profit for year	2,600

BRANCH CURRENT

1–1	Balance	$ 8,400	1–3	Remittance received	$ 2,500
1–8	Merchandise shipped	12,600	12–4	Cash received from Branch	36,600
4–10	Merchandise shipped	18,400			
8–10	Merchandise shipped	20,600			
10–1	Equipment shipped to Branch	6,300			
12–26	Cash to Branch for Expenses	5,200			

Required:

(1) Prepare a statement reconciling the current accounts as of the end of the year.

(2) Prepare any adjusting entries necessary on the books of the branch and of the home office.

Problem 8–5. The Irish Sales Company has had a branch in a nearby city for several years. At the end of each year the branch submits to the home office a copy of its trial balance to be used in preparation of combined financial statements. The trial balances of the home office and branch are presented below:

The home office regularly bills shipments to the branch at 125% of cost.

Required:

(1) Prepare closing entries for the branch, adjusting entries for the home office pertaining to the branch, and home office closing entries.

(2) Prepare a work sheet to produce a combined balance sheet.

IRISH SALES COMPANY
TRIAL BALANCE DECEMBER 31, 1967

	Home Office		Branch	
Cash	$ 6,000		$ 1,500	
Accounts receivable	14,000		6,000	
Branch current	18,600			
Inventory, December 31, 1966	15,000		5,000	
Unrealized profit in Branch inv.		$ 1,000		
Equipment (net)	26,000		8,000	
Accounts payable		12,000		$ 900
Capital stock		50,000		

	Home Office		Branch	
Earned surplus		10,000		
Sales		236,600		82,000
Purchases	260,000			
Expenses	45,000		6,000	
Shipments to Branch		75,000		
Home Office current				18,600
Merchandise from Home Office			75,000	
	$384,600	$384,600	$101,500	$101,500
Inventory, December 31, 1967	$17,000		$6,000	

Problem 8–6. The Covington Sports Store operates a branch in Appleton. The trial balances for the branch and the home office at December 31, 1967, are presented below:

COVINGTON SPORTS STORE
HOME OFFICE TRIAL BALANCE

Cash	$ 2,000	
Accounts receivable	6,000	
Inventory 1/1/67	22,000	
Fixtures (net)	10,000	
Branch current	16,000	
Accounts payable		$ 4,000
Covington, capital		40,000
Sales		180,000
Shipments to Branch		42,000
Purchases	172,000	
Selling expenses	18,000	
Administrative expenses	20,000	
	$266,000	$266,000

COVINGTON SPORTS STORE
BRANCH TRIAL BALANCE

Cash	$ 2,500	
Inventory, 1/1/67	6,480	
Fixtures (net)	7,800	
Accounts payable		$ 1,000
Home Office current		16,000
Purchases	3,000	
Shipments from Home Office	42,000	
Sales		50,000
Selling expenses	4,000	
Administrative expenses	1,220	
	$67,000	$67,000

All merchandise shipped to the branch by the home office was priced out at cost plus 20%. The home office reduced their inventory account directly at December 31, 1966, for any unrealized profit in the branch inventory at that date.

All the branch inventory at January 1, 1967, had been acquired from the home office, but at December 31, 1967, the inventory of $7,500 was 20% acquired from outsiders and 80% acquired from the home office. The home office inventory at December 31, 1967 was $20,000.

Required:
(1) Prepare entries to adjust and close the books of the branch and of the home office.
(2) Prepare a work sheet to produce a combined balance sheet.

Problem 8–7. The following trial balances were taken from the records of the Bowers Company and its branch at Springfield on December 31, 1967:

	Home Office Dr.	Home Office Cr.	Branch Dr.	Branch Cr.
Cash	$ 4,200		$ 1,500	
Receivables	16,000		4,000	
Inventory 1/1/67	25,000		7,500	
Branch current	21,000			
Equipment (net)	60,000		6,500	
Accounts payable		$ 13,000		
Unreal. Profit in Branch Inv.		1,500		
Home Office Current				$18,500
Capital Stock		70,000		
Surplus		28,700		
Sales		180,000		63,000
Merchandise from Home Office			46,000	
Purchases	190,000		5,000	
Merchandise to Branch		48,000		
Advertising	10,000		6,000	
Utilities	7,000		1,800	
Other Expenses	6,000		2,000	
Discounts (net)	2,000		1,200	
	$341,200	$341,200	$81,500	$81,500

Other pertinent facts available:
1. Cash remitted by the branch at December 31, 1967, not received by the home office, was $4,500.
2. Approximately 1/4 of the branch accounts receivable are uncollectible.
3. Merchandise shipped by the home office at 12/29/67, not received by the branch at 12/31/67, $2,000.
4. Branch advertising bill paid by the home office and charged to "Advertising" was $4,000. The branch bookkeeper recorded this properly upon receipt of interoffice memo.
5. Home office inventory at December 31, 1967, $27,500.
6. Branch inventory on hand at December 31, 1967, was $6,000, of which $4,000 was received from the home office.
7. The branch had failed to record $500 depreciation at year end.

8. For the past several years all merchandise shipped from the home office had been marked on a standard "cost-plus" basis. At 1/1/67, 80% of the branch inventory consisted of home office shipments.

Required:
(1) Prepare a work sheet to reflect the adjustments necessary at year end and to prepare a combined profit and loss statement and a combined balance sheet.
(2) Prepare the combined statements for the year.

Problem 8–8. The trial balance of the Mexican Branch of the Swingin Machine Co. as of December 31, 1967, is presented below:

MEXICAN BRANCH—SWINGIN MACHINE CO.

TRIAL BALANCE, DECEMBER 31, 1967

	Pesos	
Cash	40,800	
Receivables	6,200	
Reserve for bad debts		400
Inventory 1/1/67	8,000	
Equipment	12,000	
Res. for depr. of equipment		2,400
Accounts payable		800
Home Office current		60,600
Mdse. from Home Office	36,000	
Sales		52,000
Purchases	2,000	
Selling expenses	4,000	
Depreciation on equipment	1,200	
Administrative expenses	6,000	
	116,200	116,200

Additional data:

A. Exchange rates of dollars per peso at various dates were:

December 31, 1967	$ .32
December 31, 1966	.36
Average rate for 1967	.35
January 2, 1965 (date equipment acquired)	.38

B. Balances per home office books, December 31, 1967:

Branch current	$21,000
Shipments to Branch	12,500

Required:
Convert the 12/31/67 trial balance of the Mexican Branch into dollars.

Problem 8–9. The Beach Company has a branch in England, and at December 31, 1967, the branch submitted the following trial balance in pounds sterling to the home office:

THE BEACH CO.—LONDON BRANCH
TRIAL BALANCE, DECEMBER 31, 1967

	Dr.	Cr.
Cash	£ 2,000	
Receivables	6,000	
Inventory, 1/1/67	10,000	
Equipment	40,000	
Prepaid insurance	600	
Accounts payable		£ 3,000
Reserve for depr. of equipment		10,000
Home Office current		60,200
Sales		180,000
Purchases	130,000	
Insurance expense	600	
Depreciation expense	2,000	
Selling expense	20,000	
Other expense	12,000	
Remittances to Home Office	30,000	
	£253,200	£253,200
Inventory, 12/31/67	£ 12,000	

The exchange rates at various dates were determined to be:

December 31, 1967	$2.80 per £1
December 31, 1966	2.85 per £1
Date equipment was acquired	3.20 per £1
Average rate for 1967	2.82 per £1

Reciprocal account balances on the home office books at 12/31/67 are found to be:

Branch Current	$168,000
Remittances from Branch	75,200

Required:

Convert the above trial balance into dollars and prepare financial statements in dollars for the London Branch at December 31, 1967.

Problem 8–10. On January 2, 1967, the Bakle Company established a branch in Catlin. All merchandise to be sold through the Catlin branch was to be sent from the home office and was to be billed to the branch at cost plus 20%. At December 31, 1967, the branch submitted the following trial balance:

Cash	$ 800	
Receivables	4,200	
Fixtures (net)	3,000	
Accounts payable		$ 600
Home Office current		9,400
Sales		100,000
Shipments to Branch	90,000	
Expenses	12,000	
	$110,000	$110,000

At the same date the home office bookkeeper drew off the following trial balance from his ledger:

Cash	$18,000	
Receivables	30,000	
Inventory	38,000	
Prepaid expenses	2,000	
Machinery (net)	92,000	
Fixtures (net)	16,000	
Branch current	14,400	
Payables		$ 4,800
Capital stock		120,000
Surplus		45,200
Sales		475,000
Purchases	420,000	
Shipments to Branch		93,000
Expenses	107,600	
	$738,000	$738,000

The home office bookkeeper, recognizing that certain adjustments appeared necessary prior to preparation of combined financial statements, ascertained the following:

1. Ending inventories, per physical count, at 12/31/67:

Home Office	$36,000
Branch	6,600

2. Shipments to Branch, 12/31/67, not received by branch until 1/3/68, $3,000.
3. Expenses paid by the home office for the branch and charged to "Expenses" on home office books, $2,400. No entry made by branch.
4. Receipt of cash by home office from branch, credited to "Accounts Receivable" by home office, $2,000.

Required:

(1) Prepare a work sheet to reflect any necessary adjusting entries based upon the above information and to prepare a combined profit and loss statement and a combined balance sheet.

(2) Prepare the combined statements for the year.

Problem 8–11. The trial balances of the home office and branch office of The Illioskee Company appear below:

THE ILLIOSKEE COMPANY

For the Year Ended December 31, 1967

Debits	Home	Branch
Cash	$ 17,000	$ 200
Inventory	23,000	11,550
Sundry assets	200,000	48,450
Branch account	60,000	
Purchases	190,000	
Purchases from home office		105,000

Freight in from home office		5,500
Sundry expenses	42,000	24,300
	$532,000	$195,000

Credits		
Sundry liabilities	$ 35,000	$ 3,500
Home office account		51,500
Sales	155,000	140,000
Sales to branch	110,000	
Allowance for mark-up in branch inventory	1,000	
Capital stock	200,000	
Retained earnings	31,000	
	$532,000	$195,000

An audit at December 31, 1967 disclosed the following:

(*a*) The branch office deposits all cash receipts in a local bank for the account of the home office. The audit worksheet for the cash cut-off revealed the following:

Amount	Deposited by Branch	Recorded by Home Office
$1,050	December 27, 1967	December 31, 1967
1,100	December 30, 1967	January 2, 1968
600	December 31, 1967	January 3, 1968
300	January 2, 1968	January 6, 1968

(*b*) The branch office pays expenses incurred locally from an imprest bank account that is maintained with a balance of $2,000. Checks are drawn once a week on this imprest account and the home office is notified of the amount needed to replenish the account. At December 31 an $1,800 reimbursement check was mailed to the branch office.

(*c*) The branch office receives all of its goods from the home office. The home office bills the goods at cost plus a mark-up of 10% of cost. At December 31 a shipment with a billing value of $5,000 was in transit to the branch. Freight costs are typically 5% of billed values. Freight costs are considered to be inventoriable costs.

(*d*) The trial balance opening inventories are shown at their respective costs to the home office and to the branch office. The inventories at December 31, excluding the shipment in transit, are:

Home office, at cost	$30,000
Branch office, at billing value	10,400

Required:

Prepare a worksheet which will be useful in the preparation of a combined statement of financial position, a branch income statement, and a home office income statement. The branch income statement should be prepared on the home office cost. Disregard income taxes.   (AICPA adapted)

CHAPTER 9

Expansion by subsidiary companies

The methods by which business organizations expand vary considerably. In some instances expansion is accomplished by merely eliminating competition through the process of attracting the customers of another organization. This method of expansion, frequently referred to as "intensive" expansion, may or may not result in geographic expansion. Normally, however, expansion involves an increase in the geographic market area of the expanding organization. Such expansion may be accomplished by sending out salesmen, by establishing sales agencies and by setting up branches as discussed in the preceding chapter. This method of expansion is frequently referred to as "extensive" expansion.

Several reasons have been given for both methods of expansion. One economic reason commonly cited is the economy of large-scale operations. It is not uncommon to encounter the statement that the efforts of management to acquire the benefits of large-scale operations explain the advent of the corporation, which allowed one management to collect vast resources under one central control. Even the corporation has not proved adequate in many cases, according to some business leaders, to provide all the capital needed for desirable expansions. As a consequence other means have been developed by which management can effectively control large masses of economic resources in order to realize economies in the mass production and distribution of goods and services. The next several chapters consider some of the problems involved in accounting for expansion by corporations which acquire financial interests in other companies.

THE SUBSIDIARY COMPANY

One of the more common means used by business organizations to gather together mass resources under one central control is the acquisition of enough of the outstanding voting stock of another company to control the activities of the second company. In this manner the acquiring organization obtains command over the resources of the acquired company by a smaller investment than would be required to purchase the resources outright. The parent company (company which purchases the stock) needs to buy only enough stock of the subsidiary company (company whose stock is purchased) to elect officers who will comply with the plans of the management of the parent company. As a maximum the investment required for this type of expansion would be that needed to acquire only one share over 50% of the voting stock of the subsidiary company. Many times the cost of this investment would be a price well below the price required to purchase the assets directly from the subsidiary company.

To illustrate, assume the condensed statement of financial position of Company B on December 31, 1967, appeared as follows:

Assets	$600,000	Liabilities	$200,000
		Capital stock (3,000 shares)	300,000
		Retained earnings	100,000
Total	$600,000	Total	$600,000

Company A attempted to buy all of the assets of Company B. The price asked was $890,000. One of the stockholders of Company B agreed to sell 1,600 shares of B stock to Company A for $300,000. By buying the 1,600 shares of stock, Company A could place on the board of directors enough members to control Company B and all of its assets.

Reasons for Subsidiary Companies

Although expansion can and does take place by methods other than through the acquisition or creation of subsidiaries, several reasons exist, nevertheless, why subsidiaries (separate legal entities) are used in the expansion process. They include:

(1) The enhancement of competitive position by acquiring capital stock of a competitor.
(2) The assurance of a constant supply of raw materials by obtaining control of a supplying company.
(3) The legal provisions of some states or nations. These provisions may be such as to make it desirable to acquire an existing or create a new corporation in the particular state or nation rather than to register as a foreign corporation in that state or nation.
(4) The acquisition of assets in an amount equal to those owned by a subsidiary may require a greater investment than is necessary to obtain control of the subsidiary.
(5) Income tax regulations. Such regulations may make it desirable to acquire or create several corporations rather than to have one large corporation.
(6) The acquisition of control of an existing company may bring with it the management of the existing organization, and the background and experience of this management may make the acquisition of control advantageous.
(7) The acquisition of a subsidiary may provide additional customers for the products of the parent.

CONSOLIDATED STATEMENTS

Accountants frequently recognize that at times it is necessary to depart from the concept that the separate legal entity is the proper accounting entity for financial statements. One of the most obvious of the departures is to be found in a consolidated statement—a statement prepared to reflect the combined resources or activities of a parent company and its subsidiary or subsidiaries. Under consolidated reporting the resources and activities of more than one separate legal entity are combined as resources and activities of one entity—the consolidated entity. Consolidated reporting emphasizes the economic entity rather than the legal entity.

As indicated by the American Institute of Certified Public Accountants in *Accounting Research Bulletin* 51, the purpose of consolidated statements is to present (primarily for the benefit of the stockholders and creditors of the parent company) the financial position and results of operations of a parent company and its subsidiaries as if the group were a single company with one or more branches or divisions. There is a presumption in the Institute's position that consolidated statements are more meaningful than separate company statements and that they are normally necessary for a fair presentation when one of the companies in the group directly or indirectly has a controlling financial interest in the other companies.

When to Consolidate

As indicated above, consolidation is normally appropriate when one of the companies in the group directly or indirectly has a controlling financial interest in the other companies. The usual condition for a controlling financial interest is ownership of a majority of the voting stock. As a general rule, therefore, ownership by one company, directly or indirectly, of over 50% of the outstanding voting shares of another company is a condition pointing toward consolidation. There are, however, exceptions to this rule. The exceptions include conditions where:

(1) Control is likely to be temporary.
(2) Control does not rest with the parent company, even though over 50% of the outstanding voting stock is owned (as, for instance, where a subsidiary is in legal reorganization or bankruptcy).
(3) The amount of the shares of a subsidiary not owned by the parent is substantial; it may be desirable to issue separate statements to provide more useful information.
(4) A subsidiary is so different in operations from the activities of other subsidiaries and the parent company (as might be the case with a finance company subsidiary and a group of manufacturing subsidiaries) it might be desirable to leave the nonhomogeneous subsidiary out of the consolidated report, though its operations should be otherwise disclosed in the report.
(5) The resources of a subsidiary (such as a bank or an insurance company) are not available for use throughout the consolidated group due to restrictions imposed by law.
(6) A subsidiary is in a foreign country under currency restrictions such that resources in the subsidiary may not be realized by the parent.

Controlling Financial Interest. A minimum criterion in deciding whether consolidation is appropriate is the existence of a centralized controlling financial interest. Such control refers to the ability of the parent company's management to direct the operational policies of the subsidiary. In this respect it is necessary to distinguish between a company which owns the stock of another company for purposes of control and a company which owns the stock of another company only as an investment.

Without the existence of a controlling financial interest, consolidation is not appropriate.

The essential question is whether or not control actually exists. Does the parent company actually possess and exercise the power to make decisions for the subsidiary? If so, consolidation is proper. The possession and exercise of such power implies an integration of activities of the two organizations into one economic unit, one business enterprise. Effective and continuing control is more likely to exist where there is substantial stock ownership. Likewise, where the interest of the controlled company is large in relation to the controlling company, separate financial statements of the parent may be of limited value.

Majority-Owned Subsidiary. As indicated previously, the usual condition for a controlling financial interest is the ownership by one company, directly or indirectly, of over 50% of the outstanding voting stock of another company. It is not uncommon for two companies to create jointly a third company with each of the promoting companies receiving 50% of the stock of the new company. If such a company were included in the consolidated reports of the two parent companies, the assets and liabilities of the third company would appear on the consolidated reports of both of the parent companies. If less than 50% owned companies are consolidated, their resources and results of operations may appear on the consolidated reports of more than two parent companies. The consolidation of only majority-owned subsidiaries eliminates the possibility of the foregoing happening.

Control without Stock Ownership. It is often recognized that control of a business enterprise may be exercised without owning any of the stock of the company. Typical of this type of control is the lease agreement, under which the lessor retains control of leased property, or bond agreement, under which the provisions of the indenture may place much of the control of the company in the hands of the bondholders' trustee. Some accountants contend that control of another company by any means requires that the controlled company be included in the consolidated report. The idea underlying this position is that a consolidated report should report on all of the resources and activities under the control of one centralized management, on the grounds that such is the economic nature of the entity in existence. Theoretically, there may be much to support this position but, from a practical standpoint, there is considerable reluctance to prepare consolidated statements except where ownership of the stock of the subsidiary does exist.

Homogeneous Operations. It is frequently suggested that companies should not be consolidated unless their operations are so interrelated as to be similar or complementary to each other. Support for this view is still found in current practice where, for example, an individual non-homogeneous subsidiary is excluded from the consolidation of a group of homogeneous companies. Actually, of course, the operations of many modern business organizations are quite diverse. In fact, diversification is to a great extent the modern trend in business organization and operation. For this and other reasons there is general recognition that companies heterogeneous in operations and structure may be reported upon more adequately in a consolidated report than by a large group of separate statements.

Different Fiscal Periods. At times it is suggested that consolidation is not appropriate when a subsidiary and its parent company have different fiscal periods. Actually the existence of different fiscal periods does not pose a particularly difficult problem. Normally interim reports may be prepared by the subsidiary for consolidation purposes. Such interim reports may be prepared by adjusting the regular annual report or by developing interim statements which conform to the fiscal period of the parent company.

Consolidation Policy. As indicated in *Bulletin* 51, in deciding upon a consolidation policy, the aim should be to make the financial presentation which is most meaningful in light of the circumstances. The statement reader should be given information which is suitable to his needs, but he should not be burdened with unnecessary detail. Thus, even though a group of companies is heterogeneous in character, it may be better to consolidate than to present a large number of separate statements. On the other hand, separate statements may be more appropriate for a subsidiary if the presentation of financial information concerning the particular subsidiary would be more informative to stockholders and creditors of the parent company than would the inclusion of the subsidiary in a consolidation. For example, separate statements may be required for a subsidiary which is a bank or an insurance company and may be more appropriate for a finance company where the parent and the other subsidiaries are engaged in manufacturing operations. Since there are no hard and fast rules governing all possible situations as to the inclusion or exclusion of a given subsidiary, the consolidation policy followed in any given situation should be disclosed. In many instances this disclosure may be presented in the headings or bodies of the statements, whereas footnote disclosure is required in other situations.

Limitations of Consolidated Statements

Although consolidated statements have a very real usefulness for purposes of presenting a composite picture of the financial position and operating results of a group of affiliated companies, they cannot be regarded as properly taking the place of statements for the individual companies for certain purposes. Consolidated statements ignore important legal relationships and present statements of an "economic entity." Where there are important interests in the individual companies, consolidated statements may be of limited usefulness to (1) minority stockholders, (2) creditors, and (3) financial analysts.

Minority Stockholders. Minority stockholders of a subsidiary can obtain very little information of value to them from consolidated statements, for such statements do not detail the assets, equities, income, and expenses of the individual subsidiary. For such information, minority stockholders must turn to the separate company statements.

Creditors. The creditors of each company in a consolidated group are primarily concerned with the financial position and earnings of the specific debtor company. Most companies having subsidiaries issue consolidated reports, and as indicated earlier, it is generally presumed that the consolidated report is the basic report with separate statements only being supplementary. Creditors of a subsidiary company, however, have rights only against the subsidiary company. As the following illustration indicates, a consolidated statement may be misleading to a creditor.

Assume Company A owns 100% of the outstanding voting stock of Company B. Condensed balance sheets of the two companies as separate entities reflect:

	Company A	Company B
Assets		
Investment in B	$ 80,000	
Other assets	810,000	$200,000
	$890,000	$200,000
Equities		
Liabilities	$290,000	$120,000
Capital stock	600,000	80,000
	$890,000	$200,000

It is apparent from the balance sheet of Company B that the outstanding debt is equal to 60% of the total assets whereas the same relationship for Company A is about 33%. Creditors are interested in the amount of asset protection they have behind loans they make. A consolidated balance sheet for the two companies would appear as follows:

CONSOLIDATED BALANCE SHEET

Assets ($810,000 and $200,000)	$1,010,000
Liabilities	$ 410,000
Capital stock	600,000
Total	$1,010,000

The consolidated balance sheet indicates that the relationship of debt to total assets is about 41%, which may suggest to the creditors of the subsidiary company that they have greater asset protection than legally exists.

Creditorship information disclosed in a consolidated statement may be inadequate or limited both from the short-term as well as long-term creditor viewpoint. For example, since a consolidated statement is a composite, a weak current position in one of the affiliated companies may be bolstered by a strong current position in another affiliate. Likewise, bond indentures frequently require the maintaining of specified ratios of current assets to current liabilities, and provide penalties for nonconformance. The ordinary consolidated balance sheet does not give the bondholders of individual companies information from which they can determine whether the requirements are being fulfilled, nor can the stockholders see whether their company is in any jeopardy because of default.

Although consolidated statements may be of limited usefulness to creditors, especially creditors of the individual subsidiaries, this is not necessarily in and of itself sufficient reason for exclusion of a subsidiary from the consolidation. Limitations of consolidated statements for creditor purposes, however, may be such as to require additional disclosure (footnote disclosure, etc.) of information useful to creditors.

Financial Analysts. By its very nature a consolidated statement may fail to reveal information pertinent to the financial analyst. For example, to include as current assets, land of a real estate company, bread of a bakery company, and finished chemicals of a chemical company in a consolidated statement of financial position—all as inventory—may disclose little to a particular investor. In part because of this situation and in part because of other limitations, many companies issue both consolidated and separate company reports.

The exclusion of banks and insurance companies from consolidation with other nonfinancial companies is sometimes based upon the distorting effect which their inclusion would presumably have upon an analysis of the financial statements. While much has been said about the distorting effect on financial ratios and relationships which could result from an analysis of only consolidated statements, the importance of this distortion may be overemphasized. For example, when top management has the power to transfer resources from one affiliated company to another in the consolidated group, financial ratios and relationships resulting from the consolidated statements may more accurately reflect the economic facts of the situation than similar ratios and relationships determined from separate company statements. The latter ratios and relationships could be unrepresentative because of the ability of top management to change quickly any one affiliate's financial condition.

Illustrative of this situation would be a subsidiary company with a current ratio of 1/2 to 1 ($50,000 of current assets to $100,000 of current liabilities) but a parent company with a current ratio of 3 to 1 ($300,000 to $100,000). The ability of the subsidiary to pay its current liabilities is not properly represented by the 1/2 to 1 ratio if the parent company is in a position to transfer any needed current assets to the subsidiary.

Consolidated statements may at times be of limited value to the financial analyst if they fail to reflect adequately the activities of top management. For example, top management (parent company's management) may for various reasons treat a given affiliate as an investment at one time and as a part of the consolidated group at another time. Or, top management may direct its energies to the development of an affiliated company less than 50% owned but very effectively controlled. In this regard, some criticism may be directed to the adequacy of the over 50% standard for inclusion, but in terms of a compromise between objectivity and subjectivity (it is an observable fact whether or not over 50% of the stock is owned while the existence of control may be subjective), it has been accepted as one of the most reasonable standards for consolidation yet suggested.

Unconsolidated Subsidiaries

It is possible to distinguish two types of unconsolidated subsidiaries: (1) companies controlled by less than a 50% ownership of the voting stock, and (2) companies over 50% owned but excluded from consolidation as exceptions to the general rule. On the consolidated report, unconsolidated subsidiaries should appear as investments. The proper valuation of these investments may be either at cost or at cost plus (minus) the parent's share of the subsidiary's undistributed earnings (losses) since acquisition. According to *Bulletin* 51, the preferable method, especially for majority-owned subsidiaries, is the second mentioned above.

To illustrate, assume the parent company owns 60% of a subsidiary company which is not included in the consolidation. The investment in the stock of the subsidiary would then appear on the consolidated statement of financial position as an investment as follows:

Investment in subsidiary $XXXXX

Assuming that subsequent to acquisition the unconsolidated subsidiary earns and does not distribute $30,000, proper valuation of the "Investment in Subsidiary" account on the consolidated statement of financial position would require that 60% of the $30,000 be added to the investment account.

Illustrative of the process by which unconsolidated subsidiaries are reported is that of the Caterpillar Tractor Company which in a recent report included in its consolidated financial statements the account "Investment in Caterpillar Credit Corporation" in the amount of $7,964,917. The assets and liabilities of all other subsidiaries were combined to provide the consolidated report. Because the Caterpillar Credit Corporation was not included in the consolidation, a separate report for the Credit Corporation was attached to the annual report. A footnote to the consolidated report disclosed the following information:

> The financial positions of the Company's wholly owned subsidiaries, except Caterpillar Credit Corporation, have been consolidated with that of the parent company. The investment in Caterpillar Credit Corporation is carried at cost plus the profit retained by the subsidiary.

Theories of Consolidated Statements

Before turning to the procedures and analyses involved in preparing consolidated statements, attention should be given to alternatives regarding the nature of consolidations which are discussed at theoretical levels. While knowledge of these theories will contribute little directly to the problem of knowing current practice, they do set forth alternative objectives. There are two essential ideas on the nature of consolidated reports, as follows:

(1) Consolidated reports are prepared from the point of view of the stockholders of the parent company. This is usually called the proprietary theory.

(2) Consolidated reports are prepared from the point of view of the total

resources under the control of the top management of the group of companies. They are, therefore, for the use of all stockholders of all of the consolidated companies. This is known as the entity theory.

The first theory dominates accounting practice and represents the theory under which the procedures and analyses outlined in this textbook are presented.

A distinction between the procedures of the two theories can best be explained by an example. Assume Company A purchased 80% of the voting stock of Company B for $80,000 and that at the date of purchase the net assets (assets less liabilities) of Company B totaled $50,000. According to the first theory, the $80,000 represents the price paid for 80% of the net assets of Company B. Since the price paid ($80,000) exceeds the book value of the net assets acquired (80% of $50,000 or $40,000), the assets acquired may be revalued upward by the amount of the excess payment. The consolidated balance sheet would report the assets at $80,000 or would report the excess over book value ($80,000 − $40,000 = $40,000) in a special account so that the full $80,000 would appear on the consolidated balance sheet as the proper valuation for 80% of the net assets of the subsidiary. From the point of view of the stockholders of the parent company, the $80,000 represents their cost of the assets.

Under this theory, however, the remaining 20% of the net assets of the subsidiary would appear on the consolidated balance sheet at their net book value of $10,000.

Under the entity theory, however, the 20% of the net assets would be revalued upward to $20,000 to make it comparable with the valuation given the other assets. This theory holds that the basis for the valuation used in reporting the assets accruing to the stockholders of the parent company should be applied to the assets accruing to the minority stockholders of Company B. Assume the following condensed financial statements:

	Separate Company Reports	
Assets	A	B
Investment in B	$ 80,000	
Other assets	430,000	$70,000
Total	$510,000	$70,000
Equities		
Liabilities	$ 60,000	$20,000
Capital stock	450,000	50,000
Total	$510,000	$70,000

Consolidated balance sheets prepared under each of the two theories would be as follows:

		Entity Theory	Proprietary Theory
Assets			
Assets of A		$430,000	$430,000
Assets of B:			
Assets claimed by B creditors	$20,000		$20,000
Assets claimed by A stockholders:			
Book value	40,000		40,000
Additional cost	40,000		40,000
Assets claimed by B stockholders:			
Book value	10,000		10,000
Write up to other assets	10,000		—
		120,000	110,000
Total		$550,000	$540,000
Equities			
Liabilities (60,000 and 20,000)		$ 80,000	$ 80,000
Capital stock (A's)		450,000	450,000
Minority interest (B's)		20,000	10,000
Total		$550,000	$540,000

Summary

The nature of consolidated reports has been described as a process of reporting on the activities of an entity larger than the separate legal company. The standard for inclusion of companies within the consolidation has been established as the ownership of over 50% of the voting stock of the subsidiary stock with exception to the rule for certain foreign subsidiaries, banks, insurance companies, and finance companies. Limitations to consolidations are not as severe as might seem at first glance. Finally, the possibility of the preparation of consolidated reports under the entity theory was presented as background for the study of the procedures, analyses, and concepts of consolidations under conventional practice.

PROBLEMS

Problem 9–1. (1) State briefly the purpose of preparing consolidated financial statements.

(2) State the relationship among business organizations which makes the preparation of consolidated financial statements advisable. (AICPA adapted)

Problem 9-2. In the preparation of consolidated financial statements of a parent corporation and its subsidiaries a decision must be reached concerning the inclusion or exclusion of each of them as a member of the consolidated group. A common criterion is the percentage of voting stock owned by the parent company.

(1) What is the significance of the percentage of voting stock ownership in justifying the inclusion of a subsidiary company in a consolidated statement?

(2) List other criteria upon which the decision to consolidate or not may also rest.   (AICPA adapted)

Problem 9-3. Consolidated statements are frequently presented for a parent company and its subsidiary or subsidiaries. There are a number of reasons for their use in presenting financial data. However, such statements are subject to several limitations in the usual situation. You are to state and explain the limitations of consolidated statements.   (AICPA adapted)

Problem 9-4. The Acme Company as of December 31, 1967, had assets of $500,000 and liabilities of $300,000. Its net earnings for 1967 amounted to $80,000. The assets included all of the stock of Excelsior Company which was acquired late in 1966 for $25,000. Excelsior sustained a net loss of $17,500 in 1967. There were no intercompany transactions except that Acme guaranteed a bank loan of Excelsior in the amount of $20,000.

In preparing statements of Acme, would you disclose the 1967 transaction concerning Excelsior Company:

(1) Not at all.

(2) By a footnote disclosing Acme's contingent liability.

(3) By setting up a receivable from Excelsior and a payable to the bank.

(4) By preparing consolidated statements.

(5) By writing down the investment in Excelsior to $7,500.

Discuss, giving reasons for the alternatives selected and those rejected by you.
                                                                        (AICPA adapted)

Problem 9-5. In 1960 the K Company purchased on the open market, for $75,000, 1,000 shares of the S Company's common stock, of which more than 100,000 shares were then outstanding. During the ensuing years dividends were paid regularly and fluctuations in the market value of the stock were relatively insignificant, with a general upward tendency. At the close of the K Company's fiscal year ended October 31, 1969, the S Company stock was quoted at 150, and the company's latest annual report for its fiscal year ended June 30, 1969, shows a book value per share of approximately $165. Although a manufacturing concern, the K Company has a substantial investment in the securities of other companies which it neither controls nor in the direction of which it participates.

The president of the K Company proposes to increase the asset value of S Company stock on the K Company's books to $150 per share.

Discuss this proposal, indicating how the K Company's financial statements would be affected if it is carried out, and the reasons for and against its adoption.
                                                                        (AICPA adapted)

Problem 9–6. Discuss in detail the distinguishing features of the entity theory of consolidated reports.

Problem 9–7. The Y & P Music Company, a Washington corporation, operates two retail music stores, one located in Seattle, Washington, and the other in Tacoma, Washington. Each store maintains a separate set of accounting records; intercompany transfers or transactions are recorded in an intercompany account carried on each set of records.

Purchases of major items of inventory, such as organs and pianos, are made under a financial arrangement with a local bank advancing 90% of the invoice price and the company paying 10%. If the bank note remains unpaid at the end of 90 days the company is required to pay an additional 10% of the invoice price as a payment on the note.

In August, the Seattle store purchased an organ for which the seller's draft in the amount of $6,300 was sent to The First National Bank of Seattle, which refused to finance the purchase of the instrument. Arrangements were made through the Tacoma store with The Citizens Bank of Tacoma to provide the financing. The bank lent Tacoma 90% of the invoice price, or $5,670, which Tacoma deposited and credited to notes payable. The Seattle store drew a check payable to the Tacoma store for $630, or 10% of the invoice price, charging Tacoma intercompany account on its books. Tacoma took up the deposit crediting the intercompany account carried with Seattle.

Tacoma, using the 10% received from Seattle and the 90% advanced by the bank, drew a check payable to The First National Bank of Seattle in full payment of the draft, charging notes payable.

In November, Seattle made the second payment of $630 directly to the Tacoma bank, charging Tacoma intercompany account, and also notified the Tacoma bookkeeper that the payment had been made. Tacoma took up the transaction charging organ purchases and crediting Seattle. In December Seattle paid off the balance of the note charging organ purchases.

Required:
Adjusting entries to be recorded on each set of books correcting the account balances.   (AICPA adapted)

Problem 9–8. The use of consolidated financial statements for reporting to stockholders is common. Under some conditions, however, it is desirable to exclude a subsidiary from consolidated reports.

Required:
List the conditions under which a subsidiary should be excluded from consolidation statements.   (AICPA adapted)

Problem 9–9. You are to select from the alternatives presented, "all" of those which correctly complete each of the numbered statements. Note that some of the questions may contain more than one correct statement.

(1) Consolidated statements are used to present the result of operations and the financial position of:

(a) A company and its branches.
(b) A company and its subcontractors.
(c) A company and its subsidiaries.
(d) Any group of companies with related interests.
(e) None of the above.

(2) Consolidated statements are intended, primarily, for the benefit of:

(a) Stockholders of the parent company.
(b) Taxing authorities.
(c) Management of the parent company.
(d) Creditors of the parent company.
(e) None of the above.

(3) A consolidated statement for X, Y, and Z is proper if:

(a) X owns 100% of the outstanding common stock of Y and 49% of Z; Q owns 51% of Z.
(b) X owns 100% of the outstanding common stock of Y; Y owns 75% of Z.
(c) X owns 100% of the outstanding common stock of Y and 75% of Z. X bought the stock of Z one month before the statement date, and sold it six weeks later.
(d) There is no interrelation of financial control among X, Y, and Z. However, they are contemplating the joint purchase of 100% of the outstanding common stock of W.
(e) X owns 100% of the outstanding common stock of Y and Z. Z is in bankruptcy.

(4) H is the parent company and would probably treat K as an investment and not a consolidated subsidiary in the proposed consolidated statement of H, J, and K if:

(a) H and J manufacture electronic equipment; K manufactures ball bearings.
(b) H and J manufacture ball-point pens; K is a bank.
(c) K has assets of $1,000,000 and an outstanding bond issue of $750,000. H holds the bonds.
(d) Same as (c), except that outsiders hold the bonds.
(e) None of the above.

(5) Parent company P has a fiscal year ending June 30, 1967. Subsidiary S's fiscal year ends May 31, 1967. Therefore:
(a) A consolidated statement cannot properly be prepared for P and S.
(b) S's May 31, 1967 statement can be used for consolidation with P's June 30, 1967 statement, provided disclosure (or some recognition) is made of any June event which materially affected S.
(c) If the consolidated statement is permissible, it will be dated June 30, 1967.

(d) If the consolidated statement is permissible, it will be dated May 31, 1967.

(e) None of the above.

(6) P owns 90% of the stock of S. W owns 10% of S's stock. In relation to P, W is considered as:

(a) An affiliate.

(b) A subsidiary not to be consolidated.

(c) A minority interest.

(d) A holding company.

(e) None of the above.

(7) Company P had 300,000 shares of stock outstanding. It owned 75% of the outstanding stock of T. T owned 20,000 shares of P's stock. In the consolidated balance sheet, Company P's outstanding stock may be shown as:

(a) 280,000 shares.

(b) 300,000 shares less 20,000 shares of treasury stock.

(c) 300,000 shares.

(d) 300,000 shares footnoted to indicate that T holds 20,000 shares.

(e) None of the above.

(8) The preferable method of presenting subsidiaries not consolidated in financial statements is:

(a) At market value, adjusted through income.

(b) At market value, adjusted through retained earnings.

(c) At cost, plus the parent's share of the subsidiaries' net income (or minus the net loss) since acquisition, adjusted annually through income.

(d) At cost, plus the parent's share of the subsidiaries' net income (or minus the net loss) adjusted annually through retained earnings.

(e) At consolidated group's equity in net realizable value of assets of subsidiaries not consolidated.

(9) P and its subsidiaries, T and V, have issued combined statements for a number of years. In connection with a proposed bank loan, P has been requested to present a statement to the bank which will indicate P's financial position at December 31, 1967. The following will supply the desired information:

(a) A copy of the consolidated statement at December 31, 1967.

(b) A copy of P's financial statement at December 31, 1967 on which the investments in T and V are reported at the current carrying value.

(c) A copy of the consolidated statement and of the separate parent company (P) statement, both at December 31, 1967.

(d) A copy of the consolidated statement at December 31, 1967, modified so that one column is used for P and other columns for T and V.

(e) A copy of separate financial statements of P, T, and V as of December 31, 1967.

(10) The stockholders of S sold all of its common stock, 1,000 shares, to Company P, receiving in return 5,000 shares of Company P stock. On the day prior to the sale, P stock sold for $40 per share; S stock sold for $195 per share. P stock has a par value of $20 per share. S stock has a par value of $50 per share. The investment by P may be recorded on its books at:

    (*a*) $200,000, only.
    (*b*) $195,000, only.
    (*c*) $100,000.
    (*d*) $50,000.
    (*e*) Either $200,000 or $195,000.   (AICPA adapted)

CHAPTER **10**

Consolidated statements at date of acquisition

The preceding chapter has pointed to a variety of consolidation policies which might be adopted by different companies. Different consolidation policies normally require different application of consolidating procedures. As a result, consolidated reports should disclose the consolidation policy followed by the company. Such disclosure may be in the report headings, revealed in information in the statements, or stated in footnotes. While policy will indicate the extent of their use and may even require alternative procedures, there are certain procedures and analyses which are used regardless of a company's policies on such questions as which subsidiary to consolidate and which to exclude from consolidation. It is to these procedures that the next several chapters are directed.

Basic Consolidating Procedures

Mechanically, the preparation of consolidated statements is based on certain basic procedures. Although the application of these procedures may vary from situation to situation, their application is essentially always the same. In summary form they are:
(1) Elimination of reciprocal elements.
(2) Consolidation of nonreciprocal elements.

Elimination of Reciprocal Elements. Since consolidated statements are prepared for the purpose of reporting the combined resources, equities, and operations of a group of closely related companies, intercompany items reciprocal in nature such as intercompany payables and receivables must be eliminated. The elimination of reciprocal elements is necessary in order to avoid double counting and in order to eliminate any profits recognized on intercompany transactions that are unrealized, at the date of consolidation, from the viewpoint of the affiliated group as an entity. For example, if Company A owns Company B, and Company B owes Company A $10,000 for merchandise which cost A $8,000 and which is still in B's possession, the $10,000 receivable and payable must be eliminated. Likewise, the $2,000 intercompany profit in the valuation of inventory at $10,000 rather than $8,000 must be eliminated when A and B are viewed as one economic unit. If these eliminations were not made, it would appear that the consolidated group owed itself $10,000, and it would also appear that the group made a profit by selling to itself.

One of the more important, if not the most important, intercompany relationships is that existing between the investment account on a parent company's statement of financial position and the shareholder's equity section on a subsidiary company's statement of financial position. Since the parent company's investment account (an asset) is merely a claim against the net assets (represented by the shareholders' equity section) of the subsidiary, they are reciprocal in nature and an elimination is in order. As was the case in Chapter 8, when the assets of the branch were substituted for the Branch Office account on the home office statement, a similar substitution is made in the case of a parent and subsidiary when consolidating. When the parent's share of a subsidiary's shareholders' equity is eliminated against the investment account, as will be noted later, in reality the parent company's share of the subsidiary's net assets is substituted for the investment account.

Establishment of Reciprocity. Before reciprocal elements can be eliminated they must, of course, be reciprocal. Consequently, if for any reason reciprocity does not exist between one or more sets of intercompany accounts in which it should exist, reciprocity must be established before the consolidating procedure, as outlined above, can be effected. Reconciliation problems may include such things as goods in transit, cash in transit, interest income and interest expense, and dividends receivable and dividends payable. As will be noted in subsequent chapters, reciprocity must frequently be established between the investment account on a parent company's statement of financial position and the shareholders' equity section on a subsidiary company's statement of financial position.

Consolidation of Nonreciprocal Elements. In order to reflect the combined resources, equities, and operations of an affiliated group, nonreciprocal elements must be included in the consolidated statements. Nonreciprocal like items are combined in the statements and nonreciprocal unlike items are shown separately. For example, if Company A has cash of $6,000 and Company B has cash of $10,000, the cash reported on the consolidated statement of financial position would be $16,000. If Company A owns U.S. Government bonds of $25,000 and Company B owns no such bonds, the bonds would be reported as a separate item of $25,000 on the consolidated statement.

Valuation Principles of Consolidating Companies. If consolidated statements, prepared by combining the resources, equities, and operations of a group of affiliated companies, are to be significant, it is essential that principles of valuation be consistently applied throughout the group. This implies a certain degree of uniformity in account classification and requires uniformity in valuing such assets as receivables, inventories, and plant and equipment.

Types of Statements Consolidated

Current financial reporting for individual business organizations emphasizes three basic statements, namely, the statement of financial position, the income statement, and the statement of retained earnings. Although differences in title, content, and form of each of these statements are found in practice, there is considerable agreement as to the basic need of each when reporting financial data. These three statements are also the ones most frequently consolidated. If consolidated statements are prepared as of the date of organization or acquisition of the subsidiary by the parent, however, the preparation of a consolidated income statement is not possible since the companies have not operated as a unit.

Regardless of when consolidated statements are prepared, the basic procedure is essentially the same, that is (1) eliminate reciprocals, and (2) consolidate nonreciprocals. However, the study of consolidations is perhaps best approached by emphasizing the time of consolidating. This approach is important because if the statements are consolidated at some date subsequent to acquisition, adjustments may be necessary in order to establish reciprocity. Consequently, this textbook emphasizes the *date* of the consolidated statements, and the technique of their preparation is studied in the following sequence:

First. At date of acquisition:
    (1) Statement of financial position.
    (2) Statement of retained earnings.
Second. At a date subsequent to acquisition:
    (1) Statement of financial position.
    (2) Income statement.
    (3) Statement of retained earnings.

Consolidated Statement of Financial Position at Date of Acquisition

A consolidated statement of financial position is a statement showing as of a given moment of time the combined financial condition of a group of closely-related companies viewed as a unit. Consequently, such a statement reflects the assets and equities of the consolidated companies as they would appear to an outsider who considered the separate legal organizations as one economic unit. The technique of combining the assets and equities as of the date of acquisition is demonstrated in the following illustrations which, since control may be obtained by less than 100% ownership, are categorized according to whether (a) 100% ownership exists, or (b) less than 100% ownership exists.

100% Ownership. In the process of acquiring 100% interest in a subsidiary, a parent company may pay:

(1) Book value for the interest acquired.
(2) More than book value for the interest acquired.
(3) Less than book value for the interest acquired.

In all of the three situations the acquisition is recorded on the books of the parent company at cost. The typical entry would be

Investment in Company B	$XXXXXX	
Cash		$XXXXXX

ILLUSTRATION A-1: *100% Ownership Acquired at Book Value.* Assume that as of January 1, 1967, Company A acquires 100% ownership in Company B for $150,000, which is also the book value of the interest acquired. The following individual company statements reflect the financial position of the respective companies as of the date of acquisition, and the consolidated statement shows the financial position after consolidation:

COMPANY A

STATEMENT OF FINANCIAL POSITION

As of January 1, 1967

Current assets	$ 80,000	Current liabilities	$ 20,000
Investment in B	150,000	Fixed liabilities	100,000
Fixed assets (net)	400,000	Shareholders' equity:	
		Capital stock	400,000
		Retained earnings	110,000
	$630,000		$630,000

COMPANY B
STATEMENT OF FINANCIAL POSITION
As of JANUARY 1, 1967

Current assets	$ 40,000	Current liabilities	$ 10,000
Fixed assets (net)	120,000	Shareholders' equity:	
		Capital stock	100,000
		Retained earnings	50,000
	$160,000		$160,000

Basic Procedure. As indicated earlier, the basic procedure involved in consolidating financial statements is (1) to eliminate reciprocals, and (2) to consolidate nonreciprocals. In this instance the only reciprocal elements involved are: (1) on the subsidiary's statement, the portion of B's ownership equity owned by A and (2) on the parent company's statement, the parent company's investment in B. The work sheet entry for the elimination expressed in journal form is:

Capital stock (Company B)	$100,000	
Retained earnings (Company B)	50,000	
Investment in B (Company A's account)		$150,000
(to eliminate Company B's shareholders'		
equity against the investment account)		

The nonreciprocal elements are consolidated by adding them together where necessary and extending them to the consolidated statement as illustrated in the following working papers:

COMPANY A AND SUBSIDIARY COMPANY B
CONSOLIDATED WORKING PAPERS
STATEMENT OF FINANCIAL POSITION
As of JANUARY 1, 1967

	Company A	Company B	Eliminations Debit	Eliminations Credit	Consolidated Financial Position
Assets					
Current assets	$ 80,000	$ 40,000			$120,000
Investment in B	150,000			$150,000	
Fixed assets (net)	400,000	120,000			520,000
	$630,000	$160,000			$640,000
Equities					
Current liabilities	$ 20,000	$ 10,000			$ 30,000
Fixed liabilities	100,000				100,000
Shareholders' equity:					
Capital stock	400,000	100,000	$100,000		400,000
Retained earnings	110,000	50,000	50,000		110,000RE
	$630,000	$160,000	$150,000	$150,000	$640,000

In statement form the last column of the working papers would be presented as follows:

COMPANY A AND SUBSIDIARY COMPANY B
CONSOLIDATED STATEMENT OF FINANCIAL POSITION
AS OF JANUARY 1, 1967

Current assets	$120,000	Current liabilities	$ 30,000
Fixed assets (net)	520,000	Fixed liabilities	100,000
		Shareholders' equity:	
		Capital stock	400,000
		Retained earnings	110,000
	$640,000		$640,000

ILLUSTRATION A-2: 100% *Ownership Acquired at More Than Book Value.* A parent company may pay more than book value for the stock it acquires when purchasing an equity in a subsidiary. Since a share of stock represents an undivided interest in the net assets and the earning power of the company, payment in excess of book value (net assets) may be due to such factors as (1) market value of stock may be related to the value of the enterprise rather than the cost of the individual assets, and (2) individual assets may be undervalued on the books. Assuming the assets have been accounted for in accordance with generally accepted accounting principles, a payment in excess of book value must be accounted for on the consolidated statement of financial position.

The difference between the purchase price and the book value of the stock acquired should be analyzed carefully. If the difference is attributed to specific assets on the books of the subsidiary, it should be allocated to them. If the difference represents the price paid for intangible assets not recorded on the books of the subsidiary, these assets should be recorded as assets of the consolidated company. Any difference not assignable to specific items should be included with consolidated assets appropriately described.

To demonstrate the procedures of consolidation, it is assumed in this textbook that any payment in excess of book value should be allocated to the intangible asset, "Goodwill." Consequently, when consolidating statements of financial position, goodwill may arise when a parent pays more than book value for the stock purchased.

Assume the same general situation as used in the preceding illustration, except that Company A acquires 100% ownership in Company B for $170,000. Since the book value acquired by Company A is only $150,000, there is an excess payment of $20,000 for "goodwill." The consolidating procedure is as follows:

COMPANY A

STATEMENT OF FINANCIAL POSITION

As OF JANUARY 1, 1967

Current assets	$ 60,000	Current liabilities	$ 20,000
Investment in Company B	170,000	Fixed liabilities	100,000
Fixed assets (net)	400,000	Shareholders' equity:	
		Capital stock	400,000
		Retained earnings	110,000
	$630,000		$630,000

COMPANY B

STATEMENT OF FINANCIAL POSITION

As OF JANUARY 1, 1967

Current assets	$ 40,000	Current liabilities	$ 10,000
Fixed assets (net)	120,000	Shareholders' equity:	
		Capital stock	100,000
		Retained earnings	50,000
	$160,000		$160,000

Basic Procedure. The basic procedure is the same as in Illustration A-1, that is, eliminate the reciprocal elements and consolidate the nonreciprocal elements. However, since there is no element reciprocal to the $20,000 payment for goodwill, it cannot be eliminated, and as a result it is extended along with other assets to the consolidated statement as the cost to the consolidated entity of purchased goodwill. The work sheet entry for the elimination is the same as in Illustration A-1, that is:

Capital stock (Company B's)	$100,000	
Retained earnings (Company B's)	50,000	
Investment in B (Company A's account)		$150,000
(to eliminate Company B's shareholders' equity against the investment account)		

The nonreciprocal elements are consolidated as they were in the preceding illustration. In the working papers which follow, note how the nonreciprocal element of the investment account is extended to the consolidated statement as (G) goodwill.

COMPANY A AND SUBSIDIARY COMPANY B
CONSOLIDATED WORKING PAPERS
STATEMENT OF FINANCIAL POSITION
AS OF JANUARY 1, 1967

	Company A	Company B	Eliminations Debit	Eliminations Credit	Consolidated Financial Position
Assets					
Current assets	$ 60,000	$ 40,000			$100,000
Investment in B	170,000			$150,000	20,000G
Fixed assets (net)	400,000	120,000			520,000
	$630,000	$160,000			$640,000
Equities					
Current liabilities	$ 20,000	$ 10,000			$ 30,000
Fixed liabilities	100,000				100,000
Shareholders' equity:					
Capital stock	400,000	100,000	$100,000		400,000
Retained earnings	110,000	50,000	50,000		110,000RE
	$630,000	$160,000	$150,000	$150,000	$640,000

ILLUSTRATION A-3: 100% *Ownership Acquired at Less Than Book Value.* A parent company may pay less than book value for the stock it acquires when purchasing an equity in a subsidiary. Assuming the assets have been accounted for in accordance with generally accepted accounting principles, payment of less than book value may arise from a variety of reasons, such as an advantageous purchase, or because the subsidiary's earning power does not justify payment of book value for its shares.

As indicated in *Accounting Research Bulletin* 51, when the cost of a parent's interest in a subsidiary is less than the book value acquired, the accounting treatment of the difference should parallel in reverse the treatment used when a parent company pays more than book value for its interest. Accordingly, to the extent that the difference is considered to be attributable to specific assets, it should be allocated to them, with corresponding adjustments of the depreciation and amortization. In some circumstances there may be a remaining difference, a sort of "negative goodwill," which the Institute recommends be shown in a credit account until taken into income in future periods on a reasonable and systematic basis.

In the past, when preparing consolidated statements, negative goodwill was frequently treated as a form of capital surplus. According to *Bulletin* 51 such procedure is not now considered acceptable.

Since it is impossible to allocate the excess—whether it be a form of positive or negative goodwill—without all of the facts, the following procedures are used in this textbook to demonstrate the basic techniques of consolidation. If any positive goodwill exists on the statements being consolidated or if any results from consolidation, negative goodwill is deducted therefrom to the extent possible. However, if no positive goodwill exists on the statements being consolidated and if none results from consolidation of other subsidiaries, the unallocated excess of book value over cost is presented in an account entitled "Excess of Subsidiary Book Value Over Cost." Likewise, if positive goodwill exists, but if it is insufficient to offset all negative goodwill, it is used to offset as much negative goodwill as possible, and the balance of the excess of book value over cost is disclosed in the account.

Assume the same facts as used in Illustration A-1, except that Company A acquires 100% ownership in Company B for $140,000. Since the book value acquired by Company A is $150,000, negative goodwill of $10,000 is assumed to exist.

COMPANY A

STATEMENT OF FINANCIAL POSITION

AS OF JANUARY 1, 1967

Current assets	$ 90,000	Current liabilities	$ 20,000
Investment in Company B	140,000	Fixed liabilities	100,000
Fixed assets (net)	400,000	Shareholders' equity:	
		Capital stock	400,000
		Retained earnings	110,000
	$630,000		$630,000

COMPANY B

STATEMENT OF FINANCIAL POSITION

AS OF JANUARY 1, 1967

Current assets	$ 40,000	Current liabilities	$ 10,000
Fixed assets (net)	120,000	Shareholders' equity:	
		Capital stock	100,000
		Retained earnings	50,000
	$160,000		$160,000

Basic Procedure. The basic procedure is the same as in the two preceding illustrations—that is, eliminate the reciprocal elements and consolidate the nonreciprocal elements. However, since there is no element in the investment account reciprocal to the $10,000 excess of book value acquired over cost, the $10,000 cannot be eliminated and therefore must be extended to the consolidated statement. The work sheet entry for the elimination is the same as in the preceding illustrations, that is:

Capital stock (Company B's)	$100,000	
Retained earnings (Company B's)	50,000	
Investment in B (Company A's account)		$150,000
(to eliminate Company B's shareholders' equity against the investment account)		

COMPANY A AND SUBSIDIARY COMPANY B
CONSOLIDATED WORKING PAPERS
STATEMENT OF FINANCIAL POSITION
AS OF JANUARY 1, 1967

	Company A	Company B	Eliminations Debit	Eliminations Credit	Consolidated Financial Position
Assets					
Current assets	$ 90,000	$ 40,000			$130,000
Investment in B	140,000			$150,000	(10,000)G*
Fixed assets (net)	400,000	120,000			520,000
	$630,000	$160,000			$640,000
Equities					
Current liabilities	$ 20,000	$ 10,000			$ 30,000
Fixed liabilities	100,000				100,000
Shareholders' equity:					
Capital stock	400,000	100,000	$100,000		400,000
Retained earnings	110,000	50,000	50,000		110,000RE
	$630,000	$160,000	$150,000	$150,000	$640,000

* The excess of book value acquired over cost, as indicated previously, is treated as either a deduction from goodwill or as a deferred credit. In this instance it is treated as a deferred credit, since no goodwill appears on the consolidated statement from which it could be deducted.

In statement form the last column of the working papers would be presented as follows:

COMPANY A AND SUBSIDIARY COMPANY B
CONSOLIDATED STATEMENT OF FINANCIAL POSITION
AS OF JANUARY 1, 1967

Current assets	$130,000	Current liabilities	$ 30,000
Fixed assets (net)	520,000	Fixed liabilities	100,000
		Excess of subsidiary book value over cost	10,000
		Shareholders' equity:	
		Capital stock	400,000
		Retained earnings	110,000
	$650,000		$650,000

Computation of Consolidated Goodwill

Consolidated goodwill consists of (a) the goodwill already appearing on the books of the constituent companies plus (b) any goodwill not recorded on the books of the constituent companies but which arises when consolidating because the parent company paid more than book value for an interest in a subsidiary, and minus (c) any negative goodwill resulting when consolidating because the parent company paid less than book value for its interest in a subsidiary. If the negative goodwill exceeds the positive goodwill, the excess is considered as a deferred credit to income.

Goodwill, either positive or negative, arising from consolidation is computed by comparing the acquisition cost with the book value of the stock acquired. If the acquisition cost exceeds the book value acquired, positive goodwill exists. If the book value acquired exceeds cost, negative goodwill exists.

Less Than 100% Ownership. When a parent company acquires less than 100% ownership in a subsidiary, it shares the ownership with the other stockholders whose stock it does not acquire. These outside stockholders (outside in the sense that they are not in the consolidated group) are usually referred to as the minority interest. Since the minority interest has a proportionate equity along with the majority interest (the parent company's interest) in the subsidiary, the subsidiary's shareholders' equity is composed essentially of two elements, namely, (1) the parent company's, and (2) the minority interest's.

When consolidating, the parent company's element of the subsidiary's shareholders' equity is eliminated and the minority interest's element thereof is consolidated. As in the case of 100% ownership, three distinct situations may arise when less than 100% ownership exists. They are:

(1) Less than 100% ownership acquired at book value.
(2) Less than 100% ownership acquired at more than book value.
(3) Less than 100% ownership acquired at less than book value.

ILLUSTRATION B-1: *Less Than 100% Ownership Acquired at Book Value.* Assume that as of January 1, 1967, Company A acquires a 90% ownership in Company B for $135,000, which is also the book value of the equity acquired. The following individual statements reflect the financial position of the respective companies as of the date of acquisition, and the consolidated statement shows how they would appear when consolidated:

COMPANY A
STATEMENT OF FINANCIAL POSITION
AS OF JANUARY 1, 1967

Current assets	$ 95,000	Current liabilities	$ 20,000
Investment in Company B	135,000	Fixed liabilities	100,000
Fixed assets (net)	400,000	Shareholders' equity:	
		Capital stock	400,000
		Retained earnings	110,000
	$630,000		$630,000

COMPANY B
STATEMENT OF FINANCIAL POSITION
AS OF JANUARY 1, 1967

Current assets	$ 40,000	Current liabilities	$ 10,000
Fixed assets (net)	120,000	Shareholders' equity:	
		Capital stock	100,000
		Retained earnings	50,000
	$160,000		$160,000

COMPANY A AND SUBSIDIARY COMPANY B
CONSOLIDATED WORKING PAPERS
STATEMENT OF FINANCIAL POSITION
AS OF JANUARY 1, 1967

	Company A	Company B	Eliminations Debit	Eliminations Credit	Consolidated Financial Position
Assets					
Current assets	$ 95,000	$ 40,000			$135,000
Investment in B	135,000			$135,000	
Fixed assets (net)	400,000	120,000			520,000
	$630,000	$160,000			$655,000
Equities					
Current liabilities	$ 20,000	$ 10,000			$ 30,000
Fixed liabilities	100,000				100,000
Shareholders' equity:					
Capital stock:					
Company A	400,000				400,000
Company B		100,000	$90,000		10,000MI*
Retained earnings:					
Company A	110,000				110,000RE
Company B		50,000	45,000		5,000MI*
	$630,000	$160,000	$135,000	$135,000	$655,000

* These two elements represent the 10% interest of the outsiders in Company B. Since Company B has a shareholders' equity of $150,000, the minority interest's claim against it is $15,000 (10% of $150,000) which is composed of two elements: $5,000 equity in retained earnings and $10,000 equity in capital stock.

Basic Procedure. Again the basic procedure involved is the same as in the previous illustrations: (1) eliminate reciprocals, and (2) consolidate nonreciprocals. In this instance the only reciprocal element is the parent company's claim against the shareholders' equity of the subsidiary, which is represented by the investment account on the parent's statement. The work sheet entry for the elimination expressed in journal form is:

Capital stock (90% of Company B's)	$90,000	
Retained earnings (90% of Company B's)	45,000	
Investment in B (Company A's account)		$135,000
(to eliminate 90% of Company B's share-		
holders' equity against the investment account)		

The nonreciprocal elements are consolidated by extending them to the consolidated statement. Note the extension of the nonreciprocal element of Company B's capital stock and retained earnings as minority interest. In statement form the consolidated statement of financial position would appear as follows:

COMPANY A AND SUBSIDIARY COMPANY B
CONSOLIDATED STATEMENT OF FINANCIAL POSITION
AS OF JANUARY 1, 1967

Current assets	$135,000	Current liabilities	$ 30,000
Fixed assets (net)	520,000	Fixed liabilities	100,000
		Minority interest	15,000
		Shareholders' equity.	
		Capital stock	400,000
		Retained earnings	110,000
	$655,000		$655,000

Statement Presentation of Minority Interest. Minority interest is usually presented either in or just above the parent company's shareholders' equity section on the consolidated statement of financial position. Current practice tends to present it just above the shareholders' equity section. In published statements it is frequently shown as one amount. The Securities and Exchange Commission, however, requires it to be detailed when reporting to them: a separation is made between the minority interest in the capital stock and in the surplus elements of the subsidiary.

Reconciliation of Illustrations B-1 and A-1. Since, before consolidating, total assets and total equities of Company A and Company B are exactly the same in Illustrations B-1 and A-1, it might seem that when consolidated the total assets and equities on the consolidated statements should be the same. However, this is not the case. In Illustration B-1 the assets and equities total $655,000, respectively, whereas in Illustration A-1 they total $640,000, respectively. The $15,000 difference in total assets is due, of course, to the fact that Company A uses only $135,000 of its assets to acquire a 90% interest instead of using $150,000 to acquire a 100% interest. The difference of $15,000 remains a part of the current assets of Company A and is included in the consolidated statement. The $15,000 difference in total equities represents the claim of the minority stockholders in the shareholders' equity of Company B. Since this is an outside claim against the consolidated group, it must be reflected on the consolidated statement.

ILLUSTRATION B-2: *Less Than* 100% *Ownership Acquired at More Than Book Value.* As in the case of 100% ownership, a parent company may pay more than book value when it acquires less than 100% ownership in a subsidiary. Again, assuming that the books have been kept in accordance with generally accepted accounting principles, this excess payment is treated as a purchase of goodwill.

Assume the same facts as in Illustration B-1, except that Company A acquires a 90% interest in Company B for $155,000. Since the book value acquired by Company A is only $135,000 (90% of $150,000) there is an excess payment of $20,000 for goodwill. The consolidating procedure is illustrated as follows:

COMPANY A

STATEMENT OF FINANCIAL POSITION

As OF JANUARY 1, 1967

Current assets	$ 75,000	Current liabilities	$ 20,000
Investment in Company B	155,000	Fixed liabilities	100,000
Fixed assets (net)	400,000	Shareholders' equity:	
		Capital stock	400,000
		Retained earnings	110,000
	$630,000		$630,000

COMPANY B

STATEMENT OF FINANCIAL POSITION

As OF JANUARY 1, 1967

Current assets	$ 40,000	Current liabilities	$ 10,000
Fixed assets (net)	120,000	Shareholders' equity:	
		Capital stock	100,000
		Retained earnings	50,000
	$160,000		$160,000

COMPANY A AND SUBSIDIARY COMPANY B

CONSOLIDATED WORKING PAPERS
STATEMENT OF FINANCIAL POSITION

AS OF JANUARY 1, 1967

	Company A	Company B	Eliminations Debit	Eliminations Credit	Consolidated Financial Position
Assets					
Current assets	$ 75,000	$ 40,000			$115,000
Investment in B	155,000			$135,000	20,000G
Fixed assets (net)	400,000	120,000			520,000
	$630,000	$160,000			$655,000
Equities					
Current liabilities	$ 20,000	$ 10,000			$ 30,000
Fixed liabilities	100,000				100,000
Shareholders' equity:					
Capital stock:					
Company A	400,000				400,000
Company B		100,000	$90,000		10,000MI
Retained earnings:					
Company A	110,000				110,000RE
Company B		50,000	45,000		5,000MI
	$630,000	$160,000	$135,000	$135,000	$655,000

Basic Procedure. Again the basic procedure is the same: (1) eliminate reciprocals and (2) consolidate nonreciprocals. In this instance, the only elimination necessary is the parent's claim in the shareholders' equity of the subsidiary against the investment account. The work sheet entry is the same as in Illustration B-1:

Capital stock (90% of Company B's)	$90,000	
Retained earnings (90% of Company B's)	45,000	
Investment in B (Company A's account)		$135,000
(to eliminate 90% of Company B's shareholders' equity against the investment account)		

The nonreciprocal elements are consolidated by adding them together where necessary and extending them to the consolidated statement as in previous illustrations. In statement form the consolidated statement would appear as follows:

COMPANY A AND SUBSIDIARY COMPANY B

CONSOLIDATED STATEMENT OF FINANCIAL POSITION

AS OF JANUARY 1, 1967

Current assets	$115,000	Current liabilities	$ 30,000
Fixed assets (net)	520,000	Fixed liabilities	100,000
Goodwill	20,000	Minority interest	15,000
		Shareholders' equity:	
		Capital stock	400,000
		Retained earnings	110,000
	$655,000		$655,000

Reconciliation of Illustrations B-2 and A-2. In Illustration B-2 the assets and equities after being consolidated total $655,000, respectively, whereas in Illustration A-2 they total $640,000, although the individual statements have exactly the same totals before consolidating and the same amount of goodwill is involved. The $15,000 difference in total assets arises from the fact that Company A pays $155,000 for a 90% interest in B instead of $170,000 for a 100% interest therein. The $15,000 difference in total equities represents the claim of the minority interest in the share-holders' equity of Company B (10% of $150,000).

ILLUSTRATION B-3: *Less Than 100% Ownership Acquired at Less Than Book Value.* As in the case of 100% ownership, a parent company may pay less than book value when it acquires less than 100% ownership. Assume the same facts as in Illustration B-1, except that Company A acquires a 90% interest in Company B for $125,000. Since the book value acquired by Company A is $135,000 (90% of $150,000), negative goodwill of $10,000 is indicated.

COMPANY A

STATEMENT OF FINANCIAL POSITION

AS OF JANUARY 1, 1967

Current assets	$105,000	Current liabilities	$ 20,000
Investment in Company B	125,000	Fixed liabilities	100,000
Fixed assets (net)	400,000	Shareholders' equity:	
		Capital stock	400,000
		Retained earnings	110,000
	$630,000		$630,000

COMPANY B

STATEMENT OF FINANCIAL POSITION

AS OF JANUARY 1, 1967

Current assets	$ 40,000	Current liabilities	$ 10,000
Fixed assets (net)	120,000	Shareholders' equity:	
		Capital stock	100,000
		Retained earnings	50,000
	$160,000		$160,000

COMPANY A AND SUBSIDIARY COMPANY B

CONSOLIDATED WORKING PAPERS

STATEMENT OF FINANCIAL POSITION

AS OF JANUARY 1, 1967

	Company A	Company B	Eliminations Debit	Eliminations Credit	Consolidated Financial Position
Assets					
Current assets	$105,000	$ 40,000			$145,000
Investment in B	125,000			$135,000	(10,000)G
Fixed assets (net)	400,000	120,000			520,000
	$630,000	$160,000			$655,000
Equities					
Current liabilities	$ 20,000	$ 10,000			$ 30,000
Fixed liabilities	100,000				100,000
Shareholders' equity:					
Capital stock:					
Company A	400,000				400,000
Company B		100,000	$90,000		10,000MI
Retained earnings:					
Company A	110,000				110,000RE
Company B		50,000	45,000		5,000MI
	$630,000	$160,000	$135,000	$135,000	$655,000

Basic Procedure. The basic procedure is still essentially the same: eliminate the parent company's claim in the subsidiary's shareholders' equity against the investment account, and consolidate nonreciprocals. The work sheet entry for the elimination remains exactly the same as Illustrations B-1 and B-2:

Capital stock (90% of Company B's)	$90,000	
Retained earnings (90% of Company B's)	45,000	
Investment in B (Company A's account)		$135,000
(to eliminate 90% of Company B's shareholders' equity against the investment account)		

In statement form the consolidated statement of financial position would appear as follows:

COMPANY A AND SUBSIDIARY COMPANY B

CONSOLIDATED STATEMENT OF FINANCIAL POSITION

AS OF JANUARY 1, 1967

Current assets	$145,000	Current liabilities	$ 30,000
Fixed assets (net)	520,000	Fixed liabilities	100,000
		Excess of subsidiary book	
		value over cost	10,000
		Minority interest	15,000
		Shareholders' equity:	
		Capital stock	400,000
		Retained earnings	110,000
	$665,000		$665,000

Reconciliation of Illustrations B-3 and A-3. In Illustration B-3 the assets and equities total $665,000, respectively, on the consolidated statement, whereas in Illustration A-3 they total $650,000, although the individual statements have exactly the same totals before consolidating and the same amount of negative goodwill is involved. The $15,000 difference in total assets arises from the fact that Company A pays $125,000 for 90% interest in B instead of $140,000 for 100% interest. The $15,000 difference in total equities represents the minority interest's claim against the shareholders' equity of Company B (10% of $150,000), and since all outside equities are reflected on the consolidated statement this claim must be presented.

Miscellaneous Intercompany Items

As indicated earlier, intercompany pairs of accounts, reciprocal in nature, must be eliminated in order to avoid double-counting from the point of view of the affiliated group as an entity. Among the types of intercompany accounts that must be eliminated in order to avoid double-counting are receivable-payable accounts, such as accounts receivable and accounts payable, notes receivable and notes payable, and dividends receivable and dividends payable.

In the preparation of a consolidated statement of financial position intercompany receivables and payables are eliminated by work sheet entries which debit the payables and credit the receivables. The effect of such elimination is to restrict consolidated receivables and payables to those resulting from transactions with parties outside the affiliated group. The work sheet entries may be illustrated by using a partial work sheet and assuming that Company A (parent) and Company B (90% owned subsidiary) are being consolidated and that (*a*) Company A owes Company B $5,000 on open account (*b*) Company A holds Company B's note for $10,000, and (*c*) Company B has declared but not paid a $20,000 dividend.

COMPANY A AND SUBSIDIARY COMPANY B

CONSOLIDATED WORKING PAPERS
STATEMENT OF FINANCIAL POSITION
AS OF JANUARY 1, 1967

	Company A	Company B	Eliminations Debit	Eliminations Credit	Consolidated Financial Position
Assets					
Accounts receivable		$6,000		$ 5,000A	$1,000
Notes receivable	$10,000			10,000B	
Dividends receivable	18,000			18,000C	
Equities					
Accounts payable	$7,000		$ 5,000A		$2,000
Notes payable		$10,000	10,000B		
Dividends payable		20,000	18,000C		2,000

It should be noted that when only a portion of the intercompany account is reciprocal, only that portion is eliminated and the nonreciprocal element is consolidated. For example, in entry (C), since Company A has only a 90% interest in Company B, only 90% or $18,000 of B's Dividends Payable account is eliminated. The other 10% or $2,000 is not eliminated.

Consolidated Statements of Surplus at Acquisition Date

Unconsolidated surplus statements provide supporting detail for two successive unconsolidated statements of financial position. Likewise, consolidated surplus statements provide supporting detail for two successive consolidated statements of financial position. For example, a consolidated statement of retained earnings provides an analysis of the changes in consolidated retained earnings in a given fiscal period. Since at the date of acquisition the consolidated entity has had no period of operations, consolidated retained earnings is identical with the parent company's retained earnings. This is due to the elimination of the parent's share of the subsidiary's retained earnings, and the inclusion of the minority interest's share in the consolidated statement of financial position as minority interest. Likewise, consolidated capital surplus at the date of acquisition is composed entirely of the parent company's capital surplus.

When the subsidiary stock is acquired with one purchase at one time, it should be noted that no element of subsidiary surplus (retained earnings or capital surplus) is included as such in consolidated statements of surplus prepared at the date of acquisition. To illustrate, assume the same conditions as given in Illustration A-1. Also assume that the following retained earnings statements were prepared as of the date of acquisition.

	COMPANY A STATEMENT OF RETAINED EARNINGS AS OF JANUARY 1, 1967	COMPANY B STATEMENT OF RETAINED EARNINGS AS OF JANUARY 1, 1967
Retained earnings 1/1/66	$100,000	$44,000
Net income (1966)	10,000	6,000
Retained earnings 1/1/67	$110,000	$50,000

Since 100% of Company B's retained earnings is eliminated, the consolidated retained earnings is composed entirely of Company A's retained earnings of $110,000.

Assume the same basic situation as in Illustration B-1 which, in essence, is that Company A acquires 90% ownership in Company B at book value. Also assume that the same retained earnings statements were prepared as used in the preceding illustration. Ninety per cent of the subsidiary's retained earnings is eliminated, as follows:

Capital stock (90% of Company B's)	$90,000	
Retained earnings (90% of Company B's)	45,000	
Investment in B (Company A's account)		$135,000
(to eliminate 90% of Company B's shareholders'		
equity against the investment account)		

Although only $45,000 is eliminated from the subsidiary's retained earnings, it will be recalled that the other $5,000 is consolidated as minority interest (see page 274). Consequently, the consolidated retained earnings is the same as the parent company's retained earnings of $110,000.

Accounting for the Difference between Cost and Book Value of Subsidiary Stock Acquired

Accounting for the difference between the cost of the investment in a subsidiary and the book value of the stock acquired is somewhat more involved than that suggested in the preceding demonstrations of the consolidating procedures.

Proponents of the cost theory of asset valuation maintain that the proper cost of assets is their cost to the consolidated entity. This view, which generally conforms to current practice, provides for the following treatment of the difference between cost of the investment and the book value of the assets acquired:

If cost exceeds book value:

(1) Assign the excess to specific assets for which it is evident a price in excess of their book value was paid.
(2) Recognize as assets those intangible items for which it is evident a price was paid.
(3) Treat any difference not assignable to specific assets as a general valuation and include it with the consolidated assets under an appropriately described account.

If the difference is assigned to depreciable or amortizable assets in the allocation process, expenses of the consolidated entity will include appropriate depreciation or amortization of the allocated difference.

If book value exceeds cost:

(1) Assign the difference to specific assets in those cases where it is evident the price paid for the asset was below its book value.
(2) Any difference attributable to anticipated future losses should be provided for in specific accounts.
(3) Treat any difference not accounted for by either (1) or (2) as a balance to be allocated on some reasonable basis, normally the adjusted valuation of the specific assets, to the specific assets of the subsidiary.

Use of this method for accounting for the difference between cost and book value of the stock acquired provides for a more realistic treatment of that amount than the questionable practice of always treating it as either "positive" or "negative" goodwill. The procedures involved in accounting for the difference will be illustrated in a subsequent chapter.

PROBLEMS

Problem 10–1. From the following data prepare a consolidated statement of financial position at the date of acquisition of 80 per cent of the subsidiary's stock, showing the amount of goodwill and the minority interest:

At the date of acquisition the subsidiary's shareholders' equity was composed of $100,000 capital stock and $40,000 retained earnings. The parent company paid $130,000 for its investment in the subsidiary. The capital stock of the parent was $1,000,000; retained earnings, $200,000; and total net assets (including the investment in the subsidiary), $1,200,000.

Problem 10–2. Determine the amount of goodwill in each of the following cases:

	Cost of Investment	Per Cent of Ownership	Subsidiary's Shareholders' Equity* Retained Earnings	Capital Stock
Case 1	$120,000	100%	$20,000	$100,000
Case 2	140,000	100%	30,000	100,000
Case 3	132,000	100%	40,000	100,000
Case 4	135,000	90%	50,000	150,000
Case 5	195,000	90%	60,000	150,000
Case 6	195,000	90%	70,000	150,000

* At date of acquisition.

Problem 10–3. In each of the following cases the data were compiled at the date of acquisition. In each situation determine:
(1) The amount of goodwill involved in the acquisition.
(2) The amount of minority interest at the date of acquisition.

	Cost of Investment	Per Cent of Ownership	Subsidiary's Shareholders' Equity Retained Earnings	Capital Stock
Case 1	$230,000	100%	$35,000	$200,000
Case 2	240,000	100%	40,000	200,000
Case 3	190,000	100%	(18,000)*	200,000
Case 4	276,000	80%	40,000	300,000
Case 5	288,000	80%	60,000	300,000
Case 6	240,000	80%	(10,000)*	300,000

* Deficit.

Problem 10–4. Consolidate the following statements of financial position of Companies A and B, assuming that:
(1) Company A purchases all of the stock of Company B for $100,000 cash.
(2) Company A purchases all of the stock of Company B for $108,000 cash.
(3) Company A purchases 90% of the stock of Company B for $100,000 cash.
(4) Company A purchases 80% of the stock of Company B for $75,000, paying $25,000 cash and giving a note for the balance.

STATEMENT OF FINANCIAL POSITION
As of December 31, 1967

Assets	Co. A	Co. B	Equities	Co. A	Co. B
Current assets	$350,000	$ 20,000	Current liabilities	$ 50,000	$ 10,000
			Fixed liabilities	100,000	
Fixed assets (net)	400,000	90,000	Shareholders' equity:		
			Capital stock	500,000	80,000
			Retained earnings	100,000	20,000
	$750,000	$110,000		$750,000	$110,000

Problem 10–5. Prepare a consolidated statement of financial position for A Company and its subsidiaries, B Company and C Company. The following condensed statements show the financial position of the three companies as of September 30, 1967, the date A Company acquired its interests in the subsidiaries.

A COMPANY

Assets	$249,000	Liabilities	$150,000
Stock of B (par)	60,000	Capital stock	225,000
Stock of C (par)	81,000	Retained earnings	15,000
	$390,000		$390,000

B COMPANY

Assets	$175,000	Liabilities	$ 80,000
		Capital stock	75,000
		Retained earnings	20,000
	$175,000		$175,000

C COMPANY

Assets	$100,000	Liabilities	$ 20,000
Deficit	10,000	Capital stock	90,000
	$110,000		$110,000

Problem 10–6. On December 31, 1967, A Company purchased 90% of B Company for $280,000, 80% of C Company for $284,000, and 75% of D Company for $60,000. The statements of financial position of the various companies immediately following the acquisitions were:

Assets	A Company	B Company	C Company	D Company
Cash	$1,256,000	$ 50,000	$ 20,000	$ 25,000
Accounts receivable (net)	300,000	10,000	4,000	8,000
Inventories	900,000	125,000	70,000	150,000
Land	1,000,000	20,000	30,000	25,000
Buildings (net)	2,000,000	300,000	400,000	100,000
Investment in B Company	280,000			
Investment in C Company	284,000			
Investment in D Company	60,000			
	$6,080,000	$505,000	$524,000	$308,000
Equities				
Accounts payable	$ 200,000	$ 30,000	$ 20,000	$ 20,000
Notes payable	180,000	70,000	50,000	200,000
Bonds payable	100,000	100,000	100,000	
Capital stock	5,000,000	200,000	250,000	100,000
Retained earnings (deficit)	600,000	105,000	104,000	(12,000)
	$6,080,000	$505,000	$524,000	$308,000

Prepare a consolidated statement of financial position as of the date of acquisition.

Problem 10-7. Using the following data taken from the records of companies A, B, and C on March 1, 1967, the date Company A acquired its investment in B and C, prepare a consolidated statement of financial position.

Assets	A Company	B Company	C Company
Current assets	$ 770,000	$440,000	$490,000
Investments:			
4,200 shares of B stock	550,000		
5,520 shares of C stock	700,000		
Fixed assets (net)	1,780,000	400,000	460,000
	$3,800,000	$840,000	$950,000

Equities			
Current liabilities	$ 600,000	$120,000	$ 80,000
Fixed liabilities	200,000	80,000	120,000
Capital stock (par $100)	2,500,000	500,000	600,000
Paid-in surplus	100,000	40,000	60,000
Retained earnings	400,000	100,000	90,000
	$3,800,000	$840,000	$950,000

Problem 10-8. When a business is purchased as an entity, the price paid often differs from the equity shown by the records of the vendor.

Explain fully why the sale value of a going business may differ from the book value even where acceptable accounting practices have been followed in keeping the accounts of the business. (AICPA adapted)

Problem 10-9. What is "negative goodwill"? Explain the conditions under which it is found and its treatment on the financial statements, indicating at least two methods of presentation, and the circumstances under which each would be appropriate. (AICPA adapted)

Problem 10-10. On December 31, 1967, P Company acquired all of the capital stock of S-1, and 95% of the capital stock of S-2. Immediately after the acquisitions the statements of financial position appeared as follows:

Assets	P Company	S-1	S-2
Cash	$ 180,000	$ 25,000	$ 20,000
Accounts receivable	95,000	45,000	40,000
Notes receivable	30,000	20,000	10,000
Inventories	100,000	30,000	50,000
Investment in S-1	140,000		
Investment in S-2	160,000		
Land	80,000	30,000	40,000
Buildings (net)	200,000	130,000	120,000
Goodwill	30,000		
	$1,015,000	$280,000	$280,000

Equities	P Company	S-1	S-2
Accounts payable	$ 120,000	$ 38,000	$ 80,000
Notes payable	20,000	90,000	40,000
Bonds payable	100,000		
Capital stock	500,000	100,000	100,000
Paid-in surplus	115,000	62,000	
Retained earnings (deficit)	160,000	(10,000)	60,000
	$1,015,000	$280,000	$280,000

Intercompany relationships:

> S-1 owed S-2 $5,000 on an open account.
> S-2 owed P Company $4,000 on open account.
> P Company owed S-1 $7,000 on open account.
> S-2 held S-1's note for $10,000.

Prepare a consolidated statement of financial position.

Problem 10–11. At December 31, 1967, the balance sheet of Company A was as follows:

Cash	$ 50,000	Payables	$1,750,000
Receivables, less reserves	300,000	Accruals	450,000
Inventories	1,600,000	Common stock, 10,000 shares	1,000,000
Prepayments	47,000	Retained earnings	800,000
Fixed assets, less reserves	2,003,000		
	$4,000,000		$4,000,000

An appraisal as of that date, which was carefully considered and approved by the boards of directors of Company A and Company B, placed a total replacement value, less sustained depreciation, of $3,203,000 on the fixed assets of Company A.

Company B's condensed balance sheet at December 31, 1967, showed:

Cash and investments	$ 7,000,000	Payables	$ 7,872,000
(including stock of A)			
Receivables, less reserves	2,400,000	Accruals	1,615,000
Inventories	11,200,000	Common stock, 100,000	10,000,000
Prepayments	422,000	shares	
Fixed assets, less reserves	18,978,000	Retained earnings	20,513,000
	$40,000,000		$40,000,000

Company B offered to purchase all the assets of Company A, subject to its liabilities, as of December 31, 1967, for $3,000,000. However, 40% of the stockholders of Company A objected to the price on the ground that it did not include any consideration for goodwill, which they believed to be worth at least $500,000. A counter-proposal was made and final agreement was reached on the basis that Company B acquired 60% of the common stock of Company A at a price of $300 a share.

Prepare a consolidating statement as at December 31, 1967, of the two companies. (AICPA adapted)

Problem 10–12. You are engaged to audit the Apex Company and its subsidiary, Apex Sales Co., as of December 31, 1967. During the course of the audit you discover the balances of the intercompany accounts do not agree.

The Apex Company manufactures fountain pens which it sells to its subsidiary at cost plus 20 per cent. The subsidiary then sells the fountain pens to jewelry stores.

Shown below is a copy of the intercompany account ledger sheets.

Discussion with company employees developed the following explanation of references found on the ledger accounts:

> SR—Sales register and invoice number.
> CR—Cash receipts book.
> CD—Cash disbursements book.
> VR—Voucher register, receiving report number and Apex Company invoice number.
> RG—Returned goods register and debit memo number.

A review of the inventory observation working papers discloses the following information:

Observation at Apex Company on December 31, 1967:
(1) Last shipment prior to the physical inventory was billed on invoice number 17882 dated December 31, 1967.
(2) No returned merchandise was received from the Apex Sales Co. during the month of December 1967.
(3) The last receiving report used in December 1967 was number 59742 dated December 30, 1967.

Observation at Apex Sales Co. on December 31, 1967:
(1) Last shipment prior to the physical inventory was billed on invoice number 77843 dated December 31, 1967.
(2) The last shipment of merchandise returned to the Apex Company in December 1967 was entered on debit memo number 74 dated December 31, 1967.
(3) The last receiving report *used* in December 1967 was number 34337 dated December 31, 1967 for merchandise billed on Apex invoice 17879.

You are to prepare in good form:
  (1) A reconciliation of the intercompany accounts.
  (2) The journal entries required by each company to:
    (*a*) Adjust the intercompany accounts.
    (*b*) Adjust the inventories which are based on physical inventories taken December 31, 1967 valued by each of the two companies at its cost.

ACCOUNT IN THE APEX COMPANY GENERAL LEDGER
INTERCOMPANY ACCOUNT—APEX SALES CO.

Date	Reference	Amount	Date	Reference	Amount
Total Forwarded		$178,683.00	Total Forwarded		$123,867.00
Dec. 26	SR 17877	1,950.00	Dec. 26	CR	3,567.00
27	SR 17878	1,194.00	29	CR	31,127.00
28	SR 17879	2,183.00	31	Balance	28,189.00
29	SR 17880	849.00			
31	SR 17882	1,891.00			
		$186,750.00			$186,750.00

ACCOUNT IN THE APEX SALES CO. GENERAL LEDGER
INTERCOMPANY ACCOUNT—APEX COMPANY

Date	Reference	Amount	Date	Reference	Amount
Total Forwarded		$127,434.00	Total Forwarded		$176,508.00
Dec. 28	CD	31,127.00	Dec. 26	VR 34333–17876	2,175.00
31	CD	19,777.00	28	VR 34334–17877	1,950.00
31	RG 74	2,329.00	29	VR 34335–17878	1,194.00
31	Balance	6,318.00	31	VR 34336–17881	3,647.00
			31	VR 34340–17883	1,511.00
		$186,985.00			$186,985.00

(AICPA adapted)

Problem 10–13. From the following information prepare a consolidated statement of financial position of Holding Co. and its wholly owned subsidiary as of July 31, 1967.

On June 30, 1967, A & Co. partnership (profits and losses shared equally), and X Corp. consummated a consolidation agreement pursuant to the terms of which Consolidated Co., newly organized and incorporated with an authorized capital of 20,000 shares of $100 par value common stock, acquired for its common stock issued in the amount of $950,000 to A & Co. and $550,000 to X Corp. certain net assets of the respective companies as follows:

A & Co.—All net assets (including buildings at an appraised sound value of $1,100,000), excluding notes payable.

X Corp.—All net assets, excluding buildings.

The statements of financial position of A & Co. and X Corp. as of June 30, 1967, before consolidation are condensed as follows:

Assets	A & Co.	X Corp.
Cash	$ 25,000	$ 125,000
Accounts receivable	165,000	500,000
Inventory	150,000	435,000
Land	50,000	
Buildings, less reserves	1,000,000	125,000
Machinery, less reserves	250,000	15,000
Patents	10,000	
	$1,650,000	$1,200,000

Equities	A & Co.	X Corp.
Accounts payable	$ 300,000	$ 500,000
Notes payable	100,000	
Mortgage payable	600,000	
Capital accounts:		
Partner A	450,000	
Partner B	200,000	
Capital Stock		800,000
Retained earnings (deficit)		(100,000)
	$1,650,000	$1,200,000

On July 1, 1967, A & Co. conveyed 1,000 shares of common stock of Consolidated Co. to the note holders in full settlement of their claims and immediately thereafter distributed the remaining shares of such common stock to the partners in dissolution. On the same date, after the consolidation, in order to provide Consolidated Co. with working capital, A alone (the recipient of his partnership share of Consolidated stock) contributed to Consolidated Co. 10% of the stock so received by him. Such contributed stock was sold by Consolidated Co. on July 25, 1967, for $105 per share.

During July 1967, as a result of operations, the net assets of Consolidated Co. increased by $25,000 represented by increase in cash. For purposes of this problem, assume other balance-sheet accounts did not change during July.

On July 31, 1967, the stockholders of Consolidated Co. sold their interests to Holding Co. A statement of financial position of Holding Co. at July 31, 1967, after acquisition of 100% of the issued and outstanding stock of Consolidated Co. was as follows:

HOLDING CO.

STATEMENT OF FINANCIAL POSITION

JULY 31, 1967

Assets		*Equities*	
Investment in		Capital Stock	$2,000,000
Consolidated Co.	$1,600,000	Retained Earnings	350,000
Securities—other	600,000		
Cash	150,000		
	$2,350,000		$2,350,000

(AICPA adapted)

CHAPTER 11

Consolidated statements subsequent to date of acquisition—investment carried at cost

The preparation of consolidated statements subsequent to the date of acquisition is essentially the same as when consolidating statements at the date of acquisition, that is (1) eliminate reciprocals, and (2) consolidate nonreciprocals. However, when consolidating subsequent to the date of acquisition, it is frequently necessary to establish reciprocity between the parent company's investment account and the subsidiary's sharcholders' equity before it is possible to eliminate reciprocals. The establishment of reciprocity in any given situation is dependent upon the parent company's method of carrying the investment account. Although the method used for carrying the investment account will affect the unconsolidated statements and likewise the consolidating procedure, it will not affect the consolidated statements.

Methods of Carrying Investments in Subsidiaries. Although many variations exist, the investment account is carried cither at (1) cost, or (2) at something other than cost. The cost method is illustrated in this chapter.

COST METHOD

When the cost method is being used, cost is recorded in the investment account when the investment is originally made and remains the basis of the account until it is either partially or completely disposed of or until some fundamental change in conditions makes it clearly apparent that the value originally assigned can no longer be justified. Under this method the parent's share of the increases and decreases in the subsidiary's shareholders' equity is not recognized in the accounting records. This procedure is used in the case of investments in general.

The following entries, which would be recorded in the *parent company's books*, illustrate the accounting involved when the investment account is carried at cost:

(1) January 1, 1967, Company A purchases an 80% interest in Company B for $140,000.

Investment in Company B	$140,000	
Cash		$140,000

(2) December 31, 1967, Company B reports $40,000 net income for 1967. No entry made by parent.

(3) March 15, 1968, Company B pays $10,000 dividend.

Cash	$8,000	
Dividend income		$8,000

(4) December 31, 1968, Company B reports $20,000 net loss for 1968. No entry made by parent.

Should the subsidiary sustain a loss which appears to be a permanent loss, it is appropriate to adjust the investment account accordingly. Also, should the subsidiary pay a cash dividend out of earnings existing prior to the date the parent acquired the stock, the investment account should be adjusted. To continue the above illustration, assume that in 1969 Company B pays dividends of $20,000 and later in the year suffers an uninsured fire loss of $70,000. The entries on the *books of Company A* would be:

(1) Cash $16,000

Dividend income		$8,000
Investment in Company B		8,000

(to record 80% of cash dividend paid by B of which $8,000 was from retained earnings created prior to January 1, 1967, and not earned by Company A)

(2) Fire loss by Company B $56,000

Investment in Company B		$56,000

(to recognize A's share of the permanent loss sustained by B as a result of a fire: 80% of $70,000)

Consolidated Statement of Financial Position
Investment Carried at Cost

Basic Consolidating Procedure. As indicated earlier, the basic procedure when consolidating statements subsequent to acquisition is essentially the same as when consolidating at the date of acquisition, except that it may be necessary to establish reciprocity before it is possible to eliminate reciprocals. For example, if the parent company carries the investment account at cost, and if the shareholders' equity of the subsidiary has changed since acquisition, the investment account on the parent's statement and the parent's claim against the shareholders' equity of the subsidiary will not have the same relationship as existed at acquisition. Consequently, before eliminations can be properly made, reciprocity must be established. The basic consolidating procedure when consolidating subsequent to the date of acquisition, therefore, includes:

(1) The establishment of reciprocity, if necessary.
(2) The elimination of reciprocals.
(3) The consolidation of nonreciprocals.

Establishment of Reciprocity. Reciprocity is established by a work sheet entry or entries which are frequently referred to as adjusting entries. When the investment account is carried at cost and the subsidiary's shareholders' equity has changed (either increased or decreased) since acquisition, reciprocity could conceivably be established by either (1) adjusting the subsidiary's shareholders' equity back to the date of acquisition, or (2) adjusting the investment account up to the date of consolidation. For example, assume that Company A acquired 100% ownership of Company B for $100,000 at a time when Company B's shareholders' equity was $100,000. If at the end of one year Company B's shareholders' equity has increased to $120,000 (assume the entire increase is currently reflected in retained earnings) and Company A carries the investment account at cost ($100,000), reciprocity could be established by either of the following work sheet entries:

(1) Retained earnings (Company B's)	$20,000	
Retained earnings (Company A's)		$20,000
(2) Investment in B	$20,000	
Retained earnings (Company A's)		$20,000

Although both methods produce the same end result, the latter approach is the one generally used and is the one presented in this textbook. It should be noted that if reciprocity were not established in this case, when making the elimination, $120,000 of the subsidiary's shareholders' equity would be eliminated against the investment account of $100,000. The result would reflect $20,000 negative goodwill; actually, there was no goodwill of any type associated with the purchase since Company A paid $100,000 for a book value of $100,000.

The technique of consolidating the assets and equities of two or more related companies subsequent to the date of acquisition, when the investment is carried at cost, is examined in this chapter. As in the preceding chapter, the presentation distinguishes between (1) whether 100% ownership exists, or (2) whether less than 100% ownership exists.

100% Ownership

Illustration A-1₁: 100% Ownership Acquired at Book Value. Assume that as of January 1, 1967, Company A acquired 100% ownership in Company B for $150,000, which was also the book value of the interest acquired (see Illustration A-1, page 266). The following individual statements reflect the financial positions of the respective companies one year later, and the consolidated statement column of the working papers shows the financial position after consolidation:

COMPANY A

STATEMENT OF FINANCIAL POSITION
As of December 31, 1967

Current assets	$100,000	Current liabilities	$ 30,000
Investment in Company B	150,000	Fixed liabilities	100,000
Fixed assets (net)	450,000	Shareholders' equity:	
		Capital stock	400,000
		Retained earnings	170,000
	$700,000		$700,000

COMPANY B

STATEMENT OF FINANCIAL POSITION
As of December 31, 1967

Current assets	$ 80,000	Current liabilities	$ 20,000
Fixed assets (net)	110,000	Shareholders' equity:	
		Capital stock	100,000
		Retained earnings	70,000
	$190,000		$190,000

COMPANY A AND SUBSIDIARY COMPANY B
CONSOLIDATED WORKING PAPERS
STATEMENT OF FINANCIAL POSITION
AS OF DECEMBER 31, 1967

	Company A	Company B	Adjustments Debit	Adjustments Credit	Eliminations Debit	Eliminations Credit	Consolidated Financial Position
Assets							
Current assets	$100,000	$ 80,000					$180,000
Investment in B	150,000		$20,000			$170,000	
Fixed assets (net)	450,000	110,000					560,000
	$700,000	$190,000					$740,000
Equities							
Current liabilities	$ 30,000	$ 20,000					$ 50,000
Fixed liabilities	100,000						100,000
Shareholders' equity:							
Capital stock:							
Company A	400,000						400,000
Company B		100,000			$100,000		
Retained earnings:							
Company A	170,000			$20,000			190,000RE
Company B		70,000			70,000		
	$700,000	$190,000	$20,000	$20,000	$170,000	$170,000	$740,000

BASIC PROCEDURE. As indicated earlier, the basic procedure when consolidating subsequent to the date of acquisition includes:

(1) The establishment of reciprocity, if necessary.
(2) The elimination of reciprocals.
(3) The consolidation of nonreciprocals.

The Establishment of Reciprocity. Since the investment account on the parent company's statement reflects acquisition cost and since the subsidiary statement reflects the subsidiary's shareholders' equity at a date subsequent to acquisition, reciprocity must be established. This is accomplished by adjusting the investment account so that it will reflect the parent company's share of any increase or decrease in the subsidiary's shareholders' equity since acquisition. Company B's shareholders' equity has increased $20,000 (from $150,000 to $170,000) since acquisition. In order to establish reciprocity, because Company A owns 100% of Company B, the entire increase must be taken into consideration. Reciprocity is established through the following *work sheet* entry:

Investment in B $20,000
    Retained earnings (Company A's) $20,000
(to recognize the parent company's share of the
increase in the subsidiary's shareholders' equity
since acquisition)

The Elimination of Reciprocals.

Capital stock (Company B's)	$100,000	
Retained earnings (Company B's)	70,000	
Investment in B		$170,000
(to eliminate 100% of B's shareholders' equity		
against the investment account)		

The Consolidation of Nonreciprocals. The nonreciprocal elements are consolidated by adding them together where necessary and extending them to the consolidated statement, as is done in the case of consolidating at the date of acquisition. It should be recognized that the consolidated statement of financial position is prepared from the final column of the consolidated working papers.

Illustration A-2$_1$: 100% Ownership Acquired at More Than Book Value. Assume that as of January 1, 1967, Company A acquired 100% ownership in Company B for $170,000, which was $20,000 more than the book value acquired (see Illustration A-2, page 268). In the following work sheet, the first two columns reflect the financial positions of the respective companies *two* years later, and the final column reflects the financial position after consolidation.

COMPANY A AND SUBSIDIARY COMPANY B

CONSOLIDATED WORKING PAPERS
STATEMENT OF FINANCIAL POSITION

AS OF DECEMBER 31, 1968

	Company A	Company B	Adjustments Debit	Adjustments Credit	Eliminations Debit	Eliminations Credit	Consolidated Financial Position
Assets							
Current assets	$120,000	$ 90,000					$210,000
Investment in B	170,000		$15,000			$165,000	20,000G
Fixed assets (net)	440,000	105,000					545,000
	$730,000	$195,000					$775,000
Equities							
Current liabilities	$ 40,000	$ 30,000					$ 70,000
Fixed liabilities	90,000						90,000
Shareholders' equity:							
Capital stock:							
Company A	400,000						400,000
Company B		100,000			$100,000		
Retained earnings:							
Company A	200,000			$15,000			215,000RE
Company B		65,000			65,000		
	$730,000	$195,000	$15,000	$15,000	$165,000	$165,000	$775,000

BASIC PROCEDURE

(1) *Establishment of reciprocity:*

Investment in B	$15,000	
Retained earnings (Company A's)		$15,000

(work sheet entry to recognize A's 100% interest in
B's $15,000 increase in shareholders' equity since
date of acquisition)

(2) *Elimination of reciprocals:*

Capital stock (Company B's)	$100,000	
Retained earnings (Company B's)	65,000	
Investment in B		$165,000

(work sheet entry to eliminate 100% of B's shareholders' equity against the investment account)

(3) *Consolidation of nonreciprocals:*

Nonreciprocal items are consolidated as they have been in previous illustrations. However, it should be noted that the nonreciprocal portion of the investment account is extended to the consolidated statement as goodwill. It should be noted that this is the same amount of goodwill computed at the date of acquisition. This relationship is proper since none of the goodwill has been disposed of by sale or otherwise. It should also be noted that consolidated retained earnings is composed of the parent company's retained earnings plus the parent company's share of the increase in the subsidiary's retained earnings since the date of acquisition.

Illustration A-3₁: 100% Ownership Acquired at Less Than Book Value. Assume that as of January 1, 1967, Company A acquired 100% ownership in Company B for $140,000 which was $10,000 less than the book value acquired (see Illustration A-3, page 270). In the work sheet on page 298, the first two columns reflect the financial position of Companies A and B *three* years after acquisition, and the final column reflects the financial position after consolidation.

BASIC PROCEDURE

(1) *Establishment of reciprocity:*

Retained earnings (Company A's)	$14,000	
Investment in B		$14,000

(work sheet entry to recognize A's 100% interest in
B's $14,000 decrease in shareholders' equity since
acquisition)

(2) *Elimination of reciprocals:*

Capital stock (Company B's)	$100,000	
Retained earnings (Company B's)	36,000	
Investment in B		$136,000

(work sheet entry to eliminate 100% of B's shareholders' equity against the investment account)

(3) *Consolidation of nonreciprocals:*

Nonreciprocals are consolidated as before. However, it should be noted that the nonreciprocal portion of the investment account is extended to the consolidated statement as negative goodwill. This is also the amount computed at the date of acquisition.

COMPANY A AND SUBSIDIARY COMPANY B

CONSOLIDATED WORKING PAPERS
STATEMENT OF FINANCIAL POSITION

AS OF DECEMBER 31, 1969

	Company A	Company B	Adjustments Debit	Adjustments Credit	Eliminations Debit	Eliminations Credit	Consolidated Financial Position
Assets							
Current assets	$100,000	$ 70,000					$170,000
Investment in B	140,000			$14,000		$136,000	(10,000)G
Fixed assets (net)	430,000	100,000					530,000
	$670,000	$170,000					$690,000
Equities							
Current liabilities	$ 50,000	$ 34,000					$ 84,000
Fixed liabilities	80,000						80,000
Shareholders' equity:							
Capital stock:							
Company A	400,000						400,000
Company B		100,000			$100,000		
Retained earnings:							
Company A	140,000		$14,000				126,000RE
Company B		36,000			36,000		
	$670,000	$170,000	$14,000	$14,000	$136,000	$136,000	$690,000

Less Than 100% Ownership

When a parent company acquires less than 100% ownership in a subsidiary, as indicated in the preceding chapter, it shares the ownership with the minority interest. When consolidating subsequent to the date of acquisition, as well as at the date of acquisition, the parent company's equity in the subsidiary's shareholders' equity is eliminated and the minority interest's equity therein is consolidated. Again, as in the case of

100% ownership, three distinct situations may arise when less than 100% ownership exists, namely:

(1) Less than 100% ownership acquired at book value.
(2) Less than 100% ownership acquired at more than book value.
(3) Less than 100% ownership acquired at less than book value.

Illustration B-1₁: Less Than 100% Ownership Acquired at Book Value. Assume that as of January 1, 1967, Company A acquired a 90% interest in Company B for $135,000, which was also the book value of the interest acquired at that date (see Illustration B-1, page 273). The following individual statements reflect the financial positions of the respective companies one year later, and the consolidated statement column of the working papers the financial position after consolidation:

COMPANY A
STATEMENT OF FINANCIAL POSITION
AS OF DECEMBER 31, 1967

Current assets	$115,000	Current liabilities	$ 30,000
Investment in B	135,000	Fixed liabilities	100,000
Fixed assets (net)	450,000	Shareholders' equity:	
		Capital stock	400,000
		Retained earnings	170,000
	$700,000		$700,000

COMPANY B
STATEMENT OF FINANCIAL POSITION
AS OF DECEMBER 31, 1967

Current assets	$ 80,000	Current liabilities	$ 20,000
Fixed assets (net)	110,000	Shareholders' equity:	
		Capital stock	100,000
		Retained earnings	70,000
	$190,000		$190,000

BASIC PROCEDURE
(1) *Establishment of reciprocity:*

Investment in B	$18,000	
Retained earnings (Company A's)		$18,000

(work sheet entry to recognize A's 90% interest in the $20,000 increase in B's shareholders' equity since acquisition)

(2) *Elimination of reciprocals:*

Capital stock (Company B's)	$90,000	
Retained earnings (Company B's)	63,000	
Investment in B		$153,000

(work sheet entry to eliminate 90% of B's shareholders' equity against the investment account)

(3) *Consolidation of nonreciprocals:*

In this illustration it should be noted that the nonreciprocal elements of the subsidiary's shareholders' equity are extended to the consolidated statement as minority interest. If the minority interest of Illustration B-1 is compared with this illustration, it will be seen that the minority interest has increased $2,000, from $15,000 to $17,000. This is, of course, due to the minority interest's 10% claim against the $20,000 increase in B's shareholders' equity.

COMPANY A AND SUBSIDIARY COMPANY B

CONSOLIDATED WORKING PAPERS
STATEMENT OF FINANCIAL POSITION

AS OF DECEMBER 31, 1967

	Company A	Company B	Adjustments Debit	Adjustments Credit	Eliminations Debit	Eliminations Credit	Consolidated Financial Position
Assets							
Current assets	$115,000	$ 80,000					$195,000
Investment in B	135,000		$18,000			$153,000	
Fixed assets (net)	450,000	110,000					560,000
	$700,000	$190,000					$755,000
Equities							
Current liabilities	$ 30,000	$ 20,000					$ 50,000
Fixed liabilities	100,000						100,000
Shareholders' equity:							
Capital stock:							
Company A	400,000						400,000
Company B		100,000			$ 90,000		10,000MI
Retained earnings:							
Company A	170,000			$18,000			188,000RE
Company B		70,000			63,000		7,000MI
	$700,000	$190,000	$18,000	$18,000	$153,000	$153,000	$755,000

Illustration B-2$_1$: Less Than 100% Ownership Acquired at More Than Book Value. Assume that on January 1, 1967, Company A acquired a 90% interest in Company B for $155,000. At the date of acquisition Company B had a shareholders' equity of $150,000. Since Company A acquired a 90% interest it acquired book value of $135,000 (90% of $150,000) for its investment (see Illustration B-2, page 276). The following working paper shows how the individual statements of financial position would be consolidated *two* years later:

COMPANY A AND SUBSIDIARY COMPANY B
CONSOLIDATED WORKING PAPERS
STATEMENT OF FINANCIAL POSITION
AS OF DECEMBER 31, 1968

	Company A	Company B	Adjustments Debit	Adjustments Credit	Eliminations Debit	Eliminations Credit	Consolidated Financial Position
Assets							
Current assets	$135,000	$ 90,000					$225,000
Investment in B	155,000		$13,500			$148,500	20,000G
Fixed assets (net)	440,000	105,000					545,000
	$730,000	$195,000					$790,000
Equities							
Current liabilities	$ 40,000	$ 30,000					$ 70,000
Fixed liabilities	90,000						90,000
Shareholders' equity:							
Capital stock:							
Company A	400,000						400,000
Company B		100,000			$90,000		10,000MI
Retained earnings:							
Company A	200,000			$13,500			213,500RE
Company B		65,000			58,500		6,500MI
	$730,000	$195,000	$13,500	$13,500	$148,500	$148,500	$790,000

BASIC PROCEDURE
(1) *Establishment of reciprocity:*

Investment in B	$13,500	
Retained earnings (Company A's)		$ 13,500

(work sheet entry to recognize A's 90% interest in the $15,000 increase in B's shareholders' equity since acquisition)

(2) *Elimination of reciprocals:*

Capital stock (Company B's)	$90,000	
Retained earnings (Company B's)	58,500	
Investment in B		$148,500

(work sheet entry to eliminate 90% of B's shareholders' equity against the investment account)

(3) *Consolidation of nonreciprocals:*

All nonreciprocal elements are consolidated as usual. However, in this instance the nonreciprocal portion of the investment account is extended to the consolidated statement as goodwill, and the nonreciprocal elements of Company B's shareholders' equity are extended as minority interest. It should be noted that the amounts of goodwill in Illustrations B-2 and B-2$_1$ are the same. However, the minority interest has increased from $15,000 to $16,500 which is due, of course, to 10% of the $15,000 increase in Company B's shareholders' equity since acquisition.

Illustration B-3$_1$: Less Than 100% Ownership Acquired at Less Than Book Value. Assume that as of January 1, 1967, Company A acquired a 90% interest in Company B for $125,000. At the date of acquisition Company B had a shareholders' equity of $150,000. Since Company A acquired a 90% interest, it acquired book value of $135,000 (90% of $150,000) for its investment (see Illustration B-3, page 278). In the following work sheet, the first two columns reflect the financial positions of the respective companies *three* years after acquisition, and the final column reflects the financial position after consolidation:

COMPANY A AND SUBSIDIARY COMPANY B

CONSOLIDATED WORKING PAPERS
STATEMENT OF FINANCIAL POSITION
AS OF DECEMBER 31, 1969

Assets	Company A	Company B	Adjustments Debit	Adjustments Credit	Eliminations Debit	Eliminations Credit	Consolidated Financial Position
Current assets	$115,000	$ 70,000					$185,000
Investment in B	125,000			$12,600		$122,400	(10,000)G
Fixed assets (net)	430,000	100,000					530,000
	$670,000	$170,000					$705,000
Equities							
Current liabilities	$ 50,000	$ 34,000					$ 84,000
Fixed liabilities	80,000						80,000
Shareholders' equity:							
Capital stock:							
Company A	400,000						400,000
Company B		100,000			$ 90,000		10,000MI
Retained earnings:							
Company A	140,000		$12,600				127,400RE
Company B		36,000			32,400		3,600MI
	$670,000	$170,000	$12,600	$12,600	$122,400	$122,400	$705,000

BASIC PROCEDURE

(1) *Establishment of reciprocity:*

Retained earnings (Company A's)	$12,600	
Investment in B		$12,600

(work sheet entry to recognize A's 90% interest in B's $14,000 decrease in shareholders' equity since acquisition)

(2) *Elimination of reciprocals:*

Capital stock (Company B's)	$90,000	
Retained earnings (Company B's)	32,400	
Investment in B		$122,400

(work sheet entry to eliminate 90% of B's shareholders' equity against the investment account)

(3) *Consolidation of nonreciprocals:*

Nonreciprocal elements are extended to the consolidated statement as usual. However, it should be noted that the nonreciprocal portion of the investment account is extended to the consolidated statement as negative goodwill, and the nonreciprocal elements of Company B's shareholders' equity are extended as minority interest. The $10,000 negative goodwill is the same amount as computed at the date of acquisition (see Illustration B-3). It should also be noted that the minority interest has decreased $1,400 ($15,000 minus $13,600). This is due to the minority interest's 10% of the $14,000 decrease in the subsidiary's shareholders' equity since the date of acquisition.

Consolidated Statement of Income and Retained Earnings; Investment Carried at Cost

When reporting for a group of affiliated companies, a consolidated income statement, frequently accompanied by a consolidated statement of retained earnings, is usually prepared and presented along with the consolidated statement of financial position. The consolidated income statement, of course, shows how the consolidated income arose, whereas the consolidated statement of retained earnings serves as a link between the consolidated statement of financial position and the consolidated income statement. These statements may be prepared and presented separately or they may be combined. Combined preparation and presentation is used in this textbook since this approach permits ease of comparison and reconciliation of the two statements.

In order to prepare a consolidated income or retained earnings statement for a group of affiliated companies composed of legally separate entities and to reflect therein the group as one economic unit, all intercompany income and retained earnings transactions must be eliminated. The remaining transactions will then reflect transactions with outsiders. The basic consolidating procedure, therefore, is essentially the same as that used when preparing consolidated statements of financial position: (1) eliminate intercompany transactions through work sheet entries and (2) consolidate nonintercompany transactions. However, after consolidating the nonintercompany transactions, an additional step is required when preparing consolidated income statements. Total net income must be apportioned between the majority or controlling interest and the minority interest.

The following illustrations show how this basic procedure is applied under varying conditions. Although the general facts remain the same, certain specific conditions are changed in each instance. The general situation is the one used in Illustrations B-1 and B-1$_1$: that Company A acquired 90% of the outstanding stock of Company B as of January 1, 1967.

Illustration C-I. *Specific Assumptions:*

A. Company A sold Company B $20,000 worth of merchandise.

B. Company B paid Company A $400 interest.

C. Company B reported a net income of $20,000 for 1967.

COMPANY A AND SUBSIDIARY COMPANY B

CONSOLIDATED WORKING PAPERS
STATEMENT OF INCOME AND RETAINED EARNINGS

YEAR ENDED DECEMBER 31, 1967

Credits	Company A	Company B	Eliminations	Consolidated Income	Consolidated Retained Earnings
Net sales	$800,000	$200,000	$20,000A	$980,000	
Interest income	6,000		400B	5,600	
Totals	$806,000	$200,000	$20,400	$985,600	
Debits					
Cost of sales	$590,000	$130,000	$20,000A	$700,000	
Depreciation	80,000	26,000		106,000	
Interest expense	6,000	2,000	400B	7,600	
Other expenses	10,000	2,000		12,000	
Federal income taxes	60,000	20,000		80,000	
Net income	60,000	20,000		80,000	
Totals	$806,000	$200,000	$20,400	$985,600	
Retained earnings					
1/1/67	$110,000	$50,000			$110,000*
Net income (1967)	60,000	20,000			
Retained earnings					
12/31/67	$170,000	$70,000			

Apportionment of net income:		
Net income	$80,000	
Minority interest (10% of $20,000)	2,000	
Consolidated interest (remainder)	$78,000	78,000
Consolidated retained earnings 12/31/67		$188,000†

* *Note:* Consolidated retained earnings at date of acquisition is composed entirely of the parent company's retained earnings.

† *Proof:* Parent company's $170,000 plus 90% of B's $20,000 increase since acquisition.

BASIC PROCEDURE

(1) *Elimination of intercompany transactions:*

A

Sales	$20,000	
Cost of sales		$20,000

(work sheet elimination of intercompany sales)

B

Interest income	$ 400	
Interest expense		$ 400

(work sheet elimination of intercompany interest)

(2) *Consolidation of nonintercompany transactions:*

Nonintercompany items are consolidated by extending them to the consolidated income statement.

(3) *Apportionment of net income:*

Minority interest (10% of Company B's $20,000).
Majority interest (90% of Company B's $20,000 plus Company A's $60,000).

The last two columns of the above working papers may be presented in statement form as follows:

COMPANY A AND SUBSIDIARY COMPANY B

CONSOLIDATED STATEMENT OF INCOME
AND RETAINED EARNINGS

YEAR ENDED DECEMBER 31, 1967

Income:		
Net sales	$980,000	
Interest income	5,600	
Gross income	$985,600	$985,600
Costs and Expenses:		
Cost of sales	$700,000	
Depreciation	106,000	
Interest expense	7,600	
Other expenses	12,000	
Federal income taxes	80,000	
Total costs and expenses	$905,600	905,600
Total net income		$ 80,000
Minority interest		2,000
Consolidated Net Income		$ 78,000
Consolidated retained earnings 1/1/67		110,000
Consolidated retained earnings 12/31/67		$188,000

Illustration C-2. *Specific Assumptions:*

A. Company A sold Company B $20,000 worth of merchandise.
B. Company B paid Company A $400 interest.
C. Company B declared and paid $10,000 dividends.
D. Company B reported a net income of $30,000 for 1967.

COMPANY A AND SUBSIDIARY COMPANY B

CONSOLIDATED WORKING PAPERS
STATEMENT OF INCOME AND RETAINED EARNINGS

YEAR ENDED DECEMBER 31, 1967

Credits	Company A	Company B	Eliminations	Consolidated Income	Consolidated Retained Earnings
Net sales	$791,000	$210,000	$20,000A	$981,000	
Interest income	6,000		400B	5,600	
Dividend income	9,000		9,000C		
Totals	$806,000	$210,000	$29,400	$986,600	
Debits					
Cost of sales	$590,000	$130,000	$20,000A	$700,000	
Depreciation	80,000	26,000		106,000	
Interest expense	6,000	2,000	400B	7,600	
Other expenses	10,000	2,000		12,000	
Federal income taxes	60,000	20,000		80,000	
Net income	60,000	30,000	9,000C	81,000	
Totals	$806,000	$210,000	$29,400	$986,600	
Retained earnings 1/1/67	$110,000	$50,000			$110,000*
Dividends paid (1967)		(10,000)			
Net income (1967)	60,000	30,000			
Retained earnings 12/31/67	$170,000	$70,000			

Apportionment of net income:		
Net income	$81,000	
Minority interest (10% of $30,000)	3,000	
Consolidated interest (remainder)	$78,000	78,000
Consolidated retained earnings 12/31/67		$188,000†

* *Note:* Consolidated retained earnings at date of acquisition is composed entirely of the parent company's retained earnings.

† *Proof:* Parent company's $170,000 plus 90% of B's $20,000 increase since acquisition.

BASIC PROCEDURE.

(1) *Elimination of intercompany transactions:*

A

Sales	$20,000	
Cost of sales		$20,000

(work sheet elimination of intercompany sales)

B

Interest income	$ 400	
Interest expense		$ 400

(work sheet elimination of intercompany interest)

C

Dividend income	$9,000	
Net income		$9,000

(work sheet elimination of intercompany dividend)

(2) *Consolidation of nonintercompany transactions:*

Nonintercompany items are consolidated by extending them to the consolidated income statement.

(3) *Apportionment of net income:*

Minority interest (10% of Company B's $30,000).

Majority interest (90% of Company B's $30,000 plus Company A's $60,000 minus $9,000 intercompany income).

The last two columns of the working papers may be presented in statement form as follows:

COMPANY A AND SUBSIDIARY COMPANY B

CONSOLIDATED STATEMENT OF INCOME AND RETAINED EARNINGS

YEAR ENDED DECEMBER 31, 1967

Income:		
Net sales	$981,000	
Interest income	5,600	
Gross income	$986,600	$986,600
Costs and Expenses:		
Cost of sales	$700,000	
Depreciation	106,000	
Interest expense	7,600	
Other expenses	12,000	
Federal income taxes	80,000	
Total costs and expenses	$905,600	905,600
Total net income		$ 81,000
Minority interest		3,000
Consolidated Net Income		$ 78,000
Consolidated retained earnings 1/1/67		110,000
Consolidated retained earnings 12/31/67		$188,000

Trial Balance Approach

In the preceding illustrations consolidated statements have been prepared from the financial statements of the respective companies involved. This procedure is frequently used in practice. However, consolidated statements may be prepared from trial balances as well as from the financial statements. Regardless of the approach used, the basic procedure remains the same: establish reciprocity when necessary, eliminate reciprocals, and consolidate nonreciprocals.

The following examples illustrate the basic procedure involved in three slightly different, but fundamentally important, situations:

Illustration D-1. This illustration is based on the same basic data used in Illustrations B-1, B-1$_1$, and C-1.

Illustration D-2. The general situation in this illustration is the same as that used in Illustration D-1: that Company A acquired 90% of the outstanding stock of Company B as of January 1, 1967. However, in this instance consolidation is taking place at the end of 1968 instead of at the end of 1967. It is also assumed that no intercompany transactions arose in 1968.

In this illustration particular attention should be given to the establishment of reciprocity. When the trial balance approach is used, reciprocity must be established as of the beginning of the period rather than as of the end of the period, as is the procedure when the statement approach is used. This modification in the basic procedure is necessary because consolidated net income is added to the beginning balance of consolidated retained earnings in the working papers. If reciprocity were established as of the end of the period, the parent company's share of a subsidiary's earnings for the period would be taken into consolidated retained earnings twice. The basic procedure when using the trial balance approach, therefore, includes:

(1) the establishment of reciprocity, if necessary, as of the beginning of the period.
(2) The elimination of reciprocals.
(3) The consolidation of nonreciprocals.

Illustration D-3. The general situation in this illustration is the same as the one used in Illustrations D-1 and D-2: that Company A acquired 90% of the outstanding stock of Company B as of January 1, 1967. However, in this instance consolidation is taking place at the end of 1969 rather than 1967 or 1968, and Companies A and B submit unadjusted trial balances rather than adjusted ones. Particular attention should be given not only to the establishment of reciprocity but also to the treatment of inventories. In addition to the data in the respective trial balances, Company A reports an ending inventory of $90,000 and Company B one of $60,000.

COMPANY A AND SUBSIDIARY COMPANY B

CONSOLIDATED WORKING PAPERS

DECEMBER 31, 1967

Debits	Company A	Company B	Eliminations Debit	Eliminations Credit
Current assets	$115,000	$ 80,000		
Investment in B	135,000			$135,000*C*
Fixed assets (net)	450,000	110,000		
Cost of sales	590,000	130,000		20,000*A*
Depreciation	80,000	26,000		
Interest expense	6,000	2,000		400*B*
Other expenses	10,000	2,000		
Federal income taxes	60,000	20,000		
	$1,446,000	$370,000		
Credits				
Current liabilities	$ 30,000	$ 20,000		
Fixed liabilities	100,000			
Net sales	800,000	200,000	$ 20,000*A*	
Interest income	6,000		400*B*	
Capital stock:				
Company A	400,000			
Company B		100,000	90,000*C*	
Retained earnings:				
Company A 1/1/67	110,000			
Company B 1/1/67		50,000	45,000*C*	
	$1,446,000	$370,000	$155,400	$155,400

Income credits
Income debits

Net income
Apportionment of net income:
  Minority interest:

Subsidiary income credits	$200,000	
Subsidiary income debits	$180,000	
Subsidiary net income	$ 20,000	
Minority interest (10%)	2,000	

Consolidated net income (remainder)

Retained earnings 12/31/67

Minority interest 12/31/67

A: To eliminate intercompany sales.
B: To eliminate intercompany interest.
C: To eliminate 90% of B's shareholders' equity against the investment account.

COMPANY A AND SUBSIDIARY COMPANY B
CONSOLIDATED WORKING PAPERS
(Continued—Illustration D-1)

Consolidated Income	Consolidated Retained Earnings	Minority Interest	Consolidated Financial Position
			$195,000
			560,000
$700,000			
106,000			
7,600			
12,000			
80,000			
$905,600	–0–	–0–	$755,000
			$ 50,000
			100,000
$980,000			
5,600			
			400,000
		$10,000	
	$110,000		
		5,000	
$985,600			
905,600			
$ 80,000			
2,000		2,000	
$ 78,000	78,000		
	$188,000		188,000RE
		$17,000	17,000MI
			$755,000

311

COMPANY A AND SUBSIDIARY COMPANY B

CONSOLIDATED WORKING PAPERS

DECEMBER 31, 1968

Debits	Company A	Company B	Adjustments and Eliminations* Debit	Adjustments and Eliminations* Credit
Current assets	$ 205,000	$154,000		
Investment in B	135,000		$18,000(1)	$153,000*A*
Fixed assets (net)	460,000	100,000		
Cost of sales	650,000	170,000		
Depreciation	85,000	28,000		
Interest expense	6,000			
Other expenses	14,000	3,000		
Federal income taxes	75,000	45,000		
	$1,630,000	$500,000		
Credits				
Current liabilities	$ 60,000	$ 30,000		
Fixed liabilities	100,000			
Net sales	900,000	300,000		
Capital stock:				
Company A	400,000			
Company B		100,000	90,000*A*	
Retained earnings:				
Company A 1/1/68	170,000			18,000(1)
Company B 1/1/68		70,000	63,000*A*	
	$1,630,000	$500,000	$171,000	$171,000

Income credits
Income debits

Net income
Apportionment of net income:
  Minority interest:

Subsidiary income credits	$300,000	
Subsidiary income debits	246,000	
Subsidiary net income	$ 54,000	
Minority interest (10%)	5,400	

Consolidated net income (remainder)

Retained earnings 12/31/68

Minority interest 12/31/68

(1): To establish reciprocity by recognizing A's 90% interest in the $20,000 increase in B's shareholders' equity from the date of acquisition to the beginning of the current period.

A: To eliminate 90% of B's shareholders' equity (as of the beginning of the period) against the investment account.

Consolidated Income	Consolidated Retained Earnings	Minority Interest	Consolidated Financial Position
			$359,000
			560,000
$ 820,000			
113,000			
6,000			
17,000			
120,000			
$1,076,000	–0–	–0–	$919,000
			$ 90,000
			100,000
$1,200,000			
			400,000
		$10,000	
	$188,000		
		7,000	
$1,200,000			
1,076,000			
$ 124,000			
5,400		5,400	
$ 118,600	118,600		
	$306,600		306,600RE
		$22,400	22,400MI
			$919,000

* Here and in subsequent chapters adjustments and eliminations will be placed in the same work sheet columns. In order to distinguish between them, adjustments will be *numbered* and eliminations will be *lettered*.

Company A and Subsidiary Company B
CONSOLIDATED WORKING PAPERS
December 31, 1969

Debits	Company A	Company B	Adjustments and Eliminations Debit	Credit
Inventories 1/1/69	$ 70,000	$ 40,000		
Other current assets	208,000	158,000		
Investment in B	135,000		$ 66,600(2)	$201,600*B*
Fixed assets (net)	490,000	105,000		
Purchases	700,000	200,000		
Depreciation	84,000	30,000		
Other expenses	100,000	70,000		
Dividends paid	32,000	10,000		9,000*A*
	$1,819,000	$613,000		
Inventories 12/31/69			150,000(1)	
Credits				
Current liabilities	$ 90,000	$ 39,000		
Fixed liabilities	100,000			
Net sales	980,000	350,000		
Dividend income	9,000		9,000*A*	
Capital stock:				
Company A	400,000			
Company B		100,000	90,000*B*	
Retained earnings:				
Company A 1/1/69	240,000			66,600(2)
Company B 1/1/69		124,000	111,600*B*	
	$1,819,000	$613,000		
Inventories 12/31/69	$ 90,000	$ 60,000		150,000(1)
			$427,200	$427,200

Income credits
Income debits

Net income
Apportionment of net income:
  Minority interest:

Subsidiary income credits	$410,000		
Subsidiary income debits	340,000		
Subsidiary net income	$ 70,000		
Minority interest (10%)	7,000		

Consolidated net income (remainder)

Retained earnings 12/31/69

Minority interest 12/31/69

(1): To record ending inventories.
(2): To establish reciprocity by recognizing A's 90% interest in the $74,000 increase in B's shareholders' equity from the date of acquisition to the beginning of the current period.
A: To eliminate intercompany dividends.
B: To eliminate 90% of B's shareholders' equity against the investment account.

CONSOLIDATED WORKING PAPERS
(Continued—Illustration D-3)

Consolidated Income	Consolidated Retained Earnings	Minority Interest	Consolidated Financial Position
$ 110,000			
			$ 366,000
			595,000
900,000			
114,000			
170,000			
	$ 32,000	$ 1,000	
			150,000
$1,294,000	$ 32,000	$ 1,000	$1,111,000
			$ 129,000
			100,000
$1,330,000			
			400,000
		$10,000	
	$306,600		
		12,400	
150,000			
1,480,000			
1,294,000			
$ 186,000			
7,000		7,000	
$ 179,000	179,000		
	$485,600		
	32,000		
	$453,600		453,600RE
		$29,400	
		1,000	
		$28,400	28,400MI
			$1,111,000

PROBLEMS

Problem 11–1. Using the following basic data and the specific assumption given in each instance, for each case:

(*a*) Prepare the work sheet entry(ies) necessary when establishing reciprocity as of 12/31/68.

(*b*) Prepare the work sheet entry(ies) necessary when eliminating reciprocals as of 12/31/68.

(*c*) Determine the amount of goodwill (positive or negative) as of 12/31/68.

(*d*) Determine the amount of minority interest as of 12/31/68.

(*e*) Determine the amount of consolidated retained earnings as of 12/31/68.

BASIC DATA

	Company X	Company Y	Company Z
Balances as of 1/1/66			
Capital stock	$200,000	$75,000	$60,000
Retained earnings (deficit)	100,000	40,000	(10,000)
Paid-in surplus	20,000	15,000	5,000
Balances as of 12/31/68			
Capital stock	$200,000	$75,000	$60,000
Retained earnings	190,000	75,000	15,000
Paid-in surplus	20,000	15,000	5,000

Case 1. Assume that Company X acquired 90% of the stock of Company Y for $120,000 as of 1/1/66. Company X carries its investment in Y at *cost*.

Case 2. Assume that Company X acquired 80% of the stock of Company Z for $40,000 as of 1/1/66. Company X carries its investment in Z at *cost*.

Case 3. Assume that Company X acquired 80% of the stock of Company Y and 90% of the stock of Company Z for $105,000 and $46,000, respectively, as of 1/1/66. Company X carries these investments at *cost*.

Case 4. Assume that Company Y acquired 75% of the stock of Company Z for $35,000 as of 1/1/66. Company Y carries its investment in Z at *cost*.

Note: All cases are independent.

Problem 11–2. From the following data determine in each case:

(1) Minority interest at date of acquisition and at the date of consolidation.

(2) Goodwill (either positive or negative) at date of acquisition and at the date of consolidation.

(3) Consolidated retained earnings at date of acquisition and at the date of consolidation.

Assume that the parent company's retained earnings amount to $200,000 in all cases.

Subsidiary Company

			Acquisition Date		Consolidation Date	
	Company and % Owned	Cost	Capital Stock	Retained Earnings	Capital Stock	Retained Earnings
Case 1	A 90%	$140,000	$100,000	$50,000	$100,000	$70,000
Case 2	B 85%	104,000	100,000	30,000	100,000	20,000
Case 3	C 80%	56,000	50,000	20,000	50,000	20,000
Case 4	D 100%	100,000	50,000	40,000	50,000	55,000

Problem 11–3. XYZ, Incorporated, purchased an 80% interest in the ABC Company on January 1, 1966, for $140,000. The shareholders' equity of the ABC Company on January 1, 1966, was composed of capital stock, $100,000, and retained earnings, $60,000. XYZ, Incorporated, carries the investment account at cost. On December 31, 1966, the ABC Company announced a profit of $20,000 for 1966 and at the same time declared and paid a dividend of $30,000.

Required:
(1) Show in entry form how the dividend should be recorded on the books of XYZ, Incorporated.
(2) What is the amount of goodwill from consolidation as of (*a*) January 1, 1966, and (*b*) December 31, 1966?
(3) What is the amount of minority interest as of (*a*) January 1, 1966, and (*b*) December 31, 1966?

Problem 11–4. Company A purchases 80% of the stock of Company B for $160,000. Company B has outstanding stock of $100,000 and surplus of $100,000. Company B subsequently earns a profit of $10,000 and distributes a dividend of $30,000. Company A records the receipt of dividends by a debit to Cash and a credit to Retained Earnings of $24,000.

Required:
(1) Assuming that the investment is carried at cost, give the correct entry which should have been made on Company A's books to record the receipt of the dividend.
(2) Discuss fully the faults of the original entry.
(3) Assume that Company A purchased only 5 per cent of the stock of B as a temporary investment and that B subsequently earns $10,000 and distributes a dividend of $30,000. State how Company A should record receipt of the dividend. If the principle applicable is different from in (1) give the reason.
(AICPA adapted)

Problem 11–5. From the following statements and data:
(1) Prepare a consolidated statement of financial position, and
(2) Prove the goodwill elements.

Assets	A Company	B Company	C Company	D Company	E Company
Current assets	$ 960,000	$ 50,000	$ 80,000	$ 76,000	$ 60,000
Subsidiaries (cost):					
B Company (90%)	88,000				
C Company (80%)	42,000				
D Company (70%)	60,000				
E Company (60%)	35,000				
Other assets	410,000	80,000	75,000	35,000	45,000
	$1,595,000	$130,000	$155,000	$111,000	$105,000
Equities					
Current liabilities	$ 310,000	$ 24,000	$ 85,000	$ 16,000	$ 61,000
Fixed liabilities	200,000				
Capital stock	500,000	75,000	60,000	60,000	50,000
Retained earnings					
(deficit)	585,000	31,000	10,000	35,000	(6,000)
	$1,595,000	$130,000	$155,000	$111,000	$105,000

Shareholders' equities as of date of acquisition:

	B	C	D	E
Capital stock	$ 75,000	$ 60,000	$ 60,000	$ 50,000
Retained earnings				
(deficit)	21,000	(5,000)	14,000	12,000

Problem 11–6. Company A acquired a 90% interest in Company B and an 80% interest in Company C on January 1, 1967. Company A carries its investments in these companies at cost. From the following data prepare working papers in columnar form showing (1) consolidated income for 1967, and (2) consolidated retained earnings as of December 31, 1967.

STATEMENT OF INCOME
FOR THE YEAR ENDED DECEMBER 31, 1967

	Company A	Company B	Company C
Income:			
Sales (net)	$1,478,000	$150,800	$162,000
Dividends	20,000		
Interest	12,000	1,200	
	$1,510,000	$152,000	$162,000
Deductions:			
Cost of sales	$ 750,000	$ 74,000	$ 77,000
Selling expenses	300,000	29,000	32,000
General expenses	150,000	14,000	13,000
Taxes	166,000	15,000	16,000
	$1,366,000	$132,000	$138,000
Net Income	$ 144,000	$ 20,000	$ 24,000

STATEMENT OF RETAINED EARNINGS
As of December 31, 1967

	Company A	Company B	Company C
Balance 1/1/67	$463,000	$68,000	$51,000
Net income for year	144,000	20,000	24,000
Dividends paid	(30,000)	(10,000)	(12,000)
Balance 12/31/67	$577,000	$78,000	$63,000

Intercompany transactions:
(1) Company A purchased merchandise from Company B for $50,000.
(2) Company B purchased merchandise from Company C for $15,000.
(3) Company C paid Company A $600 interest.

Problem 11–7. From the following comparative statements of financial position prepare:
(1) A consolidated statement of financial position as of December 31, 1966, the date Company A acquired a 90% interest in Company B, and
(2) A consolidated statement of financial position as of December 31, 1967.

Company A
STATEMENT OF FINANCIAL POSITION

Assets	Dec. 31, 1966	Dec. 31, 1967
Current assets	$200,000	$240,000
Investment in Company B (Cost)	72,000	72,000
Property, plant, and equipment (net)	340,000	310,000
Other assets	4,000	5,000
	$616,000	$627,000

Equities		
Current liabilities	$200,000	$170,000
Capital stock	200,000	200,000
Retained earnings	216,000	257,000
	$616,000	$627,000

Company B
STATEMENT OF FINANCIAL POSITION

Assets	Dec. 31, 1966	Dec. 31, 1967
Current assets	$22,000	$47,000
Property, plant, and equipment (net)	45,000	42,000
Other assets	9,000	10,000
	$76,000	$99,000

Equities		
Current liabilities	$18,000	$20,000
Capital stock	50,000	50,000
Retained earnings	8,000	29,000
	$76,000	$99,000

Problem 11–8. Prepare consolidated working papers with columns for income, retained earnings, minority interest, and financial position for the year ended December 31, from the following data:

Ninety-two per cent of the stock of Co. S was acquired for $145,000 in 1966, when Co. S's shareholders' equity was composed of $50,000 retained earnings and $100,000 capital stock.

ADJUSTED TRIAL BALANCES
DECEMBER 31, 1967

Debits	Co. P	Co. S
Merchandise inventory	$ 40,000	$ 20,000
Investment in Co. S	145,000	
Other assets	520,000	270,000
Cost of sales	390,000	140,000
Expenses	110,000	65,000
Dividends paid	20,000	10,000
	$1,225,000	$505,000
Credits		
Sales	$ 620,000	$245,000
Dividend income	9,200	
Liabilities	290,000	90,000
Capital stock	200,000	100,000
Retained earnings, 1/1/67	105,800	70,000
	$1,225,000	$505,000

Problem 11–9. From the following data prepare consolidated working papers with columns for income, retained earnings, minority interest, and financial position for the year ended December 31, 1967:

TRIAL BALANCES
DECEMBER 31, 1967

Debits	Company A	Company B
Inventories 1/1/67	$ 60,000	$ 32,000
Investment in Company B	170,000	
Other assets (net)	630,000	285,000
Purchases	395,000	145,000
Expenses	125,000	68,000
Dividends paid	18,000	6,000
	$1,398,000	$536,000
Credits		
Sales	$ 605,840	$258,000
Dividend income	5,160	
Liabilities	280,000	70,000
Capital stock	300,000	100,000
Retained earnings 1/1/67	207,000	108,000
	$1,398,000	$536,000

Inventories, December 31, 1967:	Company A	$64,000
	Company B	29,000
		$93,000

Eighty-six per cent of the stock of Company B was acquired for $170,000 on January 1, 1966, when Company B's shareholders' equity was composed of $80,000 retained earnings and $100,000 capital stock.

Problem 11–10. From the following data prepare a consolidated statement of financial position as of June 30, 1968:

Assets	A Company	B Company	C Company
Cash	$ 10,000	$ 6,000	$ 2,500
Notes receivable	7,000	3,000	
Accounts receivable	36,000	15,000	7,500
Merchandise inventories	20,000	10,000	5,000
Investments:			
B Company	30,000		
C Company	28,000		
Land	18,000		5,000
Buildings, plant, and equipment	76,000	35,000	35,000
Deficit			4,000
Totals	$225,000	$69,000	$59,000
Liabilities and Capital			
Notes payable	$ 12,000	$ 6,000	$ 8,000
Accounts payable	18,000	7,500	9,000
Bonds payable	50,000	15,000	
Reserves for depreciation	25,000	9,000	7,000
Capital stock	100,000	25,000	35,000
Retained earnings	20,000	6,500	
Totals	$225,000	$69,000	$59,000

The holding company acquired 90% of the capital stock of the B Company, July 1, 1965, at a cost of $28,000, and later arbitrarily increased the book value of this asset to $30,000, crediting the increase to retained earnings. Eighty per cent of the capital stock of C Company was acquired at a cost of $28,000 when that company was organized, July 1, 1966.

The intercompany accounts at June 30, 1968, were as follows:

A Company held notes of the B Company for $3,000 and the C Company for $4,000.

B Company held a note of the C Company for $3,000.

A Company owed on open account to the B Company $4,000 and to the C Company $2,500.

The retained earnings accounts of the subsidiary companies, analyzed, were as follows:

	B Company	C Company
Balance, July 1, 1965	$4,000	
Profit, 1965–1966	3,000	
Balance, July 1, 1966	$7,000	
Profit or loss, 1966–1967	−1,500	− $5,000
Balance, July 1, 1967	$5,500	− $5,000
Profit, 1967–1968	1,000	1,000
Balance, June 30, 1968	$6,500	− $4,000

Consolidated statements subsequent to date of acquisition—investment not carried at cost

The question of when earnings and losses of a company are realized by owners of the company's stock is not clear-cut when a parent-subsidiary relationship exists. The normal accounting rule that income on a stock investment is not realized until a dividend is declared may not be applicable. Whether or not a subsidiary company pays a dividend may depend upon the orders of the parent company. In a sense the earnings of the subsidiary may be available to the parent company at any time. This has led some parent companies to carry their investment in a subsidiary as though earnings of the subsidiary applicable to the parent's investment had been realized by the parent as soon as earned by the subsidiary. This method of carrying the investment is normally referred to as the "equity" or "book value" method.

EQUITY METHOD

When the equity method is used, the investment is recorded at cost when acquired. In contrast to the cost method, however, the parent company's share of increases and decreases in the subsidiary's shareholders' equity is reflected on the parent company's books by periodic entries. Thus, if a parent company owns 90% of the outstanding stock of a subsidiary, it will debit its investment account and credit an income account for 90% of the income reported by the subsidiary.

The following example illustrates the periodic entries which would be recorded on the parent company's books when the equity method is used. For comparative purposes, the cost method is also illustrated.

   (1) January 1, 1967, Company A purchases a 90% interest in Company B for $150,000.
   (2) December 31, 1967, Company B reports $50,000 net income for 1967.
   (3) March 31, 1968, Company B pays $20,000 dividend.
   (4) December 31, 1968, Company B reports $10,000 loss for 1968.

EQUITY METHOD		COST METHOD	
(1) *Purchase*			
Investment in Co. B $150,000		Same entry	
Cash	$150,000		
(2) *1967 Net Income*			
Investment in Co. B $45,000		No entry	
Subsidiary income	$45,000		
(3) *Dividend Received*			
Cash	$18,000	Cash	$18,000
Investment in Co. B	$18,000	Dividend income	$18,000
(4) *1968 Net Loss*			
Subsidiary loss $9,000		No entry	
Investment in Co. B	$9,000		

Consolidated Statement of Financial Position
Equity Method

Basic Consolidating Procedure. As indicated in the preceding chapter, the basic procedure when consolidating statements of financial position subsequent to the date of acquisition is essentially the same as when consolidating at the date of acquisition: (1) eliminate reciprocals, and (2) consolidate nonreciprocals. When the investment is carried at cost, however, reciprocity between the parent's investment and the subsidiary shareholders' equity usually must be established before elimination is possible. This is not always the case when the equity method is used. If *all* increases and decreases in the subsidiary's shareholders' equity have been reflected on the parent company's books, reciprocity already exists. If for some reason all of the subsidiary increases and decreases have not been reflected on the parent company's books, reciprocity must be established. For example, if the subsidiary has declared but not paid a dividend, and if the parent makes no entry until the dividend is paid, an adjustment would be necessary in order to establish reciprocity. The parent would have no account on its books reciprocal to the dividend payable on the subsidiary's books, and likewise the decrease in the subsidiary's retained earnings would not be reflected on the parent's books. Thus the basic consolidating procedure is essentially the same when either the cost or the equity method is used, that is:

(1) Establish reciprocity, if necessary.
(2) Eliminate reciprocals.
(3) Consolidate nonreciprocals.

The following illustrations demonstrate the techniques of consolidating statements of financial position subsequent to the date of acquisition when the equity method is used. In these illustrations the same general conditions are assumed to exist as were used in the preceding chapter, as follows:

A. 100% Ownership:
     (1) Purchased at book value.
     (2) Purchased at more than book value.
     (3) Purchased at less than book value.

B. Less than 100% Ownership:
     (1) Purchased at book value.
     (2) Purchased at more than book value.
     (3) Purchased at less than book value.

100% Ownership

Illustration A-1$_{1(a)}$: 100% Ownership Acquired at Book Value. Assume the same facts as used in Illustration A-1$_1$ (page 294), that as of January 1, 1967, Company A acquired 100% ownership in Company B for $150,000, which was also the book value of the interest acquired. In the following work sheet the first two columns reflect the financial positions of the respective companies *one* year later, and the final column reflects the financial position after consolidation.

BASIC PROCEDURE

(1) *Establishment of reciprocity, if necessary:*

     Since Company A has taken up the $20,000 increase in Company B's shareholders' equity since acquisition ($150,000 to $170,000), reciprocity exists and no adjustment is necessary.

(2) *Elimination of reciprocals:*

A

Capital stock (Company B's)	$100,000	
Retained earnings (Company B's)	70,000	
Investment in B		$170,000

(work sheet entry to eliminate 100% of B's shareholders' equity against the investment account)

It should be noted that this is the same elimination which was made in Illustration A-1_1 when the investment account was carried at cost. This is so because the establishment of reciprocity reconciles the two methods.

(3) *Consolidation of nonreciprocals:*

The nonreciprocal elements are consolidated by extending them to the consolidated statement as is done when the investment account is carried at cost. Although the individual company statements are different, the consolidated statements are exactly the same whether the investment is carried at cost or at equity. Consolidated retained earnings under both procedures is the parent company's retained earnings.

COMPANY A AND SUBSIDIARY COMPANY B

CONSOLIDATED WORKING PAPERS
STATEMENT OF FINANCIAL POSITION
AS OF DECEMBER 31, 1967

Assets	Company A	Company B	Debit	Credit	Consolidated Financial Position
Current assets	$100,000	$ 80,000			$180,000
Investment in B	170,000			$170,000A	
Fixed assets (net)	450,000	110,000			560,000
	$720,000	$190,000			$740,000
Equities					
Current liabilities	$ 30,000	$ 20,000			$ 50,000
Fixed liabilities	100,000				100,000
Shareholders' equity:					
Capital stock:					
Company A	400,000				400,000
Company B		100,000	$100,000A		
Retained earnings:					
Company A	190,000				190,000RE
Company B		70,000	70,000A		
	$720,000	$190,000	$170,000	$170,000	$740,000

Illustration A-$2_{1(a)}$: 100% Ownership Acquired at More Than Book Value. Assume the same facts as used in Illustration A-2_1 (page 296), that as of January 1, 1967, Company A acquired 100% ownership in Company B for $170,000 which was $20,000 more than the book value acquired. The following work sheet reflects the financial position of the respective companies *two* years later and how they would appear when consolidated at that time:

COMPANY A AND SUBSIDIARY COMPANY B

CONSOLIDATED WORKING PAPERS
STATEMENT OF FINANCIAL POSITION

AS OF DECEMBER 31, 1968

Assets	Company A	Company B	Adjustments & Eliminations Debit	Adjustments & Eliminations Credit	Consolidated Financial Position
Current assets	$120,000	$ 90,000			$210,000
Investment in B	185,000			$165,000A	20,000G
Fixed assets (net)	440,000	105,000			545,000
	$745,000	$195,000			· $775,000
Equities					
Current liabilities	$ 40,000	$ 30,000			$ 70,000
Fixed liabilities	90,000				90,000
Shareholders' equity:					
Capital stock:					
Company A	400,000				400,000
Company B		100,000	$100,000A		
Retained earnings:					
Company A	215,000				215,000RE
Company B		65,000	65,000A		
	$745,000	$195,000	$165,000	$165,000	$775,000

BASIC PROCEDURE

(1) *Establishment of reciprocity:*

Since Company A has taken up its share (100% of $15,000) of Company B's increase in shareholders' equity since acquisition ($150,000 to $165,000), reciprocity exists and no adjustment is needed.

(2) *Elimination of reciprocals:*

$$A$$

Capital stock (Company B's)	$100,000
Retained earnings (Company B's)	65,000
Investment in B	$165,000

(work sheet entry to eliminate 100% of B's share-holders' equity against the investment account)

(3) *Consolidation of nonreciprocals:*

Nonreciprocals are consolidated as they have been in preceding illustrations. It should be noted, however, that, as in Illustrations A-2 and A-2_1, the nonreciprocal portion of the investment account extended to the consolidated statement is the same, $20,000.

Illustration A-3$_{1(a)}$: 100% Ownership Acquired at Less Than Book Value. The facts in Illustration A-3$_1$ (page 297), that on January 1, 1967, Company A acquired 100% ownership of Company B for $140,000 which was $10,000 less than the book value acquired, are used in the following discussion. In the work sheet the first two columns reflect the financial positions of Companies A and B *three* years after acquisition, and the final column reflects the financial position after consolidation.

COMPANY A AND SUBSIDIARY COMPANY B

CONSOLIDATED WORKING PAPERS
STATEMENT OF FINANCIAL POSITION
AS OF DECEMBER 31, 1969

	Company A	Company B	Debit	Credit	Consolidated Financial Position
Assets					
Current assets	$100,000	$ 70,000			$170,000
Investment in B	126,000			$136,000A	(10,000)G
Fixed assets (net)	430,000	100,000			530,000
	$656,000	$170,000			$690,000
Equities					
Current liabilities	$ 50,000	$ 34,000			$ 84,000
Fixed liabilities	80,000				80,000
Shareholders' equity:					
Capital stock:					
Company A	400,000				400,000
Company B		100,000	$100,000A		
Retained earnings:					
Company A	126,000				126,000RE
Company B		36,000	36,000A		
	$656,000	$170,000	$136,000	$136,000	$690,000

BASIC PROCEDURE

(1) *Establishment of reciprocity:*

No entry is necessary since reciprocity already exists.

(2) *Elimination of reciprocals:*

A

Capital stock (Company B's)	$100,000	
Retained earnings (Company B's)	36,000	
Investment in B		$136,000

(work sheet entry to eliminate 100% of B's shareholders' equity against the investment account)

(3) *Consolidation of nonreciprocals:*

Consolidation of nonreciprocals is the same as in preceding illustrations. The nonreciprocal portion of the elimination against the investment, however, is consolidated as negative goodwill as it was treated in Illustrations A-3 and A-3$_1$. This is, of course, the same amount as existed at the date of acquisition, since the goodwill element does not change unless it is disposed of, either partially or in its entirety, by sale or otherwise.

Less Than 100% Ownership

Illustration B-1$_{1(a)}$: Less Than 100% Ownership Acquired at Book Value. Assume the same basic facts as used in Illustration B-1$_1$ (page 299), that on January 1, 1967, Company A acquired a 90% interest in Company B for $135,000. This was also the book value at that date of the interest acquired. In the following work sheet the first two columns reflect the financial position of the respective companies *one* year later, and the final column reflects the financial position after consolidation.

COMPANY A AND SUBSIDIARY COMPANY B

CONSOLIDATED WORKING PAPERS
STATEMENT OF FINANCIAL POSITION

AS OF DECEMBER 31, 1967

Assets	Company A	Company B	Adjustments & Eliminations Debit	Adjustments & Eliminations Credit	Consolidated Financial Position
Current assets	$115,000	$ 80,000			$195,000
Investment in B	153,000			$153,000A	
Fixed assets (net)	450,000	110,000			560,000
	$718,000	$190,000			$755,000
Equities					
Current liabilities	$ 30,000	$ 20,000			$ 50,000
Fixed liabilities	100,000				100,000
Shareholders' equity:					
Capital stock:					
Company A	400,000				400,000
Company B		100,000	$ 90,000A		10,000MI
Retained earnings:					
Company A	188,000				188,000RE
Company B		70,000	63,000A		7,000MI
	$718,000	$190,000	$153,000	$153,000	$755,000

BASIC PROCEDURE

(1) *Establishment of reciprocity:*

Because Company A has taken up its share (90%) of the $20,000 increase in Company B's shareholders' equity since acquisition ($150,000 to $170,000), reciprocity exists and therefore no adjustment is necessary.

(2) *Elimination of reciprocals:*

A

Capital stock (Company B's)	$90,000	
Retained earnings (Company B's)	63,000	
Investment in B		$153,000

(work sheet entry to eliminate 90% of B's shareholders' equity against the investment account)

(3) *Consolidation of nonreciprocals:*

Nonreciprocals are consolidated in the usual manner. It should be noted that the nonreciprocal elements of the subsidiary's shareholders' equity are extended to the consolidated statement as minority interest. If the minority interest in this illustration is compared with that in Illustration B-1$_1$ where the cost method was in use, it will be seen that the minority interest is the same regardless of the method used for carrying the investment account.

Illustration B-2$_{1(a)}$: Less Than 100% Ownership Acquired at More Than Book Value. Assume the same basic facts as used in Illustration B-2 (page 276), that on January 1, 1967, Company A acquired a 90% interest in Company B for $155,000 which was $20,000 more than the book value acquired. The individual statements in the following work sheet reflect the financial position as reported by the respective companies on December 31, 1968. However, a $10,000 dividend declared by Company B as of December 31, 1968, is not reflected on Company A's statement.

BASIC PROCEDURE

(1) *Establishment of reciprocity:*

(1)

Dividends receivable	$9,000	
Investment in B		$9,000

(work sheet entry to recognize A's share of B's dividend declared December 31, 1968)

(2) *Elimination of reciprocals:*

A

Dividends payable	$9,000	
Dividends receivable		$9,000

(work sheet entry to eliminate dividends receivable and dividends payable)

B

Capital stock (Company B's)	$90,000	
Retained earnings (Company B's)	58,500	
Investment in B		$148,500

(work sheet entry to eliminate 90% of B's shareholders' equity against the investment account)

(3) *Consolidation of nonreciprocals:*

Nonreciprocals are consolidated in the usual manner. It should be noted that the nonreciprocal element of the subsidiary's shareholders' equity is extended to the consolidated statement as minority interest. If the minority interest in this illustration is compared with that in Illustration B-2_1 where the cost method is used, it will be seen that the minority interest is the same regardless of the method used for carrying the investment account.

COMPANY A AND SUBSIDIARY COMPANY B
CONSOLIDATED WORKING PAPERS
STATEMENT OF FINANCIAL POSITION
AS OF DECEMBER 31, 1968

	Company A	Company B	Adjustments & Eliminations Debit	Adjustments & Eliminations Credit	Consolidated Financial Position
Assets					
Cash	$ 35,000	$ 40,000			$ 75,000
Inventories	100,000	50,000			150,000
Dividends receivable			$ 9,000(1)	$ 9,000A	
Investment in B	177,500			9,000(1)	20,000G
				148,500B	
Fixed assets (net)	440,000	105,000			545,000
	$752,500	$195,000			$790,000
Equities					
Accounts payable	$ 40,000	$ 20,000			$ 60,000
Dividends payable		10,000	9,000A		1,000
Fixed liabilities	90,000				90,000
Shareholders' equity:					
Capital stock:					
Company A	400,000				400,000
Company B		100,000	90,000B		10,000MI
Retained earnings:					
Company A	222,500				222,500RE
Company B		65,000	58,500B		6,500MI
	$752,500	$195,000	$166,500	$166,500	$790,000

Illustration B-$3_{1(a)}$: Less Than 100% Ownership Acquired at Less Than Book Value.

Assume the same basic facts as used in Illustration B-3_1 (page 302), that on January 1, 1967, Company A acquired a 90% interest in Company B for $125,000, which was $10,000 less than the book value acquired. The individual statements in the following work sheet reflect the financial position as reported by the respective companies as of December 31, 1969. However, during 1969 Company B charged a $10,000 loss on disposal of fixed assets directly to retained earnings. Since Company A has taken up its share of Company B's 1969 income (loss) as reported on Company B's income statement, this item is not reflected on Company A's books.

COMPANY A AND SUBSIDIARY COMPANY B
CONSOLIDATED WORKING PAPERS
STATEMENT OF FINANCIAL POSITION
AS OF DECEMBER 31, 1969

	Company A	Company B	Adjustments & Eliminations Debit	Credit	Consolidated Financial Position
Assets					
Current assets	$115,000	$70,000			$185,000
Investment in B	121,400			{$ 9,000(1) 122,400A	(10,000)G
Fixed assets (net)	430,000	100,000			530,000
	$666,400	$170,000			$705,000
Equities					
Current liabilities	$ 50,000	$ 34,000			$ 84,000
Fixed liabilities	80,000				80,000
Shareholders' equity:					
Capital stock:					
Company A	400,000				400,000
Company B		100,000	$ 90,000A		10,000MI
Retained earnings:					
Company A	136,400			9,000(1)	127,400RE
Company B		36,000	32,400A		3,600MI
	$666,400	$170,000	$131,400	$131,400	$705,000

BASIC PROCEDURE

(1) *Establishment of reciprocity:*

(1)

Retained earnings (Company A's) $9,000
    Investment in B $9,000
(work sheet entry to recognize Company A's share
of Company B's $10,000 loss on disposal of fixed assets)

Since this item was not included in the determination of Company B's net income, and since Company A took up its share of B's reported net income this loss is not reflected on A's separate statement.

(2) *Elimination of reciprocals:*

$$A$$

Capital stock (Company B's)	$90,000	
Retained earnings (Company B's)	32,400	
Investment in B		$122,400

(work sheet entry to eliminate 90% of B's shareholders' equity against the investment account)

(3) *Consolidation of nonreciprocals:*

Nonreciprocals are consolidated in the usual manner. It should be noted that the nonreciprocal element of the subsidiary's shareholders' equity is extended to the consolidated statement as minority interest. If the minority interest in this illustration is compared with that in Illustration B-3_1 where the cost method is used, it will be seen that the minority interest is the same regardless of the method used for carrying the investment account.

COST AND EQUITY METHODS COMPARED

COST METHOD	EQUITY METHOD
(1) Stock acquisition is recorded at cost.	(1) Stock acquisition is recorded at cost.
(2) Subsidiary earnings are *not* recorded on parent company's books.	(2) Subsidiary earnings accruing to parent are recorded on parent company's books.
(3) Subsidiary earnings accruing to parent are recognized on the consolidated working papers by an adjusting entry.	(3) Subsidiary earnings are already recorded.
(4) Consolidated statements are the same as if the equity method had been used.	(4) Consolidated statements are the same as if the cost method had been used.

Consolidated Statement of Income and Retained Earnings; Investment Carried at Equity

The technique involved in the preparation of consolidated statements of income and retained earnings when the equity method is used is essentially the same as when the cost method is used, that is (1) eliminate intercompany transactions, and (2) consolidate nonintercompany transactions. However, since the parent recognizes the increases and decreases in subsidiary's shareholders' equity by periodic entries, there may be more intercompany accounts to eliminate than when the cost method is used.

The following illustrations are based on the same data as used in Chapter 11 in Illustrations C-1 and C-2. The general situation is that Company A acquired 90% of the outstanding stock of Company B as of January 1, 1967.

Illustration C-1₁. *Specific Assumptions:*

A. Company A sold Company B $20,000 worth of merchandise.
B. Company B paid Company A $400 interest.
C. Company B reported a net income of $20,000 for 1967.

COMPANY A AND SUBSIDIARY COMPANY B

CONSOLIDATED WORKING PAPERS
STATEMENT OF INCOME AND RETAINED EARNINGS
YEAR ENDED DECEMBER 31, 1967

	Company A	Company B	Eliminations	Consolidated Income	Consolidated Retained Earnings
Credits					
Net sales	$800,000	$200,000	$20,000*A*	$980,000	
Interest income	6,000		400*B*	5,600	
Income from B	18,000		18,000*C*		
Totals	$824,000	$200,000	$38,400	$985,600	
Debits					
Cost of sales	$590,000	$130,000	$20,000*A*	$700,000	
Depreciation	80,000	26,000		106,000	
Interest expense	6,000	2,000	400*B*	7,600	
Other expenses	10,000	2,000		12,000	
Federal income taxes	60,000	20,000		80,000	
Net income	78,000	20,000	18,000*C*	80,000	
Totals	$824,000	$200,000	$38,400	$985,600	
Retained earnings 1/1/67	$110,000	$ 50,000			$110,000*
Net income (1967)	78,000	20,000			
Retained earnings 12/31/67	$188,000	$ 70,000			

Apportionment of net income:
Net income	$80,000	
Minority interest (10% of $20,000)	2,000	
Consolidated interest (remainder)	$78,000	78,000
Consolidated retained earnings 12/31/67		$188,000

* *Note:* Consolidated retained earnings at date of acquisition is composed entirely of the parent company's retained earnings.

BASIC PROCEDURE

(1) *Elimination of intercompany transactions:*

A

Sales	$20,000	
Cost of Sales		$20,000

(work sheet elimination of intercompany sales)

$$B$$

Interest income	$ 400	
Interest expense		$ 400

(work sheet elimination of intercompany interest)

$$C$$

Income from B	$18,000	
Net income		$18,000

(work sheet elimination of intercompany income)

(2) *Consolidation of nonintercompany transactions:*

Nonintercompany items are consolidated by extending them to the consolidated income statement.

(3) *Apportionment of net income:*

Minority interest (10% of Company B's $20,000).
Majority interest (90% of Company B's $20,000 plus Company A's $78,000 minus $18,000 intercompany).

As is the case when the investment is carried at cost, the last two columns of the working papers may be presented in statement form as follows:

COMPANY A AND SUBSIDIARY COMPANY B
CONSOLIDATED STATEMENT OF INCOME
AND RETAINED EARNINGS
YEAR ENDED DECEMBER 31, 1967

Income:		
Net sales	$980,000	
Interest income	5,600	
Gross income	$985,600	$985,600
Costs and Expenses:		
Cost of sales	$700,000	
Depreciation	106,000	
Interest expense	7,600	
Other expenses	12,000	
Federal income taxes	80,000	
Total costs and expenses	$905,600	905,600
Total net income		$ 80,000
Minority interest		2,000
Consolidated Net Income		$ 78,000
Consolidated retained earnings 1/1/67		110,000
Consolidated retained earnings 12/31/67		$188,000

Illustration C-2$_1$. *Specific Assumptions:*

A. Company A sold Company B $20,000 worth of merchandise.
B. Company B paid Company A $400 interest.
C. Company B reported a net income of $30,000 for 1967.
D. Company B declared and paid $10,000 dividends.

COMPANY A AND SUBSIDIARY COMPANY B

CONSOLIDATED WORKING PAPERS
STATEMENT OF INCOME AND RETAINED EARNINGS

YEAR ENDED DECEMBER 31, 1967

	Company A	Company B	Eliminations	Consolidated Income	Consolidated Retained Earnings
Credits					
Net sales	$791,000	$210,000	$20,000*A*	$981,000	
Interest income	6,000		400*B*	5,600	
Income from B	27,000		27,000*C*		
Totals	$824,000	$210,000	$47,400	$986,600	
Debits					
Cost of sales	$590,000	$130,000	$20,000*A*	$700,000	
Depreciation	80,000	26,000		106,000	
Interest expense	6,000	2,000	400*B*	7,600	
Other expenses	10,000	2,000		12,000	
Federal income taxes	60,000	20,000		80,000	
Net income	78,000	30,000	27,000*C*	81,000	
Totals	$824,000	$210,000	$47,400	$986,600	
Retained earnings 1/1/67	$110,000	$50,000			$110,000
Dividends paid (1967)		(10,000)			
Net income (1967)	78,000	30,000			
Retained earnings 12/31/67	$188,000	$70,000			

Apportionment of net income:		
Net income	$81,000	
Minority interest (10% of $30,000)	3,000	
Consolidated interest (remainder)	$78,000	78,000
Consolidated retained earnings 12/31/67		$188,000

COMPANY A AND SUBSIDIARY COMPANY B

CONSOLIDATED STATEMENT OF INCOME AND RETAINED EARNINGS

YEAR ENDED DECEMBER 31, 1967

Income:

Net sales	$981,000	
Interest income	5,600	
Gross income	$986,600	$986,600

Costs and Expenses:

Cost of sales	$700,000	
Depreciation	106,000	
Interest expense	7,600	
Other expenses	12,000	
Federal income taxes	80,000	
Total costs and expenses	$905,600	905,600
Total net income		$ 81,000
Minority interest		3,000
Consolidated Net Income		$ 78,000
Consolidated retained earnings 1/1/67		110,000
Consolidated retained earnings 12/31/67		$188,000

BASIC PROCEDURE

(1) *Elimination of intercompany transactions:*

A

Sales	$20,000	
Cost of sales		$20,000

(work sheet elimination of intercompany sales)

B

Interest income	$ 400	
Interest expense		$ 400

(work sheet elimination of intercompany interest)

C

Income from B	$27,000	
Net income		$27,000

(work sheet elimination of intercompany income)

(2) *Consolidation of nonintercompany transactions:*

Nonintercompany items are consolidated by extending them to the consolidated income statement.

(3) *Apportionment of net income:*

> Minority interest (10% of Company B's $30,000).
> Majority interest (90% of Company B's $30,000 plus Company A's $78,000 minus $27,000 intercompany).

The last two columns of the working papers may be presented in statement form as shown on page 336.

Trial Balance Approach

A trial balance approach, as illustrated in Chapter 11 when the investment is carried at cost, may also be used when preparing consolidated statements if the investment is carried on some basis other than cost. Regardless of the method used in carrying the investment and regardless of the approach used when consolidating, the basic procedure remains the same: establish reciprocity if necessary, eliminate reciprocals, and consolidate nonreciprocals.

The following examples illustrate the basic procedure involved when the investment is carried at something other than cost, equity in this case. Again, three slightly different, but fundamentally important, situations are illustrated. In these examples particular attention should be given to the establishment of reciprocity.

Illustration D-1$_1$. This illustration is based on the same basic data used in Illustrations B-1, B-1$_{1(a)}$, and C-1$_1$.

Illustration D-2$_1$. The general situation in this illustration is the same as that used in Illustration D-1$_1$: that Company A acquired 90% of the outstanding stock of Company B as of January 1, 1967. However, in this instance consolidation is taking place at the end of 1968 instead of at the end of 1967.

In this illustration particular attention should be given to the establishment of reciprocity. When using the trial balance approach, reciprocity must be established as of the beginning of the period rather than at the end of the period, as is the case when using a statement approach.

Illustration D-3$_1$. The general situation in this illustration is the same as the one used in Illustrations D-1$_1$ and D-2$_1$: that Company A acquired 90% of the outstanding stock of Company B as of January 1, 1967. However, in this instance consolidation is taking place at the end of 1969, and Companies A and B submit unadjusted trial balances rather than adjusted ones. In addition to the data in the respective trial balances, Company A reports an ending inventory of $90,000 and Company B one of $60,000.

Illustration D-1$_1$

	Company A	Company B	Adjustments and Eliminations Debit	Adjustments and Eliminations Credit
Debits				
Current assets	$ 115,000	$ 80,000		
Investment in B	153,000			{$ 18,000(1)\n 135,000C
Fixed assets (net)	450,000	110,000		
Cost of sales	590,000	130,000		20,000A
Depreciation	80,000	26,000		
Interest expense	6,000	2,000		400B
Other expenses	10,000	2,000		
Federal income taxes	60,000	20,000		
	$1,464,000	$370,000		
Credits				
Current liabilities	$ 30,000	$ 20,000		
Fixed liabilities	100,000			
Net sales	800,000	200,000	$ 20,000A	
Interest income	6,000		400B	
Income from B	18,000		18,000(1)	
Capital stock:				
Company A	400,000			
Company B		100,000	90,000C	
Retained earnings:				
Company A 1/1/67	110,000			
Company B 1/1/67		50,000	45,000C	
	$1,464,000	$370,000	$173,400	$173,400

Income credits
Income debits

Net income
Apportionment of net income:
  Minority interest:

Subsidiary income credits	$200,000
Subsidiary income debits	180,000
Subsidiary net income	$ 20,000
Minority interest (10%)	2,000

Consolidated net income (remainder)

Retained earnings 12/31/67

Minority interest 12/31/67

(1): To establish reciprocity as of the beginning of the period.
A: To eliminate intercompany sales.
B: To eliminate intercompany interest.
C: To eliminate 90% of B's shareholders' equity against the investment account.

Consolidated Income	Consolidated Retained Earnings	Minority Interest	Consolidated Financial Position
			$195,000
			560,000
$700,000			
106,000			
7,600			
12,000			
80,000			
$905,600	–0–	–0–	$755,000
			$ 50,000
			100,000
$980,000			
5,600			
			400,000
		$10,000	
	$110,000		
		5,000	
$985,600			
905,600			
$ 80,000			
2,000		2,000	
$ 78,000	78,000		
	$188,000		188,000RE
		$17,000	17,000MI
			$755,000

Illustration D-2$_1$

	Company A	Company B	Adjustments and Eliminations Debit	Adjustments and Eliminations Credit
Debits				
Current assets	$ 205,000	$154,000		
Investment in B	201,600			$ 48,600(1) 153,000*A*
Fixed assets (net)	460,000	100,000		
Cost of sales	650,000	170,000		
Depreciation	85,000	28,000		
Interest expense	6,000			
Other expenses	14,000	3,000		
Federal income taxes	75,000	45,000		
	$1,696,600	$500,000		
Credits				
Current liabilities	$ 60,000	$ 30,000		
Fixed liabilities	100,000			
Net sales	900,000	300,000		
Income from B	48,600		$ 48,600(1)	
Capital stock:				
Company A	400,000			
Company B		100,000	90,000*A*	
Retained earnings:				
Company A 1/1/68	188,000			
Company B 1/1/68		70,000	63,000*A*	
	$1,696,600	$500,000	$201,600	$201,600

Income credits
Income debits

Net income				
Apportionment of net income:				
Minority interest:				
Subsidiary income credits		$300,000		
Subsidiary income debits		246,000		
Subsidiary net income		$ 54,000		
Minority interest (10%)		5,400		

Consolidated net income (remainder)

Retained earnings 12/31/68

Minority interest 12/31/68

(1): To establish reciprocity as of the beginning of the period.
A: To eliminate 90% of B's shareholders' equity against the investment account.

COMPANY A AND SUBSIDIARY COMPANY B
CONSOLIDATED WORKING PAPERS
(Continued—Illustration D-2₁)

Consolidated Income	Consolidated Retained Earnings	Minority Interest	Consolidated Financial Position
			$359,000
			560,000
$ 820,000			
113,000			
6,000			
17,000			
120,000			
$1,076,000	–0–	–0–	$919,000
			$ 90,000
			100,000
$1,200,000			
			400,000
		$10,000	
	$188,000		
		7,000	
$1,200,000			
1,076,000			
$ 124,000			
5,400		5,400	
$ 118,600	118,600		
	$306,600		306,600RE
		$22,400	22,400MI
			$919,000

341

COMPANY A AND SUBSIDIARY COMPANY B
CONSOLIDATED WORKING PAPERS
DECEMBER 31, 1969

	Company A	Company B	Adjustments and Eliminations Debits	Adjustments and Eliminations Credit
Debits				
Inventories 1/1/69	$ 70,000	$ 40,000		
Other current assets	208,000	158,000		
Investment in B	255,600		$ 9,000(2)	$ 63,000(3)
				201,600*A*
Fixed assets (net)	490,000	105,000		
Purchases	700,000	200,000		
Depreciation	84,000	30,000		
Other expenses	100,000	70,000		
Dividends paid	32,000	10,000		9,000(2)
	$1,939,600	$613,000		
Inventories 12/31/69			150,000(1)	
Credits				
Current liabilities	$ 90,000	$ 39,000		
Fixed liabilities	100,000			
Net sales	980,000	350,000		
Income from B	63,000		63,000(3)	
Capital stock:				
Company A	400,000			
Company B		100,000	90,000*A*	
Retained earnings:				
Company A 1/1/69	306,600			
Company B 1/1/69		124,000	111,600*A*	
	$1,939,600	$613,000		
Inventories 12/31/69	$ 90,000	$ 60,000		150,000(1)
			$423,600	$423,600

Income credits
Income debits

Net income
Apportionment of net income:
  Minority interest:

Subsidiary income credits	$410,000
Subsidiary income debits	340,000
Subsidiary net income	$ 70,000
Minority interest (10%)	7,000

Consolidated net income (remainder)

Retained earnings 12/31/69

Minority interest 12/31/69

(1): To record ending inventories.
(2) and (3): To establish reciprocity as of the beginning of the period.
A: To eliminate 90% of B's shareholders' equity against the investment account.

Consolidated Income	Consolidated Retained Earnings	Minority Interest	Consolidated Financial Position
$ 110,000			$ 366,000
			595,000
900,000			
114,000			
170,000			
	$ 32,000	$ 1,000	
			150,000
$1,294,000	$ 32,000	$ 1,000	$1,111,000
			$ 129,000
			100,000
$1,330,000			
			400,000
		$10,000	
	$306,600		
		12,400	
150,000			
$1,480,000			
1,294,000			
$ 186,000			
7,000		7,000	
$ 179,000	179,000		
	$485,600		
	32,000		
	$453,600		453,600RE
		$29,400	
		1,000	
		$28,400	28,400MI
			$1,111,000

PROBLEMS

Problem 12–1. Using the following data, and assuming that the equity method is being used, determine in each case:

(1) Minority interest at date of acquisition and at the date of consolidation.

(2) Goodwill (either positive or negative) at date of acquisition and at the date of consolidation.

(3) Consolidated retained earnings at date of acquisition and at the date of consolidation. Assume that the parent company's retained earnings were $100,000 at acquisition in each of the cases.

(4) Carrying value of the investment at the date of consolidation.

Company and % Owned		Cost	Acquisition Date Capital Stock	Acquisition Date Retained Earnings	Consolidation Date Capital Stock	Consolidation Date Retained Earnings
Case 1	A 90%	$200,000	$100,000	$120,000	$100,000	$130,000
Case 2	B 80%	64,000	80,000	–0–	80,000	15,000
Case 3	C 70%	59,000	40,000	50,000	40,000	30,000
Case 4	D 100%	175,000	60,000	90,000	60,000	130,000

Problem 12–2. A Company acquired an 81% interest in the B Company for $20,000 less than its book value. In the 10-year period that followed the acquisition, B Company earned profits aggregating $196,000 and paid dividends of $75,000. The minority interest at the conclusion of the 10-year period was $95,000. Assuming that A Company carries its investment in B on the equity basis, determine:

(1) The cost of the investment, and

(2) The amount at which the investment was carried at the conclusion of the 10-year period.

Problem 12–3. Using the following basic data and the specific assumptions given in each instance, for each case:

(1) Determine the carrying value of the investment account as of December 31, 1968.

(2) Prepare the work sheet entry(ies) necessary when eliminating reciprocals as of December 31, 1968.

(3) Determine the amount of goodwill (positive or negative) as of December 31, 1968.

(4) Determine the amount of minority interest as of December 31, 1968.

(5) Determine the amount of consolidated retained earnings as of December 31, 1968.

BASIC DATA

Balances as of 1/1/66:	Company X	Company Y	Company Z
Capital stock	$400,000	$150,000	$120,000
Paid-in surplus	50,000	35,000	20,000
Retained earnings (deficit)	200,000	80,000	(25,000)
Dividends paid: 1966	20,000	7,500	
1967	20,000	7,500	

Balances as of 12/31/68:

Capital stock	$400,000	$150,000	$120,000
Paid-in surplus	50,000	35,000	20,000
Retained earnings	236,000	104,000	13,000

Case 1. Assume that Company X acquired 84% of the stock of Company Y for $238,500 as of January 1, 1966. Company X carries its investment in Y on the *equity* basis.

Case 2. Assume that Company X acquired 88% of the stock of Company Z for $84,000 as of January 1, 1966. Company X carries its investment in Z on the *equity* basis.

Case 3. Assume that Company X acquired 92% of the stock of Company Y and 82% of the stock of Company Z for $250,000 and $91,000, respectively, as of January 1, 1966. Company X carries these investments on the *equity* basis.

Case 4. Assume that Company Y acquired 95% of the stock of Company Z for $105,000 as of January 1, 1966. Company Y carries its investment in Z at *cost*.

Note: All cases are independent.

Problem 12–4. From the following statements and data:
(1) Prepare a consolidated statement of financial position, and
(2) Prove the goodwill elements.

Assets	PARENT	S-1	S-2	S-3	S-4
Current assets	$ 650,000	$22,000	$40,000	$ 25,000	$ 37,000
Subsidiary investments:					
S-1* (100%)	66,000				
S-2* (95%)	59,750				
S-3* (90%)	47,000				
S-4* (80%)	72,000				
Other assets	808,000	64,000	59,000	95,000	80,000
	$1,702,750	$86,000	$99,000	$120,000	$117,000

Equities					
Current liabilities	$ 300,000	$30,000	$24,000	$ 60,000	$ 42,000
Capital stock	1,000,000	20,000	25,000	80,000	35,000
Retained earnings (deficit)	402,750	36,000	50,000	(20,000)	40,000
	$1,702,750	$86,000	$99,000	$120,000	$117,000

Shareholders' equities as of date of acquisition:

	S-1	S-2	S-3	S-4
Capital stock	$20,000	$25,000	$80,000	$35,000
Retained earnings (deficit)	40,000	45,000	(50,000)	25,000

Cost of investment at date of acquisition:

	S-1	S-2	S-3	S-4
	$70,000	$55,000	$20,000	$60,000

* Parent company uses the equity method of accounting for the investments in subsidiaries.

Problem 12–5. The Parent Company acquired a 70% interest in B Company and a 75% interest in C Company as of January 1, 1967. The Parent Company carries its investment in these companies on the equity basis. From the following data prepare working papers in columnar form showing (1) consolidated income for 1967, and (2) consolidated retained earnings as of December 31, 1967.

STATEMENT OF INCOME
YEAR ENDED DECEMBER 31, 1967

	PARENT	B Company	C Company
Income:			
Sales (net)	$1,225,000	$395,000	$202,000
Dividends	7,000	1,000	100
Income from subsidiaries	36,000		
Gross income	$1,268,000	$396,000	$202,100
Deductions:			
Cost of sales	610,000	205,000	86,000
Selling expenses	290,000	85,000	68,000
General expenses	160,000	47,000	13,100
Taxes	106,000	29,000	15,000
	$1,166,000	$366,000	$182,100
Net Income	$ 102,000	$ 30,000	$ 20,000

STATEMENT OF RETAINED EARNINGS
YEAR ENDED DECEMBER 31, 1967

	PARENT	B Company	C Company
Balance 1/1/67	$405,000	$58,000	$41,000
Net income for year	102,000	30,000	20,000
Dividends paid	(24,000)	(10,000)	(6,000)
Balance 12/31/67	$483,000	$78,000	$55,000

Intercompany transactions:

(1) B Company made sales to C Company of $40,000 and to the Parent Company of $20,000.

(2) The Parent Company borrowed $10,000 on a note from C Company and $20,000 on open account from B Company.

Problem 12–6. Prepare consolidated working papers with columns for income, retained earnings, minority interest, and financial position for the year ended December 31, 1967, from the following data:

Eighty-eight per cent of the stock of Company S was acquired for $200,000 on January 1, 1966, when Company S's shareholders' equity was composed of $100,000 retained earnings and $100,000 capital stock.

ADJUSTED TRIAL BALANCES

DECEMBER 31, 1967

	Co. P	Co. S
Debits		
Merchandise inventory	$ 80,000	$ 28,000
Investment in Co. S	217,600	
Other assets	730,000	315,000
Cost of sales	690,000	152,000
Expenses	230,000	73,000
Dividends paid	25,000	10,000
	$1,972,600	$578,000
Credits		
Sales	$1,212,000	$290,000
Liabilities	210,000	58,000
Capital stock	300,000	100,000
Retained earnings, 1/1/67	250,600	130,000
	$1,972,600	$578,000

Problem 12–7. From the following comparative statements of financial position prepare:

(1) A consolidated statement of financial position as of December 31, 1966, the date Company A acquired a 75% interest in Company B for $154,000, and

(2) A consolidated statement of financial position as of December 31, 1967.

COMPANY A

STATEMENT OF FINANCIAL POSITION

	Dec. 31, 1966	Dec. 31, 1967
Assets		
Current assets	$ 890,000	$ 960,000
Investment in Company B	154,000	190,000
Other assets	100,000	102,000
	$1,144,000	$1,252,000
Equities		
Current liabilities	$ 220,000	$ 260,000
Other liabilities	100,000	120,000
Capital stock	500,000	500,000
Retained earnings	324,000	372,000
	$1,144,000	$1,252,000

COMPANY B

STATEMENT OF FINANCIAL POSITION

	Dec. 31, 1966	Dec. 31, 1967
Assets		
Current assets	$110,000	$125,000
Other assets	260,000	270,000
	$370,000	$395,000
Equities		
Current liabilities	$120,000	$107,000
Other liabilities	50,000	40,000
Capital stock	150,000	150,000
Retained earnings	50,000	98,000
	$370,000	$395,000

Problem 12–8. From the following data prepare consolidated working papers with columns for income, retained earnings, minority interest, and financial position for the year ended December 31, 1967:

Eighty-four per cent of the stock of Company B was acquired for $325,000 on January 1, 1966, when Company B's shareholders' equity was composed of $170,000 retained earnings and $200,000 capital stock.

TRIAL BALANCES

DECEMBER 31, 1967

	Company A	Company B
Debits		
Inventories 1/1/67	$ 180,000	$ 90,000
Investment in Company B	354,400	
Other assets (net)	1,890,000	585,000
Purchases	1,187,000	425,000
Expenses	375,000	182,000
Dividends paid	45,000	15,000
	$4,031,400	$1,297,000
Credits		
Sales	$1,515,000	$ 667,000
Liabilities	996,400	210,000
Capital stock	900,000	200,000
Retained earnings 1/1/67	620,000	220,000
	$4,031,400	$1,297,000

Inventories, December 31, 1967: Company A $205,000

Company B 110,000

$315,000

Problem 12-9. P, a holding company, owns 90% of the capital stock of M and 80% of the capital stock of O. On April 15, 1966, M sold merchandise to O for $50,000, and received from O five noninterest-bearing notes of $10,000 each, due respectively on May 15, June 15, July 15, August 15, and September 15, 1966. On April 15, M discounted the notes due May 15 and June 15, respectively, with its bank, being credited with the proceeds of $19,925. The other three notes it held. In consolidating the accounts of the three companies at the close of the fiscal year ended April 30, 1966, how should the transactions involving the notes be handled? Give reasons for your answer.   (AICPA adapted)

Problem 12-10. From the following data prepare consolidated working papers with columns for income, retained earnings, minority interest, and financial position for the year ended December 31, 1968.

TRIAL BALANCES
DECEMBER 31, 1968

	Company S	Company S-1	Company S-2	Company S-3
Debits				
Inventories 1/1/68	$ 205,000	$ 60,000	$ 52,000	$ 75,000
Investments in subsidiaries (equity)	463,600			
Other assets (net)	1,600,000	270,000	245,000	265,000
Purchases	780,000	190,000	183,000	215,000
Expenses	260,000	63,000	87,000	108,000
Dividends paid	24,000	6,000		5,000
	$3,332,600	$589,000	$567,000	$668,000
Credits				
Sales	$1,210,000	$282,000	$212,000	$338,000
Liabilities	712,000	120,000	195,000	175,000
Capital stock	400,000	100,000	75,000	100,000
Retained earnings 1/1/68	1,010,600	87,000	85,000	55,000
	$3,332,600	$589,000	$567,000	$668,000

Inventories, December 31, 1968:	Company S	$228,000
	Company S-1	67,000
	Company S-2	65,000
	Company S-3	87,000
		$447,000

Ninety-five per cent of the stock of S-1 was acquired for $142,000 on April 1, 1964, when S-1's shareholders' equity was composed of $100,000 capital stock and $42,000 retained earnings.

Ninety per cent of the stock of S-2 was acquired for $138,000 on July 1, 1964, when S-2's shareholders' equity was composed of $75,000 capital stock and $63,000 retained earnings.

Eighty-five per cent of the stock of S-3 was acquired for $148,000 on October 1, 1964, when S-3's shareholders' equity was composed of $100,000 capital stock and $75,000 retained earnings.

CHAPTER **13**

Consolidated statements— intercompany profit transactions

In the preceding chapters intercompany accounts reciprocal in nature were eliminated in the consolidating process. For example, intercompany payables were eliminated against intercompany receivables and inter-company sales against intercompany cost of sales. In many instances, however, intercompany transactions result in a profit or loss to the selling affiliate. This chapter will consider this aspect of the transactions as it affects the consolidating process.

Intercompany profits or losses may be defined as those profits or losses which, on sales to affiliates, have not been actually realized from the consolidated viewpoint through subsequent sales to parties outside the affiliated group. If the consolidated statements are to reflect the financial position and the operating results of a group of affiliated companies as one economic unit, intercompany profits and losses not realized from the consolidated standpoint must be eliminated. Strictly speaking this would require the elimination of only the net income or loss recognized on the sale. Most accountants, however, assume that intercompany profit or loss for consolidation purposes refers to gross profit, and it is this amount rather than the net amount which is normally eliminated on consolidation. A reasonable position seems to be that gross profit may be eliminated unless evidence indicates that certain cost elements, such as transportation charges, should be included in the inventory. In that event elimination of less than the full gross profit may be appropriate.

Since different types of intercompany-profit transactions have differing effects upon subsequent consolidated statements, the problems involved in eliminating intercompany profits or losses can best be examined by classifying and studying them in accordance with their sources, such as:

(1) Intercompany inventory transactions.
(2) Intercompany fixed asset transactions.
(3) Intercompany bond transactions.

INTERCOMPANY INVENTORY TRANSACTIONS

When merchandise is sold by one affiliate to another, it may be necessary not only to eliminate the intercompany sale and purchase, and the receivable and payable, if appropriate, but also to eliminate the profit as well. Any profit or loss recognized by the selling affiliate on merchandise which has not been subsequently sold to customers outside the affiliated group has not been realized from a consolidated standpoint and should be eliminated. For example, if affiliate A sells $100,000 worth of merchandise to affiliate B at a $10,000 profit, A would recognize the $10,000 profit on the sale in its separate statements for the period. From the standpoint of A as a separate legal entity this is realistic. When the consolidated group is being considered as one economic unit, however, the entire $10,000 profit cannot be recognized as having been earned unless all of the intercompany merchandise has been sold to outsiders. If any of the merchandise is in B's inventory at the date of consolidation, some of the profit recognized by A has not been realized from the standpoint of the consolidated group and an elimination of it must be made.

Although there is more or less unanimity among accountants as to the necessity for eliminating intercompany profits in inventories, there is not complete agreement as to the amount of gross profit that should be eliminated or how it should be eliminated. If the affiliate reporting the profit is 100% owned (from the consolidated standpoint the parent is considered as 100% owned), there is general agreement that 100% of the intercompany gross profit should be eliminated. However, if the affiliate reporting the profit is less than 100% owned, there are at least two distinct views as to the amount to be eliminated.

100% Ownership of Selling Affiliate

In the case of 100% ownership of the selling affiliate, accountants are more or less in agreement that all of the intercompany gross profit should be eliminated when consolidating. For example, if affiliate B has in its inventory $40,000 of merchandise purchased from 100% owned affiliate A, on which A made a 10% gross profit, $4,000 intercompany profit should be eliminated.

Theoretically the elimination should result in a reduction of the selling company's income or retained earnings and the buying company's inventory. Practically the elimination is usually made against the consolidated retained earnings and the buying company's inventory. Either procedure will give the same result. When the parent company takes up the $4,000 profit (directly if it were the selling company or when establishing reciprocity if it were not the selling company) consolidated retained earnings is increased. Consequently, the elimination may be made against the consolidated retained earnings and the appropriate inventory account. Both are overstated from the standpoint of the consolidated group as one economic unit. In lieu of a direct credit to the inventory account a special contra account such as "Provision for Intercompany Profit in Inventory" may be used. The work sheet entry would be:

Retained earnings (Parent company's) $4,000
    Inventory (Company B's) or Provision
    for intercompany profit in inventory $4,000
  (to eliminate unrealized intercompany profit
  in Company B's inventory)

This elimination would reduce Company B's inventory to consolidated cost. It would also remove $4,000 of unrealized profit from consolidated retained earnings. Although this $4,000 has been realized from the standpoint of Company A as a separate legal entity, it has not been realized from the standpoint of the consolidated group as a single economic unit.

Less Than 100% Ownership in Selling Affiliate

Although accountants generally agree on the amount of the elimination in the case of 100% ownership in the selling affiliate, they do not always agree completely on the amount to be eliminated when the selling affiliate is less than 100% owned. There are at least two distinct views. One group of accountants would eliminate 100% of the intercompany profit, whereas another group would eliminate only that amount represented by the percentage of the selling company which is owned by the consolidated group. Although the latter view has received a certain amount of support in the past, *Accounting Research Bulletin* 51 recommends 100% elimination, and that approach is advocated in this textbook.

One Hundred Per Cent Elimination

The view that accountants should eliminate 100% of unrealized intercompany gross profits when a minority interest is present finds much support in practice as well as in *Bulletin* 51. For example, a recent survey of consolidation practices conducted by the American Institute of Certified Public Accountants (AICPA) indicates a great majority of companies eliminate all of the intercompany profit, regardless of the existence of a minority interest. Although 100% elimination can be supported from the practical viewpoint on such bases as conservatism and materiality, it can also be supported theoretically on the grounds that an entity should not be permitted to write up assets when merchandise is transferred from one department or division to another. From a consolidated entity point of view, the separate companies are similar to departments or divisions of a single company.

According to *Bulletin* 51, the elimination of all of the intercompany profit in the case of less than 100% ownership may be charged against consolidated retained earnings, or may be divided between the consolidated retained earnings and the minority interest. Both procedures are illustrated in the following examples.

Entire Amount Eliminated from Consolidated Retained Earnings. The elimination of the entire amount of the intercompany profit from consolidated retained earnings finds much support in practice, probably because it is expedient and simple in application. From another point of view, however, this may not be the better approach. For example, should 100% of the profit be eliminated from consolidated retained earnings when only 90% has been taken up? Assume Company A has $50,000 worth of merchandise purchased at 25% above cost from Company B, a 90% owned subsidiary. When establishing reciprocity the parent company would take up 90% of the $10,000 intercompany profit or $9,000. Assuming for illustrative purposes that the only profit reported by Company B is the $10,000 intercompany profit, the work sheet entry establishing reciprocity would be:

Investment in Company B	$9,000	
Retained earnings (Parent's)		$9,000
(to recognize Company A's share of the increase in Company B's shareholders' equity since the date of acquisition)		

However, $10,000 would be eliminated if the entire amount of intercompany profit is eliminated from consolidated retained earnings by:

Retained earnings (Parent's)	$10,000	
Inventory (Company A's)		$10,000
(to eliminate intercompany profit in inventories)		

It may not seem correct to eliminate more from consolidated retained earnings than has been entered therein. Although this approach may not be logically sound, from the practical standpoint, based on expediency and materiality, it may be justified.

Elimination Divided between Consolidated Retained Earnings and the Minority Interest. Some accountants advocate dividing the elimination of 100% of the intercompany profit between consolidated retained earnings and the minority interest. For example, assuming the facts noted previously where, at the time of consolidating, Company A has $50,000 worth of merchandise purchased at 25% above cost from Company B, a 90% owned affiliate, the work sheet eliminating entry would be:

Retained earnings (Parent's)	$9,000	
Retained earnings (Company B's)	1,000	
Inventory (Company A's)		$10,000
(to eliminate intercompany profit in inventories)		

Theoretically this approach appears to be more appropriate since the portion eliminated from consolidated retained earnings is the same as that included therein. When establishing reciprocity, $9,000 was credited to consolidated retained earnings, and if the elimination is prorated, only $9,000 is removed. This is in contrast to the $10,000 elimination in the case where all intercompany profit is eliminated from consolidated retained earnings.

Some accountants object to charging the minority interest for its pro rata share of intercompany profits. They contend that from the standpoint of the minority interest (as part of a separate legal entity) its share of the intercompany profit has been realized. Granted the intercompany profit has been realized from the standpoint of the separate legal entities, it has not been realized from the standpoint of the consolidated group as one economic unit. When consolidating, regardless of where they are currently reflected, *all* intercompany profits recognized but not realized should be eliminated.

Work Sheet Illustration. Assume Company A owns 80% of Company B and 90% of Company C, and that C sells merchandise to B at a $10,000 profit and B sells it to A at another $8,000 profit. All of the merchandise is in A's inventory at the end of the year, and the inventory reported by A is overstated by $18,000 from the point of view of the consolidated entity.

If the entire gross profit were eliminated against the retained earnings of the parent company, the work sheet entry would be:

Retained earnings (Parent's)	$18,000	
Inventory		$18,000

If the gross profit is to be allocated to the minority interests for their share of the intercompany profit, it would be necessary to compute the appropriate eliminations, as follows:

<table>
<tr><td></td><td></td><td colspan="3">To Be Eliminated Against
Retained Earnings</td></tr>
<tr><td></td><td>Total</td><td>A</td><td>B</td><td>C</td></tr>
<tr><td>First Sale</td><td>$10,000</td><td>$9,000</td><td></td><td>$1,000</td></tr>
<tr><td>Second Sale</td><td>8,000</td><td>6,400</td><td>$1,600</td><td></td></tr>
<tr><td>Total</td><td>$18,000</td><td>$15,400</td><td>$1,600</td><td>$1,000</td></tr>
</table>

In journal form the work sheet eliminations would be:

Retained earnings (Parent's)	$15,400	
Retained earnings (B's)	1,600	
Retained earnings (C's)	1,000	
Inventory		$18,000

To illustrate the elimination procedure, the working papers for the consolidated statement of financial position in which separate company statements are included is presented below. The separate statements are based on the assumption that all profits on the intercompany sales have been recorded. Reciprocity has been established.

<table>
<tr><td></td><td></td><td></td><td></td><td colspan="2">Eliminations</td><td>Consolidated
Statement of</td></tr>
<tr><td>Assets</td><td>A</td><td>C</td><td>B</td><td>Debit</td><td>Credit</td><td>Financial Position</td></tr>
<tr><td>Investment in C</td><td>$160,000</td><td></td><td></td><td></td><td>$135,000B</td><td>$ 25,000G</td></tr>
<tr><td>Investment in B</td><td>240,000</td><td></td><td></td><td></td><td>224,000C</td><td>16,000G</td></tr>
<tr><td>Inventory</td><td>160,000</td><td>$ 80,000</td><td>$ 30,000</td><td></td><td>18,000A</td><td>252,000</td></tr>
<tr><td>Other assets</td><td>350,000</td><td>110,000</td><td>270,000</td><td></td><td></td><td>730,000</td></tr>
<tr><td></td><td>$910,000</td><td>$190,000</td><td>$300,000</td><td></td><td></td><td>$1,023,000</td></tr>
<tr><td>Equities</td><td></td><td></td><td></td><td></td><td></td><td></td></tr>
<tr><td>Liabilities</td><td>$150,000</td><td>$ 40,000</td><td>$ 20,000</td><td></td><td></td><td>$ 210,000</td></tr>
<tr><td>Capital stock—A</td><td>600,000</td><td></td><td></td><td></td><td></td><td>600,000</td></tr>
<tr><td>Retained earnings—A</td><td>160,000</td><td></td><td></td><td>$ 15,400A</td><td></td><td>144,600RE</td></tr>
<tr><td>Capital stock—C</td><td></td><td>100,000</td><td></td><td>90,000B</td><td></td><td>10,000MI</td></tr>
<tr><td>Retained earnings—C</td><td></td><td>50,000</td><td></td><td>{45,000B
{ 1,000A</td><td></td><td>4,000MI</td></tr>
<tr><td>Capital stock—B</td><td></td><td></td><td>200,000</td><td>160,000C</td><td></td><td>40,000MI</td></tr>
<tr><td>Retained earnings—B</td><td></td><td></td><td>80,000</td><td>{64,000C
{ 1,600A</td><td></td><td>14,400MI</td></tr>
<tr><td></td><td>$910,000</td><td>$190,000</td><td>$300,000</td><td>$377,000</td><td>$377,000</td><td>$1,023,000</td></tr>
</table>

Trial Balance Approach. When a trial balance approach is being used to consolidate financial statements, eliminating entries for intercompany profits in inventories are dependent upon: (1) whether a perpetual inventory system is in use, (2) whether adjusted or unadjusted trial balances are being consolidated, and (3) whether the intercompany profit is being eliminated from the beginning or ending inventory. If a perpetual inventory system is in use or if adjusted trial balances are being consolidated, the cost of goods sold is reflected in a Cost of Goods Sold or similar account, and the ending inventory is reflected on the trial balance. To eliminate $10,000 intercompany profit in the ending inventory the following entry would be made:

Cost of goods sold	$10,000	
Inventory		$10,000

If a perpetual inventory system is not in use and if unadjusted trial balances are being consolidated, it is necessary to make an adjustment in the working papers to record the ending inventory. Assuming a $100,000 ending inventory, the entry to record it on an unadjusted trial balance would be:

Inventory (statement of financial position)	$100,000	
Inventory (statement of income)		$100,000

If $10,000 intercompany profit is to be eliminated, the entry would be:

Inventory (statement of income)	$10,000	
Inventory (statement of financial position)		$10,000

The same result could be obtained by simply recording the ending inventory net of intercompany profit, such as:

Inventory (statement of financial position)	$90,000	
Inventory (income statement)		$90,000

To illustrate the elimination procedure necessary for intercompany profit in beginning inventories under a trial balance approach, assume an intercompany profit of $15,000. If a perpetual inventory system is in use or if adjusted trial balances are being consolidated, the eliminating entry would be:

Retained earnings (Parent's)	$15,000	
Cost of goods sold		$15,000

If a perpetual inventory system is not in use and if unadjusted trial balances are being consolidated, the elimination would be:

Retained earnings (Parent's)	$15,000	
Inventory (beginning)		$15,000

INTERCOMPANY FIXED ASSET TRANSACTIONS

As with intercompany inventory transactions, when fixed assets are sold by one affiliate to another at a profit, any intercompany profit unrealized at the date of consolidation should be eliminated. Intercompany profits in fixed assets, as with intercompany profits in inventories, are not considered realized from the consolidated point of view until the asset has been transferred to outsiders. Intercompany profits in nondepreciating fixed assets are not realized until a sale to an outsider takes place. However, depreciating fixed assets are different from inventories and nondepreciating fixed assets in that physical transference as such is not necessary. Intercompany profits in depreciating fixed assets are realized by the process of depreciation as well as by a sale to outsiders.

The reasoning supporting this procedure may be described as follows:

(1) Depreciation represents a portion of the useful life of the fixed assets which has been used up.
(2) Any intercompany profit on the portion of the fixed asset assigned as depreciation is realized when the goods or services produced by use of the asset are sold to outsiders.
(3) The depreciation is a measure of the contribution of the asset in making and disposing of the products sold during the period. This means that part of the payment for the products was in payment for the contribution provided by the services in the depreciation. Thus, depreciation is sold when the products are sold and intercompany profit is realized at that time.

Nondepreciating Fixed Assets

The problems created by intercompany profits in nondepreciating fixed assets are basically the same as those created by intercompany profits in inventories. As long as the nondepreciating fixed asset is held within the consolidated group, any intercompany profit on it should be eliminated in consolidated reports. As with inventories, the problems are how much to eliminate and how it should be eliminated. There is more or less unanimity among accountants that 100% of the intercompany profit should be eliminated, but there is some disagreement as to how the elimination should be effected. Theoretically, as in the case of intercompany profits in inventories, the elimination should be prorated between consolidated retained earnings and minority interest. Practically expediency, materiality, and conservatism may justify eliminating the entire amount from consolidated retained earnings. There is a small minority of accountants who would eliminate only the per cent of consolidated interest in the selling affiliate.

The following examples illustrate the work sheet entries required when eliminating (1) 100% from consolidated retained earnings, and (2) 100% prorated between consolidated retained earnings and minority interest. The similarity between these entries and those for intercompany profits in inventories should be noted. It should also be noted that in the case of nondepreciating fixed assets the elimination remains the *same* as long as the asset is held by a particular affiliate.

In each illustration, assume that the asset (land) is currently carried at a cost of $100,000 and that the seller in each instance made a 20% profit based on the selling price.

100% ELIMINATION FROM CONSOLIDATED RETAINED EARNINGS

1. Parent sells to Company B (90% owned subsidiary):

	End of 1st Year	End of 2nd Year	End of Each Subsequent Year
Retained earnings			
(Parent's)	$20,000	$20,000	$20,000
Land	$20,000	$20,000	$20,000

2. Company B (90% owned subsidiary) sells to parent:

	End of 1st Year	End of 2nd Year	End of Each Subsequent Year
Retained earnings			
(Parent's)	$20,000	$20,000	$20,000
Land	$20,000	$20,000	$20,000

3. Company B (90% owned subsidiary) sells to Company C (80% owned subsidiary):

	End of 1st Year	End of 2nd Year	End of Each Subsequent Year
Retained earnings			
(Parent's)	$20,000	$20,000	$20,000 ,
Land	$20,000	$20,000	$20,000

4. Company B (90% owned subsidiary) sells to Company C (80% owned subsidiary) which in turn sells to Company D (70% owned subsidiary):

	End of 1st Year	End of 2nd Year	End of Each Subsequent Year
Retained earnings			
(Parent's)	$36,000*	$36,000*	$36,000*
Land	$36,000	$36,000	$36,000

* 20% × $100,000 = $20,000
  20% ×   80,000 =   16,000
                    _____
                    $36,000

100% ELIMINATION PRORATED BETWEEN CONSOLIDATED
RETAINED EARNINGS AND MINORITY INTEREST

1. Parent sells to Company B (90% owned subsidiary):

	End of 1st Year	End of 2nd Year	End of Each Subsequent Year
Retained earnings (Parent's)	$20,000	$20,000	$20,000
Land	$20,000	$20,000	$20,000

2. Company B (90% owned subsidiary) sells to parent:

	End of 1st Year	End of 2nd Year	End of Each Subsequent Year
Retained earnings (Parent's)	$18,000	$18,000	$18,000
Retained earnings (B's)	2,000	2,000	2,000
Land	$20,000	$20,000	$20,000

3. Company B (90% owned subsidiary) sells to Company C (80% owned subsidiary):

	End of 1st Year	End of 2nd Year	End of Each Subsequent Year
Retained earnings (Parent's)	$18,000	$18,000	$18,000
Retained earnings (B's)	2,000	2,000	2,000
Land	$20,000	$20,000	$20,000

4. Company B (90% owned subsidiary) sells to Company C (80% owned subsidiary) which in turn sells to Company D (70% owned subsidiary):

	End of 1st Year	End of 2nd Year	End of Each Subsequent Year
Retained earnings (Parent's)	$30,400	$30,400	$30,400
Retained earnings (C's)	4,000†	4,000†	4,000†
Retained earnings (B's)	1,600*	1,600*	1,600*
Land	$36,000	$36,000	$36,000

* 10% × $16,000 = $1,600
† 20% × $20,000 = $4,000

Depreciating Fixed Assets

Since intercompany profits in depreciating fixed assets are normally realized through the depreciation process, the consolidating problems revolve around and are closely related to the depreciation process. Basically, the problem is one of determining how much of the intercompany profit has been realized through depreciation and how much has not been realized. That which has not been realized as of the date of consolidation must be eliminated.

Realization through the depreciation process means that as the asset is consumed (expiration of useful life) in production or through service, its cost, which would include intercompany profit, is passed on to outsiders through the depreciation charge. Since depreciation from an accounting standpoint is primarily a matter of allocating the cost of an asset over its useful life, realization of any intercompany profit on such asset is essentially a matter of recognizing this profit as being realized over the same period of time. For example, if, after an intercompany-profit transaction has taken place, an asset with a useful life of 10 years is depreciated on a straight-line basis, 1/10 of the intercompany profit is considered realized each year. At the end of seven years 7/10 of the intercompany profit will have been realized and 3/10 unrealized. Likewise, at the end of nine years 9/10 will have been realized and 1/10 unrealized.

When consolidating, in addition to eliminating the unrealized portion from consolidated retained earnings, the asset and its related accrued depreciation must be reduced to cost from a consolidated standpoint. This may be illustrated by assuming that Company P (parent) sells to Company A (100% owned subsidiary) for $100,000 (cost to Company P, $80,000) equipment with an estimated useful life of 10 years. At the end of the fourth year 40% of the intercompany profit has been realized and 60% has not been realized. To reduce all accounts to a consolidated cost basis, $12,000 (60% of $20,000) unrealized profit must be eliminated from consolidated retained earnings; $20,000 must be removed from the asset account; and the depreciation taken on the intercompany profit element of the asset during the four-year period must also be removed from the accrued depreciation account. In entry form the elimination would be:

Retained earnings (Parent's) (60% of $20,000)	$12,000	
Accrued depreciation (40% of $20,000)	8,000	
Equipment (100% of $20,000)		$20,000

When entered in the work sheet this entry would eliminate the $12,000 unrealized profit from consolidated retained earnings, leaving in it the $8,000 realized portion. The $8,000 charged to accrued depreciation reduces this account to $32,000 ($40,000 − $8,000) which states it on a consolidated cost basis. Finally the $20,000 credit to the asset account reduces it to $80,000, which is consolidated cost. After this entry the book value of the asset is $48,000 ($80,000 − $32,000) which is the same as it would have been if no intercompany profit had been made. However, if no elimination had been made, the book value would have been $60,000 ($100,000 − $40,000).

Here, as in the case of intercompany profits in inventories and in nondepreciating fixed assets, there is some disagreement among accountants as to how much profit to eliminate and in some cases how it should be eliminated. While most accountants agree that 100% of the unrealized profit should be eliminated, there is not complete agreement as to exactly how the elimination should be made. As in the case of inventories and nondepreciating fixed assets, theory would seem to require a proration between consolidated retained earnings and minority interest. From the practical standpoint simplicity and materiality warrant total elimination from consolidated retained earnings. Although the authors favor (especially from a logical standpoint) the theoretical treatment, both methods are illustrated in the examples on pages 362–365.

Assume in each illustration that the asset (equipment) is currently carried at a cost of $100,000 and that the seller in each instance made a 20% profit based on the selling price. Also assume that depreciation is computed on a straight-line basis, using an estimated useful life of 10 years. In each of the examples the elimination accomplishes three things: (1) it eliminates the unrealized profit from consolidated retained earnings, (2) it reduces the accrued depreciation account to a consolidated cost basis, and (3) it reduces the asset to the consolidated basis.

Elimination for Consolidated Income. To illustrate the elimination needed to prepare a consolidated statement of income as well as a consolidated statement of financial position, assume (1) Company A owns 80% of Company B, (2) Company A has a $40,000 asset purchased from B on which B made a profit of $10,000, (3) the asset has a life of 10 years from the date of sale and A has depreciated it for 4 years, and (4) the books of Company A have not been closed at the end of the fourth year.

The overstatement of depreciation expense on fixed assets, including intercompany profits, is eliminated by the following work sheet entry:

Accrued depreciation	$1,000	
Depreciation expense		$1,000

(This entry would be required each year over the life of the asset because the depreciation charged by the buying affiliate on its separate books would be $1,000 too high each year.)

Abbreviated trial balance working papers for consolidated statements would appear as is shown on page 366.

This example illustrates that when the trial balance approach is used, the current year's portion of the elimination is made against the expense account rather than against the Retained Earnings account. Had the

100% ELIMINATION FROM CONSOLIDATED RETAINED EARNINGS

1. Parent sells to Company B (90% owned subsidiary):

	Date of Sale	End of 1st Year	End of 2nd Year	End of 10th Year
Retained earnings (Parent's)	$20,000*	$18,000*	$16,000*	$——*
Accrued depreciation	——*	2,000*	4,000*	20,000
Equipment	$20,000	$20,000	$20,000	$20,000

* The relationship between the amount of intercompany profit realized and the amount of depreciation taken on the intercompany cost as of any particular date should be noted. For instance at the date of sale no depreciation has been taken and none of the intercompany profit has been realized, whereas at the end of the first year $2,000 of depreciation has been taken and $2,000 of the intercompany profit has been realized. By the end of the tenth year all the depreciation has been taken and all of the profit has been realized.

2. Company B (90% owned subsidiary) sells to the parent:

	Date of Sale	End of 1st Year	End of 2nd Year	End of 10th Year
Retained earnings (Parent's)	$20,000	$18,000	$16,000	$——
Accrued depreciation	——	2,000	4,000	20,000
Equipment	$20,000	$20,000	$20,000	$20,000

3. Company B (90% owned subsidiary) sells to Company C (80% owned subsidiary):

	Date of Sale	End of 1st Year	End of 2nd Year	End of 10th Year
Retained earnings (Parent's)	$20,000	$18,000	$16,000	$——
Accrued depreciation	——	2,000	4,000	20,000
Equipment	$20,000	$20,000	$20,000	$20,000

4. Company B (90% owned subsidiary) sells to Company C (80% owned subsidiary) which in turn sells to Company D (70% owned subsidiary):

	Date of Sale	End of 1st Year	End of 2nd Year	End of 10th Year
Retained earnings (Parent's)	$36,000†	$32,400	$28,800	$——
Accrued depreciation	——	3,600‡	7,200	36,000
Equipment	$36,000	$36,000	$36,000	$36,000

† 20% × $100,000 = $20,000
  20% × $ 80,000 = 16,000
                   $36,000

‡ 10% × $36,000 = $3,600

100% ELIMINATION PRORATED BETWEEN CONSOLIDATED RETAINED EARNINGS AND MINORITY INTEREST

1. Parent sells to Company B (90% owned subsidiary):

	Date of Sale	End of 1st Year	End of 2nd Year	End of 10th Year
Retained earnings (Parent's)	$20,000	$18,000	$16,000	$——
Accrued depreciation	———	2,000	4,000	20,000
Equipment	$20,000	$20,000	$20,000	$20,000

The parent is considered to be 100% owned from the standpoint of the consolidation. Consequently, since the parent is making the sale in this situation, there is no minority interest involved.

2. Company B (90% owned subsidiary) sells to parent:

	Date of Sale	End of 1st Year	End of 2nd Year	End of 10th Year
Retained earnings (Parent's)	$18,000	$16,200	$14,400	$——
Retained earnings (B's)	2,000	1,800	1,600	
Accrued depreciation	———	2,000	4,000	20,000
Equipment	$20,000	$20,000	$20,000	$20,000

In this situation is should be noted that the unrealized portion of the intercompany profit is divided between the consolidated retained earnings and the minority interest in proportion to the consolidated interest and the minority interest in the selling affiliate—90% and 10%.

3. Company B (90% owned subsidiary) sells to Company C (80% owned subsidiary):

	Date of Sale	End of 1st Year	End of 2nd Year	End of 10th Year
Retained earnings (Parent's)	$18,000	$16,200	$14,400	$——
Retained earnings (B's)	2,000	1,800	1,600	——
Accrued depreciation Equipment	——	2,000	4,000	20,000
	$20,000	$20,000	$20,000	$20,000

It should be noted that illustrations 2 and 3 are identical. This condition exists because Company B is the seller in both cases.

4. Company B (90% owned subsidiary) sells to Company C (80% owned subsidiary) which in turn sells to Company D (70% owned subsidiary):

	Date of Sale	End of 1st Year	End of 2nd Year	End of 10th Year
Retained earnings (Parent's)	$30,400*	$27,360	$24,320	$——
Retained earnings (B's)	1,600†	1,440	1,280	——
Retained earnings (C's)	4,000‡	3,600	3,200	——
Accrued depreciation Equipment	——	3,600	7,200	36,000
	$36,000	$36,000	$36,000	$36,000

* $90\% \times \$16,000 = \$14,400$
  $80\% \times \$20,000 = \$16,000$
  $\$30,400$

† $10\% \times \$16,000 = \$1,600$
‡ $20\% \times \$20,000 = \$4,000$

A AND B

CONSOLIDATED WORKING PAPERS FOR YEAR 4

	Trial Balance		Eliminations		Consolidated	
	A	B	Debit	Credit	Income Statement	Financial Position
Debits						
Fixed asset	$40,000			$10,000B		$30,000
Depreciation expense	4,000			1,000A	$ 3,000	
Other debits	XXXX	XXXX			XXXX	XXXX
	$XXXX	$XXXX			$XXXX	$XXXX
Credits						
Retained earnings–A	$100,000		$7,000B			$93,000
Accrued depreciation	16,000		1,000A			12,000
			3,000B			
Other credits	XXXX	XXXX			$XXXX	XXXX
	$XXXX	$XXXX			$XXXX	$XXXX

books been closed, the retained earnings of A would have absorbed the additional $1,000 of excess depreciation. The eliminating entry would then have been:

Retained earnings (A's)	$6,000	
Accrued depreciation	4,000	
Fixed asset		$10,000

INTERCOMPANY BOND TRANSACTIONS *ne pas lire*

Intercompany bond transactions are considered separately from short-term debtor-creditor relationships because there is a greater likelihood that gains or losses may be recognized on these transactions. Since gains or losses may arise, the consolidating problem is composed basically of two elements: (1) the intercompany receivable and payable, and (2) the intercompany profit or loss.

When one affiliate holds bonds of another affiliate, the intercompany-held bonds are essentially treasury bonds and from the standpoint of the consolidated group should be treated as such. The consolidation problem is one of offsetting the asset account of the bondholder against the liability account of the issuer. Since treasury bonds are normally deducted from the liability account on the statement of financial position, the bond investment account would normally be extended to the consolidated column on the work sheet and presented on the consolidated statement of financial position in a manner similar to the following illustration:

Bonds Payable	$600,000	
Less: Bonds held by affiliated company	100,000	
Bonds outstanding		$500,000

When intercompany bonds are both issued and acquired at par no unusual problems occur, other than treating them as treasury bonds. This is true, of course, because the carrying value (par) is the same (and therefore reciprocal) on both the issuer's and buyer's books. Bonds are not always bought and sold at par, however, and the intercompany accounts may not be reciprocal. When this condition exists, reciprocity must be established before eliminating (i.e., "offsetting") the asset account against the liability account. In addition, whenever bonds of an affiliate are acquired from an outsider at some price other than the carrying value on the selling affiliate's books, a gain or loss from the consolidated standpoint has been realized and must be recognized when consolidating. For example, if Company A (100% owned affiliate) sells $100,000 worth of bonds at par to an outsider and Company B (100% owned affiliate) acquires one-half of them immediately for 102, there has been a $1,000 loss from the consolidated standpoint because $51,000 ($50,000 @ 102) was used to reduce a debt to an outsider of $50,000.

Selected portions of the working papers for consolidated statements would appear as follows:

	A	B	Eliminations Debit	Credit	Consolidated Financial Position
Debits					
Bonds of A	—	$51,000		$1,000A	$ 50,000TB
Credits					
Bonds payable	$100,000				100,000
Retained earnings (Parent's)				$1,000A	

When studying intercompany-bond transactions it should be recognized that when bonds are purchased as an investment they are normally recorded at cost. As a result any premium or discount involved is reflected in the cost. On the other hand when bonds are issued they are normally recorded at par and any premium or discount involved is recorded separately. As a consequence the amortization of any premium or discount on bonds purchased is accomplished by writing the bond investment account up or down to par over the remaining life of the bonds; whereas any premium or discount on the issuance of bonds is amortized by writing off the separately recorded premium or discount over the life of the bonds. In both instances the amortization results in either a charge or a credit to the income account of the individual company. As a consequence of the amortization process, a gain or loss on intercompany-bond transactions will eventually find its way into consolidated retained earnings. In this respect the amortization process has an effect similar to the depreciation process as related to intercompany profits in fixed assets. That is, an intercompany gain or loss on bond transactions is realized over the amortization period. If amortization is on a straight-line basis, realization will be on a straight-line basis. If amortization is on some other basis, realization will be on that same basis.

As with intercompany profits in inventories and fixed assets, there is general agreement among accountants of the need for eliminating inter-company gains and losses on intercompany-bond transactions. However, there is not always complete agreement as to how much gain or loss should be eliminated and just how the elimination should be effected. Although there is substantial agreement that 100% of an intercompany gain or loss should be eliminated, there is some disagreement as to how the elimination should be made. Theoretically, as in the case of intercompany profits in inventories and fixed assets, the elimination should be prorated between consolidated retained earnings and minority interest. From a practical standpoint simplicity and materiality may justify eliminating the entire amount from consolidated retained earnings. Here again there is a small minority of accountants who would eliminate only the per cent of the consolidated interest in any intercompany gain or loss.

The following examples illustrate the eliminations required when eliminating: (1) 100% from consolidated retained earnings, and (2) 100% prorated between consolidated retained earnings and minority interest.

100% Elimination from Consolidated Retained Earnings.

Assume Company A owns 80% of the stock of Company B. Company B has outstanding $100,000 of bonds with an unamortized premium of $3,000. Company A purchases $50,000 of the bonds for $49,000 or at a $1,000 discount. The gain on reacquisition of the bonds may be computed as follows:

	Total	Outstanding	Reacquired
Maturity value	$100,000	$50,000	$50,000
Premium	3,000	1,500	1,500
Book value	$103,000	$51,500	$51,500
Cost of bonds acquired on A's books			49,000
Gain on reacquisition			$ 2,500

The portion of the consolidated working papers reflecting the eliminations is presented below:

	Co. A	Co. B	Adjustments & Eliminations Debit	Credit	Consolidated Financial Position
Debits					
Bonds of B	$49,000		$1,000A		$ 50,000TB
Credits					
Bonds payable		$100,000			100,000
Premium on bonds		3,000	1,500A		1,500
Retained earnings (Parent's)	XXXX			$2,500A	

100% Elimination Prorated Between Consolidated Retained Earnings and Minority Interest.

Assume the same facts as those presented in the preceding illustration. The resulting gain of $2,500 is to be prorated between the minority interest and the consolidated retained earnings. Other than this, the solution is the same.

The questions are: Did Company A make the $2,500 gain by buying? Or did Company B make the gain by having issued the bonds advantageously? Or should the gain be divided between the two and, if so, in what proportion?

(1) If the assumption is that the gain was all made by the buying company, the $2,500 accrues to A's stockholders. Because there are no minority stockholders of A's stock, all of the gain should be reflected in consolidated retained earnings. The work sheet entry for the elimination would be:

Premium on bonds payable	$1,500	
Bonds of B	1,000	
Retained earnings (A's)		$2,500

(2) If the assumption is that the gain was all made by the issuing company, the $2,500 accrues to B's stockholders, only 80% of which is owned by A. The minority interest of 20% should share in the gain. The appropriate elimination entry on a work sheet for consolidation purposes would be:

Premium on bonds payable	$1,500	
Bonds of B	1,000	
Retained earnings (A's)		$2,000
Retained earnings (B's)		500

(3) If the assumption is that the gain was made by both the issuing company and the buying company, the $2,500 would have to be allocated between the two. The usual procedure is to take recognition of the fact that the premium and discount will be recognized as a gain by the separate companies over the life of the bonds. That is, the $1,500 premium would be amortized on the books of B, and the $1,000 discount would be amortized on the books of A. Since this procedure results in a proration on the separate companies' books, some accountants hold that the gain or loss should be allocated to the separate companies on this basis. The schedule below illustrates the procedure for allocating the gain and determining the amount to be credited or charged to the minority interest.

A AND B

COMPUTATION OF GAIN OR LOSS ON INTERCOMPANY BOND HOLDINGS

	Co. A	Co. B	Total
Issue price of bonds		$51,500	$51,500
Maturity value of bonds	$50,000	50,000	
Purchase price of bonds	49,000		49,000
Gain on reacquisition	$ 1,000	$ 1,500	$ 2,500
Minority interest per cent	—	20%	
Minority interest	—	300	300
Consolidated gain	$ 1,000	$ 1,200	$ 2,200

The entry on the consolidated work sheet would be:

Premium on bonds payable	$1,500	
Bonds of B	1,000	
Retained earnings (A's)		$2,200
Retained earnings (B's)		300

Elimination for Consolidated Income. To illustrate the work sheet procedure for intercompany gains or losses in preparing the consolidated income statement and the consolidated statement of financial position, assume the same facts as those used above and assume in addition that the bonds had a remaining life of 10 years after the date of reacquisition. One year after A acquired the bonds, assuming the bonds were purchased at the start of the fiscal year in the example, the accounts would have the balances revealed in the following work sheet.

| | Trial Balance | | Eliminations | | Consolidated | |
	Co. A	Co. B	Debit	Credit	Income Statement	Financial Position
Debits						
Bonds of B	$49,100			$ 900*A*		$ 50,000TB
Credits						
Bonds payable		$100,000				$100,000
Premium on bonds		2,700	1,080*A*			
			270*C*			1,350
Bond premium amortized		300	30*C*			
			120*B*		$150	
Income-amortization						
of bonds	100		100*B*			
Retained earnings–A	XXXX			$1,980*A*		
				220*B*		XXXX
Retained earnings–B		XXXX		300*C*		XXXX

A: To write the investment in bonds of B up to par and to write off appropriate premium on bonds sold (80% of 50% of $2,700) and to credit the sum of the two to retained earnings of A.

B: To eliminate the one year's amortization of the bond investment and to eliminate the appropriate portion of the one year's premium on bonds sold (80% of 50% of $300) and to credit the sum of the two to retained earnings of A.

C: To eliminate the minority shareholders' interest in the bond premium amortized in the year (20% of 50% of $300) and in the premium on bonds sold (20% of 50% of $2,700) and to credit the sum of the two to retained earnings of B (minority interest).

The above solution eliminates 100% of the intercompany gain and prorates it to consolidated retained earnings and minority interest. Assuming 100% elimination from consolidated retained earnings, the work sheet entries would be:

A

Bonds of B	$ 900	
Premium on bonds payable	1,350	
Retained earnings (A's)		$2,250

B

Income-amortization of bonds	$ 100	
Bond premium amortized	150	
Retained earnings (A's)		$ 250

C

No entry

PROBLEMS

Problem 13–1. Company A owns 80% of the stock of Company B and 90% of the stock of Company C. Company A carries the investment accounts at cost. Intercompany sales of merchandise are made at a gross profit of 25% on cost unless otherwise indicated. Show in journal entry form the eliminations that would be necessary for intercompany profits on merchandise in each case below assuming that:

(1) One hundred per cent is eliminated from consolidated retained earnings.

(2) One hundred per cent is eliminated prorata from consolidated retained earnings and minority interest.

Case 1. Merchandise owned by Co. A, sold by Co. B, $20,000.

Case 2. Merchandise owned by Co. B, sold by Co. A, $25,000.

Case 3. Merchandise owned by Co. C, sold by Co. B, $30,000.

Case 4. Merchandise owned by Co. A, sold by Co. B, $20,000; Co. C originally sold this merchandise to Co. B for $15,000.

Problem 13–2. On December 31, 1966, the Barr Company completed the construction of a building for the Able Company. The charge for the construction was $900,000. Cost of the construction was $720,000. The useful life of the building was estimated at 40 years.

Indicate in journal entry form the elimination that would be necessary for intercompany profit when preparing a consolidated statement of financial position as of December 31, 1976, in each case below assuming that:

(1) One hundred per cent is eliminated from consolidated retained earnings.

(2) One hundred per cent is eliminated prorata from consolidated retained earnings and minority interest.

Case 1. Barr is the parent owning 100% of Able.

Case 2. Barr is the parent owning 90% of Able.

Case 3. Able is the parent owning 100% of Barr.

Case 4. Able is the parent owning 90% of Barr.

Problem 13–3. The Baker Company issued $100,000 par value 4% bonds on January 1, 1965, at 97, interest payable June 30 and December 31. The bonds mature on January 1, 1975.

The Alpha Company acquired 40% of the bonds in the open market on December 31, 1965, for $40,450.

Indicate in journal entry form the eliminations that would be necessary for intercompany gain or loss when preparing a consolidated statement of financial position as of December 31, 1966, in each case below assuming that:

(1) One hundred per cent is eliminated from consolidated retained earnings.

(2) One hundred per cent is eliminated prorata from consolidated retained earnings and minority interest.

Case 1. Baker is the parent owning 100% of Alpha.

Case 2. Baker is the parent owning 90% of Alpha.

Case 3. Alpha is the parent owning 100% of Baker.

Case 4. Alpha is the parent owning 90% of Baker.

Problem 13–4. Company P owns 80% of the stock of Company Y and 90% of the stock of Company Z. Both holdings were acquired prior to 1960 and are carried at *cost*. From the following information prepare in journal entry form any adjustments and eliminations necessary when preparing a consolidated statement of financial position as of December 31, 1967:

(1) Company P has in its inventory merchandise of $48,300 acquired from Company Z. Merchandise is sold by Company Z at 15% above cost.

(2) Company Y has in its inventory merchandise of $7,000 acquired from Company P. The cost of the merchandise to Company P was $4,000.

(3) Company P owns $10,000 (par value) of Company Y bonds. The investment in bonds as of December 31, 1967, is carried at $9,600. Bonds are carried at this date by Company Y at $103\frac{1}{2}$.

(4) Company P owns equipment of $40,000 acquired from Company Y at the end of March, 1967. The equipment was constructed by Company Y and was sold to Company P at a gross profit of 25% based on the selling price. The equipment is being depreciated on a 10-year basis. Depreciation is computed to the nearest month.

Problem 13–5. From the following data prepare working papers for consolidated statements for the year ended December 31, 1968:

Eighty per cent of the capital stock of Company B was acquired for $148,000 in 1966, when Company B had retained earnings of $70,000. Company A carries its investment in Company B by the equity method.

Company A regularly buys merchandise from Company B. The December 31, 1967, inventory of Company A included merchandise acquired from Company B for $24,000; the December 31, 1968, inventory of Company A includes merchandise acquired from Company B for $21,000. During 1968 Company A made purchases from Company B totaling $63,000. Company B sells merchandise to Company A at 20% above cost.

TRIAL BALANCES
DECEMBER 31, 1968

	Company A	Company B
Debits		
Inventories 1/1/68	$ 130,000	$ 110,000
Investment in Company B	176,000	
Other assets (net)	780,000	460,000
Purchases	570,000	330,000
Expenses	185,000	110,000
Dividends paid	16,500	5,000
	$1,857,500	$1,015,000
Credits		
Sales	$ 890,000	$ 530,000
Liabilities	417,500	275,000
Capital stock	300,000	100,000
Retained earnings 1/1/68	250,000	110,000
	$1,857,500	$1,015,000
Inventories, December 31, 1968: Company A	$ 105,000	
Company B	80,000	
	$ 185,000	

Problem 13–6. From the following data prepare working papers for consolidated statements for the year ended December 31, 1968:

Stock of Company S was acquired for $160,000 in 1966, when Company S had retained earnings of $60,000. During 1968 Company P made purchases from Company S totaling $45,000. The December 31, 1967, inventory of

Company P included merchandise acquired from Company S at $22,500; the December 31, 1968, inventory of Company P includes merchandise acquired from Company S at $10,500. Company S sells merchandise to Company P at 25% above cost.

TRIAL BALANCES
DECEMBER 31, 1968

	Company P	Company S
Debits		
Inventories	$ 90,000	$ 70,000
Investment in Company S (90%)	160,000	
Other assets (net)	740,000	410,000
Cost of goods sold	530,000	290,000
Expenses	165,000	95,000
Dividends paid	21,000	6,000
	$1,706,000	$871,000
Credits		
Sales	$ 770,000	$370,000
Dividend income	5,400	
Liabilities	430,000	320,000
Capital stock	300,000	100,000
Retained earnings 1/1/68	200,600	81,000
	$1,706,000	$871,000

Problem 13–7.

ITEM A—Corporation X manufactures at a finished cost of $20.00 per unit and sells to Corporation Y @ $25.00 per unit. Corporation Y leaves its inventory in the warehouse of Corporation X, withdrawing only as needed and pays to Corporation X storage at the rate of 50¢ per unit per month. The quantity in the inventory of Corporation Y at December 31 was purchased six months previously. Corporation Y resells at $40.00, F.O.B. shipping point, which is the same price at which Corporation X sells to others.

ITEM B—Corporation X owns and operates a mine from which Item B is extracted. The average cost of mining Item B is $5.00 per ton. The cost of the mine and development thereof is subject to depletion at the rate of $2.50 per ton. The cost of loading on freight cars averages $1.00 per ton. Corporation Y purchases from Corporation X at cost, F.O.B. the mine, and transports to its plant, paying freight of $1.50 per ton. Corporation X sells approximately 75% of its mined product to others at a price of $15.00 per ton, F.O.B. the mine, and Corporation Y sells at a substantial profit after refinement.

ITEM C—Corporation X buys manufacturing supplies at a price of $50.00 per unit less trade discounts of 10/10/20. A portion of the supplies purchased by Corporation X are resold to Corporation Y at a price of $41.00, F.O.B. Corporation Y's plant. The freight, paid by Corporation X, amounts to 50¢ per unit. Corporation Y does not have access to the market from which Corporation X buys.

ITEM D—Corporation X manufactures this item at the average cost of $29.00 per unit and sells its total output to Corporation Y @ $35.00 per unit, F.O.B. Corporation X's plant, under terms of a firm contract. The freight amounts to

$2.00 per unit. The amount obtainable from Corporation X is only about 50% of the quantity required by Corporation Y. The balance of Corporation Y's requirements are obtained from other sources at a price of $32.50 per unit, F.O.B. Y's plant. Y resells this item at a price which yields $34.00 per unit after allowing for sales and handling expense.

ITEM E—Corporation X manufactures at a cost of $6.00 per unit and sells to Corporation Y and others @ $5.00 per unit, F.O.B. Corporation X's plant. The freight to Y's plant amounts to 75¢ per unit. Corporation Y processes this item and sells at a profit.

Required:
Consider that there were 10 units of each of the five items in the inventory of *each corporation* at the end of their concurrent fiscal years. You are to show the proper valuation at the lower of cost or market for inventory purposes in the financial statements and to explain in connection with each valuation the reason for using it. Answer for each item separately.

(1) In the financial statements of Corporation X and Corporation Y assuming there is no relation between the two corporations.

(2) In the consolidated financial statements assuming Corporation Y is a wholly-owned subsidiary of Corporation X. (AICPA adapted)

Problem 13–8. Company P, a manufacturer of earth-moving equipment, sells 10 units at its regular selling price of $18,000 each (cost is $12,000 each) to its wholly owned subsidiary, Company S, on September 1, 1966. Company S is an *unconsolidated subsidiary*, carried on Company P's books as an investment at a value adjusted for Company S earnings.

Both Company P and Company S are on the accrual basis and use a calendar year accounting period.

Company S was incorporated on July 1, 1966, and its capital stock of $25,000 was sold to P at par. It paid for the equipment purchased from Company P by obtaining a four-year, 6% bank loan on September 1, 1966 for the entire purchase price. The units purchased were leased to Company O, a nonaffiliated company, and the lease was assigned as collateral for the bank loan. The loan is payable in equal monthly principal installments on the first of each month plus interest for the preceding month, starting October 1, 1966. (Interest is computed on a 30-day, 360-day year basis.)

Company S depreciates the equipment on the basis of actual hours used, using a 12,000-hour operating life per unit.

The lease agreement with Company O is dated September 1, 1966, and runs for four years. It provides for rental payments starting October 1, 1966, based on the actual number of hours used the preceding calendar month. Rent is to be computed at the rate of $1.80 per hour, with a minimum monthly rental of $2,500, and a maximum total rental of $216,000. Hours operated were: September, 4,000; October, 5,000; November, 5,500; December, 3,500.

Do not consider federal income taxes in connection with this problem.

(1) What is the amount of gross profit that Company P should report on its income statement for 1966 as realized from the sale? State your reasoning.

(2) Assuming that this is Company S's only business activity, what is its net income for 1966? (Give your supporting computations in good form.)

(3) What is the carrying value of Company S on Company P's books at December 31, 1966? (AICPA adapted)

Problem 13–9. During its fiscal year ended October 31, 1967, the S Company, a wholly owned subsidiary of the P Company, sold to the latter, at a profit, materials which it used in constructing a new building for its own use.

State (1) how the profit on the sales of these materials should be treated in preparing the consolidated financial statements of the P Company and its subsidiary as of October 31, 1967, and for the year then ended respectively, and (2) how it should be treated in preparing financial statements in subsequent years.

(AICPA adapted)

Problem 13–10. From the following trial balances and additional information as of December 31, 1966, you are to prepare working papers showing the consolidated income of P and its subsidiary.

	P COMPANY		S COMPANY	
	Debit	Credit	Debit	Credit
Cash	$ 23,000		$ 30,000	
Accounts receivable	94,000		60,000	
Inventory 1/1/66	105,000		51,000	
Investment in stock of S	175,000			
Investment in bonds of S	51,800			
Other assets	445,000		210,000	
Current liabilities		$ 163,000		$ 17,100
Bonds payable, 5%				200,000
Deferred bond premium				5,400
Sales		630,000		340,000
Purchases	485,000		300,000	
Operating expenses	92,000		70,000	
Other expenses	22,000		15,500	
Interest and dividends		12,800		
Dividends paid	20,000		10,000	
Retained earnings 1/1/66		107,000		84,000
Common stock		600,000		100,000
	$1,512,800	$1,512,800	$746,500	$746,500

Additional information:

(1) The investment in stock of S Co. represents a 90% interest which was acquired January 1, 1966, for $175,000. At the same time $50,000 face amount of bonds of S was acquired for $52,000. These bonds had been issued in 1956 at 106 and are due January 1, 1976. S Co. has recorded the amortization of the bond premium applicable to 1966 as an adjustment of interest expense. The stock and the bonds were not purchased from the S Co. but from the public.

(2) Included in the Purchases Account of S Co. is a total of $180,000 of goods bought from P Co. at 120% of cost to P Co. The closing inventory of S Co. is estimated to include the same proportion of these purchases as of other purchases.

(3) Inventories at December 31, 1966, at cost to each company, were:

P Co.—$80,000
S Co.—$45,000

(AICPA adapted)

Problem 13–11. To facilitate its production of signal flares and equipment, Flare, Inc., on January 1, 1967, purchased the entire capital stock of Metals, Inc., for $875,000, and Tool, Inc., for $1,200,000.

The trial balances of the three companies at December 31, 1967, were as follows:

	Flare, Inc.	Metals, Inc.	Tool, Inc.
Debits			
Cash	$ 80,000	$ 58,000	$ 70,000
Notes receivable	100,000	50,000	25,000
Notes receivable, Flare, Inc.			15,000
Accounts receivable:			
Customers	420,000	190,000	380,000
Metals, Inc.	25,000		30,000
Inventories, January 1, 1967:			
Raw materials	150,000	105,000	160,000
Work in process	80,000	70,000	75,000
Finished goods	90,000	65,000	80,000
Investments:			
Flare, Inc., bonds		102,000	
Metals, Inc., stock	875,000		
Tool, Inc., stock	1,200,000		
Land	150,000	35,000	90,000
Buildings	400,000	100,000	280,000
Machinery and equipment	350,000	165,000	380,000
Purchases	650,000	400,000	510,000
Labor	450,000	320,000	370,000
Manufacturing expenses	235,000	210,000	242,500
Selling expenses	70,000	35,000	80,000
Administrative expenses	60,000	30,000	30,000
Dividends paid	150,000	25,000	40,000
Totals	$5,535,000	$1,960,000	$2,857,500
Credits			
Notes payable to:			
Banks	$ 72,000	$ 30,000	$ 20,000
Tool, Inc.	15,000		
Accounts payable:			
Trade	120,000	135,000	290,000
Flare, Inc.		25,000	
Tool, Inc.		30,000	
Bonds payable	306,000		
Reserve for depreciation	145,000	80,000	150,000
Sales	1,750,000	1,000,000	1,507,500
Dividends received	65,000		
Capital stock	3,000,000	500,000	800,000
Retained earnings, January 1, 1967	62,000	160,000	90,000
Totals	$5,535,000	$1,960,000	$2,857,500

For a number of years, the three companies had traded with each other, and at December 31, 1966, there were included in the raw material inventory of Flare, Inc., goods purchased from Metals, Inc., valued at $60,000 which cost Metals, Inc., $40,000. Likewise, on that date, the raw material inventory of Metals, Inc., included goods purchased from Tool, Inc., for $75,000 which cost the latter company $50,000 to produce.

The intercompany sales for the year ended December 31, 1967, were as follows:

	Selling Price	Cost to Produce
Tools, Inc., to Metals, Inc.	$200,000	$160,000
Metals, Inc., to Flare, Inc.	375,000	300,000

An analysis of the December 31, 1967, inventories revealed the following information:

	Raw Materials	Work in Process	Finished Goods
Flare, Inc.	$280,000	$95,000	$135,000
Intercompany profit included in above	20,000	5,000	4,000
Metals, Inc.	$175,000	$80,000	$145,000
Intercompany profit included in above	30,000	6,000	5,000
Tool, Inc.	$210,000	$85,000	$105,000

On July 1, 1967, Flare, Inc., sold to Metals, Inc., $100,000 first-mortgage 5% bonds at 102. At the same time the remainder of the issue, or $200,000, was sold through a broker for $204,000. The bonds mature June 30, 1972. The interest, payable semi-annually, had not been paid at December 31, 1967.

Required:

Consolidated working papers at December 31, 1967, with columns for income, retained earnings, and financial position.

Problem 13–12. The individual and consolidated statements of companies X and Y for the year ending December 31, 1966, are as shown on page 361.

X Company purchased its 70% interest in Y Company several years ago. X Company sells its product in part to Company Y for further processing, and in part to other firms. The inventories of Y Company included an intercompany mark-up at both the beginning and end of the year. Cash transfers are made between the companies according to working capital needs.

Early in 1966, Y Company purchased $100,000 face value of the bonds of X Company as a temporary investment. These are carried on Y's books at cost.

Required:

On the basis of the information you can develop from an analysis of the individual and consolidated statements, answer the following questions. Show clearly all computations necessary to support your answers.

(1) Does X Company carry its "Investment in Y" on the cost or equity (accrual) basis? State the reason for your conclusion.

	X Company	Y Company	Consolidated
Cash and receivables	$ 35,000	$108,000	$ 97,400
Inventories	40,000	90,000	122,000
Plant (net)	460,000	140,000	600,000
Appraisal increase in plant (net)			50,000
Investment in Y	245,000		–0–
X bonds owned		103,000	–0–
	$780,000	$441,000	$869,400
Current payables	$ 70,000	$ 23,000	$ 53,000
Dividends payable	10,000	8,000	12,400
Mortgage bonds	200,000	50,000	150,000
Capital stock	300,000	200,000	300,000
Retained earnings	200,000	160,000	231,000
Minority interest			123,000
	$780,000	$441,000	$869,400
Sales	$600,000	$400,000	$760,000
Cost of sales	360,000	280,000	403,000
Gross profit	240,000	120,000	357,000
Operating expense	130,000	54,000	184,000
Operating profit	110,000	66,000	173,000
Interest income	1,800	5,000	1,800
Dividend income	11,200	–0–	–0–
Total	$123,000	$ 71,000	$174,800
Interest expense	10,000	3,000	8,000
Provision for income taxes	56,000	34,000	90,000
Nonrecurring loss			3,000
Minority share			5,400
Net income	$ 57,000	$ 34,000	$ 68,400
Dividends	20,000	16,000	24,800
Transfer to retained earnings	$ 37,000	$ 18,000	$ 43,600

(2) The "Appraisal increase" represents a revaluation of the *total* of Y Company's assets on the basis of the price paid by X Company for its interest in Y. What was the balance of Y's "Retained earnings" at date of acquisition?

(3) Prepare a reconciliation schedule which will explain clearly the difference between X Company's "Retained earnings" at December 31, 1966, $200,000, and the "Consolidated retained earnings" at December 31, 1966, $231,000.

(4) What is the nature of the "Nonrecurring loss" on the consolidated income statement? Show the consolidating elimination entry from which it originated.

(5) Show the amounts of intercompany debts, excluding the bonds, and show which company is the debtor and which is the creditor in each instance.

(6) Prepare a schedule reconciling the sum of the "Cost of Sales" of X and

Y individually with the "Consolidated cost of sales." Show clearly the intercompany mark-up in the beginning and ending inventories of Y Company and
how you determined the amounts.   (AICPA adapted)

Problem 13–13. The P Corporation bought from its wholly-owned subsidiary
for $16,000 certain equipment which was carried on the books of the subsidiary
at a cost of $31,000 with accumulated depreciation of $17,000.

State the effect on the consolidated balance sheet of the purchase of equipment
from the subsidiary. State specifically what eliminating entries, if any, should
be made on the consolidating work sheet used for preparation of the consolidated
financial statements.

On January 1, 1965, the S Corporation issued $200,000 of 10-year 4%
bonds. These were sold at 98, and expenses of issue were $2,400. Interest is
payable January 1 and July 1. In March 1968, the P Corporation acquired 80%
of the outstanding stock of S. On March 31, 1969 the P Corporation purchased
on the market $100,000 face value of S Corporation's 4% bonds at 90 and
accrued interest.

You are to state what eliminating entries should be made as a result of the
bond transactions on the consolidating work sheets used for preparation of the
consolidated statements at December 31, 1969. *Give a brief explanation of the
purpose or reason for each entry you make.*   (AICPA adapted)

Problem 13–14. The Ohio Manufacturing Company on January 1, 1966,
acquired 90% of the capital stock of the Wabash Company and on January 1,
1968, 80% of the capital stock of Company X. Following are the trial balances
of the companies at December 31, 1968:

	Ohio Mfg. Co.	90% Wabash Co.	80% Company X
Debits			
Cash	$ 70,500	$ 8,000	$ 28,500
Accounts receivable, customers	132,500	87,000	50,000
Current account, Wabash Co.	10,000		
Current account, Company X	7,500	6,000	
Inventories, January 1, 1968:			
Raw materials	175,000	30,000	22,000
In process	140,000	20,000	20,000
Finished goods	130,000	25,000	15,000
Investments:			
Wabash Company stock (90%)	200,000		
Company X stock (80%)	50,000		
Bonds, Company X		10,000	
Land	20,000	5,000	10,000
Buildings	50,000	40,000	20,000
Machinery and equipment	225,000	180,000	100,000
Prepaid accounts	5,000	4,000	2,000
Material purchases	1,300,000	550,000	320,000
Direct labor	800,000	400,000	100,000
Indirect manufacturing labor	50,000	30,000	10,000
Taxes (other than federal taxes on income)	6,000	4,000	2,000

	Ohio Mfg. Co.	Wabash Co.	Company X
Debits			
Insurance	$ 800	$ 600	$ 200
Repairs	4,700	3,000	1,800
Manufacturing supplies and expense	5,000	4,000	2,500
Sales returns and allowances	10,000	4,000	2,000
Selling expense	100,000	60,000	25,000
General and administrative expense	75,000	40,000	25,000
Bond interest			6,000
Dividends paid		20,000	5,000
Totals	$3,567,000	$1,530,600	$767,000
Credits			
Accounts payable	$ 75,000	$ 70,000	$ 38,000
Current account, Ohio Mfg. Co.		10,000	7,500
Current account, Wabash Co.			6,000
Accrued accounts	154,500	46,500	9,500
Bonds payable			100,000
Reserve for bad debts	2,500	1,500	1,000
Reserve for depreciation	75,000	60,000	45,000
Sales	2,600,000	1,120,000	500,000
Interest income		600	
Rent of factory equipment to Company X		2,000	
Capital stock	500,000	200,000	50,000
Retained earnings, January 1, 1968	160,000	20,000	10,000
Totals	$3,567,000	$1,530,600	$767,000

Inventories at December 31, 1968 were as follows:

	Ohio Mfg. Co.	Wabash Co.	Company X
Raw materials	$190,000	$40,000	$20,000
In process	150,000	25,000	25,000
Finished goods	140,000	30,000	20,000
Totals	$480,000	$95,000	$65,000

During the year 1968 Company X sold to the Ohio Manufacturing Company $150,000 worth of goods and to the Wabash Company $100,000. The Wabash Company sold to the Ohio Manufacturing Company goods to the amount of $400,000.

The inventories at January 1, 1968, contained profits as follows on sales by the Wabash Company to the Ohio Manufacturing Company:

Raw materials	$2,000
In process	1,000
Finished goods	600

The inventories at December 31, 1968, contained the following profits made on intercompany sales:

	On sales by Wabash Co. to Ohio Mfg. Co.	On sales by Company X to Ohio Mfg. Co.	On sales by Company X to Wabash Co.
Raw materials	$2,500	$1,000	$ 800
In process	1,200	800	600
Finished goods	800	600	400
Totals	$4,500	$2,400	$1,800

Each prior year the parent company had taken up in the investment account its share of the subsidiary's profit. Such entry had not yet been made for 1968. All dividends received, including those received from both companies in 1968, had been credited to the respective investment accounts.

Depreciation and prepaid and accrued accounts have been properly accounted for. Federal taxes on income may be ignored. Reserves for bad debts are considered sufficient.

Prepare consolidated financial statements, submitting complete working papers showing the consolidating process.

Problem 13–15. On January 1, 1964, the X Manufacturing Company acquired for $1,000,000 in cash all the capital stock of the Y Coal Company. On that date the statement of financial position of the Y Coal Company was as follows:

Assets

Coal lands, less depletion	$400,000
Other assets (valued in accordance with the accounting practice of both companies)	300,000
	$700,000

Liabilities and Capital

Liabilities	$100,000
Capital stock	500,000
Retained earnings	100,000
	$700,000

The operations of the Y Coal Company are confined to the mining of coal for the exclusive use of the X Manufacturing Company. No inventories of coal are carried by the Y Coal Company, as all coal mined is immediately charged to the X Manufacturing Company at a profit of 50¢ a ton after charging 10¢ a ton to the mining cost for depletion.

The books of the two companies are kept on the same accounting basis but independent of each other and without regard to the requirements of possible consolidation of the statements of financial position.

On December 31, 1969, such a consolidation was contemplated for the first time, and on that date the statement of financial position of the Y Coal Company was as follows:

Assets

Coal lands, less depletion	$300,000
Amount due from X Company	200,000
Other assets	250,000
	$750,000

Liabilities

Liabilities	$100,000
Capital stock	500,000
Retained earnings	150,000
	$750,000

Depletion provided by the Y Company was based on the cost of the coal land to Y at the date of acquisition ($500,000) and the estimated number of tons of coal in the lands (5,000,000). The estimated number of tons of coal in the lands at January 1, 1964, was 4,000,000. Between that date and December 31, 1969, 1,000,000 tons were mined.

The investment by X Company in Y Company was carried at December 31, 1969, at cost to the X Company ($1,000,000). On that date the accounts of X Company showed that an amount of $150,000 was due to the Y Company, and the difference between this amount and the amount of $200,000 shown as receivable by the Y Company was accounted for as follows:

Cash in transit	$40,000
Inventory in transit (5,000 tons at $2)	10,000
	$50,000

The inventory of the X Company contains 5,000 tons of coal (exclusive of the 5,000 tons in transit) at $2 a ton, plus transportation cost, which includes the profit of 50 cents a ton (already mentioned) to the Y company.

There are no intercompany accounts, relations, or transactions other than those indicated in this problem.

Prepare in journal entry form the adjustments and eliminations necessary when preparing consolidated statements on December 31, 1969.

(AICPA adapted)

CHAPTER **14**

Consolidated statements— intercompany stock transactions

In the preceding chapters dealing with consolidated statements it has been assumed, either expressly or by implication, that the controlling interest in a particular subsidiary was obtained as the result of a single purchase or by parental formation. It was also assumed that this interest remained constant throughout the period(s) reported upon. This approach has been used in order to simplify the development of the basic problems involved when preparing consolidated statements. However, in any given situation these assumptions may or may not be valid. Control may not always be obtained by a single purchase or by formation. Control of a particular subsidiary may be obtained by piecemeal acquisition of its stock. Likewise, the controlling interest may not always remain unchanged. It may change at any time not only because of particular actions by the parent but also occasionally by certain actions of the subsidiary involved. For example, the parent may acquire additional stock in a subsidiary or dispose of some already owned. In addition, a subsidiary may issue additional stock which may or may not affect the controlling interest, depending upon the given situation. Likewise, treasury stock transactions by a subsidiary may affect the controlling interest.

In this chapter several of the problems arising from intercompany stock transactions are considered. The effect of such transactions on the parent company's investment account, on the resultant minority interest, and on consolidated retained earnings will be emphasized. The student should relate the methods of analysis of these problems with those methods used in the preceding chapters.

ACQUISITION OF SUBSIDIARY STOCK

Acquisition of Control and the Date of Acquisition

As has been stressed throughout the preceding chapters, the "date of acquisition" is an important time reference, and the periods of time prior to and subsequent to this date are important time frames in the preparation of consolidated statements. The date of acquisition must be known in order to determine the difference between the cost and the book value of the shares acquired, and to segregate the subsidiary's shareholders' equity into its pre- and post-acquisition components.

When control is obtained by one block acquisition of subsidiary company stock, either by purchase or formation, there is general unanimity among accountants as to what the date of acquisition is—the date that control was obtained.

When stock is acquired piecemeal, however, there is not as complete agreement. Some accountants contend the date of acquisition is the date that control is obtained; others maintain that it is the several dates of acquisition. While recognizing the possibility of the former approach being acceptable under some circumstances, in *Accounting Research Bulletin* 51 the Institute recommends that, as a general rule, the latter approach be used.

The use of the date that control is obtained is supported, even when the subsidiary stock has been acquired in small amounts over a period of time, because of its relative simplicity. However, this approach can also be supported on the theoretical grounds that subsidiary stock acquired prior to the acquisition of control is similar to and should be treated as an investment in any other nonaffiliated company. In theory the use of the several dates of acquisition can be justified, especially if the intent of the parent when acquiring the stock on a piecemeal basis was to acquire eventually a controlling interest.

For comparative purposes both approaches are illustrated in the following example. Particular attention should be given to the effect the approach chosen has on the computation of goodwill and consolidated retained earnings.

Assume that Company A makes the following purchases of Company B stock at the times indicated and under the conditions given on page 386.

Date of Purchase	Per Cent Purchased	Cost	Company B's Shareholders' Equity	
			Retained Earnings	Capital Stock
January 1, 1966	10%	$15,000	$20,000	$100,000
January 1, 1967	20%	32,000	30,000	100,000
January 1, 1968	40%	65,000	40,000	100,000

Company A's retained earnings as of January 1, 1968, is $200,000.

(1) Date of acquisition considered to be the *date control acquired:*

    (*a*) Computation of goodwill:

Amount paid	$112,000	
Book value acquired	98,000	(70% of $140,000)
Goodwill	$ 14,000	

    (*b*) Consolidated retained earnings as of January 1, 1968:

        Company A's $200,000

(2) Date of acquisition considered to be the *several dates of acquisition:*

    (*a*) Computation of goodwill:

First purchase:

Amount paid	$ 15,000		
Book value acquired	12,000	(10% of $120,000)	
Goodwill	$ 3,000		$ 3,000

Second purchase:

Amount paid	$ 32,000		
Book value acquired	26,000	(20% of $130,000)	
Goodwill	$ 6,000		6,000

Third purchase:

Amount paid	$ 65,000		
Book value acquired	56,000	(40% of $140,000)	
Goodwill	$ 9,000		9,000
Total goodwill			$ 18,000

    (*b*) Consolidated retained earnings as of January 1, 1968:

Company A's	$200,000
10% of Company B's increase since January 1, 1966.	2,000
20% of Company B's increase since January 1, 1967.	2,000
Consolidated retained earnings as of January 1, 1968	$204,000

The consolidating problem created when the several dates are used is illustrated on the next page. For comparative purposes both approaches are illustrated.

(1)

COMPANY A AND SUBSIDIARY COMPANY B

CONSOLIDATED WORKING PAPERS
STATEMENT OF FINANCIAL POSITION
AS OF JANUARY 1, 1968

	Company A	Company B	Adjustments & Eliminations Debit	Adjustments & Eliminations Credit	Consolidated Financial Position
Current assets	$ 400,000	$ 50,000			$ 450,000
Investment in Co. B (carried at cost)	112,000			$98,000A	14,000G
Fixed assets (net)	610,000	100,000			710,000
	$1,122,000	$150,000			$1,174,000
Current liabilities	$ 22,000	$ 10,000			$ 32,000
Fixed liabilities	100,000				100,000
Shareholders' equity:					
Company A:					
Capital stock	800,000				800,000
Retained earnings	200,000				200,000RE
Company B:					
Capital stock		100,000	$70,000A		30,000MI
Retained earnings		40,000	28,000A		12,000MI
	$1,122,000	$150,000	$98,000	$98,000	$1,174,000

A: To eliminate 70% of Company B's shareholders' equity against the investment account.

(2)

COMPANY A AND SUBSIDIARY COMPANY B

CONSOLIDATED WORKING PAPERS
STATEMENT OF FINANCIAL POSITION
AS OF JANUARY 1, 1968

	Company A	Company B	Adjustments & Eliminations Debit	Adjustments & Eliminations Credit	Consolidated Financial Position
Current assets	$ 400,000	$ 50,000			$ 450,000
Investment in Co. B (carried at cost)	112,000		$ 4,000(1)*	$ 98,000A	18,000G
Fixed assets (net)	610,000	100,000			710,000
	$1,122,000	$150,000			$1,178,000
Current liabilities	$ 22,000	$ 10,000			$ 32,000
Fixed liabilities	100,000				100,000
Shareholders' equity:					
Company A:					
Capital stock	800,000				800,000
Retained earnings	200,000			4,000(1)	204,000RE
Company B:					
Capital stock		100,000	70,000A		30,000MI
Retained earnings		40,000	28,000A		12,000MI
	$1,122,000	$150,000	$102,000	$102,000	$1,178,000

(1): To recognize Company A's share of the increase in Company B's retained earnings prior to the acquisition of controlling interest.

A: To eliminate 70% of Company B's shareholders' equity against the investment account.

* If the investment account were carried on the equity basis this entry would have been entered in Company A's books. However, since the cost method is in use, it is a work sheet entry only.

In these examples the selection of the several dates of acquisition, rather than the date on which control is acquired, results in an additional $4,000 of goodwill with an offsetting $4,000 in consolidated retained earnings. When consolidating (as illustrated in set (2) of working papers on page 387) it is necessary to make an adjustment which increases both goodwill and consolidated retained earnings. Set (2) of working papers (where date of acquisition is considered to be the *several dates of acquisition*) should be compared to set (1) (where the date of acquisition is considered to be the *date control is acquired*).

Purchase of Subsidiary Stock Subsequent to Acquisition of Control

If a parent company purchases additional subsidiary stock after a controlling interest has been acquired, no new problems are encountered. Although the basic procedure remains the same, the establishment of reciprocity and the proof of goodwill may become a little more complicated.

When establishing reciprocity through a work sheet adjustment if the investment account is carried at cost, or a book entry if the equity method is in use, the problem is still one of recognizing the parent's share of any increase or decrease in the subsidiary's shareholders' equity since acquisition. To establish reciprocity for any given period of time the parent should recognize as the increase or decrease the per cent it owned during that time and still owns at the date of consolidation. For example, assume the parent owned an 80% interest during the entire first half of 1967 and a 90% interest during the entire second half. When establishing reciprocity as of December 31, 1967, the amount of the adjustment would equal 80% of any increase or decrease during the first six months plus 90% for the second six months.

Although several purchases of subsidiary stock may complicate the proving of goodwill, the problem is still a matter of determining the amount involved in each purchase by comparing the amount paid with the book value acquired as of the purchase date. The usual elimination whereby goodwill is determined by eliminating the parent's share of the subsidiary's shareholders' equity against the investment account remains the same. To prove the goodwill, however, the amount involved on each individual purchase must be determined.

The following examples as of December 31, 1966, January 1, 1967, and December 31, 1967, illustrate (1) the establishment of reciprocity, and (2) the proof of goodwill where several purchases have taken place subsequent to the acquisition of control. In addition to the specific facts given in the individual statements of financial position also assume:

Company B's Shareholders' Equity

Date of Purchase	Per Cent Purchased	Cost	Retained Earnings	Capital Stock
January 1, 1965	70%	$105,000	$20,000	$100,000
January 1, 1966	10%	16,000	30,000	100,000
January 1, 1967	10%	16,250	40,000	100,000
December 31, 1967	5%	9,000	48,000	100,000

As of December 31, 1966, the work sheet would be:

COMPANY A AND SUBSIDIARY COMPANY B

CONSOLIDATED WORKING PAPERS
STATEMENT OF FINANCIAL POSITION
AS OF DECEMBER 31, 1966

	Company A	Company B	Adjustments & Eliminations Debit	Adjustments & Eliminations Credit	Consolidated Financial Position
Current assets	$ 391,000	$ 50,000			$ 441,000
Investment in Co. B (carried at cost)	121,000		$ 15,000(1)	$112,000A	24,000G*
Fixed assets (net)	610,000	100,000			710,000
	$1,122,000	$150,000			$1,175,000
Current liabilities	$ 22,000	$ 10,000			$ 32,000
Fixed liabilities	100,000				100,000
Shareholders' equity:					
Company A:					
Capital stock	800,000				800,000
Retained earnings	200,000			15,000(1)	215,000RE
Company B:					
Capital stock		100,000	80,000A		20,000MI
Retained earnings		40,000	32,000A		8,000MI
	$1,122,000	$150,000	$127,000	$127,000	$1,175,000

(1): To establish reciprocity by recognizing Company A's share of the increase in Company B's shareholders' equity since acquisition. Computed:

Either	*Or*
70% × $10,000 = $ 7,000†	70% × $20,000 = $14,000
80% × 10,000 = 8,000†	10% × 10,000 = 1,000
$15,000	$15,000

A: To eliminate 80% of Company B's shareholders' equity against the investment account.

* Goodwill proof:

First purchase:

Amount paid	$105,000	
Book value acquired	84,000	(70% of $120,000)
Goodwill	$ 21,000	$21,000

Second purchase:

Amount paid	$ 16,000	
Book value acquired	13,000	(10% of $130,000)
Goodwill	$ 3,000	3,000
Goodwill as of December 31, 1966		$24,000

† Recorded periodically when the equity method is used.

As of January 1, 1967, the work sheet would be:

COMPANY A AND SUBSIDIARY COMPANY B
CONSOLIDATED WORKING PAPERS
STATEMENT OF FINANCIAL POSITION
AS OF JANUARY 1, 1967

	Company A	Company B	Adjustments & Eliminations Debit	Credit	Consolidated Financial Position
Current assets	$ 374,750	$ 50,000			$ 424,750
Investment in Co. B					
(carried at cost)	137,250		$ 15,000(1)	$126,000A	26,250G*
Fixed assets (net)	610,000	100,000			710,000
	$1,122,000	$150,000			$1,161,000
Current liabilities	$ 22,000	$ 10,000			$ 32,000
Fixed liabilities	100,000				100,000
Shareholders' equity:					
Company A:					
Capital stock	800,000				800,000
Retained earnings	200,000			15,000(1)	215,000RE
Company B:					
Capital stock		100,000	$ 90,000A		10,000M
Retained earnings		40,000	36,000A		4,000M
	$1,122,000	$150,000	$141,000	$141,000	$1,161,000

(1): To establish reciprocity by recognizing Company A's share of the increase in Company B's shareholders' equity since acquisition. Computed:

Either	*Or*
70% × $10,000 = $ 7,000†	70% × $20,000 = $14,000
80% × 10,000 = 8,000†	10% × 10,000 = 1,000
$15,000	$15,000

A: To eliminate 90% of Company B's shareholders' equity against the investment account.

* Goodwill proof:

First purchase:
Amount paid	$105,000	
Book value acquired	84,000	
Goodwill	$ 21,000	$21,000

Second purchase:
Amount paid	$ 16,000	
Book value acquired	13,000	
Goodwill	3,000	3,000

Third purchase:
Amount paid	$ 16,250	
Book value acquired	14,000	(10% of $140,000)
Goodwill	$ 2,250	2,250
Goodwill as of January 1, 1967		$26,250

† Recorded periodically when the equity method is used.

As of December 31, 1967, the work sheet would be:

COMPANY A AND SUBSIDIARY COMPANY B

CONSOLIDATED WORKING PAPERS
STATEMENT OF FINANCIAL POSITION

As OF DECEMBER 31, 1967

	Company A	Company B	Adjustments & Eliminations Debit	Credit	Consolidated Financial Position
Current assets	$ 400,750	$ 53,000			$ 453,750
Investment in Co. B					
(carried at cost)	146,250		$ 22,200(1)	$ 140,600A	27,850G*
Fixed assets (net)	650,000	100,000			750,000
	$1,197,000	$153,000			$1,231,600
Current liabilities	$ 77,000	$ 5,000			$ 82,000
Fixed liabilities	100,000				100,000
Shareholders' equity:					
Company A:					
Capital stock	800,000				800,000
Retained earnings	220,000			22,200(1)	242,200RE
Company B:					
Capital stock		100,000	95,000A		5,000MI
Retained earnings		48,000	45,600A		2,400MI
	$1,197,000	$153,000	$162,800	$162,800	$1,231,600

(1): To establish reciprocity by recognizing Company A's share of the increase in Company B's shareholders' equity since acquisition. Computed:

Either			*Or*		
70% × $10,000 =	$ 7,000†		70% × $28,000 =	$19,600	
80% × 10,000 =	8,000†		10% × 18,000 =	1,800	
90% × 8,000 =	7,200†		10% × 8,000 =	800	
	$22,200			$22,200	

A: To eliminate 95% of Company B's shareholders' equity against the investment account.

* Goodwill proof:

First purchase: (as computed above)			$21,000
Second purchase: (as computed above)			3,000
Third purchase: (as computed above)			2,250
Fourth purchase:			
Amount paid	$9,000		
Book value acquired	7,400	(5% of $148,000)	
Goodwill	$1,600		1,600
Goodwill as of December 31, 1967			$27,850

† Recorded periodically when the equity method is used.

Purchase of Subsidiary Stock at Interim Dates

Only the parent's share of post-acquisition earnings of a subsidiary is properly included in consolidated retained earnings. Thus whenever stock of a subsidiary is acquired at some date other than the subsidiary's closing date, whether it be the acquisition of a controlling interest or additional stock acquisition after control has been acquired, a proration of the subsidiary's income may be necessary. Proration may be necessary not only to determine the subsidiary's income subsequent to the date of acquisition, but it may also be necessary in order to determine the amount of subsidiary's retained earnings as of the date of acquisition and the amount of any goodwill involved. If the subsidiary has an adequate system of interim reporting, the problem is simplified. However, if statement preparation by the subsidiary is not feasible as of the date of an interim purchase, proration based on approximation may be necessary.

When preparing consolidated statements once the subsidiary's income for a period has been prorated between the pre- and post-acquisition periods, the problem of statement presentation arises. One of two methods may be used. The first includes both the pre- and post-acquisition earnings of the subsidiary in the consolidated statement of income as if the purchase had been made either prior to or as of the beginning of the year. The pre-acquisition earnings of the subsidiary are then deducted when proration takes place. The second method includes only the post-acquisition earnings of the subsidiary in the consolidated statement of income. The first method is generally preferred, not only because it facilitates comparison with subsequent statements, but also because the resultant statement is more indicative of the earning power of the affiliated group. This method is illustrated in the following examples.

Since the problems involved in interim acquisitions pertain not only to the acquisition of control but also to the acquisition of additional stock subsequent to the acquisition of control, both situations are illustrated. For comparison purposes a continuing situation is used.

Interim Acquisition of Control. In addition to the facts given in the respective statements assume:

(1) On April 30, 1967, Company A purchases 80% of Company B's capital stock for $125,000.

(2) As of December 31, 1966, Company B had retained earnings of $40,000.

(3) During 1967 Company B's earnings of $30,000 were earned more or less uniformly throughout the year.

CONSOLIDATED WORKING PAPERS
STATEMENT OF FINANCIAL POSITION
As of December 31, 1967

	Company A	Company B	Adjustments & Eliminations Debit	Adjustments & Eliminations Credit	Consolidated Financial Position
Current assets	$200,000	$ 90,000			$290,000
Investment in Co. B (carried at cost)	125,000		$ 16,000(1)	$136,000A	5,000G*
Fixed assets (net)	500,000	100,000			600,000
	$825,000	$190,000			$895,000
Current liabilities	$ 65,000	$ 20,000			$ 85,000
Fixed liabilities	100,000				100,000
Shareholders' equity:					
Company A:					
Capital stock	500,000				500,000
Retained earnings	160,000			16,000(1)	176,000RE
Company B:					
Capital stock		100,000	80,000A		20,000MI
Retained earnings		70,000	56,000A		14,000MI
	$825,000	$190,000	$152,000	$152,000	$895,000

(1): To establish reciprocity by recognizing Company A's share of the increase in Company B's shareholders' equity since acquisition (80% × $30,000 × 2/3).

A: To eliminate 80% of Company B's shareholders' equity against the investment account.

* Goodwill proof:

Amount paid	$125,000	
Book value acquired	120,000	(80% of $150,000)†
Goodwill	$ 5,000	

† $100,000 + $70,000 − (2/3 of $30,000) = $150,000
or $100,000 + $40,000 + (1/3 of $30,000) = $150,000

Company A and Subsidiary Company B
CONSOLIDATED WORKING PAPERS
STATEMENT OF INCOME
For the Year 1967

	Company A	Company B	Eliminations	Consolidated Income
Credits:				
Net sales	$800,000	$200,000	$10,000A	$990,000
Interest income	6,000			6,000
Totals	$806,000	$200,000	$10,000	$996,000
Debits:				
Cost of sales	$560,000	$110,000	$10,000A	$660,000
Depreciation	80,000	20,000		100,000
Selling expense	46,000	10,000		56,000
Taxes	60,000	30,000		90,000
Net income	60,000	30,000		90,000
Totals	$806,000	$200,000	$10,000	$996,000

Apportionment of net income:

Net income		$ 90,000
Minority interest (20% of $30,000)	$ 6,000	
Parent's share of B's income earned prior to acquisition (80% of $10,000)	8,000	14,000
Consolidated net income (remainder)		$ 76,000

A: To eliminate intercompany sales.

393

COMPANY A AND SUBSIDIARY COMPANY B
STATEMENT OF INCOME
Income: FOR THE YEAR 1967

Net sales	$990,000	
Interest income	6,000	
	996,000	$996,000
Deductions from Income:		
Cost of sales	$660,000	
Depreciation	100,000	
Selling expense	56,000	
Taxes	90,000	
	906,000	906,000
Net income		90,000
Deduct:		
Minority interest	$ 6,000	
Parent's share of B's income prior to acquisition	8,000	$ 14,000
Consolidated net income		$ 76,000

Interim Purchase Subsequent to Acquisition of Control.

In addition to the specific facts given in the respective statements and those given in the preceding example, assume that:

(1) On April 30, 1968, Company A purchases an additional 10% of Company B's capital stock for $20,000.
(2) During 1968 Company B earned $36,000 which was earned uniformly throughout the year.

COMPANY A AND SUBSIDIARY COMPANY B
CONSOLIDATED WORKING PAPERS
STATEMENT OF FINANCIAL POSITION
As of DECEMBER 31, 1968

	Company A	Company B	Adjustments & Eliminations Debit	Adjustments & Eliminations Credit	Consolidated Financial Position
Current assets	$225,000	$126,000			$351,000
Investment in Co. B (carried at cost)	145,000		$ 47,200(1)	$185,400A	6,800G*
Fixed assets (net)	530,000	90,000			620,000
	$900,000	$216,000			$977,800
Current liabilities	$ 70,000	$ 10,000			$ 80,000
Fixed liabilities	100,000				100,000
Shareholders' equity:					
Company A:					
Capital stock	500,000				500,000
Retained earnings	230,000			47,200(1)	277,200RE
Company B:					
Capital stock		100,000	90,000A		10,000MI
Retained earnings		106,000	95,400A		10,600MI
	$900,000	$216,000	$232,600	$232,600	$977,800

Footnotes on opposite page

COMPANY A AND SUBSIDIARY COMPANY B
CONSOLIDATED WORKING PAPERS
STATEMENT OF INCOME
FOR THE YEAR 1968

	Company A	Company B	Eliminations	Consolidated Income
Credits:				
Net sales	$840,000	$210,000	$20,000*A*	$1,030,000
Interest income	6,000			6,000
	$846,000	$210,000	$20,000	$1,036,000
Debits:				
Cost of sales	$570,000	$115,000	$20,000*A*	$ 665,000
Depreciation	80,000	15,000		95,000
Selling expense	56,000	8,000		64,000
Taxes	70,000	36,000		106,000
Net income	70,000	36,000		106,000
	$846,000	$210,000	$20,000	$1,036,000

Apportionment of net income:

Net income		$ 106,000
Minority interest (10% of $36,000)	$ 3,600	
Parent's share of B's income earned prior to acquisition (10% × $36,000 × 1/3)	1,200	4,800
Consolidated net income (remainder)		$ 101,200

A: To eliminate intercompany sales.

---

(1): To establish reciprocity by recognizing Company A's share of the increase in Company B's shareholders' equity since acquisition. Computed:

Either

80% ($106,000 − $50,000) = $44,800
10% × $36,000 × 2/3   = 2,400
                        $47,200

Or

1967 (80% × $30,000 × 2/3) = $16,000
1968 (80% × $36,000 × 1/3) = 9,600
    (90% × $36,000 × 2/3) = 21,600
                            $47,200

A: To eliminate 90% of Company B's shareholders' equity against the investment account.

* Goodwill proof:

First purchase (as computed above)		$5,000
Second purchase:		
Amount paid	$20,000	
Book value acquired	18,200 (10% of $182,000)†	
Goodwill	$ 1,800	1,800
Goodwill as of December 31, 1968		$6,800

† $100,000 + $70,000 + (1/3 of $36,000) = $182,000.

COMPANY A AND SUBSIDIARY COMPANY B
STATEMENT OF INCOME
FOR THE YEAR 1968

Income:

Net sales	$1,030,000	
Interest income	6,000	
	1,036,000	$1,036,000
Deductions from Income:		
Cost of sales	$ 665,000	
Depreciation	95,000	
Selling expense	64,000	
Taxes	106,000	
	930,000	930,000
Net income		$ 106,000
Deduct:		
Minority interest	$ 3,600	
Parent's share of B's income prior to acquisition	1,200	4,800
Consolidated net income		$ 101,200

DISPOSAL OF SUBSIDIARY STOCK

The disposal of subsidiary stock, whether it be complete or partial, is similar to the disposal of any other asset. As in the case of any asset disposal, the problem includes (1) recording any asset(s) received, (2) removing the carrying value of the asset disposed of from the appropriate account(s), and (3) recording any gain or loss on disposal. Since the determination of the value of the asset(s) received is normally not too difficult, and since the gain or loss is the difference between the value of the asset(s) received and the carrying value of the asset disposed of, the basic problem involved is one of determining the carrying value of the subsidiary stock disposed of.

In order to illustrate some of the ramifications involved when accounting for disposal of subsidiary stock, several different examples are presented. Although the cost method of carrying the investment is the one usually used, for comparison purposes the equity method is also illustrated. When comparing the two methods it should be recognized that since the carrying value may vary, depending upon the method used, any gain or loss on disposal will also vary. However, the ultimate effect on consolidated retained earnings will be the same. When the equity method is in use the ultimate effect will include not only any gain or loss on disposal but also the parent's share of all increases and decreases in the subsidiary's shareholders' equity since acquisition. Under the cost method the ultimate effect would include only the gain or loss on disposal. Reconciliation of the consolidated retained earnings is illustrated in the first example. In addition it should be noted that a proportionate amount of goodwill is also disposed of since goodwill arising from consolidation attaches to the individual shares owned. When some of the shares are sold, goodwill on consolidation is also sold.

In addition to specific conditions given in each illustration, assume also the following general conditions. It should be emphasized that the illustrations are *not* continuous. Each is a separate situation based on the general and specific facts given.

(1) As of January 1, 1966, Company A purchases 80% of Company B's capital stock for $80,000. As of that date Company B had capital stock of $100,000 and a deficit of $10,000.
(2) During 1966, Company B earns $20,000.
(3) As of January 1, 1967, Company A purchases an additional 10% interest in Company B for $11,000.
(4) As of May 1, 1967, Company A purchases another 10% interest in Company B for $11,000.
(5) During 1967, Company B earns $30,000.
(6) Assume that yearly earnings by Company B are earned more or less uniformly throughout the year.

Complete Disposal

In addition to the general conditions, assume that Company A sells all of its interest (80%) in Company B as of December 31, 1966, for $88,000. The entry to reflect the sale would be:

Cost method:

Cash	$88,000	
Investment in Company B (cost)		$80,000
Gain on disposal of subsidiary stock		8,000*

Equity method:

Cash	$88,000	
Loss on disposal of subsidiary stock	8,000*	
Investment in Company B		$96,000
[$80,000 + (80% × $20,000)]		

* The ultimate effect on consolidated retained earnings would be:

	Cost	Equity
Recognition of B's increase or (decrease) in shareholders' equity	–0–	$16,000
Recognition of gain or (loss) on disposal	$8,000	(8,000)
Ultimate effect	$8,000	$ 8,000

Partial Disposal

In addition to the general conditions, assume that on December 31, 1967, Company A sells a 10% interest in Company B for $15,000. The gain or loss on disposal may vary depending upon the accounting policy adopted for pricing out the stock investment sold. Since specific identification is one method which may be used to price the investment sold, the amount of gain or loss reported may be regulated to a certain extent by selecting the certificates delivered. In the following example, the specific identification method is assumed, and entries for all three blocks of stock are included:

		Certificates Delivered		
		1st Purchase	2nd Purchase	3rd Purchase
Cost method:				
Cash	$15,000			
Investment in Company B		$10,000	$11,000	$11,000
Gain on disposal of stock		5,000	4,000	4,000
Equity method:				
Cash	$15,000			
Investment in Company B		$15,000*	$14,000*	$13,000*
Gain on disposal of stock		–0–	1,000	2,000*

* Computation of carrying value:

First purchase:
$(1/8 \times \$80,000) + (1/10 \times \$50,000) =$ $15,000

Second purchase:
$\$11,000 + (1/10 \times \$30,000)$ $=$ 14,000

Third purchase:
$\$11,000 + (1/10 \times \$30,000 \times 2/3)$ $=$ 13,000

Partial Disposal at an Interim Date. Disposal at an interim date creates no unusual problem if the investment account is carried at cost. However, if the equity method is in use, a proration of income similar to the proration problem involved when subsidiary stock is acquired at an interim date may be necessary. In addition to the general conditions, assume that as of July 1, 1967, Company A sells a 10% interest in Company B for $11,000.

		Certificates Delivered		
		1st Purchase	2nd Purchase	3rd Purchase
Cost method:				
Cash	$11,000			
Investment in Company B		$10,000	$11,000	$11,000
Gain (loss)		1,000	–0–	–0–
Equity method:				
Cash	$11,000			
Investment in Company B		$13,500*	$12,500*	$11,500*
Gain (loss)		(2,500)	(1,500)	(500)

Footnote at top of page 399

* Computation of carrying value:

First purchase:
$(1/8 \times \$80,000) + (1/10 \times \$20,000) + (1/10 \times \$30,000 \times 1/2) =$ $\$13,500$

Second purchase:
$\$11,000 + (1/10 \times \$30,000 \times 1/2)$ $=$ $12,500$

Third purchase:
$\$11,000 + (1/10 \times \$30,000 \times 1/6)$ $=$ $11,500$

Effect of Partial Disposals on Consolidated Goodwill.

As emphasized throughout the work on consolidated statements, the amount of goodwill determined at the date of purchase remains the same unless it is amortized or unless there is a change in the per cent of ownership. As seen earlier in this chapter an increase in the per cent of ownership will affect the amount of consolidated goodwill, if the purchase price is anything other than book value of the interest acquired. A disposal of subsidiary stock likewise will affect consolidated goodwill, if there was any goodwill associated with the acquisition of the stock being disposed.

In addition to the general conditions given on page 397, assume also that a 10% interest in Company B is sold by Company A for $14,000 on October 31, 1967. Assume further that the stock certificates delivered are from the January 1, 1966, purchase. The entry to record the sale would be:

		Cost	*Equity*
Cash	$14,000		
Investment in Company B		$10,000	$14,500*
Gain (loss) on disposal		4,000	(500)

* Computation of carrying value:
$1/8 \times (\$80,000 + \$16,000 + \$20,000)$

Goodwill prior to the disposal:

First purchase (1/1/66):		
Paid	$80,000	
Book value acquired	72,000 [80% × ($100,000 − $10,000)]	
Goodwill	$ 8,000	$8,000

Second purchase (1/1/67):		
Paid	$11,000	
Book value acquired	11,000 [10% × ($100,000 + $10,000)]	
Goodwill	$ –0–	–0–

Third purchase (5/1/67):		
Paid	$11,000	
Book value acquired	12,000 [10% × ($100,000 + $20,000)]	
Goodwill	$(1,000)	(1,000)

Consolidated goodwill as of October 31, 1967, prior to sale	$7,000

Since the stock certificates delivered were identified as being from the first purchase, one-eighth of the goodwill associated with that purchase was disposed of. Consequently, consolidated goodwill after the disposal should be $1,000 (1/8 × $8,000) less or a total of $6,000. Proof of this both under the cost and equity method follows:

Goodwill after disposal:

	Cost	*Equity*
Carrying value after disposal (10/31/67)	$ 92,000[1]	$127,500[2]
Establishment of reciprocity (10/31/67)	35,500[3]	–0–
	$127,500	$127,500
Elimination (90% × $135,000)	121,500	121,500
Goodwill	$ 6,000	$ 6,000

[1] INVESTMENT IN COMPANY B (Cost)

1st Purchase	$80,000	Disposal	$10,000
2nd Purchase	11,000		
3rd Purchase	11,000		

[2] INVESTMENT IN COMPANY B (Equity)

1st Purchase	$80,000	Disposal	$14,500
1966 Profit	16,000		
2nd Purchase	11,000		
3rd Purchase	11,000		
1967 Profit as of			
10/31/67	24,000		

[3] Establishment of reciprocity:

Either		*Or*	
1966 Profits 70% × $20,000	= $14,000	70% × $20,000	= $14,000
1967 Profits 80% × 30,000 × 5/6 =	20,000	80% × 30,000 × 1/3 =	8,000
10% × 30,000 × 1/2 =	1,500	90% × 30,000 × 1/2 =	13,500
	$35,500		$35,500

Effect of Partial Disposals on Subsequent Consolidations. When illustrating the effect of a partial disposal on consolidated goodwill in the preceding section, it was observed that a partial disposal affects subsequent consolidations if the cost method is in use. For example, when establishing reciprocity in the immediately preceding illustration, it will be noted that under the cost method the establishment of reciprocity is dependent not upon the percentage of subsidiary stock owned during a given period but upon the percentage owned during the period and retained to the date of consolidation. For instance, during 1966 Company A owned an 80% interest in Company B. However, since the 10% disposal was assumed to have been from the first purchase, when establishing reciprocity after the disposal only 70% of the profits for 1966 were recognized. Likewise, Company A owned a 90% interest during the first four months and a 100% interest during the next six months of 1967, but only 80% and 90% respectively were recognized when establishing reciprocity after the sale.

Had the certificates delivered been identified as having been from the second or third purchase, the percentages to use in establishing reciprocity would have been as follows (for comparison purposes the first purchase is also included):

Certificates Delivered

	1st Purchase	2nd Purchase	3rd Purchase
1966 Profits	70%	80%	80%
1967 Profits: First 4 months	80%	80%	90%
Next 6 months	90%	90%	90%

If the investment account is carried on the equity method, a partial disposal creates no unusual problem as far as subsequent consolidations are concerned. This is because increases and decreases in a subsidiary's shareholders' equity are recognized on the books of the parent, and the resulting gain or loss on disposal is affected accordingly.

Continuing the illustration from the preceding section, the consolidating process as of December 31, 1967, would reflect the following:

	Cost	Equity
Carrying value	$ 92,000	$132,000[1]
Establishment of reciprocity	40,000[2]	–0–
	$132,000	$132,000
Elimination (90% × $140,000)	126,000	$126,000
Goodwill	$ 6,000	$ 6,000

[1] $127,500 + (90% × $30,000 × 1/6).

[2]
$$\begin{array}{rcl} 70\% \times \$20{,}000 &=& \$14{,}000 \\ 80\% \times 30{,}000 \times 1/3 &=& 8{,}000 \\ 90\% \times 30{,}000 \times 2/3 &=& 18{,}000 \\ \hline && \$40{,}000 \end{array}$$

Assuming the 10% disposal to have been from the second or third purchase rather than the first, the consolidating process as of December 31, 1967, would reflect the following:

Certificates Delivered

	2nd Purchase		3rd Purchase	
	Cost	Equity	Cost	Equity
Carrying value	$ 91,000	$133,000	$ 91,000	$134,000
Establishment of reciprocity	42,000	–0–	43,000	–0–
	$133,000	$133,000	$134,000	$134,000
Elimination (90% of $140,000)	126,000	126,000	126,000	126,000
Goodwill*	$ 7,000	$ 7,000	$ 8,000	$ 8,000

* The goodwill determined here should be reconciled with the goodwill determined prior to the disposal on page 399.

SUBSIDIARY STOCK TRANSACTIONS

Preceding sections of this chapter have been concerned with inter-company-stock-transaction problems created primarily by parental action, namely: (1) the acquisition of, or (2) the disposal of, subsidiary stock. However, some intercompany-stock-transaction problems are created primarily by subsidiary action. For instance, intercompany-stock-transaction problems may be created by a subsidiary through (1) the issuance of additional shares of stock, or (2) treasury stock transactions. Likewise, a problem may arise by the existence or creation of subsidiary preferred stock. These and similar problems are considered in this section.

Issuance of Additional Shares of Subsidiary Stock

The issuance of additional shares of stock by a subsidiary may take the form of (1) a sale, or (2) a stock distribution.[1] When additional shares are sold by a subsidiary subsequent to the date of acquisition, the parent's equity in the subsidiary held prior to the sale may be affected depending upon circumstances. Although the parent's equity in a subsidiary is generally not affected by a subsidiary stock distribution, the composition of the subsidiary's shareholders' equity is affected.

Issuance by Sale. If subsequent to the date of acquisition a subsidiary sells additional stock at *book value*, a change in the per cent of

[1] Both stock dividends and stock split-ups are included in the term "stock distribution" as used in this section.

ownership by the parent may take place. No change, however, would take place in the parent company's equity held prior to the sale, and no particular problem arises. If an additional issue of stock is sold by a subsidiary subsequent to the date of acquisition at a price *other than book value*, however, not only may the per cent of ownership change but a dilution or an increase in the parent company's equity held prior to the sale may result. The particular effect will depend upon the circumstances.

The following examples, although not exhaustive, illustrate the effect of an additional issue of a subsidiary stock by sale and the adjustments which may be necessary. Although only three general possibilities exist from the standpoint of the price received (at, above, or below book value), many possibilities exist from the standpoint of who acquires the new issue. For instance, the parent may buy some, none, or all of the stock issued. Since so many possible combinations exist, for illustrative purposes it is assumed that the parent buys either all or none. Assume also that Company A (the parent) acquired 80% of Company B's stock for $110,000 at a time when Company B had capital stock outstanding of $100,000 (par value—$100 per share) and retained earnings of $20,000. At the time of the additional issue of $20,000 par value stock Company B's retained earnings was $60,000.

Sale at Book Value. If Company B issues $20,000 par value stock at book value, it will receive $32,000 [($160,000 ÷ 100,000) × 20,000].

	NEW ISSUE ACQUIRED BY			
	Company A		Outsiders	
	Prior to Issuance	After Issuance	Prior to Issuance	After Issuance
Company B's shareholders' equity:				
Capital stock	$100,000	$120,000	$100,000	$120,000
Retained earnings	60,000	60,000	60,000	60,000
Capital surplus		12,000		12,000
Total shareholders' equity	$160,000	$192,000	$160,000	$192,000
Company A's interest	80%	83⅓%	80%	66⅔%
Minority interest	20%	16⅔%	20%	33⅓%
Company A's equity	$128,000	$160,000	$128,000	$128,000
Pertaining to new issue		32,000*		
Pertaining to old issue	128,000	128,000	128,000	128,000
Increase (decrease)	–0–		–0–	

* 16⅔% of $192,000

Although Company A's per cent of ownership will change unless it acquires a proportionate amount of the new issue, the equity of the stock held prior to the new issue will not be affected. This is true whether Company A or outsiders acquire the new issue.

Sale above Book Value. If Company B issues $20,000 par value stock at $175 per share, it will receive $35,000. In this instance Company A's per cent of ownership will change unless it acquires a proportionate amount of the new issue. In addition, the equity of the shares held prior to the new issue will also change. As a consequence the basic procedure involved when establishing reciprocity will include an adjustment for this change.

| | NEW ISSUE ACQUIRED BY | | | |
| | Company A | | Outsiders | |
	Prior to Issuance	After Issuance	Prior to Issuance	After Issuance
Company B's shareholders' equity:				
Capital stock	$100,000	$120,000	$100,000	$120,000
Retained earnings	60,000	60,000	60,000	60,000
Capital surplus		15,000		15,000
Total shareholders' equity	$160,000	$195,000	$160,000	$195,000
Company A's interest	80%	83⅓%	80%	66⅔%
Minority interest	20%	16⅔%	20%	33⅓%
Company A's equity	$128,000	$162,500	$128,000	$130,000
Pertaining to new issue		32,500*		
Pertaining to old issue	128,000	130,000	128,000	130,000
Increase or (decrease)	$2,000		$2,000	

   * 16⅔% of $195,000

BASIC PROCEDURE. Since Company A's equity in Company B as represented by the interest held prior to the additional issue has increased, the following entry (a work sheet entry if the investment is carried at cost, and a book entry if the equity method is in use) is necessary when establishing reciprocity:

        Investment in Company B $2,000
               Consolidated capital surplus $2,000

The above entry recognizes the increase in the parent's equity in the subsidiary arising from the subsidiary's issuance of additional stock at more than book value. While it may be contended that the above credit should be to retained earnings, the credit to capital surplus appears to be more appropriate because the amount involved arose from a capital stock transaction. The need for the adjustment is clearly evident when the goodwill elements in existence prior to and after the additional issue are reconciled.

GOODWILL RECONCILIATION

		New Issue Acquired by	
		Company A	Outsiders
Goodwill determined at date of purchase:			
Original issue:			
Paid	$110,000		
Book value acquired	96,000		
Goodwill involved	$ 14,000	$ 14,000 .	$ 14,000
Additional issue:			
Paid	$ 35,000		
Book value acquired	32,500		
Goodwill involved	$ 2,500	2,500	–0–
Total goodwill		$ 16,500	$ 14,000
Goodwill determined by work sheet elimination: *			
Carrying value:			
Cost		$145,000	$110,000
(80% × $40,000 increase in B's retained earnings since acquisition—needed to establish reciprocity)		32,000	32,000
		$177,000	$142,000
Elimination		162,500[1]	130,000[2]
Goodwill		$ 14,500	$ 12,000

* Assuming no adjustment for the increase in equity.
[1] $83\frac{1}{3}\%$ of $195,000
[2] $66\frac{2}{3}\%$ of $195,000

Since the amount of goodwill determined by comparing cost with book value acquired on the purchase date, as compared to the amount determined by elimination after the additional stock issue, differs by $2,000 ($16,500 as compared to $14,500, and $14,000 as compared to $12,000), an adjustment is necessary.

To illustrate the overall effect on consolidated statements of a sale of subsidiary stock to *outsiders*, two work sheets in abbreviated form are presented below.

CONSOLIDATED WORKING PAPERS

BEFORE SALE OF NEW STOCK

	Company A	Company B	Adjustments & Eliminations Debit	Adjustments & Eliminations Credit	Consolidated Financial Position
Investment in B, at cost (80%)	$110,000		$32,000(1)	$128,000*A*	$ 14,000G
Other assets	702,000	$160,000			862,000
	$812,000	$160,000			$876,000
Capital stock, A	$800,000				$800,000
Retained earnings, A	12,000			32,000(1)	44,000RE
Capital stock, B		$100,000	80,000*A*		20,000MI
Retained earnings, B		60,000	48,000*A*		12,000MI
	$812,000	$160,000	$160,000	$160,000	$876,000

CONSOLIDATED WORKING PAPERS

AFTER SALE OF NEW STOCK

	Company A	Company B	Adjustments & Eliminations Debit	Adjustments & Eliminations Credit	Consolidated Financial Position
Investment in B, at cost (66⅔%)	$110,000		$ 34,000(1)	$130,000*A*	$ 14,000G
Other assets	702,000	$195,000			897,000
	$812,000	$195,000			$911,000
Capital stock, A	$800,000				$800,000
Consolidated Capital Surplus				2,000(1)	2,000
Retained earnings, A	12,000			32,000(1)	44,000RE
Capital stock, B		$120,000	80,000*A*		40,000MI
Retained earnings, B		60,000	40,000*A*		20,000MI
Capital surplus, B		15,000	10,000*A*		5,000MI
	$812,000	$195,000	$164,000	$164,000	$911,000

Sale below Book Value. If Company B issues $20,000 par value stock at $130 per share, it will receive $26,000. In this instance, as in the preceding one, Company A's per cent of ownership will change unless it acquires a proportionate amount of the new issue, and the equity of the shares held prior to the new issue will also change. As a consequence the basic procedure involved when establishing reciprocity will again include an adjustment for this change. In this case, however, the change is a dilution in equity instead of an increase.

NEW ISSUE ACQUIRED BY

	Company A		Outsiders	
	Prior to Issuance	After Issuance	Prior to Issuance	After Issuance
Company B's shareholders' equity:				
Capital stock	$100,000	$120,000	$100,000	$120,000
Retained earnings	60,000	60,000	60,000	60,000
Capital surplus		6,000		6,000
Total shareholders' equity	$160,000	$186,000	$160,000	$186,000
Company A's interest	80%	$83\frac{1}{3}\%$	80%	$66\frac{2}{3}\%$
Minority interest	20%	$16\frac{2}{3}\%$	20%	$33\frac{1}{3}\%$
Company A's equity	$128,000	$155,000	$128,000	$124,000
Pertaining to new issue		31,000*		
Pertaining to old issue	128,000	124,000	128,000	124,000
Increase or (decrease)		($4,000)		($4,000)

* $16\frac{2}{3}\%$ of $186,000

BASIC PROCEDURE. Since Company A's equity, as represented by the interest held prior to the additional issue, has decreased, the following entry (a work sheet entry if the investment is carried at cost and a book entry if the equity method is in use) is necessary when establishing reciprocity.

Consolidated capital surplus	$4,000	
Investment in Company B		$4,000

(to recognize dilution in equity resulting from the issuance of additional stock at less than book value)

GOODWILL RECONCILIATION

		New Issue Acquired by	
		Company A	Outsiders
Goodwill determined at date of purchase:			
Original issue:			
Paid	$110,000		
Book value acquired	96,000		
Goodwill involved	$ 14,000	$ 14,000	$ 14,000
Additional issue:			
Paid	$ 26,000		
Book value acquired	31,000		
Goodwill involved	(5,000)	$ (5,000)	$ –0–
Total Goodwill		$ 9,000	$ 14,000
Goodwill determined by work sheet elimination:			
Carrying value:			
Cost		$136,000	$110,000
(80% × $40,000 increase in B's retained earnings since acquisition—needed to establish reciprocity)		32,000	32,000
		$168,000	$142,000
Elimination		155,000*	124,000†
Goodwill		$ 13,000	$ 18,000

* $83\frac{1}{3}$% of $186,000
† $66\frac{2}{3}$% of $186,000

Since the amount of goodwill determined by comparing purchase price and book value acquired, as contrasted with the amount determined by the elimination process, differs by $4,000 ($9,000 as compared to $13,000, and $14,000 as compared to $18,000), an adjustment is necessary.

Subsidiary Stock Distributions

If, subsequent to acquisition, a subsidiary capitalizes part or all of its retained earnings, accumulated since acquisition, by means of a stock distribution or otherwise,[2] a problem arises as to the proper treatment of the amount so capitalized. Some accountants would consider the amount capitalized as part of consolidated capital, whereas others would treat it as part of consolidated retained earnings. According to one line of

[2] Capitalization of retained earnings may be effected by a change in par or stated value as well as by a stock dividend or split-up. However, since the basic problem involved is similar in each instance, all possibilities will not be covered.

reasoning the amount capitalized should be considered as a part of consolidated capital because the capitalization is a legal fact. Other accountants maintain that, regardless of the form of account in which the subsidiary keeps the amount, it represents earnings to the combined entity and the amount so capitalized is properly included in consolidated retained earnings. Since the consolidating process varies slightly, depending upon the approach used, the basic procedure involved in both instances is illustrated.

In addition to the specific facts given in the illustration, assume that Company A purchased an 80% interest in Company B at a time when Company B's retained earnings were $40,000. In addition, assume that, subsequent to acquisition, Company B issued a 20% stock dividend and made the following entry:

Retained earnings	$20,000	
Capital stock		$20,000

Capitalization Considered as Part of Consolidated Capital.

COMPANY A AND SUBSIDIARY COMPANY B

CONSOLIDATED WORKING PAPERS
STATEMENT OF FINANCIAL POSITION
AS OF (DATE)

	Company A	Company B	Adjustments & Eliminations Debit	Adjustments & Eliminations Credit	Consolidated Financial Position
Current assets	$200,000	$ 90,000			$290,000
Investment in Co. B (carried at cost)	125,000		$ 24,000(1)	$136,000A	13,000G*
Fixed assets	500,000	100,000			600,000
	$825,000	$190,000			$903,000
Current liabilities	$ 65 000	$ 20,000			$ 85,000
Fixed liabilities	100,000				100,000
Shareholders' equity:					
Company A:					
Capital stock	500,000				500,000
Capital surplus	60,000			16,000(1)	76,000
Retained earnings	100,000			8,000(1)	108,000RE
Company B:					
Capital stock		120,000	96,000A		24,000MI
Retained earnings		50,000	40,000A		10,000MI
	$825,000	$190,000	$160,000	$160,000	$903,000

(1): To establish reciprocity by recognizing Company A's share of Company B's increase in shareholders' equity since acquisition.

A: To eliminate 80% of Company B's shareholders' equity against the investment account

* Goodwill proof:

Paid	$125,000	
Book value acquired	112,000	[80% × ($100,000 + $40,000)]
Goodwill	$ 13,000	

Capitalization Considered as Part of Consolidated Retained Earnings.

COMPANY A AND SUBSIDIARY COMPANY B

CONSOLIDATED WORKING PAPERS

STATEMENT OF FINANCIAL POSITION

AS OF (DATE)

	Company A	Company B	Adjustments & Eliminations Debit	Adjustments & Eliminations Credit	Consolidated Financial Position
Current assets	$200,000	$ 90,000			$290,000
Investment in Co. B					
(carried at cost)	125,000		$ 24,000(1)	$136,000A	13,000G*
Fixed assets (net)	500,000	100,000			600,000
	$825,000	$190,000			$903,000
Current liabilities	$ 65,000	$ 20,000			$ 85,000
Fixed liabilities	100,000				100,000
Shareholders' equity:					
Company A:					
Capital stock	500,000				500,000
Capital surplus	60,000				60,000
Retained earnings	100,000			24,000(1)	124,000RE
Company B:					
Capital stock		120,000	96,000A		24,000MI
Retained earnings		50,000	40,000A		10,000MI
	$825,000	$190,000	$160,000	$160,000	$903,000

While there is not complete unanimity among accountants as to whether or not the capitalization of retained earnings accumulated by a subsidiary after acquisition requires a transfer to capital surplus on consolidation, *Bulletin* 51 indicates that it is not required.

Treasury Stock Transactions

When a subsidiary either acquires some of its own stock or sells some stock previously acquired, the parent company's per cent of ownership will increase or decrease, depending upon whether the transaction is a sale or purchase. Likewise, as in the case of the issuance of additional stock, the parent company's equity in the subsidiary will change unless the treasury stock is purchased or sold at book value. If a change in the parent's equity results from a treasury stock transaction, an adjustment of the investment account is necessary in order to establish reciprocity. The following examples illustrate the effect of (1) a purchase of treasury stock by a subsidiary, and (2) a sale of treasury stock by a subsidiary. Although the adjusting entries, as such, and the proof of goodwill are not included, the same procedure would apply as was illustrated in the preceding examples of additional stock issues.

In addition to the specific facts given in the illustrations, assume 100 shares of treasury stock were *acquired* at:

(1) $120 per share, or book value.
(2) $210 per share, or above book value.
(3) $75 per share, or below book value.

and 100 shares of treasury stock were *sold* at:

(1) $120 per share, or book value.
(2) $160 per share, or above book value.
(3) $80 per share, or below book value.

PURCHASE OF TREASURY STOCK

	At Book Value		Above Book Value		Below Book Value	
	Prior to Purchase	After Purchase	Prior to Purchase	After Purchase	Prior to Purchase	After Purchase
Company B's shareholders' equity:						
Capital stock	$100,000	$100,000	$100,000	$100,000	$100,000	$100,000
Retained earnings	20,000	20,000	20,000	20,000	20,000	20,000
Treasury stock		(12,000)		(21,000)		(7,500)
Total shareholders' equity	$120,000	$108,000	$120,000	$ 99,000	$120,000	$112,500
Company A's interest	80%	8/9	80%	8/9	80%	8/9
Minority interest	20%	1/9	20%	1/9	20%	1/9
Company A's equity	$ 96,000	$ 96,000	$ 96,000	$ 88,000	$ 96,000	$100,000
Increase or (decrease)		–0–		($8,000)		$4,000

SALE OF TREASURY STOCK

	At Book Value		Above Book Value		Below Book Value	
	Prior to Sale	After Sale	Prior to Sale	After Sale	Prior to Sale	After Sale
Company B's shareholders' equity:						
Capital stock	$100,000	$100,000	$100,000	$100,000	$100,000	$100,000
Retained earnings	20,000	20,000	20,000	20,000	20,000	20,000
Premium (discount) on treasury stock				4,000		(4,000)
Treasury stock	(12,000)		(12,000)		(12,000)	
Total shareholders' equity	$108,000	$120,000	$108,000	$124,000	$108,000	$116,000
Company A's interest	8/9	80%	8/9	80%	8/9	80%
Minority interest	1/9	20%	1/9	20%	1/9	20%
Company A's equity	$ 96,000	$ 96,000	$ 96,000	$ 99,200	$ 96,000	$ 92,800
Increase or (decrease)		–0–		$3,200		($3,200)

Preferred Stock

When consolidating a subsidiary that has both common and preferred shares outstanding, an additional problem arises. Since both the common and preferred interests have a claim against the shareholders' equity of the subsidiary, their respective claims must be recognized in order to prepare consolidated statements.

The following four cases, although not exhaustive (especially since there are so many different types of preferred claims), illustrate the problem

At Date of Acquisition.

	Company B's Shareholders' Equity	Case 1	
		Common	Preferred
Company B's shareholders' equity:			
Common stock	$200,000	$200,000	
Preferred stock, 6%	100,000		$100,000
Retained earnings	60,000	60,000	–0–
Total equities	$360,000	$260,000	$100,000
Company A's interest		90%	70%
Minority interest		10%	30%
Company A's equity		$234,000	$ 70,000
Computation of goodwill:			
Paid		$240,000	$ 80,000
Book value acquired		234,000	70,000
Goodwill (Negative goodwill)		$ 6,000	$ 10,000

Subsequent to Date of Acquisition.*

	Company B's Shareholders' Equity	Case 1	
		Common	Preferred
Company B's shareholders' equity:			
Common stock	$200,000	$200,000	
Preferred stock, 6%	100,000		$100,000
Retained earnings	90,000	90,000	–0–
Total equities	$390,000	$290,000	$100,000
Company A's interest		90%	70%
Minority interest		10%	30%
Company A's equity		$261,000	$ 70,000
Computation of goodwill:			
Investment in Co. B (cost)		$240,000	$ 80,000
Establishment of reciprocity		27,000	–0–
Investment account as adjusted		$267,000	$ 80,000
Eliminate Co. A's equity		261,000	70,000
Goodwill (Negative goodwill)		$ 6,000	$ 10,000

* One year later

	Case 2		Case 3		Case 4	
	Common	Preferred	Common	Preferred	Common	Preferred
	$200,000		$200,000		$200,000	
		$100,000		$100,000		$100,000
	40,000	20,000	48,000	12,000	32,000	28,000
	$240,000	$120,000	$248,000	$112,000	$232,000	$128,000
	90%	70%	90%	70%	90%	70%
	10%	30%	10%	30%	10%	30%
	$216,000	$ 84,000	$223,200	$ 78,400	$208,800	$ 89,600
	$240,000	$ 80,000	$240,000	$ 80,000	$240,000	$ 80,000
	216,000	84,000	223,200	78,400	208,800	89,600
	$ 24,000	$ (4,000)	$ 16,800	$ 1,600	$ 31,200	$ (9,600)

	Case 2		Case 3		Case 4	
	Common	Preferred	Common	Preferred	Common	Preferred
	$200,000		$200,000		$200,000	
		$100,000		$100,000		$100,000
	60,000	30,000	72,000	18,000	48,000	42,000
	$260,000	$130,000	$272,000	$118,000	$248,000	$142,000
	90%	70%	90%	70%	90%	70%
	10%	30%	10%	30%	10%	30%
	$234,000	$ 91,000	$244,800	$ 82,600	$223,200	$ 99,400
	$240,000	$80,000	$240,000	$ 80,000	$240,000	$ 80,000
	18,000	7,000	21,600	4,200	14,400	9,800
	$258,000	$ 87,000	$261,600	$ 84,200	$254,400	$ 89,800
	234,000	91,000	244,800	82,600	223,200	99,400
	$ 24,000	$ (4,000)	$ 16,800	$ 1,600	$ 31,200	$ (9,600)

involved when allocating the shareholders' equity of a subsidiary between its common and preferred interests. Although the procedure is essentially the same whether consolidating at the date of acquisition or subsequent to that date, for comparative purposes both are illustrated.

In addition to the specific facts given in the illustrations also assume that in:

Case 1, the preferred shares are noncumulative and nonparticipating.
Case 2, the preferred shares are noncumulative but fully participating.
Case 3, the preferred shares are cumulative but nonparticipating.*
Case 4, the preferred shares are cumulative and fully participating.*

The consolidating procedure at *date of acquisition* is illustrated in the following work sheet. Although the approach is the same in all cases, Case 4, in which the preferred stock is cumulative and fully participating, is selected for illustrative purposes.

COMPANY A AND SUBSIDIARY COMPANY B
CONSOLIDATED WORKING PAPERS
STATEMENT OF FINANCIAL POSITION
AS OF (DATE)

	Company A	Company B	Adjustments & Eliminations Debit	Credit	Consolidated Financial Position
Current assets	$ 400,000	$150,000			$ 550,000
Investment in Co. B common (cost)	240,000			$208,800A	31,200G
Investment in Co. B preferred (cost)	80,000			89,600B	(9,600)G
Fixed assets (net)	1,580,000	240,000			1,820,000
	$2,300,000	$390,000			$2,391,600
Current liabilities	$ 100,000	$ 30,000			$ 130,000
Shareholders' equity:					
Company A:					
Capital stock	2,000,000				2,000,000
Retained earnings	200,000				200,000RE
Company B:					
Common stock		200,000	$180,000A		20,000MI
Preferred stock		100,000	70,000B		30,000MI
Retained earnings		60,000	19,600B		
			28,800A		11,600MI
	$2,300,000	$390,000	$298,400	$298,400	$2,391,600

A: To eliminate 90% of common stock equity against the investment account.
B: To eliminate 70% of preferred stock equity against the investment account.

Subsequent to the Date of Acquisition. Assuming that during the next year Company B earns $30,000 and distributes no dividends, the

* Preferred dividends two years in arrears at date of acquisition.

same four cases are analyzed on pages 412–413 and, as above, Case 4 is used for the statement of financial position illustration.

COMPANY A AND SUBSIDIARY COMPANY B

CONSOLIDATED WORKING PAPERS
STATEMENT OF FINANCIAL POSITION

AS OF (DATE)

	Company A	Company B	Adjustments & Eliminations Debit	Credit	Consolidated Financial Position
Current assets	$ 660,000	$230,000			$ 890,000
Investment in Co. B common (cost)	240,000		$14,400(1)	$223,200A	31,200G
Investment in Co. B preferred (cost)	80,000		9,800(2)	99,400B	(9,600)G
Fixed assets (net)	1,400,000	210,000			1,610,000
	$2,380,000	$440,000			$2,521,600
Current liabilities	$ 80,000	$ 50,000			$ 130,000
Shareholders' equity:					
Company A:					
Capital stock	2,000,000				2,000,000
Retained earnings	300,000			14,400(1)	324,200RE
Company B:				9,800(2)	
Common stock		200,000	180,000A		20,000MI
Preferred stock		100,000	70,000B		30,000MI
Retained earnings		90,000	43,200A		
			29,400B		17,400MI
	$2,380,000	$440,000	$346,800	$346,800	$2,521,600

(1): To establish reciprocity by recognizing Company A's share in the increase in Company B's shareholders' equity pertaining to the common stock investment.

(2): To establish reciprocity by recognizing Company A's share in the increase in Company B's shareholders' equity pertaining to the preferred stock investment.

A: To eliminate 90% of Company B's common stock equity against the investment account.

B: To eliminate 70% of Company B's preferred stock equity against the investment account.

PROBLEMS

Problem 14–1. Company S had capital stock issued and outstanding of $50,000 and retained earnings of $30,000. Additional stock of a par value of $150,000 was issued to Company H which had previously owned none of the Company S stock. Company H paid $250,000 for the stock.

Determine the amount of (1) goodwill or deduction from goodwill, and (2) minority interest which would appear in a consolidated statement of financial position prepared as of the date of acquisition.

Problem 14–2. From the following data, and assuming that each company has $100,000 capital stock of $100 par and that profits are earned uniformly throughout the year, determine:

(1) The amount which should be credited to the investment account for the May 1, 1967, sale if the investment is carried by:

    (*a*) The cost method, and

    (*b*) The equity method.

(2) The amount of goodwill or deduction from goodwill that should be shown in the consolidated statement of financial position as of:

    (*a*) December 31, 1966, and

    (*b*) December 31, 1967.

INVESTMENT IN COMPANY S

Jan. 1, 1966 (800 shares)	$116,000	May 1, 1967 (175 shares)	???
Sept. 1, 1966 (100 shares)	18,000		

RETAINED EARNINGS (Company S)

Dec. 31, 1966 (dividends)	$12,000	Jan. 1, 1966 balance	$60,000
Dec. 31, 1967 (dividends)	12,000	Profits, 1966	15,000
		Profits, 1967	15,000

Problem 14–3. The following facts were taken from the records of a parent company and its subsidiary on the dates indicated:

	Jan. 1 1966	Dec. 31 1966	Dec. 31 1967	Dec. 31 1968
Parent Company:				
Investment in subsidiary	$288,000	$315,000	$308,000	$347,500
Retained earnings	240,000	290,000	276,000	280,000
Subsidiary Company				
Capital stock ($100 par)	$200,000	$200,000	$200,000	$200,000
Retained earnings	100,000	130,000	170,000	190,000

The parent company purchased 1,800 shares of subsidiary stock on January 1, 1966, sold 200 shares on January 1, 1967, and purchased 100 shares on January 1, 1968. Assuming that the investment account is carried on the *equity* basis and that it was *credited* for the *proceeds* of the stock sold, prepare statements showing the amounts of (1) goodwill, (2) retained earnings, and (3) minority interest that would appear on the consolidated statements of financial position as of January 1, 1966, and December 31, 1966, 1967, and 1968.

Problem 14–4. P Corporation acquired control of S Co. on June 30, 1964, by purchase in the market of 2,800 shares of its 4,000 issued shares of $100 par value common stock. At that time S had 500 shares of its own stock held as treasury stock and carried at par.

On January 1, 1966, P acquired 200 additional shares from a minority stockholder. On December 31, 1966, by agreement with the minority stockholders, P acquired the 500 shares held in the treasury of S.

The Investment account of P, carried at cost, shows the following debits:

June 30, 1964, 2,800 shares of S	$394,800
January 1, 1966, 200 shares of S purchased from outside interests	35,000
December 31, 1966, 500 shares of S obtained from S	90,000
Total	$519,800

The accounts of S contained the following items:

Credits	Paid-in Surplus	Retained Earnings
June 30, 1964	$ 74,300	$ 43,745
Earnings 6/30 to 12/31/64	—	35,306
Earnings 1965	—	65,754
Earnings 1966	—	51,025
Premium on sale of treasury stock	40,000	—
Total	$114,300	$195,830

Debits		
Dividends paid 12/1/64	—	$ 35,000
Dividends paid 12/5/65	—	35,000
Dividends paid 12/15/66		40,000
Total		$110,000
Balance 12/31/66	$114,300	$ 85,830

Required:
(1) Goodwill from consolidation as of 7/1/64.
(2) Minority interest as of 7/1/64.
(3) Goodwill from consolidation as of 1/2/66.
(4) Minority interest as of 1/2/66.
(5) Goodwill from consolidation as of 1/1/67.
(6) Minority interest as of 1/1/67.

Problem 14–5. From the following data, prepare a consolidated statement of financial position as of December 31, 1966:

On January 1, 1966, the A Company purchased 90% of the stock of Company B and 80% of the stock of Company C. Wishing to acquire the remaining stock of the more profitable company (Company C), Company A on June 30, 1966, disposed of 200 shares of its holdings in Company B at a price of $160 per share, and on that date was successful in acquiring an additional 10% of the stock of Company C in consideration of the entire proceeds from the shares of Company B stock disposed of.

The investment accounts on the books of Company A are carried at cost, except the account representing the investment in capital stock of Company B. This account has been credited with the proceeds of the 200 shares sold.

STATEMENTS OF FINANCIAL POSITION
December 31, 1966

	A	B	C
Assets			
Current assets	$152,500	$150,000	$105,000
Investment in subsidiary companies:			
Company B:			
Capital stock	220,000		
Advances	25,000		
Company C:			
Capital stock	214,000		
Advances	40,000		
Buildings and equipment (net)		170,000	235,000
	$651,500	$320,000	$340,000
Equities			
Capital stock:			
Company A, 3,000 shares	$300,000		
Company B, 2,000 shares		$200,000	
Company C, 1,000 shares			$100,000
Due to parent company		25,000	40,000
Accounts payable	235,000	40,000	25,000
Retained earnings at beginning of year	166,500	60,000	145,000
Profit for the year	20,000*	15,000	40,000
Dividends (paid December 31, 1966)	(70,000)	(20,000)	(10,000)
	$651,500	$320,000	$340,000

* Dividends received from subsidiary companies, less expenses of parent company. It is assumed that the profits of the companies for the year 1966 were earned uniformly throughout the year. (AICPA adapted)

Problem 14–6. From the following data, prepare consolidated working papers with separate columns for adjustments and eliminations.

The date on which A acquired capital stock of subsidiary companies was, in each case, the date on which the subsidiary company was organized. All investments are carried at cost.

A Company

Investment in B Company:	
Common stock, 800 shares, 80% interest	$ 80,000
Preferred stock, 400 shares, 40% interest	40,000
Investment in C Company:	
Common stock, 600 shares, 60% interest	60,000
Investment in D Company:	
Common stock, 1,000 shares, $66\frac{2}{3}$% interest	100,000
Preferred stock, 800 shares, 80% interest	80,000
Investment in E Company:	
Common stock, 1,900 shares, 95% interest	190,000
Preferred stock, 400 shares, 80% interest	40,000

Accounts receivable, C Company	300,000
Other assets	10,000
Capital stock	500,000
Retained earnings	400,000

B Company

Assets	$350,000
Preferred stock, 6% noncumulative	100,000
Common stock	100,000
Retained earnings	150,000

C Company

Assets	$420,000
Accounts payable, A Company	300,000
Common stock	100,000
Retained earnings	20,000

D Company

Assets	$244,000
Preferred stock, 6% cumulative	100,000
Common stock	150,000
Retained earnings (deficit)	(6,000)

E Company

Assets	$285,000
Preferred stock, 6% cumulative	50,000
Common stock	200,000
Retained earnings	35,000

Dividends have not been paid on preferred stock outstanding as follows:

D	for 3 years
E	for 4 years

(AICPA adapted)

Problem 14-7. The following balances appear on the books of a parent company and its subsidiary on the dates stated:

	Jan. 1, 1966	Dec. 31, 1966	Dec. 31, 1967	Dec. 31, 1968
Parent Company:				
Investment in subsidiary	$128,000	$128,000	$119,000	$140,000
Retained earnings	135,000	160,000	148,000	155,000
Subsidiary:				
Capital stock	100,000	100,000	100,000	100,000
Retained earnings	50,000	62,000	70,000	80,000

The subsidiary's capital stock consists of 1,000 shares of $100 par each. The parent company purchased 800 shares on January 1, 1966, sold 50 shares on January 1, 1967, and purchased 100 shares on January 1, 1968. Investment account was charged with the cost of stock purchased and credited with the proceeds from the stock sold. The parent company has made no other entries in the investment account and has credited income with all dividends received from the subsidiary.

Prepare statements showing the composition of the amounts of goodwill, retained earnings, and minority interest that would appear on the consolidated statements of financial position at December 31, 1966, 1967, and 1968.

(AICPA adapted)

Problem 14–8. Four years ago The American Company acquired 50% of the preferred stock of the Banner Corporation for $55,000, and 90% of that corporation's common stock for $195,000. At acquisition date the Banner Corporation had retained earnings of $60,000, and dividends on the 5% cumulative preferred stock were not in arrears. The investments were recorded by The American Company at the book value shown by the Banner Corporation at date of acquisition.

Consolidated statements are now being prepared as of December 31, 1966, for The American Company and its subsidiary. The financial position of the individual companies was as follows on that date:

THE AMERICAN COMPANY

Miscellaneous assets	$116,000	Liabilities	$ 50,000
Investments:		Preferred stock (4%)	100,000
Banner preferred	50,000	Common stock	100,000
Banner common	234,000	Retained earnings	150,000
	$400,000		$400,000

BANNER CORPORATION

Miscellaneous assets	$400,000	Liabilities	$ 60,000
		Preferred stock (5%)*	100,000
		Common stock	200,000
		Retained earnings	40,000
	$400,000		$400,000

* The preferred stock dividends are three years in arrears. No dividends have been paid on common since acquisition by The American Company. Profit in 1963 was $8,000 but losses during the past three years have totalled $23,000.

You are to prepare a consolidated statement of financial position of the above companies as of December 31, 1966, in which all significant details given in the above information are fully disclosed. Present in good form schedules showing all computations needed.

Comment on any item which you feel requires explanation.

(AICPA adapted)

Problem 14–9. On January 1, 1966, A Company purchased 800 shares of the stock of B Company @ 118. On January 1, 1967, A Company purchased an additional 150 shares of B's stock @ 125, and on January 1, 1968, sold 100 shares @ 130.

On December 31, 1968, the following data were obtained from the records of the two companies:

	A Company	B Company
Inventories, 1/1/68	$ 80,000	$ 30,000
Investment in B Company	101,350	
Other assets (net)	450,000	255,000
Purchases	520,000	275,000
Expenses	133,425	65,000
Dividends	10,000	6,000
	$1,294,775	$631,000
Sales	$ 754,000	$375,000
Dividends	5,100	
Liabilities	136,000	76,000
Capital stock ($100 par)	200,000	100,000
Retained earnings	199,675	80,000
	$1,294,775	$631,000
Inventories, 12/31/68	$ 86,000	$ 28,000

RETAINED EARNINGS

	A Company	B Company
Balances, 1/1/66	$ 26,675	$50,000
Profits, 1966	107,000	17,000
Dividends, 1966	(10,000)	(6,000)
Balances, 12/31/66	123,675	61,000
Profits, 1967	86,000	25,000
Dividends, 1967	(10,000)	(6,000)
Balances, 12/31/67	$199,675	$80,000

During 1968, B Company sold to A Company for $100,000 merchandise which cost $50,000. Fifty per cent of the merchandise remains in A's inventory on December 31, 1968.

Required:
Consolidated financial statements for the year ended December 31, 1968.

Problem 14–10. From the following information, prepare a consolidated statement of financial position of H Co. and subsidiaries, A Co. and B Co., as of December 31, 1966.

H. Co., an operating company, acquired 90% of the outstanding stock of B Co. on March 31, 1966, for $162,000. Previously H Co. acquired 30% of the outstanding stock of A Co. on January 1, 1965, for $25,000. On July 1, 1966, H Co. purchased an additional 40% of the outstanding stock of A Co. for $42,000, thereby gaining effective control of A Co. as of that date. In order further to increase its stockholdings in A Co. without impairing working capital, H Co. sold 100 shares of B Co. stock on October 1, 1966, for $20,500 and immediately used $13,800 of the proceeds to secure an additional 15% of A Co. outstanding stock.

The statements of financial position of the respective companies as of December 31, 1966, are set forth as follows:

	H Co.	A Co.	B Co.
Assets			
Cash in banks	$ 86,000	$ 12,500	$ 35,000
Notes receivable	18,000	6,000	8,000
Accounts receivable (less reserve)	52,000	13,000	34,000
Inventories	89,500	16,000	51,000
Investment in Company A (at cost)	80,800		
Investment in Company B (at equity)	149,320		
Plant and equipment (less reserves)	225,000	56,500	101,000
	$700,620	$104,000	$229,000
Equities			
Notes payable	$ 9,000	$ 8,000	$ 12,000
Accounts payable	73,600	22,400	46,200
Accrued liabilities	5,320	2,600	4,800
Capital stock, common, $100 par	400,000	60,000	100,000
Retained earnings	212,700	11,000	66,000
	$700,620	$104,000	$229,000

A summary of retained earnings (deficit) from January 1, 1965, to December 31, 1966, is as follows:

	H Co.	A Co.	B Co.
Balance at January 1, 1965	$150,000	$(10,000)	$40,000
Net profit (or loss), 1965:			
1st quarter	7,000	(2,000)	3,000
2nd quarter	9,000	1,000	4,000
3rd quarter	15,000	3,000	6,000
4th quarter	12,000	6,000	5,000
Total	$193,000	$ (2,000)	$58,000
Dividends declared and paid on July 1, 1965	12,000		3,000
Balance at January 1, 1966	$181,000	$ (2,000)	$55,000
Net profit (or loss), 1966:			
1st quarter	6,000	2,500	4,500
2nd quarter	11,500	3,000	7,000
3rd quarter	13,000	3,600	6,200
4th quarter	16,200	5,900	5,300
Total	$227,700	$ 13,000	$78,000
Dividends declared June 1, 1966 and paid on June 15, 1966	15,000		12,000
Dividends declared December 1, 1966 and paid on December 15, 1966		2,000	
Balance, December 31, 1966 — Retained earnings	$212,700	$ 11,000	$66,000

Net profit of H Co. for the fourth quarter of 1966 includes $2,500 representing the gain on the sale of 100 shares of B Co. stock. (Proceeds $20,500, less March 31, 1966, cost, $18,000.)

Inventories at December 31, 1966, include intercompany items as follows:

Date of Transaction	Company Purchaser	Seller	Amount Inventory	Seller's Cost
April 5, 1966	H	A	$ 3,600	$ 3,000
August, 15, 1966	H	B	5,000	4,500*
October 5, 1966	H	A	10,000	9,000
May 15, 1966	A	B	7,000	6,200
September 26, 1966	A	B	6,000	4,800
November 12, 1966	B	A	16,000	14,000

* Acquired on July 20, 1966, by B from A, A's cost then being $4,200.

(AICPA adapted)

Problem 14–11. Following are the statements of financial positions of Company A and its subsidiaries B and C as at December 31, 1969:

	Companies A	B	C
Assets			
Investments:			
Preferred capital stock of Company B, 60%	$ 300,000		
Common capital stock of Company B, 90%	800,000		
Common capital stock of Company C, 90%	1,300,000		
Bonds of Company B at cost	270,000		
Notes receivable:			
Company B	20,000		
Other assets	2,000,000	$2,180,000	$2,000,000
	$4,690,000	$2,180,000	$2,000,000
Equities			
Capital stock:			
Preferred, 6%	$ 500,000	$ 500,000	$ 500,000
Common	1,100,000	150,000	500,000
	$1,600,000	$ 650,000	$1,000,000
Surplus:			
Balance, January 1, 1969	$1,100,000	$ 150,000	$ 300,000
Net profits for the year 1969	400,000	200,000	300,000
	$1,500,000	$ 350,000	$ 600,000
Dividends deducted	$ 12,000	$ 30,000	$ 30,000
	$1,488,000	$ 320,000	$ 570,000
First mtge., 6% bonds outstanding	$1,000,000	$ 600,000	
Notes receivable discounted, Company B	10,000		
Notes payable, Company A		20,000	
Other liabilities	592,000	590,000	$ 430,000
	$4,690,000	$2,180,000	$2,000,000

The dividends on the preferred stocks of the respective companies have all been paid through the year 1968.

The bonds of Company B, which mature December 31, 1976, were acquired by Company A on December 31, 1969, at 90.

Company A acquired its holdings of the stock in Companies B and C at the date of their incorporation and has taken up its share of the surplus and earnings of these companies.

From the foregoing, prepare a consolidated statement of financial position as of December 31, 1969.   (AICPA adapted)

Problem 14–12. Prepare a consolidated statement of financial position and a consolidated statement of income from the following data:

TRIAL BALANCES, DECEMBER 31, 1966

	A Company	B Company
Debits		
Cash	$ 100,000	$ 25,000
Accounts receivable	150,000	75,000
Plant—cost less depreciation	350,000	200,000
Inventories		
Raw materials	60,000	40,000
Work in process	75,000	50,000
Finished goods	45,000	30,000
Raw materials purchased	400,000	250,000
Manufacturing labor and expenses	300,000	200,000
Operating expenses	225,000	150,000
Dividends paid December 15, 1966	90,000	20,000
Investment in stock of B Company (cost)	275,000	
Totals	$2,070,000	$1,040,000
Credits		
Sales	$1,095,000	$ 750,000
Dividends received	18,000	
Capital stock	900,000	200,000
Retained earnings January 1, 1966	57,000	90,000
Totals	$2,070,000	$1,040,000

A Company acquired 80% of the stock of B Company on January 1, 1966, for $240,000, and an additional 10% on July 1, 1966, for $35,000.

In solving the problem, assume that profits were earned uniformly throughout the year and that the inventories on December 31, 1966, were as follows:

	A Company	B Company
Raw materials	$50,000	$35,000
Work in process	65,000	25,000
Finished goods	35,000	10,000

CHAPTER 15

Consolidated statements— indirect ownership and mutual stockholdings

Occasionally a parent company may have an interest in a subsidiary(ies) that in turn has an interest in a subsidiary(ies) of its own, or a parent company may have two or more subsidiaries, one or more of which in turn has an interest in one of the other subsidiaries. For example, Company A may own a 90% interest in Company B which in turn owns an 80% interest in Company C, or Company A may own a 90% interest in Company B and a 70% interest in Company C with Company B, in turn, owning a 20% interest in Company C. These and similar types of ownership are usually described as indirect ownership. Thus Company A's 72% indirect ownership of Company C in the first instance is a result of A's owning 90% of B which in turn owns 80% of C. In the second situation, Company A's 88% effective interest in Company C is a result of Company A owning 70% directly and 18% (90% × 20%) indirectly through Company B. In the first situation, Company A is usually referred to as the major parent and Company B the minor parent; whereas in the second situation, Company B is usually referred to as a connecting affiliate.

In addition to problems dealing with indirect ownership, the accountant may also occasionally be faced with situations where two or more affiliates in a consolidated group have an interest, represented by stockholdings, in each other. For example, Company A may own a 90% interest in Company B which in turn owns a 5% interest in Company A. This and similar types of relationships are usually referred to as mutual stockholdings.

Some of the problems involved in consolidating companies where indirect ownership and mutual stockholdings exist are considered in this chapter. Although there is no attempt to exhaust all of the possibilities that may arise in the case of indirect ownership or mutual stockholdings, sufficient coverage is given to enable one to acquire an understanding of the particular problems involved. The basic consolidating procedure of (1) establishing reciprocity, (2) eliminating reciprocals, and (3) consolidating nonreciprocals remains the same although the establishment of reciprocity may become a little more involved. Likewise, the apportionment of net income may become a little more difficult. For these reasons special emphasis is placed on the process of establishing reciprocity and the apportionment of net income in this chapter. The elimination and the consolidation of nonreciprocals, once reciprocity has been established, are somewhat routine and will not be emphasized.

As has been stressed throughout the preceding chapters, the date of acquisition is an important reference point when preparing consolidated statements. Although the date of acquisition assumes no additional significance when consolidating a group of companies in which indirect ownership or mutual stockholdings exist, its determination in a particular situation may require additional analysis. Since the date of acquisition in any given situation refers to the date of acquisition for consolidating purposes, this may or may not be the date on which a particular subsidiary was acquired by an affiliate. For example, assume that Company A owns a 95% interest in Company B which in turn owns an 85% interest in Company C. If Company B acquired its interest in Company C on or before the date on which Company A acquired its interest in Company B, the date of acquisition of Company C when consolidating A, B, and C is the date on which Company A acquired its interest in Company B. However, if Company B acquired its interest in Company C subsequent to the date Company A acquired its interest in Company B, the date of acquisition when consolidating C with A and B is the date Company B acquired its interest in Company C. It should be noted that the important date in situations of this nature, from a consolidating standpoint, is the date a particular affiliate enters the consolidated group. In the illustrations presented in this chapter when the date of acquisition is referred to, it is assumed to be the date of acquisition for consolidating purposes.

INDIRECT OWNERSHIP

When consolidating a group of companies in which some form of indirect ownership exists, whether it be a major and minor parent situation, a connecting affiliate relationship, or a combination of the two, it is essential that establishment of reciprocity start on the lowest strata or tier of subsidiaries. The establishment of reciprocity should then progress up to the top tier or apex where the major parent is found. It is likewise better to progress up the consolidation ladder rung by rung rather than to by-pass some of the rungs. For example, if Company A owns 90% of Company B and if Company B in turn owns 80% of Company C, the first step should be to establish reciprocity between B and C by recognizing B's 80% interest in C's increase or decrease in shareholders' equity since acquisition. Then reciprocity should be established between A and B by recognizing A's 90% interest in B's increase or decrease in shareholders' equity since acquisition, which would include B's appropriate share of C's increase or decrease.

Major and Minor Parents

First Illustration. Assume Company A owns a 90% interest in Company B which, in turn, owns an 80% interest in Company C; that B's shareholders' equity has increased $20,000 (from its own operations) since date of acquisition; that C's shareholders' equity has increased $10,000 since the date of acquisition; and that all investment accounts are on the cost basis. Reciprocity would be established when consolidating by the following work sheet entries:

First:

Investment in Company C	$ 8,000	
Retained earnings (B's)		$ 8,000
(to recognize Company B's 80% interest in the increase in Company C's shareholders' equity)		

Second:

Investment in Company B	$25,200	
Retained earnings (A's)		$25,200
[to recognize Company A's 90% interest in the increase in Company B's shareholder's equity—90% × ($20,000 + $8,000)]		

Assuming that in any given period Company A earns $100,000; Company B, $20,000; and Company C, $10,000 from their respective operations, net income would be apportioned as follows:

	Company A	Company B	Company C	Total
Net income before apportionment	$100,000	$20,000	$10,000	$130,000
Apportionment:				
B's share of C's (80%)		8,000	(8,000)	
A's share of B's (90%)	25,200	(25,200)		
Balances	$125,200	$ 2,800	$ 2,000	$130,000
Consolidated net income	125,200			$125,200
Minority interest, B		2,800		2,800
Minority interest, C			2,000	2,000
Total				$130,000

Second Illustration. Assume Company A owns a 90% interest in Company B which, in turn, owns a 90% interest in Company C and a 70% interest in Company D; that from individual operations B's shareholders' equity has increased $30,000 and C's, $20,000 while D's has decreased $10,000 since the respective dates of acquisition; and that all investment accounts are on the cost basis. Reciprocity would be established by the following work sheet entries:

First:

Retained earnings (B's)	$ 7,000	
Investment in Company D		$ 7,000

(to recognize Company B's 70% interest in the
decrease in Company D's shareholders' equity)

Second:

Investment in Company C	$18,000	
Retained earnings (B's)		$18,000

(to recognize Company B's 90% interest in the
increase in Company C's shareholders' equity)

Third:

Investment in Company B	$36,900	
Retained earnings (A's)		$36,900

[to recognize Company A's 90% interest in the
increase in Company B's shareholders' equity
—90% × ($30,000 + $18,000 — $7,000)]

Assuming that in any given period Company A earns $100,000; Company B, $30,000; Company C, $20,000; and that Company D loses $10,000 from their respective operations, net income would be apportioned as follows:

	Company A	Company B	Company C	Company D	Total
Net income before apportionment	$100,000	$30,000	$20,000	($10,000)	$140,000
Apportionment:					
B's share of D's (70%)		(7,000)		7,000	
B's share of C's (90%)		18,000	(18,000)		
A's share of B's (90%)	36,900	(36,900)			
Balances	$136,900	$ 4,100	$ 2,000	($3,000)	$140,000
Consolidated net income	136,900				$136,900
Minority interest, B		4,100			4,100
Minority interest, C			2,000		2,000
Minority interest, D				(3,000)	(3,000)
Total					$140,000

Diagrams are frequently useful in following through various consolidated relationships and should be used whenever helpful. For instance, with arrows indicating the direction from which ownership flows, the afore-mentioned situations might be diagramed as follows:

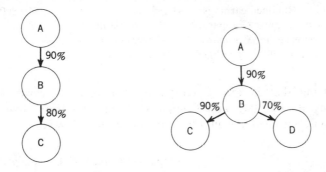

First Illustration   Second Illustration

Connecting Affiliates

First Illustration. Assume Company A owns a 90% interest in Company B and a 70% interest in Company C, while Company B owns 20% of C; that B's shareholders' equity has increased $20,000 from its own operations since acquisition and that C's shareholders' equity has increased $10,000 since acquisition; that all investment accounts are on the cost basis; and that Company A and Company B acquired their interests in Company C at the same time. Reciprocity would be established by the following work sheet entries:

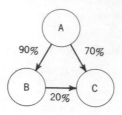

Connecting Affiliates

First:

Investment in Company C (A's)	$ 7,000	
Investment in Company C (B's)	2,000	
Retained earnings (A's)		$ 7,000
Retained earnings (B's)		2,000

(to recognize Company A's 70% and Company B's 20% interest in the increase in Company C's shareholders' equity)

Second:

Investment in Company B	$19,800	
Retained earnings (A's)		$19,800

[to recognize Company A's 90% interest in increase in Company B's shareholders' equity—90% × ($20,000 + $2,000)]

Assuming that in any given period Company A earns $100,000; Company B, $20,000; and Company C, $10,000 from their separate operations, net income would be apportioned as follows:

	Company A	Company B	Company C	Total
Net income before apportionment	$100,000	$20,000	$10,000	$130,000
Apportionment:				
A's share of C's (70%)	7,000		(7,000)	
B's share of C's (20%)		2,000	(2,000)	
A's share of B's (90%)	19,800	(19,800)		
Balances	$126,800	$ 2,200	$ 1,000	$130,000
Consolidated net income	126,800			$126,800
Minority interest, B		2,200		2,200
Minority interest, C			1,000	1,000
Total				$130,000

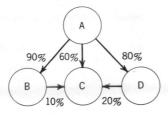

Connecting Affiliates

Second Illustration. Assume that Company A owns a 90% interest in Company B, a 60% interest in Company C, and an 80% interest in Company D; that Company B owns a 10% interest in Company C; that Company D owns a 20% interest in Company C; and that Company B's shareholders' equity has increased $30,000, C's, $20,000, and D's, $10,000 since acquisition from their own operations. Reciprocity would be established by the following work sheet entries:

First:

Investment in Company C (A's)	$12,000	
Investment in Company C (D's)	4,000	
Investment in Company C (B's)	2,000	
Retained earnings (A's)		$12,000
Retained earnings (D's)		4,000
Retained earnings (B's)		2,000

(to recognize Company A's 60%, D's 20%, and B's 10% interest in the increase in Company C's shareholders' equity)

Second:

Investment in Company D	$11,200	
Retained earnings (A's)		$11,200

[to recognize Company A's 80% interest in the increase in Company D's shareholders' equity—80% × ($10,000 + $4,000)]

Third:

Investment in Company B	$28,800	
Retained earnings (A's)		$28,800

[to recognize Company A's 90% interest in the increase in Company B's shareholders' equity—90% × ($30,000 + $2,000)]

Assuming that in any given year (period) Company A earns $100,000; B, $30,000; C, $20,000; and D, $10,000 from their separate operations, net income would be apportioned as follows:

	Company A	Company B	Company C	Company D	Total
Net income before apportionment	$100,000	$30,000	$20,000	$10,000	$160,000
Apportionment:					
A's share of C's (60%)	12,000		(12,000)		
D's share of C's (20%)			(4,000)	4,000	
B's share of C's (10%)		2,000	(2,000)		
A's share of D's (80%)	11,200			(11,200)	
A's share of B's (90%)	28,800	(28,800)			
Balances	$152,000	$ 3,200	$ 2,000	$ 2,800	$160,000
Consolidated net income	152,000				$152,000
Minority interest, B		3,200			3,200
Minority interest, C			2,000		2,000
Minority interest, D				2,800	2,800
Total					$160,000

Combination of Major and Minor Parents and a Connecting Affiliate

Assume Company A owns a 90% interest in Company B and an 80% interest in Company C; that Company B, in turn, owns an 80% interest in Company D; that Company C owns a 70% interest in Company E; that Company D owns a 20% interest in Company E; that Company B's shareholders' equity has increased $20,000, C's, $30,000, D's, $20,000, and E's, $10,000 from their own operations since their respective acquisitions; that all investments are on the cost basis; and that Company C and Company D acquired their interests in Company E on the same date. Reciprocity would be established by the following work sheet entries:

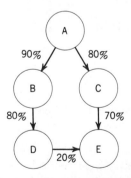

Combination of Major and Minor Parents and a Connecting Affiliate

First:

Investment in Company E (D's)	$2,000	
Investment in Company E (C's)	7,000	
Retained earnings (D's)		$ 2,000
Retained earnings (C's)		7,000

(to recognize Company D's 20% and Company C's 70% interest in the increase in Company E's shareholders' equity)

Second:

Investment in Company D	$17,600	
Retained earnings (B's)		$17,600

[to recognize Company B's 80% interest in the increase in Company D's shareholders' equity—80% × ($20,000 + $2,000)]

Third:

Investment in Company B	$33,840	
Investment in Company C	29,600	
Retained earnings (A's)		$63,440

[to recognize Company A's 90% interest— 90% × ($20,000 + $17,600)—in Company B's and 80% interest—80% × ($30,000 + $7,000)—in Company C's increases in shareholders' equities]

Assuming that in any given period Company A earns $100,000; B, $40,000; C, $30,000; D, $20,000; and E, $15,000 from their respective operations, net income would be apportioned as follows:

	Company A	Company B	Company C	Company D	Company E	Total
Net income before apportionment	$100,000	$40,000	$30,000	$20,000	$15,000	$205,000
Apportionment:						
C's share of E's (70%)			10,500		(10,500)	
D's share of E's (20%)				3,000	(3,000)	
B's share of D's (80%)		18,400		(18,400)		
A's share of B's (90%)	52,560	(52,560)				
A's share of C's (80%)	32,400		(32,400)			
Balances	$184,960	$ 5,840	$ 8,100	$ 4,600	$ 1,500	$205,000
Consolidated net income	184,960					$184,960
Minority interest, B		5,840				5,840
Minority interest, C			8,100			8,100
Minority interest, D				4,600		4,600
Minority interest, E					1,500	1,500
Total						$205,000

MUTUAL STOCKHOLDINGS

The establishment of reciprocity and the apportionment of net income may be complicated slightly by the existence of mutual stockholdings. When establishing reciprocity, the increase or decrease in the shareholders' equity of one particular affiliate may depend upon the increase or decrease in the shareholders' equity of a second affiliate, and the second affiliate's change may depend upon the change in the first affiliate's increase or decrease. Likewise, when apportioning net income, one affiliate's income may be dependent upon another's, and vice versa. Although there are roundabout ways to handle problems of this kind, the most direct approach is to solve them algebraically.

Mutual Stockholdings between Subsidiaries

First Illustration. Assume Company A owns an 80% interest in Company B and a 90% interest in Company C directly; that Company C owns a 20% interest in Company B, and Company B, in turn, owns a 10% interest in Company C; that from their respective operations Company B's shareholders' equity has increased $12,000 and Company C's $27,000 since acquisition; and that all investment accounts are on the cost basis. Reciprocity would be established by the following work sheet entries:

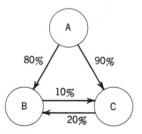

Mutual Stockholdings between Subsidiaries

Investment in Company C (A's)	$27,000	
Investment in Company C (B's)	3,000	
Retained earnings (A's)		$27,000
Retained earnings (B's)		3,000

(to recognize Company A's 90% and Company B's 10% interest in the increase in Company C's shareholders' equity)*

Investment in Company B (A's)	$12,000	
Investment in Company B (C's)	3,000	
Retained earnings (A's)		$12,000
Retained earnings (C's)		3,000

(to recognize Company A's 80% and Company C's 20% interest in the increase in Company B's shareholders' equity)*

* Let B = Company B's increase in shareholders' equity on a consolidated basis.
Let C = Company C's increase in shareholders' equity on a consolidated basis.

$$B = \$12{,}000 + .1C$$
$$C = \$27{,}000 + .2B$$

$$B = \$12{,}000 + .1 (\$27{,}000 + .2B)$$
$$B = \$12{,}000 + \$2{,}700 + .02B$$
$$.98B = \$14{,}700$$
$$B = \$15{,}000$$

$$C = \$27{,}000 + .2B$$
$$C = \$27{,}000 + .2 (\$15{,}000)$$
$$C = \$27{,}000 + \$3{,}000$$
$$C = \$30{,}000$$

Assuming that in any given period Company A earns $100,000; B, $8,000; and C, $18,000 from their respective operations, net income would be apportioned as follows:

	Company A	Company B	Company C	Total
Net income before apportionment	$100,000	$10,000*	$20,000*	$130,000
Elimination of mutual income:				
C's share of B's (20%)		(2,000)		(2,000)
B's share of C's (10%)			(2,000)	(2,000)
Apportionment:				
A's share of B's (80%)	8,000	(8,000)		
A's share of C's (90%)	18,000		(18,000)	
Balances	$126,000	–0–	–0–	$126,000
Consolidated net income	$126,000			$126,000†
Minority interest, B		–0–		
Minority interest, C			–0–	
Total				$126,000

* Let B = Company B's net income on a consolidated basis.
Let C = Company C's net income on a consolidated basis.

$$B = \$ \ 8,000 + .1C$$
$$C = \$18,000 + .2B$$

$$B = \$ \ 8,000 + .1 \ (\$18,000 + .2B)$$
$$B = \$ \ 8,000 + \$1,800 + .02B$$
$$.98B = \$ \ 9,800$$
$$B = \$10,000$$

$$C = \$18,000 + .2B$$
$$C = \$18,000 + .2 \ (\$10,000)$$
$$C = \$18,000 + \$2,000$$
$$C = \$20,000$$

† Since, from the consolidated viewpoint, Company B and Company C are wholly owned, consolidated net income may be proved by merely adding arithmetically the separate incomes of the respective companies on a non-consolidated basis ($100,000 + $8,000 + $18,000).

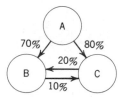

Mutual Stockholdings Between Subsidiaries

Second Illustration. Assuming the same facts as used in the preceding illustration, except that Company A owns directly only an 80% interest in Company C and a 70% interest in Company B, the establishment of reciprocity and the apportionment of net income would be accomplished as follows:

Investment in Company C (A's)	$24,000	
Investment in Company C (B's)	3,000	
Retained earnings (A's)		$24,000
Retained earnings (B's)		3,000
(to recognize Company A's 80% and Company B's 10% interest in the increase in Company C's shareholders' equity)		

Investment in Company B (A's)	$10,500		
Investment in Company B (C's)	3,000		
Retained earnings (A's)		$10,500	
Retained earnings (C's)		3,000	

(to recognize Company A's 70% and Company C's 20% interest in the increase in Company B's shareholders' equity)

	Company A	Company B	Company C	Total
Net income before apportionment	$100,000	$10,000	$20,000	$130,000
Elimination of mutual income:				
C's share of B's (20%)		(2,000)		(2,000)
B's share of C's (10%)			(2,000)	(2,000)
Apportionment:				
A's share of B's (70%)	7,000	(7,000)		
A's share of C's (80%)	16,000		(16,000)	
Balances	$123,000	$ 1,000	$ 2,000	$126,000
Consolidated net income	$123,000			$123,000
Minority interest, B (10%)		$ 1,000		1,000
Minority interest, C (10%)			$ 2,000	2,000
Total				$126,000

Mutual Stockholdings between Parent and Subsidiary

Assume Company A owns an 80% interest in Company B and that Company B, in turn, owns a 10% interest in Company A; that from their own operations Company B's shareholders' equity has increased $10,000 and Company A's $84,000 since date of acquisition; and that both investment accounts are on the cost basis. Reciprocity would be established by the following work sheet entry:

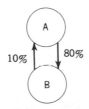

Mutual Stockholdings Between Parent and Subsidiary

Investment in Company A (B's)	$10,000		
Investment in Company B (A's)	16,000		
Retained earnings (B's)		$10,000	
Retained earnings (A's)		16,000	

(to recognize Company B's 10% interest in Company A's increase in shareholders' equity, and to recognize Company A's 80% interest in Company B's increase in shareholders' equity)*

  * Let A = Company A's increase in shareholders' equity on a consolidated basis.

  Let B = Company B's increase in shareholders' equity on a consolidated basis.

$$A = \$ 84{,}000 + .8B$$
$$B = \$ 10{,}000 + .1A$$

$$B = \$ 10{,}000 + .1 \, (\$84{,}000 + .8B)$$
$$B = \$ 10{,}000 + \$8{,}400 + .08B$$
$$.92B = \$ 18{,}400$$
$$B = \$ 20{,}000$$

$$A = \$ 84{,}000 + .8B$$
$$A = \$ 84{,}000 + .8 \, (\$20{,}000)$$
$$A = \$ 84{,}000 + \$16{,}000$$
$$A = \$100{,}000$$

Assuming that in any given period Company A earns $42,000, and Company B, $5,000 from their respective operations, net income would be apportioned as follows:

	Company A	Company B	Total
Net income before apportionment	$50,000*	$10,000*	$60,000
Elimination of mutual income:			
A's share of B's (80%)		(8,000)	(8,000)
B's share of A's (10%)	(5,000)		(5,000)
Balances	$45,000	$ 2,000	$47,000
Consolidated net income	$45,000		$45,000
Minority interest, B (20%)		$ 2,000	2,000
Total			$47,000

* Let A = A's net income on a consolidated basis.
  Let B = B's net income on a consolidated basis.

$$A = \$42,000 + .8B$$
$$B = \$ 5,000 + .1A$$

$$A = \$42,000 + .8 (\$5,000 + .1A)$$
$$A = \$42,000 + \$4,000 + .08A$$
$$.92A = \$46,000$$
$$A = \$50,000$$

$$B = \$ 5,000 + .1A$$
$$B = \$ 5,000 + .1 (\$50,000)$$
$$B = \$10,000$$

Mutual Stockholdings between Subsidiaries and between the Parent and Subsidiaries

Assume Company A owns an 80% interest in Company B and a 90% interest in Company C directly; that Company B holds a 5% interest in Company A and a 10% interest in Company C; that Company C holds a 10% interest in both Company A and Company B; that from their own operations Company A's shareholders' equity has increased $100,000, Company B's, $20,000, and Company C's, $10,000 since the date of acquisition; and that all investment accounts are on the cost basis. Reciprocity would be established by the following work sheet entry:

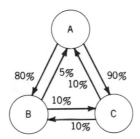

Mutual Stockholdings Between Subsidiaries and Between the Parent and Subsidiaries

(Dr.)	Investment in Company A (B's)	$ 7,469
	Investment in Company A (C's)	14,938
	Investment in Company B (A's)	24,212
	Investment in Company B (C's)	3,027
	Investment in Company C (A's)	25,168
	Investment in Company C (B's)	2,796

(Cr.)	Retained earnings (A's)	$49,380
	Retained earnings (B's)	10,265
	Retained earnings (C's)	17,965

(to recognize Company A's 80% interest in the increase in B's shareholders' equity and 90% interest in the increase in C's shareholders' equity; and Company B's 5% interest in A and 10% interest in C; and C's 10% interest in both A and B)

While problems of this nature may be solved by means of simultaneous equations, as has been illustrated, more involved holdings with a greater number of subsidiaries may make the algebraic solution unduly complex. In such situations it is not uncommon to find the "successive allocation" method used to establish reciprocity or to apportion net income. The use of this method to establish reciprocity is illustrated below:

	Company A	Company B	Company C
First allocation:			
Separate company increases	$100,000	$20,000	$10,000
Allocation of A (5% to B, 10% to C)	...	5,000	10,000
Allocation of B (80% to A, 10% to C)	20,000	...	2,500
Allocation of C (90% to A, 10% to B)	20,250	2,250	...
Total	$140,250	$27,250	$22,500
Second allocation:			
Separate company increases	$100,000	$20,000	$10,000
Allocation of A (140,250)	...	7,012	14,025
Allocation of B (27,250)	21,800	...	2,725
Allocation of C (26,750)	24,075	2,675	...
Total	$145,875	$29,687	$26,750
(Third through seventh allocation omitted.)			
Eighth allocation:			
Separate company increases	$100,000	$20,000	$10,000
Allocation of A (149,376)	...	7,469	14,938
Allocation of B (30,264)	24,211	...	3,026
Allocation of C (27,964)	25,168	2,796	...
Total	$149,379	$30,265	$27,964
Ninth allocation:			
Separate company increases	$100,000	$20,000	$10,000
Allocation of A (149,379)	...	7,469	14,938
Allocation of B (30,265)	24,212	...	3,027
Allocation of C (27,964)*	25,168	2,796	...
Total	$149,380	$30,265	$27,965

* Discrepancy of $1.00 due to rounding.

Since further allocations will give the same result, no further allocations are necessary. The work sheet entry to establish reciprocity would be based on the amounts determined in the ninth allocation.

Mutual Stockholdings as Treasury Stock

A procedure well accepted in accounting practice is to treat the subsidiary's holdings of a parent company's stock as treasury stock. Supporting this treatment is the view that subsidiary ownership of parent company's stock is an investment by the subsidiary. As with any other investment, such stock should be valued at cost.

Consolidation procedure under this concept is simplified. Eliminations would be limited to the consolidated interest in the subsidiaries. A subsidiary's investment in the parent company's stock would be carried on the consolidated statement of financial position as treasury stock.

There is considerable support for the treasury stock point of view in practice. Its use is also recommended in *Accounting Research Bulletin* 51. The work sheet on page 442 and accompanying explanation illustrate.the procedure involved. The amounts in the individual company statements are assumed and the adjustments to establish reciprocity are.based on the illustration in the preceding section.

The increases in the shareholders' equities for Companies B and C on a consolidated basis, since acquisition, may be computed as follows:

Let B = Company B's increase in shareholders' equity on a consolidated basis.
Let C = Company C's increase in shareholders' equity on a consolidated basis.

$$B = \$20,000 + .1C$$
$$C = \$10,000 + .1B$$

$$B = \$20,000 + .1\,(\$10,000 + .1B)$$
$$B = \$20,000 + \$1,000 + .01B$$
$$.99B = \$21,000$$
$$B = \$21,212.12$$

$$C = \$10,000 + .1B$$
$$C = \$10,000 + 2,121.21$$
$$C = \$12,121.21$$

When subsidiary holdings of parent stock are treated as treasury stock, the results differ from the results obtained under the assumption of a mutual holding. The extent of this difference is revealed by a comparison

COMPANY A AND SUBSIDIARIES
CONSOLIDATED WORKING PAPERS
STATEMENT OF FINANCIAL POSITION
AS OF DECEMBER 31, 1968

	Company A	Company B	Company C	Adjustments Debit	Adjustments Credit	Eliminations Debit	Eliminations Credit	Consolidated Financial Position
Current assets	$120,000	$40,000	$15,000					$175,000
Investment in A (Cost)— 5%		35,000						35,000T/S
Investment in A (Cost)—10%			90,000					90,000T/S
Investment in B (Cost)—80%	125,000			$16,970(3)			$136,970A	5,000G
Investment in B (Cost)—10%			15,000	2,121(1)			17,121B	...
Investment in C (Cost)—90%	120,000			10,909(4)			127,909C	3,000G
Investment in C (Cost)—10%		13,000		1,212(2)			14,212D	...
Fixed assets	535,000	112,000	30,000					677,000
Total	$900,000	$200,000	$150,000					$985,000
Current liabilities	$100,000	$30,000	$10,000					$140,000
Capital stock—A	500,000							500,000
Retained earnings—A, 12/31/68	300,000				$16,970(3) 10,909(4)			327,879RE
Capital stock—B		100,000				$ 80,000A 10,000B		10,000MI
Retained earnings—B (at date A acquired stock)		50,000				40,000A 5,000B		
Retained earnings (since acquisition)		20,000			1,212(2)	16,970A 2,121B		5,000MI
Capital stock—C			90,000			81,000C 9,000D		
Retained earnings—C (at date A acquired stock)			40,000			36,000C 4,000D		
Retained earnings (since acquisition)			10,000		2,121(1)	10,909C 1,212D		2,121MI
Total	$900,000	$200,000	$150,000	$31,212	$31,212	$296,212	$296,212	$985,000

of the work sheet entries to establish reciprocity in the two immediately preceding illustrations.

Effect of Indirect Ownership and Mutual Stockholdings on Intercompany-Profit Eliminations

Intercompany-profit transactions, in the case of direct ownership, were discussed in Chapter 13. Recognition was given to the general unanimity among accountants for the need to eliminate intercompany profits and to the lack of agreement as to the amount to be eliminated or how it should be eliminated. Most accountants eliminate 100% of any intercompany profit unrealized at the date of consolidation. Some accountants, however, eliminate the entire amount from consolidated retained earnings. Others prorate the elimination between consolidated retained earnings and the minority interest.

The effect of indirect and mutual stockholdings upon the elimination of intercompany profits is illustrated in the following examples. In all cases, assume that as of the consolidating date Company B has merchandise in its inventory valued at $10,000 which it purchased from Company C. The merchandise had cost Company C $6,000.

Indirect Ownership—Major and Minor Parent. Assume, in addition to the general assumptions given above, that Company A owns a 90% interest in Company B, and that Company B, in turn, owns an 80% interest in Company C. The intercompany-profit elimination under the two basic approaches would be made as follows:

	100% Elimination Not Prorated		100% Elimination Prorated	
	Debit	Credit	Debit	Credit
Consolidated retained earnings	$4,000[4]		$2,880[1]	
Minority interest, C	–0–		800[2]	
Minority interest, B	–0–		320[3]	
Inventory		$4,000[4]		$4,000[4]

$$[1] \quad 72\% \times \$4,000 = \$2,880$$
$$[2] \quad 20\% \times \$4,000 = 800$$
$$[3] \quad 8\% \times \$4,000 = 320*$$
$$[4] \quad 100\% \times \$4,000 = \$4,000$$

* When establishing reciprocity, Company B would recognize $3,200 (80% × $4,000) of the intercompany profit and, in turn, Company A would recognize $2,880 (90% × $3,200), leaving $320 pertaining to the minority interest in Company B.

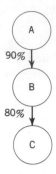

Indirect Ownership—Major and Minor Parent

Indirect Ownership—Connecting Affiliate. Assume, in addition to the general assumptions, that Company A owns a 90% interest in Company B and an 80% interest in Company C, and that Company B, in turn, owns a 10% interest in Company C. The intercompany-profit eliminations would be made as follows:

	100% Elimination Not Prorated		100% Elimination Prorated	
	Debit	Credit	Debit	Credit
Consolidated retained earnings	$4,000[4]		$3,560[1]	
Minority interest, C	–0–		400[2]	
Minority interest, B	–0–		40[3]	
Inventory		$4,000		$4,000

$$[1] \quad 89\% \times \$4,000 = \$3,560$$
$$[2] \quad 10\% \times \$4,000 = \quad 400$$
$$[3] \quad 1\% \times \$4,000 = \quad 40*$$
$$[4] \quad 100\% \times \$4,000 = \underline{\$4,000}$$

* When establishing reciprocity, Company B would recognize $400 (10% × $4,000) of the intercompany profit, and Company A in turn would recognize $360 (90% × $400) of this, leaving $40 pertaining to the minority interest in Company B. This represents 1% (10% × 10%) of the intercompany profit.

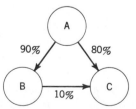

Indirect Ownership—Connecting Affiliate

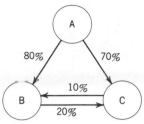

Mutual Stockholdings

Mutual Stockholdings. Assume, in addition to the general assumptions, that Company A owns an 80% interest in Company B and a 70% interest in Company C, that Company B holds a 20% interest in Company C, and that Company C, in turn, holds a 10% interest in Company B. The intercompany-profit eliminations would be made as follows:

	100% Elimination Not Prorated		100% Elimination Prorated	
	Debit	Credit	Debit	Credit
Consolidated retained earnings	$4,000		$3,510.21[1]	
Minority interest, C	–0–		408.16[2]	
Minority interest, B	–0–		81.63[3]	
Inventory		$4,000		$4,000

[1] The amount recognized by Company A when consolidating (see calculations below).

[2] 10% of $4,081.63, the amount recognized by Company C when consolidating (see calculations below).

[3] 10% of $816.33, the amount recognized by Company B when consolidating (see calculations below).

Elimination algebraically determined:
Let A = A's share of C's intercompany profit on a consolidated basis.
Let B = B's share of C's intercompany profit on a consolidated basis.
Let C = C's intercompany profit on a consolidated basis.

$$C = \$4,000 + .1B$$
$$B = .2C$$
$$A = .8B + .7C$$

$$B = .2 (\$4,000 + .1B)$$
$$B = \$800 + .02B$$
$$.98B = \$800$$
$$B = \$816.33$$

$$C = \$4,000 + .1B$$
$$C = \$4,081.63$$

$$A = .8 (\$816.33) + .7 (\$4,081.63)$$
$$A = \$653.07 + \$2,857.14$$
$$A = \$3,510.21$$

Successive allocation method:

	A	B	MI (B)	C	MI (C)
Intercompany profit				$4,000	
Allocation of intercompany profit	$2,800	$800		(4,000)	$400
Allocation of B's share	640	(800)	$80	80	
Reallocation of C's share	56	16		(80)	8
Reallocation of B's share	13	(16)	1	2	
Second reallocation of C's share	2			(2)	
Total	$3,511	–0–	$81	–0–	$408

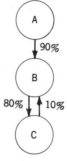

Combination of Indirect Ownership and Mutual Stockholdings

Combination of Indirect Ownership and Mutual Stockholdings.

Assume, in addition to the general assumptions, that Company A owns a 90% interest in Company B, that Company B owns an 80% interest in Company C, and that Company C, in turn, holds a 10% interest in Company B. The intercompany-profit eliminations would be made as follows:

	100% Elimination Not Prorated		100% Elimination Prorated	
	Debit	Credit	Debit	Credit
Consolidated retained earnings	$4,000		$3,130.43[1]	
Minority interest, C	–0–		869.57[2]	
Minority interest, B	–0–		–0–	
Inventory		$4,000		$4,000

[1] The amount recognized by Company A when consolidating (see calculations below).

[2] 20% of $4,347.83, the amount recognized by Company C when consolidating (see calculations below).

Elimination algebraically determined:

Let C = C's intercompany profit on a consolidated basis.

Let B = B's share of C's intercompany profit on a consolidated basis.

Let A = A's share of C's intercompany profit on a consolidated basis.

$$C = \$4,000 + .1B$$
$$B = .8C$$
$$A = .9B$$

$$B = .8\,(\$4,000 + .1B)$$
$$B = \$3,200 + .08B$$
$$.92B = \$3,200.00$$
$$B = \$3,478.26$$

$$C = \$4,000 + .1B$$
$$C = \$4,347.83$$

$$A = .9B$$
$$A = \$3,130.43$$

Successive allocation method:

	A	B	MI (B)	C	MI (C)
Intercompany profit				$4,000	
Allocation of intercompany profit		$3,200		(4,000)	$800
Allocation of B's share	$2,880	(3,200)	–0–	320	
Reallocation of C's share		256		(320)	64
Reallocation of B's share	230	(256)		26	
Second reallocation of C's share		21		(26)	5
Second reallocation of B's share	19	(21)		2	
Third reallocation of C's share	2			(2)	
Total	$3,131	–0–	–0–	–0–	$869

PROBLEMS

Problem 15–1. From the following data determine (1) the minority interest in the net income or loss of each company, and (2) consolidated net income.

Company A owns 90% of Company B and 80% of Company C. Company B owns 80% of Company D, and Company C owns 90% of Company E. During the current year the companies *individually* reported net income or loss as follows:

Company	Net Income or Loss	Amount
A	Income	$50,000
B	Income	20,000
C	Income	22,000
D	Income	14,000
E	*Loss*	*8,000*

Problem 15–2. From the following data determine (1) the minority interest in the net income or loss of each company, and (2) consolidated net income.

A Company owns 90% of B Company, 80% of C Company, and 70% of D Company. B Company owns 10% of D Company, and C Company owns 10% of D Company. During the current year the companies *individually* reported net income or loss as follows:

Company	Net Income or Loss	Amount
A	Income	$40,000
B	*Loss*	*10,000*
C	Income	10,000
D	Income	20,000

Problem 15–3. From the following data determine (1) the minority interest in the net income or loss of each company, and (2) consolidated net income.

Company A owns 80% of Company B and 90% of Company C. Company B owns 70% of Company D, and Company C owns 80% of Company E. Company E owns 20% of Company D. During the current year the companies *individually* reported net income or loss as follows:

Company	Net Income or Loss	Amount
A	Income	$100,000
B	*Loss*	*20,000*
C	Income	45,000
D	*Loss*	*6,000*
E	Income	9,000

Problem 15–4. From the following data determine (1) the minority interest in the net income of each company, and (2) consolidated net income.

Company A owns 90% of Company B and 80% of Company C. Company B owns 10% of Company C, and Company C owns 10% of Company B. During the current year the companies *individually* reported net income or loss as follows:

Company	Net Income or Loss	Amount
A	Income	$100,000
B	Income	19,000
C	Income	8,000

Problem 15–5. Company A controls Company B through the ownership of 75,600 shares of the latter's capital stock, out of a total of 96,000 shares outstanding at June 30, 1967. The authorized capital stock of Company B is 150,000 shares, all of one class.

Company B controls Company C through the ownership of 6,250 shares of the latter's capital stock, out of a total of 10,000 shares outstanding at June 30, 1967.

The sum of the capital stock and surplus of Company B at June 30, 1967, is $5,894,706, and of Company C, $2,132,470.

Company B wishes to acquire the minority interest in Company C through the issuance of shares of its capital stock at a value equal to its book value at June 30, 1967, taking into account the book value of capital stock of Company C. Company B's investment is carried on Company B's books at a total cost of $687,500.

Required:
(1) You are to determine the number of shares to be issued by Company B, ignoring fractional shares.
(2) You are to compute the percentage of control held by Company A after such shares have been issued.   (AICPA adapted)

Problem 15–6. The financial facts shown in Exhibit I below pertain to corporations R and S which had mutual holdings during and at the end of the fiscal year 1967.
There was no change in the mutual holdings during the year. Each corporation carries its investment account at cost.

EXHIBIT I

	Corporation	
	R	S
Of the issued capital stock,		
R owns	10%	50%
S owns	20%	10%
Net assets (exclusive of investment accounts),		
December 31, 1967	$540,000	$590,000
Dividends declared during 1967	?	18,000
1967 net income (after taxes), exclusive of dividends	53,000	60,000

Required:
(1) Compute the dollar equity of outside shareholders in the total net assets of R and S, respectively.
(2) Compute the dollar amount of dividends declared in 1967 to which the outside shareholders of R are entitled, assuming that R declared as dividends its *total* 1967 net income after taxes.   (AICPA adapted)

Problem 15–7. From the following condensed statements of financial position of Company A, Company B, and Company C, prepared as of December 31, 1967, prepare a consolidated statement of financial position.

	Company A	Company B	Company C
Current assets	$1,234,567	$ 731,282	$340,274
Investments:			
80% of B stock, at cost	1,400,000	...	...
75% of C stock, at cost	...	540,200	...
Fixed assets, net	3,030,933	1,322,607	514,987
Total	$5,665,500	$2,594,089	$855,261
Current liabilities	$ 400,500	$ 275,389	$ 93,261
Bonds payable	...	750,000	...
Surplus reserve for redemption of bonds	...	250,000	...
Common stock, $100 par value	3,000,000	1,000,000	600,000
Capital surplus	710,300	...	45,600
Retained earnings	1,554,700	318,700	116,400
Total	$5,665,500	$2,594,089	$855,261

The stock of Company C was acquired by Company B on January 31, 1966. Since that date Company C has had total earnings of $28,400 and paid cash dividends of $40,000. Company B has credited all dividends received to its income account.

Company A acquired the stock of Company B on December 31, 1967.

(AICPA adapted)

Problem 15–8. From the following financial statements and other data, prepare consolidated working papers with columns for income, retained earnings, minority interests, and financial position.

STATEMENTS OF FINANCIAL POSITION
DECEMBER 31, 1969

Assets	Phoenix Co.	Eastern Airports, Inc.	Potomac Airport Co.
Cash	$ 428,000	$ 14,500	$ 500
Accounts receivable		45,000	8,500
Prepayments and supplies	5,000	26,500	
Investment in U.S. Airlines Co. stock	630,000		
Investment in Eastern, Inc., stock	270,000		
Loans to Eastern, Inc.	370,000		
Investment in Potomac Co. common stock		180,000	
Land		284,000	215,500
Buildings and equipment		310,000	
Reserve for depreciation		50,000*	
	$1,703,000	$810,000	$224,500
Liabilities			
Accounts payable		$ 10,000	
Taxes and other accruals	$ 15,000	24,000	
Due Phoenix Co.		370,000	
Due Potomac Co.		8,500	
Capital stock—preferred			$ 40,000
Capital stock—common	500,000	225,000	200,000
Paid-in surplus	500,000	150,000	
Retained earnings	688,000	22,500	15,500*
	$1,703,000	$810,000	$224,500

*Deductions

INCOME STATEMENTS—1969

Income:	Phoenix Co.	Eastern Airports, Inc.	Potomac Airport Co.
Rent			$8,500
Profit on sales of securities	$165,000		
Revenue from port activities		$75,000	
Dividends	25,000		
Interest	48,000		
	$238,000	$75,000	$8,500

Expenses:

Interest		$18,000	
General, including taxes	$ 75,000	46,000	$2,000
Loss on sale of hangar			3,000
	$ 75,000	$64,000	$5,000
Net Income	$163,000	$11,000	$3,500

Other data:

(1) Phoenix Co. owns 36,000 shares of the stock of Eastern Airports, Inc. Of this holding, 21,000 shares were acquired at $10 per share by subscription at the time Eastern was organized (January 1, 1966). An additional 3,000 shares of Eastern stock were purchased on December 31, 1967, at $20 per share; immediately after this transaction the shareholders' equity of Eastern stood as follows:

Capital stock—stated value ($5 per share)	$150,000
Paid-in surplus	150,000
Retained earnings	100,000
	$400,000

As of January 1, 1968, Eastern Airports, Inc. declared a stock dividend of $75,000 (15,000 shares at $5 per share), which was appropriated from retained earnings.

(2) Eastern Airports, Inc., owns 90% of the common stock of Potomac Airport Co. acquired on December 31, 1967, at a total cost of $180,000. At this time the accumulated operating deficit of Potomac was $14,000, but preferred dividends had been paid to date.

(3) No dividends were paid by Phoenix Co. in 1969.

(4) No dividends (other than the stock dividend referred to above) were declared by Eastern Airports, Inc., during the years 1968 and 1969.

(5) No dividends were declared on the preferred stock of Potomac Airport Co. for the two years, 1968–1969. This is a 6% cumulative stock.

(6) The interest charge on the books of Eastern Airports, Inc. is entirely applicable to the advances made by the Phoenix Co.

(7) All of the revenues of Potomac Airport Co. for 1969 are based on charges to Eastern Airports, Inc., not yet collected.

(8) All investment accounts are recorded on a cost basis, with no adjustments for intercompany profit, loss, or dividends.   (AICPA adapted)

Problem 15–9. From the data shown on page 452 prepare a consolidated statement of financial position of the Top Holding Company and its subsidiaries R Company and S Company.

The investments in R Company stock are carried at cost less applicable portions of net losses since acquisition; the investments in S Company stock are carried at cost. The bonds were acquired at $1,500 discount and are carried at cost. The investments in R Company were made at a time when R Company had retained earnings of $1,500; the investments in S Company were made at a time when S Company had retained earnings of $5,000.   (AICPA adapted)

STATEMENTS OF FINANCIAL POSITION

Assets	Top Holding Company	R Company	S Company
Current assets	$150,000	$30,000	$118,110
Property, less reserves	47,000	5,500	130,000
Investment in R Company stock:			
90%	18,000		
10%			2,500
Investment in S Company stock:			
75%	45,000		
15%		9,000	
Investment in S Company bonds	41,500		
	$301,500	$44,500	$250,610
Equities			
Current liabilities	$ 80,000	$23,000	$ 70,000
Bonds payable			100,000
Capital stock	200,000	30,000	50,000
Retained earnings (deficit)	21,500	(8,500)	30,610
	$301,500	$44,500	$250,610

Problem 15–10. From the following statements of financial position and additional data, prepare consolidated working papers as of December 31, 1967:

On December 31, 1966, the Rockford Electronics Company bought 90% of the $500,000 capital stock of the Elgin Supply Company for $370,080, and 80% of the $200,000 7% preferred stock of the Peoria Radio Company for $176,000.

The Elgin Supply Company had acquired previously (December 31, 1965) 90% of the $200,000 common stock of the Peoria Radio Company for $126,000.

ROCKFORD ELECTRONICS COMPANY

STATEMENT OF FINANCIAL POSITION

DECEMBER 31, 1967

Assets		Equities	
Investments		Accounts payable	
Elgin Co.	$ 397,080	Peoria Co.	$ 10,000
Peoria Co.	187,200	Capital stock	
Notes receivable		Preferred	400,000
Peoria Co.	20,000	Common	800,000
Other assets (net)	708,520	Retained Earnings	102,800
	$1,312,800		$1,312,800

(1) Rockford consistently takes up on its books its share of Elgin's book profits.

(2) The difference of $5,000 between the current accounts of Rockford and Peoria represents Peoria merchandise in transit to Rockford.

ELGIN SUPPLY COMPANY

STATEMENT OF FINANCIAL POSITION

DECEMBER 31, 1967

Assets		Equities	
Investments			
Peoria Co.	$126,000	Notes receivable	
Notes receivable		discounted	$ 10,000
Peoria Co.	10,000	Capital stock	500,000
Other assets (net)	400,000	Retained earnings	26,000
	$536,000		$536,000

(3) Elgin does not take up on its books its share of the Peoria profits but credits to income the Peoria dividends when received.

(4) Elgin made a profit of $50,000 in 1967, before considering income from its investment in Peoria, and on December 20, 1967, paid a dividend of 4% ($20,000) on its $500,000 capital stock.

PEORIA RADIO COMPANY

STATEMENT OF FINANCIAL POSITION

DECEMBER 31, 1967

Assets		Equities	
Goodwill	$ 20,000	Notes payable	
Accounts receivable		Rockford Co.	$ 20,000
Rockford Co.	15,000	Elgin Co.	10,000
Other assets (net)	425,000	Dividends payable	
		Preferred	14,000
		Common	16,000
		Capital Stock	
		7% Preferred	200,000
		Common	200,000
	$460,000		$460,000

(5) Peoria made a profit of $20,000 in 1966, which was paid out in dividends that were duly received by the shareholders before December 31, 1966

(6) Peoria made a profit of $30,000 in 1967 and on December 20, 1967, declared dividends of 7% on the preferred and 8% on the common stock, both payable January 10, 1968.

(AICPA adapted)

Problem 15–11. From the following data prepare a consolidated statement of financial position as of December 31, 1968:

Assets	A	B	C
Investment in Company B 4,000 shares	$ 480,000		
Investment in Company C 1,500 shares		$ 150,000	
Other assets	3,201,000	965,000	$269,000
	$3,681,000	$1,115,000	$269,000
Liabilities and Capital			
Liabilities	$ 425,000	$ 191,000	$ 36,000
Capital stock:			
Number of shares	22,000	6,000	2,000
Par or declared value	$ 100	$ 90	$ 100
Amount	$2,200,000	$ 540,000	$200,000
Capital surplus		$ 60,000	
Retained earnings:			
At January 1, 1968	$ 937,000	$ 288,000	$ 38,000
Profit for 1968	559,000	54,000	3,000
Total	$1,496,000	$ 342,000	$ 41,000
Dividends declared in 1968	440,000	18,000	8,000
At December 31, 1968	$1,056,000	$ 324,000	$ 33,000
	$3,681,000	$1,115,000	$269,000

The investments in Companies B and C were acquired at the close of the year 1967, and the 1968 dividends paid or declared thereon have been credited to income. The capital surplus of Company B arose through the sale of its no-par capital stock at $100 per share, of which $90 was designated as its declared value, and the balance of $10 was credited to capital surplus.

There are no intercompany accounts or relations other than those that are indicated above.

(AICPA adapted)

CHAPTER **16**

Consolidated statements—
comprehensive review

In the preceding chapters particular problems of preparing consolidated statements have received special attention. As a result, at any one time the reader's attention has been focused primarily on the solving of a particular type of problem. In order to provide an overall picture of consolidations, a comprehensive review is presented in this chapter. The problem follows approximately the same sequence as used previously, namely:

(1) Consolidation at the date of acquisition.
(2) Consolidation subsequent to the date of acquisition.
(3) Intercompany-profit transactions.
(4) Intercompany-stock transactions.
(5) Indirect ownership and mutual stockholdings.

CONSOLIDATION AT DATE OF ACQUISITION

The review is predicated upon the assumption that as of January 1, 1967, The Parent Company purchases an 80% interest in The Cost Company and a 90% interest in The Equity Company for $100,000 and $72,000, respectively. Immediately after the acquisitions the following statements of financial position are presented for consolidation:

THE PARENT COMPANY
STATEMENT OF FINANCIAL POSITION
As of January 1, 1967

Assets		*Equities*	
Current assets	$ 290,000	Current liabilities	$ 62,000
Investment in Cost Company	100,000	Fixed liabilities	100,000
Investment in Equity Company	72,000	Shareholders' equity:	
		Capital stock	1,000,000
Fixed assets (net)	900,000	Retained earnings	200,000
	$1,362,000		$1,362,000

THE COST COMPANY
STATEMENT OF FINANCIAL POSITION
As of January 1, 1967

Assets		*Equities*	
Current assets	$ 40,000	Current liabilities	$ 10,000
Fixed assets (net)	130,000	Fixed liabilities	40,000
		Shareholders' equity:	
		Capital stock	100,000
		Retained earnings	20,000
	$170,000		$170,000

THE EQUITY COMPANY
STATEMENT OF FINANCIAL POSITION
As of January 1, 1967

Assets		*Equities*	
Current assets	$ 30,000	Current liabilities	$ 20,000
Fixed assets (net)	130,000	Fixed liabilities	50,000
		Shareholders' equity:	
		Capital stock	100,000
		Retained earnings	(10,000)
	$160,000		$160,000

Summary. Since reciprocity usually exists at the date of acquisition, consolidation at that time is primarily a matter of (1) eliminating the reciprocal elements, and (2) consolidating the nonreciprocal elements. However, if reciprocity does not exist (for instance, one or more of the

THE PARENT COMPANY AND SUBSIDIARIES
CONSOLIDATED WORKING PAPERS
STATEMENT OF FINANCIAL POSITION
AS OF JANUARY 1, 1967

	The Parent Company	The Cost Company	The Equity Company	Adjustments & Eliminations		Consolidated Financial Position
Assets						
Current assets	$ 290,000	$ 40,000	$ 30,000			$ 360,000
Investment in C	100,000				$ 96,000A	4,000G
Investment in E	72,000				81,000B	(9,000)G
Fixed assets (net)	900,000	130,000	130,000			1,160,000
	$1,362,000	$170,000	$160,000			$1,515,000
Equities						
Current liabilities	$ 62,000	$ 10,000	$ 20,000			$ 92,000
Fixed liabilities	100,000	40,000	50,000			190,000
Shareholders' equity:						
Capital stock:						
Parent Company	1,000,000					1,000,000
Cost Company		100,000		$ 80,000A		20,000MI
Equity Company			100,000	90,000B		10,000MI
Retained earnings:						
Parent Company	200,000					200,000RE
Cost Company		20,000		16,000A		4,000MI
Equity Company			(10,000)		9,000B	(1,000)MI
	$1,362,000	$170,000	$160,000	$186,000	$186,000	$1,515,000

A: To eliminate 80% of The Cost Company's shareholders' equity against the investment account.
B: To eliminate 90% of The Equity Company's shareholders' equity against the investment account.

Goodwill proof:

THE COST COMPANY		THE EQUITY COMPANY	
Paid	$100,000	Paid	$72,000
Book value acquired	96,000	Book value acquired	81,000
Goodwill	$ 4,000	Goodwill	$ (9,000)

affiliated group may not have recorded an intercompany transaction), it must be established before eliminating. It should also be remembered that consolidated retained earnings at the date of acquisition is composed of the parent company's retained earnings only.

CONSOLIDATION SUBSEQUENT TO DATE OF ACQUISITION

In the work sheets on page 458 the individual statements reflect the financial position of the respective companies as of December 31, 1967, and the operating results of the respective companies for the year ending December 31, 1967. The consolidated statement columns show how the financial position and operating results would appear on a consolidated basis at that time.

Summary. When consolidating subsequent to the date of acquisition, it may be necessary to establish reciprocity before consolidating. This is especially the case when the investment is carried on the cost basis as

THE PARENT COMPANY AND SUBSIDIARIES
CONSOLIDATED WORKING PAPERS
STATEMENT OF FINANCIAL POSITION
AS OF DECEMBER 31, 1967

	The Parent Company	The Cost Company	The Equity Company	Adjustments & Eliminations		Consolidated Financial Position
Assets						
Current assets	$ 348,000	$ 55,000	$ 50,000			$ 453,000
Investment in C	100,000			$ 18,400(1)	$114,400*A*	4,000G
Investment in E	90,000				99,000*B*	(9,000)G
Fixed assets (net)	920,000	120,000	120,000			1,160,000
	$1,458,000	$175,000	$170,000			$1,608,000
Equities						
Current liabilities	$ 50,000	$ 12,000	$ 10,000			$ 72,000
Fixed liabilities	110,000	20,000	50,000			180,000
Shareholders' equity:						
Capital stock:						
Parent Company	1,000,000					1,000,000
Cost Company		100,000		80,000*A*		20,000MI
Equity Company			100,000	90,000*B*		10,000MI
Retained earnings:						
Parent Company	298,000				18,400(1)	316,400RE
Cost Company		43,000		34,400*A*		8,600MI
Equity Company			10,000	9,000*B*		1,000MI
	$1,458,000	$175,000	$170,000	$231,800	$231,800	$1,608,000

(1): To recognize P's 80% interest in C's increase in shareholders' equity since acquisition 80% (143,000 − 120,000).
A: To eliminate 80% of C's shareholders' equity against the investment account.
B: To eliminate 90% of E's shareholders' equity against the investment account.

THE PARENT COMPANY AND SUBSIDIARIES
CONSOLIDATED WORKING PAPERS
STATEMENT OF INCOME AND RETAINED EARNINGS
YEAR ENDED DECEMBER 31, 1967

	The Parent Company	The Cost Company	The Equity Company	Eliminations	Consolidated Income	Consolidated Retained Earnings
Credits						
Net sales	$800,000	$210,000	$200,000		$1,210,000	
Interest income from C	400			$ 400*C*		
Income from E	18,000			18,000*D*		
	$818,400	$210,000	$200,000	$18,400	$1,210,000	
Debits						
Cost of sales	$556,200	$154,000	$150,000		$ 860,200	
Depreciation	80,000	10,000	10,000		100,000	
Interest expense	4,200	800	2,000	400*C*	6,600	
Federal income taxes	80,000	22,200	18,000		120,200	
Net income	98,000	23,000	20,000	18,000*D*	123,000	
	$818,400	$210,000	$200,000	$18,400	$1,210,000	
Retained earnings, 1/1/67	$200,000	$ 20,000	$ (10,000)			$200,000*
Net income	98,000	23,000	20,000			
Retained earnings, 12/31/67	$298,000	$ 43,000	$ 10,000			

Apportionment of net income:			
Net income			$ 123,000	
Minority interest, C (20% × 23,000)		$ 4,600	
Minority interest, E (10% × 20,000)		2,000	6,600
Consolidated net income—remainder (P's 98,000 + 80% of C's 23,000)		$ 116,400	116,400
Consolidated retained earnings, 12/31/67			$316,400

C: To eliminate intercompany interest income and interest expense.
D: To eliminate intercompany income.
* Parent's retained earnings at date of acquisition.

illustrated in entry (1). In the foregoing situation reciprocity existed between the Parent Company and the Equity Company, since the Parent Company had recognized on its books its share of the increase in the Equity Company's shareholders' equity since the date of acquisition.

It should be noted that the goodwill elements ($4,000 positive as related to the investment in the Cost Company, and $9,000 negative as related to the investment in the Equity Company) remain the same. This condition should exist because there has been no change in the per cent of ownership since the date of acquisition and no amortization has taken place.

It should also be noted that the consolidated retained earnings is composed of the retained earnings of the Parent Company and the Parent Company's share of the retained earnings which the subsidiaries have earned since acquisition.

	Retained Earnings 1/1/67	Earnings Retained Since 1/1/67	Parent's Share	Consolidated Retained Earnings 12/31/67
The Parent Company	$200,000	$80,000	$80,000	$280,000
The Cost Company	20,000	23,000	18,400	18,400
The Equity Company	(10,000)	20,000	18,000	18,000
Consolidated retained earnings 12/31/67				$316,400

INTERCOMPANY-PROFIT TRANSACTIONS

Intercompany profits and losses are defined as those profits and losses recognized by the selling affiliate at the time of sale, but which have not been realized from the consolidated viewpoint by transference to parties outside the affiliated group. It should be remembered that the Institute, in *Accounting Research Bulletin* 51, recommends that intercompany profits be (1) eliminated entirely from consolidated retained earnings, or (2) prorated between consolidated retained earnings and minority interest.

Intercompany Profits in Inventories. Assume that as of December 31, 1967, the inventories of the respective companies contain the following intercompany-profit elements:

	P's Inventory	C's Inventory	E's Inventory	Total
Purchased from P		$10,000	$15,000	$ 25,000
Purchased from C	$18,000		20,000	38,000
Purchased from E	25,000	12,000		37,000
Totals	$43,000	$22,000	$35,000	$100,000

Work sheet entries to eliminate the intercompany profit in inventories under each of the alternatives are presented below:

(1) One hundred per cent elimination against consolidated retained earnings:

Consolidated retained earnings	$100,000	
Inventory, Company P		$43,000
Inventory, Company C		22,000
Inventory, Company E		35,000

(2) One hundred per cent elimination prorated between consolidated retained earnings and the minority interest:

Consolidated retained earnings	$88,700*	
Minority interest, C (20% × $38,000)	7,600	
Minority interest, E (10% × $37,000)	3,700	
Inventory, Company P		$43,000
Inventory, Company C		22,000
Inventory, Company E		35,000

$$
\begin{aligned}
* \ \$25,000 \times 100\% &= \$25,000 \\
38,000 \times 80\% &= 30,400 \\
37,000 \times 90\% &= \underline{33,300} \\
& \ \underline{\underline{\$88,700}}
\end{aligned}
$$

Intercompany Profits in Fixed Assets. Although the treatment necessary for the elimination of intercompany profits in nondepreciating fixed assets and inventories is basically the same, the elimination necessary for intercompany profits in the case of depreciating fixed assets is somewhat different. The intercompany profit in depreciating assets is considered earned over the useful life of the asset as it is consumed and charged to production or to the cost of sales. The procedure involved is reviewed by assuming that as of the date of the intercompany-fixed-asset transactions, December 31, 1967, the assets of the respective companies contained the following intercompany-profit elements. Assume also that a 10-year useful life remained for all assets involved.

	P's Assets	C's Assets	E's Assets	Total
Purchased from P (12/31/67)		$20,000	$30,000	$ 50,000
Purchased from C (12/31/67)	$35,000		40,000	75,000
Purchased from E (12/31/67)	50,000	25,000		75,000
Totals	$85,000	$45,000	$70,000	$200,000

Work sheet entries to eliminate the intercompany profit in fixed assets under each of the alternatives are presented on the next page.

(1) One hundred per cent elimination against consolidated retained earnings:

	Date of Sale		End of 1st Year		End of 2nd Year		End of 10th Year	
	Debit	Credit	Debit	Credit	Debit	Credit	Debit	Credit
Consolidated retained earnings	$200,000		$180,000		$160,000			
Accrued depreciation (P)			8,500		17,000			
Accrued depreciation (C)			4,500		9,000			
Accrued depreciation (E)			7,000		14,000			
Fixed assets (P)		$85,000		$85,000		$85,000		$85,000
Fixed assets (C)		45,000		45,000		45,000		45,000
Fixed assets (E)		70,000		70,000		70,000		70,000

(2) One hundred per cent elimination prorated between consolidated retained earnings and minority interest:

	Date of Sale		End of 1st Year		End of 2nd Year		End of 10th Year	
	Debit	Credit	Debit	Credit	Debit	Credit	Debit	Credit
Consolidated retained earnings	$177,500		$159,750		$142,000			
Minority interest (C)	15,000		13,500		12,000			
Minority interest (E)	7,500		6,750		6,000			
Accrued depreciation (P)			8,500		17,000			
Accrued depreciation (C)			4,500		9,000			
Accrued depreciation (E)			7,000		14,000			
Fixed assets (P)		$85,000		$85,000		$85,000		$85,000
Fixed assets (C)		45,000		45,000		45,000		45,000
Fixed assets (E)		70,000		70,000		70,000		70,000

Summary. Although there is general unanimity among accountants as to the necessity for eliminating intercompany profits in inventories and fixed assets, there is not always agreement as to the amount that should be eliminated nor as to how it should be eliminated. If the cost principle is to be followed, 100% elimination seems to be appropriate. Realistically, the elimination should be prorated between consolidated retained earnings and the minority interest (where appropriate). For practical reasons based on materiality, however, complete elimination from consolidated retained earnings may be justified in many instances.

INTERCOMPANY-STOCK TRANSACTIONS

Although intercompany-stock transactions may take many different forms, the problems involved are perhaps best reviewed by an examination of the:

(1) Disposal of subsidiary stock.
(2) Acquisition of additional subsidiary stock.
(3) Effect(s) of intercompany-stock transactions upon subsequent consolidations.

Disposal of Subsidiary Stock. As of January 1, 1968, when contemplating investing in the Foreign Company, the Parent Company sells a 10% interest in the Cost Company for $15,000 and a 10% interest in the Equity Company for $14,000. As was pointed out in Chapter 14, the disposal of subsidiary stock is recorded, as is any asset disposal, by (1) recording any asset(s) received, (2) removing the carrying value of the asset disposed of from the appropriate account(s), and (3) recording any gain or loss on disposal. The following entries would be made to record the above sales.

Sale of the Cost Company stock:

Cash	$15,000	
Investment in Cost Company		$12,500
Gain on disposal of stock		2,500
(to record sale of stock: carrying value		
1/8 of $100,000 original cost)		

Sale of the Equity Company stock:

Cash	$14,000	
Investment in Equity Company		$10,000
Gain on disposal of stock		4,000

[to record sale of stock: carrying value
1/9 of $90,000 ($72,000 original cost +
$18,000 increase)]

It should also be noted that when disposing of subsidiary stock a proportionate amount of any goodwill associated with the acquisition of the stock is also disposed of. For example, 1/8 of the original $4,000 goodwill associated with the investment in the Cost Company and 1/9 of the original $9,000 negative goodwill associated with the investment in the Equity Company has been disposed of.

Acquisition of Additional Subsidiary Stock. Although the recording of an acquisition of additional shares of subsidiary stock is more or less routine, for subsequent illustrative purposes assume that as of July 1, 1968, the Parent Company purchases an additional 5% interest in the Cost Company for $7,000. The purchase would be recorded by:

Investment in Cost Company	$7,000	
Cash		$7,000

Effect(s) of Intercompany-Stock Transactions upon Subsequent Consolidations. The following example reviews the effect(s) of sales or purchases of subsidiary stock upon subsequent consolidations. The individual statements reflect the financial position of the respective companies as of December 31, 1968, and the operating results of the respective companies for the year then ended. The consolidated statement columns show how the financial position and operating results would appear on a consolidated basis at that time.

As of 1/1/67   As of 12/31/67

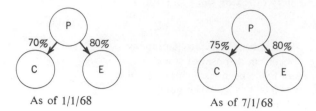

As of 1/1/68   As of 7/1/68

THE PARENT COMPANY AND SUBSIDIARIES

CONSOLIDATED WORKING PAPERS
STATEMENT OF FINANCIAL POSITION

AS OF DECEMBER 31, 1968

	The Parent Company	The Cost Company	The Equity Company	Adjustments & Eliminations		Consolidated Financial Position
Assets						
Current assets	$ 344,500	$ 80,000	$ 66,000			$ 490,500
Investment in C	94,500			$ 30,600(1)	$122,250*A*	2,850G
Investment in E	96,000				104,000*B*	(8,000)G†
Fixed assets (net)	910,000	110,000	114,000			1,134,000
	$1,445,000	$190,000	$180,000			$1,619,350
Equities						
Current liabilities	$ 23,500	$ 7,000	$ 10,000			$ 40,500
Fixed liabilities	55,000	20,000	40,000			115,000
Shareholders' equity:						
Capital stock:						
Parent Company	1,000,000					1,000,000
Cost Company		100,000		75,000*A*		25,000MI
Equity Company			100,000	80,000*B*		20,000MI
Retained earnings:						
Parent Company	366,500				30,600(1)	397,100RE
Cost Company		63,000*		47,250*A*		15,750MI
Equity Company			30,000	24,000*B*		6,000MI
	$1,445,000	$190,000	$180,000	$256,850	$256,850	$1,619,350

* Assume that C's income for 1968 was earned uniformly throughout the year.
(1): To recognize P's interest in C's increase in shareholders' equity since acquisition.

$$
\begin{aligned}
\$33,000 \times 70\% &= \$23,100 \\
10,000 \times 75\% &= 7,500 \\
\hline
& \$30,600
\end{aligned}
$$

A: To eliminate 75% of C's shareholders' equity against the investment account.
B: To eliminate 80% of E's shareholders' equity against the investment account.
† *Proof of goodwill:*

Company E, (8/9 × $9,000) original =		($8,000)
Company C:		
7/8 × $4,000 original =		$3,500
5% acquisition:		
Cost	$7,000	
Acquired (5% × $153,000)	7,650	(650)
		$2,850

THE PARENT COMPANY AND SUBSIDIARIES
CONSOLIDATED WORKING PAPERS
STATEMENT OF INCOME AND RETAINED EARNINGS

YEAR ENDED DECEMBER 31, 1968

	The Parent Company	The Cost Company	The Equity Company	Eliminations	Consolidated Income	Consolidated Retained Earnings
Credits						
Net sales	$790,000	$200,000	$195,000		$1,185,000	
Interest income from C	400			$ 400C		
Income from E	16,000			16,000D		
	$806,400	$200,000	$195,000	$16,400	$1,185,000	
Debits						
Cost of sales	$560,000	$150,000	$145,000		$ 855,000	
Depreciation	80,000	10,000	10,000		100,000	
Interest expense	4,200	800	2,000	$ 400C	6,600	
Federal income taxes	80,200	19,200	18,000		117,400	
Net income	82,000	20,000	20,000	16,000D	106,000	
	$806,400	$200,000	$195,000	$16,400	$1,185,000	
Retained earnings, 12/31/67	$298,000	$ 43,000	$ 10,000			$314,100†
Net income	82,000	20,000	20,000			
Dividends	(20,000)					(20,000)
Gain on sale of stock	6,500					6,500
Retained earnings, 12/31/68	$366,500	$ 63,000	$ 30,000			

Apportionment of net income:			
Net income			$ 106,000
Minority interest—C (25% × 20,000)		$ 5,000	
P's 5% claim earned prior to acquisition (5% × 20,000 × 1/2)		500	
Minority interest—E (20% × 20,000)		4,000	9,500
Consolidated net income—remainder			$ 96,500* 96,500
Consolidated retained earnings, 12/31/68			$397,100

C: To eliminate intercompany interest income and interest expense.
D: To eliminate P's share of E's income.
* Consolidated net income:

P's own earnings ($82,000 − $16,000) =		$66,000
C's: 70% × $20,000 −	$14,000	
5% × $20,000 × 1/2 =	500 =	14,500
E's own earnings (80% × 20,000)	=	16,000
		$96,500

† Consolidated retained earnings as of 12/31/67 as shown on page 440 is $316,400. However, when disposing of a 10% interest in C, a 10% claim against the 1967 earnings of $23,000 was also disposed of. Therefore, consolidated retained earnings as of 12/31/67 after disposing of C stock was 314,100 [316,400 − (10% × 23,000)]. No problem of reconciliation is involved as far as the disposal of Equity stock is concerned since the carrying value reflects the claim against the 1967 earnings and when the appropriate amount is removed from the investment account, this claim is reflected in the gain or loss on disposal.

Summary. The disposal of a portion of a subsidiary's stock or the acquisition of additional subsidiary stock is recorded as any other asset disposal or acquisition. A disposal is recorded by (1) recording any asset(s) received, (2) removing the carrying value of the asset from the appropriate account(s), and (3) recording any gain or loss on disposal. The recording of the acquisition of additional shares of subsidiary stock is merely a matter of debiting and crediting the appropriate accounts. When consolidating subsequent to a change in the per cent of ownership in a subsidiary, the earnings of the subsidiary in any given period can be reflected in consolidated retained earnings only to the extent of the ownership existing in that period that has been retained to the date of consolidation. It should also be emphasized that goodwill (either positive or negative) involved when acquiring subsidiary stock is disposed of proportionately when disposing of the stock.

Indirect Ownership and Mutual Stockholdings

Although the basic procedure remains the same in consolidating when indirect ownership or mutual stockholdings exist, as pointed out in Chapter 15 the establishment of reciprocity may become a little more complicated. As a consequence, this phase of consolidated work is emphasized in the review at this time. The establishment of reciprocity is considered primarily from the standpoint of:

(1) Major and minor parent.
(2) Connecting affiliate.
(3) Mutual stockholdings.

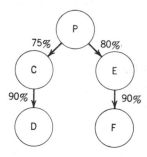

Major and Minor Parent

Major and Minor Parent. Assume that as of January 1, 1969, the Cost Company purchases a 90% interest in the D Company for $50,000 and the Equity Company purchases a 90% interest in the F Company for $40,000. Also assume that as of that date the D Company had net assets of $48,000 and the F Company $50,000. The following example illustrates the consolidating procedure as of December 31, 1969. The Equity Company carries the investment in the F Company on the equity basis, and the Cost Company carries the investment in the D Company on the cost basis.

THE PARENT COMPANY AND SUBSIDIARIES
CONSOLIDATED WORKING PAPERS. STATEMENT OF INCOME AND RETAINED EARNINGS
YEAR ENDED DECEMBER 31, 1969

	P	C	D	E	F	Eliminations	Consolidated Income	Consolidated Retained Earnings
Credits								
Net sales	$800,000	$210,000	$50,000	$200,000	$30,000		$1,290,000	
Interest income from C	400					$ 400E		
Income from E	17,200					17,200F		
Income (less) from F				(4,500)		(4,500)F		
	$817,600	$210,000	$50,000	$195,500	$30,000	$13,100	$1,290,000	
Debits								
Cost of sales	$565,900	$152,200	$36,900	$147,000	$28,100		$ 930,100	
Depreciation	82,000	10,000	4,500	10,000	6,000		112,500	
Interest expense	4,200	800	600	2,000	900	$ 400E	8,100	
Federal income taxes	80,000	20,000	2,000	15,000	-0-		117,000	
Net income	85,500	27,000	6,000	21,500	(5,000)	12,700F	122,300	
	$817,600	$210,000	$50,000	$195,500	$30,000	$13,100	$1,290,000	
Retained earnings, 1/1/69	$366,500	$ 63,000	$ (2,000)	$ 30,000	10,000			$397,100*
Net income	85,500	27,000	6,000	21,500	(5,000)			
Dividend	(20,000)							(20,000)
Retained earnings, 12/31/69	$432,000	$ 90,000	$ 4,000	$ 51,500	$ 5,000			

Apportionment of net income:

	Eliminations	Consolidated Income	Consolidated Retained Earnings
Net income		$ 122,300	
Minority interest in C (25% × 27,000) and (25% × 90% × 6,000)	$ 8,100		
Minority interest in D (10% × 6,000)	600		
Minority interest in E (20% × 21,500)	4,300		
Minority interest in F [10% × (5,000)]	(500)	12,500	
Consolidated net income—remainder		$ 109,800	109,800
Consolidated retained earnings, 12/31/69			$486,900

* See page 465. E: To eliminate intercompany income and expense. F: To eliminate intercompany income.

THE PARENT COMPANY AND SUBSIDIARIES
CONSOLIDATED WORKING PAPERS
STATEMENT OF FINANCIAL POSITION
As of DECEMBER 31, 1969

	P	C	D
Assets			
Current assets	$ 350,000	$ 50,000	$25,000
Investment in C	94,500		
Investment in D		50,000	
Investment in E	113,200		
Investment in F			
Fixed assets (net)	950,000	120,000	45,000
	$1,507,700	$220,000	$70,000
Equities			
Current liabilities	$ 25,700	$ 10,000	$ 6,000
Fixed liabilities	50,000	20,000	10,000
Shareholders' equity:			
Capital stock:			
Company P	1,000,000		
Company C		100,000	
Company D			50,000
Company E			
Company F			
Retained earnings:			
Company P	432,000		
Company C		90,000	
Company D			4,000
Company E			
Company F			
	$1,507,700	$220,000	$70,000

(1): To recognize C's interest in D's increase in shareholders' equity since acquisition (90% × $6,000).

(2): To recognize P's interest in C's increase in shareholders' equity since acquisition: $33,000* × 70% = $23,100

42,400† × 75% = 31,800

$54,900

* Increase from 1/1/67 to 6/30/68.

† $10,000 increase from 7/1/68 to 12/31/68 and $32,400 ($27,000 + $5,400) increase during 1969.

THE PARENT COMPANY AND SUBSIDIARIES
CONSOLIDATED WORKING PAPERS
STATEMENT OF FINANCIAL POSITION
(Continued)

| E | F | Adjustments & Eliminations | | Consolidated Financial Position |
		Debit	Credit	
$ 40,000	$20,000			$ 485,000
		$ 54,900(2)	$146,550A	2,850G
		5,400(1)	48,600B	6,800G
			121,200C	(8,000)G
35,500			40,500D	(5,000)G
129,500	60,000			1,304,500
$205,000	$80,000			$1,786,150
$ 13,500	$20,000			$ 75,200
40,000	15,000			135,000
				1,000,000
		75,000A		25,000MI
		45,000B		5,000MI
100,000		80,000C		20,000MI
	40,000	36,000D		4,000MI
			54,900(2)	486,900RE
		71,550A	5,400(1)	23,850MI
		3,600B		400MI
51,500		41,200C		10,300MI
	5,000	4,500D		500MI
$205,000	$80,000	$417,150	$417,150	$1,786,150

A: To eliminate 75% of C's shareholders' equity against the investment account.

B: To eliminate 90% of D's shareholders' equity against the investment account.

C: To eliminate 80% of E's shareholders' equity against the investment account.

D: To eliminate 90% of F's shareholders' equity against the investment account.

Connecting Affiliate. Assume that as of January 1, 1970, the Equity Company acquires a 10% interest in the Cost Company for $20,000. As of December 31, 1970, the financial statements would be consolidated as shown on pages 471 and 473.

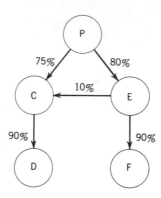

Connecting Affiliate

Mutual Stockholdings. Assume that as of January 1, 1971, the F Company acquires a 10% interest in the D Company for $7,000 and that the D Company, in turn, acquires a 10% interest in the F Company for $6,000. As of December 31, 1971, the financial statements would be consolidated as shown on pages 474–477.

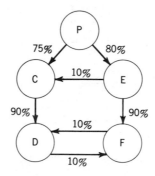

Mutual Stockholdings

The Parent Company and Subsidiaries
CONSOLIDATED WORKING PAPERS
STATEMENT OF INCOME AND RETAINED EARNINGS
Year Ended December 31, 1970

Credits	P	C	D	E	F	Eliminations	Consolidated Income	Consolidated Retained Earnings
Net sales	$820,000	$214,000	$70,000	$210,000	$50,000		$1,364,000	
Interest income from C	400					$ 400F		
Income from E	23,200			9,000		23,200G		
Income from F						9,000G		
	$843,600	$214,000	$70,000	$219,000	$50,000	$32,600	$1,364,000	
Debits								
Cost of sales	$587,400	$151,200	$48,900	$158,000	$32,100		$ 977,500	
Depreciation	80,000	10,000	4,500	10,000	6,000		110,500	
Interest expense	4,200	800	600	2,000	900	$ 400F	8,100	
Federal income tax	82,000	22,000	4,000	20,000	1,000		129,000	
Net income	90,000	30,000	12,000	29,000	10,000	32,200G	138,800	
	$843,600	$214,000	$70,000	$219,000	$50,000	$32,600	$1,364,000	
Retained earnings, 1/1/70	$432,000							$486,900
Net income	90,000	$90,000	$4,000	$51,500	$5,000			
Dividends	(20,000)	30,000	12,000	29,000	10,000			(20,000)
Retained earnings, 12/31/70	$502,000	$120,000	$16,000	$80,500	$15,000			

Apportionment of net income:

		Consolidated Income	Eliminations
Net income		$ 138,800	
Minority interest in C (15% × 30,000) + (15% × 90% × 12,000)			$ 6,120
Minority interest in D (10% × 12,000)			1,200
Minority interest in E (20% × 29,000) + (20% × 10% × 30,000) + (20% × 10% × 90% × 12,000)			6,616
Minority interest in F (10% × 10,000)			1,000
		14,936	
Consolidated net income—remainder		$ 123,864	123,864
Consolidated retained earnings, 12/31/70			$590,764

F: To eliminate inter-company income and expense.
G: To eliminate intercompany income.

	P	C	D
Assets			
Current assets	$ 410,000	$ 90,000	$40,500
Investment in C	94,500		
Investment in C			
Investment in D		50,000	
Investment in E	136,400		
Investment in F			
Fixed assets (net)	930,000	110,000	40,500
	$1,570,900	$250,000	$81,000
Equities			
Current liabilities	$ 18,900	$ 10,000	$ 5,000
Fixed liabilities	50,000	20,000	10,000
Shareholders' equity:			
Capital stock:			
Company P	1,000,000		
Company C		100,000	
Company D			50,000
Company E			
Company F			
Retained earnings:			
Company P	502,000		
Company C		120,000	
Company D			16,000
Company E			
Company F			
	$1,570,900	$250,000	$81,000

(1): To recognize C's interest in D's increase in shareholders' equity since acquisition (90% × $18,000).

(2): To recognize P's interest in C's increase in shareholders' equity since acquisition: $33,000* × 70% = $23,100
83,200† × 75% =   62,400
$85,500

* Increase from 1/1/67 to 6/30/68.

† $10,000 increase from 7/1/68 to 12/31/68, $32,400 ($27,000 + $5,400) increase during 1969, and $40,800 ($30,000 + $10,800) increase during 1970.

(3): To recognize E's interest in C's increase in shareholders' equity since acquisition. Since E only owns a 10% interest in C its interest in C's change in shareholders' equity has not been recognized (10% × $40,800) = $4,080.

472

CONSOLIDATED WORKING PAPERS
STATEMENT OF FINANCIAL POSITION
(Continued)

E	F	Adjustments & Eliminations		Consolidated Financial Position
$ 35,000	$36,000			$ 611,500
		$85,500(2)	$177,150A	2,850G
20,000		4,080(3)	23,620B	460G
		16,200(1)	59,400C	6,800G
		3,264(4)	147,664D	(8,000)G
44,500			49,500E	(5,000)G
136,000	54,000			1,270,500
$235,500	$90,000			$1,879,110
$ 15,000	$20,000			$ 68,900
40,000	15,000			135,000
				1,000,000
		10,000B		
		75,000A		15,000MI
		45,000C		5,000MI
100,000		80,000D		20,000MI
	40,000	36,000E		4,000MI
			3,264(4)	
			85,500(2)	590,764RE
		13,620B	16,200(1)	
		102,150A		20,430MI
		14,400C		1,600MI
80,500		67,664D	4,080(3)	16,916MI
	15,000	13,500E		1,500MI
$235,500	$90,000	$566,378	$566,378	$1,879,110

(4):To recognize P's 80% interest in E's 10% interest in C's increase in shareholders' equity (80% × $4,080).

A: To eliminate 75% of C's shareholders' equity against the investment account.
B: To eliminate 10% of C's shareholders' equity against the investment account.
C: To eliminate 90% of D's shareholders' equity against the investment account.
D: To eliminate 80% of E's shareholders' equity against the investment account.
E: To eliminate 90% of F's shareholders' equity against the investment account.

CONSOLIDATED WORKING PAPERS
STATEMENT OF FINANCIAL POSITION
AS OF DECEMBER 31, 1971

	P	C	D
Assets			
Current assets	$ 489,900	$114,000	$48,000
Investment in C	94,500		
Investment in C			
Investment in D		50,000	
Investment in D			
Investment in E	166,520		
Investment in F			
Investment in F			6,000
Fixed assets (net)	900,000	110,000	40,000
	$1,650,920	$274,000	$94,000
Equities			
Current liabilities	$ 20,000	$ 11,000	$ 5,000
Fixed liabilities	50,000	10,000	10,000
Shareholders' equity:			
Capital stock:			
Company P	1,000,000		
Company C		100,000	
Company D			50,000
Company E			
Company F			
Retained earnings:			
Company P	580,920		
Company C		153,000	
Company D			29,000
Company E			
Company F			
	$1,650,920	$274,000	$94,000

(1): To recognize D's 10% interest in the increase in F's shareholders' equity since acquisition (10% × $20,000*).

* Let F = Company F's increase in shareholders' equity since acquisition on a consolidated basis.
  Let D = Company D's increase in shareholders' equity since acquisition on a consolidated basis.

$F = \$18,500 + .1D$
$D = \$13,000 + .1F$

$F = \$18,500 + .1 (13,000 + .1F)$ | $D = \$13,000 + .1F$
$F = \$18,500 + \$1,300 + .01F$ | $D = \$13,000 + .1 (20,000)$
$.99F = \$19,800$ | $D = \$13,000 + \$2,000$
$F = \underline{\$20,000}$ | $D = \underline{\$15,000}$

(2): To recognize C's 90% interest in the increase in D's shareholders' equity since acquisition:

Prior to 1971, 90% × $18,000 = $16,200
1971, 90% × $15,000 = 13,500
$29,700

(3): To recognize P's 75% interest in the increase in C's shareholders' equity since acquisition:

Prior to 1971, $ 85,500
1971, 24,750 ($33,000 × 75%)
10,125 ($13,500 × 75%)
$120,375

THE PARENT COMPANY AND SUBSIDIARIES
CONSOLIDATED WORKING PAPERS
STATEMENT OF FINANCIAL POSITION
(Continued)

E	F	Adjustments & Eliminations		Consolidated Financial Position
$ 52,000	$ 45,000			$ 748,900
		$120,375(3)	$212,025D	2,850G
20,000		8,730(7)	28,270F	460G
		29,700(2)	72,900C	6,800G
	7,000	1,500(4)	8,100A	400G
		6,984(8)	182,584G	(8,000)G
		1,080(6)		
61,150		1,350(5)	67,500E	(5,000)G
		2,000(1)	7,500B	500G
130,000	50,000			1,230,000
$263,150	$102,000			$1,976,910
$ 15,000	$ 13,500			$ 64,500
30,000	15,000			115,000
				1,000,000
		10,000F		15,000MI
		75,000D		
		45,000C		
		5,000A		
100,000		80,000G		20,000MI
	40,000	36,000E		
		4,000B		
			6,984(8)	709,359RE
			1,080(6)	
			120,375(3)	
		18,270F	29,700(2)	27,405MI
		137,025D		
		27,900C	2,000(1)	
		3,100A		
118,150		102,584G	8,730(7)	25,646MI
			1,350(5)	
	33,500	31,500E	1,500(4)	
		3,500B		
$263,150	$102,000	$750,598	$750,598	$1,976,910

(4): To recognize F's 10% interest in the increase in D's shareholders' equity since acquisition (10% × $15,000).

(5): To recognize E's 90% interest in F's 10% interest in the increase in D's shareholders' equity since acquisition (90% × $1,500).

(6): To recognize P's 80% interest in E's 90% interest in F's 10% interest in the increase in D's shareholders' equity since acquisition [see (5) above].

(7): To recognize E's 10% interest in C's increase in shareholders' equity since acquisition. Since E has only a 10% interest in C this interest has not been recognized by E.

Prior to 1971, $4,080
1971,   3,300 ($33,000 × 10%)
        1,350 ($13,500 × 10%)
        ————
        $8,730

(8): To recognize P's 80% interest in E's 10% interest in C. [Same reason as (7) above.] 80% × $8,730 = $6,984.

A: To eliminate 10% of D's shareholders' equity against the investment account (F's investment in D).
B: To eliminate 10% of F's shareholders' equity against the investment account (D's investment in F).
C: To eliminate 90% of D's shareholders' equity against the investment account (C's investment in D).
D: To eliminate 75% of C's shareholders' equity against the investment account (P's investment in C).
E: To eliminate 90% of F's shareholders' equity against the investment account (E's investment in F).
F: To eliminate 10% of C's shareholders' equity against the investment account (E's investment in C).
G: To eliminate 80% of E's shareholders' equity against the investment account (P's investment in E).

THE PARENT COMPANY AND SUBSIDIARIES
CONSOLIDATED WORKING PAPERS
STATEMENT OF INCOME AND RETAINED EARNINGS
YEAR ENDED DECEMBER 31, 1971

	P	C	D
Credits			
Net sales	$840,000	$220,000	$70,000
Interest income from C	400		
Income from E	30,120		
Income from F			
	$870,520	$220,000	$70,000
Debits			
Cost of sales	$599,400	$151,400	$47,200
Depreciation	78,000	10,000	4,200
Interest expense	4,200	600	600
Federal income tax	90,000	25,000	5,000
Net income	98,920	33,000	13,000
	$870,520	$220,000	$70,000
Retained earnings, 1/1/71	$502,000	$120,000	$16,000
Net income	98,920	33,000	13,000
Dividends	(20,000)		
Retained earnings, 12/31/71	$580,920	$153,000	$29,000

Apportionment of net income:
Net income
Minority interest in C
Minority interest in E
Consolidated net income—remainder
Consolidated retained earnings, 12/31/71
H: To eliminate intercompany income and expense.
I: To eliminate intercompany income.
* Minority interest in C has a claim against the following earnings:
    15% × $33,000 (earned by C) $4,950
    15% × 90% × $15,000 (D's earnings on a consolidated
      basis)
                                                    2,025
                                                  $6,975

Summary. When consolidating a group of companies in which some form of indirect ownership or mutual stockholdings exists, it is essential that the establishment of reciprocity start on the lowest strata or tier of subsidiaries. The establishment of reciprocity should then progress up to the top tier or apex where the major parent is found. It is likewise better to progress up the consolidation ladder rung by rung rather than to by-pass some of the rungs.

Trial Balance Approach

The preceding illustrations in this chapter have been based primarily upon the assumption that the consolidated statements were being prepared from the financial statements of the companies involved. The trial

THE PARENT COMPANY AND SUBSIDIARIES
CONSOLIDATED WORKING PAPERS
STATEMENT OF INCOME AND RETAINED EARNINGS
(Continued)

E	F	Eliminations	Consolidated Income	Consolidated Retained Earnings
$230,000	$60,000		$1,420,000	
		$ 400*H*		
		30,120*I*		
16,650		16,650*I*		
$246,650	$60,000	$47,170	$1,420,000	
$175,700	$28,600		$1,002,300	
9,800	6,000		108,000	
1,500	900	$ 400*H*	7,400	
22,000	6,000		148,000	
37,650	18,500	46,770*I*	154,300	
$246,650	$60,000	$47,170	$1,420,000	
$80,500	$15,000			$590,764
37,650	18,500			
				(20,000)
$118,150	$33,500			
			$ 154,300	
		$ 6,975*		
		8,730†	15,705	
			$ 138,595	138,595
				$709,359

† Minority interest in E has a claim against the following earnings:
20% × $37,650 (recognized by E) — $7,530
20% × 10% × $33,000 (earned by C) — 660
20% × 10% × 90% × $15,000 (D's earnings on a consolidated basis) — 270
20% × 90% × $1,500 [F's earnings on a consolidated basis not initially recognized by E (see adjustment 5)] — 270
$8,730

balance approach is reviewed in the working papers on pages 478–479. For comparative purposes, the situation illustrated is the same as the immediately preceding one where the statements were being consolidated for the year ending December 31, 1971.

Summary. When the trial balance approach is used, reciprocity must be established as of the beginning of the period rather than as of the end of the period, as is the procedure when the statement approach is used. This modification in the basic procedure is necessary because consolidated net income is added to the beginning balance of consolidated retained earnings in the working papers. If reciprocity were established as of the end of the period, the parent company's share of a subsidiary's earnings for the period would be taken into consolidated retained earnings twice.

THE PARENT COMPANY AND SUBSIDIARIES
CONSOLIDATED WORKING PAPERS
DECEMBER 31, 1971

Debits	P	C	D	E
Current assets	$ 489,900	$114,000	$ 48,000	$ 52,000
Investment in C	94,500			
Investment in C				20,000
Investment in D		50,000		
Investment in D				
Investment in E	166,520			
Investment in F				61,150
Investment in F			6,000	
Fixed assets (net)	900,000	110,000	40,000	130,000
Cost of sales	599,400	151,400	47,200	175,700
Depreciation	78,000	10,000	4,200	9,800
Interest expense	4,200	600	600	1,500
Federal income taxes	90,000	25,000	5,000	22,000
Dividends paid	20,000			
	$2,442,520	$461,000	$151,000	$472,150
Credits				
Sales (net)	$ 840,000	$ 220,000	$ 70,000	$ 230,000
Interest income from C	400			
Income from E	30,120			
Income from F				16,650
Current liabilities	20,000	11,000	5,000	15,000
Fixed liabilities	50,000	10,000	10,000	30,000
Shareholders' equity:				
Capital stock:				
Company P	1,000,000			
Company C		100,000		
Company D			50,000	
Company E				100,000
Company F				
Retained earnings, 1/1/71:				
Company P	502,000			
Company C		120,000		
Company D			16,000	
Company E				80,500
Company F				
	$2,442,520	$461,000	$151,000	$472,150

Income credits
Income debits

Net income
Apportionment of net income:
    Minority interest:
        C's 15%
        E's 20%

    Consolidated net income (remainder)

Consolidated retained earnings, 12/31/71

Minority interest

The Parent Company and Subsidiaries
CONSOLIDATED WORKING PAPERS
(Continued)

F	Adjustments & Eliminations*		Consolidated Income	Consolidated Retained Earnings	Minority	Consolidated Financial Position
$ 45,000						$ 748,900
	$ 85,500(3)	$177,150D				2,850G
	4,080(7)	23,620F				460G
	16,200(2)	59,400C				6,800G
7,000		6,600A				400G
		30,120(9)				
	3,264(8)	147,664G				(8,000)G
		16,650(10)				
		49,500E				(5,000)G
		5,500B				500G
50,000						1,230,000
28,600			$1,002,300			
6,000			108,000			
900		400H	7,400			
6,000			148,000			
				$20,000		
$143,500			$1,265,700	$20,000	–0–	$1,976,910
$ 60,000			$1,420,000			
	400H					
	30,120(9)					
	16,650(10)					
13,500						$ 64,500
15,000						115,000
						1,000,000
	75,000D					
	10,000F				$15,000	
	45,000C					
	5,000A					
	80,000G				20,000	
40,000						
	36,000E					
	4,000B					
		3,264(8)		$590,764		
		85,500(3)				
	102,150D	16,200(2)			20,430	
	13,620F					
	14,400C					
	1,600A					
	67,664G	4,080(7)			16,916	
15,000	13,500E					
	1,500B					
$143,500	$625,648	$625,648				
			$1,420,000			
			1,265,700			
			$154,300			
			6,975		6,975	
			8,730		8,730	
			$138,595	138,595		
				$729,359		
				20,000		
				$709,359		709,359RE
					$88,051	88,051MI
						$1,976,910

* The eliminations are lettered to correspond with the lettering in the preceding illustration. The adjustments are numbered where possible as the adjustments were numbered in the preceding illustration. However, on the work sheet there are no adjustments similar to 1, 4, 5, and 6 on the preceding statement approach. Likewise, the adjustments numbered 9 and 10 are peculiar to the trial balance approach.

PROBLEMS

Problem 16–1. During the current year Company P acquired an 80% interest in the capital stock of two existing companies: S and T. Company P issued 100,000 shares of its $50 par value common stock in exchange for 40,000 shares of the $25 par value common stock of Company S. P Company acquired 800 shares of T Company no-par common for $400,000 in cash. The investment in S was recorded at the par value of the stock issued and the investment in T at the cash price.

In the process of consolidating the three companies, it is determined that as of the date of acquisition the book value of the investment in S and in T is smaller than the book value of an 80% interest in the net assets of the respective companies as follows: S Company—$800,000; T Company—$160,000. At the time of the acquisition the approximate quoted market values of the common shares of the three companies were as follows: P—$60–65; S—$150–160; T—$480–495.

(1) Explain the possible reasons for the cost of stock of a subsidiary being less than the book value of the underlying net assets on the books of the subsidiary, and recommend how these amounts should be handled on the consolidated financial statements in each situation, giving reasons for your recommendation.

(2) Discuss the specific situation of consolidating S Company and T Company in view of the data given and the reasons you present in (1) above.

(AICPA adapted)

Problem 16–2. A corporation with one wholly owned subsidiary does not wish to prepare consolidated financial statements primarily on the grounds that the investment in the capital stock of the subsidiary is less than 1% of the total assets of the parent. Indicate circumstances under which it would be proper to follow the parent's wishes, and circumstances under which it would be necessary to insist upon consolidation of statements. Give particular thought to the financial affairs of the subsidiary and the relations between parent and subsidiary.

(AICPA adapted)

Problem 16–3. The P Corporation has made substantial advances of cash to S Corporation, its wholly owned subsidiary. S uses some of the cash to purchase a block of P Corporation stock in the open market. S also issues some of its own stock, which it sells to P, using the cash received to repay the advances received from P.

You are to give your opinion of each of the following practices:

(1) The stock of P owned by S is shown as an "Investment" on the consolidated statement of financial position of P and S.

(2) Dividends on the stock of S are shown as a nonoperating income on the income statement of P.

(3) The total of dividends declared but not paid on the stock of P are shown as a current liability on the consolidated statement of financial position of P and S.

(AICPA adapted)

Problem 16–4. The following data pertain to a parent company and its subsidiary on the dates indicated:

	Jan. 1, 1966	Dec. 31, 1966	Dec. 31, 1967	Dec. 31, 1968
Parent Company:				
Investment in subsidiary	$256,000	$256,000	$238,000	$280,000
Retained earnings	270,000	320,000	296,000	310,000
Subsidiary Company:				
Capital stock ($100 par)	200,000	200,000	200,000	200,000
Retained earnings	100,000	124,000	140,000	160,000

The parent company purchased 1,600 shares of subsidiary stock on January 1, 1966, sold 100 shares on January 1, 1967, and purchased 200 shares on January 1, 1968. The investment account was charged with the cost of stock purchased and credited with the proceeds from the stock sold. The parent company has made no other entries in the investment account.

Required:
Prepare statements showing the amounts of (1) goodwill, (2) retained earnings, and (3) minority interest that would appear on the consolidated statements of financial position as of January 1, 1966, and December 31, 1966, 1967, and 1968.

Problem 16–5. The following data pertain to a parent company and its subsidiaries on the dates indicated:

	Jan. 1, 1966	Dec. 31, 1966	Dec. 31 1967	Dec. 31, 1968
Parent Company:				
Investment in S-1	$198,000	$198,000	$138,000	$183,000
Investment in S-2	180,000	164,000	206,000	142,000
Retained earnings	420,000	470,000	460,000	490,000
Subsidiary S-1:				
Capital stock ($100 par)	100,000	100,000	100,000	100,000
Retained earnings	110,000	110,000	140,000	165,000
Subsidiary S-2:				
Capital stock ($100 par)	100,000	100,000	100,000	100,000
Retained earnings	110,000	90,000	120,000	100,000

The parent company purchased 900 shares of S-1 stock on January 1, 1966, sold 150 shares on January 1, 1967, and purchased 100 shares on January 1, 1968. The S-1 investment account was charged with the cost of the stock purchased and credited with the proceeds from the stock sold. The parent company has made no other entries in the S-1 investment account.

The parent company purchased 800 shares of S-2 stock on January 1, 1966, and 100 shares on January 1, 1967. The parent company sold 200 shares of S-2 stock on January 1, 1968. The S-2 investment account is carried on the *equity* basis, except that it was credited with the proceeds from the stock sold.

Required:
Prepare statements showing the amounts of (1) goodwill, (2) retained earnings, and (3) minority interest that would appear on the consolidated statements of financial position as of January 1, 1966, and December 31, 1966, 1967, and 1968.

Problem 16–6. From the following information relative to the X Company and its wholly owned subsidiary, the Y Company, prepare:

(1) A consolidated statement of financial position, and (2) a consolidated statement of income and retained earnings.

	X Company	Y Company
Cash	$ 250,000	$ 130,000
Marketable securities	400,000	150,000
Accounts receivable, customers	1,250,000	540,000
Allowance for doubtful accounts	(25,000)	(10,000)
Subsidiary current account	100,000	
Inventories	1,100,000	600,000
Treasury stock	50,000	
Stock of Y company (at cost)	150,000	
Advances to subsidiary	420,000	
Plant, property, and equipment (net)	1,525,000	710,000
	$ 5,220,000	$2,120,000
Accounts payable	$ 575,000	$ 185,000
Accrued expenses	350,000	100,000
Due to X Company		90,000
Estimated federal taxes	525,000	275,000
Advances from parent		420,000
Capital stock	1,000,000	150,000
Retained earnings, 1/1/66	2,420,000	825,000
Net income	650,000	250,000
Dividends paid	(300,000)	(175,000)
	$ 5,220,000	$2,120,000
Net sales	$10,000,000	$4,600,000
Cost of goods sold	(6,700,000)	(3,210,000)
Selling, general and administrative	(2,400,000)	(900,000)
Other income (net)	250,000	20,000
Estimated federal income taxes	(500,000)	(260,000)
Net income	$ 650,000	$ 250,000

Additional information:

(1) Marketable securities of the subsidiary includes $20,000 cost of shares of the parent company's stock acquired for payment of bonuses.

(2) There is merchandise billed at $10,000 in transit from the parent to the subsidiary which has not been recorded by the subsidiary.

(3) It has been determined that there is intercompany profit of $20,000 in the portion of the subsidiary's inventory purchased from the parent. The equivalent figure at December 31, 1965 was $10,000.

(4) The parent's equity in the subsidiary was $200,000 at the date of acquisition.

(5) Sales by the parent to the subsidiary in 1966 totaled $1,700,000.

(6) The parent has made a service charge of $50,000 to the subsidiary which is included in other income of the parent and in administrative expenses of the subsidiary.   (AICPA adapted)

Problem 16–7. Following are trial balances of A Company and its subsidiary, B Company, as of December 31, 1966. From them and the other information given, prepare consolidated working papers.

Debits	A Company	B Company
Cash	$ 545,200	$ 267,300
Receivables, customers	187,000	375,400
Temporary investments	1,575,300	556,000
Inventories	398,200	146,800
Investment, B Company:		
Bonds	198,000	
Capital stock	300,000	
Advances	226,600	
Investment, A Company bonds (at par)		30,000
Fixed assets	2,311,000	714,700
Unamortized bond discount		2,700
Goodwill		90,000
Cost of sales	3,280,500	1,676,100
Selling and administrative expense	333,000	261,000
Depreciation expense	184,000	42,600
Interest expense	24,000	19,700
Bond discount amortized		300
Amortization of premium on B Company bonds owned	2,000	
Provision for income taxes	600,000	420,000
Dividends paid	100,000	20,000
	$10,264,800	$4,622,600

Credits		
Accounts payable	$ 79,200	$ 69,500
Accrued income taxes	624,800	431,400
Other accrued expense	10,000	4,000
Advances from A		226,600
Reserve for bad debts	2,500	3,200
Reserve for depreciation	1,420,600	302,300
Reserve for product warranty	1,000,000	445,000
First-mortgage 3% bonds	800,000	
First-mortgage 4% bonds		200,000
Capital stock	1,000,000	200,000
Paid-in surplus	50,200	
Retained earnings, 12/31/65	424,700	90,200
Sales	4,797,300	2,644,500
Interest: temporary investments	20,400	5,000
intercompany bonds	7,200	900
advances to B	11,700	
Dividend received	16,200	
	$10,264,800	$4,622,600

A Company on January 1, 1958, purchased from security holders its 81% interest in the capital stock of B Company and 90% interest in B Company bonds, the total consideration being $516,000 of which $216,000 was allocated to the bonds. The purpose of the purchase was to obtain additional manufacturing facilities and B Company's established markets for products similar to A Company's regular line. The retained earnings of B Company as shown by its books on December 31, 1957, was $150,000. The 25-year first-mortgage 4% bonds had been originally marketed on December 31, 1950 to net 96¼.

For several years a part of the output of B Company has been an intermediate product sold to A Company at a uniform markup of 20% (on sales). Sales of this character recorded on B Company's books were $258,000 for 1966, of which $64,500 remained in A Company's inventory at the end of the year; the corresponding amount in A Company's inventory at the beginning of the year was $82,000.

A Company has made advances to B Company on which the latter pays interest semi-annually at the rate of 6% per annum. During 1966 (on July 1) an additional $50,000 was advanced.

A Company constructed a building, at a cost of $100,000, which, on January 1, 1961, was turned over to B Company for its use at a price of $120,000. Depreciation of 3% has been accrued thereon since that date.   (AICPA adapted)

Problem 16–8. Midway Sales, Inc., and Kent Realty Corp. are wholly owned subsidiaries of the Davis Manufacturing Co., Inc. The parent corporation manufactures electric refrigerators, electric ranges, and various other electric appliances. The refrigerators and ranges are sold only to Midway Sales, Inc., which acts as a distributor. Other appliances are sold directly to outside distributors.

The parent and the subsidiary sales corporation are tenants of property owned by Kent Realty Corp.

The intercompany accounts on the books of each company as at December 31, 1966, were as follows:

DAVIS MANUFACTURING CO., INC.

	Debit	Credit
Investment in Midway Sales, Inc. (at cost)	$100,000.00	
Investment in Kent Realty Corp. (at cost)	175,000.00	
Due from Midway Sales, Inc.	86,175.97	
Due to Kent Realty Corp.		$ 1,475.00
Capital stock issued and outstanding, 100,000 shares, no par value		1,000,000.00
Retained earnings		410,169.50

MIDWAY SALES, INC.

	Debit	Credit
Due to Kent Realty Corp.		$ 800.00
Due to Davis Manufacturing Co., Inc.		33,910.00
Capital stock issued and outstanding, 1,000 shares, par value $100 per share		100,000.00
Retained earnings		62,501.10

KENT REALTY CORP.

	Debit	Credit
Due from Davis Manufacturing Co., Inc.	$6,575.00	
Due to Midway Sales, Inc.		$ 2,800.00
Capital stock issued and outstanding, 1,000 shares, no par value		175,000.00
Retained earnings		34,109.50

An audit of the books of the three companies for the year ended December 31, 1966, revealed the following:

(1) The minute books of the three companies indicate the following with respect to dividends:

(*a*) The Board of Directors of Davis Manufacturing Co., Inc., at a meeting on January 4, 1967, declared a regular quarterly dividend of 50 cents per share, payable January 31, 1967, to stockholders of record on January 23, 1967.

(*b*) The Board of Directors of Midway Sales, Inc., at a meeting on December 28, 1966, declared a 1% dividend payable in cash on January 15, 1967, to stockholders of record on December 31, 1966.

(*c*) The Board of Directors of Kent Realty Corp. at a meeting on December 1, 1966, declared a dividend of $1.00 per share, payable January 2, 1967, to stockholders of record on December 15, 1966.

No effect has been given to these dividend declarations on the books of the parent company as at December 31, 1966. The subsidiary companies recorded the dividend declarations pertaining to their respective companies at date of declaration.

(2) Midway Sales received from one of its customers a check for $4,200 covering its own invoices aggregating $2,400 and invoices of Davis Manufacturing aggregating $1,800. The sales corporation recorded this transaction as follows:

Cash	$4,200	
Accounts receivable		$4,200

(3) Midway Sales, Inc., advanced $5,000 in cash to Kent Realty Corp. and made the following entry:

Davis Manufacturing Co., Inc.	$5,000	
Cash		$5,000

(4) On September 15, 1966, Davis Manufacturing shipped 100 appliances of a new design on consignment at $20 each to Midway Sales. Midway made no entry upon receipt of the goods. During October, 1966, Midway sold all of these appliances at $25 each, crediting sales for the total thereof. Davis Manufacturing made no entries on its books, but included the 100 appliances in its inventory at December 31, 1966, at its cost of $14 each.

(5) The parent corporation filed a consolidated federal income-tax return for the year ended December 31, 1965. The results of operations for the respective companies that year, before consolidation, were as follows:

Davis Manufacturing Co., Inc., net loss	$13,280
Midway Sales, Inc., net profit	42,260
Kent Realty Corp., net profit	21,130

The federal income tax, amounting to $21,000, was paid by the parent corporation which recorded the transaction as follows:

Federal income taxes payable	$21,000	
Cash		$21,000

An agreement in the files indicates that federal income taxes should be apportioned among the companies based upon consolidated net profit. A company having a loss year is to pay no tax nor charge the other companies for the benefit derived from the use of its loss in the return. The proper liability of each company was recorded as at December 31, 1965.

(6) Kent Realty sold certain of its furniture to Midway Sales at current market value, which was 75 per cent of net book value. The realty corporation had purchased the furniture for $3,500 exactly two years prior to the date of sale and had taken depreciation at the rate of 10 per cent per annum. It billed Midway Sales, Inc., for $2,800 and recorded the transaction as follows:

Midway Sales, Inc.	$2,800	
Furniture and fixtures		$2,800

Midway Sales recorded the purchase as follows:

Furniture and fixtures	$2,800	
Kent Realty Corp.		$2,800

(7) As at December 31, 1966, the books of the parent corporation and the sales subsidiary do not reflect rent for the month of December, 1966, in the amounts of $6,100 and $1,400, respectively, due to Kent Realty Corp.

(8) Midway Sales, Inc., had not recorded December, 1966, purchase invoices submitted by the parent corporation in the amount of $48,265.97.

Required:

(1) Prepare an itemized reconciliation of the intercompany accounts.

(2) Prepare the adjusting journal entries necessary to correct each set of books.

Problem 16–9. *Required:*   (AICPA adapted)

From the data below prepare:

a. A worksheet for a consolidated statement of financial position as of December 31, 1966.

b. A consolidated statement of financial position as of December 31, 1966.

(1) Post-closing trial balances as of December 31, 1966:

	Company P	Company S-1	Company S-2
Investment in Company S-1 (acquired January 1, 1965)			
Common stock (90%)	$200,000		
Preferred stock (40%)	40,000		
Investment in Company S-2 (70% acquired January 1, 1966)	59,300		
Current assets	50,000	$50,000	$40,000
Machinery & equipment	40,000	20,000	30,000
Allowance for depreciation			
Machinery & equipment	(20,000)	(15,000)	(10,000)
Bonds of company S-2			
(Par $10,000)	10,100		
All other assets	600	313,000	70,180
Current liabilities	(20,000)	(20,000)	(20,000)
Bonds payable—10 yrs., 4%, due December 31, 1971			(30,000)
Premium on bonds payable			(180)
Capital stock—Common, par $100	(300,000)	(250,000)	(60,000)
Capital stock—Preferred, 5%, par $100, cumulative & nonparticipating		(100,000)	
Premium on preferred stock		(10,000)	
Retained earnings	(60,000)	12,000	(20,000)
	–0–	–0–	–0–

(2) The investment accounts are carried at cost.

(3) At acquisition, dividends on preferred stock for 1963 and 1964 were in arrears. Preferred stock has a liquidation value of par plus dividends in arrears and is nonvoting.

(4) On January 1, 1966, Company S-1 declared a common stock dividend of $50,000 from Premium on Preferred Stock accounts.

(5) The Retained Earnings accounts showed the following:

	S-1	S-2
January 1, 1965 Balance	$(10,000)	$14,000
Profits 1965	7,000	7,000
Cash dividends 1966—		
on January 1, 1966	(5,000)	
on December 31, 1966		(6,000)
Profit & loss 1966	(4,000)	5,000
Balance December 31, 1966	(12,000)	20,000

(6) Inventory of Company P includes $5,000 merchandise purchased from S-2; cost to S-2 is marked up 25%.

(7) Inventory of Company S-2 includes $2,000 merchandise purchased from S-1; markup by S-1 is 10% on selling price.

(8) Current Liabilities include the following: Company S-1 owes Company P $1,000; Company S-2 owes Company P $2,000; Company S-1 owes Company S-2 $3,000; and Company P owes Company S-1 $2,000.

(9) Machinery having a life of 10 years was purchased by Company P from Company S-1 on January 1, 1965, for $10,000. Cost to S-1 was $7,000.

(10) Company S-2 neglected to amortize Premium on Bonds Payable for 1966.   (AICPA adapted)

Problem 16–10. The financial statements of John Doe Manufacturing Company and its wholly owned subsidiary, Blank Sales Company, were submitted as shown on pages 488 and 489.

Also the following information was given:

(1) In June, 1966, the authorized capital stock of John Doe Manufacturing Company was changed from 100,000 shares of $10 to 250,000 shares of $5 each and the shareholders agreed to exchange their stock on the basis of $1\frac{3}{4}$ shares of the new for each share of the old stock. Accordingly, all the 75,000 outstanding shares of the old $10 stock were exchanged for 131,250 shares of the new $5 stock on July 1, 1966.

(2) On July 1, 1966, the company acquired all the outstanding 15,000 shares of Blank Sales Company for 75,000 shares of its new $5 stock.

(3) Immediately after July 1, 1966, certain shareholders of John Doe Manufacturing Company disposed of a portion of their holdings to an underwriter, receiving $20 per share. The shares were offered to the public at $22.50.

In view of the wider distribution of its stock after the public offering, the company arranged to list its common shares on the stock exchange and agreed to pay all expenses of listing and of registering the stock under the Securities Act of 1933, amounting to $15,000.

STATEMENTS OF FINANCIAL POSITION
DECEMBER 31, 1966

Assets	John Doe Mfg. Co.	Blank Sales Co.	Combined
Cash	$ 150,000	$ 75,000	$ 225,000
U.S. Government bonds, at cost	300,000	100,000	400,000
Trade accounts receivable:			
Customers, less reserves	10,000	650,000	660,000
Blank Sales Co.	490,000		490,000
Inventories	600,000	200,000	800,000
Investment in Blank Sales Co.	375,000		375,000
Investment in 1,000 shares of John Doe Mfg. Co., $5 par stock, at cost		20,000	20,000
Other assets	25,000	30,000	55,000
Property, plant, and equipment, at cost	950,000	275,000	1,225,000
Prepaid expenses	35,000	25,000	60,000
Expenses of registration and listing of stock	15,000		15,000
	$2,950,000	$1,375,000	$4,325,000

Equities			
Notes payable	$ 200,000	$ 100,000	$ 300,000
Accounts payable	325,000	665,000	990,000
Federal taxes on income	150,000	35,000	185,000
Reserve for depreciation	250,000	75,000	325,000
Common stock, $10 par value	750,000	150,000	900,000
Common stock, $5 par value	375,000		375,000
Retained earnings			
At January 1, 1966	$ 596,250		
At July 1, 1966		355,000	$ 951,250
Net profit per income statement	510,000	115,000	625,000
	$1,106,250	$ 470,000	$1,576,250
Dividends paid	206,250	120,000	326,250
	$ 900,000	$ 350,000	$1,250,000
	$2,950,000	$1,375,000	$4,325,000

(4) The inventories of Blank Sales Company included merchandise bought from John Doe Manufacturing Company at the latter's regular sales prices, as follows:

January 1, 1966	$50,000
June 30, 1966	30,000
December 31, 1966	40,000

(5) The net sales of John Doe Manufacturing Company included net sales to Blank Sales Company as follows:

January 1 to June 30, 1966	$1,500,000
July to December 31, 1966	2,500,000

STATEMENTS OF INCOME

	John Doe Mfg. Co. Year ended Dec. 31, 1966	Blank Sales Co. Six months to Dec. 31, 1966	Combined
Net sales	$4,200,000	$3,300,000	$7,500,000
Cost of goods sold	3,570,000	3,025,000	6,595,000
	$ 630,000	$ 275,000	$ 905,000
Selling and administrative expenses	75,000	140,000	215,000
	$ 555,000	$ 135,000	$ 690,000
Other income:			
Commission earned		25,000	$ 25,000
Dividends received	$ 120,000	1,000	121,000
Miscellaneous	5,000	4,000	9,000
	$ 125,000	$ 30,000	$ 155,000
	$ 680,000	$ 165,000	$ 845,000
Miscellaneous deductions from income	$ 20,000	$ 15,000	$ 35,000
Federal taxes on income	150,000	35,000	185,000
	$ 170,000	$ 50,000	$ 220,000
Net income	$ 510,000	$ 115,000	$ 625,000

(6) Commissions earned by the Blank Sales Company included $2,000 received from John Doe Manufacturing Company and charged to the latter's selling expenses.

(7) Dividends received had been credited to income.

(8) Throughout the year the rate of gross profit on sales remained the same.

(9) All depreciation had been charged to production cost, the office equipment having been written down to nominal value in previous years.

(10) No entries had been made to record the conversion of the John Doe Manufacturing Company capital stock.

From the foregoing data prepare a columnar work sheet distinctly showing the consolidated income and financial position of John Doe Manufacturing Company and its wholly owned subsidiary, Blank Sales Company. Show or mention how the 1,000 shares of John Doe Manufacturing Company stock owned by the Blank Sales Company should be treated.   (AICPA adapted)

Problem 16–11. From the information given, you are required to furnish the following:

(1) Consolidated statement of retained earnings for P Company and subsidiary for the year ended December 31, 1967.

(2) Eliminating and consolidating entries.

(3) Any footnote or disclosure which you consider to be needed for statement presentation.

Submit all supporting computations in good form.

Consolidated retained earnings at December 31, 1966, were $12,347,300. Of this amount, $11,613,170 represented retained earnings of the parent and $734,130 represented retained earnings of the subsidiary. Book income of the parent company for the year ended December 31, 1967, was $487,537 and income for the subsidiary was $134,540.

Under government Certificates of Necessity, portions of the costs of the parent's expansion program, which was completed and put into operation on January 1, 1967, are being amortized for both book and income tax purposes over a period of sixty months. Depreciation computed at normal rates based on the estimated useful life of the properties was $1,143,350 less than the amount of amortization and depreciation taken into the accounts. The prevailing income tax rate is assumed to be 52%.

The parent company's investment in its 100% owned subsidiary (a Delaware corporation) is recorded at cost of $100,000. During the year the subsidiary paid the parent $150,000 in cash dividends, together with a stock dividend of one new share of common stock for each share outstanding. The amount transferred from retained earnings to the capital stock account on the books of the subsidiary was $100,000, based on 1,000 shares with a par value of $100 a share. There were no other intercompany accounts or transactions.

During the year the parent company issued a stock dividend of one share for each 10 shares outstanding, or a total of 100,000 shares with a par value of $10 a share. The fair value of the additional shares issued was $15 a share. The issuance of the additional shares did not materially reduce the share market value.

The company, in order to state consolidated retained earnings on a realistic basis and to provide for all income taxes, both known and contingent, wants you to set up a separate reserve out of consolidated retained earnings equal to the amount of taxes that would be due at the prevailing income tax rates if the retained earnings as shown on the books of the subsidiary was distributed to the parent in the form of cash dividends. For income tax purposes separate returns are filed and the dividends received credit is assumed to be 85%.

The bond indenture, relating to the long-term debt of the parent company imposes a restriction on the payment of cash dividends and provides that no cash dividends can be paid out of the parent's earned surplus accumulated at December 31, 1967.   (AICPA adapted)

CHAPTER 17

Consolidated statements re-examined

In the preceding chapters, consolidated statements have been viewed primarily from the standpoint of technique and methodology. In this chapter the basic reasoning underlying the technique and methodology is re-examined. In addition legal and economic considerations affecting consolidated statements are examined.

As indicated in *Accounting Research Bulletin* 51, and elaborated on in Chapter 9, the primary justification for consolidated statements is based on the assumption that more meaningful information is disclosed by consolidated reports than that revealed by the financial statements of the separate companies. The reasoning in support of this assumption holds that the assets and equities underlying the investment account of a parent company should be revealed since these items are effectively used by top management in earning an income for the company as a consolidated group.

Limitations. Although consolidated statements have many advantages over separate company reports, such statements also have their limitations. For example, the variety and volume of data collected and reported upon in a consolidated statement may have to be condensed to such a degree that the brevity and conciseness afforded by the consolidated report may be misleading. The extent of the condensation in a typical consolidated report is often not realized. It may appear unusual, however, that roughly the same accounts and the same amount of space are needed for a statement of financial position on General Motors as for the Korner Grocery Store. If the growth and diversification of large companies are recognized, it becomes evident that an item such as inventory in a large company may encompass a much greater variety and volume of items than would be contained in the somewhat homogeneous inventory account of a typical small company. The question may well be raised as to whether the growth of large business organizations, even if a composition of a group of separate legal companies, suggests that accounting reports should be expanded in scope to provide more information for interested parties.

Disclosure. Most limitations of consolidated statements revolve around the problem of adequate disclosure of enterprise activity. As business organizations become more decentralized and as stock ownership becomes more widespread the disclosure problem becomes a topic of increasing concern to accountants. In an attempt to overcome the disclosure limitation inherent in typical financial statements, footnotes and other supplementary data have been used to an increasing degree. Especially has this development been reflected in the use of footnotes. In part the use and development of footnotes reflects an improvement in accounting reporting. In part, however, it has been used merely as a device enabling accountants to meet the demands placed upon accounting for additional information.

It is the opinion of the authors that footnotes may become an undesirable method for reporting if overused. Without suggesting any change in the direction of omitting the information typically revealed in a footnote, it is suggested that improvements in financial reporting are needed. For example, possible additional statements or supplementary data could be developed to enhance interpretation of the conventional reports. When the disclosure problem is examined, it is apparent that it applies to accounting reports in general but particularly to consolidated statements. Although there has been an increase in the amount of supplementary data included in the annual reports of a number of companies, such as financial reviews and financial statistics over a period of years, such data as are reported are frequently not uniform or systematic either in content or in form of presentation.

Additional Problems. In addition to the disclosure problem common to all reporting, other problems are unique to the consolidated area. For purposes of re-examination, the following problems special to the area of consolidation are considered further:

(1) Problems related to consolidation policies:
    a. Criteria for consolidation.
    b. Meaning of control.

(2) Problems related to statement presentation:
   a. Valuation of assets.
   b. Intercompany gains and losses.
   c. Minority interests.
   d. Retained earnings.
   e. Change in composition of the consolidated entity.
   f. Unconsolidated subsidiaries.

CONSOLIDATION POLICIES

Criteria for Consolidation

As indicated previously, consolidation is normally considered appropriate whenever the resulting information is more useful than if it were presented in unconsolidated statements. By more useful is meant:

(1) More informative for investors and prospective investors.
(2) More informative for creditors and others interested in limited investment in the company.
(3) More informative for top management which is concerned with reports on the results of over-all operations.
(4) More informative for governmental agencies concerned with problems of anti-trust regulation, fair trade regulation, and similar problems.

A number of limiting factors, however, bear on the problem of when consolidation is appropriate. For example, legal considerations may encourage or discourage consolidation under certain situations. In addition, economic considerations, including accepted accounting conventions, may preclude consolidation for which one group, such as a governmental agency, may feel a need. While usefulness is the underlying objective, the limiting factors have considerable force in establishing a consolidation policy on the appropriate consolidated accounting entity.

Legal Considerations. The Clayton Act of 1914, as amended, prohibits the acquisition of stock of another company where the result might be a lessening of competition. Section 7 provides:

. . . No corporation shall acquire, directly or indirectly, the whole or any part of the stock or other share capital and no corporation subject to the jurisdiction of the Federal Trade Commission shall acquire the whole or any part of the assets of one or more corporations engaged in commerce, where in any line of commerce in any section of the country, the effect of such acquisition, of such stock or assets, or the use of such stock by the voting or granting of proxies or otherwise, may be substantially to lessen competition, or to tend to create a monopoly.

The effect of this act appears to be to allow noncompeting companies to be consolidated, but to discourage the purchase of stock of competing companies. In effect this law seems to allow vertical combinations through stock ownership, but discourages horizontal combinations.

The idea that a combination of an integrated economic entity is necessary before consolidation is appropriate is reflected in Section 11 of the Public Utility Act of 1935, as follows:

To require by order, after notice and opportunity for hearing, that each registered holding company, and each subsidiary company thereof, shall take such action as the Commission shall find necessary to limit the operations of the holding-company system of which such company is a part to a single integrated public-utility system, and to such other businesses as are reasonably incidental, or economically necessary or appropriate to the operations of such integrated public-utility system . . .

The implication of these two acts appears to be that a consolidated entity should not be allowed to come into existence unless it represents an integrated economic unit.

Rule 4-20(a) of Regulation S-X issued by the Securities and Exchange Commission states the basic rule for consolidation, which requires over 50% ownership of the stock of the subsidiary as justification for consolidation, as follows:

The registrant shall not consolidate any subsidiary which is not a majority-owned subsidiary.

Throughout the legal considerations the idea prevails that consolidation is not appropriate unless the subsidiary is controlled through stock ownership. Unless control exists, the stock ownership is considered an investment. The distinction made by the Clayton Act between an investment and acquisition of control is revealed by the following portion of section 7:

. . . This section shall not apply to corporations purchasing such stock solely for investment and not using the same by voting or otherwise to bring about, or in attempting to bring about, the substantial lessening of competition.

The distinction between an investment and control is found in other areas of the law as well. The significance of the distinction is to invalidate the concept that consolidation is appropriate merely because the parent *effectively owns* the subsidiary.

Economic Considerations. The main economic considerations on consolidation policy revolve around the distinction between effective ownership and control. The concept of effective ownership is that stock ownership represents a claim to the assets of the subsidiary. When the stock ownership is such that the parent company effectively owns the assets of the subsidiary, from the economic standpoint consolidation is essentially the process of replacing the investment account with the underlying assets of the subsidiary. The distortion resulting from bringing into the consolidated statement the assets and equities represented by outside ownership of the subsidiary, as well as the assets and equities represented by the parent ownership, is assumed not to be material. Effective ownership might exist even though control is not applicable, as for example when an insurance company buys a substantial portion of the stock of a particular company. Effective ownership might exist but control might not be applicable because the stock owned is held as an investment, and no action is taken by the owners of the stock to control operations of the company. Since in situations of this kind it does not appear that effective ownership is in itself a proper basis for consolidation, some other criteria for consolidation must be appropriate. From an economic point of view the major criterion for consolidation is the existence of control or right to control the subsidiary rather than effective ownership.

As indicated in Chapter 9, various other economic considerations may influence a decision on the appropriateness of consolidation. Some of these considerations are:

(1) Subsidiary not an integral part of operating group, such as a realty corporation owned by a department store or a railroad owned by a cement company.
(2) Foreign subsidiary with economic restrictions, such as a restriction on the transfer of currency.
(3) Difference in accounting periods.
(4) Senior securities of subsidiary outstanding.
(5) Insolvent or bankrupt subsidiary.

The Meaning of Control

A distinction is normally drawn between the ability to control a subsidiary by ownership of over 50% of the voting stock, and the exercise of control over the subsidiary. The ability to control is not necessarily sufficient basis for consolidation, as noted in the preceding section. Control must be exercised. To be exercised, control requires election or retention of a sufficient number of the board of directors of the subsidiary company to dictate policy for the subsidiary. It does not require that the operating actions of the subsidiary be planned and controlled by the parent company.

In those instances where the board of directors effectively surrenders its power to set policies for the subsidiary, such as might be the case under bankruptcy, it is assumed that control does not exist and consolidation is inappropriate.

The insistence on over 50% voting stock ownership before control may be assumed to exist is obviously not always in accord with the facts of the situation. In many cases control is effected with far less than 50% stock ownership.

Re-Examination of the Control Concept. It may be difficult to justify the elimination from a consolidated report of assets effectively owned and completely controlled under a lease agreement and at the same time include in a consolidated report assets controlled through ownership of the stock of a subsidiary. What is the nature of the difference in the two types of control? In both cases the controlling company has control of the *uses* to which the assets can be directed. In both cases the company may have the right to sell the assets or the rights to the assets. The similarity is definite, yet the procedures of preparing consolidated statements are such that only the assets controlled by stock ownership of a subsidiary are included in the consolidated reports. Assets controlled by a lease agreement have not been generally included in consolidated reports.

On legal grounds, the concept of ownership may be used to justify inclusion of assets owned by a subsidiary and exclusion of those not owned although controlled by a lease agreement. Thus the control concept as used in consolidated reports appears to be influenced by legal as well as economic considerations.

Large Block of Minority Interest. There appears to be a reluctance on the part of some companies to consolidate whenever there is a large block of minority interest of a size relatively equal to the equity of the parent company stockholders. Such a situation may exist when a parent company uses substantially all of its assets to buy a fraction over 50% of the stock of a subsidiary. Upon consolidation the minority interest may be almost equal to the parent company's shareholders' equity in the consolidated report. Normally separate statements are considered appropriate in such situations. This appears to represent a partial departure from the accepted control concept for consolidations.

Conclusion on Consolidation Policy

The need for objective standards in deciding whether or not consolidation is appropriate is well recognized. It is true that the current rule of over 50% ownership of the voting stock meets the requirement of being objective. It is also evident that were the standard lowered to less than 50% ownership, the assets of one company might appear on the consolidated statements of two or more companies. For example, if the percentage of ownership required for consolidation were reduced to 20%, the assets and liabilities of a given company could well appear on the consolidated statements of five different companies.

Thus if control with less than 50% stock ownership were to be accepted as the standard for consolidation, control would have to be defined on some basis other than the per cent of voting stock owned by the parent company. In general, current accounting practice supports consolidation for those subsidiaries in which over 50% voting stock ownership exists, *providing* the existence of various economic considerations does not make such consolidation appear inappropriate.

STATEMENT PRESENTATION

The question is at times raised as to when a parent company should issue separate statements if a consolidated report is rendered. In general, three of the major reasons for preparation of separate statements are:

(1) To provide useful information for management.
(2) To comply with statement requirements of bonds and other indentures.
(3) To comply with Regulation S-X of the SEC where the parent company does not qualify to use consolidated statements only.

The preparation of separate company statements is generally based upon the needs of the various users of such statements. As a general rule no particular problems of statement presentation arise for the separate company statement except for the presentation of investment accounts. In the preparation of consolidated statements, however, various special problems of statement presentation must be resolved. Some of these problems are considered in the following sections.

Valuation of Consolidated Assets

Dual Valuation. A problem may arise in the valuation of consolidated assets when a parent company acquires an interest in a subsidiary at a price other than the book value of the stock acquired. When consolidating, the subsidiary assets may be valued at either their cost to the subsidiary or at their cost to the consolidated entity. For example, if

Company A pays $80,000 to acquire net assets of a subsidiary carried at $60,000, on a consolidated statement of financial position the specific assets could be valued at the $60,000 cost to the subsidiary and supported by a separate goodwill item of $20,000. Alternatively the specific assets could be valued at their cost to the consolidated entity of $80,000. In the latter event, the excess of cost over subsidiary book value would be allocated to the specific assets and would not appear as a separate item on the consolidated statement of financial position.

When less than 100% of the outstanding stock of a subsidiary is acquired, the procedure of allocating the excess of cost over book value of stock acquired to specific assets may give a dual valuation basis to the consolidated assets. To illustrate, assume Company A acquired 60% of the voting stock of Company B at a price of $50,000 above the book value of the stock acquired. In such a purchase it must be assumed that the net assets acquired were worth their book value plus $50,000. An objective investigation may reveal that the $50,000 excess should be allocated to specific assets in order to reflect properly their cost to the consolidated entity. If the excess were allocated, some assets would be valued on a dual basis on the consolidated statement of financial position. The portion of the assets to which the allocation has been made would be valued at cost to the consolidated entity, while the portion to which no allocation was made would be valued at cost to the subsidiary.

Imputed Valuation. Some accountants support a third valuation based on the fair value of the assets at the time they become a part of the consolidated entity. Continuing the above illustration, assume that an examination indicates that $3,000 of the $50,000 excess should be allocated to a particular asset carried by the subsidiary at a book value of $20,000. This means that Company A paid $15,000 for book value of $12,000 (60% × $20,000). Accountants supporting the imputed valuation concept would support a $25,000 valuation of the particular asset, determined as follows:

	Fair Value (Imputed from Cost to the Parent)
Valuation of 60% of the asset	$15,000
Valuation of 40% of the asset	10,000
(40/60 × $15,000)	
Total	$25,000

The $25,000 valuation of the asset might be justified on the grounds that it represents an approximation of the value of the asset at the time the consolidated entity was formed and that it therefore conforms to the basic rule that assets should be valued at their fair value at the time they are contributed to a new entity (the consolidated entity). Although this position has merit, it becomes unrealistic when the parent's investment is acquired over a period of time by a series of purchases of subsidiary stock. Under these conditions parent company cost may not be representative of the fair value prevailing on the date when the consolidated entity came into existence.

Unresolved Valuation Problems. The view that the consolidated entity is a separate and distinct entity from the underlying legal entities appears not to be entirely accepted by the accounting profession. At least this appears to be true on questions regarding the proper valuation of consolidated assets. Considerable support exists for the view that assets should be valued either at their cost to the subsidiary entity or at their cost to the parent company. For assets acquired after the consolidated entity has come into existence, consolidated cost and separate company cost may be identical, but for assets acquired by the separate companies prior to emergence of a consolidated entity, problems may exist. Questions which may well be raised regarding the valuation of consolidated assets include·

(1) Why should subsidiary assets be revalued upward upon consolidation (by an allocation of the excess of cost of an investment over the book value of the subsidiary stock acquired) when parent company assets continue to be carried at cost?
(2) Why should part of an asset be valued on one basis and part of the asset on another basis?
(3) Why is it assumed that because a parent company pays more for the stock of a subsidiary company than can be allocated to the valuation of the underlying assets the excess payment represents goodwill?

Amortization of Goodwill. Implicit in the traditional procedure of preparing consolidated reports is the view that any "goodwill" arising when subsidiary stock is purchased at a cost above book value should not be written off. The reluctance to amortize consolidated "goodwill" is claimed by some accountants to result in an understatement of the expense of the consolidated entity.

If the excess of cost over book value of assets acquired were apportioned to specific assets, the gradual absorption of these assets as operating charges would produce an expense not recognized if the "goodwill" element remains unamortized. Thus, the reasoning follows, understatement of expense arises from nonamortization of goodwill. On the other hand, other accountants claim that since the goodwill exists only to the consolidated entity, amortization would result in an expense not recorded by the separate entities.

According to some accountants, there does not appear to be any justification for treating goodwill from consolidation differently from any other type of purchased goodwill. Because the general conception of purchased goodwill is that it represents a payment for excess earnings which will accrue to the buying company in the future, proper matching of cost and revenue would require that goodwill, like any other cost, be amortized against the appropriate earnings of the future as they are realized. If this reasoning is followed, an amortization entry similar to the following would be required periodically.

Amortized consolidated goodwill	$xxxxx	
Investment in subsidiary		$xxxxx

Re-Examination of the Valuation of Consolidated Assets. As indicated in the foregoing discussion, the generally accepted basis for valuing consolidated assets appears to be cost to the parent company. For those assets not acquired by the parent company, i.e., the assets of the subsidiary company(ies) represented by equities not acquired by the parent company (subsidiary company liabilities and minority interest), cost to the subsidiary is accepted as the appropriate valuation.

An exception to the foregoing rule is generally recognized when an asset is acquired directly from an affiliated company. In those instances cost to the affiliate, adjusted for transportation and other costs normally capitalized when an item is transferred from one segment of an enterprise to another, is the accepted valuation basis.

The dual valuation basis for consolidated assets creates some rather unusual situations. For example, assume a 60% owned subsidiary whose only asset is an apartment building with a book value of $100,000. If the parent company pays $70,000 for 60% of the subsidiary's stock, the asset might be valued at $110,000 on the consolidated report, assuming the excess of cost over book value is allocated to the asset on the consolidated report. The $110,000 has limited meaning since part (60%) of the building is valued at cost to the parent and another part (40%) at cost to the subsidiary.

Intercompany Gains and Losses

Another unusual situation might arise if a subsidiary traded machinery it has on its own books at $50,000 for machinery the parent has on its books at $60,000. To the parent company the machinery might be inventory. To the subsidiary the machinery might represent fixed assets. The parent would record the new asset at $60,000, thus recognizing no loss, while the subsidiary would enter its new asset at $50,000 and would recognize no gain on the sale of the exchange. No intercompany profit or loss is recognized, but it is evident that the proper valuation of the assets would require a decrease of inventory by $10,000 and an increase in fixed assets by $10,000.

A somewhat similar situation arises in the classification of inventories as materials, work-in-process, and finished goods when the finished product of the subsidiary is used as raw material by the parent company. Should the finished goods of the subsidiary be included as part of the consolidated finished goods? In general, a negative answer is appropriate. The finished goods of the subsidiary are in reality work-in-process from a consolidated point of view. A work sheet adjustment would be necessary to reclassify the finished goods of the subsidiary as work-in-process or as raw materials, depending upon the nature of the parent's manufacturing operations.

Valuation of Minority Interest

Traditionally, minority interest has been valued on the basis of its equity as revealed on the separate company report of the subsidiary. In addition, minority interest traditionally has been classified on the statement of financial position as a separate item between the liability section and the parent company shareholders' equity section.

Recently the views have shifted. Today, as indicated in Chapter 13, it is not uncommon to find the minority interest valued at the separate company equity after adjustment for any intercompany profit eliminations which might apply to the minority interest. Also there appears to be growing recognition of the fact that the minority interest, as with preferred stock of the parent company, is part of the shareholders' equity section of the consolidated statement of financial position. In a sense, it represents a special class of stock outstanding.

In those rare instances where the minority interest is negative, there is a supposition that it should be deducted from the consolidated equity of the parent company. The reasoning involved is that the parent company will normally make good to subsidiary creditors any deficit in their "buffer" as represented by the shareholders' equity section.

Although minority interest is normally valued at its equity in the separate subsidiary company report, adjusted for intercompany profit or loss which might apply to the minority interest, one type of intercompany transaction should be considered further. It is the consolidated gain or loss which accrues to a parent or subsidiary when a liability of the other company is liquidated at an amount different from the amount at which it is carried on the books.

Illustration. To illustrate the above situation, assume Company A has bonds payable outstanding at par of $50,000. Company B, 60% owned by A, acquires $30,000 of these bonds in the open market for $27,000. From the consolidated point of view, a gain of $3,000 has been realized. The question is: To whom does the gain accrue and when should it be recognized? If B holds the bonds to maturity, $30,000 will be received from A so that ultimately the $3,000 gain may be said to accrue to B's stockholders. It is often contended that the gain should be recognized immediately and not deferred until A pays B at maturity. To treat the gain as immediate income of the subsidiary would increase the minority interest by 40% of $3,000 or $1,200. To treat the gain as deferred income of the subsidiary would result in an allocation of the gain over the remaining life of the bonds. Many accountants would recognize immediately the portion of the $3,000 gain accruing to the parent company (60% of $3,000) and would defer the portion accruing to minority interest ($1,200) to future periods.

Valuation of Consolidated Retained Earnings

As emphasized in preceding sections, retained earnings in a consolidated statement properly includes:

(1) All undistributed retained earnings of the parent company.
(2) The parent company's share of the increase or decrease in shareholders' equity of the subsidiary since the date of acquisition.

It does not include that portion of subsidiary retained earnings which pertains to the minority interest. However, consolidated retained earnings may include as earnings an element that might normally be treated as unrealized income from the point of view of the parent company. That is, income from investments in general is considered as unrealized until a distribution in the form of dividends is received. However, from the point of view of the parent company's stockholders, the consolidated report advances the date when earnings of subsidiaries are treated as income.

Another aspect of consolidated retained earnings is that it may change if the parent company increases or decreases its per cent of equity in a subsidiary company. It should be the function of the statement of changes in consolidated retained earnings to show all changes in this account from one period to the next.

Statement of Changes in Consolidated Retained Earnings— Illustrated. Assume Company A acquires an 80% interest in Company B on January 1, 1967, when B's shareholders' equity is composed of $100,000 of capital stock and $40,000 of retained earnings. At that time

A's retained earnings as a separate company were $70,000. On a consolidated statement of financial position prepared on the date of acquisition, the $40,000 of retained earnings of the subsidiary would be partially eliminated ($32,000) and partially consolidated as minority interest ($8,000). As a result, consolidated retained earnings on that date would be $70,000.

Assume that during 1967 Company A earns an income from its own operations of $50,000 and pays a $40,000 dividend, and during the same period Company B reports an income of $30,000 and pays a $20,000 dividend.

STATEMENT OF CHANGES IN CONSOLIDATED RETAINED EARNINGS
COMPANIES A AND B

Balance, January 1, 1967			$ 70,000
Add: Income for 1967:			
A's operations		$50,000	
80% of B's dividend	$16,000		
80% of B's equity increase, 1967	8,000	24,000	74,000
Total			$144,000
Deduct: A's dividends paid, 1967			40,000
Balance, December 31, 1967			$104,000
Add: Income for 1968:			
A's income		$40,000	
70% of B's dividend	$14,000		
70% of B's equity increase, 1968	17,500	31,500	71,500
Total			$175,500
Deduct: Loss on sale of investment in B		$ 3,000	
Loss of 10% of B's equity increase since January 1, 1967 (10% × $10,000)		1,000	
A's dividends paid, 1968		40,000	44,000
Balance, December 31, 1968			$131,500
Add: A's income for 1969		$52,000	
70% of B's dividend	$21,000		
70% of B's equity increase, 1969	7,000	28,000	80,000
Total			$211,500
Deduct: A's dividends paid, 1969			50,000
Balance, December 31, 1969			$161,500*

* If the stock dividend received by A (70% of $25,000) were to be excluded from consolidated retained earnings, the December 31, 1969, balance would be $144,000.

On January 1, 1968, Company A sells a 10% interest in Company B at a loss of $3,000, the difference between cost and selling price of the stock. During 1968 Company A earns an income from its own operations of $40,000 and pays a $40,000 dividend. During the same period Company B reports an income of $45,000 and pays a $20,000 dividend.

On January 1, 1969, B distributes a stock dividend which transfers $25,000 from retained earnings to the Capital Stock account. During 1969 Company A earns an income from its own operations of $52,000 and pays a $50,000 dividend, and during the same period Company B reports an income of $40,000 and pays a $30,000 dividend.

A continuing statement of changes in consolidated retained earnings would reflect the above information as shown on page 503.

PROOF: Retained Earnings
                                             Separate Company Statements

	Company A		Company B
Balance, January 1, 1967	$ 70,000		$ 40,000
1967 income	50,000		30,000
Dividends received	16,000		
Total	$136,000		$ 70,000
Deduct: dividends paid, 1967	40,000		20,000
Balance, December 31, 1967	$ 96,000		$ 50,000
1968 income	40,000		45,000
Dividends received	14,000		
Total	$150,000		$ 95,000
Deduct: Dividends paid, 1968 $40,000			20,000
Loss on sale of B's stock 3,000	43,000		
Balance, December 31, 1968	$107,000		$ 75,000
1969 income	52,000		40,000
Dividends received	21,000		
Total	$180,000		$115,000
Deduct: Stock dividend paid, 1969		$25,000	
Dividends paid, 1969	50,000	30,000	55,000
Balance, December 31, 1969	$130,000		$ 60,000
Elimination:			
Retained earnings at acquisition		40,000	
Minority interest 30% of increase			
since acquisition		6,000	46,000
To consolidated retained earnings	14,000		$ 14,000
Add: A's share of B's stock dividend	17,500		
Consolidated retained earnings,			
December 31, 1969	$161,500		

Change in Parent Company's Per Cent of Ownership of Subsidiary. The impact of a change in the parent company's proportionate interest in a subsidiary can best be re-examined by an illustration. Assume abbreviated statements of financial position of Company A and Company B, on January 1, 1967, were as follows:

COMPANY A

Assets	$1,000,000	Capital stock	$1,000,000

COMPANY B

Assets	$ 300,000	Capital stock	$ 300,000

On January 2, 1967, Company A purchases an 80% interest in Company B for $264,000. The statements immediately after the purchase would be:

COMPANY A

Investment in B	264,000		
Other assets	736,000	Capital stock	$1,000,000
	$1,000,000		$1,000,000

COMPANY B

Assets	$ 300,000	Capital stock	$ 300,000

A consolidated statement of financial position prepared as of January 2, 1967, would reflect the following:

CONSOLIDATED STATEMENT OF FINANCIAL POSITION

Assets	$1,036,000	Minority interest	$ 60,000
Goodwill	24,000	Capital stock	1,000,000
	$1,060,000		$1,060,000

Following one acceptable consolidation procedure, the "Goodwill" of $24,000 might be allocated to other assets. As a result, the consolidated statement on January 2, 1967, might be:

CONSOLIDATED STATEMENT OF FINANCIAL POSITION

Assets	$1,060,000	Minority interest	$ 60,000
		Capital stock	1,000,000
	$1,060,000		$1,060,000

For illustrative purposes assume that during 1967 the only consolidated activity was Company B's operations which provided an income of $40,000, all of which was retained by Company B. Assuming Company A carries the investment at cost, the statements on December 31, 1967, would appear as follows:

COMPANY A

Investment in B	$ 264,000	Capital stock	$1,000,000
Other assets	736,000		
	$1,000,000		$1,000,000

COMPANY B

Assets	$ 340,000	Capital stock	$ 300,000
		Retained earnings	40,000
	$ 340,000		$ 340,000

CONSOLIDATED

Assets	$1,100,000	Minority interest	$ 68,000
		Capital stock	1,000,000
		Consolidated retained earnings	32,000
	$1,100,000		$1,100,000

Assume on January 2, 1968, Company A sells one-eighth of its holdings of Company B stock for $33,000, the same price which Company A paid for the stock. Statements prepared on this date would appear as follows:

COMPANY A

Investment in B	$ 231,000	Capital stock	$1,000,000
Other assets	769,000		
	$1,000,000		$1,000,000

COMPANY B

Assets	$ 340,000	Capital stock	$ 300,000
		Retained earnings	40,000
	$ 340,000		$ 340,000

CONSOLIDATED

Assets (including $21,000 of allocated "goodwill")		$1,130,000	Minority interest (30%)	$ 102,000
			Capital stock	1,000,000
			Consolidated retained earnings	28,000
		$1,130,000		$1,130,000

Two pertinent observations may be drawn from the preceding illustration:

(1) The consolidated statement of financial position on December 31, 1967, values the subsidiary assets at $24,000 above their cost to the subsidiary company, whereas the January 2, 1968, consolidated statement values the same assets at only $21,000 above the subsidiary company's cost. Allocated "Goodwill" was reduced from $24,000 to $21,000 by the sale of one-eighth of Company A's holdings in Company B.

(2) Consolidated retained earnings declined from $32,000 on December 31, 1967, to $28,000 on January 2, 1968. The $4,000 decline was due to:

(a) Revaluation of consolidated assets downward—allocated "Goodwill" declined from $24,000 to $21,000. $3,000

(b) Minority interest acquired an additional $34,000 book value equity in exchange for $33,000.   1,000

Total decline in consolidated retained earnings $4,000

Change in Composition of Consolidated Entity

The impact of the sale by the parent of a substantial amount of the stock of a subsidiary may be such that it changes the composition of the consolidated entity. As a result, successive consolidated statements of financial position, income, and retained earnings may not be comparable over a period of time.

To illustrate, assume Company A on January 1, 1967, owns 90% of Company B, 80% of Company C, and B owns 70% of Company D. These investments have been held for some time. On January 1, 1968, Company A sells eight-ninths of its investment in B, thus eliminating B and D from the consolidated group. For simplification purposes, assume operating incomes for the separate companies in 1968 were identical with the 1967 earnings. Abbreviated consolidated statements of financial position and income might appear as follows:

CONSOLIDATED INCOME STATEMENTS

	1967	1968
Sales	$890,000	$490,000
Cost of sales	510,000	300,000
Margin	$380,000	$190,000
Operating expenses	230,000	120,000
Income	$150,000	$ 70,000
Minority interest	21,400	8,000
Consolidated income	$128,600	$ 62,000

CONSOLIDATED STATEMENTS OF FINANCIAL POSITION

	1967	1968
Current assets	$190,000	$400,000
Investment in B (cost)		14,000
Fixed assets	641,000	431,000
Goodwill	61,000	25,000
Total	$892,000	$870,000
Current liabilities	$120,000	$ 80,000
Fixed liabilities	20,000	20,000
Minority interest	83,400	36,000
Capital stock	500,000	500,000
Retained earnings	168,600	234,000
Total	$892,000	$870,000

Any attempt to draw conclusions from comparative statements when a change in the composition of the consolidated entity has resulted between the dates of the two statements is questionable. Various suggestions have been made to overcome the problems arising from a change in the composition of a consolidated entity. As a minimum, it is suggested that footnotes be used to explain major changes in the composition of the entity. If data are available, adjusted statements which are comparable might be appropriate.

Disclosure of the effect of the disposition of a subsidiary on consolidated retained earnings should be disclosed in the statement of changes in consolidated earnings, if material, as shown on page 509.

There should be no attempt to restate the December 31, 1967, balance of retained earnings to the amount it would have been had the composition of the 1967 entity been the same as the composition of the 1968 entity. Instead, all changes in consolidated retained earnings should be reflected

COMPANY A

CONSOLIDATED STATEMENT
OF RETAINED EARNINGS

FOR 1968

Balance, December 31, 1967	$168,600
Add: Gain on sale of 80% of B's stock	3,400
Balance, after adjustment for disposition of 80% of B's stock	$172,000
Add: 1968 consolidated income	62,000
Balance, December 31, 1968	$234,000

in the consolidated statement of retained earnings. In computing the gain or loss on the sale of B's stock, it may be desirable to disclose the elements of the gain or loss in the following manner.

Sale price of 80% of B's stock		$xxxx
Less:		
Cost of 80% of B's stock	$xxx	
80% of B's increase in stockholders' equity since acquisition	xxx	
10% of B's increase in stockholders' equity since acquisition	xxx	xxx
Net increase in consolidated retained earnings due to sale of B's stock		$3,400

Unconsolidated Subsidiaries

Although the proper valuation of investments in general is at cost, as indicated in *Bulletin* 51, there are two methods of dealing with investments in unconsolidated subsidiaries in consolidated statements.

To illustrate, assume Company A carries two investments on its books, as follows:

(1) "Investment in B" acquired on January 1, 1967, when 60% of B's voting stock was acquired for $120,000. On that date B's shareholders' equity was $190,000, composed of $150,000 of capital stock and $40,000 of retained earnings.
(2) "Investment in C" acquired on January 1, 1968, when 90% of C's voting stock was acquired for $380,000.

On January 1, 1968, the statements of financial position of the three companies were as follows:

	Company A	Company B	Company C
Assets			
Investment in B (60%)	$120,000		
Investment in C (90%)	380,000		
Other assets	440,000	$250,000	$400,000
Total	$940,000	$250,000	$400,000
Equities			
Liabilities	$100,000	$ 40,000	$ 20,000
Capital stock	800,000	150,000	300,000
Retained earnings	40,000	60,000	80,000
Total	$940,000	$250,000	$400,000

Assume Company B does not meet the standards for consolidation required by the consolidation policy of Company A. When Company C is acquired and does meet the standards for consolidation, however, consolidated statements may be prepared. In a consolidated statement of financial position, the investment in B may be reported as $120,0C0 with a footnote disclosure that the undistributed earnings of B since acquisition of the stock by A amounts to $20,000 ($210,000 — $190,000), and that 60% of this amount or $12,000 accrues to the investment. The preferred method, however, is to adjust the $120,000 investment upward by $12,000 with an offsetting credit through income to the retained earnings of Company A. A consolidated statement of financial position prepared on January 1, 1968, could be developed as follows:

COMPANY A AND SUBSIDIARY
CONSOLIDATED WORKING PAPERS
STATEMENT OF FINANCIAL POSITION
As of January 1, 1968

	Company A	Company C	Adjustments & Eliminations Debit	Adjustments & Eliminations Credit	Consolidated Financial Position
Assets					
Investment in B	$120,000		$ 12,000(1)		$ 132,000
Investment in C	380,000			$342,000A	38,000G
Other assets	440,000	$400,000			840,000
Total	$940,000	$400,000			$1,010,000
Equities					
Liabilities	$100,000	$ 20,000			$ 120,000
Capital stock	800,000				800,000
Retained earnings	40,000			12,000(1)	52,000RE
Capital stock		300,000	270,000A		30,000MI
Retained earnings		80,000	72,000A		8,000MI
Total	$940,000	$400,000	$354,000	$354,000	$1,010,000

(1): To revalue upward the investment in the unconsolidated subsidiary by the amount of the parent's share of the subsidiary's undistributed earnings since January 1, 1967.

A: To eliminate 90% of C's shareholders' equity against the investment account.

PROBLEMS

Problem 17-1. The problem of consolidated working paper adjustments for intercompany bond holdings may be solved in accordance with a variety of assumptions, such as:
1. The consolidated gain or loss on reacquiring bonds may be assumed to accrue to both the purchasing company and the issuing company.
2. The consolidated gain or loss on reacquiring bonds may be assumed to accrue entirely to the issuing company (company having the bonds outstanding).
3. The consolidated gain or loss on reacquiring bonds may be assumed to accrue entirely to the purchasing company (company carrying the bonds as an investment).

Required:
(1) In the case below, give the journal entry or entries required to adjust for intercompany bondholding in the consolidated working papers under the three assumptions.
(2) How is consolidated retained earnings affected under each procedure?

STATEMENTS OF FINANCIAL POSITION
DECEMBER 31, 1968

	Company A	Company B
Investment in B Stock (80%)	$110,000	
Investment in A Bonds ($10,000)		$ 9,600
Bond Discount	6,000	
Other Assets	244,000	130,400
	$360,000	$140,000
Bonds Payable	$100,000	
Capital Stock	200,000	$100,000
Retained Earnings	60,000	40,000
	$360,000	$140,000

Problem 17-2. Company P acquired control of Company S over a 15-year period, as follows:

			Subsidiary	
Date	Stock Acquired	Price Paid	Capital Stock	Retained Earnings
1/1/51	10%	$ 45,000	$500,000	$100,000
1/1/55	2%	12,000	500,000	130,000
1/1/57	10%	75,000	500,000	160,000
1/1/61	10%	90,000	500,000	210,000
1/1/63	13%	120,000	500,000	250,000
1/1/66	20%	200,000	500,000	300,000

On January 1, 1966, the retained earnings of Company P was $160,000. Having acquired control of Company S on January 1, 1966, the Company has decided to prepare a consolidated statement of financial position. Two amounts have been suggested for consolidated retained earnings: $160,000 and $212,900.

Required:

(1) Give the theory supporting each amount.

(2) How much "goodwill" should be recognized on the consolidated statement of financial position?

(3) Would your answer be different if the acquisitions were made as follows; 1/1/51 (10%), 1/1/55 (2%); 1/1/66 (53%). The price paid for the last acquisition was $530,000. The other prices were as given in the above data.

Problem 17–3. On January 1, 1967, Company P acquired 80% of the stock of Company S for $55,000. On that date the statements of financial position of the two companies appeared as follows:

	Company P		Company S	
	Dr.	Cr.	Dr.	Cr.
Investment in S (80%)	$ 55,000			
Other assets	545,000		$210,000	
Liabilities		$ 60,000		$165,000
Capital stock		500,000		100,000
Retained earnings		40,000		(55,000)
Total	$600,000	$600,000	$210,000	$210,000

During 1967 neither company paid dividends. Financial statements of the separate companies on December 31, 1967, contained the following information.

	Company P		Company S	
	Dr.	Cr.	Dr.	Cr.
Investment in S (80%)	$ 55,000			
Other assets	585,000		$180,000	
Liabilities		$ 50,000		$200,000
Capital stock		500,000		100,000
Retained earnings		90,000		(120,000)
Total	$640,000	$640,000	$180,000	$180,000

Required:

Prepare a consolidated statement of financial position as of December 31, 1967.

Problem 17–4. Company P owns 60% of Company S. Statements of financial position, as of December 31, 1966, reveal the following information:

	Company P		Company S	
	Dr.	Cr.	Dr.	Cr.
Investment in S (60%)	$480,000			
Other assets	35,000		$990,000	
Liabilities		$115,000		$ 90,000
Capital stock		400,000		800,000
Retained earnings		—		100,000
Total	$515,000	$515,000	$990,000	$990,000

Company P acquired the 60% interest in Company S on January 1, 1966, for $480,000 when Company S's retained earnings were zero. (Separate earnings of Company P for 1966 were zero.)

Required:
(1) Prepare a consolidated statement of financial position.
(2) Point out some limitations to the consolidated report which would be overcome by separate company reports

Problem 17–5. Company P acquired 90% of the stock of Company S by issuing its own stock in payment. The market value of the stock issued was $120,000; the market value of the stock acquired was $118,000; and the book value of the stock acquired was $54,000. The par value ($100 per share) of the stock issued was $100,000. Total assets of Company S were $75,000. The stock issued by Company P represents 10% of its total stock outstanding which has been issued on an average at 15% above par. Liabilities of Company P are $400,000.

Required:
Prepare a consolidated statement of financial position under each of the following assumptions:
(1) Subsidiary assets are to be valued at cost to the subsidiary.
(2) Subsidiary assets are to be valued at the cost prevailing when the parent company acquired the subsidiary.
(3) Assets claimed by parent company stockholders are valued at cost to the parent. Assets claimed by minority interest are valued at cost to the subsidiary.

Problem 17–6. Company A purchased on January 1, 1967, 80% of Company S for $100,000 when Company S's stockholders' equity was $100,000 of capital stock and $10,000 of retained earnings. On this same date S acquired a 10% interest in Company A for $40,000. At this time Company A's stockholders' equity was capital stock of $300,000 and retained earnings of $60,000. Liabilities of the two companies on this date were: A, $70,000; S, $20,000. Earnings for 1967, all retained by each company, were: A, $30,000; S, $10,000. Liabilities on December 31, 1967, were A, $80,000; S, $25,000.

Required:
(1) Prepare a consolidated statement of financial position as of 12/31/67.

(*a*) Assuming the investment of S in A is considered a mutual holding.

(*b*) Assuming the investment of S in A is considered treasury stock.

(2) Prepare a statement reconciling the two views.

Problem 17–7. Company A purchased 90% of Company S on January 1, 1966, for $160,000 when S's stockholders' equity was capital stock, $100,000 and retained earnings, $50,000. On this date A's retained earnings were $70,000.

During 1966, S earned $20,000 and paid a cash dividend of $10,000. A earned from its own operations $15,000.

On January 1, 1967, A sold 2/9 of its holdings of S's stock for $32,000. During 1967 earnings and dividends were as follows:

	A	S
1967 earnings	$20,000	$24,000
Cash dividend paid	30,000	10,000
Stock dividend paid (12/31/67)		20,000

Required:

Prepare a statement of changes in consolidated retained earnings for 1966 and 1967.

Problem 17–8. Comparative consolidated statements of financial position for Companies A and B on January 2 and January 3 were as follows. The change is due entirely to A's sale of 10% of B's stock.

	Jan. 2	Jan. 3
Assets (includes $16,000 goodwill on Jan. 2)	$880,000	$905,000
Minority interest	48,000	72,000
Capital stock	700,000	700,000
Retained earnings	132,000	133,000
Total	$880,000	$905,000

Required:

Prepare a statement explaining the change in consolidated retained earnings.

Problem 17–9. Condensed statements of financial position of Company P and Company S on January 1, 1967, appear as follows:

	Company P	Company S
Assets	$600,000	$300,000
Capital stock	500,000	200,000
Retained earnings	40,000	50,000
Liabilities	60,000	50,000
Total	$600,000	$300,000

On January 2, Company P purchased 80% of the stock of Company S for $160,000. An examination of the difference between the price paid for the stock and its book value reveals the following information:

(1) Assets of S are overvalued by	$30,000
(2) Additional costs required (none of which can be capitalized) for integrating the operations of P and S to be paid by P	25,000
(3) Unrecorded liability of Company S	5,000

Required:

Prepare a consolidated statement of financial position as of January 2, 1967.

Problem 17–10. Company S has 1,000 shares of stock outstanding. On January 2, 1967, H acquired 800 of these shares for $320,000. On that date S's stockholders' equity was

Capital stock (1,000 shares)	$100,000
Retained earnings	250,000
Total	$350,000

Consolidated retained earnings on January 2, 1967, was $280,000.

During 1967, Company S earned an income of $50,000, all of which was retained in the business.

On January 2, 1968, Company S issued an additional 200 shares of stock to investors. None of this was purchased by Company H.

Required:

(1) Compute consolidated retained earnings as of January 2, 1968 and explain the changes in it since January 2, 1967, assuming

        (*a*) The new stock is sold at $200 per share.
        (*b*) The new stock is sold at $400 per share.
        (*c*) The new stock is sold at $500 per share.

CHAPTER **18**

Expansion by foreign operations

History shows that as an economy matures and its business enterprises expand, businessmen often look abroad for wider markets and additional investment possibilities. The economy of the United States has been no exception. Today American business organizations operate throughout the world with some form of an organization in practically every country of the world.

The problems involved when accounting for foreign operations can best be examined by studying the problems peculiar to the various types of foreign operations. Foreign operations, as a general rule, can be classified in one of the following categories:

(1) Domestic company with foreign transactions.
(2) Foreign branches.
(3) Foreign subsidiaries.

Domestic Company with Foreign Transactions

When a domestic company sells or buys merchandise abroad, it may bill or be billed either in the domestic currency or in the foreign currency. If the domestic company bills or is billed in domestic currency, there is no problem involved accountingwise as far as the domestic company is concerned. However, if the domestic company bills or is billed in the foreign currency, there may be an exchange gain or loss involved due to fluctuations in the exchange rates between the date of sale or purchase and the date of settlement. If the exchange rate in effect at the date of settlement is the same as it was at the date of sale or purchase, no exchange gain or loss is involved. If the rates at these dates are not the same, an exchange gain or loss will arise.

Foreign Sales. Assuming a United States company sells merchandise for $10,000 to a British company and bills the British company in dollars, no exchange gain or loss is involved from the standpoint of the United States company as the following entries illustrate:

Date of sale:
    British company $10,000
        Sales (foreign) $10,000

Date of settlement:
    Cash $10,000
        British company $10,000

However, if the United States company bills the British company in pounds, an exchange gain or loss will arise if the rate of exchange at the date of settlement is not the same as it was at the date of sale. For example, assume, in addition to the facts used above, that the rate of exchange at the date of sale was 2.828 (that is, $2.828 per pound) and at the date of settlement 2.800.

Date of sale:
    British company (£3,536) $10,000
        Sales (foreign) $10,000

Date of settlement:
    Cash (£3,536) $ 9,901
    Exchange gain or loss   99
        British company $10,000

Foreign Purchases. Assuming a United States company buys $28,000 worth of merchandise from a British company and is billed by the British company in dollars, no exchange gain or loss is involved from the standpoint of the United States company, as the following entries illustrate:

Date of purchase:
    Purchases $28,000
        British company $28,000

Date of settlement:
    British company $28,000
        Cash $28,000

If, however, the United States company is billed in pounds instead of dollars, an exchange gain or loss will arise if the rate of exchange at the date of settlement is not the same as it was at the date of purchase. For example, assume a United States company purchases merchandise worth 10,000 pounds from a British company at a time when the exchange rate is 2.800 and settles the obligation when the rate is 2.828.

Date of purchase:		
Purchases	$28,000	
British company (£10,000)		$28,000
Date of settlement:		
British company	$28,000	
Exchange gain or loss	280	
Cash (£10,000)		$28,280

Realized vs. Unrealized Exchange Gain or Loss. The foregoing illustrations have dealt with realized exchange gains and losses. In contrast to realized exchange gains and losses are unrealized exchange gains and losses which come into being when financial statements are prepared before a transaction has been completed.

To illustrate, assume a United States company sells to a British company on December 18, merchandise for $10,000 billed in pounds when the exchange rate was $2.828 per pound. The account was settled on April 15 when the exchange rate was $2.813 per pound ($9,947). The United States company prepared financial statements on December 31 when the exchange rate was $2.800 per pound ($9,901). On December 31, the United States company has an unrealized loss of $99 ($10,000 − $9,901). The realized loss of $53 ($10,000 − $9,947) will not be reported until the settlement date.

In summary form, the calculations would be as follows:

	Date of Sale	December 31	April 15
Sale recorded in United States	$10,000	$10,000	$10,000
Billed in pounds (3,536)			
Cash to be received if 3,536 pounds were collected	10,000	9,901	9,947
Sales dollars not collected:			
Unrealized on December 18	–0–		
Unrealized on December 31		$ 99	
Realized on April 15			$ 53

Realized exchange gains and losses are normally recognized as non-operating income items. Unrealized exchange gains and losses should be provided for in a suspense account unless the amounts involved are substantial and the fluctuation appears to be permanent. Application of these rules to the above illustration will give the following results:

Date of sale:
Due from British Company (£3,536)	$10,000	
Sales		$10,000

December 31:
Provision for exchange fluctuations	$ 99	
Due from British Company		$ 99

April 15:
Cash (£3,536)	$ 9,947	
Exchange gain or loss	53	
Due from British Company		$ 9,901
Provision for exchange fluctuations		99

When a company has a number of foreign transactions in process, the above entries might more conveniently be recorded as follows:

Date of sale—Same entry as above
December 31, 1966— Same entry as above
April 15:
Cash	$ 9,947	
Due from British Company		$ 9,901
Exchange gain or loss		46

December 31, 1967—Assuming analysis reveals no balance is needed in the "Provision for Exchange Fluctuations" account, the following entry should be made:

Exchange gain or loss	$ 99	
Provision for exchange fluctuations		$ 99

The "Exchange Gain or Loss" account is an income statement account and the balance of $53 ($99 — $46) would reflect the realized exchange loss for 1967.

The "Provision for Exchange Fluctuations" account is a suspense account and would be reported on the statement of financial position as a deferred item.

Assets Transmitted for Sale in a Foreign Country. At times, a domestic company may ship goods to a foreign country for subsequent sale in the foreign country. Normally this involves the use of an associated firm in the foreign country which will handle the goods for the domestic company.

It is normally assumed for accounting purposes that the goods shipped for sale will be sold at a price other than the cost valuation which was attached to them at the time of shipment. This raises a problem regarding any unrealized exchange gain or loss on unsold goods at any reporting date. Some accountants contend that no unrealized exchange gain or loss comes into existence until there is definite reason to believe a currency exchange is involved. These accountants maintain that no realized or unrealized exchange gain or loss is possible until the goods are sold and the probability of currency transmission increased. Essentially this group contends that the proper conversion rate for unsold goods is the rate which prevailed when the goods were shipped.

To illustrate, assume a United States company ships to a British company goods which had cost the United States company $10,000. The British Company picked up the goods at £3,536 (exchange rate of 2.828). On December 31, the British company reports one-half of the goods had been sold as a net price of £2,500 on November 19 when the exchange rate was $2.790 per pound. On December 31, the rate of exchange is $2.800 per pound. On April 15, the British Company transmits the £2,500 when the exchange rate is $2.813 and reports the other half of the goods are unsold. Assuming unsold goods are converted at the rate prevailing when the goods were shipped, the following entries would record the above transactions:

Date shipped:

Goods shipped to British associate	$10,000	
Merchandise		$10,000

November 19, 1967:

Due from British company (£2,500 × 2.79)	$ 6,975	
Cost of sales	5,000	
Goods shipped to British associate		$ 5,000
Sales		6,975

[to record the sale reported by the British company and the related cost of sales. The British company report would be:

Sales	£ 2,500	
Cost of sales (one-half £3,536)	1,768	
Gross margin	£ 732	

If these amounts were converted to dollars at the exchange rate prevailing at the date of sales the converted amounts would be:

Sales £2,500 at 2.79	$ 6,975	
Cost of sales £1,768 at 2.79	4,933	

Recording cost of sales at $5,000 instead of $4,933 is supported on the reasoning that the cost of sales should be converted at the exchange rate prevailing at the date the goods were shipped:
£1,768 at $2.828 = $5,000]

December 31, 1967:
    Due from British company $ 25
        Provision for exchange fluctuations $ 25
[to record the increase in cash since the sale date which would be received if the British company were to pay on December 31 the £2,500 owed the United States Company. The computation would be:
Valuation of receivable from British:
    December 31, 1967—£2,500 @ 2.800 = $7,000
    November 19, 1967—£2,500 @ 2.790 = 6,975

    Increase in receivable since November
    19 because of exchange fluctuation $ 25

Because the $25 is an unrealized exchange gain, the offsetting credit is to the suspense account. While it may be suggested that an unrealized exchange exists on the unsold merchandise (£1,768 recorded at $5,000), accountants who believe unsold merchandise should be converted at the exchange rate prevailing when the goods were shipped would give no recognition to the exchange fluctuations of the unsold goods.]

April 15, 1968:
    Cash $7,032.50
    Provision for exchange fluctuations   25.00
        Due from British Company $7,000.00
        Exchange gain or loss   57.50
    (to record the realized exchange gain when the British company pays the £2,500. The computations would be:
        Cash received £2,500 @ 2.813 = $7,032.50
        Valuation of receivable on
          date of sale £2,500 @ 2.790 = 6,975.00
        Realized exchange fluctuation
          gain $ 57.50

Because of the provision for the unrealized exchange gain on December 31, which revalued the receivable to $7,000, it is necessary to eliminate the balance in the Provision for Exchange Fluctuation account.)

Other accountants maintain that the unsold goods on any reporting date should be converted at the exchange rate prevailing at that date. This procedure is based on the reasoning that normally the goods will be sold and will not be returned. These accountants contend that the exchange rate existing at the reporting date gives a more realistic basis for recognition of the normal relationship which exists between cost and selling price. Acceptance of this position would suggest the following *additional* entries:

November 19, 1967:

Exchange fluctuation loss	$ 67	
Cost of sales		$67

(to remove from cost of sales the element of exchange fluctuation loss on the goods sold, which arose due to changes in the exchange rate between the date the goods were shipped and the date when they were sold. The computation of this amount as a realized loss would be:)

Valuation at shipping date	$5,000
Valuation at sales date:	
1/2 of goods 1,768 × $2.79 =	4,933
Loss	$ 67

December 31, 1967:

Provision for exchange fluctuation	$50	
Goods shipped to British associate		$50

[to record the unrealized exchange loss on the unsold merchandise on December 31 in the inventory of the British associate. The computation would be:

Total shipment	$10,000
Sold (one-half)	5,000
Unsold	$ 5,000

The $5,000 would be picked up by the British associate in pounds determined by the rate of exchange prevailing at the date the goods were shipped in an amount of £1,768 ($5,000 ÷ 2.828). As a result the valuation of the unsold merchandise would be:

    £1,768 at 2.828 = $5,000

If the merchandise were converted at the rate prevailing on December 31, the amount would be:

    £1,768 at 2.800 = 4,950

Decline in valuation of unsold merchandise due to exchange rate fluctuation $ 50

Because this exchange rate fluctuation is unrealized it may be charged to the suspense account rather than as a realized loss.]

Assets Transmitted for Use in a Foreign Country. Machinery and other fixed assets may be shipped by a domestic company to a foreign country for use by a branch or foreign associate and not for sale. Since these assets may have long lives and their contribution to sales in the foreign country may extend over a long period of time, the rate at which they are converted is normally the rate prevailing on the date these assets are shipped. This position on conversion of fixed assets is consistent with the valuation of fixed assets at acquisition cost. Fluctuations in the values of assets committed to relatively long periods of use are normally not reflected in accounting records. It has also been contended that conversion at exchange rates prevailing on the reporting date implies this is the rate at which the fixed assets will be converted to currency and transmitted to the domestic country. Since it is obvious that this rate is not proper, it appears logical to conclude that the rate prevailing at the reporting date should not be used. Likewise since it is impossible to forecast future exchange rates which will prevail when these assets are converted to currency, expected future rates should not be used. The most objective basis for conversion appears to be the rate prevailing on the date the resources were shipped.

Assets Transmitted vs. Assets Acquired in a Foreign Country. No distinction should be drawn between assets shipped by a domestic company to a foreign associate for sale or use and similar assets acquired by the associate for sale or use for the benefit of the domestic company. Assets should be converted at similar exchange rates whether shipped from the domestic country or acquired in the foreign country. The exchange rate on the acquisition date is substituted for the exchange rate on the shipment date for acquired assets.

Foreign Operations. Before discussing the procedures for converting branch accounts and subsidiary company accounts, certain aspects of foreign operations should be noted. First, many domestic companies have experienced difficulty in getting funds out of some foreign countries due to a variety of restrictions. Inclusion of income earned in a foreign country as part of the income of the United States company may be misleading if such income cannot be transmitted to the domestic company.

In some instances, different foreign exchange rates will exist at the same time. A foreign government may decree an official exchange rate but the free market may establish another rate. The selection of the most appropriate rate for conversion should be realistic in terms of the rate which will prevail for the particular company.

Foreign Branches

In Chapter 8, when discussing domestic branches, it was pointed out that it is not uncommon for a company to establish a branch(es) in a foreign country(ies). Attention was also directed to the accounting procedures to be followed for such a branch. Essentially the same procedures apply as for a domestic branch, except when preparing combined statements. On that date it is necessary to convert branch account balances from the foreign currency into the domestic currency.

Conversion Rates. In general, the American Institute of Certified Public Accountants in *Accounting Research Bulletin* 43 recommends the use of the following rates when converting foreign accounts into domestic currency:

Current Assets. Cash, accounts receivable, and other current assets, unless covered by some type of hedging contract, should be converted at the rate prevailing on the reporting date. This rate is frequently referred to as the *current rate*.

Noncurrent Assets. Fixed assets, permanent investments, and long-term receivables should be converted at the rates prevailing when such assets were acquired or constructed. Since fixed assets are converted at the rate prevailing when such assets were acquired. or constructed, depreciation (not only the charge for the period but also the accumulated amount) should be converted similarly.

Current Liabilities. Current liabilities like current assets should be converted at the rate prevailing at the reporting date, the *current rate*.

Noncurrent Liabilities. Long-term liabilities should be converted at the rate prevailing when the liabilities were originally incurred.

Reciprocal Accounts. Branch accounts that are reciprocal to home office accounts should be converted to the balances as shown by the respective home office accounts. For example:

"Home Office" account is converted to the same amount as shown in "Branch Office" account.

"Merchandise from Home Office" is converted to the same amount as shown in the "Merchandise Shipments to Branch" account.

"Remittances to Home Office" is converted to the same amount as shown in the "Remittances from Branch" account.

"Remittances from Home Office" is converted to the same amount as shown in the "Remittances to Branch" account.

Nominal Accounts. Income and expense accounts, except for depreciation, should be converted at the average rate applicable to each month or, if this procedure is impractical, on the basis of a carefully weighted average. This rate is usually referred to as the *average rate*. Depreciation, as was pointed out above, should be converted at the rates prevailing when the related assets were acquired or constructed.

Exchange Gain or Loss. When converting foreign accounts into domestic currency, the use of several rates usually results in a discrepancy between the total debits and credits. This represents an exchange gain or loss, depending upon whether the debits exceed the credits (a gain) or whether the credits exceed the debits (a loss).

The American Institute of Certified Public Accountants recommends that realized gains or losses on foreign exchange be credited or charged to operations, and that unrealized losses be charged against operations but that unrealized gains should be carried to a suspense account, except to the extent that they offset prior provisions for unrealized losses, in which case they may be credited to the account previously charged.

Realized Gains and Losses. Realized gains or losses result if the rate of exchange prevailing when the cash transfer is made differs from the rate of exchange prevailing when the cash was advanced or earned. For example, a realized gain or loss would result if a branch made sales and incurred expenses which were converted at an average rate. When the cash arising from any income reported is transmitted to the home office, the rate of exchange may be different from the average rate at which the income was originally converted. In general, realized gains or losses arise from a delay in transmitting earnings after the date earned or in returning cash advances. The earlier illustrations of exchange gain or loss arising on foreign sales or purchases suggest the nature of realized gains and losses.

To illustrate more fully, assume Branch B transferred £2,000 of income to the home office in the United States when the exchange rate was $2.80 per pound. The earnings were the result of £5,000 of sales and £3,000 of expenses. The average exchange rate during the period when the sales were made and the expenses incurred was $2.78 per pound. The converted income statement in abbreviated form would appear as follows:

	Pounds	Rate	Dollars
Sales	5,000	2.78	13,900
Expenses	3,000	2.78	8,340
Income	2,000	2.78	5,560

Upon receipt of the report, the home office would record the income by the following entry:

Branch office (foreign)	$5,560	
Branch income		$5,560

When the cash resulting from the operations (£2,000) is transmitted, however, the home office would receive a total of $5,600 (£2,000 @ $2.80). The entry to record the cash receipt would be:

Cash	$5,600	
Branch office (foreign)		$5,560
Exchange gain or loss		40

Unrealized Gains and Losses. Unrealized gains or losses result from the conversion of the accounts of a foreign branch to domestic currency. Since different rates may be used in converting various inter-related accounts, an unrealized gain or loss may result. Typical examples of unrealized gains or losses are:

(1) Unremitted cash (converted at the rate prevailing at the reporting date) may be valued differently from the offsetting credit. (If the credit were to an income account, the conversion rate would *not* necessarily be that prevailing at the reporting date.)
(2) An asset may be converted at one rate and the credit at another, as might result if a fixed asset were purchased with the credit going to a current liability, or if a current asset arose as a result of a credit to the Home Office account, as when the home office ships merchandise to the branch.

Thus various transactions may result in unrealized gains or losses. If a loss results, it is charged as an expense or as a direct charge to retained earnings. If a gain results the credit is to a "Provision for Exchange Fluctuations" account.

To illustrate, assume the same facts as those in the above example except that the cash was not transmitted to the United States and the conversion rate was $2.77 on the reporting date. In work sheet form, assuming these are the only items to be converted, the result would be:

	Pounds		Conversion	Dollars	
Account	Dr.	Cr.	Rate	Dr.	Cr.
Cash	2,000		2.77	5,540	
Income		2,000	2.78		5,560
Exchange gain or loss				20	
Total	2,000	2,000		5,560	5,560

The exchange loss would be charged to operations and the entry to pick up branch earnings would be:

Branch office (foreign)	$5,540	
Exchange gain or loss	20	
Branch income		$5,560

Of course, in an actual case, many other accounts would exist. The unrealized gain or loss is the amount needed to balance the converted amounts.

Foreign Branch Accounting Illustrated

Assume a United States company establishes a branch in England and that the following transactions occur during the first month of operation:

(1) January 1.   The home office establishes the English branch by transferring $7,500 cash and $10,000 worth of merchandise to the branch.
(2) January 2.   The home office purchases in England and turns over to the branch equipment costing £2,000.
(3) January 5.   The branch purchases merchandise costing £1,000.
(4) January 10.   The branch sells merchandise for £3,000 cash.
(5) January 20.   The branch purchases £2,000 worth of merchandise on account.
(6) January 20.   The branch sells merchandise on account for £4,000.
(7) January 31.   The branch pays expenses for January totaling £2,000.
(8) January 31.   The branch remits £1,000 to the home office.
(9) January 31.   The branch submits its trial balance as of January 31 to the home office.
(10) January 31.   The home office converts the branch trial balance and combines it with that of the home office.

The following rates of exchange were in effect during the month:

January 1	2.500
January 2	2.510
January 5	2.512
January 10	2.515
January 20	2.520
January 31	2.528
Average January rate	2.515

	BRANCH BOOKS				HOME OFFICE BOOKS		
Jan. 1	Cash	£3,000			Branch office	$17,500	
	Merchandise from				Cash		$ 7,500
	home office	£4,000			Merchandise ship-		
	Home office		£7,000		ments to branch		$ 10,000
Jan. 2	Equipment	£2,000			Branch office	$ 5,020	
	Home office		£2,000		Cash		$ 5,020
Jan. 5	Purchases	£1,000			No entry		
	Cash		£1,000				
Jan. 10	Cash	£3,000			No entry		
	Sales		£3,000				
Jan. 20	Purchases	£2,000			No entry		
	Accounts payable		£2,000				
Jan. 20	Accounts receivable	£4,000			No entry		
	Sales		£4,000				
Jan. 31	Expenses	£2,000			No entry		
	Cash		£2,000				
Jan. 31	Remittances to				Cash	$ 2,528	
	home office	£1,000			Remittances from		
	Cash		£1,000		branch		$ 2,528

As of January 31, the branch submits the following trial balance to the home office:

BRANCH TRIAL BALANCE
As of January 31

Cash	£ 2,000	
Merchandise from home office	4,000	
Equipment	2,000	
Purchases	3,000	
Accounts receivable	4,000	
Expenses	2,000	
Remittances to home office	1,000	
Home office		£ 9,000
Sales		7,000
Accounts payable		2,000
	£18,000	£18,000

Merchandise on hand January 31, £2,000.

Conversion of the branch trial balance would be as follows:

BRANCH TRIAL BALANCE
As of January 31

	Pounds Dr.	Pounds Cr.	Conversion Rate	Dollars Dr.	Dollars Cr.
Cash	2,000		2.528C	5,056	
Merchandise from home office	4,000		R	10,000	
Equipment	2,000		2.510D	5,020	
Purchases	3,000		2.515A	7,545	
Accounts receivable	4,000		2.528C	10,112	
Expenses	2,000		2.515A	5,030	
Remittances to home office	1,000		R	2,528	
Home office		9,000	R		22,520
Sales		7,000	2.515A		17,605
Accounts payable		2,000	2.528C		5,056
	18,000	18,000			
Exchange gain or loss					110
				45,291	45,291

Merchandise on hand January 31, £2,000   2.528C 5,056

A: Average rate.
C: Current rate.
D: Rate prevailing at date equipment was acquired.
R: Reciprocal.

Combination of the converted branch trial balance with the home office accounts would be as follows:

U. S. COMPANY AND ENGLISH BRANCH
COMBINED WORKING PAPERS

JANUARY 31

	U. S. Company	English Branch	Adjustments and Eliminations	Income	Combined Financial Position
Debits					
Cash	$ 20,000	$ 5,056			$ 25,056
Accounts receivable	30,000	10,112			40,112
Inventory, January 1	40,000			$ 40,000	
Branch office	22,520		$22,520A		
Merchandise from home office		10,000	10,000B		
Remittances to home office		2,528	2,528C		
Equipment		5,020			5,020
Other assets	49,952				49,952
Purchases	140,000	7,545		147,545	
Expenses	25,056	5,030		30,086	
	$327,528	$45,291			
Inventories, January 31			$35,056(1)		35,056
				$217,631	$155,196
Credits					
Accounts payable	$15,000	$ 5,056			$ 20,056
Home office		22,520	22,520A		
Merchandise shipments to branch	10,000		10,000B		
Remittances from branch	2,528		2,528C		
Sales	200,000	17,605		$217,605	
Exchange gain or loss		110		110	
Capital stock	80,000				80,000
Retained earnings	20,000				20,000
	$327,528	$45,291			
Inventories, January 31	$ 30,000	$ 5,056	35,056(1)	35,056	
			$70,104	$70,104	
Income credits				$252,771	
Income debits				217,631	
Combined net income				$ 35,140	35,140
					$155,196

The illustration provides for no distinction between realized and unrealized gain. The entire $110 was treated as a realized gain. When the amount involved is not significant such treatment is acceptable. In principle, however, the $110 should be analyzed as realized and unrealized, as follows:

Cash remittance £1,000 converted at $2.528, or	$2,528.00
Equivalent rate at which the offsetting income should be converted would be £1,000 at the average rate of 2.515, or	2,515.00
Realized exchange gain	$ 13.00
The unrealized portion would be $110 minus $13, or	$ 97.00

In principle, the $97 should appear on the statement of financial position as an unrealized exchange gain under the account "Provision for Exchange Fluctuations." The $13 should be treated as realized income and be reported in the income report for the period.

Foreign Subsidiaries

As indicated earlier, domestic companies may have subsidiaries in countries all over the world. These subsidiaries may be formed by their respective parent companies or they may be obtained through acquisition by the parent companies. In general, accounting for a foreign subsidiary is similar to accounting for a foreign branch. Consequently, only such areas as are peculiar to the subsidiary are stressed here.

Conversion Rates. As a general rule, foreign subsidiary accounts are converted into domestic currency by using the same rates as are used when converting foreign branch accounts. However, there are certain accounts that are peculiar to the home office-branch relationship, whereas others are peculiar to the parent-subsidiary relationship. For instance, the branch office and home office accounts are replaced by the parent company's investment account and subsidiary's shareholders' equity section. In general, the following rates are used when converting the accounts of a foreign subsidiary into domestic currency:

(1) *Current assets* and *current liabilities* at the current rate.
(2) *Noncurrent assets* and *noncurrent liabilities* at the rates prevailing when the assets were acquired and the liabilities were incurred. Although noncurrent assets and liabilities are normally converted at historical rates, there are circumstances, as indicated by the Accounting Principles Board in *Opinion 6*, which warrant translation of long-term receivables and long-term liabilities at current rates.
(3) *Nominal accounts* (income and expense), except depreciation, at the average rate. Depreciation, as indicated earlier, should be converted on the same basis as the related asset.
(4) *Shareholders' equity accounts:*
    a. Capital stock. As a general rule, capital stock should be converted at the rate prevailing when the subsidiary was formed, if formed by the parent company, or at the date of acquisition, if acquired by the parent subsequent to formation.
    b. Capital surplus. If a parent company forms a foreign subsidiary, any capital surplus created by the formation should be converted at the rate prevailing at the date of formation. If the parent acquires a foreign subsidiary subsequent to its formation, any

capital surplus in existence as of the date of acquisition should be converted at the rate prevailing at that time. Capital surplus created subsequent to either formation or acquisition should be converted at the rate(s) prevailing when such surplus was created.

c. *Retained earnings.* When using a statement approach, retained earnings may be either forced or converted using the current rate. If forced after converting all other real accounts, retained earnings is considered to be the balancing amount. However, any exchange gain or loss is hidden when this method is used. If, when using a statement approach, retained earnings is converted at the current rate, the balancing amount is the exchange gain or loss. When using a trial balance approach, retained earnings at the beginning of a period must be the same as it was at the end of the preceding period.

Consolidation of Foreign Subsidiaries Illustrated

As is the case in consolidation of a domestic subsidiary with its parent, when consolidating a foreign subsidiary with its parent, either a statement or trial balance approach may be used. Both methods are illustrated, using for comparison purposes the same basic data.

Assume Company A, an American company, acquired a 90% interest in a British firm, Company B, for $130,000 on January 1, 1967, when Company B's $150,000 converted shareholders' equity was composed of $100,000 of capital stock and $50,000 retained earnings. In addition to the specific data given in the statements and trial balances, assume also the following exchange rates prevailed during the period:

> *Prevailing rates*
> | | |
> |---|---|
> | January 1, 1967 | 2.5000 |
> | December 31, 1967 | 2.5300 |
> | Average | 2.5150 |
> | At date fixed assets acquired | 2.5100 |
> | At date fixed liabilities incurred | 2.5200 |

STATEMENT APPROACH

COMPANY A AND SUBSIDIARY COMPANY B
CONSOLIDATED WORKING PAPERS
STATEMENT OF FINANCIAL POSITION
As of DECEMBER 31, 1967

	Co. B Pounds	Conversion Rate	Co. B Converted	Company A	Adjustments and Eliminations		Consolidated Financial Position
Assets							
Current assets	30,000	2.530	$ 75,900	$ 100,000			$ 175,900
Investment in Company B				130,000	$ 46,080(1)	$181,080A	(5,000)G
Fixed assets (net)	80,000	2.510	200,800	800,000			1,000,800
	110,000		$276,700	$1,030,000			$1,171,700
Equities							
Current liabilities	20,000	2.530	$ 50,600	$ 60,000			$ 110,600
Fixed liabilities	10,000	2.520	25,200	100,000			125,200
Shareholders' equity:							
Capital stock:							
Company A				500,000			500,000
Company B	40,000	2.500	100,000		90,000A		10,000MI
Retained earnings:							
Company A				370,000	270(2)	46,080(1)	415,810RE
Company B	40,000	2.530	101,200		91,080A		10,120MI
Exchange gain (loss)			(300)			270(2)	(30)MI
	110,000		$276,700	$1,030,000	$227,430	$227,430	$1,171,700

(1): To recognize A's share of the increase in B's shareholders' equity (90% of $51,200).
(2): To recognize A's share of the exchange loss (90% of $300).
A: To eliminate 90% of B's shareholders' equity against the investment account.

STATEMENT APPROACH (Continued)

COMPANY A AND SUBSIDIARY COMPANY B
CONSOLIDATED WORKING PAPERS
STATEMENT OF INCOME AND RETAINED EARNINGS
YEAR ENDED DECEMBER 31, 1967

	Co. B Pounds	Conversion Rate	Co. B Converted	Company A	Income	Retained Earnings
Credits						
Sales	100,000	2.515	$251,500	$900,000	$1,151,500	
	100,000		$251,500	$900,000	$1,151,500	
Debits						
Cost of sales	60,000	2.515	$150,900	$500,000	$ 650,900	
Depreciation	10,000	2.510	25,100	90,000	115,100	
Other expenses	10,000	2.515	25,150	40,000	65,150	
Net income	20,000	balance	50,350	270,000	320,350	
	100,000		$251,500	$900,000	$1,151,500	
Retained earnings, 1/1/67	20,000	2.500	$ 50,000			$100,000
Net income	20,000	as above	50,350			
Exchange gain or loss			850			495*
Balance, 12/31/67	40,000	2.530	$101,200			
Apportionment of net income:						
Net income					$320,350	
Minority interest (10% of $50,350)					5,035	
Consolidated net income (remainder)					$315,315	
Retained earnings						315,315
						$415,810

* 90% of $850 gain minus $300 loss (see statement of financial position).

TRIAL-BALANCE APPROACH

Company A and Subsidiary Company B
CONSOLIDATED WORKING PAPERS
As of December 31, 1967

	Co. B Pounds	Conversion Rate	Co. B Converted	Company A
Debits				
Current assets	30,000	2.530	$ 75,900	$ 100,000
Investment in Company B				130,000
Fixed assets (net)	80,000	2.510	200,800	800,000
Cost of sales	60,000	2.515	150,900	500,000
Depreciation	10,000	2.510	25,100	90,000
Other expenses	10,000	2.515	25,150	40,000
	190,000		$477,850	$1,660,000
Credits				
Current liabilities	20,000	2.530	$ 50,600	$ 60,000
Fixed liabilities	10,000	2.520	25,200	100,000
Sales	100,000	2.515	251,500	900,000
Shareholders' equity:				
Capital stock:				
Company A				500,000
Company B	40,000	2.500	100,000	
Retained earnings:				
Company A, 1/1/67				100,000
Company B, 1/1/67	20,000	2.500	50,000	
Exchange gain or loss			550	
	190,000		$477,850	$1,660,000

Income credits

Income debits

Net income
Apportionment of net income:
  Minority interest:

Income credits, Co. B		$251,500
Income debits, Co. B		201,150
Net income, Co. B		50,350
Minority interest (10%)		5,035
Consolidated net income (remainder)		

Retained earnings

Minority interest

TRIAL-BALANCE APPROACH (Continued)

COMPANY A AND SUBSIDIARY COMPANY B
CONSOLIDATED WORKING PAPERS
(Continued)

Adjustments & Eliminations		Income	Retained Earnings	Minority Interest	Consolidated Financial Position
					$ 175,900
$135,000*A*					(5,000)G
					1,000,800
		$ 650,900			
		115,100			
		65,150			
		$ 831,150	–0–	–0–	$1,171,700
					$ 110,600
					125,200
		$1,151,500			
					500,000
$ 90,000*A*				$10,000	
			$100,000		
45,000*A*				5,000	
			495	55	
$135,000	$135,000				
		$1,151,500			
		831,150			
		$ 320,350			
		5,035		5,035	
		$ 315,315	315,315		
			$415,810		415,810RE
				$20,090	20,090MI
					$1,171,700

A: To eliminate 90% of B's shareholders' equity against the investment account.

PROBLEMS

Problem 18–1. During the year the Domestic Company (an American organization) made the following purchases from the British Company:

		Rate of Exchange*	
Date of Purchase	Amount	Date of Purchase	Date of Payment
January 15	$14,000	2.80	2.80
April 15	21,000	2.80	2.81
July 15	28,100	2.81	2.82
October 15	56,400	2.82	2.80

* Dollars per pound.

Required:
Journal entries on the Domestic Company's books to record the payments of the above purchases, assuming that the billings were:
(1) In dollars.
(2) In pounds.

Problem 18–2. Prepare in journal entry form all entries necessary to record the following transactions on the books of the American Company and its branch in Spain:

(1) January 1.   American establishes the Spanish branch by transferring $10,000 cash to the branch.
(2) January 5.   Home office purchases in Spain and turns over to the branch equipment costing 735,000 pesetas.
(3) January 10.   The branch purchases merchandise for 200,000 pesetas.
(4) January 15.   The branch sells merchandise for 100,000 pesetas.
(5) January 15.   The branch purchases 120,000 pesetas worth of merchandise on account.
(6) January 20.   The branch sells merchandise on account for 60,000 pesetas.
(7) January 30.   The branch pays expenses for January totaling 40,000 pesetas.
(8) January 30.   The branch remits 100,000 pesetas to the home office.
The following rates of exchange were in effect during the month:

	Pesetas Per Dollar
January 1	50
January 5	49
January 10	48
January 15	46
January 20	48
January 30	52

Problem 18–3. On the basis of the following information, convert the branch trial balance of the English Company into dollars:

	Pounds	Pounds
Cash	1,400	
Accounts receivable	2,800	
Inventory, Jan. 1	1,800	
Remittances to home office	36,500	
Accounts payable		1,100
Remittances from home office		3,000
Home office		33,300
Sales		46,500
Merchandise from home office	24,000	
Purchases	2,400	
Expenses	15,000	
	83,900	83,900

Inventory, Dec. 31   3,400 pounds

BRANCH OFFICE

Balance, Jan. 1	$26,956	Remittances	$103,112
Shipments to branch	67,320		
Remittances	7,475		

Rates of exchange:	January 1	2.83
	December 31	2.80
	Average for year	2:81

Problem 18–4. (1) State the rule followed by a company in converting foreign currency into U.S. Dollars on:
  (a) Fixed assets of branches in foreign countries.
  (b) Inventory of merchandise bought by the foreign branch in that country.
  (2) If your basis of conversion differs as to the two items listed in (1), explain why there is such difference, including a discussion of the accounting principles that are involved.   (AICPA adapted)

Problem 18–5. Convert the following trial balances into dollars prior to consolidating them with the parent company—The U.S. Company. When converting, round off to the nearest dollar.

	Argentina Company (pesos)	Brazil Company (cruzeiros)	Panama Company (balboas)	Venezuela Company (bolivares)
Debits				
Inventories, 1/1/67	1,600,000	3,300,000	40,000	99,000
Other current assets	4,800,000	9,900,000	50,000	136,000
Fixed assets	8,000,000	16,100,000	130,000	603,000
Purchases	6,000,000	12,200,000	120,000	525,000
Expenses	1,500,000	3,350,000	30,000	140,000
	21,900,000	44,850,000	370,000	1,503,000

	Argentina Company (pesos)	Brazil Company (cruzeiros)	Panama Company (balboas)	Venezuela Company (bolivares)
Credits				
Sales	8,000,000	16,080,000	140,000	720,000
Current liabilities	600,000	1,100,000	30,000	130,000
Reserve for depreciation	2,000,000	4,200,000	20,000	200,000
Capital stock	10,000,000	20,000,000	100,000	300,000
Retained earnings, 1/1/67	1,300,000	3,470,000	80,000	153,000
	21,900,000	44,850,000	370,000	1,503,000
Inventories 12/31/67	2,100,000	3,900,000	70,000	110,000
Prevailing rates:	Pesos*	Cruzeiros*	Balboas*	Bolivares*
Jan. 1, 1967	37.00	68.00	1.00	3.30
Dec. 31, 1967	40.00	66.00	1.00	3.40
Average	38.00	67.00	1.00	3.36
Date fixed assets acquired	36.00	70.00	1.00	3.35
Date investment acquired	37.00	68.00	1.00	3.30

* In terms of dollars.

Problem 18–6. Using the data in problem 5 and the following facts, prepare consolidated working papers for the U.S. Company and its foreign subsidiaries for the year ended December 31, 1967. The U.S. Company carries the investments at *cost*.

U.S. COMPANY

TRIAL BALANCE

As OF DECEMBER 31, 1967

Debits

Inventories, 1/1/67	$ 600,000
Other current assets	900,000
Investments in foreign subsidiaries (90% acquired 1/1/67)	930,000
Fixed assets	2,000,000
Purchases	1,600,000
Expenses	200,000
	$6,230,000

Credits

Sales	$2,400,000
Current liabilities	1,200,000
Reserve for depreciation	800,000
Capital stock	1,000,000
Retained earnings, 1/1/67	830,000
	$6,230,000
Inventories 12/31/67	$ 500,000

Problem 18–7. (1) The ABC Manufacturing Corporation during the current year opened a manufacturing and selling branch in X country. At the year-end the official rate of currency exchange with country X was 12 to $1 and the

unofficial free market rate was 15 to $1. In combining the statements of the branch with those of the parent at year-end, at what value would the following branch accounts be reflected in the combined statement of financial position?

(a) Accounts receivable.
(b) Fixed assets.
(c) Inventories.
(d) Short-term debt.
(e) Long-term debt.

(2) How is the gain or loss resulting from the translation of the foreign currency into U.S. currency reflected in the financial statements of ABC Corporation at year-end?

(3) On June 30, 1966, ABC sold merchandise costing $75,000 to Z located in Y country, taking a note payable in Y currency. At the official rate of exchange on the date of sale the note had a fair market value of $100,000. On December 31, 1966, the note was worth $75,000 due to a change in the rate of exchange. On March 15, 1967, the note was paid in full and when immediately converted to U.S. dollars, ABC received $125,000. What journal entries are required at June 30, 1966, December 31, 1966, and March 15, 1967? Explain.

(AICPA adapted)

Problem 18–8. Company A (an American company) owns 90% of the stock of Company B (a British company) which it acquired January 1, 1967. Company A bought the stock from various stockholders in England and carries the investment at *cost*. The following data were taken from the books and records of the respective companies as of December 31, 1967:

	Co. A (dollars)	Co. B (pounds)
Inventories, 1/1/67	120,000	20,000
Other current assets	200,000	20,000
Investment in Company B	240,000	
Fixed assets	860,000	30,000
Purchases	700,000	120,000
Depreciation	34,400	1,200
Other expenses	400,000	90,000
	2,554,400	281,200
Sales	1,700,000	182,200
Reserve for depreciation	344,000	9,000
Capital stock	300,000	80,000
Retained earnings, 1/1/67	210,400	10,000
	2,554,400	281,200
Inventories, 12/31/67	140,000	70,000

Company A regularly sells merchandise to Company B. There was no intercompany profit in inventories at the beginning of the year, but Company B's inventory at the end of the year contained merchandise acquired from Company A at $25,000 above A's cost. During the year, Company A sold merchandise to Company B at a billed price of $210,000.

Rates of exchange were as follows:

January 1, 1967	2.85
December 31, 1967	2.88
Date of purchase of fixed assets	2.84
Average rate for the year	2.86

Required:

Prepare consolidated working papers with columns for income, retained earnings, minority interest, and financial position for the year ended December 31, 1967.

Problem 18-9. Trial balances as of December 31, 1967, of the parent company and its two subsidiaries were:

	Parent Company		Domestic Subsidiary		Mexican Subsidiary Pesos	
	Dr.	Cr.	Dr.	Cr.	Dr.	Cr.
Cash	$ 10,000		$ 1,500		10,000	
Accounts receivable, trade	30,000		8,000		35,000	
Accounts receivable, merchandise in transit to domestic subsidiary	4,000					
Inventories	20,000				83,000	
Investments at cost:						
Domestic subsidiary 900 shares acquired 12/31/66	9,000					
Foreign subsidiary 1,000 shares acquired 12/31/66	12,000					
Fixed assets	45,000		3,500		175,000	
Goodwill			2,000			
Cost of sales	300,000		15,000		300,000	
Depreciation	3,000		200		7,000	
Taxes	15,000		400		15,000	
Selling expenses	42,000		2,400		27,000	
Administrative and general expenses	35,000		2,000		18,000	
Dividends declared			1,000			
Sales, trade		$400,000		$21,000		381,000
Sales, domestic subsidiary		10,000				
Accounts payable, trade		25,000				7,000
Dividend payable				1,000		
Long-term debt due 1/1/70						100,000
Reserve for depreciation		15,000		2,000		75,000
Capital stock		50,000		*10,000		*100,000
Retained earnings, 1/1/67		25,000		2,000		7,000
	$525,000	$525,000	$36,000	$36,000	670,000	670,000

* 1,000 shares issued and outstanding.

Data:
In April 1967, the Mexican peso was devalued from U.S. $.12, the prevailing rate of exchange on December 31, 1966, to $.08 which was also the prevailing rate of exchange on December 31, 1967.

Required:
(1) Prepare working trial balance in U.S. dollars for the Mexican subsidiary.
(2) Prepare working papers for consolidated statements.   (AICPA adapted)

Problem 18-10. The Wiend Corporation acquired The Dieck Corporation on January 1, 1967 by the purchase at book value of all outstanding capital stock. The Dieck Corporation is located in a Central American country whose monetary unit is the peso. The Dieck Corporation's accounting records were continued without change; a trial balance, in pesos, of the balance sheet accounts at the purchase date follows:

THE DIECK CORPORATION
TRIAL BALANCE (IN PESOS)
JANUARY 1, 1967

	Debit	Credit
Cash	P 3,000	
Accounts receivable	5,000	
Inventories	32,000	
Machinery and equipment	204,000	
Allowance for depreciation		P 42,000
Accounts payable		81,400
Capital stock		50,000
Retained earnings		70,600
	P244,000	P244,000

The Dieck Corporation's trial balance, in pesos, at December 31, 1967 follows:

THE DIECK CORPORATION
TRIAL BALANCE (IN PESOS)
DECEMBER 31, 1967

	Debit	Credit
Cash	P 25,000	
Accounts receivable	20,000	
Allowance for bad debts		P 500
Due from The Wiend Corporation	30,000	
Inventories, December 31, 1967	110,000	
Prepaid expenses	3,000	
Machinery and equipment	210,000	
Allowance for depreciation		79,900
Accounts payable		22,000
Income taxes payable		40,000
Notes payable		60,000
Capital stock		50,000
Retained earnings		100,600
Sales—domestic		170,000
Sales—foreign		200,000

	Debit	Credit
Cost of sales	207,600	
Depreciation	22,400	
Selling and administrative expenses	60,000	
Gain on sale of assets		5,000
Provision for income taxes	40,000	
	P728,000	P728,000

The following additional information is available:

(1) All of The Dieck Corporation's export sales are made to its parent company and are accumulated in the account, Sales—Foreign. The balance in the account, Due from The Wiend Corporation, is the total of unpaid invoices. All foreign sales are billed in U.S. dollars. The reciprocal accounts on the parent company's books show total 1967 purchases as $471,000 and the total of unpaid invoices as $70,500.

(2) Depreciation is computed by the straight-line method over a ten-year life for all depreciable assets. Machinery costing P20,000 was purchased on December 31, 1966, and no depreciation was recorded for this machinery in 1966. There have been no other depreciable assets acquired since January 1, 1966, and no assets are fully depreciated.

(3) Certain assets that were in the inventory of fixed assets at January 1, 1966 were sold on December 31, 1967. For 1967 a full year's depreciation was recorded before the assets were removed from the books. Information regarding the sale follows:

Cost of assets	P14,000
Accumulated depreciation	4,900
Net book value	9,100
Proceeds of sale	14,100
Gain on sale	P 5,000

(4) Notes payable are long-term obligations that were incurred on December 31, 1966.

(5) No entries have been made in the Retained Earnings account of the subsidiary since its acquisition other than the net income for 1966. The Retained Earnings account at December 31, 1966 was converted to $212,000.

(6) The prevailing rates of exchange follow:

	Dollars per Peso
January 1, 1966	2.00
1966 average	2.10
December 31, 1966	2.20
1967 average	2.30
December 31, 1967	2.40

Required:

Prepare a worksheet to convert the December 31, 1967 trial balance of The Dieck Corporation from pesos to dollars. The worksheet should show the unconverted trial balance, the conversion rate, and the converted trial balance. (Do not extend the trial balance to statement columns. Supporting schedules should be in good form.)   (AICPA adapted)

CHAPTER 19

Expansion by combination

Expansion of a business enterprise may be accomplished in various ways. Some of these methods have been discussed in preceding chapters. In addition, expansion may be effected by what is called a "business combination." This term, as used in accounting, encompasses certain types of more rigorously defined combinations, such as merger, consolidation, pooling of interests, acquisition, and purchase. Generally a business combination is "any transaction whereby one economic unit obtains control over the assets and properties of another economic unit, regardless of the legal avenue by which such control is obtained and regardless of the resultant form of the economic unit emerging from the combination transaction."[1]

When two or more business entities are joined together by means of a combination, one of the predecessor entities (commonly referred to as the surviving entity) normally takes over the assets and liabilities of the other entities in the combination (hence, the term "takeover" is sometimes used to describe the transaction). The entities that have been "taken over" may lose their identity, as when they are legally merged into the surviving entity or when their former legal structure is eliminated by liquidation. Frequently, the entities taken over remain in existence as operating subsidiaries of the surviving entity. On occasion, an entirely new entity may be formed to take over the assets and liabilities of all the combining organizations.

[1] Wyatt, Arthur R., *A Critical Study of Accounting for Business Combinations*, American Institute of Certified Public Accountants, New York, 1963, p. 12.

The accounting problems created by a business combination transaction are often complex.   One problem is the classification of the transaction according to the type of business combination involved. The decision on classification has consequences of an accounting nature which have a long-run impact on financial results of the enterprise. Another problem involves recording and valuation decisions for the combination transaction.   If a given entity which has been taken over remains in existence as a subsidiary, many of the problems discussed in the several preceding chapters will assume importance.   The emphasis in the ensuing sections centers on the classification of a business combination and on the accounting problems which must be resolved once a classification has been made.

Types of Business Combinations

While any type of business organization—proprietorship, partnership, or corporation—may be a constituent of a business combination, by far the majority are corporations.   Thus, the discussion and examples that follow are in terms of corporations.

For accounting purposes business combinations are generally classified in one of two broad categories:

(1) Pooling of interests.
(2) Purchase.

As these two concepts emerged in the 1940's, business combinations were classified at the time of the transaction as either a pooling of interests or as a purchase, and this classification determined the appropriate accounting treatment.   Starting in the 1950's, however, the difference in concept between the two classes of business combinations became less well defined.   At the same time, two clearly different methods of accounting for business combinations emerged in practice.   These two accounting methods, also called pooling of interests and purchase, soon came to be determinative of the classification of a given business combination. Thus, while we may view the business combination accounting problem as, first, a determination of the kind of combination which has been consummated and, then, as a determination of the appropriate accounting treatment, the two parts are commonly reversed in practice.   That is, the accounting treatment decision is made first, and this decision governs the classification of the transaction.   The difference between the two types of business combinations insofar as accounting treatment is concerned is covered in some detail in a later section.

Definitions. In concept, a *pooling of interests* is a business combination in which the holders of all or substantially all of the ownership interests in the combining entities continue as holders of ownership interests in the entity that results or emerges from the combination. The resultant enterprise owns the assets and businesses of the constituent organizations, either directly or through ownership of the stock. A *purchase* is a business combination in which all or an important part of the ownership interests in one or more of the constituent entities is eliminated, that is, is no longer in an ownership position via ownership of stock.

Basic Accounting Distinctions

Two principal accounting distinctions exist between the accounting entries for a pooling of interests and those used for a purchase. One distinction lies in the accounting for the assets of the taken-over company, and the other concerns the accounting for retained earnings, or more broadly, shareholders' equity. These accounting distinctions both rest on a concept underlying the distinction between a pooling of interests and a purchase. This concept is that in a pooling-of-interests type of combination nothing of real economic substance has occurred. That is, the people who were shareholders prior to the business combination are still shareholders; the assets in use are unchanged; the relative interests of the various parties, if changed, are changed only in relatively minor respects. In a purchase combination, on the other hand, changes of economic substance have occurred. One group of stockholders has actually bought out another. Some previous ownership interests have been replaced, and one or more other quite substantive changes has occurred. These conceptual distinctions lead rather naturally to the two important differences in accounting treatment.

Pooling-of-Interests Accounting

Since nothing of real substance is deemed to have occurred in a pooling of interests, the accounting entries necessary to give effect to the combination leave existing relationships basically undisturbed. The basis of accountability for the taken-over entity is the book value of the net assets of the taken-over entity at the date of combination. This means that the company effecting the takeover will either debit various asset accounts for amounts as stated in the taken-over entity's ledger (in the situation in which the taken-over entity goes out of existence) or debit an investment account for the book value of the net assets (in the situation in which the taken-over entity will continue to operate as a subsidiary). The fair market value of the shares issued to effect the combination is of no consequence to the accounting entries. Certain exceptions to the above generalizations are permitted in order to place like assets on each company's books on a consistent basis. For example, inventories may be restated to move from LIFO to FIFO if this is the pricing basis used by the dominant company in the combination.

The credit entries emerging from the transaction likewise tend to continue existing relationships. Here, however, some adjustments are commonly necessary because of legal requirements. In general, however, the retained earnings of the taken-over entity become a credit to Retained Earnings on the dominant or surviving company's books. Capital Stock is credited for the par or stated value of the shares issued to effect the combination. Any additional credit necessary to make the entry balance goes to a capital surplus account. If the credits to Retained Earnings and Capital Stock as determined above exceed the book value of the net assets, the amount credited to Retained Earnings is scaled down to balance the entry. We can conclude that in a pooling of interests the retained earnings of the taken-over entity become retained earnings of the resultant enterprise in the absence of changes caused by legal requirements or adjustments to achieve consistency in asset bases.

Purchase Accounting

A combination classified as a purchase is accounted for like any other purchase or acquisition. The fair value of the consideration given or the fair value of the consideration acquired, whichever is more clearly evident, becomes the basis of accountability. In most business combinations the fair value of the consideration given, cash or shares of stock with a ready marketability, provides a valid starting point for determining the basis of accounting. In some situations a thorough consideration of all negotiations leading to the eventual combination may provide a more valid basis of accountability than the market value of shares given.

While this principle has many applications and is fairly simple in concept, in practice its application to a business combination may involve certain difficulties. The most significant difficulty probably lies in a determination of the proper accounting for the difference between the fair market value of the shares issued, or other basis of accountability, and the book value of the net assets acquired. Commonly the simple expedient of calling this difference "goodwill" is followed.

The overall problem is one that arises any time a group of different assets is purchased at a lump-sum price. Little justification appears to exist for the acquiring company to use the book values of the assets on the acquired company's books in accounting for the purchase. Rather, serious effort should be made to determine the fair values of the various assets acquired, and these values should become the basis of accountability on the acquiring company's books. Any difference between the purchase price and the sum of the fair values of the various identifiable assets, tangible and intangible, acquired could be labeled "goodwill." If the acquired company is to remain in existence as a subsidiary, the acquiring company should debit an Investment account for the fair value of the consideration given. The problem of allocating this cost to specific assets will become important at the date of consolidation.

The credit entries for a purchase combination are relatively simple to make. No portion of the credit can be made to Retained Earnings in a purchase combination. A long-standing and widely accepted rule of the American Institute of Certified Public Accountants states that the retained earnings of a subsidiary created prior to acquisition does not form a part of the consolidated retained earnings.[2]

The justification for crediting Retained Earnings in a pooling combination, as discussed above, lies in the concept that the pooling combination is not an acquisition, but merely the continuation of formerly separate entities as one entity. In a purchase combination Capital Stock is credited for the par or stated value of the shares given, and any amount necessary to balance the entry is credited to Capital Surplus. Of course, if cash or other assets are used to consummate the transaction, rather than stock, those assets would be credited.

Summary. The accounting treatment distinctions between a pooling-of-interests combination and a purchase combination are rather well defined and widely accepted. One should recognize, however, that significantly different results may be determined from the accounting records if a given combination is considered a pooling of interests rather than a purchase, or vice versa. The example to follow on pages 551–554 highlights this difference.

Classification of the Combination Transaction

The primary importance of the classification of a given combination transaction becomes clear once we grasp the implications of the two methods of accounting and recognize that the methods produce quite different results in accounting records and reports. Several attempts have been made to develop guidelines useful for classifying a combination

---

[2] American Institute of Certified Public Accountants, Committee on Accounting Procedure", *Accounting Research Bulletin 43*, Chapter 1a, "Rules Adopted by the Membership", p. 11, 1953. However, in a merger or consolidation effected legally at a date subsequent to acquisition retained earnings of the subsidiary accumulated since acquisition may become part of the consolidated retained earnings.

as a purchase or as a pooling of interests. The official pronouncement of the American Institute of Certified Public Accountants on this topic is *Accounting Research Bulletin 48*. *Bulletin 48* sets forth a number of criteria that we should consider in the classification of a combination transaction. *Opinion 6* of the Accounting Principles Board in effect supports the positions taken in *Bulletin 48*.

Principal emphasis is attached to the "attendant circumstances" of the transaction rather than to the legal form which is used or which emerges. One of the attendant circumstances concerns the continuity of ownership. As a general rule, if all ownership interests prior to the combination continue in ownership positions after the combination,[3] a pooling of interests classification is suggested. Thus, a combination effected by means of cash is a purchase combination since some former ownership interests hold cash rather than stock after the transaction. In the absence of factors indicating otherwise, a combination effected entirely by means of common stock suggests a pooling combination, since all stockholders prior to the combination continue as stockholders.

Another attendant circumstance is the relative voting rights. If the relative voting rights of the shareholders of the constituent companies of a combination are materially altered, the transaction takes on appearances of a purchase. This alteration can arise by using debt or nonvoting preferred stock rather than common stock to effect the combination. In addition, if a plan exists to retire a substantial part of the outstanding common stock or if substantial changes in ownership of one or more of the constituents occurs or is planned to occur, the combination takes on appearances of a purchase.

Other attendant circumstances include:

(1) Continuity of operations. The abandonment or sale of a large part of the business of one or more constituents suggests that the transaction is a purchase combination.
(2) Continuity of management. If the management of one of the constituents is eliminated or if its influence on overall management is small, a purchase combination is suggested.
(3) Relative size of the constituents. Where one of the constituent companies is clearly dominant, for example, where shareholders of one of the companies have 90 to 95% or more of the shares in the

---

[3] As used in *Accounting Research Bulletin 48*, the term "ownership interests" normally refers to common stock. However, in some cases the term may also include other classes of stock having senior or preferential rights, as well as classes whose rights may be restricted in certain respects.

resultant enterprise, a presumption exists that the combination is a purchase.[4]

As might be expected, many combinations have characteristics of both a pooling of interests and a purchase. In determining which classification is appropriate, no one factor is necessarily determinative. The absence of one of the conditions for a pooling of interests does not mean that the transaction is not necessarily classifiable as a pooling of interests. All the attendant circumstances are to be considered in deciding the classification of a given combination.

Practice Since *Accounting Research Bulletin 48*

In the several years since *Bulletin 48* was issued, accounting practice in the business combination area has tended to move away from the guidelines set forth in the *Bulletin*. Many of the criteria set forth now appear to have little influence on the classification of a combination. This is particularly true of the relative size criterion, and to a lesser degree it is true for the continuity of management and continuity of operations criteria. Even the continuity of ownership interests criterion has fallen by the wayside in some instances.

By 1967 most business combinations effected through the exchange of equity securities, common or preferred, were classified as poolings of interests if management so desired. The *Bulletin 48* criteria had little significance. As a result, the pooling-of-interests concept was applied to a substantial number of business transactions for which its propriety was questionable. The motivations of management for widespread application of this concept are discussed further in subsequent sections.

Proforma Statements

"Proforma" statements are often called "as if" or "giving effect" statements. While the rules of professional conduct of the public accounting profession generally prohibit a public accountant from attaching his name to financial statements which involve predictions of future earnings or events, proforma statements are acceptable in some circumstances. Most generally they are used to report the accounting effect of some contemplated specific transaction or set of transactions. They come into use in the business combination area when securities are to be issued to effect the combination. Requirements of the New York Stock Exchange and of the Securities and Exchange Commission deal with the issuance of a prospectus prior to the issuance or sale of a block of stock.

---

[4] American Institute of Certified Public Accountants, Committee on Accounting Procedure, *Accounting Research Bulletin 48*, 1957, pp. 2–3.

When a proposed business combination is to be effected by an exchange of shares, one part of the prospectus is a proforma balance sheet. Accountants serving management also commonly provide financial data and projections on an "as if" basis to provide information for making decisions.

A typical proposal to consummate a business combination may involve presentation in columnar form of:

(1) The financial statements of the combining companies
(2) The changes to be effected in the combination process
(3) Proforma statements giving effect to the proposed combination.

Proforma Statement—Illustrated. Companies A, B, and C decided to pool their resources and continue operations on a combined basis. To effect the combination Company A agreed to issue its capital stock in exchange for the outstanding capital stock of the other two companies. The basis for the exchange of stock was determined by considering relative market values, relative profitability of the three companies, and various other factors. The combination agreement provided that 1 share of A's stock would be issued for each 3 shares of B's, and that 1 share of A's would be issued for each 2 shares of C's stock. The combination was considered to have met the requirements necessary to be classified as a pooling of interests.

COMPANIES A, B, AND C
STATEMENT OF FINANCIAL POSITION
PROPOSED COMBINATION

Items	Co. A	Co. B	Co. C	Adjustments	Proforma
Cash	$ 30,000	$ 20,000	$ 25,000		$ 75,000
Receivables	60,000	50,000	40,000		150,000
Merchandise	70,000	40,000	50,000		160,000
Fixed assets (net)	240,000	315,000	196,000		751,000
Total assets	$400,000	$425,000	$311,000		$1,136,000
Payables	$ 50,000	$ 40,000	$ 60,000		$ 150,000
Capital stock (1,000 shares)	100,000			+500,000	600,000
Capital stock (par $50)		300,000		−300,000	—
Capital stock (par $50)			200,000	−200,000	—
Retained earnings	250,000			+136,000	386,000
Retained earnings		85,000		− 85,000	—
Retained earnings			51,000	− 51,000	—
Total equities	$400,000	$425,000	$311,000		$1,136,000

In some reports the data in the right-hand column are presented in statement form.

Accounting for Business Combinations—an Example

Agreement has been reached in principle for a business combination involving the Pitcher Company and the Vaughn Company. Negotiations have taken place over a period of months. The combination is to be effected by an exchange of common shares, and subsequent to the exchange the Vaughn Company is to be dissolved. The following data along with various other information were considered in the negotiations:

	Price Range of Common Stock		Earnings per Share	
	Pitcher	Vaughn	Pitcher	Vaughn
1965	26–32	7–11	$2.10	$ .70
1966	31–54	10–18	2.60	1.05
1967	46–65	16–33	3.00	1.45

Agreement was reached that the Pitcher Company would issue 800,000 shares of its $5 stated value common stock in exchange for the 2,000,000 outstanding shares of the Vaughn Company's $3 par value common stock, the exchange to be made on the basis of .4 share of Pitcher for each share of Vaughn stock exchanged. The exchange ratio of .4 to 1 was determined after lengthy negotiations. The relative price ranges of the common stock and the relative earnings per share were particularly important in the determination of the exchange ratio.

Other aspects of the combination were such that the independent certified public accountants for the Pitcher Company have indicated that the transaction can be accounted for either as a purchase or as a pooling of interests. An understanding has been reached with the Securities and Exchange Commission which will permit pooling-of-interests accounting.

The condensed statements of financial position of the two companies presented below were prepared just prior to the effective date of the combination. A proforma statement of financial position giving effect to the combination under each accounting alternative is to be prepared. Under the purchase alternative, the board of directors of the Pitcher Company has determined that a fair value for the shares to be issued in the combination is $51.25 per share.

In the pooling-of-interests column of the proforma statement all items except Capital Stock and Paid-in Surplus have been determined by combining (or pooling) like items in the separate company statements of financial position. This result is consistent with the pooling concept that nothing of economic substance happens in a combination. Even

PITCHER COMPANY AND VAUGHN COMPANY
CONDENSED STATEMENTS OF FINANCIAL POSITION
DECEMBER 31, 1967

Assets	Pitcher Co.	Vaughn Co.
Cash	$ 2,500,000	$ 800,000
Receivables	12,500,000	3,200,000
Inventories	21,000,000	6,000,000
Investments	14,000,000	—
Fixed assets (net)	42,000,000	12,000,000
Goodwill	2,400,000	—
Other assets	3,600,000	800,000
	$98,000,000	$22,800,000
Equities		
Current payables	$14,000,000	$ 3,800,000
Long-term debt	22,000,000	—
Capital stock	36,000,000	6,000,000
Paid-in surplus	4,200,000	4,000,000
Retained earnings	21,800,000	9,000,000
	$98,000,000	$22,800,000

PITCHER-VAUGHN COMBINATION
PROFORMA STATEMENT OF FINANCIAL POSITION
DECEMBER 31, 1967

Assets	Pooling of Interests	Purchase
Cash	$ 3,300,000	$ 3,300,000
Receivables	15,700,000	15,700,000
Inventories	27,000,000	27,000,000
Investments	14,000,000	14,000,000
Fixed assets (net)	54,000,000	54,000,000
Goodwill	2,400,000	24,400,000
Other assets	4,400,000	4,400,000
	$120,800,000	$142,800,000
Equities		
Current payables	$ 17,800,000	$ 17,800,000
Long-term debt	22,000,000	22,000,000
Capital stock ($5 stated value)	40,000,000	40,000,000
Paid-in surplus	10,200,000	41,200,000
Retained earnings	30,800,000	21,800,000
	$120,800,000	$142,800,000

the new balance of Retained Earnings combines the balances of Retained Earnings on the separate company statements. The noncombination of the Capital Stock and Paid-in Surplus items for each company results from legal rather than from accounting considerations. The Pitcher Company gave up 800,000 shares of $5 stated value stock and, therefore, should credit Capital Stock for $4,000,000. However, the par value of the Vaughn Company stock was $6,000,000. The excess of the par value of the Vaughn Company stock over the stated value of the Pitcher Company stock given in exchange ($2,000,000) is classified as Paid-in Surplus on the proforma statement. Under the pooling concept the agreed fair value per share of the Pitcher stock given in the combination has no bearing on the accounting procedures. It is apparent in the proforma statement that the objective of pooling is to effect a statement of financial position as similar as possible to the combined precombination statements.

Several differences appear in the column presenting the combination as a purchase on a proforma basis. Among the assets, the only item of difference is the Goodwill amount. On a proforma basis, it is stated at $22,000,000 greater than the combined Goodwill of the two companies (and also $22,000,000 greater than the Goodwill on a proforma pooling basis). This $22,000,000 is determined as follows: the fair value of the 800,000 shares of the Pitcher Company stock transferred in the combination, $41,000,000 (800,000 × $51.25), less the book value of the net assets of the Vaughn Company, $19,000,000. In many actual combinations effected during periods of rising prices, the difference between the fair value of the shares given in the combination transaction and the book value of the net assets acquired is substantial. In the illustration, this excess is classified as Goodwill in accounting for the combination.

Another difference exists in the amount reported as Retained Earnings. Under the purchase assumption the proforma statement shows $21,800,000 as Retained Earnings, or the same amount as reported separately by the Pitcher Company. The $9,000,000 Retained Earnings of the Vaughn Company is not carried forward as retained earnings, but is classified as Paid-in Surplus. The Paid-in Surplus amount under the purchase assumption is $41,200,000 on a proforma basis, whereas it was $10,200,000 on a proforma pooling basis. The difference of $31,000,000 is accounted for by the Goodwill increase ($22,000,000) and by the Retained Earnings decrease ($9,000,000) under the purchase assumption.

The proforma statement under the purchase assumption gives effect to the purchase concept by recording assets on the basis of the fair value of the consideration given and by carrying forward as retained earnings only the amount so reported on the acquiring company's statements.

This illustration of the proforma statement under the purchase assumption is oversimplified. The oversimplification lies in the treatment of the entire excess of the fair value of the shares transferred over the book value of the net assets acquired as Goodwill. While this conclusion is reached many times in practice, a better approach is to attempt to allocate any excess among specific assets, tangible and intangible, that appear undervalued. In a purchase combination little justification exists for carrying forward the asset book values which appear on the acquired company's books. For example, assume that an appraisal of the Vaughn Company assets indicated that replacement values for inventories and fixed assets (net) were $9,000,000 and $23,000,000 respectively. We might conclude that the undervaluation on the books for these assets could be one of the causes of the price difference between the value of the shares given and the book value of the assets. If this were the case, the proforma statement of financial position might appear as follows:

PITCHER VAUGHN COMBINATION
PROFORMA STATEMENT OF FINANCIAL POSITION (PURCHASE)
DECEMBER 31, 1967

Assets		Equities	
Cash	$ 3,300,000	Current Payables	$ 17,800,000
Receivables	15,700,000	Long-term Debt	22,000,000
Inventories	30,000,000	Common Stock	40,000,000
Investments	14,000,000	Paid-in Surplus	41,200,000
Fixed Assets (net)	65,000,000	Retained Earnings	21,800,000
Goodwill	10,400,000		
Other Assets	4,400,000		
	$142,800,000		$142,800,000

As previously noted, any adjustments necessary to place the accounting records of the two companies on a uniform basis are permissible under both the purchase and the pooling concepts.

Since the assumption was made that the Vaughn Company was to be dissolved, the Pitcher Company would make entries in its ledger accounts to give effect to the combination transaction. The entries made would result in new account balances as represented in the proforma statements. This is true under either the pooling or the purchase accounting treatment.

If the Vaughn Company were to be operated as a subsidiary, on the other hand, the Pitcher Company would debit a new account—Investment in Vaughn Company—for the appropriate exchange value. In the pooling case the debit to the investment account would be $19,000,000, while in the purchase example the debit would be for $41,000,000. In each situation a consolidated balance sheet would be prepared at the end of each fiscal period, following procedures discussed in earlier chapters.

Impact on Subsequent Financial Statements

From the examples presented in the preceding section it is apparent that for some business combinations the two alternative methods of accounting produce widely different statements of financial position. This conclusion is true in practice for a substantial portion of the combinations effected by American businesses. While the differences in financial position as illustrated can lead to different interpretations of financial position, the significance of the alternative accounting methods lies in the impact each has on the operating results of subsequent fiscal periods.

The results of operations subsequent to a business combination can vary, of course, from the sum of the results of the separate companies for a wide variety of reasons. Managerial efficiencies, production efficiencies, marketing efficiencies, and many other factors may improve operating results in periods subsequent to the combination. The reverse can also result from a variety of unanticipated inefficiencies or uneconomical events. Disregarding all of these for the moment, the results of operations may be influenced purely by the accounting treatments accorded the combination transaction.

If the combination is accounted for as a pooling of interests, the accounting treatment will have a minimal effect on operating results of future periods. All deferred items carried forward as assets on the combined balance sheet would be the same as would have been reported on the separate company statements. Amortizations and other charges to operations in future periods would not be affected by the accounting entries. Since the accounting entries for the pooling did not alter previously existing book values, subsequent earnings statements on a combined basis would approximate the aggregate of the separate company earnings statements, disregarding other effects which the combination event could produce on the operations of the various companies.

A similar conclusion can be reached in some instances in which the combination transaction is accounted for as a purchase. In the initial example of purchase accounting presented in the preceding section all deferred items carried forward as assets in the combined balance sheet are the same as would have been reported on the separate company statements, with the exception of goodwill. If the resulting company determines that the proper accounting treatment for the goodwill is to carry it forward intact as an asset, the subsequent earnings statements on a combined basis would also approximate the aggregate of the separate company earnings statements, disregarding the other effects on operations which the combination event might produce. In effect, the only asset difference as between purchase and pooling accounting is sterilized in that it has no impact on future earnings.

If the amount of goodwill which is recognized at the time of, or is created by, a business combination is amortized by charges to income, however, operating results subsequent to the combination will be affected by the purchase or pooling accounting decision. Earnings subsequent to the combination will be lower if the combination is accounted for as a purchase than they will be if the combination is accounted for as a pooling. The amount of the difference will be directly attributable to the decision made on the manner of accounting for the combination transaction.

A similar result will follow if the combination is accounted for as a purchase and the difference between the fair value of the assets given in exchange and the book value of the net assets acquired is allocated among specific tangible and intangible assets. To the extent that the specific tangible or intangible assets are subject to periodic amortization, results of operations in subsequent periods will be affected by the amortization.

Referring to the Pitcher-Vaughn combination, the following comparisons can be made:

| | | | Purchase Accounting | |
| | | | New Goodwill Amortized— 10 Years | |
	Pooling Accounting	No Goodwill Amortization		New Fixed Asset Life—15 Years. Inventory on FIFO Basis
Shares outstanding after combination	8,000,000	8,000,000	8,000,000	8,000,000
1967 combined net income	$24,500,000	$24,500,000	$24,500,000	$24,500,000
1967 earnings per share combined basis	$3.06	$3.06	$3.06	$3.06
1968 proforma net income	$24,500,000	$24,500,000	$22,300,000	$19,966,667
1968 proforma earnings per share	$3.06	$3.06	$2.79	$2.50

The impact on subsequent earnings of the decision on how to account for a business combination should be apparent from this oversimplified illustration. Considerable evidence exists that awareness of these subsequent effects has had a significant impact on decisions on how to account for a given business combination.

Accounting for Combinations—a Reevaluation

Any discussion of accounting for business combinations embodies a number of issues:

(1) *Proper accounting for goodwill.* Once goodwill has been determined to exist in a given transaction, a problem arises in accounting for this item in subsequent periods. Present accounting practice permits goodwill to be carried forward as an asset indefinitely so long as no apparent limitation on its useful life exists, permits direct charge-offs of goodwill to retained earnings when abrupt loss of value arises, and permits amortization of goodwill by charges to income when a period of limited useful life is evident (See Chapter 5, *Accounting Research Bulletin 43*). Pressure brought by the Securities and Exchange Commission subsequent to World War II for the write-off of goodwill had a noticeable effect on accounting practice. A considerable portion of these write-offs was made through the income statement because of the SEC's policy against direct charges and credits to retained earnings.

(2) *Determination of value in exchange transactions.* As previously indicated, accountants have long followed a principle of valuation in noncash transactions which stipulates the appropriate value of assets received as the fair value of the consideration given or the fair value of the consideration received, whichever is more clearly evident. When the consideration given is stock which is traded in a reasonably broad market, the value of this stock provides an apparently valid basis for valuing the consideration received. However, even in a reasonably broad market, prices of shares of stock may have rather wide variations for obscure reasons. Further, listed prices commonly relate to the trading value of shares in relatively small quantities, certainly smaller than the number of shares issued to effect a combination. When purchase accounting is appropriate, serious consideration should be given to establishing a fair value for accountability. The fair value of the shares issued as determined from the stock market should be no more than a point of departure in determining the exchange value.

(3) *The nature of a transaction.* Insofar as accounting entries are concerned, accountants are principally concerned with business transactions. Business transactions generally embody some exchange of values, and the accountant must explain this exchange. Most accountants would agree that a business combination is a business transaction

and that it involves an exchange of values. Those accountants who support pooling-of-interests accounting, however, hold that in the combination transaction nothing of economic substance has happened. As a result, these accountants account for the combination *as if* no transaction occurred.

(4) *Existence of alternative accounting principles.* The business combination area is one of several examples in current accounting practice in which alternative accounting principles exist. In some areas the alternatives are supportable as being properly applicable in differing circumstances. In the combination area, however, the situation is that two alternative procedures are generally accepted and have come to be considered appropriate for similar situations. That is, either alternative may be used for most noncash business combinations. As the preceding illustration showed, the use of one alternative rather than the other leads to differing operating results in subsequent periods. The existence of this type of acceptable alternative in accounting practice does little to increase the understandability of accounting reports.

Distribution of Securities

In some business combinations various types of securities are issued. To illustrate different methods for distributing securities in exchange when a combination is formed, assume the following facts:

	Company A	Company B	Company C	Total
Adjusted book value of assets contributed:				
Fixed assets	$100,000	$300,000	$100,000	$500,000
Current assets	100,000	100,000	200,000	400,000
Total assets	$200,000	$400,000	$300,000	$900,000
Book value of equities:				
Current liabilities	$ 50,000	$ 50,000	$100,000	$200,000
Fixed liabilities	—	100,000	—	100,000
Shareholders' equity	150,000	250,000	200,000	600,000
Total equities	$200,000	$400,000	$300,000	$900,000
Annual earnings:				
1967	$ 25,000	$ 20,000	$ 21,000	$ 66,000
1966	23,000	18,000	17,000	58,000
1965	19,500	22,000	14,500	56,000
Average annual earnings	$ 22,500	$ 20,000	$ 17,500	$ 60,000
Average rate of return on shareholders' equity	15%	8%	8.75%	10%

It is estimated that total average earnings will increase to $75,000 per year and that the competitive position of the three companies will be improved by the combination.

Plans under consideration for distributing securities to the three companies by a newly formed Company D, in exchange for the stockholders' rights in the separate companies, are:

(1) Common stock with a par value of $600,000 to be issued in the ratio of relative shareholder equity contributed.

(2) Common stock with a par value of $600,000 to be issued in the ratio of former earning power.

(3) Excess earning power (over 8%) to be capitalized at 16% and treated as goodwill, and common stock to be issued in the ratio of relative shareholder equity plus the goodwill contributed. Total capital of the three companies was $600,000, and an 8% return on this would have been $48,000. Since $60,000 was earned, the excess is $12,000, to be capitalized at 16%. Common stock to be issued is $600,000 plus $75,000 ($12,000 ÷ .16), or $675,000.

(4) Preferred stock (6%), to be issued in payment for the shareholder equity contributed, and common stock to be issued for the earning power contributed (earnings in excess of 6% to be capitalized at 16%). Here the excess earnings are $24,000 ($60,000 − 6% of $600,000). When capitalized at 16%, $24,000 = $150,000.

(5) Bonds to be issued in payment for 50% of the portion of the shareholder equity represented by fixed assets; preferred stock to be issued in payment for any balance of the shareholder equity contributed; Class A Common Stock to be issued for the goodwill, computed as excess of past earnings over 8% capitalized at 8%, contributed by each company ($60,000 − 8% of $600,000 = $12,000 ÷ .08 = $150,000); and Class C Common Stock to be issued equally to each company for the anticipated increase in earnings due to the combination, capitalized at 20%.

The proposed distribution of securities under each plan would be as shown on page 560. Any evaluation of the relative merits of the five plans for distributing securities should as a minimum give consideration to the following analysis:

Plan 1. While this plan gives an equitable allocation of the net assets to the contributing companies, future earnings of the combined companies will not be allocated to stockholder interests in the manner they would have been if the companies had not merged. Companies B and C

	Company A	Company B	Company C	Total
Plan 1:				
Common stock	$150,000	$250,000	$200,000	$600,000
Plan 2:				
Common stock	$225,000	$200,000	$175,000	$600,000
Plan 3:				
Common stock				
For equity	$150,000	$250,000	$200,000	$600,000
For goodwill (excess earnings over 8% capitalized at 16%)	65,625	–0–	9,375	75,000
Total	$215,625	$250,000	$209,375	$675,000
Plan 4:				
Preferred stock (6%)	$150,000	$250,000	$200,000	$600,000
Common stock (excess earnings over 6% capitalized at 16%)	84,375	31,250	34,375	150,000
Total	$234,375	$281,250	$234,375	$750,000
Plan 5:				
Bonds (50% of fixed assets)	$ 50,000	$150,000	$ 50,000	$250,000
Preferred stock	100,000	100,000	150,000	350,000
Class A, Common	131,250	–0–	18,750	150,000
Class B, Common	25,000	25,000	25,000	75,000
	$306,250	$275,000	$243,750	$825,000

would receive a greater proportion while Company A's share would be reduced.

Plan 2. This plan will allocate earnings on an equitable basis as represented by past earnings of the separate companies, but the stockholdings acquired by each company will not be in proportion to the assets contributed by each company. If the combination were to be liquidated, Company B might not receive an equitable share of the assets distributed whereas Company A might receive an excessive share of the distributed assets.

Plan 3. Unless the goodwill can be realized in case the combination is liquidated, this plan is subject to the same reservation as Plan 2. In addition, it may involve including an amount of goodwill as an asset of the combination. If goodwill is not recorded on the books of the combination, this plan is a compromise between Plan 1 and Plan 2.

Plan 4. Provided the preferred stock is participating, this plan has merit. It provides a means of giving the new stockholders an equity claim for assets contributed which will be returned to them upon dissolution of the business through the preferred stock. By making the preferred stock preferred as to dividends in an amount equal to a fair earnings rate on assets, common stock needs to be distributed only to companies contributing earning power in excess of the basic rate. As a result of this arrangement, earnings will be distributed among the various stockholder interests in the same proportion as they would have if the combination had not been formed. Should the combined entity produce income in excess of what had previously been the total normal earnings of the separate companies, it is equitable that such excess earnings should be distributed to both the new preferred stockholders and the new common stockholders. This can be accomplished by making the preferred stock participating with the common stock in all distributions of earnings in excess of the amount which it appears would have been earned had the companies remained as separate entities.

A variation of this plan used by one company was to issue common stock on the basis of relative earning power contributed by the separate companies, and to issue convertible preferred stock to stockholders for the book value of the assets not covered by the common stock. To illustrate the procedure, assume Companies A, B, and C contribute net assets of $100,000 each to a new company and earning power of $1,000, $5,000, and $10,000, respectively. The distribution of the common stock would be on the ratio of 1:5:10. The earnings of the company with the highest rate of return is C with a 10% return. Capitalizing the earnings of each company at 10% indicates the amount of common stock to be issued as follows:

	Earnings	Capitalized Value
A	$ 1,000	$ 10,000
B	5,000	50,000
C	10,000	100,000
Common stock to be issued		$160,000

If the $160,000 of common stock is distributed as indicated and earnings are paid only on common stock (the preferred stock would normally be assigned a dividend rate but to keep the illustration simple assume the preferred receives no dividend and is preferred as to assets on dissolution only) earnings of the combination will be distributed in accordance with the earning power contributed by the separate companies.

To provide for the assets contributed by the separate companies for which common stock is not issued, convertible preferred stock may be issued, as follows:

	A	B	C
Assets contributed	$100,000	$100,000	$100,000
Common stock issued	10,000	50,000	100,000
Preferred stock	$ 90,000	$ 50,000	$ -0-

The idea involved in this plan was that if the assets not covered by the common stock should start earning greater income, the market price of the common stock would react accordingly, and by converting the preferred stock the preferred stockholders would receive the earnings arising due to their contribution of assets.

Plan 5. This plan represents an attempt to equalize the risk of loss, provide for equitable rights to assets contributed on liquidation, distribute future earnings equal in amount to past earnings of the separate companies as such earnings would have been distributed had the combination not taken place, and provide for an equal distribution of excess earnings due to the combination. It is based on an assumption that future earnings will be greater than, or at least equal to, past combined earnings.

Under the plan the bonds provide the greatest protection against loss for the company contributing proportionately more fixed assets than the other companies. The preferred stock assures the various stockholders of protection against unfair distribution at liquidation of their contributed assets. The Class A common stock assures a fair distribution of earning power contributed by each company, while the class B common stock provides for a fair distribution of excess earnings among the stockholders.

A variation of this plan, when only one class of common stock is issued, was used by a company a few years ago. Under this plan the common stock was issued for the goodwill but a provision in the combination agreement provided that the additional shares would be issued on the basis of future excess earnings attributable to the combined contributed assets. This method was used because it was felt that the record of past earnings was not representative of earning power.

There are, of course, many variations from these five plans to be found in practice. The selection and presentation of a suitable plan for the distribution of securities in a business combination requires considerable experience and judgment.

PROBLEMS

Problem 19–1. The balance sheets of the J. K. Foster Co. and the P. C. Baker Co. as of October 31, 1967 are presented below. On that date, following a lengthy period of negotiations, a merger of the two companies was effected, with the resulting company to be known as Foster-Baker, Inc. In the merger, the J. K. Foster Co. was to exchange 250,000 of its authorized, but unissued, shares in exchange for all the shares of the Baker Co., on the basis of $1\frac{1}{4}$ shares of Foster for each share of Baker. Market values of the respective shares on October 31 were:

J. K. Foster Co. stock,   20
P. C. Baker Co. stock,   25

During the preceding three months the respective shares had traded in the following ranges: Foster, $18\frac{1}{2}$–22; Baker 22–$26\frac{3}{4}$.

	Foster Co.	Baker Co.
Cash	$ 1,200,000	$ 400,000
Receivables	1,400,000	600,000
Inventories	4,000,000	800,000
Fixed assets (net)	11,400,000	2,000,000
	$18,000,000	$3,800,000
Payables	$ 3,000,000	$ 800,000
Common stock (par $100)	10,000,000	2,000,000
Paid-in surplus	1,000,000	–0–
Retained income	4,000,000	1,000,000
	$18,000,000	$3,800,000

Required:

(1) Present a statement of financial position for Foster-Baker, Inc., on the assumption that the business combination is a pooling of interests.

(2) Present a statement of financial position of Foster-Baker, Inc., on the assumption that the business combination is a purchase.

Problem 19–2. The Bess Co. has been negotiating several months to effect a combination with the Tate Co. The book value of the net assets of the Tate Co. at the present time is $8,000,000. At current market prices the Bess Co. would issue about $12,000,000 in common stock in exchange for all the common stock of the Tate Co. Of this difference about one half can be attributed to under-valued assets (inventory and properties) on the Tate Co. books, and the other half represents the Tate Co.'s favorable earning capacity. Several unresolved questions remain, including whether to operate Tate as a subsidiary, how to account for the combination, and effect on future earnings.

Required:

Write a brief discussion which might be helpful to the Bess Co. management on the following points:

(1) How would the Bess Co. statement of financial position differ if the Tate Co. were operated as a subsidiary as opposed to being a division in a merged company?

(2) What would be the principal differences in accounting if the combination were considered to be a pooling of interests as opposed to a purchase?

(3) Would the decision made as to a pooling of interests or a purchase affect subsequent income statements? Why?

Problem 19–3. Presented below are condensed balance sheets of three companies as of May 31, 1967. All companies are in the same industry. Effective as of that date, the Regis Co. obtained control of both the Tippit Co. and the Peoples Co. through exchanges of stock with the respective shareholders. In both instances, the managements of the two acquired companies were to continue to operate their former companies as departments of the Regis Co. The shareholders of both Tippit and Peoples agreed not to sell their newly acquired Regis Co. shares for a period of at least two years.

	Regis Co.	Tippit Co.	Peoples Co.
Cash	$ 2,000,000	$ 200,000	$ 400,000
Receivables	18,000,000	600,000	700,000
Inventories	42,000,000	1,400,000	1,000,000
Investments	30,000,000	300,000	–0–
Plant, property, and equipment	85,000,000	2,600,000	1,500,000
Other assets	6,000,000	400,000	–0–
Goodwill	8,000,000	–0–	–0–
	$191,000,000	$5,500,000	$3,600,000
Current liabilities	$ 20,000,000	$1,300,000	$ 500,000
Bonds payable	40,000,000	–0–	–0–
Common stock—par $20	100,000,000	–0–	–0–
Common stock—par $100	–0–	3,000,000	2,500,000
Paid-in surplus	4,000,000	900,000	–0–
Retained earnings	27,000,000	300,000	600,000
	$191,000,000	$5,500,000	$3,600,000

Separate negotiations were conducted with the boards of directors of the Tippit Co. and the Peoples Co. Each agreement indicated that the Regis Co. would issue 140,000 shares of its $20 par value common stock to the shareholders of the respective companies in exchange for their shares. During the 90 days prior to May 31, 1967 the common stocks of the three companies had traded in the following ranges:

Regis Co.	28–32
Tippit Co.	90–124
Peoples Co.	116–163

The board of directors of the Regis Co. decided: (1) to account for the Tippit combination as a purchase, using the average of the range of market prices for the Regis Co. stock during the 90 days prior to May 31, 1967 as a basis for the accounting; and (2) to account for the Peoples combination as a pooling of interests. The Regis Co.'s independent auditors and the SEC approved these decisions.

Required:
(1) Prepare a statement of financial position of the Regis Co. giving effect to the Tippit Co. combination only.
(2) Prepare a statement of financial position of the Regis Co. giving effect to the Peoples Co. combination only.

(3) Prepare a statement of financial position for the Regis Co. giving effect to both the Tippit and Peoples combinations.

(4) Why would the board of directors of the Regis Co. decide to account for the two combinations in the manner indicated? As their independent auditor how would you support your decision to approve the board actions?

(5) Why might the Regis Co. pay the same price for both companies?

Problem 19–4. On January 1, 1967 Corporation Z acquired all of the outstanding stock of Corporation M in order to combine the two businesses. Z issued $100,000 par value of its stock (which had a market value of $300,000) to the stockholders of M in exchange for their stock. Immediately upon the exchange of the stock, Corporation M was dissolved and Z took over the net assets. As of January 1, 1967 Corporation M had $100,000 of stock outstanding; $100,000 of paid-in surplus; and $100,000 of retained earnings.

Required:
(1) Give two ways that these transactions may be recorded on the books of Corporation Z.
(2) State the circumstances under which each of the two treatments would be appropriate and give the reasoning supporting each treatment.

(AICPA adapted)

Problem 19–5. Effective December 31, 1967 Wesco Corporation proposes to acquire, in exchange for common stock, all of the assets and liabilities of Southco Corporation and Eastco Corporation, after which Southco and Eastco will distribute the Wesco stock to their shareholders in complete liquidation and dissolution. Wesco proposes to increase its outstanding stock for purposes of these acquisitions. Balance sheets of each of the corporations immediately prior to merger on December 31, 1967 are given below. The assets are deemed to be worth their book values.

	Wesco	Southco	Eastco
Current assets	$ 2,000,000	$ 500,000	$ 25,000
Fixed assets (net)	10,000,000	4,000,000	200,000
	$12,000,000	$4,500,000	$225,000
Current liabilities	$ 1,000,000	$ 300,000	$ 20,000
Long term debt	3,000,000	1,000,000	105,000
Capital stock ($10 par)	3,000,000	1,000,000	50,000
Retained earnings	5,000,000	2,200,000	50,000
	$12,000,000	$4,500,000	$225,000
Other data relative to acquisition:			
Shares outstanding	300,000	100,000	5,000
Fair market value per share	$40	$40	$30
Number of shares Wesco stock to be exchanged:			
for Southco assets		100,000	
for Eastco assets			5,000
Old management to continue		Yes	No
Old shareholders to elect director on Wesco board		Yes	No

Required:

(1) The terms *purchase* and *pooling of interests* describe two methods designating the results of bringing together two or more corporations into a combination for the purpose of carrying on the previously conducted businesses. Define the terms *purchase* and *pooling of interests* as used to designate business combinations.

(2) Describe the accounting treatment in each case.

(3) Prepare Wesco's journal entries from the above data to record the combination of Wesco, Southco, and Eastco.   (AICPA adapted)

Problem 19–6. Mr. J. T. Hendrix owns three corporations, A, B, and C. The three companies are in different industries, have different managements, and operate completely independently of each other. At times Mr. Hendrix has borrowed money from one company and loaned it to another company. Also, he sold 10% of his interest in B to C for $20,000 and loaned that money to B. The financial statements of the three companies on December 31, 1967, are as follows:

	A	B	C
Due from J. T. Hendrix	$ 10,000		
Investment in B (10%)			$ 20,000
Due from A		$ 6,000	
Other assets	370,000	184,000	430,000
Total assets	$380,000	$190,000	$450,000
Due to J. T. Hendrix		$ 25,000	$ 5,000
Other liabilities	$ 40,000	15,000	95,000
Capital stock	300,000	100,000	300,000
Retained earnings	40,000	50,000	50,000
Total equities	$380,000	$190,000	$450,000

Required:

Prepare a combined statement of financial position, showing Mr. Hendrix a composite picture of his holdings.

Problem 19–7. A news release of the SEC is presented below:

Futterman-Dupont Hotel Company, 580 Fifth Ave., *New York*, filed a registration statement (File 2–15148) with the SEC, seeking registration of $1,706,900 of Limited Partnership Interests.

The company is a limited partnership consisting of Robert A. Futterman, I. Theodore Leader and M. Joshua Aber, as General Partners, and Rosalie Futterman, Beatrice Leader, and eight other individuals as original Limited Partners. The partnership has purchased the land and the Dupont Plaza Hotel at Dupont Circle in Washington, D.C., from Sidney B. Fink as trustee for the stockholders of Dupont Plaza, Inc. The purchase price was $4,565,000, of which $1,565,000 was paid in cash and the balance by taking title subject to a $3,000,000 mortgage. The partnership is offering $975,000 of Limited Partnership interests to repay monies borrowed for the purposes of closing title and paying incidental acquisition costs. The original Limited Partners also are offering their Limited Partnership interests in the amount of $731,900. The offering is to be made in $25,000 units. The properties are leased for slightly over 21 years to Dupont Plaza, Inc., The Babin Company, Clinton B. Snyder, Max Siegal and Paul M. Schreibman.

Required:
(1) What effect will the consummation of this plan have on the financial position of Dupont Plaza, Inc.?

(2) Should this be considered a business combination for reporting purposes? Would your answer be the same if the Futterman-Dupont Hotel Company held other assets besides the hotel?

Problem 19–8. Company A and Company B have considered a merger. At issue is the proper ratio at which their shares shall be exchanged. Neither stock is listed on any stock exchange. Earnings and book value of the two companies are:

	A	B
Book value of capital stock (10,000 shares for A and 5,000 shares for B)	$900,000	$400,000
Average annual earnings	80,000	80,000

In addition A has an asset which will reduce B's future annual expenses by $20,000 a year for 5 years, if the merger is accomplished. A requests and receives B's approval to treat the $20,000 annual cost savings as an asset, by discounting it at the rate of earnings currently enjoyed by B.

Required:
Suggest a basis for exchanging the stock for the merger. Assume A's stock is to be surrendered for new stock of B.

Problem 19–9. The Argonat Company and the Bassilla Company are considering a merger under which all of the Bassilla outstanding stock would be sold to Argonat in exchange for stock of Argonat. The basis of exchange of the stock is 1 share of Argonat for 1.3 shares of Bassilla. Fractional shares shall be paid in cash at $130 per share. The agreement has to be approved by the stockholders. Condensed financial statements of the two companies are:

	Argonat	Bassilla
Cash	$ 60,000	$ 50,000
Receivables	100,000	180,000
Merchandise	100,000	200,000
Fixed assets	800,000	400,000
Allowance for depreciation	(300,000)	(100,000)
Total assets	$760,000	$730,000
Liabilities	$150,000	$200,000
Capital stock (par $100)	500,000	500,000
Retained earnings	110,000	30,000
Total equities	$760,000	$730,000

Adjustments needed to value the assets of both companies on a consistent basis are:

(1) Increase Bassilla's merchandise by $20,000.
(2) Decrease Argonat's accumulated depreciation by $10,000.
(3) Increase Argonat's liabilities by $20,000.

Required:

Prepare a report showing adjustments and eliminations and a proforma statement of financial position, assuming a pooling of interest.

Problem 19–10. Company A purchased 90% of the stock of Company B, paying for the stock by issuing 2 shares of A's stock for 1 share of B's stock. Financial statements of the two companies immediately prior to the exchange of stock, in condensed form, were:

	A	B
Assets	$800,000	$400,000
Liabilities	$100,000	$ 20,000
Capital stock (no par)	600,000	200,000
Retained earnings	100,000	180,000
Total	$800,000	$400,000

The market prices of the stock on the date agreed upon for the exchange were:

	Price per Share	Number of Shares Outstanding
Company A	$ 80	12,000
Company B	160	4,000

Required:

(1) Prepare a consolidated statement of financial position assuming:
   (*a*) The merger is considered a purchase by A.
   (*b*) The merger is considered a pooling of interests of the two companies.
(2) Which procedure is more realistic?

Problem 19–11. On April 30, 1967 Investment Co. agrees to purchase the common stock of Consolidated Co. for a tentative price of $180,000. The purchase price is to be reduced by the amount, if any, by which the total book value of the shares of Consolidated Co. as of January 31, 1967 exceeded the total book value as of April 30, 1967.

The balance sheets of Consolidated Co. were as follows:

Assets	April 30, 1967	January 31, 1967
Current assets	$ 55,000	$ 56,000
Fixed assets, less accumulated depreciation	76,000	78,000
Investment in and advances to Industries, Inc.	20,200	14,100
	$151,200	$148,100
Liabilities and Owners' Equity		
Current liabilities	$ 27,000	$ 30,000
Capital stock	17,000	17,000
Retained earnings	107,200	101,100
	$151,200	$148,100

The balance sheets of Industries, Inc., subsidiary of Consolidated Co., were as follows:

Assets	April 30, 1967	January 31, 1967
Current assets	$ 10,000	$ 18,100
Other assets	1,200	1,200
Fixed assets, less accumulated depreciation	4,300	18,600
	$ 15,500	$ 37,900
Liabilities and Owners' Equity		
Notes payable	$ 5,000	$ 14,300
Accounts payable—trade	5,800	8,600
Accrued liabilities	2,000	2,200
	$ 12,800	$ 25,100
Long-term debt:		
Notes payable	18,500	19,400
Advance from Consolidated Co.	250	6,400
	$ 18,750	$ 25,800
Capital stock	700	1,000
Paid-in capital	19,250	10,000
Deficit	(36,000)	(24,000)
	$ 15,500	$ 37,900

The agreement provided that the book value of Consolidated Co. should be determined in accordance with generally accepted accounting principles except that the shares of Industries, Inc., should be included at their book value, if any. In the absence of a book value, the liabilities of Consolidated Co. are to be increased by a proportionate amount of the excess of the liabilities of Industries, Inc., over its assets; the proportion shall be the percentage of outstanding stock owned. The excess of liabilities over assets shall be reduced by any loss sustained by Industries, Inc., in the transfer of certain assets to its sole minority stockholder in cancellation of its promissory note.

During the period from January 31, 1967 to April 30, 1967 accumulated advances made by Consolidated Co. in the amount of $12,250 were transferred to Paid-in Capital by Industries, Inc.

On March 31, 1967 Industries, Inc., sold certain assets to its minority stockholder in consideration of the cancellation of a note payable to him. The transaction resulted in a book loss of $6,100. As part of this transaction the minority stockholder surrendered all of his stock, 30% of the outstanding stock, to Industries, Inc., for cancellation.

Required:

(1) Prepare schedules showing the net book value of Consolidated Co. at January 31, 1967 and April 30, 1967, computed in accordance with the terms of the sales agreement.

(2) Compute the adjustment, if any, to the tentative purchase price.

(AICPA adapted)

Problem 19-12. Financial statements of the Orange Corporation and the Blue Corporation appear below:

STATEMENTS OF FINANCIAL POSITION
JUNE 30, 1967

Assets	Orange Corporation	Blue Corporation
Cash	$ 25,500	$ 1,500
Receivables, net	24,500	7,500
Inventories	42,000	8,800
Due from Blue Corporation	7,600	
Fixed assets, less depreciation	59,500	35,800
Other assets	4,500	200
	$163,600	$ 53,800

Liabilities		
Accounts and notes payable	$ 22,600	$ 35,400
Due to Orange Corporation		7,600
Accrued expenses	1,500	2,200
Federal income tax payable	9,500	
Total liabilities	33,600	45,200
Capital stock, $10 par value	50,000	
Capital stock, $100 par value		25,000
Capital contributed in excess of par value	30,000	32,000
Retained earnings, December 31, 1966	43,000	(42,300)
Net income (loss) from January 1, 1967	9,500	(6,100)
Dividends paid	(2,500)	
Total stockholders' equity	130,000	8,600
	$163,600	$ 53,800

STATEMENTS OF INCOME AND EXPENSE
FOR THE SIX MONTHS ENDED JUNE 30, 1967

	Orange Corporation	Blue Corporation
Sales	$150,000	$ 60,000
Cost of sales	105,000	54,000
Gross profit	45,000	6,000
Operating expenses	31,000	8,200
Operating profit (loss)	14,000	(2,200)
Other income (deductions)	5,000	(3,900)
Net income (loss) before taxes	19,000	(6,100)
Provision for income taxes	9,500	
Net income after taxes	$ 9,500	$ (6,100)

The net incomes (losses) before income taxes for the two corporations for the last six years are as follows (net income per books and net taxable income are the same):

	Orange Corporation	Blue Corporation
1961	$18,000	$(10,000)
1962	(7,500)	4,000
1963	12,600	(15,000)
1964	14,900	(6,000)
1965	31,200	(7,000)
1966	28,900	(11,100)

On July 1, 1967 the Blue Corporation transferred to Orange Corporation all of its assets, subject to all liabilities, in exchange for unissued Orange Corporation capital stock. Both corporations have been owned since their inceptions in 1961 by the same group of stockholders, although in different proportions as to individuals. The terms of the merger provided that the fair value of the stock in each case is to be its book value except that an allowance is to be made for the value of any net operating carry-forward losses. Obtaining the benefit of the loss carry-over deduction was not the principal purpose for the merger. (Assume a 50% tax rate.)

Required:

(1) Compute (*a*) the number of shares of Orange Corp. to be distributed to shareholders of Blue Corp., and (*b*) the number of shares of Orange Corp. stock to be exchanged for each share of Blue stock.

(2) Prepare the journal entry for the books of Orange Corp. recording the merger with Blue Corp. as a pooling of interests.

(3) Prepare the journal entries for the books of Blue Corp. recording the merger with Orange Corp. and the distribution of Orange Corp. stock to the stockholders of Blue Corp. (AICPA adapted)

Problem 19–13. Prior to January 1, 1968 the stockholders of Large Co. and Small Co. approved the merger of the two companies. On January 1, 1968, 5,000 shares of Large Co. common stock were issued to the Small Co. stockholders in exchange for the 3,000 shares of Small Co. common stock outstanding.

The December 31, 1967 postclosing statements of financial position of the two companies are as follows:

LARGE COMPANY AND SUBSIDIARY
POSTCLOSING STATEMENTS OF FINANCIAL POSITION
DECEMBER 31, 1967

	Large Company	Small Company
Cash	$ 36,400	$ 28,200
Notes receivable	22,000	9,000
Accounts receivable	20,900	21,700
Accruals receivable	13,000	3,300
Inventories	81,200	49,600
Plant and equipment	83,200	43,500
Accumulated depreciation	(12,800)	(9,300)
Investment in Small Co.	50,000	
	$293,900	$146,000

LARGE COMPANY AND SUBSIDIARY—continued

Notes payable	$ 4,000	$ 12,000
Accounts payable	42,000	19,600
Dividends payable		4,500
Accruals payable	2,600	2,100
Notes receivable discounted	8,100	
Capital stock, $10 par value	120,000	
Capital stock, $20 par value		60,000
Capital in excess of par	28,500	20,000
Retained earnings	88,700	27,800
	$293,900	$146,000

The following additional information is available:

(a) Net income for 1967 (disregard income taxes):

Large Company	$21,700
Small Company	10,200

(b) On December 31, 1967 Small Co. owed Large Co. $16,000 on open account and $8,000 in interest bearing notes. Large Co. discounted $3,000 of the notes received from Small Co. with the First State Bank.

(c) On December 31, 1967 Small Co. accrued interest payable of $120 on the notes payable to Large Co.; $40 on the notes of $3,000 discounted with the bank and $80 on the remaining notes of $5,000. Large Co. did not accrue interest receivable from Small Co.

(d) During 1967 Large Co. sold merchandise which cost $30,000 to Small Co. for $40,000. Small Company's December 31st inventory included $10,000 of this merchandise priced at Small Company's cost.

(e) On July 1 Small Co. sold equipment that had a book value of $15,000 to Large Co. for $17,000. Large Co. recorded depreciation on it in the amount of $850 for 1967. The remaining life of the equipment at the date of sale was 10 years.

(f) Small Co. shipped merchandise to Large Co. on December 31, 1967 and recorded an account receivable of $6,000 for the sale. Small Company's cost for the merchandise was $4,800. Because the merchandise was in transit, Large Company did not record the transaction. The terms of the sale were FOB shipping point.

(g) Small Co. declared a dividend of $1.50 per share on December 30, 1967 payable on January 10, 1968. Large Co. made no entry for the declaration.

Required:

Prepare a consolidated statement of financial position worksheet. The consolidation is to be accounted for as a pooling of interests. Formal journal entries are not required.   (AICPA adapted)

IV

CONTRACTION OF THE BUSINESS ORGANIZATION

CHAPTER 20

Disinvestment

The earlier sections of this textbook have dealt with some of the important accounting problems involved in the formation, maintenance, and expansion of a business enterprise. There are times, however, when even the best managements find that the wisest course of action is to retrench the scope of operations. At times such retrenchment may actually be the first step in total liquidation of the enterprise. Other situations may arise in the life cycle of the enterprise, such as improper management, unsettled economic conditions in general, changes in customer habits, failure to meet competition, and many other specific detrimental occurrences which may bring about a period of contraction, or even of eventual liquidation, for a business enterprise. This section of the book will consider some of the accounting problems incident to the contraction of a going enterprise. The following section of the book will treat some of the accounting problems arising from business liquidations.

Enterprise Contraction. A business enterprise may contract the scope of its operations voluntarily, wherein management (board of directors or owners) may decide that, of several alternatives available under the circumstances, contraction is the most desirable. On occasion the enterprise may find that, in effect, contraction has been decreed involuntarily through the working of outside forces upon the enterprise. In any event, such contraction may be a temporary condition in a long-run growth pattern of the enterprise, it may be the turning point of past growth and the start of a more stabilized period of operations, or it may presage the eventual liquidation of the enterprise in the reasonably near future. Thus, a contraction of the scope of operations does not necessarily indicate a decision to liquidate the enterprise. Frequently, long-run growth patterns may be achieved only by living through periods of retrenchment in which the basic strengths of the enterprise are further developed and past weaknesses are eliminated. Thus, while contraction of the firm nearly always precedes actual liquidation of the firm, contraction does not necessarily mean that liquidation will be forthcoming in the near future.

Accounting for Contraction. In accounting for decisions to contract the scope of operations the accountant should, in general, be governed by the same basic theory which is applicable to maintenance and expansion decisions of a business enterprise. During the period of contraction one cannot know with a high degree of certainty what the events of the future will bring. Thus, it is generally unwise to use predictions of future events to any great extent in determining accounting actions during a contraction phase of the enterprise. The accounting actions taken must strive to account for the decisions made, and the guiding principles previously discussed are generally applicable to most business contraction situations.

Previous discussion has pointed out that during the maintenance and expansion phases of the life of an enterprise accounting actions may occasionally deviate from a strictly theoretical soundness. Likewise, during the contraction phase of an enterprise it may be necessary to modify some of the guiding principles of accounting. This section and the following section will deal with some of the modifications of the guiding principles. Generally such modifications are necessitated by an alteration in one of the basic assumptions upon which accounting for the enterprise is based. For example, if full or partial liquidation is imminent, the going-concern concept of accounting for enterprise actions may no longer be valid. Those principles which rest primarily upon this assumption may therefore require modification in such situations.

In the discussion which follows it must be recognized that the accounting treatment accorded the various events in contraction and in liquidation may involve departures from the concepts previously presented. Attempts will be made to justify these departures in relation to the conditions involved and to support the deviations as being proper or suitable under the circumstances.

ASSET REALIZATION

An enterprise may dispose of a portion of its assets in various ways and for a variety of reasons. The sale of a plant site or a producing facility may be dictated by over-expansion in the past. Likewise, the disposition of productive facilities, or even an operating division, may be necessary because of the loss of a key customer or because of changes in government procurement. At times the sale of productive facilities may develop from changing consumer habits, from lack of raw materials, or from an absence of a favorable labor market. While these are only a few of the reasons for contraction of productive facilities, the important problem from the accountant's point of view involves the accounting treatment to be accorded the various dispositions.

Accounting for Asset Realization

Sale for Cash and for Interest-Bearing Securities. The accounting problems are fairly simple if the disposition involves an outright sale for cash or for interest-bearing securities. Thus, if the A Corporation were to dispose of its plant and part of its equipment at Danville, Illinois, by a sale to the Bell Corporation, the basis of the property sold would be removed from the records, and a gain or loss would arise based upon the difference between such basis and the assets received in exchange. If the assets sold were carried on the books as follows:

Plant	$450,000	
Reserve for depreciation of plant		$288,000
Machinery	122,000	
Reserve for depreciation of machinery		90,000

and if these assets were sold for $100,000 in cash and $60,000 of notes receivable due in four years at 5% interest, the following entry would be made:

Cash	$100,000	
Notes receivable	60,000	
Reserve for depreciation of plant	288,000	
Reserve for depreciation of machinery	90,000	
Loss on disposal of fixed assets	34,000	
Plant		$450,000
Machinery		122,000

The cash received may be used for a variety of purposes, depending upon the existing needs of the business. For example, the cash may be temporarily invested until it may be employed profitably in a venture in a new field or in the development of a new plant site in a more favorable location. If the contraction is in reality the initial stage of a disinvestment or liquidation process, the cash may be used as a partial liquidating dividend to the stockholders in a corporate organization, as a partial return of invested capital for a partnership, or be applied in other ways to reduce a portion of the equities of the enterprise.

Sale for Noninterest-Bearing Securities. The problem becomes somewhat more complicated if the sale is not made for cash. Thus, if the A corporation were to sell the assets described in the above example to the Bell Corporation for 10-year, noninterest-bearing serial notes having a face value of $207,207.32, the following entry might appear to be appropriate:

Notes receivable	$207,207.32	
Reserve for depreciation of plant	288,000.00	
Reserve for depreciation of machinery	90,000.00	
Plant		$450,000.00
Machinery		122,000.00
Gain on disposal of fixed assets		13,207.32

From this entry it appears that the A Corporation made a profit on the disposal, whereas in the sale for cash and interest-bearing notes the Corporation suffered a loss. A closer study of this situation, however, leads to the conclusion that the above entry is not proper and that no profit was earned.

In the sale for cash and interest-bearing notes the A Corporation receives assets having a present value of $160,000, assuming that 5% is the market rate of interest. In the sale for noninterest-bearing serial notes in the face amount of $207,207.32, the A Corporation receives no immediate cash, but will receive cash over a 10-year period at $20,720.73 per year. It appears logical to conclude that the face amount of the notes includes an interest element, since no interest is explicit in the transaction.

Determination of Cash Equivalent of Securities. Referring to Chapter 2 and the concepts on the valuation of assets discussed at that point, it appears that the serial notes might be more properly valued at their cash equivalent value at the date of receipt than at their face value. If the present value of the notes becomes the basis for the assets, the interest implicit in the face of the notes may be taken up as income as the serial notes are paid. If the present value of the notes received is to be used as the basis for their valuation, a problem arises in the determination of their value. The problem is to determine the present value of 10 payments of $20,720.73 each, assuming that 5% is the market rate of interest. Referring to the Present Value of an Annuity of 1 Table in the Appendix, the present value of an annuity of $1 at 5% for 10 periods is found to be 7.72173493. If this value is multiplied by the $20,720.73 payments that will be made each year, the result should be the value today of an annuity of 10 payments of $20,720.73 at 5%. The present value of the notes received which results from the multiplication is $160,000. Using this amount as the basis of the notes, the following entry would be made:

Notes receivable	$160,000	
Reserve for depreciation of plant	288,000	
Reserve for depreciation of machinery	90,000	
Loss on disposal of fixed assets	34,000	
Plant		$450,000
Machinery		122,000

The above entry results in the same dollar loss from disposal of the assets that resulted when it was assumed the assets were sold for a cash equivalent of $160,000 composed of cash and interest-bearing notes. If the present value of the serial notes received is also $160,000, the above entry would appear to result in the proper loss on disposal.

Interest Earned—Straight-Line Approach. Assuming that $160,000 is the proper basis for the notes received in the sale transaction, another problem arises at the end of the first year when the first payment is received. The amount received will be 1/10 of the face amount of the serial notes, or $20,720.73. The entry to record the receipt of cash could be:

Cash	$20,720.73	
Notes receivable		$16,000.00
Interest income		4,720.73

The credit to the Notes Receivable account equals 1/10 of the basis upon which the notes were recorded, since 1/10 of the face value was received. The above entry would be made for each of the 10 payments on the serial notes.

Interest Earned—Actuarial Approach. One criticism of the above entry is that the interest income reported would be the same for each of the 10 years, even though the amount of the debt unpaid decreases each year. It does not appear logical to conclude that the interest earned on $160,000 during the first year should be the same as the interest earned on roughly one-tenth of this amount during the tenth year. One method of overcoming this criticism is to take up as income the interest earned on the amount of debt unpaid. Under this method of determining the interest earned the present value of the serial notes is determined at the start of the year and also at the end of the year. The difference represents the interest income for the period.

The above discussion indicates that the present value of an annuity of 10 payments of $20,720.73 at 5% is $160,000. One year later the present value would have to be increased by the amount of interest for the one year. Thus, the present value of the serial notes just prior to the payment of the first installment would equal $168,000 or $160,000 plus one year's interest on the $160,000 at 5%. The increase in present value from the start of the year, $8,000, represents the interest income for that year. Actuarially the present value could be determined as follows:

Present value of an annuity of 9 payments of $20,720.73 at 5% = (20,720.73 × 7.10782168) =		$147,279.27
Present value of one payment of $20,720.73 due immediately	=	20,720.73
Total present value	=	$168,000.00

If the increase in present value during the year is considered to be the interest earned, the following entry would be made:

Cash	$20,720.73	
Notes receivable		$12,720.73
Interest income		8,000.00

At the end of the second year a similar entry would be made, but the interest earned would be less since the second year's interest would be based upon the present value of the unpaid notes at the start of the second year, or $147,279.27 ($160,000 − $12,720.73). Thus the credit to interest income would be progressively less in each of the 10 years, and the credit to notes receivable would increase in each of the 10 years. The total interest income over the 10 years would be $47,207.32, or the same total income that would be reported if the interest income were recorded at $4,720.73 per year.

By recording the notes at their present value at the date of their receipt in exchange for the assets, and by determining interest income as a percentage of the present value of the notes at the start of the year, the accounting records will provide more accurate information both on asset bases and on income earned.

Sale for Stock of Acquiring Corporation. Another possibility in the sale of assets is to receive stock of the acquiring enterprise in exchange for the assets sold. The problem here is somewhat different from that arising if cash, interest-bearing notes, or noninterest-bearing notes or bonds are involved. Assume the A Corporation sells the assets in the above example for 2,000 shares of Bell Corporation $50 par value common stock. At the date of the sale the Bell Corporation stock has a market value of $80 per share and the fair value of the assets exchanged is $156,000. Once again the problem involves determination of the proper accounting basis for the asset received in exchange for the operating assets sold. At least four alternative methods for valuing the stock received may be considered.

(1) Record the stock on the basis of the book value of the assets exchanged for the stock:

Stock of Bell Corporation	$194,000	
Reserve for depreciation of plant	288,000	
Reserve for depreciation of machinery	90,000	
Plant		$450,000
Machinery		122,000

If this entry is made no gain or loss is recognized on the sale of the assets. In the absence of objective evidence as to the fair value of the assets sold, *and* in the absence of a ready market and therefore an existing market value for the stock, the above entry would be satisfactory. In the entry it is assumed that the value, or basis, of the stock is equal to the book value, or undepreciated cost, of the assets sold. If this relationship is known not to exist, the above entry may not be advisable.

(2) Record the stock on the basis of the fair value of the assets exchanged for the stock:

Stock of Bell Corporation	$156,000	
Reserve for depreciation of plant	288,000	
Reserve for depreciation of machinery	90,000	
Loss on sale of assets	38,000	
Plant		$450,000
Machinery		122,000

Valuation of the stock received at the fair value of the assets given up in exchange for the stock may be appropriate when the fair value has an objective basis. The use of fair value would appear to be more appropriate than the use of book value of the assets exchanged whenever the fair value may be determined with a reasonable degree of objectivity, as by an independent appraisal, for example.

(3) Record the stock on the basis of the par value of the stock:

Stock of Bell Corporation	$100,000	
Reserve for depreciation of plant	288,000	
Reserve for depreciation of machinery	90,000	
Loss on sale of assets	94,000	
Plant		$450,000
Machinery		122,000

Valuation of stock received in the sale transaction at par value will result in recognition of a loss or a gain, depending on whether the book value of the assets sold exceeds or is less than the par value of the stock. Other than some minor legal justification, the use of par value as a basis for recording stock has little support. Par value bears no necessary relationship to the inherent worth of the stock, and therefore its use as a basis for asset recordation is not recommended.

(4) Record the stock on the basis of the market value of the stock at the date of the sale:

Stock of Bell Corporation	$160,000	
Reserve for depreciation of plant	288,000	
Reserve for depreciation of machinery	90,000	
Loss on sale of assets	34,000	
Plant		$450,000
Machinery		122,000

If the above entry is made, the assets received are recorded on the basis of their value existing at the date of the transaction. The loss or gain which may arise is determined by comparison of the value of the assets received and the book value of the assets sold. Recognition of loss or gain in such a manner is commonly the most appropriate procedure to follow.

If a sound basis exists to determine the value of the consideration given up in a sale transaction, such basis should be used as the basis for recording the assets received. If a sound basis for valuation of the consideration given up does not exist, the fair value of the assets received in the transaction may be the most appropriate basis to use. If neither the fair value of the consideration given up nor the fair value of the assets received is available, the book value of the assets given up in exchange may be the most appropriate basis to use. Rarely, if ever, is par value appropriate as a basis for valuation of stock received and held as an asset.

From the above discussion the conclusion can be drawn that there is little relationship between the reason supporting a disinvestment situation through the realization of assets and the accounting for the disinvestment. Of far more importance from an accounting viewpoint is the manner in which the disinvestment is consummated. The objective in accounting for disinvestments through asset realization is consistent with the objectives of accounting for assets as previously discussed. That is, the entry to reflect the disinvestment should remove from the accounting records the bases of the properties disposed of and should record any assets received in exchange at the cash or cash equivalent value of the assets at the date of the transaction.

ASSET REVALUATION

A few of the accounting problems arising when an enterprise purposely disposes of a portion of its productive facilities were considered in the preceding section. At this point a different type of disinvestment situation will be considered. Not only may a disinvestment be accomplished by management plan or decision, but disinvestment may also arise without the awareness of management or in spite of management planning. In fact, an erosion of asset values may develop so slowly that management may become aware of the disinvestment only after it has become rather severe.

Decline in Economic Values. A decline in economic values in the economy generally, or a decline in economic values within an industry, or even a decline in economic values in a locality affecting various industries in the locality may produce a noticeable, or even a substantial, decline in the value of the assets of a given enterprise. The decline in value may be rather abrupt, or it may be a relatively slow process requiring several years. Regardless of the degree of abruptness of the change in economic value, at any time when such a decline has occurred and when the extent of the decline is subject to reasonably objective measurement, accounting recognition of the decline may be appropriate.

Accounting for Decline in Economic Values. As previously discussed, assets are normally recorded at the cash or cash equivalent value of the asset at the date of its acquisition. Changes in the acquisition value of an asset are not commonly reflected in the accounting records except for those changes which are closely related to the passage of time or to the physical consumption or utilization of the asset. Recognizing that the accountant assumes the enterprise is a going concern, periodic fluctuations in economic values in general are not recorded in the accounting records. This fact alone may contribute to a rather sudden awakening as to the degree of decline in economic values that may have developed over a period of years. Thus, if the economic values of the assets of an enterprise have been declining for a number of years, and if no accounting recognition has been made of this situation, after several years the extent of the decline could be substantial. While adherence to acquisition costs in the accounting records is generally a sound valuation policy for service resources, in circumstances indicating a relatively permanent decline in economic values of such resources, revaluation may well produce more significant and more useful accounting data and reports.

If the decline in economic values has been substantial, if the decline appears to have a relative degree of permanence, and if the decline may be measured quantitatively in some relatively objective manner, recognition of the decline in economic values in the accounting records may be advisable. At times the recording of such a decline in values is accomplished as a part of a quasi-reorganization of the enterprise. The subject of quasi-reorganizations is discussed more fully in the next chapter. In other instances, the decline in economic values may be recorded to put the accounting bases in more realistic terms. In any event, the recording of a decline in economic values gives accounting recognition to a disinvestment process that may have been developing for several years.

Once sufficient evidence as to the nature and extent of the decline in economic values has been accumulated, the actual accounting entries are not very complicated. The various asset accounts which are being carried at excessive values would be credited to reflect their decline in value. The total (or net) effect of the decline would be charged to a loss account, appropriately named, or to the Retained Earnings account. Full disclosure would require complete discussion of the action taken in any reports issued for public consumption.

Decline in Value Due to Obsolescence. In addition to a general decline in economic values, an enterprise may find that a specific asset has lost its economic usefulness rather abruptly or at least somewhat in advance of previous expectations. Thus a given asset or unit of productive facilities may become obsolete under a variety of circumstances. If an asset becomes obsolete, the enterprise has in reality suffered a disinvestment of assets, and this disinvestment should receive accounting recognition.

The possibility of obsolescence may have some effect upon the depreciation policy which an enterprise adopts in its fixed asset accounting. Thus, an asset with a physical life of 15 years, but which is expected to have a useful life to the enterprise of eight years because of technological progress or other causes of obsolescence, would be depreciated over the eight-year period. At times, however, the economic usefulness of the asset may disappear even more quickly than had originally been anticipated. Or, after usage for a few years it may become evident that the remaining period of useful life will be somewhat less than had been previously expected.

Accounting for Decline Due to Obsolescence. Under either of these situations the accounting records should reflect the decline in economic usefulness. If the obsolescence occurs rather suddenly so that the asset is scrapped, sold, or traded in on a newer asset, the entry to be made would be as follows:

Cash (or other asset)	$xxxx	
Reserve for depreciation of asset	xxxx	
Loss on disposal of fixed asset	xxxx	
Fixed asset		$xxxx

If obsolescence is recognized in advance of its actual final impact, an entry may be prepared at the date of recognition to reflect the reduced economic usefulness of the asset. This entry is normally considered to be an adjustment of prior years' depreciation on the reasoning that, had the obsolescence been foreseen at the date of acquisition, the depreciation charges in the past years would have been greater. Thus the entry to recognize the obsolescence might appear as follows:

Loss from obsolescence of fixed assets	$xxxx	
Reserve for depreciation of fixed assets		$xxxx

Each of the above entries produces a decrease in the book value of the assets of the enterprise, and therefore recognizes a disinvestment for the firm. It should be noted at this point that obsolescence of fixed assets does not necessarily produce a disinvestment, because on some occasions the obsolete assets are replaced with more modern equipment. The net result of the change may be an additional investment in assets for the firm.

DEBT RETIREMENT

The preceding two sections have dealt briefly with some of the accounting problems arising from contraction of the operations of an enterprise through asset realizations or revaluations. As was noted, realization of assets does not necessarily result in enterprise contraction nor in disinvestment. The realization of operating assets in cash or cash equivalent may be an early phase of an expansion program or change in product mix. On the other hand, the cash received from the realization of assets may be applied to the retirement of various equity interests—claims of short-term creditors, bonds outstanding, partnership contributions, or all or portions of one or more classes of stock outstanding. Use of the proceeds of realization to effect equity retirements normally accomplishes firm contraction or disinvestment.

Retirement of Short-term Debt. While debt retirement is commonly a characteristic of disinvestment, the accounting problems arising from some debt retirements are not too complicated. In particular, the retirement of short-term obligations normally involves an entry similar to the settlement of payables in the normal course of business.

Retirement of Bonds Outstanding—at Par. The early retirement of bonds outstanding may create a few more problems, however. For example, assume the Y Corporation sold $1,000,000 of 4% bonds on January 2, 1960. The bonds were due December 31, 1979, were sold at 97, and the interest on them was payable on January 2 and July 1. The entry to record the sale, under usual accounting practice, would have been:

Cash	$970,000	
Unamortized bond discount	30,000	
Bonds payable		$1,000,000

On April 1, 1969, the Y Corporation completes the sale, for cash, of certain productive facilities and desires to use the proceeds of the sale to retire the bonds outstanding. At this date the Unamortized Bond Discount account contains a balance of $16,125 ($30,000 less $9\frac{1}{4}$ annual amortization entries of $1,500 each). The entry to record the retirement, assumed in this instance to be accomplished at face value, would be:

Bonds payable	$1,000,000	
Interest expense	10,000	
Loss on retirement of bonds	16,125	
Unamortized bond discount		$ 16,125
Cash		1,010,000

The loss on retirement would be reported in the income statement or in a surplus analysis, depending upon the materiality of the amount.

Retirement of Bonds Outstanding—at a Premium. If the bond indenture provided that the bonds could be retired prior to maturity only by payment of a call premium, the loss on retirement would be increased by the amount of the premium. Thus, if the above bonds were callable in the January 1, 1969, to January 1, 1971, period at $102\frac{1}{2}$, the following entry would reflect the retirement on April 1, 1969:

Bonds payable	$1,000,000	
Interest expense	10,000	
Loss on retirement of bonds (16,125 + 25,000)	41,125	
Unamortized bond discount		$ 16,125
Cash		1,035,000

A more thorough treatment of the accounting problems arising from the retirement of long-term indebtedness prior to maturity date is to be found in most intermediate accounting textbooks.

Alternatives to Debt Retirement. As with most areas of accounting, accountants may be called upon in the area of disinvestment, and particularly in the debt retirement phase, to provide the bases upon which to make decisions among alternative plans of action. For example, in the illustration above, alternative uses could have been made of the cash realized from the sale of the assets. It is possible that one or more of these alternatives would prove to be more advisable than the retirement of the bonds outstanding.

After completing the asset retrenchment previously decided upon, company officials may be faced with these alternatives, among others: (1) retirement of outstanding indebtedness, as described above; (2) retirement of portions of equity interests or payment of a partial liquidating dividend, as discussed in the following section; (3) acquisition of new assets or the controlling interest in a going concern, as described in Part III of this textbook; (4) acquisition of temporary investments to hold until a more permanent decision is made or until debt retirement conditions become more favorable.

In the above illustration, for example, an investment alternative may exist which would be more favorable to the enterprise than would be debt retirement. If the Y Corporation officials are able to invest the $1,000,000 necessary to retire the bonds outstanding to enable them to earn a return greater than the 4% interest which they are currently paying on their bonds, it may be advisable to make such investment. The investment alternative would become even more advisable when the existence of the call premium is considered. Most bond indentures which contain a call premium provision provide for a declining premium to maturity. Thus, the $102\frac{1}{2}$ call price existing at April 1, 1969, for the Y Corporation bonds might gradually decline to 102 for the period January 1, 1971, to January 1, 1973, to $101\frac{1}{2}$ from January 1, 1973, to January 1, 1975, and so on. The acquisition of temporary investments producing more than 4% income may be more advisable when considered in the light of the gradual call premium reduction if retirement of the indebtedness is delayed a few years.

A similar situation may exist if the bonds do not have a callable provision, but may be retired prior to maturity only through acquisitions on the open market. Because of the vagaries of the market situation, company officials may deem it advisable to hold off making open-market acquisitions until market prices for the bonds are more favorable. During the interim, a period of unknown duration, temporary investments of the cash available to retire the bonds may be advisable.

The decision on which of the various alternative uses of the cash is most advisable must be made by the responsible management officials; however, the accounting staff may be expected to provide management with dollar evaluations of the alternatives available.

RESIDUAL EQUITY RETIREMENTS

As already mentioned, the realization in cash of assets previously committed to operations may result in the retirement of portions of the residual equity interests, among other possibilities. For purposes of this discussion we can divide residual equity retirements into the following areas: (1) retirement or sale of partnership interest; (2) payment of corporate liquidating dividends; (3) acquisition by the corporation of its own shares; and (4) acquisition and elimination of one or more classes of outstanding stock.

Retirement or Sale of Partnership Interest. In Chapter 2 the accounting for the purchase of an interest and for the purchase of an investment in a partnership was discussed. At that point the most important problem raised concerned the proper valuation of the assets of the partnership at the date of admission of a new partner. Since the admission of a new partner creates a new partnership, adjustments of existing asset values to correspond to their value to the new entity are generally advisable. In the sale of a partnership interest the same problem arises, since the sale is merely the other side of the purchase transaction.

It has been also noted previously that the true profit or loss of an enterprise can be known only at the time that enterprise is liquidated or dissolved. When a partner sells his interest or when a partner retires, in reality a dissolution of an enterprise has occurred, and it would seem desirable to determine as accurately as possible the final profit of that enterprise. This is particularly true when a partner retires, since there may not be an objective bargaining basis upon which to base the retirement settlement. When a partner sells his interest, on the other hand, a buyer exists, and the worth of the interest being transferred is at least indicated by the exchange price.

Since the sale of a partnership interest has been discussed previously, and since the sale does not generally result in a contraction of the firm's operations or in a disinvestment situation, only the problems of accounting for a retirement of a partner will be considered here.

Basis of Settlement with Retiring Partner. The basic problem when a partner retires lies in the determination of the proper settlement to him. While it might appear simple enough to settle with a partner on the basis of the equity represented by his capital, drawing, and loan accounts, various reasons could exist to cause the fair value of this equity to be different from the value as reflected in these accounts. For example, the existing market values of the assets in use may be somewhat different from the acquisition costs or amortized-acquisition costs (book value) of those assets. Likewise, either excessively conservative or excessively liberal accounting policies in areas involving estimates may, at the date of retirement, result in the statement of financial position providing an improper basis for determining the value of the retiring partner's equity. Unrecorded assets may exist, the most commonly noted of which is goodwill. Any of these conditions may require that the statement values of the partnership be modified in order to achieve an equitable settlement with a retiring partner.

When a partner retires it would seem that the settlement with him by the partnership should be based upon the value of the partnership at the date of retirement. While the theory of using this value as a settlement basis is usually acceptable, its application may be accomplished only by solving some of the problems in valuing assets that were discussed in Chapter 2. If at the date of retirement inventories, fixed assets, or other properties of the partnership have current values different from their book values, some adjustment of the book values may be necessary to achieve an equitable settlement with the retiring partner. Even if the partners who continue in the partnership are agreeable to a settlement with the retiring partner based on current values of the assets, the recognition of these values in the accounting records of the partnership may still pose some problems.

ILLUSTRATION. To illustrate the accounting treatment of some of the problems that may arise from partner retirement, assume the following partnership situation:

ABC PARTNERSHIP
FINANCIAL POSITION
DECEMBER 31, 1966

Cash	$110,000	Payables	$ 30,000
Receivables	40,000	A, Capital	90,000
Inventory (Fair value, $68,000)	60,000	B, Capital	90,000
Fixed assets (Fair value, $109,000)	90,000	C, Capital	90,000
	$300,000		$300,000

Partner A desires to withdraw from the partnership for personal reasons, and in anticipation of this withdrawal the partnership has conserved its working capital so that it is now in a position to effect the retirement. At the date of retirement, December 31, 1966, the fair market value of the inventory is $8,000 in excess of the cost, and the fair market value of the fixed assets is $19,000 in excess of amortized cost. The partners agree that settlement with A should be based upon the current values. The partners share profits and losses equally, so that one-third of the increase in the market value of $27,000 is allocable to A. Therefore, A will be paid $99,000—$90,000 for his book equity plus $9,000 for his share of the increase in market value of the assets.

Adherence to Cost Principle. The accounting treatment of the $9,000 excess over book equity paid to A and of the market value increases in general is open to some differences of opinion. On one hand, there is support for the following entry when settlement is effected with A:

A, Capital	$90,000	
Inventory	2,667	
Fixed assets	6,333	
Cash		$99,000

This entry would find support from those who place considerable emphasis on the cost principle. Since a going business will remain in operation, the cost of the inventory and fixed assets to B and C has increased by a total of $9,000 because of the retirement settlement with A. Recognition of the additional increase in market values of $18,000 would introduce unrealized profit into the accounts and result in an overstatement of assets.

Revaluation of Assets. On the other hand some accountants would argue that the following entry is proper to record the retirement of A:

A, Capital	$90,000	
Inventory	8,000	
Fixed assets	19,000	
Cash		$99,000
B, Capital		9,000
C, Capital		9,000

This entry would find support from those who would view the new partnership involving B and C as a new enterprise. In accordance with the principles of valuation of assets for a new enterprise, as previously discussed, each partner is entitled to receive credit for his share of the proper value of the assets contributed. Here recognition of the entire increase in market value is necessary to value properly the assets of the new business and to credit the new partners for the fair value of the assets contributed at the date of organization of the enterprise. Modification of the cost principle is justified on the basis that a new enterprise is established and the going-concern assumption which existed previously is now inapplicable as far as these assets are concerned.

It appears that the latter reasoning is preferable, providing the fair market values determined for the assets are subject to reasonably objective verification. If the remaining partners must pay the retiring partner an amount in excess of his book equity because of increases in market values of assets of the enterprise, it appears that the remaining partners are entitled to capital credits in the new enterprise based upon the values of the assets agreed upon in the settlement with the retiring partner.

3 **Recognition of Goodwill.** A problem similar to that discussed above arises if the partners agree that goodwill, previously unrecognized, exists at the time a partner retires. Thus, if in the above illustration the current values for the various assets were unknown, or if the current values were essentially the same as the book values, the partners might agree to recognize the existence of goodwill in effecting the settlement with A. Assume that the goodwill is valued at $27,000. Since the general rule is that goodwill should be divided among the partners in their profit and loss sharing ratio, each partner would be entitled to $9,000 of the goodwill. Two alternatives exist as to the recognition of the goodwill:

Goodwill	$9,000	
A, Capital		$9,000

This entry records on the books A's portion of the goodwill since this is the only portion which the enterprise is paying for at this time.

Goodwill	$27,000	
A, Capital		$9,000
B, Capital		9,000
C, Capital		9,000

This entry records on the books the goodwill agreed upon and credits the partners for their appropriate portions of the goodwill.

The determination of which of these two entries is the more acceptable rests very largely upon the degree of objectivity with which the goodwill value has been determined. In the two preceding sections it was assumed that the fair values determined for the inventory and fixed assets were subject to reasonably objective verification. The determination, objectively, of a fair value for goodwill is frequently a more difficult problem than is such a determination for tangible assets. The second entry above would be preferable if the goodwill value were subject to objective verification. However, the first entry would likely be preferred by most accountants because of the subjective nature of the valuation of goodwill in most instances. Thus, the choice between the alternatives appears to rest upon the degree of objectivity with which the goodwill value has been determined.

Bonus to Retiring Partner. Another alternative is available to A, B, and C at the date that A retires. The partners may agree that A is to receive $99,000 for his equity in the partnership, but they may agree that no increases in asset values are appropriate and that no goodwill exists, or if it exists it is to remain unrecognized. In this alternative B and C are in reality paying a $9,000 bonus to A, and the entry to effect A's retirement would be:

A, Capital	$90,000	
B, Capital	4,500	
C, Capital	4,500	
Cash		$99,000

So long as B and C continue to share profits in the same relationship after the retirement of A as they did prior to his retirement, neither will be affected by the decision to use the bonus treatment rather than goodwill, or vice versa. After recording the bonus in the above entry each partner has a balance of $85,500 in his capital account. If the goodwill recorded in either of the entries above subsequently proves to be non-existent and is written off, B and C will each have a capital balance of $85,500. If the goodwill is recorded and if B and C change their profit and loss relationship prior to the date that the goodwill is written off, the end result will be different from that produced by the use of the bonus treatment, as noted in Chapter 2.

Deferred Settlement upon Retirement. In the above illustrations it has been assumed that the partnership had sufficient assets to effect the settlement with retiring partner A. The settlement, of course, reduces the properties and the equities of the enterprise, and thus results in a disinvestment by the firm. On some occasions a partner may decide to retire, but the partnership may not have sufficient assets to pay the retiring partner in full for his agreed settlement price. In some instances the settlement may be deferred until the value of certain assets can be determined with finality through their actual realization. In either instance, when the agreed settlement is deferred it would seem preferable to eliminate the retiring partner's capital account and to transfer the amount due him in settlement to a payable account, clearly described.

Payment of Corporate Liquidating Dividend

In a corporate disinvestment situation the contraction of the assets of an enterprise may proceed in various ways, one of which involves a distribution to the stockholders of a portion of their capital contributions. Such a distribution is commonly referred to as a liquidating dividend. The main point of distinction between the normal corporate dividend distribution and a liquidating dividend is that the former is paid from earned income of the enterprise, while the latter is paid from some form of capital contribution and not from income from operations.

While the term "liquidating dividend" might seem to imply that this type of distribution would be made only during the actual liquidation phase of the enterprise, the term might also be used properly to describe a distribution of assets arising from asset realizations in a disinvestment phase of the life of the enterprise. Since a liquidating dividend is paid from capital contribution rather than from earnings, certain legal requirements must be satisfied prior to the payment of the dividend. While the legal requirements will vary from state to state, these requirements generally would provide for action by the board of directors, ratification by the various classes of stockholders, and full disclosure to all dividend recipients that they were receiving a return of their invested capital and not a distribution from earnings of the corporation.

Accounting for a Liquidating Dividend. When a liquidating dividend is paid it would appear to be preferable to record the distribution as a charge to a special account rather than as a charge against the existing capital accounts. The dividend does not redeem any shares of stock, but merely involves a pro-rata return to the stockholders of a portion of the contributed capital. Thus, if a corporation declares a $90,000 dividend and notifies the stockholders that $30,000 of the dividend comes from earnings of the business and $60,000 involves a return of contributed capital no longer needed in the operations of the enterprise, the following entry could be made:

Retained earnings	$30,000	
Capital distribution to stockholders	60,000	
Dividends payable (Cash)		$90,000

The special account charged for the $60,000 return of contributed capital could be reported in the shareholders' equity section of the statement of financial position as a deduction from the contributed capital items.

In making a liquidating dividend distribution a corporation should take care to notify the stockholders as to the nature of the dividend checks they are receiving. Dividends received from earnings of the corporation are income to the stockholders, while dividends received from capital contributions are reductions in the basis of the investment carried by the stockholder.

It should also be noted at this point that corporate officials must be conversant with the appropriate income tax regulations in arriving at a decision to declare a liquidating dividend. Certain provisions of the tax law stipulate the requirements which must be met for a distribution to be considered a liquidating dividend from an income tax point of view. These requirements should be considered in arriving at a decision as to the form of the distribution.

A liquidating dividend may effect a disinvestment by an enterprise, since assets realized in cash are returned to the investors through the medium of the dividend. The distribution may be made in contemplation of eventual liquidation or it may be made at a time when the corporate officials intend to continue operations of the enterprise.

Reacquisition of Corporation's Own Stock

The various reasons why a corporation might reacquire its own shares and the possible accounting treatments for the reacquired shares are discussed rather thoroughly in most intermediate accounting textbooks. At this point the discussion will be limited to the reacquisition of a corporation's own stock in order to effect a disinvestment.

As an alternative to the payment of a liquidating dividend, the board of directors of a corporation which has excess cash assets available may decide to acquire on the open market, or directly from some of the existing stockholders, a portion of the stock outstanding. The stock so acquired, generally referred to as treasury stock, might be retired in a legal sense, although legal retirement of the shares would not be necessary.

Reporting of Stock Reacquired. While there may be some justification under certain circumstances for reporting treasury stock as an asset, it would not appear that such reporting would be proper for treasury stock acquired in order to effect a disinvestment for the enterprise. If the intention of the board of directors is to acquire the shares in order to retire them, either legally or effectively, proper reporting of the reacquired shares would be as a deduction in the shareholders' equity section of the statement of financial position. Likewise, any legal restriction on dividend distributions resulting from the acquisition of the treasury shares should be reported.

While remaining stockholders may have a gain or loss when stock is reacquired above or below *book value*, for recording purposes accountants are concerned primarily with a comparison of the reacquisition price with the *issue price*.

To illustrate, assume the Bow Corporation has the following share-holders' equity section on May 31, 1966:

Shareholders' equity:

Common stock, 300,000 shares, $100 par	$30,000,000
Excess of issue price over par value	6,000,000
Total contributed capital	36,000,000
Retained earnings	14,000,000
Total shareholders' equity	$50,000,000

The board of directors of the Bow Corporation decides to acquire 50,000 shares of its own stock in order to effect a disinvestment and to strengthen the market position of the shares which will remain out-standing. In acquiring these shares three possibilities may arise. The Bow Corporation may:

(1) Acquire 50,000 shares for exactly $6,000,000, the pro-rata portion of the contributed capital applicable to the 50,000 shares.
(2) Acquire 50,000 shares for less than $6,000,000, for example, $5,000,000.
(3) Acquire 50,000 shares for more than $6,000,000, for example, $8,000,000.

Stock Reacquired at Issue Price. In the first possibility above, the cost of the treasury shares, $6,000,000, should be deducted from the total of the contributed capital on the statement of financial position. The resulting balance of $30,000,000 might be labeled "contributed capital of outstanding shares." If the effective disinvestment is completed from a legal point of view by retiring the shares, the Common Stock account would be reduced by $5,000,000 and the "Excess" account would be reduced by $1,000,000.

Stock Reacquired at Less Than Issue Price. In the second possibility above, many accountants maintain that the $5,000,000 cost of the treasury shares should be deducted from the total of the contributed capital, leaving $31,000,000 contributed capital applicable to the out-standing shares. The excess of the contributed capital applicable to the shares reacquired over the acquisition cost of those shares should still be properly labeled contributed capital. A problem arises, however, if these shares are retired. Should the $1,000,000 excess of contributed capital over the cost of the shares retired remain in the "Excess" account, or should this amount be removed from the "Excess" account and be credited to Retained Earnings? Some accountants would argue that the $1,000,000 is contributed capital and the fact that the shares to which it applies have been retired does not change this fact. Following this reasoning the $1,000,000 should remain as a part of the contributed capital. Other accountants would argue that, upon retirement of stock which cost less to reacquire than the initial contribution, the difference becomes an addition to retained earnings. The sale and acquisition of the stock was accomplished at a profit to the corporation, and this is as much a profit as income from operations. Hence, the $1,000,000 should be transferred out of contributed capital into retained earnings following this line of reasoning. The weight of authority, however, at present supports the reporting of the $1,000,000 as a part of contributed capital. Accountants generally do not approve inclusion of "profit" on treasury stock transactions in the income statement, and likewise are hesitant to treat such "profits" as a part of retained earnings.

Stock Reacquired at More Than Issue Price. When treasury stock is acquired for more than the portion of contributed capital attributable to such stock, as in the third possibility above, the reporting of the cost of the treasury stock is not so clear as in the above situations. Some accountants would argue that the total cost, $8,000,000 in the illustration, should be deducted from contributed capital, leaving $28,000,000 as contributed capital. Other accountants would limit the amount of the deduction from contributed capital to the pro-rata portion of the contributed capital applicable to the shares reacquired. Any excess would be charged against retained earnings and be considered as a partial distribution of such retained earnings. In the above example, this treatment would result in reporting $30,000,000 contributed capital and $12,000,000 retained earnings.

The deduction of the total price paid to reacquire the shares from the contributed capital is consistent with the discussion above regarding the excess of contributed capital over the cost of reacquired shares. The resulting balance of contributed capital would then represent the original contributions, less amounts paid to reacquire a portion of the shares sold. The amount would not indicate the contributed capital attributable to the shares remaining outstanding. Those accountants supporting this procedure would argue that if profits from reacquiring (and retiring) a corporation's own shares are not included in retained earnings, it would hardly appear to be logical to charge "losses" from such acquisitions to the retained earnings account.

However, most authorities support the charge to retained earnings of any excess paid to reacquire the shares.[1] Presumably, the action by the

[1] *Accounting and Reporting Standards for Corporate Financial Statements and Preceding Statements and Supplements*, American Accounting Association, 1957 Revision, p. 7 "Preferably, the outlay by a corporation for its own shares is reflected as a reduction of the aggregate of contributed capital, and any excess of outlay over the pro-rata portion of contributed capital as a distribution of retained earnings."

board of directors to reacquire the shares was in the best interests of the remaining stockholders, and if the price paid to effect the retirement was greater than the amount previously paid in for those shares, the difference may be looked upon as a distribution of retained earnings for the benefit of the remaining stockholders. The authors support this alternative as being the preferable treatment when shares have been reacquired at a cost in excess of the capital contributed applicable to the shares.

In the third possibility discussed above, a reporting problem arises at the time the shares are reacquired, whether or not they are retired. At the date of retirement the problem must be resolved in the accounting records as well as in the reports. It appears preferable to charge the excess discussed above to the Retained Earnings account at the date of retirement.

In each of the three possibilities discussed the accountant must be cognizant of applicable state incorporation laws. If the state law so provides, either a parenthetical notation, a footnote, or a segregation of retained earnings must be made to indicate the extent to which the retained earnings is restricted as to dividends because of the treasury stock acquisitions.

Retirement of One or More Classes of Stock

Another method of effecting a disinvestment of a corporation is the retirement or elimination of one or more of the classes of stock outstanding. This method is related to the acquisition of treasury shares discussed above, but differs in that *all* of the shares of a class are retired, not just a portion of the class.

If the corporation has liquid assets which will not be required for operating purposes in the foreseeable future, such assets may be applied to the retirement of one class of stock for various reasons. A given class of stock may have certain objectionable features, such as a fixed dividend rate, a high dividend rate, or possibly an unfavorable conversion feature which may become operative in the near future. Retirement of a class of stock may be desired to simplify the corporate capital structure. At times the retirement might eliminate from "nuisance control" those individuals holding the shares of the class to be retired. Thus retirement of a class of stock may be desirable even though disinvestment is not particularly desirable. The coexistence of excess liquid assets and the desire to eliminate a given class of stock may result in both disinvestment and elimination of the objectionable capital element.

Exercise of Call Option. The retirement of a class of stock may arise under two conditions. The covenants of the stock issue may provide that the stock be callable at a certain price or prices at various dates in the future. If such a covenant exists, and if the board of directors calls the stock for redemption, the stock issue will be retired with a minimum of inconvenience. Thus, if the Arrow Corporation has outstanding 1,000 shares of Class A Stock, par value $100, and if the stock is presently callable at 103, the following entry could be made at retirement:

Class A stock	$100,000	
Stock retirement expense (Retained earnings)	3,000	
Cash		$103,000

The $3,000 excess of redemption price over par (assuming here par was also the amount paid in upon the original sale) may be charged to income or to retained earnings, depending upon the materiality of the item. If the stock had been sold at more or less than par originally, any paid-in surplus account should be removed in the entry to record the redemption.

Use of an Agent to Effect Retirement. At times a corporation may avail itself of an agent to handle the details of the retirement. If the Class A Stock above were retired through an agent, and if the agent's fee for handling such retirement were set at $2,500, the following entry would record the deposit with the agent:

Stock retirement fund deposit	$105,500	
Cash		$105,500

As the canceled stock certificates are turned over to the company, or as the disposal certificates are received, the following entry would be made:

Class A stock	$xxxx	
Stock retirement expense	xxxx	
Stock retirement fund deposit		$xxxx

After a reasonable period of time any cash deposited for shares not redeemed should be returned to the corporation.

Retirement without a Call Option. A given class of stock may also be retired even though the covenants of the stock do not provide for calling the stock for redemption. If the callable feature does not exist, the actual retirement of the entire class of stock may involve more time and also more problems. The board of directors may vote to retire the Class A Stock, and if the various classes of stockholders approve (depending on the law of the various states) the retirement could proceed. A general announcement would be made of the retirement plans and of the price set for redemption. In addition, specific notices would normally be sent to the stockholders involved. Each would be urged to submit his shares for redemption immediately. However, for various reasons some of the stockholders may refuse to send in their stock for redemption. Thus, although a large percentage of the shares may be redeemed in a short period of time, total retirement could take several years.

As in the above illustration when the stock was callable, the corporation may avail itself of the services of an agent to handle the redemption. The entries to be made would be similar to those above.

Retirement of a class of stock might also proceed on a piecemeal basis over a period of years through the purchase by the corporation of shares of the given class of stock on the open market. In some instances these shares might be carried as treasury shares until a substantial amount is accumulated. This might be particularly true if the corporation officials did not want to disclose their intentions to retire the class of stock. Accounting for treasury acquisitions and the reporting procedures when treasury stock is held were discussed in the preceding section.

Regardless of the accounting and reporting procedures followed for treasury stock during the period prior to retirement of the shares, it would appear proper to account for the retirement of the shares in the manner discussed above. That is, any excess of the retirement outlay over the original capital contribution attributable to the class of stock involved should be charged against retained earnings upon retirement of the shares. Logically, it would appear proper to credit retained earnings for any excess of the original capital contribution over the cost of acquiring the shares at retirement. However, the hesitancy of the accounting profession to recognize an increase in retained earnings, whether through the income statement or not, from dealings in the enterprise's own stock is likely to persist for some time in the future.

SUMMARY

Disinvestment by an enterprise normally involves the realization in cash of some of the existing operating assets. The cash so realized is then used to eliminate or reduce a portion of the equities of the enterprise, either creditorship or ownership. Upon completion of the realization-equity retirement cycle the enterprise may well be in a strong financial and operating condition. On the other hand, a given disinvestment situation may be merely one in a chain of events leading to reorganization or liquidation. In the following chapters some of the problems of reorganization and liquidation will be considered.

PROBLEMS

Problem 20–1. The Barclay Corporation has the following balance sheet as of June 30, 1966, at which date the books have been closed:

THE BARCLAY CORPORATION
BALANCE SHEET, JUNE 30, 1966

Cash	$ 400,000	Payables	$ 2,200,000
Receivables	600,000	Current accruals	250,000
Finished goods	1,200,000	5% First Mortgage bonds,	
Work in process	500,000	due June 30, 1981	1,750,000
Raw materials	800,000	Preferred stock	2,500,000
Buildings (net)	3,540,000	Common stock, 50,000 shares	
Machinery (net)	4,500,000	auth., 38,000 outstanding	3,800,000
Unamortized bond discount	60,000	Retained income	1,100,000
	$11,600,000		$11,600,000

Profits in recent years have been declining, and the management is now planning more aggressively for the future. Certain nonprofitable operations are to be sold or otherwise disposed of, the capital structure is to be modified, and possible new acquisitions are to be studied, although none is presently under consideration.

The glass-making facilities at Portsmouth have been a particularly heavy loser, and the sale of these facilities has been decided upon. The facilities to be sold include:

Buildings, at cost	$1,700,000	
Less reserve	800,000	$ 900,000
Machinery, at cost	2,000,000	
Less reserve	800,000	1,200,000
Finished goods, at cost		400,000
Raw materials, at cost		300,000
Book value of facilities to be sold		$2,800,000

None of the glass-making facilities is subject to the mortgage.

The Acme Glass Co. has evidenced an interest in acquiring these facilities and has presented four optional plans for the acquisition:

1. Cash of $2,500,000.
2. Acme Glass Co. Common stock, 100,000 shares of $20 par, market value currently ranging from $25\frac{1}{2}$ to 27. Acme is largely controlled by one family, and this block of stock would represent about 5% of the total outstanding stock and about 12% of the stock generally considered available for trading on the market.
3. A serial note issue, face value $3,600,000, with interest included in the face, the notes maturing $300,000 per year beginning June 30, 1970.
4. Convertible bonds, face value $2,800,000, interest at 4%, due on June 30, 1981, and convertible into Acme Co. Common stock at prices ranging from 38 to 50, beginning January 1, 1970. During the five years prior to June 30, 1966, Acme Common traded in a range of $12 to $36 per share.

The Barclay management is undecided as to which option to accept, part of the indecision arising from a lack of agreement on the use of any proceeds from the sale. The "Payables" balance contains $750,000 of 6% bank notes which have been outstanding for 18 months. The notes have a six-month maturity, but they have been renewed each six months, on January 1 and July 1, for the past two years. The First Mortgage bonds are callable at 103 until January 1, 1968, and at declining call premiums thereafter until maturity. The Preferred stock pays dividends of $5 per year on a cumulative basis, has no arrearage, and is redeemable at 105 until January 1, 1971, and at declining call premiums thereafter.

Required:
The management of the Barclay Corporation would like an evaluation of the options presented by the Acme Glass Co., assuming they decide (1) to make no equity adjustments presently, but to invest any cash received at an expected market rate of interest of 5%; (2) to eliminate the bank notes and bonds from the balance sheet; or (3) to redeem the preferred stock. They would also like a recommendation on the total course of action to follow.

Problem 20–2. The William Saw Co. has accepted an offer from the Morten Tool Co. for the sale of its plant and facilities at Menasha. The William Saw Co. will receive 25,000 shares of Morten Tool $100 par value common stock in exchange for the facilities. The assets sold are carried on the William Saw Co. books at the date of sale as follows:

Building	$2,500,000	
Less accrued depreciation	1,600,000	$ 900,000
Machinery and equipment	3,750,000	
Less accrued depreciation	2,250,000	1,500,000
Inventories		600,000
		$3,000,000

Operations at the Menasha plant had not been as profitable to the William Saw Co. as desired, and it was felt the sale of these facilities would remove a drain on profits. Review of the asset values shortly before the date of the sale indicated the following appraised values for the Menasha facilities:

Building (net)	$1,000,000
Machinery and equipment (net)	1,200,000
Inventories	450,000

The Morten Tool Co. common stock trades in a rather narrow market, with a price range during the two years preceding the sale of $90 to $135 per share. Just prior to announcement of the acquisition of the Menasha facilities the stock was quoted at $112. On the sale date the stock had fallen back to $105 per share.

Required:
Consider the several possible bases for recording the receipt of the Morten Tool Co. stock and prepare a journal entry to record the sale of assets in exchange for the stock. Justify your entry as best reflecting the valuation of the stock received.

Problem 20–3. The Niblick Corporation has been carrying on negotiations for the sale of one of its operating divisions at Greenbriar. The negotiations have reached a point where the Niblick management must decide which of several alternative offers to accept. The basic decision to sell has already been reached. The offers available and under consideration are:

1. Cash of $1,500,000, payable one-third at date of sale and the balance in quarterly installments, the first due three months after date of sale.
2. Cash of $300,000 and $1,250,000 in 8-year 4% notes, the notes due in full eight years from the date of sale.
3. Cash of $500,000 and $1,200,000 in 8-year non interest-bearing serial notes, the first series payable one year from the date of sale.

The assets involved in the sale negotiations have a book value of $1,350,000. The management has no specific plans in mind for employment of cash derived from the sale, but investment of such cash to earn 5% is considered the most likely usage. You agree that 5% appears to be a reasonable market rate of interest.

Required:
Determine which of the three options is most advisable from the viewpoint of the Niblick Co., disregarding all considerations other than the sale price.

Problem 20–4. During the last months of 1967 the Sawbill Co. reviewed carefully its various asset values and determined that of total assets of $1,000,000 the inventories were overvalued $80,000 on a lower of cost or market basis and the fixed properties were overvalued $140,000 on a depreciated cost basis. The company had capital stock outstanding of $400,000 stated value and retained income of $160,000. Fixed assets totaled $620,000 at cost on which depreciation of $200,000 had been recorded by the end of 1967. These assets had an average estimated life of 10 years.

Company officials cannot agree on the action to take with regard to the overvalued assets. Profits for the past three years have averaged $20,000 on sales averaging $1,000,000.

You have been asked by the Sawbill management to discuss with them some of the implications of their overvalued asset condition, including consideration of recording the write downs indicated, effects on retained income and dividend possibilities, and effects on future earnings.

Problem 20–5. The Waldie Corporation recently completed the sale of a plant site and various assets for cash. The balance sheet at December 31, 1967, appears below:

THE WALDIE CORPORATION
BALANCE SHEET, DECEMBER 31, 1967

Cash	$2,500,000	Accounts payable	$ 400,000
Receivables	500,000	20-year, 6% Notes payable,	
Inventories	1,300,000	due 12/31/1977	2,000,000
Plant and machinery (net)	4,000,000	$5.50 Preferred stock,	
Other assets	200,000	$100 par	2,000,000
		Common stock	2,500,000
		Retained income	1,600,000
	$8,500,000		$8,500,000

Several alternative uses are available for the cash on hand. The management feels that approximately $2,000,000 in cash is not required for business purposes at the existing level of operations. No immediate acquisitions or expansion plans are contemplated, although the management is not opposed to considering such plans as they might develop.

The present rate of interest for short-term investments is approximately 5%. The notes payable are redeemable at 103 prior to December 31, 1969, at 101.5 prior to December 31, 1972, and at par thereafter. The preferred stock is callable at par.

Required:

Prepare a summary for management evaluating several possible uses of the excess cash available, placing primary emphasis on cost savings.

Problem 20–6. The partnership of Bolstad, Kepler, and Fitch has the following balance sheet at December 31, 1967:

BOLSTAD, KEPLER, & FITCH

BALANCE SHEET, DECEMBER 31, 1967

Cash	$120,000	Payables	$ 50,000
Receivables	40,000	Bolstad, Capital (50%)	120,000
Inventories	60,000	Kepler, Capital (30%)	70,000
		Kepler, Drawing	(10,000)
Fixed assets (net)	80,000	Fitch, Capital (20%)	65,000
		Fitch, Drawing	5,000
	$300,000		$300,000

The partners share profits in the ratios indicated above. Fitch desires to withdraw from the partnership, and the partners agree to settle with him in cash for his equity. Prior to the settlement the following facts are determined as of December 31, 1967:

1. Purchases in transit and unrecorded, 12/31/67 $6,000
2. Inventory pricing errors, understatement, net   5,000
3. Miscellaneous accrued expenses unrecorded   3,000
4. Salary unrecorded for Fitch, an expense of the
   partnership   2,000

Settlement with Fitch is to be based on his equity, after considering any adjustments in the above, at 12/31/1967.

Required:

Prepare a schedule to determine the amount of the settlement with Fitch. If Fitch were paid $74,000, how much "Goodwill" might be recorded? How much bonus would be involved in a settlement of $74,000, assuming no goodwill is to be recorded?

Problem 20–7. Black, Boots, and Drake have been operating a partnership in which profits and losses have been shared equally. On October 31, 1967, the balances in their capital accounts appeared as follows:

Black, Capital	$30,000
Boots, Capital	36,000
Drake, Capital	38,000

In addition, during 1967 Black and Boots had each drawn $6,000 from the business, while Drake had withdrawn $2,000. Drake's salary for September and October, which is normally recorded as an expense of the partnership and an adjustment of his drawing account, had not been recorded. His salary is $1,000 per month.

On October 31, Black desires to withdraw from the partnership. If the partners agree to pay him on the basis of his equity as of October 31, and if he is paid $29,000, how much profit had the partnership earned in the first 10 months of 1967?

If the partners agree to pay Black $32,000, and if the profits per the books as of closing on October 31, 1967, were $20,000, prepare journal entries to record Black's retirement, assuming:

(1) That inventories have been improperly valued to the extent reflected in the settlement price with Black.

(2) That goodwill is to be recorded for Black only.

(3) That goodwill is to be recorded on the basis of the amount indicated by the settlement with Black.

(4) That a "bonus" entry is to be made.

Problem 20–8. Roddy, Rees, and Rowe have been in partnership for several years, sharing profits in the ratio of 2:4:4. Rowe, the senior partner and founder of the firm, is to retire as of December 31, 1967. On this date the following balance sheet is prepared:

RODDY, REES, & ROWE
BALANCE SHEET, DECEMBER 31, 1967

Cash	$ 80,000	Accounts payable	$ 20,000
Receivables	30,000	Due to Rowe	20,000
Inventory	60,000	Roddy, Capital	40,000
Fixed assets (net)	75,000	Rees, Capital	80,000
Goodwill	5,000	Rowe, Capital	90,000
	$250,000		$250,000

The partners agree that no specific asset values require modification. They also agree that Rowe is to receive $120,000 in full settlement of his partnership claims, one-half of which is payable in cash and one-half in notes payable in five equal annual installments, beginning January 1, 1969, with interest at 5% on the unpaid balance.

Required:

Prepare three alternative entries possible to record the retirement of Rowe. Evaluate the propriety of each solution.

Problem 20–9. Brewer, Swain, and Brown had been operating as a partnership for several years, and at December 31, 1967, the partners agreed that Brown would retire from active interest in the partnership. Profits and losses had been shared equally. The following balance sheet was prepared at December 31, 1967:

BREWER, SWAIN, & BROWN

BALANCE SHEET, DECEMBER 31, 1967

Cash	$ 58,000	Payables	$ 40,000
Receivables	20,000	Brewer, Capital	148,000
Inventories	60,000	Swain, Capital	130,000
Buildings (net)	180,000	Swain, Drawing	25,000
Equipment (net)	120,000	Brown, Capital	125,000
Autos and trucks (net)	30,000	Brown, Drawing	10,000
Other assets	10,000		
	$478,000		$478,000

The terms of settlement with Brown are as follows: Inventories, at lower of cost or market, are valued at $50,000; the Buildings account, which relates to two buildings, should contain a net value of $95,000 for Building A and $100,000 for Building B; Equipment has an appraisal value of $107,000; Autos and trucks contains 5 trucks, each with a net value of $4,200, and 3 autos, each with a value of $2,400; Other assets are worthless. Brown is to receive one auto, Building A (which he had owned prior to formation of the partnership), and cash of $35,000. The partners agree that the settlement with Brown involves a goodwill element and desire to recognize on their books the total goodwill implied in the settlement with Brown.

Required:
Prepare journal entries to reflect the above facts. Prepare a balance sheet giving effect to your entries.

Problem 20–10. The Bradford Corporation had the following stockholder equities at December 31, 1967:

Class A Common, 10,000 shares, par value $100		$1,000,000
Excess of issue price over par of Class A Common		600,000
		1,600,000
Class B Common, 150,000 shares, $10 stated value	$1,500,000	
Excess of issue price over stated value	400,000	1,900,000
Retained income		1,000,000
Total		$4,500,000

The Class A Common is nonvoting, and management's desire is to retire gradually this class of stock. On January 3, 1968, the management acquired on the open market 2,000 shares of the Class A Common at $125 per share. The shares were not immediately retired. The state of incorporation limits dividend payments if treasury stock is held.

Required:

(1) Prepare a journal entry to record the acquisition of the treasury shares. Prepare an equity section of the Bradford Corporation balance sheet subsequent to the acquisition of the treasury shares. Support your treatment.

(2) Prepare a journal entry to record the acquisition of the Class A Common shares assuming they are immediately retired. Prepare an equity section of the Bradford Corporation balance sheet subsequent to the retirement of the shares. Support your treatment.

Problem 20–11. The capital and surplus section of the Jones Company's balance sheet at December 31, 1967, was as follows:

Common stock—$100 par (Authorized 50,000 shares, issued and outstanding 10,000 shares)	$1,000,000
Paid-in surplus	200,000
Retained earnings	100,000
	$1,300,000

On January 2, 1968, having idle cash, the company repurchased 400 shares of its stock for $50,000. During the year it sold 100 of the reacquired shares at $135 per share, sold 100 shares at $122.50 per share and legally retired the remaining 200 shares.

Required:

(1) Discuss the accounting principles involved in handling these transactions, including consideration of possible alternatives.

(2) Prepare journal entries for each transaction in accordance with the principles which you believe should be applied.   (AICPA adapted)

Problem 20–12. The Ecton Company proposes to sell all of its assets except Cash and Receivables to the Jones Company on July 31, 1967. The sales price shall be $10,000,000 adjusted by the change in book value from December 31, 1966 to May 31, 1967 for Inventories and Property. The May 31 book values of Prepaid Expenses and Other Assets are to be added to the sales price.

The settlement shall be:

(*a*) Jones Company 4% note for $3,000,000 payable in semiannual installments of $150,000 commencing January 31, 1968.

(*b*) Assumption of all liabilities except the Estimated Federal Income Taxes Payable and Long-Term Debt.

(*c*) Balance payable in cash immediately.

The company intends to retire the preferred stock and establish a $300,000 reserve for contingencies. The net income for June and July is estimated at $150,000 before taxes (assume that a 50% tax rate has been in effect since 1962).

The last preferred stock dividend was declared on December 31, 1966. The regular common stock dividend was paid on June 15, 1967.

Taxable income for the past four years follows:

1963	$1,481,000
1964	412,400
1965	639,600
1966	842,500

Presented below are statements of financial position for December 31, 1966 and May 31, 1967:

ECTON COMPANY
STATEMENTS OF FINANCIAL POSITION

Assets	December 31, 1966	May 31, 1967
Cash	$ 1,038,000	$ 472,000
Receivables	2,550,000	3,105,000
Inventories	5,592,000	6,028,000
Prepaid expenses	308,000	297,000
Total current assets	9,488,000	9,902,000
Property (net)	6,927,000	6,804,000
Other assets	635,000	604,000
Total assets	$17,050,000	$17,310,000

Liabilities and Capital		
Accounts payable	$ 2,427,000	$ 3,052,500
Current maturities—long-term debt	600,000	600,000
Accrued liabilities	1,096,000	922,000
Dividends payable—preferred stock	63,000	0
Estimated federal income taxes	417,000	333,500
Total current liabilities	4,603,000	4,908,000
Long-term debt	4,200,000	4,050,000
Stockholders' equity:		
Preferred cumulative stock—21,000 shares of $100 par, 3%, outstanding. Redeemable at $102	2,100,000	2,100,000
Common stock—100,000 shares of $10 par outstanding	1,000,000	1,000,000
Capital contributed in excess of par value of common stock	587,000	587,000
Retained earnings	4,560,000	4,665,000
Total liabilities and capital	$17,050,000	$17,310,000

Note:
    The increase in Retained Earnings is net of a dividend of $.20 per share paid March 15, 1967 on common stock.

Required:

(1) Compute the total sales price and settlement to be made.

(2) Compute Ecton Company's gain or loss on the sale giving effect to income taxes.

(3) Prepare a worksheet with column headings "Per Books," "Adjustments," and "Estimated Statement of Financial Position, July 31, 1967" giving effect to the proposed sale and other information given.   Support your adjustments with schedules or computations you deem necessary.   (AICPA adapted)

CHAPTER **21**

Reorganizations

In the preceding chapter some of the accounting problems encountered when an enterprise contracts its scope of operations were considered. In most of the situations considered it was presumed that the enterprise would continue operations somewhat as it had in the past, although on a reduced scale. In addition, it was presumed that existing ownership interests would not be severely upset. At times, however, an enterprise may require a rather drastic overhauling if it is to continue as an operating enterprise. The enterprise which emerges from the overhauling may bear the same name, but it frequently will have a new look, a new management, a new financial structure, and in some instances, a substantially new ownership equity. This chapter will deal with some of the accounting problems arising from various forms of enterprise reorganization. In general, the reorganizations considered will have been preceded by a period in which the enterprise has had financial difficulties. The basic earning potential may still exist, but its emergence awaits various changes and modifications in the enterprise financial structure.

The problems to be considered could relate to all types of business organizations, and are found to some degree in proprietorships, partnerships, and corporations. The type of business organization, however, will not be an important aspect of the problem in most instances. The primary areas of interest in the reorganization area lie in the various equity interests and in the elimination of the causes of the financial difficulties of an enterprise.

The residual owners of a business which has had past financial difficulties, but which has a basic earning potential, may decide that the simplest procedure to eliminate existing problems is to dissolve the existing enterprise and to begin a new enterprise with the remains of the old. Frequently such a procedure involves certain legal requirements, considerable time, and even a diminution or gradual erosion of the basic earning potential.

The dissolution of the existing enterprise and emergence of a new enterprise may be accomplished by meeting certain legal requirements pertaining to dissolution of an existing business and formation of a new business. On the other hand, a similar end result may be obtained through the employment of certain accounting entries and without a legal dissolution.

Legal Background. A corporate enterprise may find the reorganization procedure somewhat easier to accomplish than will a proprietorship or a partnership. Thus a new corporation may be formed legally to take over the assets of an existing enterprise, the latter being legally dissolved in the process. Since the new corporation is a new entity, the values attached to the assets and the equities of the new corporation need not be related in any way to the values attached to the same assets and equities in the old enterprise. For example, the valuation of the inventories taken over by the new enterprise would depend upon the "cost" of those assets to the new enterprise, and this cost might be far different from the basis, or unrecovered cost, at which the inventories were carried on the preceding corporation's books.

One interesting example of this device to gain a fresh start involved a public utility company which found it desirable to shift from acquisition cost in order to maintain a suitable rate base upon which the rate of income was allowed by the rate-making agency. The company in question reorganized several times, and so little was the change that in one instance the new corporation differed from the dissolved corporation only in that a comma was deleted from the title used by the dissolved corporation to provide a title for the new company.

Of course, the concept underlying the coincident establishment of a new corporate entity to replace a dissolved predecessor may involve a departure from the acquisition-cost basis of the assets of the old enterprise. The device cited is a legal device, since the corporation is a legal creature. and the accountant is thereby forced to consider adjusting the existing acquisition costs. This does not mean that the assets of the new corporation may be stated at any convenient basis desired by the new equity interests. The assets are valued at new acquisition cost, however, and this is normally determined by appraisal of fair market value or in some similar manner. While it may appear that this is a devious means of avoiding adherence to the acquisition cost principle, the fact remains that legally a new entity exists, and the new entity should not necessarily be bound by decisions made by the predecessor entity.

Accounting Background. The above described procedure of legally dissolving an existing enterprise and creating a new enterprise to take its place may be somewhat costly and may also be impractical in some instances. From a practical point of view it does not appear that justification for a restatement of various asset and equity interests should turn upon a legal nicety such as the dissolution-creation procedure described. Thus in practice the revaluation of assets downward, and the resulting realignment of equity interests, has been an accepted accounting procedure when there is reason to think the enterprise might otherwise legally reorganize and find legal support for the revaluations. The process by which accountants record revaluations of assets without a formal reorganization is sometimes referred to as a quasi-reorganization. The term indicates that the same results as a formal reorganization are accomplished, but the legal processes of the formal reorganization are absent. The quasi-reorganization is also sometimes referred to as the "fresh start."

QUASI-REORGANIZATION

Characteristics. Quasi-reorganizations should be limited to rather unusual business situations and should possess all or most of the following characteristics:

(1) *A new management.* When a new management assumes control of an enterprise which has had financial difficulties, the new management should be relieved of responsibility for the mistakes of the former management if such mistakes are reflected in overstated asset values. Since the asset values carried forward would eventually flow through an income statement, the new management may be entitled to assume asset values which are more in line with actualities at the time the new management assumes control.

(2) *Overstated asset values.* If an enterprise has had a period of operating losses, but if it also has a valid potential earning capacity, and if in spite of the operating losses the asset valuations are still excessive in relation to current values, it would appear that justification exists for asset write downs. Continued adherence to the existing asset values may distort depreciation charges in the coming periods and thereby prevent the reported income from being a realistic measure of the operating efficiency of management.

(3) *Overstated equity values.* If asset values are excessive it follows that some equity interests are also overvalued. Normally, the equity of the residual owners (stockholders in the case of a corporation) is overstated. The inaccurate picture presented generally has arisen from a failure in the past to recognize all losses that have occurred.

(4) *A brighter future.* If operating losses have been incurred in the past, or if such losses have not been reported but actually exist in overstated asset and equity values, an enterprise may find that its financial statements do not disclose a fair picture of its earning potential. Development of new products, emergence of new markets, institution of new management, elimination of past inefficiencies, and other developments may make the future appear brighter, even from an objective viewpoint. While a new enterprise may not be a legal reality, the future may be so much different from the past that a new enterprise *appears* to exist. If this situation exists, accounting adjustments to effect the new enterprise may be warranted.

Upward vs. Downward Revaluations. The above discussion has not dealt with the situation where a "fresh start" is warranted and the existing asset and equity interests are undervalued. The question may be raised: Do accountants utilize the quasi-reorganization procedure to include upward revaluation of assets as well as downward adjustments? In one sense it is difficult to justify the downward adjustment and reject the upward revaluation of assets. Both represent an attempt to correct valuations on the accounting records. It has previously been emphasized, however, that accountants are reluctant to depart from the acquisition cost principle. This reluctance is reflected in the view that revaluation of assets should normally be recorded only when an objective transaction takes place. The adherence to acquisition cost appears to be more tenacious on the part of accountants when the possible revaluation is upward than when it is downward. Losses are more often recognized prior to an actual transaction occurrence than are gains. Thus many accountants at the present time support the quasi-reorganization procedure when assets are overvalued, but do not support a similar procedure to correct the accounts for assets which are undervalued.

While many reasons have been cited to support the accounting procedure of recognizing losses prior to a transaction occurrence, most of the reasons appear more in the nature of attempts to justify the procedure rather than to explain the reason for the procedure. It seems likely that the reason behind the advance recognition of losses (without a similar advance recognition of gains) lies in the historical conservatism of accountants. Most of the outside pressures on accountants during the early part of the century—the period of emergence of accounting as an important service to business—originated from conservative sources, bankers and other credit grantors. Since their primary concern was an absence of overvaluation, it is not unusual that write downs were somewhat prevalent. While accountants today do not generally approve indiscriminate write downs, the past effect of conservatism probably makes write downs to appropriate values more acceptable than write ups to appropriate values. The accountant probably has not overcome completely his past conditioning to accept conservative departures from otherwise acceptable standards.

Revaluations in a Quasi-Reorganization. If a management decides that an accounting, or quasi-, reorganization is warranted, the first step would be to determine the fair market values of the various assets that will be employed in the future operations of the enterprise. While some accountants would contend that only the fixed assets should be revalued, the quasi-reorganization procedure should probably be a thorough-going one and include revaluation of all the assets. If it is realized that the justification for the quasi-reorganization procedure lies in the "fresh start" which the enterprise is contemplating, it appears only logical that the reorganization should include a review and adjustment of all asset and equity elements. The following illustration indicates the process of revaluation in a quasi-reorganization.

Illustration of Quasi-Reorganization

Assume that the EXY Corporation has been in operation for several years, that for the past few years operating results have not been satisfactory, and that assets are presently overvalued. However, certain new products have been perfected from a marketability viewpoint, and the officers are convinced that profitable operations will exist in the coming months. The statement of financial position of the EXY Corporation on December 31, 1967, follows, on page 614, with current fair values of the assets shown parenthetically.

Adjustment of Assets. Assuming the fair market values as shown are reasonable and that the management wishes to proceed with a revaluation of the assets, the accountant would record the revaluation as follows:

Inventory	$ 1,000	
Loss on revaluation of assets	25,000	
Receivables		$ 1,000
Building		20,000
Machinery		5,000
(to record revaluation of assets to fair market value)		

EXY CORPORATION

FINANCIAL POSITION AS OF DECEMBER 31, 1967

Assets

Cash ($40,000)	$ 40,000
Receivables ($89,000)	90,000
Inventories ($21,000)	20,000
Building ($80,000)	100,000
Machinery ($45,000)	50,000
Total assets	$300,000

Equities

Current liabilities	$ 60,000
Capital stock (par value $100)	200,000
Retained earnings	40,000
Total equities	$300,000

The effect of the above entry is to place the assets at a proper value for future operating periods of the enterprise. The loss on revaluation of assets might be reflected on the 1967 income statement as a special charge; or, if material, the loss could be closed directly to retained earnings. In either case full disclosure of the treatment and of the quasi-reorganization would be essential.

Adjustment of Equities. The quasi-reorganization in the above example involved only a revaluation of assets. Now assume that the assets of the EXY Corporation as shown on the above statement of financial position at cost are proper valuations. Thus $300,000 does measure the fair value of the assets of the corporation. Also assume that the equity section of the statement appears as follows:

Equities

Current liabilities	$ 60,000
Capital stock (par value $100)	400,000
Retained earnings (Deficit)	(160,000)
Total equities	$300,000

Since the future outlook for the EXY Corporation is relatively bright, the management may decide that the existing deficit should be eliminated if possible so that the expected profits of the future may be available for dividends without having to overcome the large deficit. One means of eliminating this deficit would be to reduce the par value of the common stock from $100 a share to $60 a share. The reduction of the par value would create a paid-in surplus against which the deficit could be charged. This procedure would eliminate the deficit and permit dividends to be paid out of future earnings.

If the par value of the capital stock is reduced to $60 per share, the following entry would be made:

Capital stock	$160,000	
Paid-in surplus		$160,000
(to reduce par value per share from $100		
to $60, or $40 per share on 4,000 shares		
outstanding = $160,000)		

The existing deficit could then be charged off against the surplus created in the above entry:

Paid-in surplus	$160,000	
Retained earnings (deficit)		$160,000

After these entries have been made, the equity section of the statement of financial position of the EXY Corporation would be:

Equities

Current liabilities	$ 60,000
Capital stock (par value $60)	240,000
Retained earnings	–0–
Total equities	$300,000

It should be noted that it is not necessary for the reduction in par of the capital stock to equal exactly the deficit to be eliminated. Thus, the par value above could have been reduced to $50 per share, creating a paid-in surplus of $200,000. After eliminating the deficit, $40,000 of paid-in surplus would remain.

The above entries give effect to a quasi-reorganization even though no asset adjustments were involved. Thus a revaluation of assets is not necessary to effect a quasi-reorganization. If the assets are already properly valued and the various losses have been recorded previously through the normal accounting procedure, the result may have been to produce the deficit which was assumed to exist above. The quasi-reorganization then becomes a problem in elimination of the deficit.

Adjustments of Both Assets and Equities. Most quasi-reorganizations involve both the adjustment of asset values and the adjustment of equity interests. Thus assume that the EXY Corporation in the previous examples has a statement of financial position reporting assets at acquisition cost of $300,000, but with the fair values as indicated on page 614. Also assume the equities to be those in the preceding section, with a $160,000 deficit existing from past operations.

In this situation the EXY Corporation accountant should first record the write down of the assets to their fair values (see entry on page 613), and should charge the resulting loss to the Retained Earnings (Deficit) account. After recording the asset revaluation, the deficit would be $185,000. At this point the board of directors of the corporation would probably decide to write down the par value of the capital stock sufficiently to absorb the entire $185,000 deficit in the paid-in surplus created in the write down of par. Assuming that the par is to be reduced to $50 per share, the following series of entries would be made to record the quasi-reorganization:

Inventory	$ 1,000	
Retained earnings (deficit)	25,000	
Receivables		$ 1,000
Building		20,000
Machinery		5,000
Capital stock	$200,000	
Paid-in surplus		$200,000
Paid-in surplus	$185,000	
Retained earnings (deficit)		$185,000

The statement of financial position of the EXY Corporation after giving effect to the quasi-reorganization would be:

EXY CORPORATION
FINANCIAL POSITION AS OF DECEMBER 31, 1967

Assets

Cash	$ 40,000
Receivables	89,000
Inventories	21,000
Building	80,000
Machinery	45,000
Total assets	$275,000

Equities

Current liabilities	$ 60,000
Capital stock (par value $50)	200,000
Paid-in surplus	15,000
Total equities	$275,000

A thorough explanation of the reorganization procedure should accompany the statement to enable the reader to interpret properly the results of the reorganization.

Dating of Retained Earnings. If the EXY Corporation reports profitable operations in 1968, such profits would be closed to the Retained Earnings account in the normal manner. However, a statement of financial position prepared at December 31, 1968, should disclose that the retained earnings reported has been accumulated since December 31, 1967, the effective date of the quasi-reorganization. In order to put the statement reader on notice that a reorganization has occurred and that the amount in the Retained Earnings account represents only undistributed earnings since reorganization, the Retained Earnings account should be dated for several years. It is unlikely that the date would have significance after a period of 10 years, and in some instances the date of the amount could be discontinued at the conclusion of a period of less than 10 years.[1]

FINANCIAL REORGANIZATIONS

In addition to the accounting, or quasi-, reorganization procedure, business enterprises in financial difficulty may employ various other means to alleviate their financial problems. Certain available methods involve modifications in the financial structure of the enterprise; such modifications are implemented by the existing management or by representatives of existing equity interests, and are discussed at this point. Other procedures involve modifications in the financial structure of the enterprise; such modifications are implemented by a court, trustee, or other agency outside the existing enterprise management or equity interests, and are considered in the final portion of this chapter. Finally, some procedures involve plans to liquidate the enterprise. Accounting problems involved in liquidations will be considered in the final section of the book, beginning with Chapter 22.

Securing an Extension of Time for Payments to Creditors

When the financial difficulty arises from a temporary shortage of cash occasioned by having too much of the equity contributions tied up in noncash assets, it is often possible to secure from creditors an extension of the time period over which the debts will be paid. Creditors are aware that, if they resort to legal procedures to collect their claims against the enterprise, considerable time and expense may be involved. Thus the creditors may prefer to grant an extension of time to the debtor in the hope that the amount due will be paid in full, within a reasonable time, and without incurring the ill will that may arise in a legal action.

[1] *Accounting Research Bulletin* 46, American Institute of Certified Public Accountants, February, 1956.

The accounting personnel of an enterprise in financial difficulty may be asked to aid in the solution of problems of this nature in the following ways:

(1) The development of a cash budget or cash forecast to accompany the request for an extension of time. If the creditors can see that the enterprise in financial difficulty has a well-thought-out plan of reducing its indebtedness, they may be more amenable to the suggested extension of time.

(2) The development of a schedule for the payment of various creditors. This becomes particularly important if the extension of time is granted only by certain creditors.

Refinancing of Debt

At times financial difficulty may arise from, or at least be partially the result of, heavy interest or financing charges on existing bonds or other debt obligations. Thus a company may have a bond issue outstanding on which it is paying 6% interest, when under present conditions a similar bond issue could be sold at $3\frac{1}{2}\%$ or 4% interest. If the company could replace the existing bonds with bonds carrying the lower interest rate, at least one factor contributing to the financial difficulty would be removed. In other situations a company may have a bond issue coming due but not have available funds with which to meet the retirement of the debt. Depending upon the going rate of interest, the company might well be able to sell a new bond issue, possibly at a lower interest rate, and use the proceeds to retire the bonds which are presently maturing. This process of replacing an existing indebtedness with a new indebtedness is generally referred to as refinancing or refunding. It should be noted here that refinancing or refunding of debt may arise in enterprises which are financially sound, as well as in enterprises which are in financial difficulty. The conditions surrounding the refinancing are not significant from the accounting viewpoint.

Refinancing at Face Value. In the simplest situation, Zee Company may have outstanding $1,000,000 of first mortgage, 6% bonds, which were issued at par 10 years ago and which have 15 years remaining until maturity. In addition, the bond indenture of these bonds provides that they are callable at par any time prior to maturity. In order to reduce the interest charges, the company may decide to call this bond issue and to replace the indebtedness with an issue of $1,000,000 first mortgage bonds, with interest at 4%. Assuming that the new bond issue could be sold at exactly the face amount, the following entry summarizes the transaction:

Bonds payable	$1,000,000	
Bonds payable		$1,000,000

The net effect of the refinancing would be to reduce the interest charges by $20,000 a year (from $60,000 to $40,000). Since the old bonds have 15 years of life remaining, a saving of $300,000 may be gained over the 15 years. As this saving would build up annually in $20,000 increments, investment of the increments would produce an additional saving. Offsetting this saving would be the cost of refinancing, which would include the costs of printing and selling the new bonds, and of calling and retiring the old bonds.

Refinancing with a Call Premium. Assume that the Zee Company has outstanding $1,000,000 of first mortgage, 6% bonds, which were issued at par 10 years ago. Because of the decline in the market rate of interest, the management believes that it will be advisable to call the old bonds and to issue new bonds bearing 4% interest to replace them. However, the existing bonds are not presently callable at par. The call price at the date decided upon is 103.

Assuming that the company does not have any excess cash available to help retire the bonds, it is apparent that the new bonds will have to yield an amount in excess of $1,000,000 if the old bonds are to be retired. The sale of the new bonds must yield at least $1,030,000 (103% of par). The management of the Zee Company must evaluate several alternatives in arriving at a decision on how to retire the 6% bonds. Assume that the decision is finally made to set the interest rate at 4% on the new bonds. If at the date of sale the 4% bonds sell at 99, the Zee Company will have to sell in excess of $1,040,000 par value bonds of the new issue in order to realize enough cash to retire the old bonds. Assume they decide to issue bonds of $1,050,000 par value at 99. This would provide cash of $1,039,500, of which $1,030,000 would be necessary to retire the outstanding bonds. The entries to record these events could be made as follows:

Cash	$1,039,500	
Unamortized bond discount	10,500	
Bonds payable		$1,050,000
(to record the sale and issuance of new bonds)		
Bonds payable	$1,000,000	
Loss on retirement of bonds	30,000	
Cash		$1,030,000
(to record retirement of original issue of bonds)		

The loss on retirement of the bonds ($30,000) and the bond discount ($10,500) would in effect be recovered over the years through the reduction in interest costs from $60,000 a year to $40,000 a year.

Unamortized Discount or Premium on Issue Outstanding.
Another problem that sometimes exists in the refinancing of an existing
bond issue has to do with any unamortized discount or premium on
the original bond issuance which is still being carried at the time of the
refinancing. Thus, for example, the Zee Company might have sold
initially the $1,000,000 of first mortgage, 6% bonds at 97½, or for $975,000.
If the life of these bonds is assumed to be 25 years, and if the refinancing
arises 10 years after the initial sale, $15,000 of unamortized discount
exists at the date of the refinancing.

Three alternatives are commonly suggested as possibilities for handling
this discount:

(1) The discount (or premium if such existed) could be written off
immediately to income as a gain or loss on retirement of the bonds, or
directly to retained earnings. The decision as between a charge
(credit) in the income statement or a charge (credit) to retained
earnings normally rests upon the materiality of the amount involved.

(2) The discount (premium) could be amortized over the remaining
period of the life of the original bond issue. In the above example,
the discount would be written off over 15 years, the remaining life of
the bonds retired.

(3) The discount (premium) could be amortized over the life of the new
bonds. Thus, if the 4% bonds which the Zee Company is selling to
retire the original bonds has a life of 25 years, the $15,000 unamortized
discount would be written off over this 25-year period.

Referring to the illustration above, if the Zee Company retired at 103
their 6% bonds, which had $15,000 unamortized discount and 15 years to
maturity, and if the retirement were effected by the sale at 99 of $1,050,000
of 4% bonds, the following entry could be made under the first alternative
above:

Cash	$ 9,500	
Loss on retirement of bonds	45,000	
Unamortized bond discount	10,500	
Bonds payable	1,000,000	
Unamortized bond discount		$ 15,000
Bonds payable		1,050,000

The loss on retirement of bonds is composed of the $15,000 unamortized
discount on the bonds retired, plus the $30,000 premium required to call
the old bonds in order to retire them. If this amount were so material as to
distort the current period's net income, the amount might be charged
directly to retained earnings.

Under the second and third alternatives above, the entry at the date of retirement of the 6% bonds would not be affected by the unamortized discount. Thus the entries would be the same as those shown on page 619. Subsequent periods would be charged for a portion of the $15,000 ($1,000 per year under the second alternative, and $600 a year under the third alternative).

Immediate Write Off. Numerous arguments have been advanced over the years in support of the three alternatives. The direct charge to income or to retained earnings for the unamortized discount or premium treats this item in a manner similar to the issue cost or redemption premium on the bonds retired. The basic question seems to rest on the time when the gain or loss on retirement is to be recognized. The immediate elimination of the redemption premium, issue cost, and unamortized discount or premium on the bonds retired may be justified by reasoning that the retirement of the bonds brings to a close a series of entries arising from those bonds. Since the bonds are no longer carried forward, all costs (income) related to those bonds should also be closed to income or retained earnings. The fact that the bonds were replaced by similar bonds is not significant in determining the accounting treatment for the retirement of the old bonds.

Amortization Over Life of Original Issue. The second alternative has been supported on the grounds that the cost of borrowing money was established at the date of the issuance of the original bonds. Thus, unless future periods are charged or credited with "their share" of the gain or loss on retirement of the bonds, an overstatement or an understatement of income will exist in the future periods. The benefit to the future periods from the lower interest charges on the new bonds must be offset by the portion of the loss (gain) arising from the retirement of the original issue.

Amortization Over Life of New Issue. The third alternative does not appear to have much theoretical support. There seems to be little justification for charging unamortized costs of one bond issue over a period unrelated to that bond issue.

It is the opinion of the authors that the first alternative, the charging off of the unamortized discount as a loss on retirement, either to income or to retained earnings, is the most appropriate procedure. This procedure is consistent with other accounting procedures which recognize gains and losses at the time of their occurrence. If the second procedure were used, a logical extension of it into the area of fixed asset accounting would require that gains or losses on assets replaced should not be recognized until such time as the assets would have been fully depreciated.

Refinancing of debt may involve either an increase or a decrease in the amount of debt previously outstanding. Likewise, refinancing may well arise at times when the enterprise is in a sound financial condition. However, enterprises which are in financial difficulty may well be able to convince various equity interests that, through refinancing, the causes or some of the causes of the financial difficulty may be eliminated.

Creditor Committee

The process of turning the business over to a committee representing the creditors is, in reality, more in the nature of a change in management than it is a reorganization. Likewise, the formation of a creditor committee, and its assumption of control of the business operations, may frequently follow certain legal proceedings. At times, however, a group of creditors may organize to advise, on a voluntary basis, the existing management. In any event, the end effect desired is to eliminate the causes of financial difficulty and to rehabilitate the business prior to the resumption of control by the former management. At times a legal reorganization is effected before the business is returned to the ownership equities. No particular accounting problems arise from the existence of a creditor committee. Any actions taken or transactions entered into by the committee would be recorded in the same manner as if the previous management had taken the action or entered into the transaction.

Equity Receivership

An alternative to the formation of a creditor committee may involve the filing of a petition in a court requesting the court to protect the business during a period of financial difficulty or planning preceding reorganization. As with a creditor committee, the request for the protection of the court may be voluntary on the part of the management of the enterprise, or it may be involuntarily imposed at the request of one or more equity interests. If the court deems such action desirable, it may appoint either an individual or a corporation to act as receiver. The receiver is an agent of the court, and since the purpose of appointment of the receiver is to preserve the interests of the various equity groups of the corporation, the period during which the receiver has control of the operations of the enterprise is generally referred to as a period of equity receivership.

Legal Procedures. In an equity receivership the court appoints the receiver, provides the receiver with certain instructions, and in general assumes responsibility for the protection of the assets and of the equity interests of the corporation. The receiver is generally charged with the responsibility of attempting to eliminate the causes of financial difficulty, and at the same time he must retain the goodwill of the various equity interests. If the receiver is unable to remove the causes of difficulty, or if he is unable to get the various parties to agree to a particular plan of reorganization, he may recommend to the court that liquidation proceedings be instituted. If such action does result, the receiver may supervise the liquidation. Likewise, during the period of receivership, one or more of the equity interests may petition the court for institution of liquidation proceedings. As discussed in the following chapter, the institution of receivership proceedings, either voluntary or involuntary, when the debtor is insolvent under the terms of bankruptcy law is an act of bankruptcy. As such, any creditor who may so desire may institute bankruptcy proceedings. If the debtor business is found to be bankrupt the receivership proceedings are terminated.

Equity receiverships may proceed under state courts or under federal courts, depending upon the circumstances. While receiverships may begin in an atmosphere of cooperation, various conflicts of interest may arise as the receivership period progresses. The resolution of the conflicts to the satisfaction of the varied parties at interest is frequently a difficult and time-consuming problem. At times the parties at conflict cannot reach a suitable agreement, and, if this situation does result, complete reorganization or even liquidation may be necessary.

Accounting Procedures. Although the accounting problems of a receivership are discussed in more detail in Chapter 24, it should be noted at this point that a receiver must maintain thorough records of the various actions taken during the period of receivership. Just as business management has the responsibility of maintaining adequate records for the information of the various equity interests of the enterprise, so the receiver must maintain similarly detailed records to discharge his responsibilities to the court as well as to the existing equity interests.

In recent years, since the amendment to the Bankruptcy Act of 1933, equity receivership proceedings have become relatively uncommon. The procedure was unduly time consuming and costly, and provisions of the Bankruptcy Act afford comparable relief which, at least in theory, may be accomplished in a more economical and less time-consuming manner.

Reorganizations under Bankruptcy Act

Amendments to the Bankruptcy Act in 1938 (as well as those adopted in 1933 and 1934) dealt to a considerable degree with relief provisions for debtors. Chapter X of the 1938 amendment (Chandler Act) governs those corporate reorganizations wherein revisions of the capital structure are proposed. In general, corporate reorganizations other than those involving adjustment of unsecured obligations only fall within the framework of Chapter X.

Legal Procedures. The action preliminary to a reorganization is somewhat similar to that preceding an equity receivership. The petition to effect a reorganization plan may be filed with the court by the corporation or by any of the equity interests or their representatives. The filing of the reorganization petition is not an act of bankruptcy, however, and the court may approve the petition even though bankruptcy proceedings may be pending against the corporation. Depending upon the size of the corporation, the court may appoint one or more trustees (comparable in duties and responsibilities to receivers) to administer the assets of the corporation, or the existing management may continue in control.

After the trustee assumes control, or after management is approved to retain control under the petition, a reorganization plan is prepared and filed with the court. The court will hold a hearing on the plan, and if the plan is fair, equitable, and feasible it will be approved. At this point the plan is submitted to the various equity interests for their approval. Approval must be obtained from the holders of two-thirds of the amount of the equity in each equity class which has had its claim allowed by the court. A majority of each class of stockholders must also approve the plan if the corporation is solvent. After the approvals of the various equity interests have been obtained, the court will hold another hearing on the plan and, providing the plan is still considered to be fair, equitable, and feasible, the court will order the plan confirmed. The plan is then binding on all parties, and the trustee or management in control will execute the various terms of the plan. After the various provisions of the plan have been carried out, the court will enter an order discharging the corporation from its liabilities and discharging the trustee from his responsibilities.

As mentioned above, the reorganization provisions of Chapter X of the Chandler Act have largely rendered equity receivership obsolete. While the expected savings in time and costs under the reorganization procedure probably have not been realized, this procedure has been effective in rehabilitating financially troubled corporations. Under the equity receivership procedure the court (and the receiver) was in the position of being a guardian of the corporation, with its main duty being to preserve the rights of the various parties at issue until the management resumed control or until liquidation proceedings began. Under reorganization procedure, the court largely assumes the responsibilities of corporate management, and its main duty is to preserve the fundamental values of the various properties in order for each equity interest to obtain the fairest and most equitable adjustment of its claims possible.

Accounting Procedures. The accounting problems arising in a reorganization plan may be divided into two groups:

(1) Those arising from the assumption of control by a trustee or other court appointed official. The trustee is in a position comparable to the receiver in an equity receivership, and he should maintain such records as will permit him to render a thorough and accurate report to the court and the equity interests regarding the actions taken during the period of his control. This problem area is discussed in greater detail in Chapter 24.

(2) Those arising from the sales, disposals, or adjustments made to the various asset values of the corporation, and from the settlements, agreements, or adjustments made with the various equity interests of the corporation.

In addition to the problems in these two groups, it must be recognized that the advice and counsel of accountants are solicited on a widespread basis in reorganization planning. Problems of asset valuation, projections of future earning probabilities, and evaluations of the equity in the various phases of the reorganization plan are all areas in which the accountant may render valuable service.

While it is quite difficult to generalize regarding reorganization plans, the following example indicates a few of the readjustments in the equity structure that might be made. In the illustration it is necessary to recognize that a considerable amount of discussion, proposal, and counter-proposal preceded the plan finally decided upon. Likewise, the plan itself could have been varied in a number of respects. The primary interest here lies in the accounting treatment accorded the various provisions of the reorganization plan as agreed upon. It might also be desirable to compare the discussion in the following example with the plan of reorganization discussed on pages 611–617, to see the differences in a rather thorough-going financial reorganization and a quasi-reorganization.

ILLUSTRATION. *Reorganization of the F Corporation.* The F Corporation is a manufacturer of machine tools. During its early life the company incurred steady losses, but in 1966 and 1967 the operations generated $800,000 total profit after interest charges and taxes. The future outlook is promising, but the corporation has certain restrictive covenants in some of the equity provisions that will impede growth. Throughout 1967 representatives of the various equity interests met and finally agreed upon a reorganization plan which has been approved by the proper court officials. The plan is to be made effective on January 1, 1968. The statement of financial position of the F Corporation on December 31, 1967, appears below. Following the statement are the various provisions of the reorganization plan.

THE F CORPORATION
FINANCIAL POSITION DECEMBER 31, 1967

Assets

Cash	$ 600,000
Receivables	1,800,000
Inventories	3,440,000
Plant and equipment	10,300,000
Unamortized bond discount	60,000
Total assets	$16,200,000

Equities

Current payables	$ 2,000,000
5% First mortgage bonds payable, due 1/1/78	6,000,000
6% Cumulative preferred stock, $50 par value, 100,000 shares outstanding (Dividends in arrears since 1/1/59)	5,000,000
Common stock, no par, 120,000 shares outstanding, assigned value of $40 per share	4,800,000
Accumulated operating deficit	(1,600,000)
Total equities	$16,200,000

(1) No revision in the carrying value of the assets is to be made. Review of current values indicates the assets are reasonably stated.

(2) Current payables will be paid in full as they fall due. The corporation has been slow in paying its current debt, but has paid all such debt in full in the past. The various current payables have agreed to a reasonable extension of time of payments on a temporary basis.

(3) The bondholders have agreed to surrender their 5% first mortgage bonds on the following terms: Each $1,000 bond will be exchanged for one $1,000, $3\frac{1}{2}$% first mortgage bond, due January 1, 1978, plus five shares of new Class B common stock.

(4) Preferred stockholders have agreed that the 6% preferred stock be reduced from $50 par value per share to $40 par value; that it continue to be preferred for $3 per share dividends on a cumulative basis; and that it be preferred in liquidation at $50 per share. In settlement of the dividends in arrears, cash of $400,000 is to be paid and 125,000 shares of Class B common stock are to be issued. Class B common has a $10 par value, is nonvoting, and is not entitled to dividends. In addition,

the Class B common is redeemable at $25 per share and entitled to $25 per share after preferred but prior to Class A common in liquidation. The Class B common is to be retired through a redemption fund to be created by yearly deposits equal to 50% of net profit in excess of preferred dividend requirements. No dividend will be paid on the Class A common until the Class B common has been fully retired.

(5) The common stock is to be exchanged for Class A common on a share for share basis, but the stated value of the new Class A common is to be $10 per share.

Entries to give effect to the plan:

(a)	5% First mortgage bonds payable	$6,000,000	
	Reorganization surplus	360,000	
	$3\frac{1}{2}$% First mortgage bonds payable		$6,000,000
	Class B common stock		300,000
	Unamortized bond discount		60,000

This entry gives effect to the transfer of the 5% bonds for $3\frac{1}{2}$% bonds and Class B common stock. The unamortized discount is written off, although this amount could be carried forward on the reasoning that the bonds to which it was related are, in effect, still outstanding. However, a write off appears advisable at this time on the reasoning that a new equity structure exists and no discount arose in its formation. The Reorganization Surplus account is a temporary account used only to effect the equity changes. It is disposed of in the final entry below.

(b)	6% Cumulative preferred stock	$1,000,000	
	Reorganization surplus		$1,000,000

This entry records the reduction in the par value of the preferred stock and the reorganization surplus created by the write down in par value.

(c)	Reorganization surplus	$1,650,000	
	Cash		$ 400,000
	Class B common stock		1,250,000

This entry records the settlement of the preferred dividend arrearage. The Class B common is recorded at its par value rather than at its redemption value. The redemption value and terms of redemption must be fully disclosed on the statement of financial position.

(d)	Common stock	$4,800,000	
	Class A common stock		$1,200,000
	Reorganization surplus		3,600,000

This entry records the transfer of the old common for the new Class A common and the write down in par value from $40 per share to $10 per share.

(e) Reorganization surplus $1,600,000
      Accumulated operating deficit $1,600,000

This entry eliminates the existing operating deficit by a charge against the reorganization surplus established through the write downs of par of the preferred and common stock.

(f) Reorganization surplus $990,000
      Paid-in surplus $990,000

This entry closes the Reorganization Surplus account and transfers the balance to a Paid-in Surplus account which will be more appropriately described for financial statement reporting purposes. Any retained earnings resulting from profitable operations in the future should be dated from 1/1/68.

After the above entries have been made the statement of financial position of the F Corporation would appear as follows:

THE F CORPORATION
FINANCIAL POSITION, JANUARY 1, 1968

Assets

Cash	$ 200,000
Receivables	1,800,000
Inventories	3,440,000
Plant and equipment	10,300,000
Total assets	$15,740,000

Equities

Current payables	$ 2,000,000
$3\frac{1}{2}\%$ First mortgage bonds payable, due 1/1/78	6,000,000
6% Cumulative preferred stock, $40 par value—100,000 shares outstanding (Note 1)	4,000,000
Class B common stock, par value $10 per share, 155,000 shares outstanding (Notes 2 and 4)	1,550,000
Class A common stock, stated value $10 per share, 120,000 shares outstanding (Note 3)	1,200,000
Paid-in surplus (excess of equity write downs at reorganization of 1/1/68 over existing operating deficit)	990,000
Total equities	$15,740,000

Note 1. Stock is entitled to $50 per share in liquidation.

Note 2. Stock is not entitled to dividends, is redeemable at $25 per share, and is preferred over Class A Common as to assets in liquidation at $25 per share.

Note 3. The liquidating preference of the preferred stock amounting to $5,000,000 and of the Class B common stock amounting to $3,875,000 exceeds the entire shareholders' equity of the company and creates a deficiency to the Class A common stock amounting to $1,135,000 as of January 1, 1967. No dividends may be paid on the Class A common stock as long as any Class B common stock remains outstanding.

Note 4. The Class B common stock is to be retired through accumulation of a cash fund equal to 50% of the net profits in excess of dividend requirements on preferred stock. The stock will be retired as funds are available at a price of $25 per share.

Summary. While the above illustration is merely indicative of the treatment in the accounting records of a reorganization plan, it does indicate the thorough-going nature of such a plan. The reorganization of a business enterprise which has suffered a period of financial difficulty is a complex process. Even though a sound plan is worked out and is acceptable to all interests concerned, there is no assurance that the plan will eliminate the causes of the difficulty. Unless the basic cause or causes of the past financial difficulties are eliminated, a plan of reorganization may merely provide a short breathing period prior to eventual liquidation of the enterprise. A sound plan of reorganization accompanied by a suitable economic climate and the elimination of the causes of financial distress may well result in a rehabilitated company, one in which the various equity interests will fare far better than they would through a liquidation of the enterprise. If the enterprise does recuperate, its subsequent problems will be similar to those discussed in earlier sections of this textbook. If the enterprise is not able to re-establish a firm financial base, liquidation may be the next and final stage of its life. Some of the problems arising in the liquidation of business enterprises will be considered in the following chapters.

PROBLEMS

Problem 21-1. The Foley Company presented the following condensed balance sheet on March 31, 1967:

THE FOLEY COMPANY
BALANCE SHEET, MARCH 31, 1967

Cash and receivables	$110,000	Current payables	$130,000
Inventories	180,000	First mortgage bonds payable, 5%	250,000
Fixed assets (net)	480,000	Common stock, authorized and issued 100,000 shares at $5 par value	500,000
		Retained income (deficit)	(110,000)
	$770,000		$770,000

The Company is in need of additional cash, but the above balance sheet is not conducive to borrowing nor to the successful sale of additional stock. Thus, the directors have decided to proceed with a quasi-reorganization. By May 31, 1967, the necessary approvals of the suggested plan had been received, and the principal points of the plan are presented below:

1. The par value attaching to the shares will be eliminated, the number of shares increased to 500,000, and a stated value per share of $1.00 adopted.
2. Three shares of the new stock are to be exchanged for each share of $5.00 par value stock.
3. Inventories are to be reduced to $160,000 to bring their value down to the lower of cost or market.
4. Bondholders agreed to accept 30,000 shares of the new common stock in lieu of two years' interest accrued but unpaid.
5. Fixed assets no longer in use with a book value of $26,000 are to be written off.
6. No deficit is to exist at May 31, 1967.

Required:

Prepare journal entries to give effect to the above items and prepare a balance sheet as of May 31, 1967, after preparation of the above entries.

Problem 21–2. The Cainbrake Corporation was formed in July 1967. At date of incorporation it issued $1,000,000 of $100 par value common stock at par for cash. Operations during the remainder of 1967 resulted in $60,000 net income. As a result of its operating experience it was decided that $800,000 of contributed capital would be adequate to meet foreseeable operating needs and provide for reasonable expansion. At a directors' meeting in January, the following independent suggestions were made to take care of the excess capitalization:

1. Reduce shares from $100 to $80 par value.
2. Invest $200,000 of excess cash in the firm's own shares.
3. Distribute a cash dividend of $20 per share.
4. Resort to a quasi-reorganization and write down various assets by $200,000.

Required:

Explain the soundness and reasonableness of each of these suggestions in relation to the accomplishment of the desired purpose.   (AICPA adapted)

Problem 21–3. The Mancett Corporation had $105,000 of dividends in arrears on its preferred stock as of March 31, 1967. While retained earnings were adequate to meet accumulated dividends, the company's management did not wish to weaken its working capital position. They also realized that a portion of the fixed assets was no longer used or useful in their operation. Therefore, they proposed the following reorganization which was approved by stockholders to be effected as of April 1, 1967:

1. The preferred stock was to be exchanged for $300,000 of 5% debenture bonds. Dividends in arrears were to be settled by the issuance of $120,000 of $10 par value, 5% noncumulative preferred stock.
2. Common stock was to be assigned a value of $50 per share.
3. Goodwill was to be written off.
4. Property, plant, and equipment were to be written down, based on appraisal and estimates of useful value, by a total of $103,200 consisting of $85,400 increase in allowance for depreciation and $17,800 decrease in certain assets.

5. Current assets were to be written down by $10,460 to reduce certain items to expected realizable values.
6. The condensed balance sheet as of March 31, 1967 appears below:

Assets

Cash		$ 34,690
Other current assets		252,890
Property, plant, and equipment	$1,458,731	
Allowance for depreciation	512,481	946,250
Goodwill		50,000
		$1,283,830

Liabilities and Capital

Current liabilities	$ 136,860
7% Cumulative preferred stock ($100 par)*	300,000
Common stock (9,000 shares, no par)	648,430
Premium on preferred stock	22,470
Retained earnings	176,070
	$1,283,830

    * $105,000 dividends in arrears.

Required:
  You are to prepare:
  (1) The journal entries to give effect to the reorganization as of April 1, 1967. Give complete explanations with each entry and comment on any possible options in recording the reorganization.
  (2) A balance sheet as of April 30, 1967, assuming that net income in April was $10,320 after provision for taxes. The operations resulted in $5,290 increase in cash, $10,660 increase in other current assets, $2,010 increase in current liabilities, and $3,620 increase in allowance for depreciation.

(AICPA adapted)

Problem 21–4. The Vance Corporation encountered a series of loss years after several prior years of profits. As of January 1, 1967, the stockholders' equity section of the balance sheet of the Vance Corporation was as follows:

Preferred stock, $25 par value, authorized 10,000	
shares, outstanding 6,000 shares	$150,000
Common stock, $5 par value, authorized and out-	
standing 15,000 shares	75,000
Retained income (deficit)	(40,000)
Total	$185,000

  During the year various revisions were made in Vance's articles of incorporation, with the result that the corporation's new authorized capital consisted of 1,000 shares of $100 par value preferred stock and 50,000 shares of common stock with no par value.
  On October 1, 1967, 36,000 shares of the new common stock were issued on the following basis: 4 shares of the new common for each share of the outstanding

preferred stock; $8/10$ of a share of the new common for each share of the then outstanding common stock. The remaining authorized shares of new common were not issued. Four hundred shares of the new preferred stock were sold at par value.

An analysis of Retained Income at December 31, 1967, is presented below:

Balance, January 1, 1966	$ (5,000)
Net loss for 1966	(25,000)
	(30,000)
Provision for doubtful accounts receivables	(10,000)
Balance, December 31, 1966	(40,000)
Net loss for 1967	(12,000)
Balance, December 31, 1967	$(52,000)

At December 31, 1967, you are called in to prepare a balance sheet for the Vance Corporation. You find that no earnings information is available for any interim date during the year.

Required:

Prepare a stockholders' equity section for the Vance Corporation at December 31, 1967, assuming that the capital adjustments effected constitute a quasi-reorganization. In addition, discuss any features of the data presented which might cause you to modify your presentation or on which you would want additional information prior to preparation of the balance sheet.

Problem 21–5. The Johnson Company issued 5%, 25-year debenture bonds totaling $10,000,000 face value on January 2, 1960, at 97. The bonds were callable for redemption at 105 prior to January 1, 1966, at 104 from January 1, 1966, to January 1, 1971, and at 103 subsequently. Discount on issuance was amortized on a straight line basis to maturity.

On March 31, 1971, the company issued at 4%, 30-year convertible debentures totaling $10,000,000 face value at $101\frac{1}{2}$ plus accrued interest. The proceeds were used to call the 5%, 25-year bonds at that date.

Interest on both bond issues was payable January 2 and July 1.

Required:

Prepare all journal entries required during the year 1971, assuming the company's fiscal year ends December 31. Support your entry(ies) for March 31, 1971, as being preferable to possible alternatives.

Problem 21–6. (1) The X Company has outstanding $2,000,000 of 20-year 5% bonds which were issued 10 years ago. Unamortized discount and expense of $120,000 remains on the books. The bonds are callable at 105. The company has the opportunity to refinance, by issuing at par, $2,150,000 of 4%, 10-year bonds. Expenses which would be incurred in connection with the issue are estimated to be $50,000. Interest on both issues is payable semi-annually.

Determine whether refinancing would be desirable. Show your computations in good form and explain the basis used in reaching your conclusion. Ignore any tax difference which might arise out of the refinancing. Refer to the appropriate tables in the Appendix.

(2) If X Company carries out the refunding of the long-term debt, a decision must be made concerning the accounting treatment to be accorded the unamortized portion of discount and expense pertaining to the old bonds. Three different treatments of this item have received support from various accountants.

Describe these treatments and give a brief statement of the central argument offered in support of each of them. (AICPA adapted)

Problem 21–7. The Herbert Sherman Company issued $3,000,000 of 4% first mortgage bonds on September 30, 1960, at 96 and accrued interest. The bonds were dated June 30, 1960; interest payable semi-annually; redeemable after June 30, 1965 and to June 30, 1967 at 104, and thereafter until maturity at 102; and convertible into $100 par value common stock as follows:

Until June 30, 1965, at the rate of 6 shares for each $1,000 of bonds.

From July 1, 1965 to June 30, 1968, at the rate of 5 shares for each $1,000 of bonds.

After June 30, 1968, at the rate of 4 shares for each $1,000 of bonds.

Expenses of issue were $6,360 which is to be combined with the premium or discount, and the total is to be amortized over the life of the bonds from date of issue. The bonds mature in 10 years from their date. The company adjusts its books monthly and closes as of December 31 each year.

The following transactions occur in connection with the bonds:

(a) July 1, 1966—$500,000 of bonds were converted into stock.

(b) December 30, 1967— $500,000 face amounts of bonds were reacquired by purchase on the market at 99¼ and accrued interest. These were immediately retired.

(c) June 30, 1968—Because of favorable market conditions and interest rates the management had instituted and publicized a plan to retire the remainder of the bonds. The remaining bonds were called for redemption. A $2,000,000 issue of 2¾% bonds were sold to effect this redemption. The sale price was 98¾, the bonds were dated June 30, 1968 and were due in 20 years.

Required:

Prepare in journal form the entries necessary for the company in connection with the above transactions, including monthly adjustments where appropriate, as of each of the following dates: (1) September 30, 1960; (2) December 31, 1960; (3) July 1, 1966; (4) December 30, 1967; (5) June 30, 1968.

(AICPA adapted)

Problem 21–8. The board of directors of the Nelson Company authorized a $1,000,000 issue of 5% convertible 20-year bonds dated March 1, 1968. Interest is payable on March 1 and September 1 of each year. The conversion agreement provides that until March 1, 1973, each $1,000 of bonds may be converted into 6 shares of $100 par value common stock and that interest accrued to date of conversion will be paid in cash. After March 1, 1973, each $1,000 of bonds is convertible into 5 shares of common.

The company sold the entire bond issue on June 30, 1968, at 98 and accrued interest. Deferable costs incurred in making the sale amounted to $8,320. The company adjusts its books at the end of each month and closes them on December

31 of each year. Interest is paid as due. On February 1, 1970, a holder of $20,000 of bonds converts them into common stock.

You are to prepare entries in journal form to reflect the transactions arising out of the existence of these bonds on each of the following dates:

> June 30, 1968
> September 1, 1968
> December 31, 1969 (including closing entries)
> February 1, 1970
> December 31, 1970 (including closing entries)

In support of the above entries, prepare a summary analysis of the unamortized bond discount and expense account for the period to December 31, 1970.

(AICPA adapted)

Problem 21–9. The president of the Bankrola Company, F. A. Bank, is planning to retire. By agreement with the other stockholders of the Company he will exchange his capital stock and other voting rights for nonvoting preferred stock.

The Bankrola Company has no preferred stock in its capitalization. The capital stock is held as follows:

> 100 shares held by F. A. Bank, President
> 350 shares held by J. R. Fenn, Executive Vice-President
> 150 shares held by M. A. Rola, Vice-President in charge of sales
> 150 shares held in treasury of company
> ‾‾‾
> 750 shares, total capital stock issued

The stockholders' equity section of the Company's statement of financial position follows:

Capital stock ($100 par value)	$ 75,000
Premium on stock	37,500
Retained earnings	17,500
Total	130,000
Treasury stock, at cost	10,000
Total stockholders' equity	$120,000

Under the terms of the agreement the Company will be reorganized as follows:

(a) The treasury stock will be cancelled.

(b) Two new stock issues will be authorized, common and 5% cumulative nonvoting preferred. Both will be $100 par value per share.

(c) The stockholders will surrender their capital stock for cancellation and will receive the newly authorized issues as follows:

1. F. A. Bank will receive only preferred stock.
2. J. R. Fenn will receive 60% of the common stock and the remainder of the preferred.
3. M. A. Rola will receive 40% of the common.

(d) The combined total number of shares of common and preferred stock outstanding after the exchange will be the same as the total number of shares authorized and outstanding before the transfer (after giving effect to the retirement of the treasury stock).

Required:

(1) Prepare the journal entry to cancel the treasury stock account on the books of the Company.

(2) Prepare a schedule computing the amount of each stockholder's equity in the Company before recapitalization.

(3) Compute the number of new common stock and new preferred stock shares to be issued.

(4) Prepare a schedule computing the number of shares of each type of newly issued stock that each stockholder must receive so that he will have the same equity in the Company after the exchange as before the exchange.

(AICPA adapted)

Problem 21-10. Following a series of creditor committee meetings, stockholder meetings, and conferences with other individuals and management representatives, the Small Corporation officers agreed to the following plan of action:

1. Sale of the assets of the Hoop Division to the Downey Corporation for $300,000 cash, plus $1,500,000 in 4%, 8-year notes, due June 30, 1978. Assets of the Hoop Division taken over by the Downey Corporation include, at book value:

Inventories	$400,000
Machinery and Equipment	1,600,000
Supplies and Parts	50,000

   The Downey Company also assumed the lease terms and obligations for the building which housed the Hoop Division operations.
2. Reduction in par value of the common stock outstanding from $25 per share to $10 per share, with an increase in authorized shares from 300,000 to 600,000.
3. Redemption of the outstanding 6% serial bond issue on the following terms: Payment of six months' accrued interest; redemption of the bonds at 80% face value, in cash, plus issuance of 30 shares of new common for each $1,000 bond outstanding. Existing call price covenants of the serial issue were waived by the bondholders.
4. Redemption of the outstanding $7, $100 par value preferred stock on the following terms: 1 new share of $5 convertible $100 par value preferred stock for each share of $7 preferred outstanding, plus 3 shares of new common for each share of $7 preferred stock outstanding, in lieu of three years' dividends in arrears and reduction of the dividend rate on the new preferred.
5. Issuance of 1 share of new $10 par value common stock for each share of old $25 par value common stock.
6. Discounting of the 8-year notes received from the Downey Company, at 6%, at the First National Bank.
7. Elimination of any deficit on the books of the Small Corporation at June 30, 1970.

The above plan was properly approved by all necessary groups, including the court of jurisdiction, and became effective June 30, 1970.

The Small Corporation balance sheet, after closing, but prior to implementation of the above plan, on June 30, 1970, was as follows:

THE SMALL CORPORATION
BALANCE SHEET, JUNE 30, 1970

Cash	$ 500,000	Current payables	$ 600,000
Receivables	610,000	6% Serial bonds, due	
Inventories	1,350,000	1970	1,750,000
Supplies and parts	110,000	$7 Preferred stock, par	
Buildings (net)	1,200,000	$100	2,000,000
Machinery and equipment	4,000,000	Common stock, $25 par	
Unamort. discount on		value, 200,000 shares	
bonds	30,000	outstanding	5,000,000
		Retained income	
		(deficit)	(1,550,000)
	$7,800,000		$7,800,000

Required:

(1) Prepare a work sheet to give effect to the above plan of reorganization, including necessary journal entries.

(2) Prepare a balance sheet for the Small Corporation, after the reorganization plan has been effected.

Problem 21–11. The assets shown on the balance sheets at September 30, 1970 of three summer resorts on Waverly Lake are shown below. The appraisal data opposite the book values for land and depreciable assets summarize an independent appraisal made in September, 1970, as a basis for negotiations to combine the three resorts under one management. The appraisal was made on the basis of reproduction cost less depreciation.

Description	Book Value	Appraised Value (Reproduction Cost Less Depreciation)
ASSETS OF WAVERLY HOTEL CO.		
Current	$15,000	...
Land	5,000	$10,000
Hotel building	12,500	38,000
Boathouse	600	2,000
Kitchen equipment	1,000	1,000
Other equipment	4,000	29,000
Total	$38,100	$80,000

Description	Book Value	Appraised Value (Reproduction Cost Less Depreciation)
ASSETS OF RUSTIC CAMPS (Orville Johnsen, Proprietor)		
Current	$ 3,000	...
Land	1,000	$ 1,500
Lodge	4,000	9,500
Boathouse	600	700
Kitchen equipment	2,500	2,500
Other equipment	1,000	800
Total	$12,100	$15,000

ASSETS OF LAKEVIEW COTTAGES
(Burgess & Crayton, A Partnership)

Current	$ 6,800	...
Land	3,000	$ 1,600
Lodge	8,000	9,400
Cottages	15,000	32,000
Lodge kitchen equipment	2,000	2,000
Other equipment	3,500	5,000
Total	$38,300	$50,000

Total appraised value of land and
depreciable assets — $145,000

Operating statements for the year ended September 30, 1970 are as follows:

	Waverly Hotel	Rustic Camps	Lakeview Cottages
Revenue	$17,281	$13,698	$8,740
Deduct:			
Officers' salaries	$ 3,600	...	...
Partners' drawings	...	...	$5,500
Depreciation	1,590	$ 850	2,300
Interest on notes	600	...	...
Other expenses	8,112	5,224	1,868
Total	$13,902	$ 6,074	$9,668
Net income (loss)	$ 3,379	$ 7,624	($ 928)

The hotel's clientele had been declining in recent years so Mr. Holt, the principal stockholder and manager, decided to retire. The Rustic Camp's profit is attributable to Mr. Johnsen's facility with people and knack for organized recreation. Burgess and Crayton provide light-housekeeping cottages and serve dinner in the lodge, but provide no organized recreation.

The three businesses agree to combine by organizing a new corporation, Waverly Resorts, Inc. This corporation is to have authorized capital of 2,000 shares of 5% cumulative preferred stock of $100 par value and 1,000 shares of no-par common stock. The new corporation will take over the land and depreciable assets of the three businesses. It will also take over from the hotel at $10,000 and from the partnership at $5,000 certain assets classed as current, but which are carried on their books at $10,500 and $4,800, respectively. All liabilities are to be paid off by the separate businesses and all other current assets retained by them.

In exchange for the assets acquired, the corporation is to issue to the Hotel Company $50,000 of first mortgage 4% bonds and preferred stock having $32,500 par value. Rustic Camps is to receive $25,000 of preferred stock and Lakeview Cottages is to receive $55,000 of preferred stock. The differences between the appraisal values of the properties taken over and the bonds and stock issued are to adjust for the low income earned on the hotel property and the high income which Mr. Johnsen has been receiving from his camps as a result of his ability to attract patronage.

Common stock is all to be issued and divided to the nearest share among the three businesses in the ratio of their net operating profits for the year ended September 30, 1970, adjusted as follows:

As an approximation of correct depreciation, the depreciation charges for the past year are to be recomputed. In recomputing, use rates of 4% per annum for building and 10% for equipment applied to the September 30, 1970, appraised values. The new corporation will use the 10% and 4% annual rates, applied to the balances in the asset accounts at the first of each quarter-year period.

As a result of a specific request for information as to the adequacy of past maintenance, the appraiser reported that maintenance on the hotel had been inadequate over the past 10 years to the extent of approximately $500 per year. Adjustment is to be made for the annual deficiency.

It is also agreed that for purpose of restating profits, each business should have $3,000 a year charged as the reasonable value of the services of the officers or owners.

The businesses were combined on October 1, 1970 as planned. Transactions for the three months ended December 31, 1970 are summarized below:

Received $6,500 from guests.

Paid $1,800 to Tom and Lee Wilson whose time was spent as follows: one-half installing equipment to convert the Rustic Camp's lodge to a bar and dance pavilion; one-third moving the camp's boathouse adjacent to the hotel boathouse; and one-sixth moving wooden floors for tents from the camps to a location near the cottages.

Equipment for the pavilion was purchased for $1,500 of which $1,200 was paid.

The principal maintenance work needed on the hotel was done in December at a cost of $4,500. Payment for this work was made by issuing a 12-month note.

Three hundred dollars appraised value of kitchen equipment in the lodge by the cottages was moved to the hotel and the remaining $1,700 of equipment was sold for $550.

Orville Johnsen's monthly salary of $400 was paid for October and November.

Other expenses amounted to $3,000 of which $2,750 was paid.

You are to prepare a worksheet for the Waverly Resorts, Inc., with columns showing the acquisition of the assets on October 1, 1970; the transactions from October 1 to December 31; the Income Statement figures for the three months ended December 31 and Balance Sheet figures for December 31, 1970. In a separate schedule you are to show the distribution of the common stock among the three business units. Give an explanation and justification for your treatment of any transaction where you consider the treatment to be debatable.

(AICPA adapted)

Problem 21–12. The president of Wooddee Corporation, your client, has asked you for an explanation of a "quasi-reorganization." He is unfamiliar with the procedure and is concerned that a competitor might have an advantage since undergoing a "quasi-reorganization."

Required:

Prepare a report for the president explaining the "quasi-reorganization." Your report should include the following points:

(1) Definition and accounting features of the procedure.

(2) The purpose of the procedure. Under what conditions should it be considered?

(3) Authorization necessary.

(4) Disclosure required in financial statements.

(5) Does the competitor have an advantage? Discuss briefly.

(AICPA adapted)

Problem 21-13. The Saucer Corporation had operated on a profitable basis for a number of years prior to 1960. Starting with 1960, however, the corporation suffered a series of loss years, and by December 31, 1966, a sizable deficit existed. Representatives of the various equity interests worked out a plan to eliminate the deficit and to effect a balance sheet that might meet with favorable reaction in efforts to raise new capital investment. The reorganization group felt that the worst was past and that the operating outlook in coming months was again favorable.

At December 31, 1966, the equity portion of the Saucer Corporation balance sheet appeared as follows:

Current liabilities	$140,000
Bonds payable, 6% interest	250,000
Preferred stock, 6%, par value $100, cumulative, 2,000 shares outstanding	200,000
Common stock, $10 par value, 25,000 shares outstanding	250,000
Retained income (deficit)	(75,000)
	$765,000

The following plan was agreed upon:

1. The 6% bonds payable were exchanged for new 4% bonds payable plus 20 shares of new common stock for each $1,000, 6% bond outstanding.

2. Preferred stockholders received three shares of new common stock for each share of $100 par preferred in lieu of $12,000 dividends in arrears, and in exchange for elimination of the cumulative feature from the preferred shares outstanding.

3. Each old common share, par $10, was exchanged for 3 shares of the new no-par common, stated value $2 per share, 150,000 shares authorized.

4. No asset write downs were considered necessary at the date of reorganization, since recent review of the asset values indicated that book values were generally in line with current values. Inventory write downs had been made periodically in recent years.

Required:

Prepare entries to give effect to the above features of the quasi-reorganization. Prepare an equity section of a balance sheet as of March 31, 1967, assuming first-quarter net income for 1967 was $2,600.

V

LIQUIDATION OF THE
BUSINESS ORGANIZATION

CHAPTER 22

Proprietorship liquidation

The final stage in the life cycle of a business entity, and the ultimate in the contraction of a business organization is liquidation. While liquidation may have varied meanings, liquidation of a business enterprise includes the process of winding up business affairs, converting assets into cash, paying the various priority equity claims, and finally distributing any remaining cash or other assets among the ownership equity interests. Throughout this process the business is generally said to be in liquidation.

A business in the liquidation stage presents many peculiar accounting problems, several of which are discussed in this and succeeding chapters. By and large most of the problems arise because one of the basic assumptions underlying accounting decisions for a "going concern" is no longer valid. This assumption, that the business entity will have an indefinite life (so-called going-concern concept), is not warranted when the business is anticipating or is involved in liquidation. Because the business no longer anticipates indefinite life a new assumption is applied in lieu of the going-concern concept; an assumption of imminent liquidation. Subsequent portions of this book will consider the effect which the assumption of liquidation has on accounting actions and financial statements.

Reasons for a Business Liquidation. Liquidation of a business enterprise may take place for various reasons, some voluntary and some involuntary. A single proprietorship, for example, may well be liquidated upon the death of the owner. Death of a partner may also result in liquidation of a partnership. Completion of the predetermined term of life of a partnership or corporation will result in liquidation. In addition, the results of past business activity, if of a generally adverse nature, may produce a situation requiring liquidation. Situations such as the following may precede liquidation: (1) overextension of credit, (2) excessive stockpiling of inventories, (3) undue investment in plant and equipment, (4) excessive borrowing, and (5) continued operating losses. The results of any of the preceding situations may cause liquidation of a proprietorship, partnership, or corporation. In addition, other acts over which the business entity may not have complete control may precipitate liquidation, such as fires, floods, thefts, or fraud. Other forces working on a business organization may encourage liquidation, such as the pressure of competition, loss of markets, personality conflicts in management, and excessive government taxation or regulation. And, of course, there are times when a businessman or a group of businessmen just decide to quit and liquidate their operations and retire.

Liquidation Procedures. In general, the first step in the liquidation procedure is either a decision by the owner(s) of the business entity to liquidate or an act or series of acts by the business enterprise which will force liquidation. Thus the single proprietor, partners, or stockholders may decide to liquidate their business venture, or through the operation of the law, in situations such as those resulting from death or bankruptcy, the decision to liquidate is, in effect, made for the owners.

Once the decision to liquidate the enterprise has been made the owners must make plans to provide for the realization of the business assets. Realization of the assets may proceed on a piecemeal basis over a period of time, or it may be accomplished largely or wholly through sale to one purchaser. In either event the aim is to secure as much cash, or claims to cash, as possible for the assets of the business. It should be noted that even during the period of asset realization the enterprise may continue to conduct business somewhat as in the past, though normally on a reduced scale of operations. In fact, many times continued business activity is essential to the realization of maximum value for the assets. This is particularly true where large dollar amounts are invested in inventories at various stages of completion at the time the enterprise decides to liquidate.

Concurrent with the realization of the assets, the enterprise will gradually liquidate or pay off the various creditor claims. In some instances creditors may accept assets such as inventory, equipment, notes, or other assets in lieu of cash in settlement of their claims. Thus realization of a particular asset in cash would not occur, although realization to the extent the asset satisfies or liquidates a creditorship claim does result. No particular problems arise in the process of liquidating creditor claims, except in liquidations arising under bankruptcy statutes. Some of these problems are discussed further in a subsequent section.

When realization of assets is completed and when the various creditorship claims are settled in full, any remaining assets will be distributed among the ownership interests in the enterprise. Such distribution will be made to the owners in accordance with their various interests in the organization.

The procedure of realizing the assets, liquidating the liabilities, and distributing the excess assets among the ownership interests may take place under the supervision of the proprietor, one or several of the partners, or the management or board of directors of a corporation. Many liquidations, however, are supervised by an outside party such as an executor, a trustee, a receiver, a third party appointed by the court, or someone agreed upon by members of the business organization. The accounting problems vary somewhat with the type of supervision in a liquidation situation.

Bankruptcy

As previously noted, business enterprises may be liquidated voluntarily by the owners or involuntarily because of action of the law or because of adverse past operating results and an inability of the enterprise to pay its debts as they mature. When an enterprise is unable to pay its maturing obligations it is normally considered from a practical standpoint to be in an *insolvent* financial condition. Technical insolvency, however, within the framework of the National Bankruptcy Act embraces only those organizations whose aggregate liabilities exceed their assets at a fair valuation.

Insolvency vs. Bankruptcy. A clear distinction should be made between an insolvent business enterprise and one that is bankrupt. An organization may be insolvent in the general sense (as well as within the meaning of most state statutes) in that it cannot meet its maturing obligations. Or, it may be insolvent in the technical sense of the National Bankruptcy Act, as noted above. Neither of these conditions of insolvency means that the enterprise is necessarily bankrupt. An enterprise is not bankrupt, under the provisions of the National Bankruptcy Act, unless (1) a petition has been filed voluntarily by the enterprise, asking that it be adjudged a bankrupt, or a petition has been filed by a creditor or creditors, alleging commission of an act of bankruptcy by the enterprise; and (2) an adjudication that the enterprise is bankrupt has been delivered.

Involuntary Bankruptcy. The Bankruptcy Act permits any person except a municipal, railroad, insurance, or banking corporation or a building and loan association to file a petition asking to be adjudged a voluntary bankrupt. Likewise the law permits creditors to file a petition against any natural person, except a wage earner or a farmer, any un-incorporated company, and any moneyed business or commercial corporation, except a municipal, railroad, insurance, or banking corporation or a building and loan association, with debts of $1,000 or more, asking that the person be adjudged an *involuntary bankrupt*. Thus, under the Act, either the debtor may seek discharge from his debts or his creditors may seek a fair distribution of the bankrupt's assets. Accountingwise there is little difference between a voluntary bankrupt and an involuntary bankrupt.

Acts of Bankruptcy. The Bankruptcy Act sets forth certain *acts of bankruptcy*, one or more of which must have been committed by the debtor within four months prior to the filing of the petition requesting adjudication as a bankrupt. It should be noted that specific acts of bankruptcy are required, and the condition of technical insolvency alone is not sufficient grounds for filing a petition for bankruptcy. A debtor has committed an act of bankruptcy if he has:

(1) Conveyed, transferred, concealed, or removed, or permitted to be concealed or removed, any of his property with the intent to hinder, delay, or defraud his creditors.
(2) Transferred, while insolvent, any portion of his property to one or more of his creditors with intent to prefer such creditors over his other creditors.
(3) Suffered, or permitted, while insolvent, any creditor to obtain a lien upon any of his property through legal proceedings, and not having vacated or discharged such lien within 30 days, or at least within 5 days before the date set for any sale or other disposition of such property.
(4) Made a general assignment for the benefit of creditors.
(5) While insolvent or unable to pay his debts as they matured, procured, permitted, or suffered, voluntarily or involuntarily, the appointment of a receiver or trustee to take charge of his property.
(6) Admitted in writing his inability to pay his debts and his willingness to be adjudged a bankrupt.

General Bankruptcy Procedure. The filing of the voluntary or involuntary petition with the bankruptcy court indicates the grounds for the petition and is the initial step in the liquidation of the business. As previously noted, liquidation of a business may frequently require a considerable period of time. Liquidation through bankruptcy proceedings is no exception. While no fixed pattern follows from the filing of a petition to be adjudged a bankrupt, the normal sequence of events would be somewhat along the following line. The court appoints a receiver or custodian to take charge of the assets of the bankrupt organization and manage its operations pending action on the petition. If the debtor is adjudged a bankrupt, either the creditors agree on a trustee or the court appoints one or more. In some cases the receiver becomes the trustee. The trustee acquires all of the bankrupt's rights, titles, and interests in property, real or personal, tangible or intangible. The trustee then proceeds with the liquidation of the enterprise under the general supervision of a *referee*, an officer appointed by the court, who reviews the activities of the trustee and authorizes the distribution of the proceeds from the sale of the bankrupt's property. Liquidation of the creditorship claims according to their rights proceeds to the extent that the realized assets permit. Further discussion of the creditors' rights and priority of liquidation is presented in Chapter 24.

Adjudication as a bankrupt of any person except a corporation operates as an application for a discharge in bankruptcy. A corporate debtor, however, may file an application for a discharge within six months after the adjudication. In the absence of any valid objections to a discharge in bankruptcy filed within a time fixed by the court, the court will grant a discharge that serves to release the bankrupt from all his provable debts except for certain debts specifically not dischargeable under the Bankruptcy Act.

Throughout the liquidation proceedings the services of accountants may be utilized frequently. Accountants may be called upon to aid in the preparation and presentation of various financial reports. In addition, accountants are frequently called upon to aid the receiver and the trustee in the proper discharge of their reporting responsibilities under the law.

Summary. In summary, liquidation of an enterprise through bankruptcy proceedings consists of a judicial determination that the debtor is a bankrupt, a grouping or marshaling of the debtor's assets, the realization of these assets, the distribution of the proceeds of the realization to the creditors according to their priority, and the discharge of the bankrupt from the liabilities which cannot be paid.

While not all liquidations of business organizations arise through bankruptcy proceedings, the above discussion indicates (1) that a liquidation may be voluntary or involuntary on the part of the organization, (2) that a liquidation is a time-consuming process accomplished with due care and accountability, (3) that liquidation proceedings are sometimes handled by individuals not connected with the organization, and (4) that some reasons for liquidation apply alike to proprietorships, partnerships, and corporations. Liquidations because of bankruptcy are considered further in Chapter 24, at which time an example involving a corporate bankruptcy is considered. The legal form of the business enterprise involved in bankruptcy affects only negligibly the accounting problems involved.

LIQUIDATION OF PROPRIETORSHIPS

Single proprietorships may be liquidated for a number of reasons. The general procedure if the proprietor has been adjudged a bankrupt has already been considered. Among the other reasons for a proprietorship liquidation, death of the proprietor is probably the most prevalent. Although the proprietor's widow, children, or other relatives may continue operation of the business, death of the proprietor frequently causes liquidation of the business. This is particularly true when there are numerous heirs, each of whom is to share in the estate of the proprietor.

Liquidation Because of Death of the Proprietor

The death of any person normally creates a problem of control and administration of the property of the deceased until appropriate distribution of such property can be made. The problem may be more complicated, however, when the deceased is the owner of a going business. As in the case where a proprietor is adjudged a bankrupt, liquidation of a proprietorship because of the death of the owner frequently requires considerable time.

Various legal procedures must be observed, and during this period the property of the deceased must be conserved and administered according to the provisions of the will of the deceased and good business practice.

Role of the Accountant. Occasionally an accountant will be called upon for advice or to take charge of the accountability for the property involved. Because of his financial background the accountant is often in a position to give helpful advice on matters relating to valuation and realization of assets and on matters dealing with the optimum manner of liquidating liabilities. In addition, accountants are being called upon with increasing frequency in connection with estate planning of individuals, both with and without ownership interests in going business organizations. Thus the accountant should be familiar with the more important laws and legal decisions relating to the administration of estates.

General Legal Procedures. If the decedent has left a will directing the disposal of his estate, he is said to have died *testate*, and the property should be disposed of in accordance with the terms of the will. If he has left no will, he is said to have died *intestate*, and the property should be disposed of in accordance with the *laws of descent and distribution*. The law of descent governs the disposition of real property whereas the law of distribution governs the disposition of personal property. For a will to become operative it must be *probated* or proved in a court of probate jurisdiction. Such a court is variously known as a *probate, surrogate*, or *orphan's* court. This court governs the administration and disposition of the decedent's property.

If the decedent has left a will, he normally will have named therein an individual to serve as *executor* (or *executrix*) of the estate. The executor is expected to carry out the terms of the will. If no executor is named in the will, or if the person named is not satisfactory to the court, the court will appoint an *administrator* (or *administratress*) to settle the estate. His duties are similar to those of an executor.

DUTIES OF EXECUTOR. The executor or administrator obtains control of the property of the decedent upon admission of the will to probate. The executor must first take an inventory of the property of the decedent, as he will be accountable for such property. He must likewise establish records which will permit him to keep the estate properties separate from his own. If the decedent owned a business which is to be liquidated, the executor would normally value the business assets according to the values expressed on the books of the owner. The original valuation by the executor is made primarily to get a complete listing of the items of property owned and is later adjusted upward or downward to reflect fair values of the various inventoriable items. The eventual valuation of the business property may depend largely on whether the business is to be sold piecemeal or as a going concern.

During the administration of the estate the executor is expected to continue to seek out and take possession of any property belonging to the estate. He is expected to manage prudently all properties coming under his control and to protect and conserve such properties until they are realized and utilized in settlement of debts arising from the estate or in satisfaction of the terms of the will or laws of the state involved.

The executor also has the responsibility of paying various debts and obligations of the decedent. Most state laws fix a limited period within which creditors must file their claims or otherwise forfeit any legal rights they have against the estate. The executor should exercise care in examining all claims against the estate and should liquidate only those which are valid. If the properties of the estate are not sufficient to meet all liabilities, the applicable state laws will indicate the priority of payment. In general, the following priority is applicable: (1) funeral and administrative expenses, including expenses connected with the last illness and with the administration of the estate, (2) certain allowances to support and maintain the decedent's family for a limited period, (3) debts entitled to preference under laws of the United States and of the state, (4) government claims and taxes, (5) any judgment creditors, and (6) all other debts.

Realization and Liquidation by an Executor. The executor normally realizes the properties and liquidates the valid claims against the estate. Many times only properties sufficient to pay the claims against the estate are realized, the remaining properties being maintained for distribution among the heirs of the estate. On other occasions all properties may be realized in cash prior to distribution to the heirs. In any event, the executor pays the claims against the estate and then takes steps to distribute the remaining properties. Personal property disposed of in accordance with the will is known as a *legacy* or *bequest*. Real property so disposed of is known as a *devise*. The will may provide for *specific legacies* (e.g., an automobile to a son), *demonstrative legacies* (e.g., $1,000 out of the First National Bank account to the gardener), *general legacies* (e.g., $5,000 to the State University), and *residuary legacies* (includes all personal property remaining after payment of other legacies).

The executor normally takes title to all personal property of the decedent except life insurance proceeds when the beneficiary is other than the estate. In addition, the executor takes title to real estate of the decedent if the terms of the will so provide or if the court orders sale of the real estate to provide funds to pay existing debts. Thus the executor would take title to all business property of a proprietorship (including inventory, fixed assets, etc.) except the real estate and would, in some cases, take title to the latter as well. The executor must account for all properties with care and must also recognize that estate expenses and debts of the decedent take priority over legacies stipulated in the will. If the executor should distribute assets as legacies and then be unable to meet estate or creditor claims, he may be held personally liable to the unsatisfied creditors.

Consequently, an executor should itemize with care the various creditorship claims against the estate of a deceased, both personal and business. If the payment of various claims does not leave a sufficient amount of assets to pay all legacies provided for in the will, the terms of the will are met by a scaling down (*abatement*) of legacies in the following order: (1) residuary legacies, (2) general legacies, (3) demonstrative and specific legacies. As mentioned above, when the personal property is insufficient to satisfy the claims of the estate, the court may approve the sale, mortgage, or lease of any real property owned by the decedent.

Accounting for Estate Liquidation

As previously emphasized, an executor must maintain careful records of any property which he controls for the settlement of the estate. The accounts which an executor should maintain are based upon a different accounting equation from the one which applies to commercial operations. The executor is interested in safeguarding the property, realizing proceeds from its sale, and distributing the property or its proceeds in accordance with the will or the state law. Thus the set of accounts should show the property over which the executor has control and his disposition of that property. The equation

$$Assets = Accountability$$

is more appropriate to the executor's records than the standard equation

$$Assets = Equities$$

Opening Accountability Records. The executor opens his books by recording the properties of the estate to which he takes title. The various properties should be recorded in appropriately named asset accounts at the valuations shown by the inventory prepared by the executor and accepted by the court. Sufficient accounts should be maintained to permit a proper classification of the assets. The executor's accountability should be recorded initially in an account normally called "Estate Corpus" or "Estate Principal." Subsequent changes in his accountability should be recorded in separate accounts. Thus, if additional assets are discovered after recording the initial inventory, the executor should debit an appropriate asset account and credit an accountability account normally called "Assets Subsequently Discovered." Even though this latter account is an accountability account, similar to Estate Corpus, the use of a separate account is desirable since it facilitates the preparation of the executor's reports to the court. Instead of having to analyze several entries in the Estate Corpus account to determine how his accountability has changed during his executorship, the executor can use the various supplementary accountability accounts to provide this information. No liabilities of the decedent are recorded at the time the executor assumes control of the decedent's properties. However, liquidation of liabilities will necessitate an entry. This applies to liquidation of liabilities of the proprietorship which the deceased owned as well as to liquidation of the decedent's personal obligations.

Entries in Accountability Records. The executor's accountability changes whenever an asset is sold at a gain or a loss. When an asset is disposed of, the asset account should be credited at its carrying value, a new asset account debited, and any gain should be credited to an account such as "Gain on Realization" and any loss debited to an account such as "Loss on Realization." Both the gain and the loss accounts are accountability accounts similar in nature to Assets Subsequently Discovered.

When the executor settles or liquidates any of the claims against the deceased or claims arising from estate operations, he should credit the appropriate asset and debit an accountability account. Thus, if funeral or administrative expenses are paid, instead of charging Estate Corpus the executor should charge an appropriately named expense account. In small estates one account, sometimes titled "Funeral and Administrative Expense," is used. In large or complex estates the executor may wish to use several accounts for the several types of administrative expenses that arise.

When the executor settles liabilities incurred by the decedent, either through his business operations or his personal activities, the accountability of the executor is likewise decreased. An entry is necessary, crediting the asset used and debiting an account such as "Debts of Decedent Paid," including the name of the creditor, as "Debts of Decedent Paid—Jones Produce Co." If numerous creditors exist, the Debts of Decedent Paid account may serve as a controlling account. In any event, the account will provide the executor with information necessary to satisfy his reporting responsibilities as to the discharge of his accountability.

In addition to discharging his accountability for the decedent's property through liquidation of the various claims against the estate, the executor also decreases his accountability through payment of legacies. As legacies are paid, the executor charges an account such as "Legacies Paid" and credits the asset transferred to the legatee. Depending upon the number of legacies involved, the executor may wish to use several accounts for the legacies paid. While legacies may be paid any time after the executor takes charge of the estate, payment of legacies should normally be deferred until the executor has determined that the estate is sufficient to pay existing debts. Payment of legacies which reduce the estate below an amount sufficient to pay debts of the decedent and the estate may involve the executor in personal liability to creditors.

The new accounts discussed above—Assets Subsequently Discovered, Gain on Realization, Loss on Realization, Funeral and Administrative Expenses, Debts of Decedent Paid, Legacies Paid—are all temporary accountability accounts designed to provide the executor with necessary reporting information. After his report has been accepted by the court, the executor closes these accounts to Estate Corpus.

Proforma Entries for Estate Liquidation. The preceding sections introduced several accounts peculiar to estate accounting. The following entries summarize relatively common transactions arising in the liquidation of an estate.

(a) Dr. Assets (various)   xxxx
      Cr. Estate corpus (or Estate principal)   xxxx
    (to record assumption by the executor of responsibility for
    estate assets)

(b) Dr. Assets (specific asset discovered)   xxxx
      Cr. Assets subsequently discovered   xxxx
    (to record discovery of an asset not known to exist at inventory date)

(c) Dr. Asset (newly acquired)   xxxx
      Cr. Asset (at inventory carrying value)   xxxx
          Gain on realization   xx
    (to record disposition of an asset in inventory, at a gain)

(d) Dr. Asset (newly acquired)   xxxx
        Loss on realization   xx
      Cr. Asset (at inventory carrying value)   xxxx
    (to record disposition of an asset in inventory, at a loss)

(e) Dr. Funeral and administrative expense   xxxx
      Cr. Assets (Cash, generally)   xxxx
    (to record payment of funeral and administrative expenses)

(f) Dr. Debts of decedent paid   xxxx
      Cr. Assets (Cash, generally)   xxxx
    (to record payment of liabilities incurred by the decedent)

(g) Dr. Legacies paid   xxxx
      Cr. Assets (various)   xxxx
    (to record payment of legacies as provided in the will)

(h) Dr. Gain on realization   xx
        Estate corpus   xxxx
      Cr. Loss on realization   xx
          Funeral and administrative expense   xxxx
          Debts of decedent paid   xxxx
          Legacies paid   xxxx
    (to close temporary accountability accounts to "Estate corpus"
    after executor's report is submitted)

Estate Principal vs. Estate Income. While the primary purpose of an executor is to conserve the assets of the decedent and to liquidate the estate, the executor frequently must account for transactions which may involve income (expense) on estate assets. The distinction between estate principal (or estate corpus) and income is particularly important if the will of the decedent provides that part or all of the principal of the estate should be maintained by a trustee (the executor or a different party), with the income from the assets of the trust going to one class of beneficiaries during a given period of time and with the estate principal eventually passing over to another class of beneficiaries at a later date. While accounting for the operations of a trust is not under consideration at this time, the importance of a clear distinction between principal and income warrants further discussion.

The executor (or trustee) should maintain records which will distinguish principal and income. Thus, any income from estate assets should be credited to an income account, or accounts, the number of which will depend upon the variety of incomes which the estate generates. Likewise, expenses deductible from income may be charged to one account, generally called "Expense-Income," or to as many separate accounts as the executor deems necessary. Any cash collected from income and later distributed to beneficiaries should be charged to an account such as "Distributions to Income Beneficiaries."

Estate Principal and Income Problems. Certain problems arise in distinguishing between estate principal and income. If the trust provisions provide specifically for a method of distinguishing principal and income, the provisions of the trust must be followed. If the trust makes no provision for distinguishing principal and income, the appropriate state law or ruling of the court must be followed. While it is difficult to generalize because of the variety of state laws and court rulings, the following statements suggest some of the general rules governing the apportionment of estate property between principal and income:

(1) Interest generally accrues, with interest accrued up to and including the date of death of the decedent being principal, and interest accruing subsequent to the date of death being income.
(2) Dividends do not accrue. Cash dividends declared prior to the date of death are generally principal, while dividends in cash declared subsequent to the date of death are income. The date of collection is not significant. *Ordinary* stock dividends are commonly treated in a manner similar to cash dividends. *Extraordinary* cash or stock dividends may be similarly treated or may be subject to apportionment between principal and income. The apportionment of an extraordinary dividend is made in such a manner that the book value of the stock after the payment of the dividend, plus the portion of the dividend allocated to principal, is equal to the book value at the date of death.
(3) Rents become due on the rent date. Rents due prior to the date of death are principal, while rents falling due after death are income.
(4) Taxes generally do not accrue, but are payable out of principal if the

assessment became a lien prior to death, and payable out of income if the assessment became a lien subsequent to death.

(5) Other possible accruals are generally handled in a manner which relates the item to the passage of time. If the item involved accrues in a reasonably direct relationship to the passage of time, in general it will be accrued on this basis for estate purposes. If such accrual-time relationship does not exist, there will normally have to be a determination of the status of the item at the date of death. For example, partnership profits do not accrue but must be determined as of the date of death unless provided for otherwise in the partnership agreement.

Classification of Estate Expenditures. A problem related to the distinction between principal and income concerns the classification of certain expenditures made by the executor or the trustee. Some of the expenditures mentioned previously are properly chargeable against principal, such as debts of decedent, expenses of the decedent's last illness, and funeral and administrative expenses. Other expenditures generally chargeable to principal include various legal fees, costs of probating the will, defending it against various claimants, and preserving the principal of the estate. In addition, federal and state estate and inheritance taxes are generally chargeable against principal.

Ordinary operating expenses of the estate are normally chargeable against the income of the estate and, as mentioned earlier, these items should be charged to an account such as "Expense-Income" or to several such accounts. Expenditures falling within this area include ordinary repairs, fees for collection and distribution of income, wages of people caring for the property, legal fees arising from matters pertaining to earning income, and generally insurance premiums on income producing property.

Many varied problems may arise in the area of distinguishing principal and income because of the wide variety of properties which may comprise an estate. The proper treatment of specific items frequently requires reference to the intentions of the decedent, to applicable state and federal laws, and to court rulings. Because of the possibility of differences of opinion on the treatment of many items of receipt and expenditures for an estate, it is essential that the executor or trustee maintain careful records detailing the treatment accorded the various items.

Accounting for Proprietorship Liquidation

Proprietorships are, of course, liquidated for reasons other than bankruptcy or death of the owner as discussed in preceding sections. For example, a proprietor may merely tire of continuing in business and decide either to sell his business or to liquidate. In either situation, the accounting problems involved are not particularly complex. The liquidation process may cover a considerable period of time during which operations proceed in a more or less normal fashion, although possibly on a reduced scale. During the liquidation period sales and purchases are normally accounted for as in the usual operations. Disposal of non-inventoriable assets will normally involve gains or losses, but accounting for these gains and losses is no different from that encountered in normal business operations.

When a business proprietorship is to be liquidated because of the death of the proprietor, a dual accounting problem arises. One aspect relates to the accounting for the business assets, and the problems here are no different from those arising in a liquidation for other reasons. The other aspect relates to the accounting for personal assets. The problem here is that of estate accounting, and one of the inventoriable assets of the estate would be the decedent's equity in his business. While the illustrative situation which follows combines the two problems of accounting for the liquidation of a proprietorship and for the estate of the deceased proprietor, it should be recognized that either aspect of the problem could exist separately from the other.

The following liquidation situation illustrates some of the accounting and reporting procedures involved in the liquidation of a proprietorship because of the death of the proprietor. The accounting records of the proprietorship should be closed as of the date of death in order to establish accountability at that date. The executor should maintain records sufficient to enable the court to determine whether or not he has fulfilled the fiduciary responsibility assumed by him. Assume the following statement of financial position was taken from the ledger of James Andrews, Grocer, as of October 8, 1967, the day of the death of Mr. Andrews.

In his will Mr. Andrews named D. F. Keck, a close personal friend, as executor of his estate. Andrews was married and had four children, three of whom were married, but none of whom had an active part in his business. His widow and all children survive. His will included the following provisions:

(1) Household effects and automobile to his widow.
(2) Cash of $5,000 to each married child; cash of $3,000 to his single child; cash of $1,000 to D. F. Keck, in lieu of fee for services as executor.
(3) Remainder to his widow.

JAMES ANDREWS, GROCER

FINANCIAL POSITION

OCTOBER 8, 1967

ASSETS

Current assets:

Cash in bank		$ 3,400
Petty cash		100
Accounts receivable		1,600
Inventory		31,880
Unexpired insurance		120
Total current assets		$37,100

Fixed assets:

	Cost	Accumulated Depreciation	Net	
Showcases and fixtures	$ 2,800	$1,700	$ 1,100	
Refrigeration equipment	7,200	3,200	4,000	
Total	$10,000	$4,900		5,100
TOTAL ASSETS				$42,200

EQUITIES

Liabilities:

Accounts payable		$ 4,200
Notes payable to bank		5,000
Total liabilities		$ 9,200

Owner's equity:

James Andrews, Equity, 1/1/67	$30,470	
Net profit through 10/8/67	2,530	
James Andrews, Equity, 10/8/67		33,000
TOTAL EQUITIES		$42,200

It was decided to liquidate the grocery business. November 30, 1967, was set as a target date for completing the sale of the inventory and other assets. In order to facilitate the liquidation of the business, the heirs agreed to apply to the court to have Mr. Keck appointed temporary administrator of the estate. Approval was received and the operations of the store were continued October 9 without having to await probating of the will some 10 days later. Keck agreed that the statement of financial position as of October 8 would serve as the basis for inclusion of the business equity in the inventory of assets filed with the court subject to final approval by the executor. Keck also authorized Mr. Andrews' butcher to wind up the store affairs under his supervision.

On the following pages the events in the liquidation process are presented. The executor records the equity of the business as it is reflected on the books of the business. The executor's records need not reflect in detail each step in the liquidation process, but they should reveal what has transpired each time he makes a report to the court. On the other hand, the books of the store should reflect the step by step process in the liquidation of the grocery business. The illustration does not include consideration of any federal or state income, inheritance, or estate taxes. The tax laws applicable in the jurisdiction involved would require the attention of the executor.

EVENTS IN THE LIQUIDATION
OF THE JAMES ANDREWS ESTATE

(1) Oct.   9—Court approved D. F. Keck as temporary administrator.

(2) Oct. 19—The will was admitted to probate and D. F. Keck was duly approved (issued letters testamentary) to act as executor.

(3) Oct. 22—The executor filed the following inventory with the court:

Cash	$ 1,200
Life insurance, payable to the estate	15,000
Co. X bonds (5%)	2,400
Accrued interest on Co. X. bonds, July 1 to October 7	32
Y Co. preferred stock	1,000
Z Co. common stock	3,400
Household effects	2,600
Automobile	1,900
Equity in grocery business (a)	33,000
Total	$60,532

(a) Amount equals equity per statement of financial position as of October 8, 1967. The books of the grocery business were closed as of October 8, 1967, to establish the cut-off point for the executor's responsibility.

(4) Oct. 22—A summary of grocery store operations since death includes the following: cash sales, $9,000; collections on account, $700; purchases for cash, $1,200; payments on account, $3,000; payments of expenses, including salaries, $700.

(5) Oct. 25—The executor collected the $15,000 life insurance.

(6) Nov.   1—Y Company stock was sold for $1,100.

(7) Nov.   3—Paid various liabilities filed against the estate:

Jones Auto Repair	$65
Gorman Haberdashery	90

(8) Nov.   5—Summary of grocery store operations since 10/22/67: cash sales, $13,000; collections on account, $800; purchases for cash, $2,100; payments on account, $1,200; payment of notes, $5,000; payment of expenses, including interest on notes, $750.

(9) Nov.   8—Sold X Company bonds for $2,200, plus accrued interest of $42.

(10) Nov. 10—Received dividend on Z Company stock, declared October 10, 1967, $150.
(11) Nov. 12—Discovered a savings account having a balance of $860.
(12) Nov. 15—Paid funeral expenses, $400.
(13) Nov. 16—Paid various administrative and legal expenses, $150.
(14) Nov. 18—Executor turned over household furniture and automobile to the widow. He also paid her $100 cash.
(15) Nov. 19—Summary of store operations since November 5, 1967: cash sales, $7,000; collections on account, $60; purchases for cash, $1,600; payments of expenses, $500.
(16) Nov. 26—Received $10,000 from grocery store account.
(17) Nov. 27—Paid legacies to the four children, as provided in the will.
(18) Nov. 30—Final report on store operations showed the following: cash sales, $8,500; purchases for cash, $800; payments of expenses, $900; sale of showcases, fixtures, etc., $500; sale of refrigeration equipment, $5,500; refund on insurance, $50; cash balance transferred to Estate Cash account.
(19) Nov. 30—Executor received his $1,000 bequest and rendered his report to the court.

Presented below are cash journals and a general journal in which the executor might have recorded the above events. Events 1, 2, 4, 8, and 15 would not require any entries in the executor's journals. Entries for all other events numbered may be found by reference to the various journals. Events 4, 8, 15, 16, and 18 would require entries in the grocery store records, and these entries are presented following the executor's journal

D. F. KECK
EXECUTOR'S JOURNAL

1967		Dr.	Cr.
(3) Oct. 22 Cash—Principal	($\sqrt$)	$ 1,200	
Insurance policies		15,000	
Co. X. bonds		2,400	
Interest receivable		32	
Y Co. preferred stock		1,000	
Z Co. common stock		3,400	
Household effects		2,600	
Automobile		1,900	
Equity in grocery business		33,000	
Estate corpus			$60,532
(to record assets, per inventory)			
(14) Nov. 18 Legacies paid—Mrs. Andrews		$ 4,500	
Household effects			$ 2,600
Automobile			1,900
(payment of legacy, as provided in will)			

D. F. Keck
EXECUTOR'S CASH RECEIPTS JOURNAL

	Date	L.F.	Account Credited	Explanation
(3)	Oct.	22 (√)	Estate corpus	Cash, per inventory
(5)	"	25	Insurance policies	Face of policies collected
(6)	Nov.	1	Y Co. preferred stock	Sold
(9)	"	8	Co. X bonds	Sold
(9)	"	8	Interest receivable	Interest collected
(9)	"	8	Income	Interest from 10/8/67
(10)	"	10	Income	Dividend on Z Co. stock
(11)	"	12	Assets subsequently discovered	Savings account discovered
(16)	"	26	Equity in grocery business	Transfer of cash
(18)	"	30	Equity in grocery business	Transfer of cash (final)

D. F. Keck
EXECUTOR'S CASH DISBURSEMENTS JOURNAL

	Date	L.F.	Account Debited
(7)	Nov.	3	Debts of decedent paid
(7)		3	Debts of decedent paid
(12)		15	Funeral expenses
(13)		16	Administrative expenses
(14)		18	Distributions to income beneficiary
(17)		27	Legacies paid
(19)		30	Legacies paid

	Principal			Income
				Cash
Credit	Loss	Gain	Cash	
$ 1,200			$ 1,200	
15,000			15,000	
1,000		$100	1,100	
2,400	$ 200		2,200	
32			32	
				$ 10
				150
860			860	
10,000			10,000	
23,000	2,140		20,860	
$53,492	$2,340	$100	$51,252	$160

	Cash	
Explanation	Principal	Income
Jones Auto Repair	$ 65	
Gorman Haberdashery	90	
Funeral expenses	400	
Administrative and legal expenses	150	
Payment of cash to widow		$100
Cash payments to children, per will	18,000	
D. F. Keck, for services	1,000	
	$19,705	$100

Entries to be made on the books of the Andrews Grocery Store giving effect to the liquidation:

(4) Oct. 22	Cash		$ 9,700	
	Purchases		1,200	
	Accounts payable		3,000	
	Expenses		700	
		Cash		$ 4,900
		Sales		9,000
		Accounts receivable		700
(8) Nov. 5	Cash		$13,800	
	Purchases		2,100	
	Accounts payable		1,200	
	Notes payable		5,000	
	Expenses		750	
		Cash		$ 9,050
		Sales		13,000
		Accounts receivable		800
(15) Nov. 19	Cash		$ 7,060	
	Purchases		1,600	
	Expenses		500	
		Cash		$ 2,100
		Sales		7,000
		Accounts receivable		60
(16) Nov. 26	James Andrews, Equity		$10,000	
		Cash		$10,000
(18) Nov. 30	Cash		$14,550	
	Purchases		800	
	Expenses		900	
		Cash		$ 1,700
		Sales		8,500
		Showcases and fixtures		500
		Refrigeration equipment		5,500
		Unexpired insurance		50
30	Expenses (loss on receivables and unexpired insurance)		$ 110	
	Reserve for depreciation— Showcases and fixtures		1,700	
	Reserve for depreciation— Refrigeration equipment		3,200	
		Accounts receivable		$ 40
		Showcases and fixtures		2,300
		Refrigeration equipment		1,700
		Unexpired insurance		70
		Gain on sale of equipment		900

(to write off remaining uncollectible accounts and unexpired insurance; to remove remaining asset and reserve balances and take up gain on sale from previous transaction)

30	James Andrews, Equity	$ 2,140	
	Sales	37,500	
	Gain on sale of equipment	900	
	Inventory		$31,880
	Purchases		5,700
	Expenses		2,960

(to close the cost, expense, and income accounts and the loss on liquidation to the capital account)

30	James Andrews, Equity	$20,860	
	Cash		$20,760
	Petty cash		100

(to record transfer of cash from grocery business to executor)

Executor's Report to the Court

While the exact form of the statements which an executor will render is generally prescribed by the court to which he will report, an example of a charge and discharge statement based upon the preceding facts is presented below. Requirements of this type of report vary from state to state, and as a result several variations in form may be found. The statements presented below indicate the information which a fiduciary (executor or administrator) is generally required to submit, although not necessarily in the form in which the information would be submitted.

ESTATE OF JAMES ANDREWS

D. F. KECK, EXECUTOR

CHARGE AND DISCHARGE STATEMENT
AS TO PRINCIPAL

OCTOBER 8, 1967 TO NOVEMBER 30, 1967

I Charge Myself with:

Assets per inventory (Schedule A)	$60,532
Assets subsequently discovered—	
savings account	860
Gain on realization of assets (Schedule B)	100
Total Charges	$61,492

I Credit Myself with:

Debts of decedent paid (Schedule C)	$ 155	
Funeral expenses	400	
Administrative expenses	150	
Legacies paid (Schedule D)	23,500	
Loss on realization of assets (Schedule B)	2,340	
Total Credits		26,545
Balance as to principal		$34,947

Balance consists of:

Z Co. common stock	$ 3,400
Cash	31,547
Total	$34,947

Schedule A

ASSETS PER INVENTORY, OCTOBER 8, 1967

Cash	$ 1,200
Insurance policies	15,000
Co X bonds	2,400
Interest receivable	32
Y Co. preferred stock	1,000
Z Co. common stock	3,400
Household effects	2,600
Automobile	1,900
Equity in grocery business	33,000
Total assets per inventory	$60,532

Schedule B

REALIZATION OF ASSETS

	Per Inventory	Cash on Realization	Gain	Loss
Insurance policies	$15,000	$15,000		
Y Co. preferred stock	1,000	1,100	$100	
Co. X bonds	2,400	2,200		$ 200
Interest receivable	32	32		
Equity in grocery business (See Schedule B-1)	33,000	30,860		2,140
	$51,432	$49,192	$100	$2,340

Schedule B-1

SUMMARY OF JAMES ANDREWS GROCERY
BUSINESS LIQUIDATION
OCTOBER 8, 1967 TO NOVEMBER 30, 1967

Equity per inventory			$33,000
Sales		$37,500	
Less cost of sales:			
Inventory	$31,880		
Purchases	5,700		
Cost of goods sold		37,580	
Gross loss on sales		$(80)	
Expenses:			
Uncollectible receivables	$ 40		
Insurance expired	70		
Various	2,850		
Total expenses		$ 2,960	
Net operating loss		$(3,040)	
Gain on disposal of assets		900	
Net loss			(2,140)
Equity of grocery business, as realized			$30,860

Schedule C

DEBTS OF DECEDENT PAID

Jones Auto Repair	$ 65
Gorman Haberdashery	90
Total	$ 155

Schedule D

LEGACIES PAID

Mrs. James Andrews:		
Household Effects	$2,600	
Automobile	1,900	$ 4,500
Tom Andrews		5,000
Richard Andrews		5,000
Harry Andrews		5,000
Vernon Andrews		3,000
D. F. Keck		1,000
Total		$23,500

ESTATE OF JAMES ANDREWS
D. F. KECK, EXECUTOR

CHARGE AND DISCHARGE STATEMENT
AS TO INCOME

OCTOBER 8, 1967 TO NOVEMBER 30, 1967

I Charge Myself with:

Interest on Co. X bonds, October 8, 1967,
  to November 8, 1967 $ 10
Dividends received on Z Co., common stock   150
                                                             ─────────
    Total Charges $ 160

I Credit Myself with:

Distribution to income beneficiary,
  Mrs. J. Andrews   100
                                                             ─────────
Balance as to income $ 60
                                                             ═════════
Balance consists of: Cash $ 60

PROBLEMS

Problem 22–1. Prepare entries in general journal form to record the following events relating to the estate of L. Johnson, who died October 1, 1967.

a. Semi-annual interest is collected on the 5% bonds of the A Company, face value $30,000. One-third of this interest had accrued at the date of death and was included in the inventory of the estate.

b. The executor sold bonds of the B Company, face value $10,000, interest at 6%, for 104 and two months accrued interest. These bonds were valued at $10,250 at the date of the inventory. Date of the sale was December 1, 1967.

c. The executor sold some of the decedent's personal effects for $500. These items had been included in the inventory of the estate at a value of $125.

d. The executor sold 200 shares of the Acme Corporation common stock for $60 per share, plus a $.50 dividend. The dividend was declared on October 6, 1967. The stock was carried in the inventory at $12,400.

e. A dividend check for $100 was received on November 6 relating to 100 shares of the Greater Corporation common stock. Investigation revealed this stock was in a locked box, the existence of which was unknown until November 6. The stock had a value of $8,000 at October 1, 1967, and the dividend declaration was September 20, 1967.

Problem 22–2. On July 20, 1967, A. N. Phillip died, leaving the following items in his estate. G. Vance was named executor.

Cash in checking account	$ 1,450
Cash in savings account	2,475
Automobile	2,600
Household effects	1,750
Stock in GD Co., 400 shares	14,400
Bonds of AB Co., face value $8,000	8,075
U.S. Savings Bonds, Series E, valued at	9,275

Mr. Phillip's will provided for the following legacies:

To his son, Andrew:	Cash	$2,000
	Automobile	
	200 shares of GD Stock	
To University Achievement Fund:		$2,500
To his widow: Remainder of the estate		

During the period in which the executor administered the estate the following transactions occurred:

1. Funeral expenses were paid, $950.
2. U.S. Savings Bonds, Series E, were redeemed for $9,350.
3. Debts of the decedent were paid, $2,150.
4. A dividend of $120 was received on the GD stock.
5. The legacy to the University Achievement Fund was paid.
6. The legacy to the son, Andrew, was distributed.
7. Interest on the AB Co. bonds was collected, $200, $\frac{3}{4}$ earned subsequent to the date of death.
8. Administrative fees and expenses of the executor, $1,200 were approved and paid.
9. The balance of the estate was turned over to the widow, December 1, 1967.

Required:
Prepare journal entries to record the above events for the executor.

Problem 22–3. On June 10, 1967, J. B. Whitson, a retired businessman, died, leaving the following assets in his estate:

Cash in 2nd National Bank	$ 7,240
Preferred stock of Gable Corp., 200 shares	20,000
1966 automobile, valued at	3,100
Life insurance policies payable to the estate	25,000
U.S. Government Bonds, face value $10,000	8,975
Household Effects	1,050

The above items were included in the inventory filed with the court, and the following events subsequently took place:

a. Various liabilities owed by Whitson as of June 10, 1967, were paid, totaling $3,400.

b. An additional certificate for 20 shares of preferred stock of the Gable Corporation was discovered. The stock had a value of $100 per share at June 10, 1967.

c. Funeral and other related expenses of $1,450 were paid.

d. A dividend of $1.25 per share was received on the Gable Corporation preferred stock. The dividend was declared June 30, 1967.

e. The U.S. Government Bonds were redeemed for $9,035. The difference in redemption price and inventory value represents interest earned after the date of the inventory.

f. One-half the Gable Corporation preferred stock was sold at 101½.

g. Personal property taxes of $42 were paid. These taxes related to the automobile and had been assessed in April, 1967.

Required:

Prepare entries in general journal form to record the above events relating to the estate of Mr. Whitson.

Problem 22–4. Robert Hill died on August 10, 1967, and his will designated Richard Hill as the executor. Richard Hill established a general journal and appropriate cash journals in which to record the transactions of the estate. Record the following events as they might appear in such journals.

(1) The following items constituted the inventory of the estate filed with the probate court:

Cash	$ 4,050
Stock of ABC Co.	25,000
Bonds of ABC Co., 4%, interest A & O, par value	18,000
Automobile	1,800
Note receivable, 5%	3,000
Accrued interest on note	200
Bonds of LMN Co., 4½%, interest M & S, par value	10,000

(2) The following collections of cash were made in 1967:

a.	Sept. 1	Interest on LMN Co. bonds	$ 225
b.	Oct. 1	Interest on ABC Co. bonds	360
c.	Oct. 10	Note receivable	1,000
		Interest on note receivable	225
d.	Nov. 1	Dividend on ABC Co. stock (declared September 1, 1967)	800
e.	Nov. 10	Note receivable	500
f.	Dec. 1	Sale of automobile	1,650

(3) The following cash disbursements were made in 1967:

a.	Aug. 15	Miscellaneous debts	$1,200
b.	Sep. 1	Funeral expenses	950
c.	Sep. 10	Hospital and physician's bills	1,650
d.	Oct. 10	Legal expenses in connection with will	200
e.	Nov. 1	Safe deposit box rental to 11/1/68	10

(4) On December 10, 1967, the LMN Co. bonds were sold for $10,900, net, including interest.

(5) On December 1, 1967, special bequests were paid, as follows:

Steven Hill, a nephew	$2,000
Jackson Hill, a brother	4,000

(6) All interest income collected was transferred to the widow on the date of collection.

(7) On December 31, 1967, all cash on hand was transferred to the widow.

Problem 22–5. The following items arose in connection with the estate of B. L. Brothers, who died on August 1, 1967. For each item determine the portion of the amount properly allocable to the principal of the estate and the portion properly allocable to the income of the estate.

a. A dividend of $3,200 was received from the XYZ Realty Company in October 1967. The dividend was declared in September 1967. Attached to the dividend check was a notation that 60% of the dividend represented earnings of the company, while the remainder represented a return of capital.

b. An uncashed check for $4,500 was included in the inventory of assets. The check had been received by Mr. Brothers on July 1, 1967, and represented the rental payment for the third quarter of 1967 on a building owned by Brothers and included as a part of the estate.

c. Bonds of the Vinella Production Company were included in the inventory. Par value of the bonds was $30,000, interest rate was 5%, and the bonds were inventoried at the market value on August 1, 1967, of 98. On November 1, 1967, the bonds were sold for 100 plus accrued interest. Interest was payable February 1 and August 1.

d. Bonds of the Pinella Co., face value of $5,000, were discovered on October 1, 1967. These bonds had not been inventoried as their presence was not known at August 1, 1967. On October 1, 1967, the semi-annual interest check for $137.50 was received.

Problem 22–6. Mr. G. G. Frey, a haberdasher in Catlin, Illinois, died on February 20, 1967, leaving an estate consisiting of the following:

Cash in bank	$ 6,950
Cash on his person	120
Household goods	2,000
Building at 1 Main St., leased on a quarterly basis, at $1,800 per quarter, in advance	68,000
City of Catlin Improvement Bonds, 4%, interest payable January 1 and July 1	9,000
Equity in haberdashery, per books	52,500

The will made the following provisions: The widow was to receive $10,000 plus all household goods; a married daughter, Jane Simmer, was to receive the City of Catlin bonds; the executor, A. R. Combes, was to receive $1,500; the remaining estate was to be established as a trust fund, the income to be payable to the widow for life. The principal of the estate would pass in equal shares to the heirs of Jane Simmer upon death of the widow.

The executor paid funeral expenses of $1,100, debts existing at February 20, 1967, of $3,200, and legal and accounting fees of $1,250. Rents were collected on April 1 and July 1. Interest on the City of Catlin bonds was collected on July 1. On July 10 all legacies prescribed in the will were paid. In addition, the widow was paid $800 on March 15 and on May 15.

The executor, and the widow, decided to accept a lump sum offer for the equity in the haberdashery—cash of $30,000 received March 15, 1967, and $25,000 in 5% notes received March 15, 1967. Interest and one-fifth of the face of the notes would be due March 15, 1968, and each succeeding March 15 for 5 years.

Required:

Record the above events in the appropriate journals of the executor, A. R. Combes. List the assets to be turned over to the trustee on July 15.

Problem 22–7. The trial balance below was taken from the records of L. Landt, executor for the estate of W. Ridley, on October 31, 1967. Landt had acted as executor since the date of Ridley's death, June 12, 1967.

Required:

(1) Prepare the proper statements for the estate of W. Ridley, and

(2) Prepare journal entries as of November 1, 1967, to close the executor's accounts and to transfer the remaining assets to Helga Ridley, widow, on that date.

L. LANDT

TRIAL BALANCE

OCTOBER 31, 1967

Cash: Principal	$ 4,400	
Cash: Income	680	
Debts of decedent paid	1,120	
Loss on realization	460	
Funeral and administrative expenses	850	
Automobile	1,750	
Bonds	20,000	
Legacy paid: Martha Ridley	2,500	
Gain on Realization		$ 960
Assets Subsequently Discovered		1,450
Expense—Income	290	
Distributions to income beneficiary:		
Helga Ridley	1,070	
Estate corpus		28,670
Income		2,040
	$33,120	$33,120

Problem 22–8. William Hite died on March 31, 1967. His will provided for two executors, Paul Mortensen and William Sawtell, to administer his estate. In addition to providing for the payment of the normal funeral expenses and other debts, the will included the following bequests:

Local Church	$ 2,500
University Achievement Fund	4,000
Brother, Ernest	10,000
Executors (in lieu of fees, $2,500 each)	5,000

The inventory of assets, as presented to the court by the executors, was as follows at the date of death:

Cash in First National Bank	$ 6,500
Real property, valued by appraisal at	41,400
Convertible debenture bonds of KC Corporation, $4\frac{1}{2}\%$,	
Interest January 1 and July 1, par (and market)	60,000
Stock investments:	
KC Corporation, 600 shares common, value	36,500
GSG Mining Corp., 1,000 shares, no par, value	–0–
AD Corporation, 200 shares common, value	12,500
Furniture and household items	5,000
Accrued interest (KC Corp. bonds)	675

The following transactions relating to the estate were consummated by the executors:

April 15. Paid funeral expenses, $2,100; debts of decedent, $4,000.
April 30. Sold KC Corp. bonds at 102, plus accrued interest.
May 10.   Paid all specific bequests, except executors' fees.
May 15.   Received dividends on KC Corp. stock, $260, and on AD Corp. stock, $400, both being income items.
May 20.   Sold GSG Mining stock for $.0425 per share.
May 22.   Received check from M. Mills, $2,500 in repayment of personal loan made by Mr. Hite before death.
May 24.   Paid estate administration expenses, totaling $7,800, of which $300 was allocable to income.
May 27.   ½ furniture and household items were sold for $1,000, and other ½ donated to charitable organizations.
May 31.   Paid bequests to executors.

On May 31, the executors requested release from their charge and turned over the remainder of the estate to the trustee provided in the will. Income from the trust was to be paid equally to Mr. Hite's two children.

Required:
Prepare charge and discharge statements as to principal and income for the period March 31, 1967 to May 31, 1967. Supporting schedules should be prepared where necessary.

Problem 22-9. E. W. Smith died on January 13, 1967. His will appointed C. W. Bowen as the executor to administer the estate. At the date of death the decedent possessed the following assets: cash, $40,000; amount loaned to associates, $12,000; bonds of OC Corporation, 5%, interest payable January 1 and July 1, par $24,000, market value $26,000; Stock of SA Company, 1,000 shares, no par, cost $15,500, market value $71,000; Stock of CU Development Co, 50 shares, par value $50, cost $2,500, market value, nominal; City of Kenyon Bonds, 4%, par value $18,000, market value, $16,200, interest March 1 and September 1; clothing, $1,500; jewelry, $5,700, accrued interest, (?).

The will provided for the payment of funeral and other necessary expenses, and for the following bequests:

City Cemetery	$ 5,000
Civic Auditorium	5,000
Brother, W. E. Smith	10,000
Executor, in lieu of fees	4,000

From January 13, 1967, to March 31, 1960, the executor completed the following transactions relating to the E. W. Smith estate:

Collected amounts advanced to associates, $10,500, with the balance considered uncollectible; sold OC Corporation bonds on March 1, 1967, at 110, plus interest; received dividend of $.50 per share on SA Company stock, payable to stockholders of record on December 29, 1966, received January 21, 1967; received interest on City of Kenyon bonds March 1; paid funeral expenses, $2,000, administrative expenses, $6,150 ($6,000 applicable to principal), debts of decedent, $8,750, legal and accounting fees, $3,600; purchased SA Corporation bonds, par value $20,000, interest $5\frac{1}{2}\%$, for 103, plus 3 months interest on March 15, 1967; paid all bequests in full, with brother W. E. Smith accepting jewelry at inventory value, $4,000 in cash, and the CU Development stock in full settlement of his bequest; gave clothing to charity; sold golf equipment found in country club locker to neighbor for $150.

Required:

Prepare charge and discharge statements as to principal and income for the period January 13, 1967, to March 31, 1967. Prepare supporting schedules where necessary.

Problem 22–10. Arthur Taine died in an accident on May 31, 1967. His will, dated February 28, 1966, provided that all just debts and expenses be paid and that his property be disposed of as follows:

Personal residence—devised to Bertha Taine, widow.

United States Treasury Bonds and Puritan Company stock—to be placed in trust. All income to go to Bertha Taine during her lifetime, with right of appointment upon her death.

Seneca Co. mortgage notes—bequeathed to Elaine Taine Langer, daughter.

Cash—a bequest of $10,000 to David Taine, son.

Remainder of estate—to be divided equally between the two children, Elaine Langer and David Taine.

The will further provided that during the administration period Bertha Taine was to receive $300 a month out of estate income. Estate and inheritance taxes are to be borne by the residue. David Taine was named as executor and trustee.

An inventory of the decedent's property was prepared. The fair market value of all items as of the date of death was determined. The preliminary inventory, before the computation of any appropriate income accruals on inventory items, follows:

Personal residence property	$ 45,000
Jewelry—diamond ring	9,000
York Life Insurance Co.—term life policy on life of Arthur Taine. Beneficiary—Bertha Taine, widow.	120,000
Granite Trust Co.—3% savings bank account, Arthur Taine, in trust for Philip Langer (grandchild), interest credited January and July 1; balance May 31, 1967	400
Fidelity National Bank—checking account; balance May 31, 1967	143,000
$100,000 United States Treasury Bonds, 3%, 1999, interest payable March 1 and September 1	100,000
$9,700 Seneca Co. first mortgage notes, 6%, 1971, interest payable May 31 and November 30	9,900
800 shares Puritan Co. common stock	64,000
700 shares Meta Manufacturing Co. common stock	70,000

The executor opened an estate bank account to which he transferred the decedent's checking account balance. Other deposits, through July 1, 1968, were as follows:

Interest collected on bonds:
  $100,000 United States Treasury

September 1, 1967	$ 1,500
March 1, 1968	1,500

Dividends received on stock:
  800 shares Puritan Co.

June 15, 1967 declared May 7, 1967 payable to holders	
of record May 27, 1967	800
September 15, 1967	800
December 15, 1967	1,200
March 15, 1968	800
June 15, 1968	800
Net proceeds of June 19, 1967 sale of 700 shares of Meta	
Mfg. Co.	68,810

Payments were made from the estate's checking account through July 1, 1968 for the following:

Funeral expenses	2,000
Assessments for additional 1965 federal and state income	
tax ($1,700) plus interest ($110) to May 31, 1967	1,810
1967 income taxes of Arthur Taine for the period January 1,	
1967 through May 31, 1967, in excess of amounts paid by	
the decedent on declarations of estimated tax	9,100
Federal and state fiduciary income taxes, fiscal years ending	
June 30, 1967 ($75) and June 30, 1968 ($1,400)	1,475
Federal and state estate taxes	58,000
Monthly payments to Bertha Taine: 13 payments of $300	3,900
Attorney's and accountant's fee	25,000

The executor waived his commission. However, he desired to receive his father's diamond ring in lieu of the $10,000 specific legacy. All parties agreed to this in writing, and the court's approval was secured. All other specific legacies were delivered by July 15, 1968.

Required:

Prepare a Charge and Discharge Statement as to Principal and Income, and its supporting schedules, to accompany the attorney's formal court accounting on behalf of the executor of the estate of Arthur Taine for the period May 31, 1967 through July 1, 1968. (Arthur Taine was not a resident of a community property state.) The following supporting schedules should be included:

1. Original Capital of Estate.
2. Gain on Disposal of Estate Assets.
3. Loss on Disposal of Estate Assets.
4. Funeral, Administration and Other Expenses.
5. Debts of Decedent Paid.
6. Legacies Paid or Delivered.
7. Assets (Corpus) on Hand, July 1, 1968.
8. Proposed Plan of Distribution of Estate Assets.
9. Income Collected.
10. Distribution of Income.   (AICPA adapted)

Problem 22–11. For several years John Kibler had operated a clothing store in Central City. Aside from part time help, his only full time employee was an older brother, Sam. On February 16, 1967, John Kibler died, leaving a will in which he appointed Don MacArthur executor of his estate, provided for the payment of funeral and other expenses, and made the following special bequests:

First Church	$1,500
Sam Kibler	3,000
Susan Kibler, his wife	their home and furnishings
Marie MacArthur, his daughter	5,000
Executor, in lieu of fees	2,000

The remainder of his estate was to become a trust, the income of which was to go to his widow during her lifetime, with the trust being divided in equal shares among his grandchildren after the death of Susan Kibler.

The executor listed the following assets of John Kibler:

Home and furnishings, valued at	$26,500
Cash, personal	1,500
U.S. Govt. Bonds, Series E, redemption value	12,750
MG Corporation stock, 200 shares, value	18,600
Life insurance policy, Susan Kibler beneficiary	20,000
Equity in Kibler Clothing Store	(?)

Sam Kibler drew a trial balance from the records of the Kibler Clothing Store on February 17, 1967, the store being closed that day. This trial balance showed the following:

KIBLER CLOTHING STORE
TRIAL BALANCE, FEBRUARY 17, 1967

Cash	$ 2,100	
Accounts receivable	8,400	
Inventory as of Jan. 1, 1967	26,250	
Fixtures, net	3,600	
Prepaid expenses	400	
Accounts payable		$ 8,000
Accrued liabilities		750
Kibler, Capital		25,700
Purchases	16,000	
Sales		28,000
Advertising	1,100	
Salaries	1,400	
Rent	1,200	
Various expenses	2,000	
	$62,450	$62,450

Past experience indicated that gross profit on sales was normally 25%, and this was agreed upon as the basis for determining the inventory on February 17, 1967. It was similarly agreed that Sam Kibler would operate the store on a liquidation basis, reporting periodically to the executor. The books were not closed. It was estimated the liquidation would be completed by April 15, 1967. New purchases would be limited to fast-moving items.

On April 15, 1967, the executor disposed of the U.S. Government bonds for $13,000; collected a dividend on the MG Corporation stock, declared March 1, 1967, $200; paid all bequests, except his own. He had also given the widow $150 from the income collected. He paid funeral and administrative costs of $1,200 and paid other debts of $1,800. On April 15, Sam Kibler presented the following trial balance of the Kibler Clothing Store:

Cash	$25,520	
Accounts receivable	700	
Inventory, as of Jan. 1, 1967	26,250	
Fixtures, net	–0–	
Prepaid expenses	50	
Accounts payable		$ –0–
Accrued liabilities		20
Kibler, Capital		25,700
Purchases	24,000	
Sales		64,000
Advertising	3,100	
Salaries	3,800	
Rent	2,600	
Various expenses	3,000	
Loss on sale of fixtures	700	
	$89,720	$89,720

No further operations are contemplated, even though there is about $800 of inventory on hand. About $400 of the receivables will be collectible, but no recovery from the prepayments is anticipated. The accrued liabilities are paid by the executor, and he turns over all remaining properties to the trustee on April 17, 1967, after paying himself the bequest provided in the will.

Required:
Prepare the charge and discharge statements as to principal and income for the period February 17, 1967, to April 17, 1967. Ignore all federal and state income, estate, and inheritance taxes. Prepare supporting schedules for all necessary amounts.

Problem 22–12. The Eells Print Shop in Hamilton had been operated continuously by the Eells family since 1832. On September 15, 1967, William Eells died, leaving his widow but no children or grandchildren to succeed him in operation of the family business. Eells' will appointed Dave Brown executor of the estate and provided that, upon settlement of the estate, a trust would be established, the income from which would go to the widow, with the trust principal passing to various educational and charitable sources upon the widow's death.

In addition to his equity in the Eells Print Shop, William Eells possessed the following properties over which the executor assumed control:

Cash in personal account	$ 1,800
AB Corporation 4% bonds, face value $30,000	
interest F & A, value	31,375
Accrued interest on AB Corp. bonds	150
BO Corporation 6% cumulative preferred stock, 200	
shares, $100 par, dividends unpaid since October	
31, 1965, value	16,400
Property at One Green Street, housing Eells	
Print Shop and two other businesses, value	40,000
Personal effects	1,500
Equity in Eells Print Shop	65,000

A balance sheet of the Eells Print Shop, prepared after closing the books as of September 15, 1967, follows:

EELLS PRINT SHOP
BALANCE SHEET AS OF SEPTEMBER 15, 1967

Cash	$ 4,000	Accounts payable	$ 3,500
Accounts receivable	8,500	Note due at bank	5,000
Paper stock	16,400	Misc. accruals	2,000
Unbilled order, completed	3,600	Total liabilities	10,500
Supplies	1,500		
Mach. & equip, net	41,500	Eells, Capital	65,000
	$75,500		$75,500

During the latter part of September, negotiations were completed for the sale of the Eells Print Shop business to J. K. Foster on the following terms: Foster takes over all the assets except cash and receivables; assumes all liabilities; agrees to pay $48,000, ⅓ on October 1, 1967, ⅓ January 2, 1968, and ⅓ on June 1, 1968, with interest at 6% upon default of any payment; and agrees to a monthly rental of $240 on the Print Shop building.

The executor additionally completes the following transactions by December 1, 1967, on which date he transfers the estate to the trustee:

1. Takes control of cash and receivables of the Eells Print Shop.
2. Collects rent from other tenants, $200 on each of the following dates, a month in advance: September 15, October 15, November 15.
3. Collects $8,200 of receivables of Eells Print Shop, remainder deemed uncollectible.
4. On October 1, 1967, receives a check from J. K. Foster for $16,240.
5. Sells AB Corp. Bonds on November 15 for $32,000 and accrued interest.
6. Receives $2,400 dividend on BO Corporation stock, declared October 1, 1967.
7. Paid following items: funeral expenses, $1,500; personal debts of Eells at time of death, $2,400; legal fees, $1,500; executor's fee, determined by court, $2,500.
8. Receives rental checks of $240 on November 1 and December 1.
9. Buys, on November 15, 1967, 300 shares of TA & A stock, cost $33,675, per agreement with widow and approval of the court.

10. Personal effects were donated to charity except for a few items of little intrinsic value.
11. Pays widow three checks of $400 from income and pays $250 of expenses in connection with income.

Required:

Prepare a charge and discharge statement as to principal and as to income for the period September 15, 1967, to December 1, 1967. Ignore all federal and state income, estate, and inheritance taxes. Supporting schedules should be included where necessary.

Problem 22–13. On April 15, 1967, Craig Stewart, for many years operator of Stewart's Book Shop, died. In his will Ralph Reno was named executor of his estate. The book store had not been prospering sufficiently in recent years to attract the interest of any of Stewart's three children, James, Paul, and Larry. It was decided that the executor should proceed with the liquidation of the business, with one son, James, supervising much of the actual liquidation operation.

The executor decided to set up necessary journals and ledgers to account for the estate operations, and he assumed control of the business properties as of April 15, 1967. The balance sheet, after closing, on that date showed:

STEWART BOOK STORE
BALANCE SHEET AS OF APRIL 15, 1967

Cash in bank	$ 3,700	Due to book companies	$ 4,600
Accounts receivable	400	Misc. accrued debts	1,400
Inventory of books (net)	42,600	Rent payable	150
Inventory of novelties (net)	12,800	Total liabilities	6,150
Showcases and equipment (net)	4,200	Stewart, Capital	57,550
	$63,700		$63,700

In addition to the book store, Stewart possessed the following properties, per inventory:

Automobile	$ 2,200
Cash in bank	4,000
Real estate, per appraisal	38,400
Household effects	4,200
Bonds of XYZ Co. 4%, $30,000 par value, interest January 1 and July 1, valued at	31,000
Accrued interest	350

Mr. Stewart's will provided for certain bequests, listed below. The estate, including any income arising during the period of executorship, was to be divided equally among the three sons. It was estimated that about five months would be required to liquidate the book store. The sons agreed that James Stewart would be paid $1,500 for his services in supervising the store liquidation. The bequests provided:

University Achievement Fund	$2,500
Local hospital	5,000
Executor, in lieu of fee	2,500

Ralph Reno, executor, paid the above bequests, funeral expenses of $1,800, debts of Mr. Stewart existing at the date of death, $2,500, legal and accounting fees, $3,000. The real estate was sold for $35,000 net. The household effects were divided equally among the three sons. Bond interest of $600 was collected July 1. Paul Stewart agreed, the other brothers concurring, to accept the automobile at $2,000 in partial settlement of his legacy. On October 1, the bonds had not been sold. By that date Ralph Reno had received the following reports from James Stewart:

	Apr.–May	June	July	August	September
Sales of merchandise	$27,000	$16,000	$11,000	$ 6,500	$ 4,000
Expenses paid, incl.					
Liquidator's fee	4,000	3,000	2,600	2,000	2,000
Cash collections	26,800	16,100	10,800	6,900	6,800
Cash payouts	6,000	4,000	4,200	3,050	2,500
	May 31	June 30	July 31	Aug. 31	Sept. 30
Cash on hand	$24,500	$36,600	$43,200	$47,050	$51,350
Inventory of books	29,000	19,000	12,000	6,000	500
Inven. of novelties	6,800	3,000	2,000	800	200

Other items than the above pertaining to the business on September 30, 1967, were: Receivables estimated collectible, $200; sales value of inventory, $200. Included in September cash collections was $2,800 received from the sale of all showcases and equipment. No obligations remained outstanding, and· all cash was transferred to the executor on October 1, 1967.

Required:

(1) Determine the gain or loss on liquidation of the Stewart Book Store, accepting the above values as proper at September 30, 1967. Prepare an operating statement and a balance sheet to reflect the liquidation proceedings and results thereof.

(2) Prepare a charge and discharge statement and supporting schedules.

(3) Determine the division of the remaining properties at October 1, 1967.

CHAPTER 23

Partnership liquidation

In the preceding chapter a few of the reasons why a business might be liquidated were mentioned. In this chapter the accounting problems involved in the liquidation of a partnership are covered more completely.

In Chapter 1 it was pointed out that a partnership is an association of two or more persons to carry on a business for profit. A partnership rests upon a contractual foundation, and the life period of a partnership may therefore be somewhat hazardous, depending in part on the moods and relationships of the various partners. When the contract which establishes a partnership is terminated the partnership is dissolved. Thus dissolution of a partnership arises when the contractual relationship comes to an end. While dissolution may occur under a variety of circumstances, it should be noted that dissolution and liquidation, as related to partnerships, are not synonymous. A partnership is *dissolved* when a partner withdraws, regardless of the reason. A partnership is *liquidated* when the business is terminated with the assets being converted into cash, liabilities being paid, and the remaining cash being distributed among the partners. Thus a partnership may be dissolved without being liquidated. For example, this situation would exist when one or more of the old partners continues the operation of the business upon the withdrawal of a partner or partners.

While this chapter deals primarily with the accounting problems of liquidations, a brief digest of the causes or reasons for partnership dissolution is necessary. While dissolution *may* result in liquidation of the partnership, liquidation *always* results in dissolution. As a result, all the following causes of dissolution may also be causes for partnership liquidation.

Causes of Partnership Dissolution

The various causes of partnership dissolution may be classified as:

I. Dissolution caused by acts of the parties to the partnership agreement:
  A. Termination of the time stipulated in the contract. When a definite time for termination is stated in the partnership agreement, the passage of the agreed time terminates the contract, and the partnership dissolves. If the partners decide to continue the partnership beyond the termination time stipulated, the partnership is known as a "partnership at will" and any partner may withdraw at any time.
  B. Accomplishment of the purpose stipulated in the contract. When the contract states that the partnership was formed for the accomplishment of a specific task or purpose, the accomplishment of this stated task or purpose fulfills the contract and dissolves the partnership.
  C. Mutual agreement of the partners. As with any contract, the parties at interest may at any time mutually agree to terminate the contract.
  D. Withdrawal of a partner. A partner has the power to withdraw from a partnership at any time; that is, a partner cannot be forced to continue in a business venture against his will. However, when a partner withdraws from a partnership at a time other than when he has a *right* to do so (e.g., when agreed upon time has elapsed, when stated purpose has been accomplished, or when partners mutually agree to the withdrawal), he violates the partnership contract and thus becomes liable to his prior copartners for any damages sustained because of his withdrawal from the partnership.
II. Dissolution caused by operation of the law:
  A. Death of a partner. A partnership is automatically dissolved upon the death of any partner.
  B. Bankruptcy of the partnership or of any partner.
  C. Illegality of purpose. The partnership is dissolved when legislation is enacted which makes the business of the firm illegal.
  D. Entrance into war. If one or more of the partners of a partnership are citizens or subjects of the different warring countries, the partnership is dissolved or suspended during the war.
III. Dissolution caused by judicial decree. Any of the following circumstances may become the basis for a decree dissolving the partnership, such decree being issued by a court of equity upon the application of any partner:
  A. Insanity or other incapacity of a partner to fulfill his duties.
  B. Misconduct of a partner which tends to interfere with successful operations of the business.
  C. Internal dissension among the partners, thus interfering with successful operations of the business.
  D. Inability of the business to make profits.
  E. Fraudulent representations being the basis for inducing the complaining partner to become a partner.

Accounting for Liquidation of a Partnership

While the cause of partnership dissolution will have some effect upon the events preceding the final liquidation of a partnership, the similarities of liquidations flowing from all causes are more significant than the differences. The procedure in liquidation involves the sale or other realization of the assets into cash, the apportionment of any gains or losses upon realization to the partners in the proper ratio, the liquidation of any liabilities, and the payment of partners' interests.

Certain rules should be followed by individuals handling the liquidation of a partnership and by the accountant maintaining the records of the liquidation. The first rule involves the accounting allocation of any gain or loss arising from the realization of partnership assets. Simply stated, the rule is *always allocate any gains or losses to the proper partners' accounts prior to distributing any cash to the partners.* Violation of this rule can subject the liquidator or administrator of the partnership liquidation to liability for improper distribution of partnership assets. Profits and losses upon realization of assets are allocated to the partners in the appropriate profit and loss sharing ratios, and this allocation must be accomplished prior to any cash distributions to the partners for return of their loans, investments, or accumulated profits. After gains and losses on realization have been allocated to the partners' accounts, cash may be distributed to the various equity interests. As a general rule all outside creditors must be paid first. When these claims have been settled, the remaining cash is distributed to the partners in their latest equity ratio.

Death of a Partner

The death of a partner automatically dissolves the existing partnership. At the same time, as we have seen in the previous chapter, death creates a problem of control and administration of the property of the deceased until appropriate distribution of such property can be made. In a partnership the problem may be more complicated than with a proprietorship, since the partnership agreement may contain various provisions bearing upon events subsequent to the death of a partner. While the executor of the deceased is interested in as rapid and equitable liquidation of the estate as is feasible, the remaining partners may not be interested in actual liquidation of the partnership.

For example, a partnership agreement may provide that surviving partners are to continue in business as a new partnership. Even though this may be the situation, the estate of the decedent is entitled to a determination of the interest of the decedent partner at the date of his death. Such a valuation of the equity of the decedent may have to be tentative at the date of death, subject to later determination at the close of the partnership fiscal period, or at some other agreed upon date.

Because there is frequently a conflict of interests between the estate of the decedent, which desires a cash settlement for the equity of the deceased partner in the shortest possible time, and the surviving partners, who desire to retain the business assets for continued business operation, many partnerships carry insurance on the partners. Proceeds of the life insurance policies are used to settle the equity of the deceased partner with his estate.

When the death of a partner results in actual liquidation (as well as dissolution) of the partnership, the accounting problems of the partnership are similar to those discussed on the following pages. The accounting problems of the deceased partner's heirs or executors are similar to those discussed in the preceding chapter.

Liquidation of a Partnership After Complete Realization of Assets

In the following several examples it is assumed that the partnership is dissolved and all assets are realized in cash before any distribution of assets is made to the partners. Because various situations may arise from the realization of assets, the following illustrations are organized into three groups:

Group 1. Allocation of realization losses does not produce a debit balance in any partner's equity, as represented by his capital, loan, and drawing accounts.

Group 2. Allocation of realization losses produces a debit balance in one or more (but not all) of the partners' equities, as represented by capital, loan, and drawing accounts.

Group 3. Allocation of realization losses renders the partnership insolvent, i.e., it produces a net debit balance in partners' equities, as represented by capital, loan, and drawing accounts.

Group I Illustrations. For the two examples in this group, assume the ABC Partnership has three partners who share profits and losses as follows: A, 30%; B, 30%; and C, 40%. The following statement of financial position was prepared just prior to dissolution and subsequent liquidation.

ABC PARTNERSHIP

FINANCIAL POSITION

OCTOBER 15, 1967

Cash	$ 4,000	Liabilities	$40,000
Other assets	90,000	A, Loan	3,000
		B, Loan	6,000
		A, Capital	12,000
		B, Capital	15,000
		C, Capital	18,000
	$94,000		$94,000

ILLUSTRATION 1-1. For purposes of illustration, assume the other assets were sold for $75,000 cash. The loss to be allocated among the partners is $15,000. This loss must be allocated to the partners' equity accounts before distributing any cash. Existing cash is then applied in accordance with the general rule previously stated to outside creditors and to partners' equities. The following entries illustrate the accounting procedures involved.

(1)	Cash	$75,000	
	Loss on realization of assets	15,000	
	Other assets		$90,000
	(to record the sale of other assets at a $15,000 loss)		
(2)	A, Capital	$ 4,500	
	B, Capital	4,500	
	C, Capital	6,000	
	Loss on realization of assets		$15,000
	(to allocate the loss to partners in their profit and loss ratio)		
(3)	Liabilities	$40,000	
	Cash		$40,000
	(to record payment of liabilities)		
(4)	A, Loan	$ 3,000	
	B, Loan	6,000	
	Cash		$ 9,000
	(to record payment of partners' loans)		
(5)	A, Capital	$ 7,500	
	B, Capital	10,500	
	C, Capital	12,000	
	Cash		$30,000
	(to record payment of partners' remaining capital balances)		

A tabular arrangement to portray the liquidation of this partnership might appear as follows on page 684.

This illustration shows that the distribution of cash does not present a difficult problem when the capital of each partner is large enough to absorb his share of the loss from realization of assets. It should be noted at this point that gains or losses from realization should *always* be allocated among the partners in their profit and loss sharing ratio, or in the same manner as gains or losses from operations are allocated.

ABC PARTNERSHIP
STATEMENT OF LIQUIDATION
OCTOBER, 1967

	Cash	Other Assets	Liabilities	Loans A	Loans B	Capitals A	Capitals B	Capitals C
Profit and loss ratio						30%	30%	40%
Balances per statement	$ 4,000	$90,000	$40,000	$3,000	$6,000	$12,000	$15,000	$18,000
(1, 2) Sale of assets and allocation of loss	75,000	(90,000)				(4,500)	(4,500)	(6,000)
Balances	$79,000	...	$40,000	$3,000	$6,000	$ 7,500	$10,500	$12,000
(3) Payment to creditors	(40,000)		(40,000)					
Balances	$39,000	...	...	$3,000	$6,000	$ 7,500	$10,500	$12,000
(4) Payment of loans	(9,000)			(3,000)	(6,000)			
Balances	$30,000	...	...	...	...	$ 7,500	$10,500	$12,000
(5) Distribution to partners	(30,000)					(7,500)	(10,500)	(12,000)
Balances	-0-	-0-	-0-	-0-	-0-	-0-	-0-	-0-

ILLUSTRATION 1-2. Assume the assets were sold for $45,000. The following entries would be made:

(1)	Cash	$45,000	
	Loss on realization of assets	45,000	
	Other assets		$90,000
(2)	A, Capital	$13,500	
	B, Capital	13,500	
	C, Capital	18,000	
	Loss on realization of assets		$45,000
(3)	Liabilities	$40,000	
	Cash		$40,000
(4)	A, Loan	$ 1,500	
	A, Capital		$ 1,500
	(to transfer from A's loan account to his capital account an amount required to absorb his capital deficit)		
(5)	A, Loan	$ 1,500	
	B, Loan	6,000	
	Cash		$ 7,500
(6)	B, Capital	$ 1,500	
	Cash		$ 1,500

A tabular arrangement to portray the liquidation of this partnership would appear as follows on page 686.

From this tabular presentation the following points should be noted: (1) the loss from realization is allocated to the partners' capitals in their profit and loss ratio, even though one partner's capital balance (A) is not sufficient to absorb the loss; (2) the allocation of the loss from the realization takes place prior to any cash distributions; and (3) an adjustment of the partners' loan accounts takes place prior to the liquidation of the loans. A partner should not be paid in full for his loan if his capital account contains a debit balance. In reality the debit balance in the partner's capital account represents a debt owing to the partnership, while the loan account credit balance represents a debt owing from the partnership to the partner. In step (4) enough of the loan credit is transferred to the capital account to eliminate the debit balance in the capital account. This procedure is called exercising the *right of offset*, and after it is completed the remaining balance in the loan account represents a claim against the partnership. After the offset of part of A's loan against his capital deficit, the remaining loan balances are paid, and finally, the balances in the partners' capitals are liquidated.

ABC PARTNERSHIP
STATEMENT OF LIQUIDATION
OCTOBER, 1967

	Cash	Other Assets	Liabilities	Loans A	Loans B	Capitals A	Capitals B	Capitals C
Profit and loss ratio						30%	30%	40%
Balances per statement	$ 4,000	$90,000	$40,000	$3,000	$6,000	$12,000	$15,000	$18,000
(1, 2) Sale of assets and allocation of loss	45,000	(90,000)				(13,500)	(13,500)	(18,000)
Balances	$49,000		$40,000	$3,000	$6,000	$(1,500)	$ 1,500	....
(3) Payment to creditors	(40,000)		(40,000)					
Balances	$ 9,000		....	$3,000	$6,000	$(1,500)	$ 1,500	
(4) Offset of A's capital deficit against loan account				(1,500)		$ 1,500		
Balances	$ 9,000		....	$1,500	$6,000	....	$ 1,500	....
(5) Payment of loans	(7,500)			(1,500)	(6,000)			
Balances	$ 1,500		....	....	....	....	$ 1,500	....
(6) Distribution to partners	(1,500)						(1,500)	
Balances	-0-	-0-	-0-	-0-	-0-	-0-	-0-	-0-

Group 2 Illustrations. For the two illustrations and their alternatives in this group, assume the same statement of financial position and related facts as was used for the previous group of illustrations.

This group of illustrations portrays the accounting treatment for partnership liquidations in which allocation of loss upon realization produces a debit balance in one or more, but not all, of the partners' equities.

ILLUSTRATION 2-1. The first illustration in this group would arise whenever the loss upon realization of the assets was great enough to produce a debit balance in *one* partners' equity, the equity being the sum of the partners' capital, drawing, and loan accounts. For this example, assume a sale of the other assets for $43,000, with a resulting loss of $47,000 to be allocated to the partners. The following entries would be made:

(1)

Cash	$43,000	
Loss on realization of assets	47,000	
Other assets		$90,000

(2)

A, Capital	$14,100	
B, Capital	14,100	
C, Capital	18,800	
Loss on realization of assets		$47,000

(3)

Liabilities	$40,000	
Cash		$40,000

(The above entries are similar to those in the preceding illustrations)

A tabular arrangement to portray the liquidation events to this point would appear as on page 688.

At this point the tabulation reveals that $7,000 cash is available for distribution to the partners; and A's equity is $900 (the net balance of his $3,000 loan and the $2,100 debit in his capital account); that B's equity is $6,900 (the sum of his loan and capital accounts); and that C has a negative equity of $800. In other words, C owes the ABC Partnership $800.

Three alternative solutions are possible in this type of situation depending upon the action taken by C.

Alternative 1. C may pay the partnership the $800 which he owes. If C pays the $800, the partnership is able to proceed with the liquidation in a

ABC PARTNERSHIP

STATEMENT OF LIQUIDATION (PARTIAL)

OCTOBER, 1967

	Cash	Other Assets	Liabilities	Loans A	Loans B	Capitals A	Capitals B	Capitals C
Profit and loss ratio						30%	30%	40%
Balances per statement	$ 4,000	$90,000	$40,000	$3,000	$6,000	$ 12,000	$ 15,000	$ 18,000
(1, 2) Sale of assets and allocation of loss	43,000	(90,000)				(14,100)	(14,100)	(18,800)
Balances	$47,000	...	$40,000	$3,000	$6,000	$ (2,100)	$ 900	$ (800)
(3) Payment to creditors	(40,000)		(40,000)					
Balances (see subsequent statements)	$ 7,000	-0-	-0-	$3,000	$6,000	$ (2,100)	$ 900	$ (800)

manner similar to that in previous illustrations. The following entries would be made:

(4)

Cash	$ 800	
C, Capital		$ 800
(to record C's payment to the		
partnership)		

(5)

A, Loan	$2,100	
A, Capital		$2,100
(to offset A's capital deficit against		
his loan account)		

(6)

A, Loan	$ 900	
B, Loan	6,000	
Cash		$6,900

(7)

B, Capital	$ 900	
Cash		$ 900

The preceding tabular arrangement could then be completed as on page 690.

Alternative 2. C may be unable to pay the $800 owed the partnership. To the other partners the $800 represents a loss to the partnership and should be shared by the remaining partners in their respective profit and loss ratio. Since A and B each share in the profits and losses to the extent of 30% each, they would share the $800 loss equally (30/60 to each). The following entry would be necessary to record the additional loss suffered by A and B:

(4)

A, Capital	$400	
B, Capital	400	
C, Capital		$800
(to record A's and B's share of C's		
uncollectible equity balance)		

Entries similar to (5), (6), and (7) in alternative 1 would then be made reflecting the appropriate amounts. Completion of the tabular arrangement would proceed as on page 691.

Alternative 3. Partners A and B may decide to distribute the remaining cash ($7,000) before it is known whether Partner C will pay the partnership his $800 debt. Under this situation the problem facing the partners is how to distribute the $7,000 cash between the equity of A of $900 ($3,000 loan minus $2,100 capital deficit) and the equity of B of $6,900 ($6,000 loan plus $900 capital balance), or a total equity of $7,800.

ABC PARTNERSHIP
STATEMENT OF LIQUIDATION (COMPLETED)
OCTOBER, 1967

	Cash	Other Assets	Liabilities	Loans A	Loans B	Capitals A 30%	Capitals B 30%	Capitals C 40%
Profit and loss ratio						30%	30%	40%
Balances per preceding partial statement	$7,000	-0-	-0-	$3,000	$6,000	$(2,100)	$900	$(800)
(4) Cash from C	800							800
Balances	$7,800	...	...	$3,000	$6,000	$(2,100)	$900	-0-
(5) Offset A's capital debit against loan				(2,100)		2,100		
Balances	$7,800	...	...	$ 900	$6,000	...	$900	...
(6) Payment of loans	(6,900)			(900)	(6,000)			
Balances	$ 900	...	...	...	...		$900	
(7) Distribution to partners	(900)						(900)	
Balances	-0-	-0-	-0-	-0-	-0-	-0-	-0-	-0-

ABC PARTNERSHIP
STATEMENT OF LIQUIDATION (COMPLETED)
OCTOBER, 1967

	Cash	Other Assets	Liabilities	Loans A	Loans B	Capitals A 30%	Capitals B 30%	Capitals C 40%
Profit and loss ratio						30%	30%	40%
Balances per preceding partial statement	$7,000	-0-	-0-	$3,000	$6,000	$(2,100)	$900	$(800)
(4) Record loss on non-collection from partner C		⋯	⋯			(400)	(400)	800
Balances	$7,000	⋯	⋯	$3,000	$6,000	$(2,500)	$500	⋯
(5) Offset A's capital debit against loan		⋯	⋯	(2,500)		2,500		
Balances	$7,000	⋯	⋯	$ 500	$6,000	⋯	$500	⋯
(6) Payment of loans	(6,500)			(500)	(6,000)			
Balances	$ 500	⋯	⋯	⋯	⋯	⋯	$500	⋯
(7) Distribution to partners	(500)						(500)	
Balances	-0-	-0-	-0-	-0-	-0-	-0-	-0-	-0-

Here it must be recognized that if C cannot pay his $800 obligation, the other partners will have to absorb C's capital deficit in their relative profit and loss ratio. Therefore, before any cash distribution should be made to the partners the amount necessary to absorb any *possible* future loss must be calculated for each partner. The loss calculated must then be subtracted from each partner's equity to arrive at the balance of each partner's equity which can be paid. The cash may then be distributed accordingly. After distribution of the cash, the partners' equities on the partnership's books would contain credit balances exactly equal to their respective shares of the possible loss from nonpayment by the partner with the debit balance in his capital account.

The key to the solution of a situation where cash is to be distributed before all possible losses are known is to recognize that provision *must* be made to restrict each partner's equity for his possible loss *prior* to the distribution of any cash to the partners.

Referring again to the partial statement of liquidation on page 688, under alternative 3 the possible loss from the nonpayment by C must be computed and deducted from the remaining partners' equities. (Such deductions are calculations only and not the basis of an entry affecting the ledger accounts.) After the deduction, the amount properly payable to each partner is the balance of each partner's equity.

ABC Partnership

Schedule 1

COMPUTATION OF PAYMENTS TO PARTNERS

October, 1967

	Partners' Equities		
	A	B	C
Profit and loss ratio	30%	30%	40%
Capital account balances, per statement on page 688	$(2,100)	$ 900	$(800)
Add: Loan balances	3,000	6,000	
Partners' total equities	$ 900	$6,900	$(800)
Amount of restriction of equity for possible loss from nonpayment of C. (A and B share in a 30 : 30 ratio)	$ (400)	$ (400)	$ 800
Net equity	$ 500	$6,500	–0–

After this calculation has been made, the $7,000 cash can be distributed: $6,000 to pay B's loan, $500 to pay a portion of the remaining balance of A's loan, and $500 to pay a portion of B's remaining capital account credit balance. Entries similar to (4), (5), and (6), for the first alternative under this group would then be made. Completion of the tabular arrangement would appear as on page 694.

If C subsequently pays in the $800, A and B would use the $800 to settle their respective equities. If C subsequently finds it impossible to pay, the remaining balances would be eliminated by an appropriate entry.

This alternative also illustrates that the general rule to the effect that partners' loan accounts are to be liquidated before payments are made on capital accounts does not necessarily hold true. The only equitable distribution in the above illustration is to pay B $6,000 to liquidate his loan completely, pay B an additional $500 on his capital contribution, and pay A $500 in partial settlement of his loan. Payment of A's loan in full at this point would be inequitable to B, particularly if A subsequently refused, or was unable, to make good his capital deficit.

ILLUSTRATION 2-2. This illustration indicates the accounting procedure necessary whenever the loss upon realization of the assets is great enough to produce a deficit in *more* than *one* partners' equity accounts. This situation may arise in one of two ways. First, the loss on realization itself may produce only one equity deficit, but absorption of this deficit by the remaining partners may produce another equity deficit. Second, the loss on realization itself may produce more than one equity deficit.

Using the statement of financial position and related data previously used and assuming the other assets were sold for $41,000, the following entries would be made:

(1)		
Cash	$41,000	
Loss on realization of assets	49,000	
Other assets		$90,000
(2)		
A, Capital	$14,700	
B, Capital	14,700	
C, Capital	19,600	
Loss on realization of assets		$49,000
(3)		
Liabilities	$40,000	
Cash		$40,000

A tabular arrangement to portray the liquidation events to this point would appear as on page 695.

ABC PARTNERSHIP
STATEMENT OF LIQUIDATION (COMPLETED)
OCTOBER, 1967

	Cash	Assets	Liabilities	Loans A	Loans B	Capitals A 30%	Capitals B 30%	Capitals C 40%
Profit and loss ratio						30%	30%	40%
Balances per preceding partial statement	$7,000	-0-	-0-	$3,000	$6,000	$(2,100)	$900	$(800)
(4) No entry to be made (see computation of payment to partners)								
(5) Offset of A's capital debit against loan				$(2,100)		$2,100		
Balances	$7,000	...	...	$ 900	$6,000	...	$900	$(800)
(6, 7) Settlement of loans and capital accounts, per computation of payment to partners	(7,000)			(500)	(6,000)		(500)	
Balances	-0-	-0-	-0-	$ 400	-0-	-0-	$400	$(800)

ABC Partnership
STATEMENT OF LIQUIDATION (Partial)
October, 1967

| | Cash | Other Assets | Liabilities | Loans | | Capitals | | |
				A	B	A	B	C
Profit and loss ratio						30%	30%	40%
Balances per statement	$ 4,000	$90,000	$40,000	$3,000	$6,000	$12,000	$15,000	$18,000
(1, 2) Sale of assets and allocation of loss	41,000	(90,000)				(14,700)	(14,700)	(19,600)
Balances	$45,000	...	$40,000	$3,000	$6,000	$(2,700)	$ 300	(1,600)
(3) Payment to creditors	(40,000)		(40,000)					
Balances	$ 5,000	-0-	-0-	$3,000	$6,000	$(2,700)	$ 300	$(1,600)

At this point the tabulation reveals that there is $5,000 cash available for distribution to the partners and that the following equities (loans plus capitals) exist:

$$A = \$ \ 300$$
$$B = \ \ 6,300$$
$$C = \ (1,600)$$
$$\text{Total} = \$5,000$$

Alternative 1-A. If C pays the amount he owes, cash will be increased to $6,600, and A will receive $300 and B will receive $6,300.

Alternative 2-A. If C is unable to pay the $1,600, A and B must share this loss in their profit and loss ratio. Completion of the Statement of Liquidation for this illustration would appear as on page 697.

At this point A owes the partnership $500 and if he pays this amount into the partnership, B will receive the entire $5,500 in full settlement of the remaining balance in his loan account. If A cannot pay in this $500, B will receive only the $5,000 cash on hand.

Alternative 3-A. As in alternative 3, it is possible that partners A and B may desire to distribute the cash before it is known whether C can pay in the $1,600 balance he owes. In this situation, all possible losses to each partner must be computed before deciding how the $5,000 will be distributed. Therefore, after preparing the Statement of Liquidation (partial), the following schedule would be prepared:

ABC PARTNERSHIP
SCHEDULE 1
COMPUTATION OF PAYMENTS TO PARTNERS
OCTOBER, 1967

	Partners' Equities		
	A	B	C
Profit and loss ratio	30%	30%	40%
Capital account balance, per statement on page 695	$(2,700)	$ 300	$(1,600)
Add: loan balances	3,000	6,000	
Partners' total equities	$ 300	$6,300	$(1,600)
Allocation of possible loss from nonpayment by C (A and B now share in a 30 : 30 ratio)	$ (800)	(800)	1,600
Net equities	$ (500)	$5,500	...
Allocation of possible loss from nonpayment by A	500	(500)	
Net equity	–0–	$5,000	–0–

ABC PARTNERSHIP

STATEMENT OF LIQUIDATION (CONTINUATION)

OCTOBER, 1967

	Cash	Other Assets	Liabilities	Loans A	Loans B	Capitals A 30%	Capitals B 30%	Capitals C 40%
Profit and loss ratio						30%	30%	40%
Balances per preceding partial statement	$5,000	-0-	-0-	$3,000	$6,000	$(2,700)	$ 300	$(1,600)
(4) Allocation of C's deficit						(800)	(800)	1,600
Balances	$5,000	...	...	$3,000	$6,000	$(3,500)	$(500)	...
(5) Offset capital deficits against loan accounts				(3,000)	(500)	3,000	500	
Balances	$5,000	-0-	-0-	-0-	$5,500	$ (500)	-0-	-0-

This schedule reveals that at this point the only equitable method for distributing the $5,000 is to distribute it all to B. Although the loss on realization of assets did not eliminate A's equity in the partnership entirely, his share of that loss, plus his share of the possible loss arising from nonpayment by C, did create an equity deficit for A although perhaps of a temporary nature.

If the $5,000 were distributed to B at this time, the following completion of the Statement of Liquidation started would result, as on page 699.

If C subsequently pays in the $1,600 he owes, A and B would use the $1,600 to settle their respective equity interests. If C subsequently finds it impossible to pay, the remaining equity balances would be eliminated by an appropriate entry.

Group 3 Illustrations. For the two illustrations and their alternatives in this group, assume the same statement of financial position and related facts as was used for the previous illustrations.

This group of illustrations portrays the accounting treatment for those partnership liquidations in which the distribution of the loss upon realization of the assets renders the partnership insolvent, i.e., produces a net debit balance in partners' equities. The two basic illustrations in this group deal with the situations which exist when a partnership is insolvent and (1) all partners are individually solvent, or (2) one or more partners is individually insolvent.

ILLUSTRATION 3-1. Situations falling within Group 3 will arise, under the basic facts assumed, whenever realization of the assets produces less than $36,000 cash or, conversely, whenever realization results in a loss in excess of $54,000, the sum of the partners' equities. Assume a sale of other assets for $30,000, with a resulting loss of $60,000. The entries to record the realization and allocation of the resulting loss would be as previously illustrated, and the Statement of Partnership Liquidation would appear as on page 700.

For this illustration, assume additionally that all the individual partners are solvent. This being the case, any of the three partners may be called upon to pay the remaining $6,000 owed to the creditors, since partners are jointly and severally liable for any partnership debts.

Alternative 1-B. If A pays the $6,000 balance of liabilities, the partners' equities after the payment would appear as follows:

> A's equity = $3,000   (increased from $ −3,000 by payment)
> B's equity = 3,000
> C's equity = (6,000)

If C can pay in his negative equity, A and B can be paid in full. If C cannot pay in his negative equity, A and B will stand a $3,000 loss each.

ABC PARTNERSHIP
STATEMENT OF LIQUIDATION (COMPLETED)
OCTOBER, 1967

	Cash	Other Assets	Liabilities	Loans A	Loans B	Capitals A 30%	Capitals B 30%	Capitals C 40%
Profit and loss ratio						30%	30%	40%
Balance per preceding partial statement, p. 695	$5,000	-0-	-0-	$3,000	$6,000	$(2,700)	$300	$(1,600)
(4) No entry necessary (see Computation of payment to partners)								
(5) Offset of A's capital deficit against his loan account				(2,700)		2,700		
Balances	$5,000	...	...	$ 300	$6,000	...	$300	$(1,600)
(6, 7) Partial settlement of B's Loan, per Schedule 1	(5,000)				(5,000)			
Balances	-0-	-0-	-0-	$ 300	$1,000	-0-	$300	$(1,600)

ABC PARTNERSHIP
STATEMENT OF LIQUIDATION (PARTIAL)
OCTOBER, 1967

	Cash	Other Assets	Liabilities	Loans A	Loans B	Capitals A 30%	Capitals B 30%	Capitals C 40%
Profit and loss ratio						30%	30%	40%
Balances per statement	$ 4,000	$90,000	$40,000	$ 3,000	$ 6,000	$12,000	$15,000	$18,000
Sale of assets and allocation of loss	30,000	(90,000)				(18,000)	(18,000)	(24,000)
Balances	$34,000	...	$40,000	$ 3,000	$ 6,000	$(6,000)	$(3,000)	$ (6,000)
Payment to creditors	(34,000)		(34,000)					
Balances	...		$ 6,000	$ 3,000	$ 6,000	$(6,000)	$(3,000)	$ (6,000)
Offset of partners' capital deficits against loans				(3,000)	(3,000)	3,000	3,000	
Balances	-0-	-0-	$ 6,000	-0-	$ 3,000	$(3,000)	-0-	$ (6,000)

Alternative 2-B. If B pays the $6,000 of liabilities, the partners' equities after the payment would appear as follows:

A's equity = $(3,000)
B's equity =   9,000   (increased from $3,000 by payment)
C's equity =   (6,000)

If both A and C can make payments, B will take such payments in settlement of his $9,000 equity. However, if A can make his payment and C cannot, there must be a further division of C's loss between A and B in their profit and loss ratio. Thus, if C cannot pay, A's and B's equities would appear as below:

A's equity = $(6,000)
B's equity =   6,000

A and B would share the $6,000 loss from nonpayment by C in their profit and loss ratio or $\frac{30}{60}$ and $\frac{30}{60}$. Thus, A would owe B a total of $6,000, $3,000 for his original negative equity and $3,000 for his share of C's nonpayment.

On the other hand, if C can settle his deficit and A cannot, there must be a division of the loss from A's nonpayment between B and C in their profit and loss ratio. Thus, if A cannot pay, B's and C's equities would appear as below:

B's equity = $7,714
C's equity = (7,714)

B and C would share the $3,000 loss from nonpayment by A in their profit and loss ratio of $\frac{30}{70}$ and $\frac{40}{70}$. Thus, C would owe B a total of $7,714, $6,000 for his deficit and $1,714 for his 4/7 share of A's nonpayment.

Alternative 3-B. If C pays the $6,000 of liabilities, the partners' equities after the payment would appear as follows:

A's equity = $(3,000)
B's equity =   3,000
C's equity =   –0–   (decreased from $ –6,000
                        by payment to creditors)

If A can pay his negative equity, B will receive the $3,000 in settlement of his claim. However, if A cannot pay his $3,000 negative equity, the amount which A owes to the partnership and which he cannot pay must be shared by B and C in their profit and loss ratio. Thus, if A cannot pay, B's and C's equities would appear as follows:

B's equity = $1,714
C's equity = (1,714)

B's equity would absorb 3/7 of the $3,000 loss, or $1,286, while C's equity would be charged with 4/7, or $1,714. Thus, C would owe B $1,714, his share of the loss arising from A's inability to pay his capital deficit.

ILLUSTRATION 3-2. For this illustration, assume the same conditions with regard to realization of partnership assets as in the preceding illustrations in this group. This would leave the following balances on the partnership books:

	Dr.	Cr.
Liabilities		$6,000
B, Loan		3,000
A, Capital	$3,000	
C, Capital	6,000	

Assume also that each of the partners has personal assets and liabilities, in addition to their partnership claims and debts, as follows:

	Assets	Liabilities
A	$ 4,000	$3,000
B	4,000	9,000
C	14,000	2,000

From the above data it can be seen that A's personal assets are sufficient to settle fully his personal obligations, but the excess is not sufficient to settle his obligation as evidenced by his partnership capital account.

B's personal assets will not meet his personal debts, and the $3,000 due him from the partnership is insufficient to make up the difference. C has sufficient assets to meet his personal debts as well as to meet the obligations arising from his partnership interest.

Certain legal rules, which are generally referred to as marshaling of assets, govern situations in which a partnership and one or more of the partners are insolvent. These rules, while subject to some exceptions, in essence provide:

(1) That creditors of the partnership have the right to payment in full from partnership assets before any of the partners' personal creditors can claim partnership assets. However, if all partnership obligations have been paid, personal creditors of any partner may receive settlement from partnership assets, through a court-obtained charging order, to the extent of that partner's remaining equity.

(2) That personal creditors of a partner have the right to payment in

full from the partner's personal assets before creditors of the partnership can claim payment from these assets. However, once the personal creditors have been paid, the unpaid partnership creditors may obtain settlement from the balance of the partners' personal assets, regardless of the capital balance a given partner has in the partnership.

In this illustration all proceeds from the sale of partnership assets have been used to pay partnership creditors, and those creditors still have claims of $6,000 against the partnership. These creditors cannot look to B at this time for payment, since his assets are insufficient to cover his personal debts. They can look to A for only $1,000 of the $6,000 due, since A must apply $3,000 of his personal assets to settle his personal debts. The unsatisfied partnership creditors can, however, look to C for full payment, as his assets are sufficient to make such payment. These creditors will be able to obtain payment from C regardless of whether he has a debit or credit balance in his partnership equity account.

If the partnership creditors collect $6,000 from C, the balances on the partnership books would then be:

	Dr.	Cr.
B, Loan		$3,000
A, Capital	$3,000	

All partnership creditors would now be satisfied, but the personal obligations of each partner remain unsettled. The remaining partnership question concerns what to do about B's $3,000 loan and A's $3,000 capital deficit.

Under the Uniform Partnership Act, A's personal creditors would receive the first $3,000 from his personal assets. The remaining $1,000 of A's assets would be paid by A to the partnership in partial settlement of his $3,000 capital account deficit. Since A has no additional assets at this time, his remaining $2,000 deficit may be considered a loss by the partnership. The following table shows the accounts as they would appear on the partnership books assuming the above conditions.

	Cash	B Loan	A Capital	C Capital
Balances after C pays the partnership creditors, but before any receipt of cash from A		$3,000	$(3,000)	
Receipt of cash from A	$1,000		1,000	
Balances	1,000	3,000	(2,000)	
Loss on A's remaining balance, in profit and loss ratio of 30:40		(857)	2,000	$(1,143)
Balances	$1,000	$2,143	0	$(1,143)

This table reveals B has a $2,143 interest in the partnership. Since B owes his personal creditors $9,000 and has personal assets of only $4,000, B's personal creditors have unsatisfied claims of $5,000. In satisfaction of these claims these creditors have a right to any interest that B may have in the partnership, or $2,143 as indicated. Thus, B's personal creditors would be entitled to the $1,000 cash of the partnership and would also have a claim against the partnership for the $1,143 that C must pay in as his share of A's nonpayment. C's assets are sufficient to pay his personal creditors, to pay the $6,000 unsatisfied partnership claims, and also to allow him to contribute to the partnership his portion of any nonpayment by A, or $1,143.

B and C would each retain a claim against A, of $857 and $1,143 respectively, because of his failure to be able to meet the terms of the partnership agreement.

Liquidation of a Partnership by Installment

Frequently partnership assets are not realized through an instantaneous sale but are realized in a piecemeal fashion over a period of time. Under such circumstances the partners may prefer not to wait until realization of all assets has been completed before they begin to distribute the cash resulting from realization. Whereas the preceding illustrations have been concerned with the distribution of the cash available after all assets have been realized, the following illustrations indicate the procedure for the distribution of cash to the partners prior to the completion of the realization of all assets. This type of partnership liquidation is generally referred to as "liquidation by installments."

General Rules for Distribution of Cash. Preceding illustrations have emphasized the considerable care required in liquidation of a partnership in order to assure an equitable distribution of assets. Such care is equally important in the partial liquidation of a partnership prior to complete realization of assets. In a situation of this nature partners receive payments in installments, the payments being made before knowledge exists of the complete loss from realization. In order to assure equitable treatment among the partners, and also to protect any individuals charged with the responsibility of approving the installment payments, no payments should be made to any partner at any time when his equity (capital, loan, and drawing accounts) is insufficient to bear his share of any *possible* loss from subsequent asset realizations or from failure of a fellow partner to contribute the amount of any debit balance which may result in his equity.

In addition to the above rule, which should guide liquidations by installments, no distributions of assets to the partners should be made until all liabilities are either (1) paid in full or (2) provided for through retention of cash sufficient to complete their liquidation. Therefore, each of the following conditions must exist before a partner should receive any cash in the liquidation procedure:

(1) All liabilities should be liquidated, or cash retained sufficient to accomplish their total liquidation.
(2) The capital, loan, and drawing accounts of the partners must contain sufficient total credit balances to absorb all *possible* losses in the future.

Illustrations. Three illustrations are presented to indicate the manner in which liquidation proceeds under varying conditions. These illustrations do not, of course, cover all possible alternatives, but merely indicate some of the problems encountered and how the above rules are applied to meet these problems.

For these illustrations assume the same ABC partnership exists as was used in the previous series of illustrations. A, B, and C share profits and losses in a 30 : 30 : 40 relationship, respectively. The following statement of financial position was prepared immediately prior to the start of the liquidation process.

ABC PARTNERSHIP
STATEMENT OF FINANCIAL POSITION
OCTOBER 15, 1967

Cash	$ 4,000	Liabilities	$40,000
Other assets	90,000	A, Loan	3,000
		B, Loan	6,000
		A, Capital	12,000
		B, Capital	15,000
		C, Capital	18,000
	$94,000		$94,000

ILLUSTRATION 4-1. In the first illustration in this section assume that realization of the assets proceeds in the three stages set forth below. In addition, as cash becomes available from the realization of assets it is used to liquidate liabilities and to make distributions to the partners.

(1) Assets carried at $30,000 are sold for $25,000. All cash on hand after the sale, $29,000, is used to liquidate liabilities.
(2) Assets carried at $40,000 are sold for $30,000. Cash of $11,000 is used to liquidate remaining liabilities, and $19,000 is distributed to the partners.
(3) Remaining assets are sold for $10,000.

Entries to record these events are similar to those previously presented. A statement of partnership liquidation would appear as in Exhibit A on page 707.

The first phase of the liquidation statement, (1), should be completed without difficulty. Likewise the second phase, (2), can be completed down to the "Payment to partners" without any complications arising. In order to complete the "Payment to partners" line it is necessary to determine the total possible loss which each partner may have to bear if the remaining assets prove to be a total loss. A schedule to organize this information may be prepared as in Schedule 1 as follows:

Schedule 1

ABC PARTNERSHIP

COMPUTATION OF BALANCES AFTER PROVIDING
FOR POSSIBLE LOSSES

	Loans		Capitals		
	A	B	A	B	C
Profit and loss ratio			30%	30%	40%
(2) Balances after liquidation of liabilities	$3,000	$6,000	$7,500	$10,500	$12,000
Possible loss from nonrealization of remaining Other Assets ($20,000), per Exhibit A			(6,000)	(6,000)	(8,000)
Balances after deducting all possible losses (payment to partners)	$3,000	$6,000	$1,500	$ 4,500	$ 4,000

The balances shown, which total $19,000, represent the amount which may be safely paid to the partners. The payments are safe in that after deducting them from the partners' equities, which exist after liquidation of

Exhibit A

ABC PARTNERSHIP
STATEMENT OF LIQUIDATION
OCTOBER, 1967

	Cash	Other Assets	Liabilities	Loans A	Loans B	Capitals A 30%	Capitals B 30%	Capitals C 40%
Profit and loss ratio						30%	30%	40%
Balances per statement	$ 4,000	$90,000	$40,000	$3,000	$6,000	$12,000	15,000	$18,000
(1) Realization and loss	25,000	(30,000)				(1,500)	(1,500)	(2,000)
Balances	$29,000	$60,000	$40,000	$3,000	$6,000	$10,500	$13,500	$16,000
Payment to creditors	(29,000)		(29,000)					
Balances	....	$60,000	$11,000	$3,000	$6,000	$10,500	$13,500	$16,000
(2) Realization and loss	$30,000	(40,000)				(3,000)	(3,000)	(4,000)
Balances	$30,000	$20,000	$11,000	$3,000	$6,000	$ 7,500	$10,500	$12,000
Payment to creditors	(11,000)		(11,000)					
Balances	$19,000	$20,000	....	$3,000	$6,000	$ 7,500	$10,500	$12,000
Payment to partners (Schedule 1):								
Loans	(9,000)			(3,000)	(6,000)			
Capitals	(10,000)					(1,500)	(4,500)	(4,000)
Balances	....	$20,000	....	....	....	$ 6,000	$ 6,000	$ 8,000
(3) Realization and loss	$10,000	(20,000)				(3,000)	(3,000)	(4,000)
Balances	$10,000	....				$ 3,000	$ 3,000	$ 4,000
Payments to partners	(10,000)					(3,000)	(3,000)	(4,000)
Balances	-0-	-0-	-0-	-0-	-0-	-0-	-0-	-0-

the liabilities, each partner has a remaining equity balance equal to his share of all possible future loss from nonrealization of the assets.

The final phase of the liquidation statement, (3), poses no problem. The partners' equities at this point are sufficient to bear their respective shares of any possible loss. After each partner is charged with his share of the actual loss in the final phase, the cash realized in the final phase would be distributed, with each partner receiving the balance of his equity after deducting his share of the actual loss.

The above liquidation of the ABC partnership by installments has the same end result as if no distributions had been made to the partners until the final realization phase was completed. No party was harmed by the liquidation by installments because (1) all liabilities were liquidated before any cash was distributed to the partners, and (2) payments were made to partners only to the extent that their partnership equities were sufficient to cover all possible losses.

ILLUSTRATION 4-2. In this illustration, assume that realization of the assets proceeds in the following three stages:

(1) Assets carried at $30,000 are sold for $25,000. All cash on hand after the sale, $29,000, is used to liquidate liabilities.
(2) Assets carried at $40,000 are sold for $22,000. Cash of $11,000 is used to liquidate the remaining liabilities, and $11,000 is distributed to the partners.
(3) Remaining assets are sold for $10,000.

This illustration again indicates the exception to the general rule that partners' loan accounts are to be paid before their capital accounts. The right of offset has been dealt with in previous illustrations whereby debit balances in a partner's capital account may be offset against his loan account. When partners are to receive cash for their partnership interests prior to complete realization of the assets, care must be taken to provide for all possible losses for each partner prior to distributing any cash to the partners. The total possible loss for each partner should be compared with that partner's equity (capital, drawing, and loan) to see if the equity is sufficient to bear the loss. Only then should the liquidation proceed.

The following statement of partnership liquidation on page 709 presents the liquidation under the above assumptions.

As in the preceding illustration, the first phase of the liquidation, part (1), should be completed without difficulty. All cash realized from the partial sale of assets is used to liquidate liabilities. In the second phase, however, a problem arises after final liquidation of liabilities. The state-

Exhibit A

ABC PARTNERSHIP
STATEMENT OF LIQUIDATION
OCTOBER, 1967

	Cash	Other Assets	Liabilities	Loans		Capitals		
				A	B	A 30%	B 30%	C 40%
Profit and loss ratio						30%	30%	40%
Balances per statement	$ 4,000	$90,000	$40,000	$3,000	$6,000	$12,000	$15,000	$18,000
(1) Realization and loss	25,000	(30,000)				(1,500)	(1,500)	(2,000)
Balances	$29,000	$60,000	$40,000	$3,000	$6,000	$10,500	$13,500	$16,000
Payment to creditors	(29,000)		(29,000)					
Balances	...	$60,000	$11,000	$3,000	$6,000	$10,500	$13,500	$16,000
(2) Realization and loss	$22,000	(40,000)				(5,400)	(5,400)	(7,200)
Balances	$22,000	$20,000	$11,000	$3,000	$6,000	$ 5,100	$ 8,100	$ 8,800
Payment to creditors	(11,000)		(11,000)					
Balances	$11,000	$20,000	...	$3,000	$6,000	$ 5,100	$ 8,100	$ 8,800
Payment to partners (Schedule 1):								
Loans	(8,100)			(2,100)	(6,000)			
Capitals	(2,900)						(2,100)	(800)
Balances	...	$20,000		$ 900	...	$ 5,100	$ 6,000	$ 8,000
(3) Realization and loss	$10,000	(20,000)				(3,000)	(3,000)	(4,000)
Balances	$10,000	...		$ 900	...	$ 2,100	$ 3,000	$ 4,000
Payment to partners:								
Loans	(900)			(900)				
Capitals	(9,100)					(2,100)	(3,000)	(4,000)
Balances	-0-	-0-	-0-	-0-	-0-	-0-	-0-	-0-

ment can be completed only down to the "Payment to partners" line under (2), without making supplementary calculations to determine the safe payments to partners at this point. The schedule showing this computation would appear as follows:

Schedule 1

ABC PARTNERSHIP

COMPUTATION OF BALANCES AFTER PROVIDING
FOR POSSIBLE LOSSES

	Loans		Capitals		
	A	B	A	B	C
Profit and loss ratio			30%	30%	40%
(2) Balances, after payment of creditors	$3,000	$6,000	$ 5,100	$8,100	$8,800
Possible loss from nonrealization of remaining other assets, ($20,000) per Exhibit A			(6,000)	(6,000)	(8,000)
Balances	$3,000	$6,000	$(900)	$2,100	$ 800
Offset of capital debit of A against loan account	(900)		900		
Balances after deduction of all possible losses (payments to partners)	$2,100	$6,000	–0–	$2,100	$ 800

As the schedule reveals, partners B and C receive payment of a portion of their capitals even though partner A does not receive full return of his loan. Any other distribution of the available cash would not provide fully for the possibility of nonrealization of the remaining "Other Assets."

Phase (3) of the liquidation causes no problem in determining how much to pay the partners, regardless of the amount realized on the final $20,000 of assets. Provision was made in the above schedule to absorb a 100% loss. Any loss of less than 100% can thus be absorbed by the partners, with cash being distributed for whatever equity interests remain.

ILLUSTRATION 4-3. In each of the preceding illustrations each partner has had some equity in the partnership at the time of the first cash distribution to the partners, even after providing for possible losses from nonrealization of remaining assets. This illustration deals with the situation which arises when one or more partners do not have an equity remaining after providing for all possible loss from realization of remaining assets. In this illustration, assume realization of the assets proceeds in the following three stages:

(1) Assets carried at $30,000 are sold for $25,000. All cash on hand after the sale, $29,000, is used to liquidate liabilities.
(2) Assets carried at $40,000 are sold for $18,000. Cash of $11,000 is used to liquidate remaining liabilities, and $7,000 is distributed to the partners.
(3) Remaining assets are sold for $10,000.

In this illustration, it should be noted that after liquidation of all liabilities in phase (2) Partner C should not receive any of the $7,000 cash remaining because his partnership equity is not sufficient to bear his share of the possible loss on nonrealization of the remaining $20,000 of Other Assets. The amount to be distributed to Partners A and B cannot be determined until after provision is made in their equities for (1) their share of the possible loss from nonrealization of Other Assets, and (2) their share of the possible loss from the failure of C to make good his debit balance which would exist if a total loss on the remaining assets did arise.

The following statement of partnership liquidation, Exhibit A on page 712, illustrates the liquidation procedure under the above assumptions.

Again, no problems arise in liquidation until the point of determining payments to partners in phase (2) is encountered. Cash of $7,000 is available for distribution, and partners' equities total $27,000. Only after provision is made for the possible loss of $20,000 from nonrealization of remaining assets can the liquidation proceed. In this illustration, as the following Schedule 1 on page 713 reveals, additional provision must be made for possible nonrealization of C's debit balance before the cash can be distributed appropriately.

In this same schedule it should be noted that offsets of capital debit balances against loans should be made before providing for additional losses from noncollection of other partners' debit balances.

After payment of the amounts indicated on the final line of the cited schedule, A and B will each have remaining equities of $6,400 (see Exhibit A). This is the equity required for each to absorb his share of the possible loss from nonrealization of assets and from noncollection from C.

Exhibit A

ABC PARTNERSHIP
STATEMENT OF LIQUIDATION
OCTOBER, 1967

	Cash	Other Assets	Liabilities	Loans A	Loans B	Capitals A	Capitals B	Capitals C
Profit and loss ratio						30%	30%	40%
Balances per statement	$ 4,000	$90,000	$40,000	$3,000	$6,000	$12,000	$15,000	$18,000
(1) Realization and loss	25,000	(30,000)				(1,500)	(1,500)	(2,000)
Balances	$29,000	$60,000	$40,000	$3,000	$6,000	$10,500	$13,500	$16,000
Payments to creditors	(29,000)		(29,000)					
Balances	...	$60,000	$11,000	$3,000	$6,000	$10,500	$13,500	$16,000
(2) Realization and loss	$18,000	(40,000)				(6,600)	(6,600)	(8,800)
Balances	$18,000	$20,000	$11,000	$3,000	$6,000	$ 3,900	$ 6,900	$16,000
Payment to creditors	(11,000)	(20,000)	(11,000)					
Balances	$ 7,000	$20,000	...	$3,000	$6,000	$ 3,900	$ 6,900	$ 7,200
Payments to partners (Schedule 1):								
Loans	(6,500)			(500)	(6,000)			
Capitals	(500)						(500)	
Balances	...	$20,000		$2,500	...	$ 3,900	$ 6,400	$ 7,200
(3) Realization and loss	$10,000	(20,000)				(3,000)	(3,000)	(4,000)
Balances	$10,000	...		$2,500	...	$ 900	$ 3,400	$ 3,200
Payments to partners:								
Loans	(2,500)			(2,500)				
Capitals	(7,500)					(900)	(3,400)	(3,200)
Balances	-0-	-0-	-0-	-0-	-0-	-0-	-0-	-0-

Schedule 1

ABC PARTNERSHIP
COMPUTATION OF BALANCES AFTER PROVIDING FOR POSSIBLE LOSSES

	Loans		Capitals		
	A	B	A	B	C
Profit and loss ratio			30%	30%	40%
(2) Balances after payment to creditors	$3,000	$6,000	$3,900	$6,900	$ 7,200
Possible loss from nonrealization of remaining Other Assets of $20,000, per Exhibit A			(6,000)	(6,000)	(8,000)
Balances	$3,000	$6,000	$(2,100)	$ 900	$(800)
Offset of A's capital debit against loan account	(2,100)		2,100		
Balances	$ 900	$6,000	...	$ 900	$(800)
Possible additional loss from noncontribution by C of debit balance (in 30 : 30 ratio)	(400)			(400)	800
Balance after deduction of all possible losses (payments to partners)	$ 500	$6,000	–0–	$ 500	–0–

Miscellaneous Problems

The amounts determined to be safe payments in some of the preceding illustrations might not be agreeable to each of the partners concerned. For example, in illustration 4-3, A might feel that B was being treated preferentially if, in phase (2) of the realization and liquidation, B received return in full of his $6,000 loan and also $500 return of his capital while A was receiving only $500 of his $3,000 loan. If A objected to this proposed liquidation installment, and if the liquidator or individual charged with administering the liquidation could not convince A that the proposed payments were the only ones which could be made properly at that time, the liquidator should refrain from making any payments until the assets are fully realized. Since the liquidator may be held liable for any improper installment payments, he should not make any payments prior to full realization of assets if the partners cannot agree to his plan of payment.

Advance Planning for Cash Distributions. When a partnership's assets are realized on a piecemeal basis over a period of time, it may be desirable to determine in advance the order or priority in which any cash realized from the sale of assets will be applied in settlement of the existing claims. To develop an advance plan of cash distribution the liquidator must consider the extent of loss which would be necessary to eliminate each partner's equity. After determining the loss required to eliminate each partner from any cash distribution, the liquidator may plan his cash distribution.

For example, assume the partnership ABC has $94,000 of assets prior to realization, $40,000 in liabilities, and total equities for A, B, and C of $15,000, $21,000, and $18,000, respectively. Since A, B, and C share profits in a 30 : 30 : 40 relationship, the loss which would extinguish each partner's equity may be determined by dividing his profit and loss percentage into his equity.

A—$15,000 ÷ 30% = $50,000 loss required to extinguish A's equity.

B—$21,000 ÷ 30% = $70,000 loss required to extinguish B's equity.

C—$18,000 ÷ 40% = $45,000 loss required to extinguish C's equity.

Since C's equity would be eliminated by the smallest loss, if realization of the assets brought $49,000 cash causing a $45,000 loss, C would receive no payments on his equity. (See liquidation statement on page 715.)

From this illustration it should be noted:

(1) The general rule of priority of partners' loans in liquidation is of little consequence when installment liquidation is to be followed. In liquidation by installments, partner equity (loans, drawings, and capital) is of prime importance.

(2) The order of cash distribution is the reverse of the order of losses necessary to extinguish each partner's equity in the partnership. Before the plan can be prepared the liquidator must determine for each partnership interest, in turn, the loss necessary to extinguish such interest. This determination proceeds until all partner interests have been eliminated.

(3) By working back through the illustration, the liquidator could prepare a plan to guide his liquidation similar to the one on page 716.

ABC PARTNERSHIP
STATEMENT OF LIQUIDATION (PARTIAL)

	Cash	Other Assets	Liabilities	Loans		Capitals		
				A	B	A 30%	B 30%	C 40%
Profit and loss ratio						30%	30%	40%
Balances	$4,000	$90,000	$40,000	$3,000	$6,000	$12,000	$15,000	$18,000
Loss, as above		(45,000)				(13,500)	(13,500)	(18,000)
Balances	$4,000	$45,000	$40,000	$3,000	$6,000	$(1,500)	$ 1,500	–0–

The liquidator must now determine how much additional loss would be needed to extinguish the equities of A and B of ($1,500 and $7,500 respectively). Since they share profits in a 30 : 30 relationship or 50% each, an additional loss of $3,000 would eliminate A. The above partial Statement of Liquidation would be continued as follows:

	Cash	Other Assets	Liabilities	Loans		Capitals		
				A	B	A 30%	B 30%	C 40%
Balances, as above	$4,000	$45,000	$40,000	$3,000	$6,000	$(1,500)	$ 1,500	–0–
Loss, as above to be shared by A and B only		(3,000)				(1,500)	(1,500)	
Balances	$4,000	$42,000	$40,000	$3,000	$6,000	$(3,000)	...	...
Offset A's debit balance against loan				(3,000)		$ 3,000		
Balances	$4,000	$42,000	$40,000	–0–	$6,000	–0–	–0–	–0–

ABC PARTNERSHIP IN LIQUIDATION
PLAN FOR DISTRIBUTION OF CASH

	Total Assets	Liabilities	Partners' Equities		
			A	B	C
Balances prior to realization	$94,000	$40,000	$15,000	$21,000	$18,000
Order of distribution of cash:					
First $40,000	$40,000	$40,000			
Next $6,000	6,000			$ 6,000	
Next $3,000	3,000		$ 1,500	1,500	
Next $45,000, in profit and loss ratio*	45,000		13,500	13,500	$18,000
Total	$94,000	$40,000	$15,000	$21,000	$18,000

* Any additional cash realized in liquidation would be distributed in the profit and loss ratio.

PROBLEMS

Problem 23–1. Green, Brown, and White are partners with capital balances of $12,000, $9,000, and $7,000, respectively. On November 10, 1967, the partners agree to liquidate their business. At this date they have assets of $47,000 and liabilities of $22,000, including an amount due to Brown of $2,000. On November 10 they accept an offer of $35,000 for the assets of their business, the partners agreeing to settle all partnership obligations.

Required:
Prepare a liquidation statement for the partnership showing how the cash arising from the sale of assets is to be distributed.

Problem 23–2. Burnside and Brewer decided to liquidate their partnership business on August 1, 1967. The partners had been sharing profits and losses in a 60 : 40 ratio. The following balance sheet was prepared on the day liquidation began.

BURNSIDE AND BREWER
BALANCE SHEET, AUGUST 1, 1967

Cash	$ 6,000	Accounts payable	$14,000
Receivables	25,000	Burnside, Loan	8,000
Inventory	30,000	Burnside, Capital (60%)	34,000
Other assets (net)	28,000	Brewer, Drawing	3,000
		Brewer, Capital (40%)	30,000
	$89,000		$89,000

During August one-half the receivables were collected at a loss of $1,000; $20,000 of inventory was sold at an average of 75% of book value; all the "other assets" were sold for $20,000.

Required:
Prepare a liquidation statement and accompanying schedule to show how the cash on hand would be distributed on August 31, 1967.

Problem 23–3. Adams, Denny, and Paul operated a partnership, sharing profits in a 5 : 3 : 2 ratio. On October 31, 1967, the balance sheet of their partnership showed the following:

ADAMS, DENNY, & PAUL PARTNERSHIP

BALANCE SHEET 10/31/67)

Cash	$ 5,000	Liabilities	$ 45,000
Other Assets	145,000	Due to Adams	10,000
		Adams, Capital	35,000
		Denny, Capital	30,000
		Paul, Capital	30,000
	$150,000		$150,000

The partnership agreement also provided for a $1,000 per month salary payable to Denny and chargeable to operations as an expense. Salaries have not been paid or accrued since December 31, 1966. On October 31, 1967, the partners realize that their assets are overvalued. Because of pressing demands from creditors, they accept an offer of $79,000 for the "Other Assets" shown above.

Required:
(1) Prepare a statement of partnership liquidation which will reflect the above facts and show how the cash resulting would be distributed.

(2) How would the cash resulting from the sale have been distributed if the proceeds of the sale had been only $49,000, and if Adams were personally insolvent? Prepare a statement to support your conclusion.

Problem 23–4. Keenan, Opal, and Peters, each of whom had personal assets well in excess of their personal debts, decided to liquidate their partnership on August 31, 1967. On that date the equities of each partner were as follows:

Loan from Keenan	$15,000	
Loan from Peters	5,000	
Keenan, Capital	35,000	
Keenan, Drawing	5,000	Cr.
Opal, Capital	30,000	
Opal, Drawing	5,000	Dr.
Peters, Capital	15,000	

The partners shared profits equally. Liabilities of the partnership at August 31, 1967, exclusive of the partners' claims, were equal to 50% of the book value of the assets. Opal insisted, and the other partners agreed, that upon sale the assets of the partnership had to realize an amount sufficient to provide him with $5,000 cash. A buyer was found who agreed to buy the assets at a price just sufficient to meet Opal's demands.

Required:

Prepare a statement of partnership liquidation with supporting calculations where necessary. Show how cash from the sale of the assets would be distributed.

Problem 23–5. The partners of Sims and Company agreed to dissolve their partnership and to begin liquidation on February 1, 1967. Rowe was designated as the partner in charge of liquidation. It was agreed that distributions of cash to the partners were to be made on the last day of each month during liquidation, provided that there was sufficient cash available.

The partnership agreement provided that profits and losses were to be shared on the following basis: Quinn 20%, Rowe 30%, Sims 30%, and Toth 20%. The firm's condensed balance sheet on February 1, 1967 was as follows:

Cash	$33,440	Accounts payable	$ 7,120
Goodwill	20,000	Loan from Quinn	5,000
Other assets	44,510	Capital:	
		Quinn	8,040
		Rowe	32,160
		Sims	36,340
		Toth	9,290
	$97,950		$97,950

The liquidating transactions for February and March, other than cash distributions to partners, are summarized by months below:

	Cash	
	February	March
Realization of assets with a book value of:		
$22,020	$16,440	
$14,950		$16,110
Paid liquidation expenses as incurred	2,740	2,460
Paid to Creditors on account	5,910	1,210

Required:

Prepare a schedule showing the total amounts of cash distributed to the partners at the end of February and March, and the amounts received by each partner in each distribution. Assume that Rowe made the distributions in such a manner that eventual overpayment to any partner was precluded.

(AICPA adapted)

Problem 23–6. Kolar, Leddy, and Martin are partners sharing profits in the ratio of 4, 3, and 2 respectively. The partnership and two of the partners are currently unable to pay their creditors. The firm balance sheet and personal status of the partners are as follows:

Kolar, Leddy, & Martin Partnership
BALANCE SHEET

Assets		Liabilities	
Cash	$ 500	Accounts and Bills Payable	$37,000
Other Assets	60,500	Capital: Kolar	10,000
		Leddy	6,000
		Martin	8,000
	$61,000		$61,000

Personal Status of Partners
(Excluding Partnership Interests)

Partner	Cash and cash value of personal assets	Liabilities
Kolar	$31,000	$20,000
Leddy	9,450	11,900
Martin	4,000	5,000

Required:

(1) Prepare a worksheet showing distribution to partnership and personal creditors in the event of dissolution under the provisions of the Uniform Partnership Act, assuming that the "Other Assets" are sold for $33,500.

(2) Prepare a computation showing the minimum amount which must be realized from the sale of the partnership assets other than cash, so that the personal creditors of Leddy would receive full settlement of their claims.

(AICPA adapted)

Problem 23–7. The balance sheet of the Button, Conroy, and Tolle partnership just prior to the sale of the partnership assets is:

Button, Conroy & Tolle
BALANCE SHEET as of July 15, 1967

Cash	$ 20,000	Payables	$ 75,000
Receivables	40,000	Conroy, Loan	15,000
Inventory	60,000	Button, Capital	49,000
Fixed assets (net)	60,000	Conroy, Capital	25,000
		Tolle, Capital	16,000
	$180,000		$180,000

Button, Conroy, and Tolle share profits and losses in a 4 : 3 : 3 ratio, respectively. Sale of the noncash assets realizes a total of $60,000. The personal financial position of each partner, in addition to their partnership status, is shown below:

	Assets	Liabilities
Button	$90,000	$100,000
Conroy	70,000	30,000
Tolle	30,000	36,000

Required:

(1) Prepare a statement of partnership liquidation to show how the cash realized from the sale of the assets will be distributed, assuming (*a*) that the Uniform Partnership Act is applicable, *and* (*b*) assuming that common law is applicable.

(2) Prepare journal entries to record the above facts under assumption (*a*) in (1) above.

Problem 23–8. Sawtell, Mortensen, and Halasz have decided to dissolve their partnership. On March 1, 1967, the partners had the following equities and profit and loss sharing ratios:

Partner	Loan Acct.	Capital Acct.	P & L
Sawtell	$20,000	$42,000	40%
Mortensen	—	26,000	30%
Halasz	10,000	31,000	30%
	$30,000	$99,000	

On March 1, 1967, all liabilities except $11,000 had been paid and cash on hand amounted to $5,000. During March, assets with a book value of $65,000 were sold for $50,000; during April, additional assets with a book value of $40,000 were sold for $28,000; during May, the remaining assets were sold for $10,000. Expenses of realization were $4,000, $3,000, and $2,000 in March, April, and May, respectively. All liabilities were paid at March 31, and cash realized was distributed to partners at the end of each month. The partners had no personal assets.

Required:

(1) Prepare a liquidation statement, with supporting schedule, to show how the cash available should be paid out on March 31, April 30, and May 31.

(2) Prepare journal entries to record the events of the three months.

Problem 23– 9. The partners of the Three-Ten Company agree to dissolve their partnership and to begin the realization of assets on August 1, 1967. The partners agreed to distribute to themselves at the end of each month all cash resulting from realization of assets except any cash needed to liquidate unpaid liabilities, plus $5,000 to be reserved for the following month's expenses. Upon completion of the realization of the assets, all existing cash was distributed.

The partners had been in business for many years and had been sharing profits and losses as follows: Brown, 40%; Herman, 40%; Schwartz, 20%. A balance sheet prepared on August 1, 1967, disclosed the following financial condition:

THREE-TEN COMPANY

BALANCE SHEET, AUGUST 1, 1967

Cash	$ 6,000	Payables	$ 20,000
Other Assets	106,000	Brown, Loan	5,000
Herman, Drawing	6,000	Herman, Loan	10,000
Schwartz, Drawing	2,000	Brown, Capital	23,000
		Herman, Capital	40,000
		Schwartz, Capital	22,000
	$120,000		$120,000

The following table summarizes the results of realization over a three-month period:

	Assets Realized	Cash Received	Liabilities Paid
August	$30,000	$20,000	$12,000
September	30,000	18,000	8,000
October	46,000	22,000	

Required:

Prepare a statement of partnership liquidation and a supporting schedule to show how the cash available at the end of the three months was distributed.

Problem 23-10. On September 1, 1967, Berns, a partner in the firm of Berns, Giller, and Ulrich, discovers that the books of the partnership do not reflect an accurate state of partnership affairs. Ulrich has been in charge of the partnership records, and Berns' discovery reveals that certain personal transactions of Ulrich have been merged with the partnership affairs, while other partnership transactions have not been recorded properly. The three men began business by contributing equal capitals of $30,000, and they share profits and losses equally. A balance sheet prepared on September 1, 1967, before reflecting any of the findings of Berns, follows:

BERNS, GILLER, & ULRICH

BALANCE SHEET, SEPTEMBER 1, 1967

Cash	$ 6,000	Accounts payable	$ 55,000
Receivables	30,000	Berns, Loan	15,000
Inventory	50,000	Berns, Capital	23,000
Other assets	70,000	Giller, Capital	25,000
		Ulrich, Capital	38,000
	$156,000		$156,000

After a thorough examination of the records of the partnership, the following discrepancies are determined to exist:

1. Over a period of years Ulrich made purchases of items for his personal use through the partnership, totaling $12,000, and he charged "Purchases" for these items.
2. Ulrich has "borrowed" funds from the partnership totaling $15,000 over several years. Of this amount, $6,000 is presently included in the balance of "Receivables" above, while the other $9,000 has been charged off as a loss in previous years.
3. Giller had loaned $5,000 to the partnership, but Ulrich had taken the amount for his personal use and had not recorded the loan. This amount was unpaid at September 1, 1967.
4. Purchases of merchandise made in late August, 1967, totaling $4,500 had not been recorded prior to closing the books at the end of August, although the merchandise was on hand and included in the inventory September 1, 1967.

Berns and Giller agree to continue in business after acquiring the interest of Ulrich. The partners agree that, in addition to the corrections required from the above facts, the proper values for the other assets and inventories are $60,000 and $45,000 respectively. Ulrich is to bear no penalty for his actions.

Required:
(1) How much will Ulrich receive for his partnership interest?
(2) Prepare entries to reflect the above facts, including an entry to set up as a liability the amount due to Ulrich for liquidation of his partnership interest.
(3) What is the corrected balance of Berns' capital? Of Giller's capital?

Problem 23–11. *Part A.* The partnership of Adams, Baker, and Crane has called you to assist them in winding up the affairs of their partnership. You are able to gather the following information:

(1) The trial balance of the partnership at June 30, 1967 is as follows:

	Debit	Credit
Cash	$ 6,000	
Accounts receivable	22,000	
Inventory	14,000	
Plant and equipment (net)	99,000	
Adams, loan	12,000	
Crane, loan	7,500	
Accounts payable		$ 17,000
Adams, capital		67,000
Baker, capital		45,000
Crane, capital		31,500
	$160,500	$160,500

(2) The partners share profits and losses as follows: Adams, 50%; Baker, 30%; Crane, 20%.

(3) The partners are considering an offer of $100,000 for the accounts receivable, inventory, and plant and equipment as of June 30. The $100,000 would be paid to the partners in installments, the number and amounts of which are to be negotiated.

Required:
Prepare a cash distribution schedule as of June 30, 1967, showing how the $100,000 would be distributed as it becomes available.

Part B. Assume the same facts as in Part A except that the partners have decided to liquidate their partnership instead of accepting the offer of $100,000. Cash is to be distributed to the partners at the end of each month.

A summary of the liquidation transactions follows:
July
$16,500—collected on accounts receivable, balance is uncollectible.
  10,000—received for the entire inventory.
   1,000—liquidation expenses.
   8,000—cash retained in the business at end of the month.
August
$ 1,500—liquidation expenses paid.
           As part payment of his capital, Crane accepted a piece of special equipment that he developed which had a book value of $4,000.

The partners agreed that a value of $10,000 should be placed
on the machine for liquidation purposes.

2,500—cash retained in the business at end of the month.

September

$75,000—received on sale of remaining plant and equipment.

1,000—liquidation expenses paid.

No cash retained in the business.

Required:

Prepare a schedule of cash payments as of September 30, 1967 showing how
the cash was actually distributed.   (AICPA adapted)

Problem 23–12. You are engaged to assist in terminating the affairs of T and
A Discount Sales, a partnership under liquidation. Allen owns Toy Wholesalers
and contributed $10,000 in inventory for a 50% interest in T and A Discount
Sales on January 2, 1967. Ball owns Appliance Wholesalers and contributed
$2,000 cash and $8,000 in inventory for a 50% interest on the same date. All
profits and losses are to be shared equally.

T and A Discount Sales was an unsuccessful operation so it was decided to
dissolve the partnership after the Christmas shopping season.

In the course of your examination you determine the following facts:

(1) An incompetent part-time bookkeeper had discarded all cash register
tapes and invoices for expenses and purchases. He was also the bookkeeper
for Appliance Wholesalers.

(2) The partners state that the only existing payables are to themselves, as
follows:

Toy Wholesalers	$ 9,740
Appliance Wholesalers	5,260
	$15,000

(3) You are able to prepare the following summary of cash transactions from
bank statements and cancelled checks:

Opening cash balance		$ 2,000
Receipts:		
Sales	$70,000	
Inventory liquidation	7,000	77,000
		79,000
Disbursements:		
Purchases	36,000	
Operating expenses	26,000	
Leasehold improvements (5-year lease)	6,000	
Liquidating expense	4,000	72,000
Balance, December 31, 1967		$ 7,000

(4) On December 31, 1967 $7,000 was paid to the partners, $3,500 to each,
to apply on the $15,000 liability.

(5) The partners state that the dollar amounts of regular sales of toys and
appliances were approximately equal and that the dollar amounts of liquidating
sales of toys and appliances were also approximately equal. There was a
uniform mark-up of 40% of cost on toys and 25% of cost on appliances. All

LIQUIDATION OF THE BUSINESS ORGANIZATION

sales were for cash. The ending inventory of shopworn merchandise was liquidated on December 31, 1967 for 50% of the retail sales price.

(6) The partners believe that some appliances may have been returned to Appliance Wholesalers but the bookkeeper failed to record the returns on the books of either organization.

Required:

(1) Compute the unrecorded amount of appliances returned to Appliance Wholesalers, if any.

(2) Prepare an income statement for T and A Discount Sales for the period January 2 to December 31, 1967.

(3) Prepare a statement of partners' capital accounts.   (AICPA adapted)

Problem 23–13. The XYZ Partnership is being dissolved. All liabilities have been liquidated. The balance of assets on hand is being realized gradually. Shown below are details of partners' accounts:

	Capital Account (Original Investment)	Current Account (Undistributed Earnings Net of Drawings)	Profit and Loss Ratio
X	$20,000	$1,500 Cr.	4
Y	25,000	2,000 Dr.	4
Z	10,000	1,000 Cr.	2

Additional information:

X loaned $15,000 to the partnership and Z loaned $5,000. Y made no loan to the partnership.

Required:

Prepare a schedule showing how cash payments should be made to the partners as assets are realized.   (AICPA adapted)

Problem 23–14. Bowers, Levan, and Miller have agreed to dissolve their partnership as of November 1, 1967. They plan to proceed with a gradual liquidation of the business in hopes of reducing the loss upon realization to a minimum. As cash from realization becomes available the partners plan to have partial distributions in settlement of their interests. The following balance sheet was prepared on October 31, 1967:

BOWERS, LEVAN, & MILLER
BALANCE SHEET, OCTOBER 31, 1967

Cash	$ 10,000	Current liabilities	$ 30,000
Other assets	170,000	Bowers, Loan	20,000
		Bowers, Capital	62,000
		Levan, Capital	24,000
		Miller, Capital	44,000
	$180,000		$180,000

The partners have been sharing profits and losses in the following manner: Bowers, 50%; Levan, 30%; Miller, 20%.

Required:

Prepare a cash distribution plan showing the proper distribution of cash as it becomes available.

CHAPTER 24

Corporate
liquidation

This chapter deals primarily with some of the accounting and reporting problems faced by a corporation which is in the process of liquidation. Certain related legal and tax considerations will be noted from time to time to indicate some of the complications involved in a corporate liquidation situation.

The preceding two chapters have dealt with the liquidation problems of proprietorships and partnerships. In those chapters some of the reasons for business liquidations were noted. Corporate liquidations arise for some of the same reasons, and, in addition, for reasons peculiar to the corporate form of organization. The following situations may precipitate corporate liquidation: bankruptcy, occasioned by sustained operating losses, overinvestment in fixed assets, excessive accumulation of inventories, excessive borrowing, as well as a variety of other reasons; theft, fraud, or improper managerial manipulations; losses from floods, fires, or other "acts of God"; excessive taxation or undue legal or administrative stringencies imposed by governmental rulings; and loss of sales potential because of success of competitors, development of new products, or changes in consumer demand.

Since a corporation is in reality a creature of the state, that is, it is organized and operated only under the jurisdiction of a state law, it follows that liquidation and dissolution of a corporation would proceed according to the provision of the statutes of the state of incorporation. While a corporation is legally terminated only when its franchise is extinguished and its charter is terminated, for all practical purposes the corporation is terminated when it goes out of business.

Reasons for Corporate Dissolution. Ballantine lists the following ways in which a corporation may be legally dissolved:[1]

(1) By an act of the legislature repealing or withdrawing its charter, provided the legislature, in granting the charter, has reserved the power to repeal the same, but not otherwise.
(2) By the expiration of a time limited in its charter for the continuance of its corporate existence.
(3) By the happening of some contingency prescribed in its charter or by statute.
(4) By a surrender of its charter, provided the surrender is authorized or accepted by the state.
(5) By the forfeiture of its charter in a judicial proceeding by the state.
(6) By decree of court of equity in some states.

Corporate Liquidation vs. Dissolution. As in the two preceding chapters, the primary emphasis in this chapter will be on liquidation of the business entity rather than on its dissolution. While neither bankruptcy nor receivership in equity necessarily results in legal dissolution, each of these will frequently result in corporate liquidation. A corporation may be liquidated, that is, its assets may be sold and its liabilities liquidated, without necessarily being dissolved in a legal sense. From an accounting point of view corporate liquidation is more significant than dissolution.

The distinction between liquidation and dissolution is particularly important as far as corporations are concerned, because the period of liquidation may extend well beyond the legal date of corporate dissolution. The statutes of most states permit a corporation to continue in existence for an interval (frequently three years) after filing notice of dissolution with the state. During this period of existence certain officials are empowered to collect the corporate assets, pay its liabilities, and distribute remaining assets to the stockholders. In addition, lawsuits may be brought, continued, or defended, and any other actions undertaken which are necessary to wind up the corporate affairs.

Tax Considerations

In addition to meeting the various legal requirements of a corporate dissolution, the officers of a corporation which faces liquidation should plan their actions carefully so that the stockholders will suffer minimum tax disadvantages. The basic problem for officials of a corporation which is considering liquidation is to plan their actions leading up to liquidation, and generally legal dissolution, in such a manner that distributions to

---

[1] Ballantine's, *Manual on Corporation Law and Practice*, 1930, Callaghan & Co., p. 775.

stockholders are considered to be distributions in carrying out a "plan of liquidation" and are not considered to be distributions in the nature of dividends. Collateral problems exist in distinguishing between certain types of statutory reorganizations, stock redemption plans, and corporate liquidation plans. While no attempt is made to delve into the various facets of these problems, certain tax aspects of corporate liquidations are considered briefly.

As a general rule taxing authorities appear to take the position that the question of whether a corporation is or is not liquidating is one of intention or fact. In any questionable liquidation situation they seem to attempt to determine the intent of the corporate officials and use this intent as the basis for deciding what, in fact, has been done. An attempt is generally made to determine whether the over-all plan of liquidation is a device to deprive the taxing authority of tax revenue to which it is entitled.

Types of Corporate Liquidations. A corporate liquidation may be consummated completely in a single-step transaction with the proceeds being distributed to the stockholders, or the liquidation may proceed piecemeal with distributions being made periodically to stockholders. The latter alternative creates the greater number of problems from a tax viewpoint. When corporate liquidation is contemplated, one of the main points to be determined taxwise is whether the distribution is a liquidation distribution, wherein the stockholder-taxpayer does not include any amounts received as income until the basis of his holdings are recovered, or whether the distribution is essentially equivalent to a taxable dividend, wherein the stockholder-taxpayer includes the distribution as ordinary income from dividends. To be treated as a liquidation distribution, the amount paid out by a corporation must either be in full settlement of *all* outstanding stock or be in accordance with a plan of gradual liquidation which is directed toward eventual complete liquidation of the corporation. The existence of either of these alternatives is a matter of fact to be determined by review of the intent underlying the distributions made.

Corporate Liquidation by Trustee. Corporate liquidations, particularly when a large corporation is involved, frequently require a considerable period of time. In addition, it may be desirable for the liquidation to be carried out by trustees specifically appointed for the purpose. The trustee (or trustees) takes control of the assets and acts in the place of the regular corporate officials. The trustee(s) acts in a fiduciary capacity, being compensated for his services normally through a fee arrangement. When liquidation proceeds under the direction of a trustee, the corporation is faced with several alternative tax possibilities. For instance, its operations during the liquidation period may be taxed on a regular corporate basis, on a trust association basis, or on a strict trust arrangement basis. The detailed form of the trustee's organization, duties, and responsibilities would establish the factual situation which would be the basis for the determination of the tax method applicable.

Statement of Affairs

As previously indicated several of the reasons for corporate liquidation involve insolvency and bankruptcy. The normal procedure of liquidation under the Bankruptcy Act was presented in some detail in Chapter 22. The general bankruptcy procedure (filing of petitions by the organization or its creditors, adjudication as a bankrupt by a court of law, selection of trustees, and the realization and liquidation proceedings) is basically the same for corporations as for other bankrupts.

Significance of Current Values. When a corporation is insolvent or faces bankruptcy, a statement of financial position prepared in accordance with generally accepted principles of accounting may not present a fair representation of the financial position of the company. The primary reason for the shortcomings of regular statements of financial position under conditions of imminent liquidation lies in the fact that the statement is normally presented from a "going-concern" point of view. The assets are reported on the basis of acquisition cost, less applicable amortization, to the corporation. Little attempt is made to report the current value of the various assets, since the current value of assets committed to use by a corporation is of secondary importance. The current value of an asset assumes primary importance when the corporate officials contemplate that the asset will be severed from corporate use through sale, trade, or abandonment.

A corporation facing liquidation is more interested in the current value of its various assets than in their book value on a going-concern basis. A statement of affairs is one form of statement presenting the financial position of a corporation contemplating liquidation. While the statement is of British origin and usage and has relatively little practical use, it does provide a means by which useful financial information may be presented when conditions render some generally accepted accounting practices inapplicable.

Nature of the Statement of Affairs. On a statement of affairs the various assets of the corporation are reported at their estimated realizable values, in addition to the going-concern values (amortized costs). Furthermore, on a statement of affairs corporate liabilities are classified differently from the normal categories used on a statement of financial position.

An individual interested in the financial position of a corporation anticipating liquidation is interested in the manner of liquidation of the various equity claims and the availability of assets for satisfaction of the claims. As a consequence, on the statement of affairs liabilities are classified by their position of priority in liquidation, that is, by the degree to which specific assets are pledged to the given liability. Assets are classified so as to report clearly those assets pledged to specific creditors and those available to meet unsecured corporate obligations.

ILLUSTRATION. In the following illustration a going-concern statement of financial position is presented, along with supplementary information which indicates that the corporation is insolvent. The statement of affairs on page 730 is based on this statement and the supplementary information. While the statement of affairs may take various forms, the particular headings and the organization used are representative.

ABC CORPORATION

STATEMENT OF FINANCIAL POSITION

AS OF OCTOBER 31, 1967

Assets			Equities			
Current assets:			Current liabilities:			
Cash	$ 1,000		Accounts payable			$ 36,000
Accounts receivable	16,000		Notes payable			10,000
Inventory	24,000		Accrued wages			800
Prepayments	1,200		Accrued interest			450
Total current assets		$ 42,200	Total current liabilities			$ 47,250
Investment in stock of X Co.		12,000	5% Bonds payable			36,000
Property, plant, & equipment		56,000	Common stock	$35,000		
Goodwill		10,000	Retained earnings	1,950		36,950
		$120,200				$120,200

On October 31, 1967, the corporation contemplates liquidation because of a deteriorating sales market, poor current financial position, and recent operational losses. At this date the following data must also be considered to view properly the financial position of the company from a possible liquidation point of view:

(1) The notes payable are due to the First National Bank and are secured by the X Co. stock as collateral. Market value of the X Co. stock at October 31, 1967, is $8,000.

ABC Corporation
STATEMENT OF AFFAIRS
As of October 31, 1967

Book Value	Assets	Estimated value	Available to Unsecured Creditors
	Assets pledged with fully secured creditors:		
56,000	Property, plant, and equipment:		
	Estimated value	$40,000	
	Less: 5% bonds payable, $36,000		
	Accrued interest 450	36,450	$ 3,550
	Assets pledged with partially secured creditors:		
12,000	Stock of X Co., deducted contra, estimated value		$ 8,000
	Free assets:		
1,000	Cash		1,000
16,000	Accounts receivable		12,500
24,000	Inventory		18,000
1,200	Prepayments		400
10,000	Goodwill		
	Total free assets		$35,450
	Less: Liabilities having priority		800
	Net free assets		$34,650
	Deficiency to unsecured creditors		3,350
$120,200			$38,000

Book Value	Liabilities and Shareholders' Equity	Unsecured Creditors
	Liabilities having priority:	
$ 800	Accrued wages: Deducted from free assets	
	Fully secured liabilities:	
36,000	5% Bonds payable, deducted contra	
450	Accrued interest, deducted contra	
	Partially secured liabilities:	
10,000	Notes payable to bank $10,000	
	Less: Stock of X Co. 8,000	$ 2,000
	Unsecured liabilities:	
36,000	Accounts payable	36,000
	Shareholders' equity per books:	
35,000	Common stock	
1,950	Retained earnings	
$120,200		$38,000

(2) The bonds payable are secured by the property, plant, and equipment, which are estimated to be worth $40,000 at October 31, 1967.

(3) The receivables contain $1,500 of uncollectible accounts and $4,000 of accounts from which 50% collectibility is expected. All other accounts are considered wholly collectible.

(4) The inventory is not pledged and is estimated to be worth $18,000.

(5) The prepayments will yield about $400 cash upon sale or rebate.

In the statement of affairs on page 730 the "Book Value" columns report the balances as reflected on the statement of financial position. The column headed "Available to Unsecured Creditors" reflects the amounts which corporate officials expect to realize from the various assets and which will be available to satisfy unsecured claims.

As mentioned previously the statement of affairs is organized differently from a statement of financial position. Some of the areas of difference are discussed on the following pages.

Assets Pledged: Fully Secured Creditors. When the realizable value of an asset pledged as security for a debt equals or exceeds the amount of the debt, the debt is considered to be fully secured. In liquidation, one of two alternatives may arise. The creditor may sell the pledged assets, deduct the amount of his claim, and remit the excess to the receiver or trustee responsible for the liquidation. Or, the corporate officials may arrange for the sale of the assets, using the proceeds to liquidate the secured debt, with any remainder flowing into the corporate treasury.

In the illustration, the property, plant, and equipment are reported under the caption "Assets pledged with fully secured creditors" since the value of the assets exceeds the 5% bonds payable plus the accrued bond interest. The bond liability and the accrued interest are deducted directly from the estimated value of the property to arrive at the net amount which the asset will realize for the corporate treasury. On the right-hand side of the statement the bonds and accrued interest are reported, but no amount is extended to the "Unsecured Creditors" column, since the liability will be settled in full by realization of the property. The term "deducted contra" indicates that the amount which would normally appear opposite the bonds and interest liability has been deducted from an asset on the other side (contra) of the statement.

Assets Pledged: Partially Secured Creditors. When the realizable value of an asset pledged as security for a debt is less than the amount of the debt, the debt is considered to be partially secured. The asset pledged as security will not, upon realization, fully satisfy the creditor claims. No excess exists to be used to settle unsecured claims. A portion of the debt itself is in reality unsecured, and this portion is extended to the "Unsecured

Creditors" column to share proportionately in the free assets along with the other unsecured creditors.

In the illustration, the stock of X Co. is reported under the caption "Assets pledged with partially secured creditors," but no amount is extended to the "Available to Unsecured Creditors" column. The realizable value ($8,000) is deducted on the right-hand side of the statement from the liability for which it has been pledged. Since the liability exceeds the realizable value of the asset pledged, the liability excess is extended to the "Unsecured Creditors" column to be included among the total of the unsecured claims.

Free Assets. Assets not specifically pledged to secure liabilities are classified as free assets. The expected realizable values are extended to the "Available to Unsecured Creditors" column, the total of which is available to satisfy certain unsecured claims which have a "priority" status, as well as unsecured claims in general.

Liabilities Having Priority. Under bankruptcy law, certain liabilities have a preferential or prior claim upon liquidation. The priority order, in general, under bankruptcy law is somewhat as follows:

(1) Liabilities incurred by receivers or trustees in preserving and administering the assets of the business.
(2) Amounts due wage earners for services rendered, not to exceed $600 per employee and provided that the wages have been earned within the last three months.
(3) Amounts claimed by creditors for reimbursement of funds expended to defeat alternative, and thus presumably less reasonable, settlement plans.
(4) Taxes.
(5) Amounts owing for rent or to governmental units which have been granted priority under state or federal statute.

Since any liabilities falling within the above categories must be settled in full before any payments may be made on unsecured claims, amounts of liabilities having priority are deducted directly from the total free assets. The remainder of the free assets is available to meet unsecured claims. While liabilities having priority are not secured technically, as long as total free assets exceed the priority claims, no amount of the preferred claims will be extended to the Unsecured Creditors column.

Unsecured Liabilities. Liabilities not secured and having no priority are classified as unsecured liabilities. The amounts of these claims are extended to the Unsecured Creditors column of the statement.

Shareholders' Equity per Books. The items in this section are included in the report primarily for completeness, that is, to make the book value columns on each side of the statement balance. Conceptually, however, it indicates the degree to which the stockholders share in the realization proceeds.

Deficiency to Unsecured Creditors. This amount is normally the balancing figure on the statement of affairs. A deficiency exists when the unsecured creditors column exceeds the net free assets. If the net free assets exceed the unsecured claims, no deficiency to unsecured creditors exists and assets will be available for stockholder claims.

The deficiency to unsecured creditors may be further analyzed in terms of its causes. At times this analysis, frequently in the form of an account, accompanies the statement of affairs. In the illustration, the estimated deficiency may be analyzed as follows:

ABC CORPORATION

DEFICIENCY ACCOUNT

OCTOBER 31, 1967

Estimated loss on:		Equity interests bearing loss:	
Accounts receivable	$ 3,500	Common stock	$35,000
Inventory	6,000	Retained earnings	1,950
Prepayments	800	Unsecured creditors	
Stock of X Co.	4,000	(deficiency)	3,350
Property, plant, and			
equipment	16,000		
Goodwill	10,000		
	$40,300		$40,300

The left side of the account details the losses estimated on realization of the various assets. On the right side the equity interests which will bear the estimated loss are listed in the order in which they will bear the loss. If gains arise on the realization of particular assets, the gains would appear on the right side of the account, separately reported.

General Comments on the Statement of Affairs

At times, more than one asset may be pledged as security for a given liability. When this situation exists the assets so pledged would be reported under the appropriate heading (Assets pledged with fully secured creditors, for example), and the liability deducted from the total estimated realizable value. Likewise, more than one liability may be secured by a specific asset. An example of this situation appears in the "Assets pledged with fully secured creditors" section of the illustration, where both the 5% bonds payable and the accrued interest on the bonds are deducted from the property.

A company may pledge only a part of an asset as security for a given liability. For example, a portion of the X Co. stock may have been pledged as collateral for the note payable to the bank. If this had been done, the portion of the asset pledged would have been reported as an "Asset pledged with partially (or fully) secured creditors," and the portion not so pledged would have been reported as a "free asset." As a result, a given asset or liability may appear in more than one section of a statement of affairs.

A more difficult problem arises in the reporting of assets which will require an additional expenditure prior to their realization. This condition frequently exists when determining a realizable value for a goods in process inventory. Assume the following data:

	Book Value	Realizable Value
Goods in process	$12,000	$15,000
Raw materials	20,000	15,000

For the goods in process to realize $15,000, however, the following additional costs must be incurred:

Additional raw material, cost	
(at realizable value, $1,500)	$2,000
Additional labor cost	2,500
Additional other costs	500

Assuming neither the goods in process nor the raw materials are pledged, the above information could be reported in the following manner in a statement of affairs:

				Available to Unsecured Creditors
	Free assets:			
12,000	Goods in process:			
	Estimated realization upon completion		15,000	
	Less: Costs of completion:			
	Raw materials			
	(75% of cost)	1,500		
	Labor	2,500		
	Other costs	500	4,500	10,500
20,000	Raw materials:			
	Used in completing goods in process (cost of $2,000)			1,500
	Available for sale (cost of $18,000)			13,500

This procedure reveals the proceeds upon realization of both goods in process and the raw materials. In addition, the wages and other costs necessary to complete the goods in process are deducted directly from the estimated proceeds of the sale of this asset. It is unnecessary to deduct these wages and other costs from the free assets on the statement because they have been deducted from goods in process and will be paid in cash or other assets which are included in the statement.

In the illustration no valuation accounts were included. If valuation accounts for uncollectible accounts or estimated depreciation exist, they may be treated in one of two ways in a statement of affairs. The "reserve" may be deducted from the applicable asset balance and only the net book value reported on the statement or both the asset balance and the "reserve" balance may be reported on the statement. In either case, the realizable value would be unaffected.

Summary

In summary, it should be noted that a statement of affairs may be used as the basis for a credit application, as well as in actual liquidation situations. In addition, the statement may be used for proprietorships or partnerships as well as for corporations. The important concept involved in the preparation of the statement is that asset values used are not necessarily those existing under the generally accepted going-concern concept of accounting for unexpired costs. Rather the assets are valued at the amounts expected to be realized if liquidation takes place within a reasonable period of time.

RECEIVERSHIP IN EQUITY

The statement of affairs, as discussed in the preceding section, is prepared either in contemplation of liquidation or to provide additional data for judgment decisions on an enterprise in financial difficulty. After considering the data in a statement of affairs, or similar data, and after giving consideration to a variety of other forces bearing on the continuation or liquidation of the enterprise, a decision may be made either voluntarily or involuntarily to liquidate the enterprise. This section deals with some of the accounting problems arising if the enterprise is to be liquidated.

While some corporate liquidations are accomplished by the same corporate officials who formerly managed the organization, corporate liquidations are frequently accomplished under the supervision of a third party, often a receiver in equity. Liquidation under the direction of a receiver in equity arises through a court order and may come about from a variety of reasons. Likewise, a receiver is sometimes appointed by the courts to take charge of the operations of a going concern. In either instance it is usually advisable for the receiver to establish a new set of accounting records in order to record his activities in directing the corporate affairs. The following sections deal with the accounting procedures which a receiver should follow, with emphasis primarily directed at the liquidation proceedings.

As is the case when any person is charged with responsibility for property, a receiver should maintain records which will enable him to report clearly the results of his activities while he has control of the property. The records which a receiver should maintain are not substitutes for the regular corporate records, but are in addition to them. In general, a receiver should take up on his records the various assets over which he assumes control, as well as the related valuation reserves. The assets are recorded at the same values at which they appear on the corporate records. Normally, no existing liabilities are recorded by the receiver on his books. However, liabilities subsequently incurred by the receiver are entered on his books. Thus, a distinction is clearly drawn between debts existing prior to the receivership period and debts incurred by the receiver. The receiver also sets up an accountability account for the net assets taken over. The accountability account title frequently used includes the corporation name such as "ABC Corporation—in receivership."

On the corporate books the asset and valuation accounts turned over to the receiver are closed out, and a new receivable-type account opened for the net assets transferred such as "John Jones—receiver." No change is made in existing liability accounts.

Receivership Accounting

General Concepts. After the receiver assumes control of the corporate properties a dual accounting problem arises. Entries must be recorded on the receiver's books for any change in the assets over which he has assumed control and for any change in liabilities incurred by him. Likewise, entries must be made on the corporation's books for any change in the liability accounts existing prior to the receivership period. Some transactions, such as payments by the receiver of a prior liability, require entries in each set of records.

If the receiver is charged solely with winding up the affairs of the corporation, that is, if he is not authorized to continue the regular business activities of the corporation, the problem is relatively simple. Entries need to be made only to record cash received for assets realized, cash paid out for liabilities liquidated, and for any gains or losses on realization. Eventually all assets will be realized in cash, all liabilities will be liquidated, and appropriate cash distributions made to stockholders.

The receiver may also be charged with the responsibility of operating the corporation, pending either (1) eventual liquidation, with the continued operation primarily designed to preserve asset values, or (2) eventual improvement in financial condition, with the subsequent return of operating control to the corporate officials. Except for a difference in scale of operations and for the entries to record final liquidation under (1), the accounting problems under these two alternatives are similar.

Basic Procedures. (*1*) *Payment of liabilities existing at the date the receiver assumes control of the corporation.* As previously stated, the receiver does not record on his records any liabilities owing by the corporation at the date the receiver assumes responsibility. However, he may pay these liabilities, either in the normal course of operating the corporation or under court order to pay. The payment of liabilities of this nature reduces the assets for which the receiver is accountable, and also reduces the receiver's responsibility to the corporation. A receiver generally finds it preferable not to record changes in his accountability in "ABC Corporation—in receivership," the same account as was used to record his initial accountability. The use of a temporary accountability account facilitates the preparation of subsequent reports. For example, if a receiver pays $10,000 of accounts payable which the corporation had incurred prior to the assumption of control by the receiver, the following entry would be made on the receiver's books:

ABC Corporation—Accounts payable paid	$10,000	
Cash		$10,000

Simultaneously an entry is necessary on the corporation books to reflect the liability liquidation, as follows:

Accounts payable	$10,000	
John Jones—receiver		$10,000

It should be noted that the account credited on the corporation's books is the "receivable" account set up to record the receiver's initial accountability.

(*2*) *Incurrence and payment of liabilities incurred subsequent to the date of receivership.* No particular problems arise in this situation. If purchases are made or expenses incurred by the receiver, the appropriate purchase or expense account is charged and "accounts payable" credited on the receiver's books. No entry is necessary on the corporation's books. Like-wise, the receiver records payment of the liability in the usual manner, and no entry would be made on the corporation's books.

(*3*) *Increase in liability existing at the date receiver assumes control, and subsequent payment thereof.* Interest which accrues on a note or mortgage liability on the corporation's books should be recorded periodically. Since the liability is reflected on the corporation's books, the entry to record the accrual of interest should also be made on the corporation's books. No entry need be made on the receiver's books for the accrual. When the interest is paid, entries similar to those in (1) above would be made on both the corporation's books and the receiver's books.

(*4*) *Operating transactions.* If the corporation continues operations in a normal manner under the receivership, the receiver should record all operating transactions on his records. The account classification should follow closely that previously used by the corporation. No entries for the operating results need be recorded on the corporation's books. At the end of the accounting period the receiver closes his books and determines any profit or loss. The net profit or loss is also recorded on the corporation's books by adjusting the accountability account (receivable) with the receiver.

Receiver's Reports. Periodically the receiver may desire or be required to report on the results of corporate activities under his super-vision. Since it is generally desirable to report on total corporate activities, the receiver combines the data on his records and on the corporation records by means of a work sheet. The resulting information should afford reports, statement of financial position and income statement, which can be compared with prior corporation reports. A statement designed to report on what has been accomplished in the realization and liquidation of an insolvent business is illustrated later in this chapter.

Termination of Receivership. A receivership may be terminated when a corporation's assets have been realized. Termination may also arise when a corporation regains a solvent state while under the receiver's control. In either situation, the receiver closes his books by returning to the corporation the various assets for which he is accountable. Likewise, any unpaid liabilities incurred by the receiver are transferred to the corporation's books. The entries made on the receiver's books and on the corporation's books closely parallel the entries made to establish the receivership. The receiver's accountability account with the corporation and the corporation's receivable-type account with the receiver are closed. The corporation thereafter accounts for its transactions in the normal manner.

Realization and Liquidation Statement

As noted previously, corporate liquidations often require a considerable period of time to accomplish. Frequently it is desirable during the liquidation period to have prepared reports which indicate the progress of the liquidation. Periodic reports are particularly desirable when the corporation is continuing operations in a normal or semi-normal manner, even though on a reduced scale, during the period of liquidation. A statement of particular usefulness to report this type of information is the *realization and liquidation statement*, or, as it is commonly called because of its form of presentation, the *realization and liquidation account*.

This statement contains information concerning the events which have occurred during the liquidation operations. It is designed to indicate the initial accountability of the individual who assumed control over the assets and liabilities of the enterprise being liquidated, the effect of actions taken under his supervision in regard to these properties and liabilities, and the resultant accountability of this individual at the date the statement is prepared.

This statement, which may be prepared by a receiver, a trustee, or an individual responsible for the corporate activities during the realization of the assets and the liquidation of the liabilities, is organized in the manner shown on page 740.

Depending upon the results of operations during the period covered by the report, a net gain would appear as a balancing amount on the left side of the statement whereas a net loss would appear as a balance amount on the right side of the statement. The net gain or loss results from (1) the realization of assets at more or less than their book value, (2) the liquidation of liabilities for less (or more) than their book value, and (3) the excess of supplementary credits over supplementary charges, or vice versa.

In addition to the statement on page 740 a cash account or a summary of cash changes during the period is generally presented. A memorandum capital account would also be necessary to complete the reporting picture, as owners' equities are not included in the realization and liquidation statement.

From the information in the realization and liquidation statement, a realization profit and loss statement may be prepared. A statement of financial position as of the final date of the period covered by the realization and liquidation statement may also be prepared from the following data: (1) all items in the final sections of the statement (liabilities not liquidated and assets not realized), (2) ending cash balance from the cash account, and (3) ending capital from the memorandum capital account. The information for the realization and liquidation statement may be

ABC CORPORATION

REALIZATION AND LIQUIDATION STATEMENT

Assets to be realized:
All assets other than cash are listed at their respective book (carrying) values as of the beginning of the period covered by the statement.   xxxxx

Assets subsequently acquired:
All assets other than cash which were discovered or acquired during the period covered by the report are listed here.   xxxxx

Supplementary charges:
All expenses are listed here, *except* asset expirations and losses arising from the realization of specific assets.   xxxxx

Liabilities liquidated:
All liabilities settled are listed here.   xxxxx

Liabilities not liquidated:
All liabilities not liquidated at the end of the period covered by the statement are listed here.   xxxxx

Liabilities to be liquidated:
All liabilities as of the beginning of the period covered by the statement are listed here.   xxxxx

Liabilities subsequently assumed:
All liabilities incurred or discovered during the period covered by the report are listed here.   xxxxx

Supplementary credits:
All revenue is listed here, *except* gains on the realization of specific assets.   xxxxx

Assets realized:
The proceeds from the realization of the various assets are listed here.   xxxxx

Assets not realized:
All assets not realized at the end of the period covered by the statement are listed here at their book (carrying) values.   xxxxx

prepared from analyses of the information contained in a regular ledger maintained by a trustee or receiver, or the statement may be prepared from memoranda of various transactions made by the trustee or receiver during the period.

Illustration. In the following illustration it is assumed that the corporation, Johnson Sales Co., is placed in receivership under Vernon Griffin on March 1, 1967. Griffin operates the company for the remainder of the year, and on December 31, 1967, prepares a realization and liquidation statement and other data in order to report on the results of the corporate activities under his supervision. The following statement of financial position reveals the condition of the corporation on March 1, 1967:

JOHNSON SALES CO.

STATEMENT OF FINANCIAL POSITION

MARCH 1, 1967

Assets

Current assets:			
Cash			$ 1,060
Receivables			55,820
Finished goods			37,840
Raw materials			41,660
Total current assets			$136,380
Fixed assets:			
Land		$10,000	
Building	$100,000		
Less: Depreciation	47,000	53,000	
Equipment	$ 50,000		
Less: Depreciation	19,600	30,400	
Total fixed assets			93,400
Organization cost			6,980
			$236,760

Equities

Current liabilities:			
Accounts payable			$ 79,540
Notes payable			33,020
Accrued interest payable			520
Total current liabilities			$113,080
Fixed liabilities:			
Mortgage payable			48,000
Shareholders' equity:			
Common stock		$80,000	
Deficit		(4,320)	75,680
			$236,760

The various transactions of the receiver during the remainder of the year are summarized below. The transaction summaries, identified by the number opposite each summary, are journalized as they would appear on the records of the receiver and the corporation.

(1) March 1. The receiver takes over the assets at the values shown on the statement of financial position.

(2) The receiver purchases additional merchandise on account, $5,280.

(3) Sales on account total $137,500.

(4) Of the receivables on the books on March 1, $50,800 is collected after allowing discounts of $520.

(5) Collections are made on all accounts receivable arising from the receiver's sales, except on $14,200. Discounts of $1,900 are allowed on the accounts collected.

(6) Payments for labor and other costs total $22,400.

(7) All old accounts payable are paid; discounts amount to $1,600.

(8) All new accounts payable are paid in full.

(9) Payments on notes payable total $30,020.

(10) Payments on the mortgage total $10,000.

(11) Mortgage interest accrued from March 1 to December 31 totals $2,400. All mortgage interest is paid at December 31, 1967.

(12) Depreciation for the year is as follows: on building, $2,600; on equipment, $2,800.

(13) The receiver submits a bill for his services of $10,000, and is paid.

(14) All organization costs are written off.

(15) A reserve for uncollectibles amounting to one-half the remaining old accounts receivable is set up.

(16) The inventories on hand at December 31, 1967, are: raw materials, $6,800; finished goods, $3,560.

VERNON GRIFFIN—RECEIVER

JOURNAL

(1) Cash	$ 1,060	
Receivables—old	55,820	
Raw materials	41,660	
Finished goods	37,840	
Land	10,000	
Buildings	100,000	
Equipment	50,000	
Organization cost	6,980	
Reserve for depreciation of building		$ 47,000
Reserve for depreciation of equipment		19,600
Johnson Sales Co.—In receivership		236,760
(to open receiver's books)		

(2) Purchases	$ 5,280	
Accounts payable		$ 5,280
(to record purchase of merchandise)		
(3) Accounts receivable—new	$137,500	
Sales		$137,500
(to record sales of finished goods)		
(4) Cash	$ 50,800	
Sales discount	520	
Accounts receivable—old		$ 51,320
(to record collections of old receivables)		
(5) Cash	$121,400	
Sales discount	1,900	
Accounts receivable—new		$123,300
(to record collections of new receivables)		
(6) Labor and other costs	$ 22,400	
Cash		$ 22,400
(to record payment of labor and other costs)		
(7) Johnson Sales Co.—Accounts payable paid	$ 79,540	
Purchase discount		$ 1,600
Cash		77,940
(to record payment of old accounts payable)		
(8) Accounts payable	$ 5,280	
Cash		$ 5,280
(to record payment of new accounts payable)		
(9) Johnson Sales Co.—Notes payable paid	$ 30,020	
Cash		$ 30,020
(to record payment on notes payable)		
(10) Johnson Sales Co.—Mortage payable paid	$ 10,000	
Cash		$ 10,000
(to record payment on mortgage payable)		
(11) (No entry to record additional interest. Entry to be made on corporation's books.)		
Johnson Sales Co.—Interest paid	$ 2,920	
Cash		$ 2,920
(to record payment of interest on mortgage)		

(12) Depreciation on building $ 2,600

      Depreciation on equipment   2,800

          Reserve for depreciation of building $ 2,600

          Reserve for depreciation of equipment   2,800

          (to record depreciation provisions

          for the year)

(13) Receiver's expenses $ 10,000

      Cash $ 10,000

          (to record payment of receiver's fee)

(14) Loss on organization expense $ 6,980

      Organization cost $ 6,980

          (to write off organization costs)

(15) Bad debts expense $ 2,250

      Reserve for uncollectibles $ 2,250

          (to record estimated uncollectibles, $\frac{1}{2}$ of

          old accounts receivable)

Johnson Sales Co.
JOURNAL

(1) Vernon Griffin—Receiver $236,760

      Reserve for depreciation of building   47,000

      Reserve for depreciation of equipment   19,600

          Cash $ 1,060

          Receivables   55,820

          Raw materials   41,660

          Finished goods   37,840

          Land   10,000

          Buildings   100,000

          Equipment   50,000

          Organization cost   6,980

          (to close accounts for which receiver

          took responsibility)

(7) Accounts payable $ 79,540

      Vernon Griffin—receiver $ 79,540

          (to record payment of old accounts

          payable by the receiver)

(9) Notes payable $ 30,020

      Vernon Griffin—Receiver $ 30,020

          (to record payment of notes payable

          by receiver)

(10) Mortgage payable	$ 10,000	
Vernon Griffin—Receiver		$ 10,000
(to record payment on mortgage		
payable by the receiver)		

(11) Mortgage interest expense	$ 2,400	
Accrued interest payable		$ 2,400
(to accrue interest to December 31, 1967)		
Accrued interest payable	$ 2,920	
Vernon Griffin—Receiver		$ 2,920
(to record payment of accrued interest on		
the mortgage by the receiver)		

At this point the results of operations under the receivership have been journalized. The reports which follow are based upon the foregoing entries and are reports which Vernon Griffin might render at December 31, 1967. At this point assume the receiver continues to control the affairs of the Johnson Sales Co. beyond December 31, 1967.

THE JOHNSON CO.—IN RECEIVERSHIP

VERNON GRIFFIN, RECEIVER

ANALYSIS OF CASH ACCOUNT

MARCH 1, 1967 TO DECEMBER 31, 1967

Balance, 3/1/67	$ 1,060	(6) Labor and other costs	$ 22,400
(4) Accounts receivable—old	50,800	(7) Accounts payable—old	77,940
(5) Accounts receivable—new	121,400	(8) Accounts payable—new	5,280
		(9) Notes payable	30,020
		(10) Mortgage payable	10,000
		(11) Mortgage interest	2,920
		(13) Receiver's fees	10,000
		Balance, 12/31/67	14,700
	$173,260		$173,260

MEMORANDUM CAPITAL ACCOUNT

Deficit 3/1/67,	$ 4,320	Common stock, 3/1/67	$ 80,000
Balance, 12/31/67	88,510	Gain for the period	
		(see income statement)	12,830
	$ 92,830		$ 92,830

The Johnson Sales Co.—In Receivership
Vernon Griffin, Receiver
REALIZATION AND LIQUIDATION STATEMENT
March 1, 1967 to December 31, 1967

Debit			
Assets to be realized:			
(1) Receivables—old		$55,820	
(1) Raw materials		41,660	
(1) Finished goods		37,840	
(1) Land		10,000	
(1) Building	$100,000		
Less: reserve	47,000	53,000	
Equipment	50,000		
Less: reserve	19,600	30,400	
(1) Organization cost		6,980	$235,700
Assets subsequently acquired:			
(3) Accounts receivable—new			137,500
Supplementary charges:			
(2) Purchases		$5,280	
(4) (5) Discounts on sales		2,420	
(6) Labor and other costs		22,400	
(11) Mortgage interest expense		2,400	
(13) Receiver's expense		10,000	42,500
Liabilities liquidated:			
(7) Accounts payable—old		$79,540	
(8) Accounts payable—new		5,280	
(9) Notes payable		30,020	
(10) Mortgage payable		10,000	
(11) Interest on mortgage, to 3/1/67	$520		
Interest on mortgage, 3/1/67 to 12/31/67	2,400	2,920	127,760
Liabilities not liquidated:			
Notes payable		$3,000	
Mortgage payable		38,000	41,000
Gain for the period			12,830
			$597,290

Credit			
Liabilities to be liquidated:			
Accounts payable		$79,540	
Notes payable		33,020	
Interest on mortgage payable		520	
Mortgage payable		48,000	$161,080
Liabilities subsequently assumed:			
(2) Accounts payable for purchases		$5,280	
(11) Accrued interest on mortgage, from 3/1/67 to 12/31/67		2,400	7,680
Supplementary credits:			
(3) Sales		$137,500	
(7) Purchase discounts		1,600	139,100
Assets realized:			
(4) Accounts receivable—old		$51,320	
(5) Accounts receivable—new		123,300	174,620
Assets not realized:			
Accounts receivable—old	$4,500		
Less: reserve	2,250	2,250	
Accounts receivable—new		14,200	
Raw materials		6,800	
Finished goods		3,560	
Land		10,000	
Buildings	$100,000		
Less: reserve	49,600	50,400	
Equipment	50,000		
Less: reserve	22,400	27,600	114,810
			$597,290

THE JOHNSON SALES CO.—IN RECEIVERSHIP
VERNON GRIFFIN, RECEIVER
INCOME STATEMENT
MARCH 1, 1967 TO DECEMBER 31, 1967

Sales		
Cost of sales:		$137,500
Beginning inventory of raw materials	$ 41,660	
Add: purchases	5,280	
Cost of materials available	$ 46,940	
Ending inventory of raw materials	6,800	
Cost of materials used	$ 40,140	
Labor and other costs	22,400	
Total costs incurred	$ 62,540	
Add: Finished goods inventory, 3/1/67	37,840	
Cost of goods available for sale	$100,380	
Less: Finished goods inventory, 12/31/67	3,560	
Cost of goods sold		96,820
Gross profit on sales		$ 40,680
Operating expenses:		
Receiver's expenses	$ 10,000	
Discount on sales	2,420	
Depreciation on building	2,600	
Depreciation on equipment	2,800	
Estimated loss on bad debts	2,250	20,070
		$ 20,610
Discount on purchases		1,600
Net income on sales		$ 22,210
Write off of organization cost		6,980
Net gain before mortgage interest		$ 15,230
Less: Mortgage interest expense		2,400
Net gain for the period		$ 12,830

In reviewing the statements (including the one on page 748) and their relationship to the transactions during the period of the receivership, the following comments may help clarify certain areas:

Purchases and Sales of Products. The continued operations of the business must be reported in the Statement of Realization and Liquidation. In the above illustration the purchases were included as supplementary charges and the sales as supplementary credits. This treatment is logical since it results in the inclusion of the operating transactions in the supplementary charge and credit sections. An alternative treatment

THE JOHNSON CO.—IN RECEIVERSHIP
VERNON GRIFFIN, RECEIVER

STATEMENT OF FINANCIAL POSITION

DECEMBER 31, 1967

Assets

Current assets:

Cash			$ 14,700
Receivables—old		$ 4,500	
Less: uncollectibles		2,250	2,250
Receivables—new			14,200
Finished goods			3,560
Raw materials			6,800
Total current assets			$ 41,510

Fixed assets:

Land		$10,000	
Buildings	$100,000		
Less: reserve	49,600	50,400	
Equipment	50,000		
Less: reserve	22,400	27,600	
Total fixed assets			88,000
			$129,510

Equities

Current liabilities:

Notes payable		$ 3,000
Fixed liabilities:		
Mortgage payable		38,000
Shareholders' equity:		
Common stock	$80,000	
Retained earnings	8,510	88,510
		$129,510

would report the purchases as assets acquired, and the sales as assets realized.

Old and New Accounts. In transaction (3), the account debited was "Accounts receivable—new." The distinction between accounts receivable existing at the date the receiver assumes control and those resulting from the receiver's operation of the business is important because the receiver has a different degree of responsibility for the two types of receivables. The receiver is responsible only for diligent collection action on the old accounts receivable, but is responsible for an appraisal of credit risks in granting credit to new customers.

4. Land and buildings are mortgaged as security for bonds. They have an appraised value of $95,000. The company recently purchased $20,000 of machinery on a conditional sales contract. It still owes $12,000 principal on this contract, which is included in the notes payable. These machines have a current used value of $10,000. Depreciation taken on these machines amounts to $1,800. The remaining machinery is believed to be salable at $10,000, but cost of selling may be $1,000.

Required:
(1) Prepare a statement showing the estimated deficiency to unsecured creditors, indicating clearly the causes of the deficiency. Omit consideration of any expenses of liquidation which are not specifically mentioned.
(2) Prepare a statement of affairs and compute the per cent of probable payment to the $52,000 accounts payable.   (AICPA adapted)

Problem 24–2. The Hardhyt Corporation is in financial difficulty because of low sales. Its stockholders and principal creditors want an estimate of the financial results of the liquidation of the assets and liabilities and the dissolution of the Corporation. The Corporation's trial balance follows:

HARDHYT CORPORATION
POSTCLOSING TRIAL BALANCE
DECEMBER 31, 1967

Cash	$ 1,000	
Accounts receivable	20,500	
Allowance for bad debts		$ 350
Inventories	40,000	
Supplies inventory	3,000	
Downhill Railroad 5% bonds	5,000	
Accrued bond interest receivable	750	
Advertising	6,000	
Land	4,000	
Building	30,000	
Accumulated depreciation—building		5,000
Machinery and equipment	46,000	
Accumulated depreciation—machinery and equipment		8,000
Accounts payable		26,000
Notes payable—bank		25,000
Notes payable—officers		20,000
Payroll taxes payable		800
Wages payable		1,500
Mortgage payable		42,000
Mortgage interest payable		500
Capital stock		50,000
Retained earnings	29,100	
Reserve for product guarantees		6,200
	$185,350	$185,350

The following information has been collected in anticipation of a meeting of the stockholders and principal creditors to be held on January 2, 1968:

Separate accounts are of necessity maintained for old and new accounts payable, since the liabilities existing when the receiver assumes control remain on the corporation's books, while new liabilities incurred are recorded on the receiver's books. The separation is significant because of the priority of rights enjoyed by those creditors whose claims arise from dealings with the receiver.

Cash Discounts. Transactions (4), (5), and (7) involved cash discounts. In each transaction the amount of the discount was reported as a supplementary charge (sales discount) or as a supplementary credit (purchase discount). Reporting discounts in this manner necessitates showing the realization proceeds from collection or the liabilities liquidated by payment at the gross amounts rather than at the amount of the cash involved. An alternative treatment of discounts follows, with transaction (4) used as an example:

Supplementary Charges:	*Assets Realized:*
No entry	Accounts receivable—old
	$50,800

Under this method of reporting, the discount is not separately shown, but becomes a part of the net gain or loss on realization for the period. Entry (4) on page 743 would be the same except that the $520 discount would not be entered in a separate expense account.

Accrued Interest. Transaction (11) involves interest accrued during the receiver's period of operation. As noted previously, if the accrued interest results from a liability existing at the date the receivership began, the entry for the additional interest is made on the corporation's books. However, since the statement of realization and liquidation reflects all transactions of the receivership period, the effect of the additional interest is reported in the statement. The additional interest is reported both as a supplementary charge and as a liability assumed. Payment of the previously existing accrued interest plus the addition this period is reported under liabilities liquidated.

An alternative treatment reports the additional accrual only as a supplementary charge. When payment takes place, only the liability existing at the date the receiver took charge would be reported as liquidated. This method appears less preferable than the other.

Other accrued expenses are handled in a manner similar to interest charges while accrued incomes are reported, preferably, as assets acquired and as supplementary credits.

Depreciation. Periodic depreciation does not appear on the realization and liquidation statement although it is reported on the receiver's income statement. On the realization and liquidation statement the assets to be realized are reported, less any applicable reserves, and the assets not realized are reported similarly. The period depreciation is considered as part of the realization gain or loss for the period.

Bad Debts. Any increase in the reserve for uncollectibles is handled in a manner similar to depreciation. Write offs of specific accounts against a previously established reserve do not affect the realization and liquidation statement nor the gain or loss for the period. Such write offs were, in effect, reported as losses at the time the reserve was established.

Asset Write offs. Since gains and losses on realization of assets are not reported separately on the realization and liquidation statement, asset write offs do not appear as separate amounts. The effect of an asset write off, as illustrated in the write off of organization cost, appears in the gain or loss for the period as part of the balancing amount on the statement.

Closing Out the Receivership. When a receivership is terminated the receiver closes all accounts remaining on his books, and the corporation records the return of the various assets and liabilities in its books. In the illustration, the receiver would credit the asset accounts appearing on the statement of financial position, would debit the reserve accounts, and would debit The Johnson Co.—In Receivership for $129,510 to close that account. The corporation would make the reverse of this entry, crediting Vernon Griffin, Receiver for $129,510.

Summary. The discussion in this chapter has been directed to some of the problems encountered in corporate liquidations and to the reporting problems involved in the operations of a corporation undergoing liquidation. The statements illustrated may also be used to report the liquidation of a partnership or a proprietorship. While the causes of business liquidation may vary among the various types of business organizations, accounting for a business liquidation and the reporting involved contain far more similarities than differences. The preceding discussion on receiverships and the reporting involved should not be considered to be limited to the corporate form of business.

PROBLEMS

Problem 24–1. The Machine Manufacturing Company has been forced into bankruptcy as of April 30, 1967. The following balance sheet was prepared by the company bookkeeper as of April 30, 1967:

Assets

Cash	$ 2,700
Accounts receivable	39,350
Notes receivable	18,500
Inventories:	
Raw materials	19,600
Work in process	35,100
Finished goods	12,000
Supplies	6,450
Tools	14,700
Prepaid expenses	950
Plant and property:	
Land	20,000
Buildings	75,000
Machinery	80,900
	$325,250

Liabilities and Capital

Note payable to the First Bank	$ 15,000
Notes payable to suppliers	51,250
Accounts payable	52,000
Accrued liabilities:	
Accrued salaries and wages	8,850
Accrued property taxes	2,900
Employees' taxes withheld	1,150
Accrued wage taxes	600
Accrued interest on bonds	1,800
First mortgage bonds payable	90,000
Allowance for depreciation, Buildings	33,750
Allowance for depreciation, Machinery	32,100
Common stock ($100 par value)	75,000
Deficit	(39,150)
	$325,250

Additional information:

1. Of the total accounts receivable, $10,300 are believed to be good. The other accounts are doubtful, but it seems probable that 20% finally can be collected.
2. A total of $15,000 of the notes receivable have been pledged to secure the note payable to the First Bank. All except $2,500 of these appear to be good. Interest of $800 is accrued on the $12,500 of good notes pledged, and $300 is accrued on the $15,000 payable to the bank. The remaining notes are not considered collectible.
3. The finished machines are expected to be sold for one-third above their cost, but expenses of disposing of them will equal 20% of their sales price. Work in process can be completed at an additional cost of $15,400, of which $3,700 would be material used from the raw material inventory. The work in process, when completed, will probably sell for $40,000 and costs of selling this will be 20% of sales price. The raw material not used will realize $8,000. Most of the value of tools consists of special items. After completion of work in process, the tools should sell for $3,000. The supply inventory which will not be needed to complete work should sell for $1,000.

Separate accounts are of necessity maintained for old and new accounts payable, since the liabilities existing when the receiver assumes control remain on the corporation's books, while new liabilities incurred are recorded on the receiver's books. The separation is significant because of the priority of rights enjoyed by those creditors whose claims arise from dealings with the receiver.

Cash Discounts. Transactions (4), (5), and (7) involved cash discounts. In each transaction the amount of the discount was reported as a supplementary charge (sales discount) or as a supplementary credit (purchase discount). Reporting discounts in this manner necessitates showing the realization proceeds from collection or the liabilities liquidated by payment at the gross amounts rather than at the amount of the cash involved. An alternative treatment of discounts follows, with transaction (4) used as an example:

Supplementary Charges:	*Assets Realized:*
No entry	Accounts receivable—old
	$50,800

Under this method of reporting, the discount is not separately shown, but becomes a part of the net gain or loss on realization for the period. Entry (4) on page 743 would be the same except that the $520 discount would not be entered in a separate expense account.

Accrued Interest. Transaction (11) involves interest accrued during the receiver's period of operation. As noted previously, if the accrued interest results from a liability existing at the date the receivership began, the entry for the additional interest is made on the corporation's books. However, since the statement of realization and liquidation reflects all transactions of the receivership period, the effect of the additional interest is reported in the statement. The additional interest is reported both as a supplementary charge and as a liability assumed. Payment of the previously existing accrued interest plus the addition this period is reported under liabilities liquidated.

An alternative treatment reports the additional accrual only as a supplementary charge. When payment takes place, only the liability existing at the date the receiver took charge would be reported as liquidated. This method appears less preferable than the other.

Other accrued expenses are handled in a manner similar to interest charges while accrued incomes are reported, preferably, as assets acquired and as supplementary credits.

Depreciation. Periodic depreciation does not appear on the realization and liquidation statement although it is reported on the receiver's income statement. On the realization and liquidation statement the assets to be realized are reported, less any applicable reserves, and the assets not realized are reported similarly. The period depreciation is considered as part of the realization gain or loss for the period.

Bad Debts. Any increase in the reserve for uncollectibles is handled in a manner similar to depreciation. Write offs of specific accounts against a previously established reserve do not affect the realization and liquidation statement nor the gain or loss for the period. Such write offs were, in effect, reported as losses at the time the reserve was established.

Asset Write offs. Since gains and losses on realization of assets are not reported separately on the realization and liquidation statement, asset write offs do not appear as separate amounts. The effect of an asset write off, as illustrated in the write off of organization cost, appears in the gain or loss for the period as part of the balancing amount on the statement.

Closing Out the Receivership. When a receivership is terminated the receiver closes all accounts remaining on his books, and the corporation records the return of the various assets and liabilities in its books. In the illustration, the receiver would credit the asset accounts appearing on the statement of financial position, would debit the reserve accounts, and would debit The Johnson Co.—In Receivership for $129,510 to close that account. The corporation would make the reverse of this entry, crediting Vernon Griffin, Receiver for $129,510.

Summary. The discussion in this chapter has been directed to some of the problems encountered in corporate liquidations and to the reporting problems involved in the operations of a corporation undergoing liquidation. The statements illustrated may also be used to report the liquidation of a partnership or a proprietorship. While the causes of business liquidation may vary among the various types of business organizations, accounting for a business liquidation and the reporting involved contain far more similarities than differences. The preceding discussion on receiverships and the reporting involved should not be considered to be limited to the corporate form of business.

PROBLEMS

Problem 24–1. The Machine Manufacturing Company has been forced into bankruptcy as of April 30, 1967. The following balance sheet was prepared by the company bookkeeper as of April 30, 1967:

Assets

Cash	$ 2,700
Accounts receivable	39,350
Notes receivable	18,500
Inventories:	
Raw materials	19,600
Work in process	35,100
Finished goods	12,000
Supplies	6,450
Tools	14,700
Prepaid expenses	950
Plant and property:	
Land	20,000
Buildings	75,000
Machinery	80,900
	$325,250

Liabilities and Capital

Note payable to the First Bank	$ 15,000
Notes payable to suppliers	51,250
Accounts payable	52,000
Accrued liabilities:	
Accrued salaries and wages	8,850
Accrued property taxes	2,900
Employees' taxes withheld	1,150
Accrued wage taxes	600
Accrued interest on bonds	1,800
First mortgage bonds payable	90,000
Allowance for depreciation, Buildings	33,750
Allowance for depreciation, Machinery	32,100
Common stock ($100 par value)	75,000
Deficit	(39,150)
	$325,250

Additional information:
1. Of the total accounts receivable, $10,300 are believed to be good. The other accounts are doubtful, but it seems probable that 20% finally can be collected.
2. A total of $15,000 of the notes receivable have been pledged to secure the note payable to the First Bank. All except $2,500 of these appear to be good. Interest of $800 is accrued on the $12,500 of good notes pledged, and $300 is accrued on the $15,000 payable to the bank. The remaining notes are not considered collectible.
3. The finished machines are expected to be sold for one-third above their cost, but expenses of disposing of them will equal 20% of their sales price. Work in process can be completed at an additional cost of $15,400, of which $3,700 would be material used from the raw material inventory. The work in process, when completed, will probably sell for $40,000 and costs of selling this will be 20% of sales price. The raw material not used will realize $8,000. Most of the value of tools consists of special items. After completion of work in process, the tools should sell for $3,000. The supply inventory which will not be needed to complete work should sell for $1,000.

4. Land and buildings are mortgaged as security for bonds. They have an appraised value of $95,000. The company recently purchased $20,000 of machinery on a conditional sales contract. It still owes $12,000 principal on this contract, which is included in the notes payable. These machines have a current used value of $10,000. Depreciation taken on these machines amounts to $1,800. The remaining machinery is believed to be salable at $10,000, but cost of selling may be $1,000.

Required:

(1) Prepare a statement showing the estimated deficiency to unsecured creditors, indicating clearly the causes of the deficiency. Omit consideration of any expenses of liquidation which are not specifically mentioned.

(2) Prepare a statement of affairs and compute the per cent of probable payment to the $52,000 accounts payable.   (AICPA adapted)

Problem 24–2. The Hardhyt Corporation is in financial difficulty because of low sales. Its stockholders and principal creditors want an estimate of the financial results of the liquidation of the assets and liabilities and the dissolution of the Corporation. The Corporation's trial balance follows:

HARDHYT CORPORATION
POSTCLOSING TRIAL BALANCE
DECEMBER 31, 1967

Cash	$ 1,000	
Accounts receivable	20,500	
Allowance for bad debts		$ 350
Inventories	40,000	
Supplies inventory	3,000	
Downhill Railroad 5% bonds	5,000	
Accrued bond interest receivable	750	
Advertising	6,000	
Land	4,000	
Building	30,000	
Accumulated depreciation—building		5,000
Machinery and equipment	46,000	
Accumulated depreciation—machinery and equipment		8,000
Accounts payable		26,000
Notes payable—bank		25,000
Notes payable—officers		20,000
Payroll taxes payable		800
Wages payable		1,500
Mortgage payable		42,000
Mortgage interest payable		500
Capital stock		50,000
Retained earnings	29,100	
Reserve for product guarantees		6,200
	$185,350	$185,350

The following information has been collected in anticipation of a meeting of the stockholders and principal creditors to be held on January 2, 1968:

(1) Cash includes a $300 protested check from a customer. The customer stated that he would have funds to honor the check in about two weeks.

(2) Accounts receivable include accounts totaling $10,000 that are fully collectible and have been assigned to the bank in connection with the notes payable. Included in unassigned receivables is an uncollectible account of $150. The Allowance for Bad Debts account of $350 now on the books will adequately provide for other doubtful accounts.

(3) Purchase orders totaling $9,000 are on hand for the Corporation's products. Inventory with a book value of $6,000 can be processed at an additional cost of $400 to fill these orders. The balance of the inventory, which includes obsolete materials with a book value of $1,200, can be sold for $10,500.

(4) In transit at December 31 but not recorded on the books was a shipment of defective merchandise being returned by a customer. Mr. Hardhyt, president of the Corporation, had authorized the return and the refund of the purchase price of $250 after the merchandise had been inspected. Other than this return, Mr. Hardhyt knows of no other defective merchandise that would bear upon the appropriated Reserve for Product Guarantees account. The merchandise being returned has no salvage value.

(5) The Supplies Inventory is comprised of advertising literature, brochures, and other sales aids. These could not be replaced for less than $3,700.

(6) The Downhill Railroad bonds are recorded at face value. They were purchased in 1964 for $600, and the adjustment to face value was credited to Retained Earnings. At December 31, 1967 the bonds were quoted at 18 dealt in flat.

(7) The Advertising account represents the future benefits of a 1967 advertising campaign. Ten per cent of certain advertising expenditures were placed in the account. Mr. Hardhyt stated that this was too conservative and that 20% would result in a more realistic measure of the market that was created.

(8) The land and building are in a downtown area. A firm offer of $50,000 has been received for the land which would be used as a parking lot; the building would be razed at a cost of $12,000 to the buyer. Another offer of $40,000 was received for the real estate which the bidder stated would be used for manufacturing that would probably employ some Hardhyt employees.

(9) The highest of the offers received from used machinery dealers was $18,000 for all of the machinery and equipment.

(10) One creditor, whose account for $1,000 is included in the accounts payable, confirmed in writing that he would accept 90¢ on the dollar if the Corporation paid him by January 10.

(11) Wages payable include year-end adjustments of $325 payable to certain factory employees for their overtime during the busy season.

(12) The mortgage payable is secured by the land and building. The last two monthly principal payments of $200 each were not made.

(13) Estimated liquidation expenses amount to $3,200.

(14) For income tax purposes the Corporation has the following net operating loss carryovers: (The tax rate is 50%.)

1965	$10,000
1966	12,000
1967	8,000

Required:

(1) Prepare a statement of affairs. Assets should be classified according to their availability for secured and unsecured creditors, and liabilities should be classified according to their legal priority and secured status. The statement should have the following column headings:

> For Assets:
>> Book Value
>> Assets
>> Appraised Value
>> Estimated Amount Available
>> Loss or Gain on Realization
> For Liabilities and Capital:
>> Book Value
>> Liabilities and Capital
>> Amount Unsecured

(2) Prepare a schedule that computes the estimated settlement per dollar of unsecured liabilities.   (AICPA adapted)

Problem 24–3. The Hamilton Company entered receivership on July 31, 1967. The following trial balance is taken from the company records on that date:

THE HAMILTON COMPANY
TRIAL BALANCE, JULY 31, 1967

Cash	$ 20,000	
Notes receivable	25,000	
Accounts receivable	90,000	
Inventories	40,000	
Land	30,000	
Buildings	240,000	
Reserve for deprec. of buildings		$110,000
Equipment	200,000	
Reserve for deprec. of equipment		90,000
Unexpired insurance	5,000	
Accounts payable		150,000
Notes payable		55,000
Accrued wages		6,000
Accrued interest on bonds		2,000
First mortgage bonds, 4%		120,000
Common stock		100,000
Earned surplus		17,000
	$650,000	$650,000

Additional analyses of the Hamilton Company's financial position and discussions with responsible officials disclosed the following information:

Realizable value of assets:	
Notes receivable	$ 17,000
Accounts receivable	65,000

Inventories	45,000
Land	25,000
Buildings	100,000
Equipment	60,000
Unexpired insurance	1,000

Other Information:
1. The first mortgage bonds are secured by a mortgage on the land and buildings.
2. The company is liable under certain product guarantees. No entry has been made to reflect this contingency, but it is estimated $15,000 will be necessary to settle claims that will arise.
3. The inventories have been pledged as collateral for the notes payable.
4. All accrued wages are of recent origin.
5. Expenses of liquidation are expected to total $7,000.

Required:
(1) Prepare a statement of affairs.
(2) Prepare a deficiency account.

Problem 24–4. The partnership of Brody, Mason, and Soule was placed in receivership on September 1, 1967. At that date the receiver took control, and the following balance sheet of the partnership was prepared:

BRODY, MASON, & SOULE PARTNERSHIP
BALANCE SHEET, SEPTEMBER 1, 1967

Cash	$ 600	Accounts payable		$124,000
Accounts receivable	90,000	Notes payable		45,000
Marketable securities	30,000	Wages payable		4,400
Inventories	84,000	Taxes payable		1,500
Prepaid insurance	900	Interest payable on mortgage		600
Land	30,000	Mortgage payable		120,000
Buildings (net)	165,000	Partners' capitals:		
		Brody	$60,000	
		Mason	30,000	
		Soule	15,000	105,000
	$400,500			$400,500

Other information pertinent to the financial condition of the partnership appears below:
1. The mortgage payable is secured by the land and buildings.
2. The marketable securities have been pledged as collateral for the notes payable.
3. Upon liquidation, the assets are expected to realize the following amounts:

Accounts receivable:
1/3, fully collectible
1/2, collectible at 66⅔%
1/6, uncollectible
Marketable securities—$34,000
Inventories—$41,000
Prepaid insurance—$225
Land—$24,000
Buildings—$120,000

Required:
(1) Prepare a statement of affairs for the partnership.
(2) Prepare a deficiency account.

Problem 24–5. The Adams-Story Partnership, of which Adams is manager, has had difficulty in meeting its obligations as the debts matured. If the business is dissolved it will require six months to complete the dissolution. The book-keeper prepared the trial balance as shown on page 757.

An analysis of the accounts revealed the following:

1. Cash in First Bank, $8,000; in Second Bank, $12,000.
2. Of the accounts receivable, 60% are good and fully collectible, 30% are doubtful and considered to be only 80% collectible, the remaining 10% are worthless.
3. All notes are good and are pledged as security on notes payable to the Factor House of $50,000 with accrued interest of $500.
4. Of the notes which were discounted at the Manning Bank it is estimated that one, amounting to $2,000, will not be paid at maturity or thereafter.
5. All finished goods will be sold for 20% less than their cost. Work in process cannot be sold until finished and can be completed by incurring labor and material costs of $9,000 of which $3,000 will be from raw material inventory. The balance of raw material inventory will realize $5,000.
6. The prepaid insurance, which expires October 15, has a short-term cancellation value on April 15, 1967 of $900.
7. Property held in trust is in the form of stocks and bonds with realizable value of $24,000. The partnership is entitled to a fee of $600 per year, payable April 15, for their services. Cash was not available in the trust for the payment; therefore, the fee was not recorded.
8. The machinery and equipment with a book value of $8,000 will realize $5,000.
9. The land and building may be sold for $38,000; however, the mortgage holder has indicated a willingness to cancel the debt and assume all encumbrances for the surrender of the title to the real estate. Interest on the mortgage was paid on January 15, 1967.
10. The wages and commissions were last paid in full on December 31, 1966. Commission salesmen were dismissed on February 15, 1967. Accrued wages in the trial balance are:

Burke, bookkeeper (to April 15)	$1,400
Commission salesman (to February 15)	300
Adams, manager (to April 15)	1,750
	$3,450

ADAMS-STORY PARTNERSHIP
TRIAL BALANCE, APRIL 15, 1967

Cash in banks	$ 20,000	
Accounts receivable	100,000	
Allowance for bad debts		$ 4,000
Notes receivable	58,000	
Notes receivable discounted		12,000
Raw materials	9,000	
Work in process	20,000	
Finished goods	15,000	
Prepaid insurance	1,200	
Property held in trust	18,000	
Machinery and equipment, cost	9,000	
Building	33,000	
Land	12,000	
Accumulated depreciation		6,000
Interest receivable	700	
Payroll taxes payable		200
Real estate taxes		1,200
Wages payable		3,450
Notes payable		60,000
Accounts payable		125,700
Mortgage payable, 4%		40,000
Equipment contract payable (purchased on a conditional sales contract)		6,400
Interest payable		1,000
Adams, Capital		15,975
Story, Capital		1,975
Trust, Capital		18,000
	$295,900	$295,900

11. The partnership owes the Second Bank a note of $10,000.
12. The estimated administrative expenses are $3,000.
13. While Adams has personal liabilities which are approximately equal to his personal assets, Story's personal assets exceed his personal liabilities by $2,800.

Required:
(1) Prepare a statement in good form showing the estimated deficiency, if any, to the unsecured creditors.
(2) Prepare a schedule summarizing the estimated amounts available for each class of creditors.   (AICPA adapted)

Problem 24-6. The Alpha Corporation, currently in financial difficulty, has the following inventory amounts on hand:

Raw materials	$60,000
Work in process	45,000
Finished goods	40,000

The work in process will require the application of $12,000 of raw materials and expenditure of $14,000 for labor and other costs in order to process the goods to a finished condition. The remaining raw materials will be sold at a discount of 20% from their book value. It is estimated that all finished goods will be sold for cost plus 10%.

Required:

How would the above information be reported on a statement of affairs?

Problem 24–7. The Neversink Corporation advises you that it is facing bankruptcy proceedings. As the company's CPA you are aware of its condition.

The statement of financial position of the Neversink Corporation at June 30, 1967 and supplementary data are presented below:

Assets

Cash	$ 2,000
Accounts receivable, less allowance for bad debts	70,000
Inventory, raw material	40,000
Inventory, finished goods	60,000
Marketable securities	20,000
Land	13,000
Buildings, less allowance for depreciation	90,000
Machinery, less allowance for depreciation	120,000
Goodwill	20,000
Prepaid expenses	5,000
Total assets	$440,000

Liabilities and Capital

Accounts payable	$ 80,000
Notes payable	135,000
Accrued wages	15,000
Mortgage payable	130,000
Common stock	100,000
Retained earnings (deficit)	(20,000)
Total liabilities and capital	$440,000

Supplementary data:

(1) Cash includes a $500 travel advance which has been expended.

(2) Accounts receivable of $40,000 have been pledged in support of bank loans of $30,000. Credit balances of $5,000 are netted in the accounts receivable total.

(3) Marketable securities consisted of government bonds costing $10,000 and 500 shares of Bartlett Company stock. The market value of the bonds is $10,000 and the stock is $18 per share. The bonds have accrued interest due of $200. The securities are collateral for a $20,000 bank loan.

(4) Appraised value of raw materials is $30,000 and finished goods is $50,000. For an additional cost of $10,000, the raw materials would realize $70,000 as finished goods.

(5) The appraisal value of fixed assets is: Land, $25,000; Buildings, $110,000; Machinery, $75,000.

(6) Prepaid expenses will be exhausted during the liquidation period.

(7) Accounts payable include $15,000 withheld payroll taxes and $6,000 for creditors who had been reassured by the president they would be paid. There are unrecorded employer's taxes in the amount of $500.

(8) Wages payable are not subject to any limitations under bankruptcy laws.

(9) Mortgages payable consist of $100,000 on land and buildings, and $30,000 chattel mortgage on machinery. Total unrecorded accrued interest for these mortgages amounted to $2,400.

(10) Estimated legal fees and expenses in connection with the liquidation are $10,000.

(11) Probable judgment on a pending damage suit is $50,000.

(12) You have not rendered an invoice for $5,000 for last year's audit and you estimate a $1,000 fee for liquidation work.

Required:

(1) Prepare a statement of affairs.

(2) Compute the estimated settlement per dollar of unsecured liabilities.

(AICPA adapted)

Problem 24–8. The Sellow Furniture Company, Inc., has been finding it more and more difficult to meet its obligations. Although its sales volume appeared to be satisfactory and it was showing a profit, the requirements for capital for inventory and time contracts were greater than the company could provide. Finally, after pledging all of its installment accounts, it found itself unable to meet the bills falling due on October 10, 1967. It is the opinion of the management that if it could obtain an extension of time in which to pay its obligations it could meet its liabilities in full. The corporation has arranged for a meeting of creditors to determine if the company should be granted an extension or be forced into bankruptcy.

You have been asked to assist the company by:

(1) Preparing a statement of affairs.

(2) Preparing a statement of estimated deficiency to unsecured creditors.

(3) Computing the percentage of recovery by the unsecured creditors if the company were to be forced into bankruptcy.

You find the trial balance for the current calendar year of the company on September 30, 1967, is as shown on page 760.

From further investigation you obtain the following additional data:

a. Depreciation, bad debts, prepaid and accrued items had all been adjusted as of September 30, 1967.

b. All installment contracts had been pledged with the bank on September 30, 1967; the bank had deducted its interest to date and had increased the company loan to equal 75% of face amount of the contracts in accordance with a loan agreement. It was estimated that a forced liquidation would result in a loss of $40,000 from the face amount of the contracts.

c. Thirty-day accounts receivable were not pledged and it was estimated that they would provide $16,500 on a liquidation basis.

d. It was estimated that since January 1, 1967, the company had made a gross profit of $33\frac{1}{3}\%$, but that the inventory on hand would provide only $100,000 on a forced liquidation.

e. Cancellation of the insurance would provide $990.

f. All the autos and trucks were covered by a chattel mortgage, and their total market value was $8,000.

g. The store had been remodeled in 1966 and the furniture and equipment had been acquired on contract. Because of its special utility it was estimated that on a forced sale no more than $5,000 could be expected.

THE SELLOW FURNITURE COMPANY, INC.

TRIAL BALANCE, SEPTEMBER 30, 1967

Cash on hand	$ 500	
Cash in bank	1,620	
Installment contracts, pledged	215,000	
Allowance for bad contracts		$ 13,440
Accounts receivable, 30 days	20,830	
Allowance for bad debts		1,050
Inventories, January 1, 1967	151,150	
Unexpired insurance	1,490	
Autos and trucks	22,380	
Allowance for depreciation, autos and trucks		14,960
Furniture and equipment	12,500	
Allowance for depreciation, furniture and equipment		2,140
Buildings	89,760	
Allowance for depreciation, buildings		7,530
Land	10,240	
Organization expense	880	
Trade accounts payable		132,100
Contract payable, furniture and equipment		5,800
Chattel mortgage on autos and trucks		10,000
Bank loan, secured by installment contracts		161,250
Taxes payable		14,220
Accrued salaries and wages		4,680
Accrued interest		10,990
Notes payable, stockholder		100,000
First mortgage		49,000
Capital stock		100,000
Surplus	65,290	
Sales		708,900
Purchases	527,630	
Expenses and miscellaneous income (net)	216,790	
	$1,336,060	$1,336,060

h. The land and buildings were subject to a 6% first mortgage on which interest had been paid to July 30, 1967. It was estimated the property could be sold for $75,000.

i. The notes payable to stockholders had not been subordinated to general creditors. The notes carried a 6% rate of interest, but no interest had been paid since December 31, 1965.

j. Since prior income tax returns disclosed a large available net operating loss carry-over, no current income tax need be considered.

k. The cost of a liquidation proceedings was estimated to be $5,000.

l. There appeared to be no other values on liquidation and no unrecorded liabilities.   (AICPA adapted)

Problem 24–9. The Bielby Corporation was placed in receivership on August 31, 1967, at which date Frank Herhold was appointed receiver. Upon assuming control of the Bielby Corp., Herhold prepared the following trial balance.

THE BIELBY CORPORATION—IN RECEIVERSHIP

FRANK HERHOLD, RECEIVER

TRIAL BALANCE, AUGUST 31, 1967

Cash	$ 3,000	
Accounts receivable	18,400	
Stock of Niehus Co., at cost	12,200	
Inventory	17,600	
Machinery and equipment	42,200	
Reserve for depreciation of mach. and equip.		$27,400
Accounts payable		40,600
Accrued wages		3,600
Accrued taxes		2,800
Common stock		20,000
Retained income	1,000	
	$94,400	$94,400

During the three months ended November 30, 1967, the receiver entered into various transactions, the results of which are summarized below:

(*a*) Cash Receipts:

Collections of accounts receivable as of 8/31/67	$12,000
Collections of accounts receivable arising in receivership	31,000
Sale of equipment (cost, $10,000, 60% depreciated)	2,800

(*b*) Cash disbursements:

Payment of accrued wages	3,600
Payment of accrued taxes	2,800
Payment of accounts payable as of 8/31/67	30,000
Payment of accounts payable arising in receivership	8,200
Payment of receivership operating expenses	4,500

(*c*) Purchases on account	10,000
(*d*) Sales on account	34,000
(*e*) Inventory of unsold merchandise at November 30, 1967	1,700
(*f*) Depreciation of machinery & equipment for 3 months	1,100

(*g*) Balance of accounts receivable as of 8/31/67 is not collectible.

Required:

Prepare a statement of realization and liquidation. Analyze the net gain or loss for the period.

Problem 24–10. The Gorman Dental Equipment Co. has suffered a series of declining profit years, and the management of the company has decided to liquidate the business. On April 30, 1967, the following balance sheet was taken from the ledger of the company:

GORMAN DENTAL EQUIPMENT CO.
BALANCE SHEET, APRIL 30, 1967

Cash	$ 4,220	Accounts payable	$ 52,400
Accounts receivable	32,400	Notes payable	21,000
Notes receivable	8,600	Accrued wages	3,600
Finished goods	18,350	Interest payable on notes	150
Materials and supplies	7,480	Mortgage payable, 6%	25,000
Land and building (net)	60,000	Common stock	50,000
Equipment and tools (net)	26,800	Earned surplus	5,700
	$157,850		$157,850

During the three months ended July 31, 1967, the officers designated to supervise the liquidation operations sold all the finished goods, $6,200 for cash and $18,400 on account. The materials and supplies realized $4,000, and at July 31 an estimated $1,200 remained on hand. Collections on accounts amounted to $44,000, with only $4,200 of the receivables arising in the three-month period remaining uncollected and collectible. All accounts written off existed at April 30, 1967. Notes collected totaled $6,000, with 50% of the remaining balance estimated to be uncollectible. The major portion of the equipment and tools was sold for $16,000, with equipment on hand July 31 valued at $2,000.

Payments were made as follows: expenses during the period, $7,500; on accounts payable, $46,500; on notes and interest, $21,400, settled in full; on accrued wages, $3,600; on mortgage interest, $125.

On June 1 the land and buildings were taken over by the mortgagee in settlement of his claim. In addition, the mortgagee agreed to pay the Gorman Co. $20,000, payment to be made prior to January 1, 1968.

Accounts payable remaining unpaid totaled $4,700.

Required:

Prepare a statement of realization and liquidation for the period ended July 31, 1967.

Problem 24–11. Keenan and Mosher, a partnership, were unable to obtain working capital sufficient to carry on their business. On May 15, 1967, the creditors convened and appointed a friendly receiver to take over the business immediately. The books were closed and the following balance sheet was prepared:

KEENAN AND MOSHER
BALANCE SHEET, MAY 15, 1967

Cash		$ 356	Accounts payable		$38,560
Notes receivable		4,500	Notes payable		6,500
Accounts receivable	$32,546		Keenan, Capital	$6,986	
Less reserve	3,250	29,296	Keenan, Drawing	2,228	4,758
Furn. and fixtures	750		Mosher, Capital	7,166	
Less reserve	150	600	Mosher, Drawing	2,232	4,934
Goodwill		20,000			
		$54,752			$54,752

A review of the records discloses that an inventory of merchandise exists, totaling $3,250. This amount had not been considered when closing the books on May 15.

During the next $5\frac{1}{2}$ months the receiver operated the business and collected the following amounts on the above accounts: $3,900 on notes receivable; $27,470 on accounts receivable. At November 1, 1967, the balance of the notes and accounts were considered to be uncollectible. All notes payable were paid, and all old accounts payable were settled at $.80 on the dollar. In addition, the following summary presents other operations of the receiver:

Sales on account	$56,000
Purchases on account	28,000
Operating expenses paid	13,600
Receiver's expenses	5,600
Collections on sales made	51,600
Payments on purchases made	24,500
Unsold merchandise at 11/1/67	3,400

Required:
Prepare a realization and liquidation statement.

Problem 24–12. The Specialty Shops Company was unable to meet its obligations. As a result, John Mann was appointed receiver on February 5, 1967. The trial balance on page 764 was taken from the books as of that date.

In the period from February 5 to April 30, 1967, the receiver's actions resulted in the following:

1. An audit of the accounts receivable disclosed that there were an additional $423 of accounts receivable which had not been brought on the books.
2. Merchandise costing $8,310 was sold for cash.
3. A portion of the fixtures, which cost $5,376 and had accumulated depreciation credits of $942, was sold.
4. Accounts receivable totaling $1,882 were collected. Other accounts, amounting to $741, have been determined to be worthless.
5. Claims have been approved and paid for $903 of the wages and taxes which were accrued at February 5. Wage claims for $125 which were unrecorded

THE SPECIALTY SHOPS COMPANY
TRIAL BALANCE, FEBRUARY 5, 1967

Cash	$ 764	
Accounts receivable	5,928	
Merchandise	16,536	
Prepayment of expenses	704	
Fixtures	12,342	
Accounts payable		$15,987
Notes payable		3,500
Accrued wages, taxes, etc.		1,275
Accrued rent		600
Reserve for depreciation		3,803
Capital stock		10,000
Earned surplus		1,109
	$36,274	$36,274

on February 5 have also been approved and paid. Other claims have not yet been paid.
6. Expenses for wages and supplies used in liquidating the business to April 30 amounted to $1,245. Fees for the receiver need not be considered.
7. Rent under leases has continued to accrue in the amount of $900. Interest of $70 has accrued on notes payable.
8. Cash receipts and cash disbursements show the following:

Cash Receipts

Collection of accounts	$1,882
Sales of merchandise	9,108
Sale of fixtures	1,000

Cash Disbursements

Accrued wages and taxes	$1,028
Expenses of the receivership	1,245

Required:

Prepare a statement of realization and liquidation and related gain and loss account for the period February 5 to April 30, 1967.   (AICPA adapted)

Problem 24–13. The Deake Toy Company finds itself in financial difficulty, being unable to meet promptly its obligations to its general creditors. The following balance sheet was prepared on October 16, 1967:

DEAKE TOY COMPANY
BALANCE SHEET, OCTOBER 16, 1967

Cash	$ 15,240	Accounts payable		$156,000
Receivables	73,324	Accrued wages		8,220
Inventories	44,778	Notes payable		96,800
Prepaid insurance	7,120	Capital stock	$30,000	
Equipment (net)	151,080	Retained income	522	30,522
	$291,542			$291,542

The general creditors have been negotiating for a suitable settlement with the stockholders-managers of the company. The best offer they have received to date involves a settlement at 42½ cents on the dollar, with 20 cents payable immediately and the balance in three bi-monthly installments, beginning December 15, 1967. Acceptance of this plan may permit the Deake Company to raise additional capital and thereby to strengthen further the financial structure of the company.

Accountants for the general creditors have agreed that the following represent reasonable liquidation values for the various assets: receivables, $50,000; inventories, $40,000; prepaid insurance, $4,000; equipment, $98,000. The notes payable are secured by the equipment. Costs estimated to be incurred if liquidation materializes are $18,000.

Required:

Prepare a report which will indicate to the general creditors the advisability of accepting the offer of the Deake Co. officials, or starting liquidation proceedings.

APPENDIX

Actuarial science

An understanding of the basic ideas involved in actuarial science as applied to accounting is essential if the accountant is to perform with maximum effectiveness in his profession. Actuarial science is the mathematical science based upon compound interest and upon insurance probabilities. In accounting most of the applications of actuarial science are concerned with compound interest and with annuities. In several areas of this textbook it is assumed that the student has a working knowledge of compound interest and annuities. For those students not familiar with actuarial science as applied to accounting, it seems appropriate to provide at this point an elementary discussion of the essentials of compound interest and annuities. Students who have had previous exposure to the mathematics of finance should have less need for a thorough study of the following material.

INTEREST

Interest may be defined as the payment for the use of money. In this sense it represents an excess payment over and above the principal loaned or borrowed. For example, if A were to loan B $1,000 with the understanding that B would repay $1,100, the excess over $1,000 would represent interest, computed as follows:

Proceeds from loan	$1,100
Amount loaned	1,000
Interest on loan	$ 100

The amount of interest to be paid is generally stated as a rate over a specific period of time. For example, if B were to have the use of the money for 1 year before repaying the principal plus interest, the rate of interest would be 10% per year. That is, the interest is 10% of the principal each year. The custom of expressing interest as a rate is well established. In fact, decisions are made on the basis of the *rate* of interest involved rather than on the actual dollar amount of interest which will have to be paid.

Rate of Interest. The period of 1 year is rather well established as the period to which the rate of interest applies. Thus, a rate of interest of 6% is assumed to represent a rate of 6% per year unless stipulated otherwise. In fact, the statement that a company will pay bond interest of 6%, payable semi-annually, means a rate of 3% every 6 months, not 6% each 6 months. There is no necessary reason, of course, why the rate must be expressed at so much a year. In fact, some small finance companies generally refer to their interest rate as 1% per month to give an appearance of a low rate when it really represents a rate of around 12% a year.

To illustrate the difference in the manner in which interest rates are expressed, assume A borrowed $1,000 in cash with an interest rate of 12% payable at the end of the year, and that B borrowed $1,000 with an interest rate of 1% per month payable at the end of each month. The total repayment required to settle the debt would be:

	A	B
Payable during year:		
11 payments at $10		$ 110
Payable at end of year:		
1 payment at $10		10
1 payment at $120	$ 120	
Principal borrowed	1,000	1,000
Total payment	$1,120	$1,120

Actually, it may be noted that A will have a slight advantage over B in that A gets to keep the entire $1,000 borrowed until the end of the year, whereas B has to use $110 for interest payments during the year.

Simple Interest

Simple interest is the term used to describe interest that is computed on the amount of the principal only. The illustrations in the above sections were in terms of simple interest, since the rate was always applied to the principal. For example, if the $1,000 A borrowed in the illustration above were for a 5-year period, with a simple interest rate of 12% per year, the total interest A would have to pay would be $600 ($120 times 5 years).

Symbols for Simple Interest. The following symbols are commonly used in presenting data on simple interest:

i—rate of interest for a single period.
n—number of periods.
P—principal.

If i equals the rate of interest per period of time, n the number of periods, and P the principal, simple interest on a sum of money may be expressed as:

$$\text{Interest} = P \times i \times n$$

In the above illustration of a rate of 1% per month for 1 year, the computation would be:

$$\begin{aligned} \text{Interest} &= \$1,000 \times .01 \times 12 \\ &= \$1,000 \times .12 \\ &= \$120 \end{aligned}$$

Compound Interest

Simple interest, as indicated above, is interest on principal only. Compound interest is the term used to describe interest that is computed on principal and on any interest earned which has not been paid. To illustrate the difference, assume you borrow $1,000 from Bank A agreeing to pay simple interest of 6% per year, and you borrow another $1,000 from Bank B agreeing to pay compound interest of 6% per year compounded annually. Assume you pay no interest until the maturity date of the loan, which may be assumed to be 3 years. The calculation of the interest to be paid would be as follows:

		Simple Interest Bank A	Compound Interest Bank B
First year	($ 1,000 × 6%)	$ 60.00	$ 60.00
Second year	($ 1,000 × 6%)	60.00	60.00
	($ 60 × 6%)	...	3.60
Third year	($ 1,000 × 6%)	60.00	60.00
	($123.60 × 6%)	...	7.42
Total interest, 3-year period		$180.00	$191.02

The amount of compound interest in the above illustration is $191.02, whereas the amount of simple interest is only $180. The difference in amounts is due to the calculation of interest on interest in the case of the compound interest. Compound interest is the type of interest normally used in business. For practical purposes in computing compound interest, it may be assumed that unpaid interest earned becomes a part of the principal and is entitled to interest. In the above illustration, the computation of compound interest under this assumption would be:

	Principal	Interest Rate	Amount
First year	$1,000	6%	$ 60.00
Second year	$1,060 (1,000 plus 60)	6%	63.60
Third year	$1,123.60 (1,000 plus 60 plus 63.60)	6%	67.42
Total interest			$191.02

Compound Interest Tables. Every loan made by a lender is made on the assumption that the lender will receive back the principal loaned plus any interest. Each period the loan is outstanding the amount due increases by the amount of interest. Thus if $1.00 is loaned at a rate of 6% per year, the $1.00 will increase to $1.06 at the end of the year. Each subsequent year the previous amount due will increase to 1.06 of the amount due at the beginning of the period. In compound interest terminology, 1 plus the rate of interest expressed as a decimal (.06) gives the *ratio of increase*. Under compound interest, the interest is computed on the balance of principal and interest accumulated at the end of the previous period, so that the second year's interest will be 6% of the $1.06 to which the amount due had accumulated at the end of the first year. Stated another way, the ratio of increase for the 2 periods may be multiplied together to get the ratio of increase for the 2-year period as one amount. To illustrate:

Ratio of increase—1st year	1.06
Ratio of increase—2nd year	1.06
	636
	000
	106
Ratio of increase for 2 years	1.1236

As proof of this, assume Mr. A puts $1.00 on deposit to receive compound interest of 6% compounded annually and that he leaves the money on deposit for 2 years.

Principal	$1.00
Interest—1st year ($1.00 @ 6%)	.06
Interest—2nd year ($1.06 @ 6%)	.0636
Total amount due at end of 2 years	$1.1236

Using the computed ratio of increase, the amount to which the $1.00 will accumulate may be computed by multiplying $1.00 directly by 1.1236 to arrive at the $1.1236. Since there is a need on the part of a great number of people to know how much a sum invested at a certain rate of compound interest will amount to over a period of time, tables have been constructed to show how much $1 invested at various compound rates of interest will amount to at the end of various periods. Compound interest tables are presented at the end of this appendix. The excerpt below illustrates the nature of such tables by showing the amount of 1 at the end of each of the periods given.

AMOUNT OF 1 AT COMPOUND INTEREST

Periods	3%	4%	5%
1	1.030000	1.040000	1.050000
2	1.060900	1.081600	1.102500
3	1.092727	1.124864	1.157625
4	1.125509	1.169859	1.215506
5	1.159274	1.216653	1.276282

Interpreting the table, if $1.00 is invested for 3 periods at a compound interest rate of 3% per period, the $1.00 will amount to $1.09 (1.092727 × $1.00); if the investment were for 5 periods it would amount to $1.16. If $1 were invested at 5%, at the end of 4 periods, it would amount to $1.22; at the end of 5 periods it would equal $1.28. If the investment were $100 instead of $1.00, the amounts would be as follows:

If invested for 3 periods at 3% ($100 × 1.092727) = $109.27.
If invested for 4 periods at 5% ($100 × 1.215506) = $121.55.
If invested for 5 periods at 4% ($100 × 1.216653) = $121.67.

For any sum invested, the amount to which 1 would accumulate may be multiplied by the amount invested to determine the amount to which the sum invested would accumulate.

Symbols for Compound Interest. The following symbols are commonly used in presenting data on compound interest:

i—rate of interest for a single period.
n—number of periods.
r—periodic ratio of increase (1 plus i).
s—compound amount of 1.
P—principal.

Amount of 1

Frequently an individual or a business enterprise which has an amount available for investment will desire to know how much the investment will accumulate to at a given rate of interest compounded periodically. The amount to which 1 will accumulate may be expressed as a formula:

$$s = (1 + i)^n$$

To illustrate, assume $1.00 is invested at 6% interest for 3 periods. The amounts to which the $1.00 will accumulate at the end of each period are expressed as follows:

$s = (1.06)^1$ for the end of the 1st period.
$s = (1.06)^2$ for the end of the 2nd period.
$s = (1.06)^3$ for the end of the 3rd period.

If tables are available, there is no need to apply the formula, since the formula is the basis for the construction of the table.

Amount of 1 Tables. In using the tables for the amount of 1, care must be exercised to distinguish between the stated rate of interest per year and the actual rate of interest per period implicit in a given problem. Thus a loan which stipulates a stated rate of interest of 6% per year, the interest compounded twice a year for 10 years, is in reality a loan at an interest rate of 3% per period for 20 periods. Assuming the loan is for $1,000 at the end of the 10-year period the amount payable would be equal to:

$1,000 × amount of 1 for 20 periods at 3%,
(1.80611123), or a total of $1,806.11.

It would be incorrect to compute the future amount of the $1,000 at the stated rate of 6% per year for 10 years. Using the 6% rate for 10 years, the incorrect computation would be:

$1,000 × amount of 1 for 10 years at 6%,
(1.79084770), or a total of $1,790.85.

Because the amount is compounded semi-annually rather than annually, the future amount is $15.26 ($1,806.11 − $1,790.85) greater.

As the foregoing illustration indicates, the number of *periods* involved in a computation is not merely the number of *years* involved in the investment. For example, $1,000 invested at 6% per year compounded *monthly* for 5 years, represents 60 periods (5 × 12) at $\frac{1}{2}$% interest per period.

EXAMPLE

QUESTION: What amount will be accumulated in 5 years if $400 is loaned at 6% compounded quarterly?

Solution: Since the interest is compounded quarterly, the stated rate of 6% per year becomes an actual rate of $1\frac{1}{2}$% per quarterly period (6% divided by 4). Likewise, the 5-year period becomes 20 periods on a quarterly basis. To compute the amount to which $400 would accumulate in 5 years at 6% compounded quarterly, select the amount of 1 table for which the interest rate is $1\frac{1}{2}$% and determine the amount in this table for 20 periods. This amount would be 1.34685501 (the amount of 1 for 20 periods at $1\frac{1}{2}\%$ interest) and when it is multiplied by \$400, the result is \$538.74, or the amount to which \$400 would accumulate in 5 years at 6% interest compounded quarterly.

Present Value of 1

Sometimes an individual desires to know how much should be deposited now to amount to a given sum in the future. Thus, if an individual needs \$1,000 in 10 years, and if the current rate of interest at which money can be invested is 6% per year, the problem is to determine how much he would have to invest now to have \$1,000 in 10 years. This type of problem is known as the determination of the *present value* of a future amount. The present value is always a smaller amount than the known future amount because interest will be earned and accumulated on the present value to the future date.

The present value of an amount may be computed by dividing 1 by the amount of 1 for a like number of periods and a like rate of interest and multiplying the result by the known future amount. To illustrate, assume \$1,000 is needed in 10 years and funds can be invested currently at 6% per year. Using the table of amount of 1, it can be seen that \$1.00 invested for 10 periods at 6% will equal \$1.79084770. If \$1.00 is divided by this amount (1.79084770), the result equals the present value of 1 due in 10 years if invested at 6% per year, or \$0.55839478. This means that an investment of approximately \$0.56 now at 6% will equal approximately \$1.00 in 10 years. Since \$1,000 is needed, the amount to be invested would be 1,000 times \$0.55839478 or \$558.39.

Present Value of 1 Tables. Because there is frequently need for quick computations of present values, tables have been developed showing how much would have to be invested at various compound interest rates for various periods of time to equal 1 at a future date. Excerpts from such tables are illustrated below, and more complete tables appear at the end of this appendix:

PRESENT VALUE OF 1 AT COMPOUND INTEREST

Periods	3%	4%	5%
1	0.97087379	0.96153846	0.95238095
2	0.94259591	0.92455621	0.90702948
3	0.91514166	0.88899636	0.86383760
4	0.88848705	0.85480419	0.82270247
5	0.86260878	0.82192711	0.78352617

The present value of 1 tables may be constructed from the general formula:

$$v = 1 \div s$$

where s is the amount of 1 and v is the present value of 1. To illustrate, assume that it is desired to determine the present value of $1 at compound interest of 5% for 4 periods. Referring to the amount of 1 table on p. 731, the amount of 1 at 5% compound interest for 4 periods = 1.215506. To determine the present value, the above formula becomes:

$$v = \frac{1}{1.215506} = \$0.82270247$$

or the amount which must be invested now to equal $1.00 in 4 years at 5% compound interest. In the above table this same amount may be found in the 5% column on the 4-period line.

The tables of present value give the amount which would have to be invested at a specified rate of interest for a period of time to equal 1 at the end of the period of time. For example, the table indicates that an investment of 0.86383760 at 5% for 3 years will equal 1. As proof of the table a computation may be made of the increase which would take place each period to see if the accumulation would amount to 1 at the end of the 3-year period, as follows:

Present value at start of investment	0.86383760
Interest—1st year (5% × 0.86383760)	0.04319188
Value at end of 1st year	0.90702948
Interest—2nd year (5% × 0.90702948)	0.04535147
Value at end of 2nd year	0.95238095
Interest—3rd year (5% × 0.95238095)	0.04761905
Value at end of 3rd year	1.00000000

To illustrate the use of the table, assume a young man has the opportunity to make a substantial investment now at 6% interest compounded annually for a 42-year period. At the end of the 42-year period, the young man plans to retire. He has decided he will require $100,000 to meet his retirement needs. He wants to know how much he should invest now in order to have the $100,000 at the end of the 42 years. By referring to the tables of present value, he would find that approximately $0.08 (0.08652740) invested now will yield $1.00 in 42 years. Since he needs $100,000 instead of $1.00, he must multiply the 0.08652740 by $100,000. The multiplication indicates he should invest $8,652.74 now in order to have the needed $100,000 at retirement time.

ANNUITIES

Life insurance companies have made a great contribution to the American way of life by encouraging people to save a regular sum of money. That is, a person may pay a premium every week, month, quarter, or year which then accumulates to a given amount at the end of a specified number of periods. Such a process of periodic saving represents the accumulation through an annuity of a sum of money. By definition an annuity is a series of equal payments made at equal intervals of time. It should be emphasized that an annuity requires that the periodic payment always be the same amount and that the interval between payments always be the same.

Amount of an Annuity

The amount of an annuity is the sum of the payments (called rents) and the accumulated compound interest on them. To illustrate, assume a man starts an annuity of $1,000 a year for 3 years and earns on all investments 5% compound interest. An annuity of $1,000 a year means that this sum is invested each year for 3 years. It should be noted that the annual $1,000 investment may be made at either the *beginning* or the *end* of the year. To distinguish annuity investments under these two alternatives, an annuity is classified as either an *ordinary annuity* or an *annuity due*.

In an ordinary annuity, the payments are made at the *end* of the period. In an annuity due, the payments are made at the *beginning* of the period.

The distinction between the two kinds of annuities may be noted by the solution to the illustration noted above, as follows:

	Ordinary Annuity	Annuity Due
1st year's investment	$1,000.00	$1,000.00
1st year's interest	0	50.00
Balance at end of 1st year	$1,000.00	$1,050.00
2nd year's investment	1,000.00	1,000.00
2nd year's interest:		
$1,000 @ 5%	50.00	
$2,050 @ 5%		102.50
Balance at end of 2nd year	$2,050.00	$2,152.50
3rd year's investment	1,000.00	1,000.00
3rd year's interest:		
$2,050 @ 5%	102.50	
$3,152.50 @ 5%		157.63
Balance at end of 3rd year	$3,152.50	$3,310.13

Thus, the amount to which an annuity of $1,000 a year for 3 years at 5% will accumulate will depend upon whether it is an ordinary annuity or an annuity due. When investments are made during the middle of a calendar year, they are converted to an ordinary annuity or to an annuity due by using a fiscal year starting at the time of the investment, rather than a regular calendar year, so that the annual payment falls either at the end (ordinary annuity) or at the beginning (annuity due) of the fiscal year.

Annuity Tables. Tables have been developed similar to those used for the amount of 1 and the present value of 1 for both an ordinary annuity and an annuity due. Because an annuity due table is easily constructed from an ordinary annuity table, this textbook presents only tables for an ordinary annuity. An explanation of the process for converting an ordinary annuity table into a table for an annuity due will be presented later.

An understanding of annuities requires familiarity with the method by which compound interest tables are constructed. It will be recalled that the amount of 1 table was constructed from the general formula:

$$s = (1 + i)^n$$

Thus, if $1.00 is deposited for 4 periods at 5%, the formula becomes $s = (1.05)^4$ or $(1.05 \times 1.05 \times 1.05 \times 1.05)$ which gives 1.21550625 (the amount indicated in the amount of 1 table) or approximately $1.22.

The table for an ordinary annuity of 1 can be constructed from an amount of 1 table. The procedure is:

(1) Determine the compound amount of 1 at the given rate of interest for the number of periods involved, using the formula $s = (1 + i)^n$, or find this amount in the amount of 1 table.
(2) Compute the compound interest by subtracting 1 from the amount derived in step (1). In formula form this is $I = s - 1$.
(3) Divide the compound interest (I) by the interest rate (i) to obtain the amount of the annuity of 1. The formula is: $I \div (i) = (s_{ni})$, where s_{ni} represents the amount of an annuity of 1 for n periods at i rate of interest.
(4) Multiply the amount of an annuity of 1 by the number of dollars in each rent. In formula form this is: $R \times s_{ni}$, where R equals the amount of each rent.

EXAMPLE

QUESTION: To what amount will an ordinary annuity of $1 for 4 periods at 5% accumulate?

Solution: From the table of amount of 1:

(1) Amount of 1 for 4 periods at 5%	1.215506
(2) Deduct 1	−1.000000
(2) Compound interest	.215506
(3) Divide by the interest rate	.05
(3) Amount of annuity of 1 for 4 periods at 5%	4.310125

A table of the amount of an annuity of 1 which might be constructed from a series of solutions similar to that illustrated above is shown below:

AMOUNT OF ANNUITY OF 1

Periods	3%	4%	5%
1	1.000000	1.000000	1.000000
2	2.030000	2.040000	2.050000
3	3.090900	3.121600	3.152500
4	4.183627	4.246464	4.310125
5	5.309136	5.416323	5.525631

Relation of Compound Interest and Annuities

An analysis of compound interest tables reveals that the amount of 1 table is composed of three elements:

(1) The principal of 1.
(2) The annual regular addition of simple interest on the principal.
(3) The interest on the interest.

This may be illustrated by the following tabulation, on a 5% basis:

	Principal	Simple Interest	Interest on Interest	Total
Investment beginning of period	1.000000			1.000000
1st period:				
Simple interest		.0500		.050000
Interest on interest			...	
2nd period:				
Simple interest		.0500		.050000
Interest on interest			.0025	.002500
3rd period:				
Simple interest		.0500		.050000
Interest on interest			.005125	.005125
4th period:				
Simple interest		.0500		.050000
Interest on interest			.007881	.007881
Total	1.000000	.200000	.015506	1.215506

The sum of the three elements, 1.215506, agrees with the amount in the table of the amount of 1 for 4 periods at 5%. If the principal is deducted from this amount, the remainder is the compound interest (I) of .215506. From the tabulation it can be seen that the .215506 is accumulated by regular deposits of simple interest of $.05 each period, plus interest on the deposits. Compound interest is thus the same as an annuity of .05 each period of time. If an annuity of .05 equals a total of .215506 in 4 periods if invested at 5%, it may be concluded that an annuity of 1 could be computed by dividing the accumulation of .215506 by .05. The result would be 4.310125, which is the amount of an annuity of 1 for 4 periods at 5%. A review of this analysis will show that it followed the steps set forth in the preceding section for developing a table of an amount of ordinary annuity of 1.

Amount of an Annuity of I Tables. The uses to which an amount of an ordinary annuity table may be applied are extensive. Listed below are two illustrations of the use of annuity tables in the business world.

(1) How much should a young man deposit each year for 30 years if he wants to have $100,000 at the end of the period and if he can invest all deposits at 5% interest compounded annually?

According to the amount of an ordinary annuity table, if he were to deposit $1.00 a period for 30 periods at 5%, he would have a total of $66.43884750. If $1.00 a period gives him over $66, he may divide the $100,000 by $66.43884750 and determine that the annual deposit he should make would be $1,505.14.

(2) A borrower promises to pay back to a lender the sum of $100,000 in 30 years, if the lender will lend him $2,000 a year at the end of each year. What rate of interest would the lender earn on the investment assuming yearly compounding?

Dividing the $100,000 by 2,000, it can be seen that $1 loaned each period will return a total of $50 at the end of the 30 years. Referring to the table of the amount of an annuity of 1, it can be seen that for 30 periods at a rate of 3%, the $1 annuity would yield $47.58, whereas a rate of $3\frac{1}{2}$% will yield $51.62. If each of the values in the table is multiplied by $2,000 the following results are obtained:

At 3%, an annuity of $2,000 will yield $95,150.83.
At $3\frac{1}{2}$%, an annuity of $2,000 will yield $103,245.35.

From this, by interpolation an approximation from the table shows that the lender would obtain a rate of return on his investment of between 3% and $3\frac{1}{2}$%.

Relationship of Annuity Due to Ordinary Annuity Table. It has been noted that under an annuity due the periodic payments, termed "rents" in actuarial terminology, are made at the beginning of the period. Payments under an ordinary annuity are made at the end of the period. This means an annuity due will accumulate interest on the first year's payment in the first year, whereas an ordinary annuity payment will earn no interest during the first year. Stated in general terms, the periodic interest earnings under an ordinary annuity will always be less by one period's interest than the interest earned by an annuity due. To illustrate the relationship of the two types of annuities, the following tabulated comparison accumulates the interest and payments of $1,000 a period for 5 periods at 6%.

Period	ORDINARY ANNUITY			ANNUITY DUE		
	Payment	Interest	End of Period Accumulation	Payment	Interest	End of Period Accumulation
1	$1,000	$ 0	$1,000.00	$1,000	$ 60.00	$1,060.00
2	1,000	60.00	2,060.00	1,000	123.60	2,183.60
3	1,000	123.60	3,183.60	1,000	191.02	3,374.62
4	1,000	191.02	4,374.62	1,000	262.48	4,637.10
5	1,000	262.48	5,637.10	1,000	338.23	5,975.33

The illustration emphasizes the fact that an ordinary annuity for 5 periods earns interest for only 4 periods. This is so because the payments are always made at the end of the period. The annuity due, however, earns 4 periods' interest in 4 periods. This relationship suggests the basis for converting an ordinary annuity table to an annuity due table. If the last rent payment in an ordinary annuity is deducted from the end of period accumulation, the residual will represent the amount of an annuity due for 1 less period. For example, if 1 payment is deducted from the ordinary annuity of 5 periods at 6%, in the preceding illustration, the result will be the amount of an annuity due of 4 periods at 6%, as follows:

(1) Amount of ordinary annuity of $1,000 a period for 5 periods at 6% $5,637.10

(2) Deduct last payment   1,000.00

(3) Amount of annuity due of $1,000 a period for 4 periods at 6% $4,637.10

EXAMPLE

PROBLEM: Convert a table of the amount of an ordinary annuity of 1 to a table of the amount of an annuity due of 1 for 4 periods at an interest rate of 4%.

Solution:

Ordinary Annuity			Annuity Due	
1st period	1.000000			
2nd period	2.040000	−1	1st period	1.040000
3rd period	3.121600	−1	2nd period	2.121600
4th period	4.246464	−1	3rd period	3.246464
5th period	5.416323	−1	4th period	4.416323

Use of Annuity Due Illustrated. Mr. Zim plans to deposit $2,000 a year on each birthday, starting with his 35th birthday, at 3% interest compounded annually. He wants to know the amount he will have accumulated on his 65th birthday. He plans to make no payment on his 65th birthday.

Since the first payment is made on his 35th birthday, he will make a total of 30 payments over the life of the annuity. These payments will all be made at the beginning of the periods, so the payments represent an annuity due.

Referring to the amount of an ordinary annuity for 31 periods at 3% and deducting 1 to arrive at the annuity due for 30 periods, the solution would be as follows:

(1) Amount of an ordinary annuity of 1 for 31 periods at 3%	50.00267818
(2) Deduct 1 payment	1.00000000
(3) Amount of an annuity due of 1 for 30 periods at 3%	49.00267818
(4) Periodic payment	× $2,000
(5) Accumulated amount on 65th birthday	$98,005.36

Present Value of an Annuity

A simple way to look at the idea of the present value of an annuity is to consider what lump sum needs to be deposited now at a specified rate of interest in order to receive back an annuity of so much a period for so many periods. More formally, the present value of an ordinary annuity is the sum which, if earning compound interest, will provide the periodic rents of an annuity contract as they become due. The present value is always computed as of the beginning of the first period.

Computing Present Value of an Annuity—Method One. The future payments to be received as an annuity may be treated individually as the present value of a series of separate amounts. For example, an annuity of $1.00 a year to be received at the end of each year for 5 years may be looked upon as separate amounts and the present value of each computed from the table of present value of 1. If the interest rate is 6%, the present value of the above annuity might be computed as follows:

End of Year in Which $1.00 Is to Be Received

Present Value	1	2	3	4	5
$ .9434	$1.00				
.8900		$1.00			
.8396			$1.00		
.7921				$1.00	
.7473					$1.00
$4.2124	Total (Present value of annuity of $1.00 for 5 periods at 6% interest rate)				

Computing Present Value of an Annuity—Method Two. Method one, a variation of which can also be used for computing the amount of an annuity by using an amount of 1 table, becomes cumbersome and subject to error if the annuity covers a great number of periods. As a consequence, method two is often used. The procedure under this method is as follows:

1. Compute the compound discount (D) on 1 (this is the difference between 1 and the present value of 1) for the number of periods involved at the stated rate of interest. The formula to be used is: $(1 - v^n) = D$, where v^n represents the present value of 1 and may be taken from the table of present value of 1.

2. Divide the compound discount by the rate of interest used. The quotient will be the present value of an annuity of 1. The formula is: $D \div i = a_{ni}$, where a_{ni} represents the present value of an annuity of 1 for n periods at i rate of interest.

3. Multiply the present value of the annuity of 1 by the number of dollars in each rent. In formula form, this is: $R \times a_{ni}$.

EXAMPLE

QUESTION: What amount should be deposited now at 4% annual interest to receive an annuity of $3,000 a year, starting at the end of the first year, for 15 years?

Solution:

(1) Start with 1	1.000000
(1) Deduct the present value of 1 at 4% for 15 years (v^{15})	.555265
(1) Compound discount (D)	.444735
(2) Rate of interest (i)	.04
(2) Present value of ordinary annuity of 1 at 4% for 15 years (D divided by i)	11.118387
(3) Number of dollars in each rent (R)	3,000
(3) Present value of annuity of $3,000 at 4% for 15 periods	$33,355.16

Construction of Present Value of Annuity of 1 Table. A table of present value of an annuity of 1 may be constructed quite easily by method two, as illustrated below:

Period	Table of present value of 1 at 4%	D, or $(1 - v^n)$	Divide by i	Present value of ordinary annuity of 1 at 4%
1	.961538	.038462	.04	.961538
2	.924556	.075444	.04	1.886100
3	.888996	.111004	.04	2.775100
4	.854804	.145196	.04	3.629900

From several calculations such as this for various rates of interest and periods, the table may be constructed. Excerpts from such a table are illustrated below:

PRESENT VALUE OF ANNUITY OF 1

Periods	3%	4%	5%
1	.970874	.961538	.952381
2	1.913470	1.886095	1.859410
3	2.828611	2.775091	2.723248
4	3.717098	3.629895	3.545951
5	4.579707	4.451822	4.329477

Present Value of Ordinary Annuity of I Table. Illustrative of the many uses to which a table of present value of an ordinary annuity of 1 may be applied is the following example:

Mr. X died leaving to his wife an insurance policy contract which provided that the beneficiary (the wife) could choose any one of the three following options:

(a) $100 every three months payable at the end of each quarter, for 12 years.

(b) $1,000 immediate cash and $100 every three months for 9 years.

(c) $200 every three months for 3 years and $100 a quarter for the following 26 quarters.

If money is worth 1% per quarter, compounded quarterly, which option should the wife exercise?

Solution:

	OPTION		
	a	b	c
(1) Immediate cash	–0–	$1,000.00	–0–
(2) P.v. of $100 a quarter for 48 quarters at 1% interest per quarter	$3,797.40	–0–	–0–
(3) P.v. of $100 a quarter for 36 quarters at 1% interest per quarter	–0–	3,010.75	–0–
(4) P.v. of $100 a quarter for 38 quarters at 1% interest per quarter	–0–	–0–	$3,148.47
(5) P.v. of $100 a quarter for 12 quarters at 1% interest per quarter	–0–	–0–	1,125.51
Present value of option	$3,797.40	$4,010.75	$4,273.98

From the above facts option (c) appears to be the best option, based on the dollar amounts involved.

Present Value of an Annuity Due. In an annuity due, payments or withdrawals are made at the beginning of the period. As a result in the present value of an annuity due the first withdrawal will be withdrawn immediately and will have no opportunity to earn interest. The second withdrawal will have earned interest for one period before it is withdrawn at the start of the second period. In an ordinary annuity, however, because withdrawal takes place at the end of the period, the first withdrawal will have earned interest for one period before it is withdrawn. This means a smaller deposit will have to be made for the first period's withdrawal in an ordinary annuity than in an annuity due. The difference between the interest accumulations may be illustrated by noting the interest periods in each annuity, as follows:

	Ordinary Annuity	Annuity Due
Initial deposit (present value)	xxxxxxxx	xxxxxxxx
Beginning of period—1st withdrawal		1.00
Interest on 1st withdrawal	yes	no
End of period—1st withdrawal	1.00	
Beginning of 2nd period withdrawal		1.00
Interest on 2nd withdrawal	yes	yes
End of 2nd period withdrawal	1.00	

The presentation illustrates that in an ordinary annuity which is to be withdrawn, the number of interest periods and the number of withdrawals are the same (two in the illustration), whereas in an annuity due, the number of interest periods is always one less than the number of withdrawals. This suggests the basis for converting a table of present value of an ordinary annuity of 1 to a table of present value of an annuity due of 1. The procedure would involve adding 1 withdrawal to the present value of an ordinary annuity of one less period than that of the annuity due as follows:

Present value of an ordinary annuity of 1 for 5 rents at 6%	4.212364
Add 1	1.000000
Present value of an annuity due of 1 for 6 rents at 6%	5.212364

The steps in computing the present value of an annuity due are:
(1) Compute, or take from a table, the present value of an ordinary annuity of 1 at the specified rate of interest for one less period than the desired number of annuity periods.

(2) To the result of (1) add 1. The result is the present value of an annuity due of 1 for the desired number of periods.

(3) Multiply the present value of an annuity due of 1 by the number of dollars in each rent.

EXAMPLE

PROBLEM: Convert a table of the present value of an ordinary annuity of 1 to a table of the present value of an annuity due of 1 for 6 periods at an interest rate of 4%.

Solution:

Ordinary Annuity			Annuity Due	
		+1	1st period	1.000000
1st period	.961538	+1	2nd period	1.961538
2nd period	1.886095	+1	3rd period	2.886095
3rd period	2.775091	+1	4th period	3.775091
4th period	3.629895	+1	5th period	4.629895
5th period	4.451822	+1	6th period	5.451822

Use of Present Value of an Annuity Due. Typical of the use of present value of an annuity is the situation in which a homeowner buys a home and mortgages it, for example, for $18,000 at 5% a year interest under a direct-reduction type of loan, so that the mortgage is to be paid off in 15 annual payments of equal amounts. The first payment is to be made immediately. The problem is to determine the amount of the equal annual payments which is required.

From a table of present value of an ordinary annuity of 1:

(1) Determine the present value of 14 rents of 1 at 5%   9.898641
(2) Add   1.000000
                                                                                      ──────────
(3) Present value of an annuity due of 1 for 15 periods
      at 5%   10.898641

(4) If $10.898641 is the present value of an annuity of $1.00 for 15 periods at 5%, to determine the amount of the periodic rent of an annuity due for 15 periods at 5% for which the present value is $18,000, divide the $18,000 by $10.898641. The result is $1,651.59, the amount of each annual payment, and the first payment is due immediately.

Summary of Compound Interest Tables

(1) An amount of 1 table indicates the amount to which 1 will accumulate if it is deposited now at a specified rate of interest and left for a specified number of periods.

(2) A present value of 1 table indicates the amount which must be deposited now at a specified rate of interest to amount to 1 at the end of a specified number of periods.

(3) An amount of an annuity of 1 table indicates the amount to which periodic payments of 1 will accumulate if the payments are invested at a specified rate of interest and are continued for a specified number of periods. If the payment is made at the start of each period the series of payments is called an annuity due; if made at the end of each period, an ordinary annuity.

(4) A present value of an annuity of 1 table indicates the amount which must be deposited now at a specified rate of interest to permit withdrawals of 1 at regular periodic intervals for the specified number of periods. If withdrawal is made at the start of each period, the annuity is called an annuity due; if made at the end of each period, an ordinary annuity.

Various combinations of these tables may be used to solve such problems as (1) deferred annuities, (2) the price to pay for a bond, (3) sinking fund accumulations, (4) annuity method of depreciation, (5) valuation of leaseholds, and (6) amortization of a variety of investments.

SPECIAL APPLICATIONS

Deferred Annuity

A deferred annuity is an annuity in which the periodic payments are deferred a specified number of periods before the initial payment is made. Thus a deferred annuity of 10 periods deferred 6 periods means the annuity will not start for 6 periods.

The amount of a deferred annuity is identical to the amount of an annuity which is not deferred. This is so because the amount of any annuity does not begin to accumulate until the initial payment is made, and the initial payment in a deferred annuity will not be made until the deferred periods have passed.

The present value of a deferred annuity is the value now of an annuity in which the initial payment will be made later. Thus, it involves a deposit now, a waiting period, and then the start of the withdrawal payments. The present value of a deferred annuity will not be identical to the present value of an annuity which is not deferred, as the following two methods for computing the present value of a deferred annuity will indicate.

Method One

(1) Select from the table the present value of an ordinary annuity of 1 at the specified rate and the number of periods for which payments are to be made.
(2) Multiply the result of (1) by the amount of each rent.
(3) Multiply the result of (2) by the present value of 1 for the number of deferred periods.

ILLUSTRATION. Determine the present value of an annuity of $1,000 a year for 12 years at 6% deferred 5 years.

(1) P.v. of ordinary annuity of 1 for 12 periods at 6%	8.383844
(2) Amount of each rent	$1,000
(2) P.v. of ordinary annuity of $1,000 for 12 periods at 6%	$8,383.84
(3) P.v. of 1 at 6% for 5 periods	.747258
(3) P.v. of annuity of $1,000 a period for 12 periods at 6% deferred 5 periods ($8,383.84 multiplied by .747258)	$6,264.89

Method Two

(1) Select from the table the present value of an ordinary annuity of 1 at the specified rate and the number of periods equal to the sum of the deferred periods and the payment periods.
(2) Select from the table the present value of an ordinary annuity of 1 at the specified rate and number of periods equal to the deferred periods.
(3) Subtract (2) from (1).
(4) Multiply (3) by the amount of each payment (rent).

ILLUSTRATION. Determine the present value of an annuity of $1,000 a year for 12 years at 6% deferred 5 years.

(1) P.v. of ordinary annuity of 1 for 17 years at 6%	10.477260
(2) P.v. of ordinary annuity of 1 for 5 years at 6%	4.212364
(3) P.v. of ordinary annuity of 1 for 12 periods at 6% deferred 5 periods	6.264896
(4) Annual rent	$1,000
(4) P.v. of ordinary annuity of $1,000 for 12 years at 6% deferred 5 years	$6,264.89

Computing the Price of a Bond

Bonds are normally issued with a promise (1) to pay at a designated future date a stated sum of money called the par, maturity, or face value of the bond, and (2) to pay at regular intervals cash interest computed as a specified per cent of the face of the bond. The cash interest paid at the regular intervals is referred to as the "nominal" rate of interest.

The proper price to pay for a bond depends not upon the par or face value of the bond but upon the present value of the interest annuity and the present value of the par, maturity, or face value which the bond will provide.

To illustrate, assume the SAF Board Company issues a $1,000, 5% bond on April 1, 1960, due on April 1, 1980, with interest payable each October 1 and April 1. At the time the bond is issued investors may be earning more or less than the nominal rate which the SAF bond is to pay. If investors are earning 3% every six months on investments of risk comparable to that of the SAF bond, investors will not pay $1,000 for the SAF bond. If an investor did pay $1,000 for the bond, he would earn only $2\frac{1}{2}$% interest every six months. To realize an effective rate of interest of 3% every six months on a SAF bond the investor would have to pay something less than $1,000.

The solution to the problem of the appropriate price for the bond rests on the realization that ownership of the bond will provide $1,000 on April 1, 1980 plus $25 every six months for the 20-year period. Since the investor wants to earn 3% every six months on the investment, the price of the bond will be the present value of the future $1,000 plus the present value of the $25 annuity of 40 six-month periods. The process of discounting these amounts at 3% every six months is presented below:

(1) P.v. of $1,000 discounted at 3% for 40 periods:

P.v. of 1 @ 3% for 40 periods		.306557	
Times		$ 1,000	$306.56

(2) P.v. of annuity of $25 for 40 periods at 3%:

P.v. of annuity of 1 at 3% for 40 periods		23.11477	
Times		$ 25	577.87

Price to be paid for a $1,000, 5% bond to yield an effective rate of return of 3% every 6 months for 40 periods $884.43

Accounting for Bond Amortization—Effective Rate Method.

Proper accounting requires that the premium or discount, the difference between the face of the bond ($1,000) and the price of the bond ($884.43), be amortized over the life of the bond. The amount involved ($115.57) may be amortized on a straight-line basis, in which case the total discount ($115.57) or premium will be divided by the number of periods before maturity of the bonds (40 periods) to determine the amount to write off each period ($2.89 each six months). The entry to amortize the discount each period and to recognize the cash interest received would be:

Cash	$25.00	
Bond investment	2.89	
Interest income		$27.89

While the straight line method of amortization is widely used in accounting practice, a more accurate procedure and one that is used by many investors with large holdings of bonds is the effective rate method of amortization.

The effective rate method for amortizing bond discount or bond premium is based on the realization that bond interest income, or bond interest expense in the case of the issuing company, should be computed at the effective rate at which the bonds were purchased or issued. In the preceding illustration, the bond was purchased to yield 3% every six months on the money invested. For the first six months this would be 3% of $884.43, or $26.53. Since only $25 of this income would be in cash, the remaining $1.53 would represent the amortization of the discount for that period. The entry to record the interest for the six months would be:

Cash	$25.00	
Bond investment	1.53	
Interest income		$26.53

At the start of the second six-month period, the bond would be carried at $885.96 ($884.43 plus $1.53), and the second six months' interest income would be 3% of $885.96, or $26.58. This income would be recorded in a manner similar to that shown for the first six-month period. If the procedure of the effective rate method is followed carefully, the amortization of the bond discount in the 40th six-month period will bring the bond up to par, face, or maturity value at the maturity or due date.

When the effective rate method is used for amortizing bond discount or premium, a schedule is typically prepared to facilitate recording the

SCHEDULE OF AMORTIZATION
6% Bond Bought To Yield 5%

Date	Debit Cash	Credit Interest Income	Credit Bond Account	Carrying Value of Bond
Purchase date	—	—	—	$1,035.85
End 1st 6 mos.	$ 30.00	$ 25.90	$ 4.10	1,031.75
End 2nd 6 mos.	30.00	25.79	4.21	1,027.54
End 3rd 6 mos.	30.00	25.69	4.31	1,023.23
End 4th 6 mos.	30.00	25.58	4.42	1,018.81
End 5th 6 mos.	30.00	25.47	4.53	1,014.28
End 6th 6 mos.	30.00	25.36	4.64	1,009.64
End 7th 6 mos.	30.00	25.24	4.76	1,004.88
End 8th 6 mos.	30.00	25.12	4.88	1,000.00
	$240.00	$204.15	$35.85	

periodic income. Such a schedule, illustrating the purchase at a premium of $35.85 of a $1,000 bond paying nominal interest of 3% every six months but yielding an effective rate of only $2\frac{1}{2}$% every six months, is presented on page 790.

Sinking Fund Accumulations

It is not uncommon for business organizations to accumulate funds for specific purposes. In fact, many indentures under which bonds are issued may require a company to accumulate a fund to redeem the bonds upon their maturity. Funds built up or being accumulated are often referred to as sinking funds to indicate that the resources invested in the fund are tied up or "sunk" and not available for normal business operations.

Bond Sinking Fund Contributions. In the case of sinking funds to redeem outstanding bonds at their maturity, a third party called a trustee may be designated as the person to whom the sinking fund payments are to be made. To illustrate the problem involved, assume the Lini Book Company issues $100,000 of bonds due in 20 years. The bond indenture provides that the company shall deposit annually in a sinking fund, with the First National Bank as trustee, an amount which when invested at 4% will provide a fund of $100,000 to retire the bonds at their maturity date in 20 years.

The amount of the annual payment to be made may be computed by dividing the $100,000 by the amount of an annuity of 1 for 20 years at 4% (29.77807858). The result ($3,358.18) indicates the approximate amount which should be deposited in the fund each year. Actually, this might be rounded off to $3,350, $3,400, or $3,500 for purposes of the accumulation.

Sinking Fund Depreciation. Some accountants have suggested that the sinking fund concept be applied to the measurement of depreciation of fixed assets. In fact, some public utility companies have used the sinking fund concept to determine annual depreciation charges. Under the sinking fund concept, the annual depreciation is the amount of the periodic deposit which would have to be made *if* a sinking fund were being accumulated plus the interest on the accumulated balance. Thus, from the above illustration, the first year's depreciation entry on a $100,000 asset with a useful life of 20 years would be:

Depreciation expense	$3,358.18	
Allowance for depreciation		$3,358.18

This first year's entry would be for the amount of the periodic deposit only, since no interest would have been earned. The second year's depreciation, however, would be for the periodic deposit plus interest (at 4%) on the accumulated depreciation to date. The interest for the second year would be $134.33, and the depreciation entry at the end of the second year would be:

Depreciation expense	$3,492.51	
Allowance for depreciation		$3,492.51

The effect of this method of depreciation is to increase gradually the depreciation charge each period. It has not been used extensively in practice and when used has seldom been used along with a voluntary sinking fund accumulation.

Annuity Method of Depreciation

The sinking fund method of depreciation looks upon the cost of the asset as the amount of an annuity to be accumulated from annual deposits. Depreciation is considered to be the process of accumulating a sum of money equal to the cost of the asset (less scrap value) being depreciated. On the other hand, the annuity method of depreciation looks upon the cost of the asset as the present value of a future annuity which will be received. Depreciation is considered to be the amount of the rents foregone by investing in the asset rather than by purchasing the annuity. The distinction between the two methods may best be explained by a comparison of the procedures to be followed and the results of an illustrative example:

Procedure

Sinking Fund Method	*Annuity Method*
(1) Deduct scrap value from the cost of the asset to determine depreciable cost.	(1) Deduct scrap value from the cost of the asset to determine depreciable cost.
(2) Divide depreciable cost by the *amount* of an ordinary annuity of 1 at the sinking fund interest rate for the number of years of useful life of the asset.	(2) Divide depreciable cost by the *present value* of an annuity of 1 at the specified interest rate for the number of years of useful life of the asset.
(3) To the periodic sum determined in (2), add a sum equal to the interest on the accumulated balance in the "Allowance for Depreciation" account. This gives the periodic depreciation charge.	(3) Compute the annual interest on the scrap value for one year at the specified rate of interest.
	(4) The sum of (2) and (3) is the annual depreciation charge.
	(5) Imputed interest on the undepreciated cost is recorded reducing the credit for accumulated depreciation.

ILLUSTRATION. The Shrud-&-Coy company purchases for $11,000 a machine having an estimated useful life of four years and an estimated scrap value at the end of the four years of $1,000. Had the company not invested in the asset it could have earned interest at 5% a year and can earn this same rate on any future investments it might make. The depreciation entries which would be made over each of the four years of useful life of the machine, using both the sinking fund method and the annuity method of depreciation, are presented below:

ANNUITY METHOD

(1) Cost $11,000
  Scrap value   1,000

  Depreciable cost $10,000

(2) $10,000 divided by the present value of an ordinary annuity of 1 at 5% for 4 years (3.5459505) gives $2,820.12.

(3) Annual interest on scrap value is $1,000 × .05 or $50.00.

(4) $2,820.12 plus $50 gives $2,870.12, the annual depreciation charge.

Summary of depreciation:

Year	Depreciation Expense	Interest Income	Allowance for Depreciation
1	$2,870.12	$550.00	$ 2,320.12
2	2,870.12	433.99	2,436.13
3	2,870.12	312.19	2,557.93
4	2,870.12	184.29	2,685.83
			$10,000.01

ENTRIES

Year 1

Depreciation	$2,870.12	
Allowance for depreciation		$2,320.12
Interest income		550.00

Year 2

Depreciation	$2,870.12	
Allowance for depreciation		$2,436.13
Interest income		433.99

Year 3

Depreciation	$2,870.12	
Allowance for depreciation		$2,557.93
Interest income		312.19

Year 4

Depreciation	$2,870.12	
Allowance for depreciation		$2,685.83
Interest income		184.29

SINKING FUND METHOD

(1) Cost $11,000
    Scrap value   1,000

    Depreciable cost $10,000

(2) $10,000 divided by the amount of an ordinary annuity of 1 at 5% for 4 years (4.310125) gives $2,320.12, the first year's depreciation.

(3) The depreciation charge by years would be

1st year:		$ 2,320.12
2nd year:	$2,320.12 plus 5% of 2,320.12 ($116.01) =	$ 2,436.13
3rd year:	$2,320.12 plus 5% of 4,756.25 ($237.81) =	$ 2,557.93
4th year:	$2,320.12 plus 5% of 7,314.18 ($365.71) =	$ 2,685.83
Total		$10,000.01

ENTRIES

Year 1

Depreciation	$2,320.12	
Allowance for depreciation		$2,320.12

Year 2

Depreciation	$2,436.13	
Allowance for depreciation		$2,436.13

Year 3

Depreciation	$2,557.93	
Allowance for depreciation		$2,557.93

Year 4

Depreciation	$2,685.83	
Allowance for depreciation		$2,685.83

Valuation of Leaseholds

A leasehold arises from a tenure contract which provides for the use of property by the lessee in exchange for a specified sum of money payable at various times. The owner of the property, called the lessor, commonly has inserted in the contract a provision that a lump-sum deposit shall be made at the time of signing of the tenure contract. Such a deposit or direct advance payment of rent essentially represents a prepayment of a future rental payment(s). In reaching agreement regarding the amount to be paid in the form of a deposit for prepaid rent, the lessor and lessee not infrequently resort to the use of compound interest tables.

Illustration. To illustrate, assume Mr. A., the lessor, and Mr. B., the lessee, reach a rental agreement as follows:

(1) The rental payments shall be:
    (a) $8,000 a year for the 1st 5 years.
    (b) $10,000 a year for the next 5 years.
    (c) $12,000 a year for the last 5 years.
(2) Payments are to be made as follows:
    (a) $5,000 cash shall be paid at the beginning of each year.
    (b) A deposit shall be made immediately of an amount which, when deposited at 5% per year, shall provide for the payment of the balance of the annual rent due at the beginning of each year.

    The question of the amount of the leasehold prepayment resolves itself into one of determining the amount of the present value of annuities due for:
        (1) $3,000 a year for 5 years.
        (2) $5,000 a year for 5 years deferred 5 years.
        (3) $7,000 a year for 5 years deferred 10 years.

(1) P.v. of an annuity due of $3,000 a year for 5 years at 5%:

P.v. of ordinary annuity of 1 for 4 years at 5%	3.54595	
Add	1.00000	
P.v. of annuity due of 1 for 5 years at 5%	4.54595	
Times	$3,000	$13,637.85

(2) P.v. of an annuity due of $5,000 a year for 5 years at 5% deferred 5 years:

P.v. of ordinary annuity of 1 for 9 years at 5%	7.10782	
Add	1.00000	
P.v. of annuity due of 1 for 10 years at 5%	8.10782	
Less P.v. of annuity due of 1 for 5 years at 5% (above)	4.54595	
P.v. of annuity due of 1 for 5 years at 5% deferred 5 years	3.56187	
Times	$5,000	17,809.35

(3) P.v. of an annuity due of $7,000 a year for 5 years at 5% deferred 10 years:

P.v. of ordinary annuity of 1 for 14 years at 5%	9.89864	
Add	1.00000	
P.v. of annuity due of 1 for 15 years at 5%	10.89864	
Less P.v. of annuity due of 1 for 10 years at 5% (above)	8.10782	
P.v. of annuity due of 1 for 5 years at 5% deferred 10 years	2.79082	
Times	$7,000	19,535.74
Deposit to be made (total)		$50,982.94*

    * It should be noted that this computation is a variation of Method Two on page 788.

When the deposit or advance upon the purchase of the leasehold is made, an entry similar to the following would be made to record the acquisition of the asset, "Leasehold":

Leasehold	$50,982.94	
Cash		$50,982.94

A schedule for the amortization of the leasehold might be set up as follows:

AMORTIZATION SCHEDULE

Start of Period	Interest Earned	Withdrawal	Annual Amortization	Balance of "Leasehold"
0	...	...	...	$50,982.94
1	...	$3,000	$3,000.00*	47,982.94
2	$2,399.15	3,000	600.85	47,382.09
3	2,369.10	3,000	630.90	46,751.19
4	2,337.56	3,000	662.44	46,088.75
5	2,304.44	3,000	695.56	45,393.19
6	2,269.66	5,000	2,730.34	42,662.85
7	2,133.14	5,000	2,866.86	39,795.99
8	1,989.80	5,000	3,010.20	36,785.79
9	1,839.29	5,000	3,160.71	33,625.08
10	1,681.25	5,000	3,318.75	30,306.33
11	1,515.31	7,000	5,484.69	24,821.64
12	1,241.08	7,000	5,758.92	19,062.72
13	953.13	7,000	6,046.87	13,015.85
14	650.79	7,000	6,349.21	6,666.64
15	333.36	7,000	6,666.64	–0–

Miscellaneous Problems

Compound Interest for Fractional Part of a Period. Sometimes a deposit may be left at compound interest for a specified number of periods, plus a fraction of another period. The problem of determining the compound interest on the fractional period is settled in practice by using simple interest for the fractional period.

To illustrate, assume Mr. K. T. Belsley deposited $1,000 at 4% and plans to leave it for 8 years and 3 months, or $8\frac{1}{4}$ years. Interest is compounded annually. The solution determining the amount of the fund at the end of the 8 years and 3 months would be:

---

* Actually, the $3,000 for the first year's payment would seldom be included as a cost of the leasehold. Normally it would be charged directly to leasehold expense for the first year. As a result the initial valuation of the leasehold would be $47,982.94.

    (1) Amount of 1 for 8 periods at 4% is   1.368569
        Times $1,000

    (2) Amount of $1,000 for 8 periods at 4% $1,368.57
    (3) Interest on $1,368.57 at 4% per year
        for 3 months is   13.69

    (4) Amount of $1,000 for 8 years and 3
        months at 4% $1,382.26

Computing the Number of Periods in an Annuity. The practice of leaving a sum of money on deposit at a specified rate of interest with provision for periodic withdrawals is not uncommon. The unsolved problem in such situations may be to determine the number of periodic payments which will be made. Normally a close approximation may be made, as illustrated below.

EXAMPLE

Mr. A. T. Halsey left the sum of $27,180 on deposit at 6% annual interest with a provision that $2,000 a year could be withdrawn at the end of each year. He desired to know how many withdrawals could be made.

Solution:

(1) Divide the deposit of $27,180 by $2,000 to arrive at the present value of an annuity of 1 for x periods at 6% interest. The result is 13.59.
(2) Locate in a present value of an annuity of 1 table at 6% the amount nearest 13.59. The table indicates that for 29 periods the present value of an annuity of 1 at 6% is 13.59072102. From this the conclusion is drawn that the annuity of $2,000 a year will last approximately 29 years.

Perpetuity. A perpetuity is an annuity which is to run indefinitely. As an example, the problem involved would arise if a person wanted to leave a deposit at 5% annual interest which would provide $1,000 a year indefinitely. The solution involves dividing the annuity by the rate of interest ($1,000 ÷ .05 = $20,000), or determining the present value of $1,000 for an indefinitely long period as illustrated in Chapter 6.

The amount of the endowment fund would be $20,000 and it would remain unchanged as long as the annuity conditions remained constant. To illustrate, the $20,000 at 5% a year would increase the fund by $1,000 a year. Since the $1,000 is then withdrawn, the fund reverts to $20,000 to start the next period.

PROBLEMS

Problem AP 1. Adams borrowed $1,200 from a "friend" who agreed to loan him the money at the monthly rate of 1% of $1,200 each month ($12 a month) provided Adams paid off the loan at the rate of $100 a month. The friend then withheld $100 of the $1,200 loan as a financing charge. Adams paid the loan off ($112 a month) in the 12 month period.

Required:
What was the effective rate of interest Adams paid?

Problem AP-2. Baker invests $1,000 at 6% per year interest. After leaving the money invested without withdrawing any of the interest for 10 years, Baker withdrew the accumulated investment.

Required:
Compute the amount Baker would withdraw assuming:
(1) The investment earns simple interest.
(2) The investment earns compound interest.

Problem AP-3. Using the tables of amount of 1, compute the amount the following sums would accumulate to at compound interest by the end of the designated periods at the specified rate of interest:
(1) $1,000 for 10 years at 6% per year.
(2) $1,000 for 10 years at 3% every 6 months.
(3) $1,000 for 5 years at 1% every month.
(4) $1,000 for 5 years at 5% per year, then at 6% per year for another 5 years.
(5) $1,000 for 4 years at 2% per quarter.
(6) $633.33 for 9 years at 5% per year.
(7) $1,000 each year for 5 years at 4% per year.

Problem AP-4. Using the tables of present value of 1, compute the amount to be deposited now at compound interest to provide the desired sum at the end of the designated periods at the specified rate of interest.
(1) Invested for 10 years at 6% per year to amount to $1,000.
(2) Invested for 10 years at 3% every 6 months to amount to $1,000.
(3) Invested for 5 years at 6% per year, then invested at 5% per year for another 10 years to amount to $10,000.
(4) To be invested now at 4% per year until retirement (33 years) to have $100,000.

Problem AP-5. Compute the amount Smith would have at the end of 1985 if the following investments were made.
(1) $1,000 a year at the end of each year 1960 through 1969.
(2) Nothing in 1970.
(3) $2,000 a year at the end of each year 1971 through 1980.
(4) Nothing in 1981, 1982, and 1983.
(5) $5,000 a year at the end of each year 1984 and 1985. The investments earned compound interest at the following rates:

> 1960 through 1971—5%
> 1972 through 1982—6%
> 1983 through 1985—4%

Problem AP-6. Mr. Black wants to retire at the end of this year. His life expectancy is 20 years from the present. He wants to know how much he should deposit now at 5% to be able to withdraw $5,000 at the end of each year for the next 20 years.

Problem AP-7. Prepare (1) an amount of 1 table, (2) a present value of 1 table, (3) an amount of an annuity of 1 table, and (4) a present value of an annuity of 1 table for 5 periods at an interest rate of 8% per year.

Problem AP–8. Mr. C. A. Dorner deposits $1,000 a year, starting on his 40th birthday, until retirement on his 70th birthday at which time he starts withdrawing $3,000 a year. (His last deposit was on his 69th birthday.) Interest is constant by a contract with an insurance company at 4% per year.

Required:
For how many periods could Mr. Dorner make his $3,000 annual withdrawals?

Problem AP–9. (*a*) Compute the amount of an annuity due for $3,000 a year for 10 years at 5% interest. (*b*) What would the amount be if it were an ordinary annuity?

Problem AP–10. How much should be deposited now at 6% annual interest to provide an annuity of $10,000 a year for 20 years, if the start of the annuity is deferred 40 years?

Problem AP–11. Mr. Y wishes to accumulate a fund of $20,000. He can afford to invest $800 semiannually, and can get interest compounded semiannually at 3% per year.
How many semiannual deposits must he make, and what will be the amount of his final deposit?

Problem AP–12. Company P leases a store building to Company R on a 10-year lease. The lease calls for rent the first 5 years of $15,000 per year, and $20,000 per year for the last 5 years. Company R pays the entire 10 years' rent in advance at 4% discount. How much is the payment?

Problem AP–13. Your client has made annual payments of $2,500 into a fund at the close of each year for the past 9 years. The fund balance immediately after the ninth payment totaled $26,457. He has asked you how many more $2,500 annual payments will be required to bring the fund to $50,000, assuming that the fund continues to earn interest at 4% compounded annually. Compute the number of full payments required and the amount of the final payment, if it does not require the entire $2,500. Carefully label all computations supporting your answer.

Problem AP–14. Your client wishes to provide for the payment of an obligation of $200,000 due on July 1, 1976. He plans to deposit $20,000 in a special fund each July 1 for 8 years, starting July 1, 1969. He wishes to make an initial deposit on July 1, 1968, of an amount which, with its accumulated interest, will bring the fund up to $200,000 at the maturity of the obligation. He expects that the fund will earn interest at the rate of 4% compounded annually. Compute the amount to be deposited July 1, 1968. Carefully label all computations supporting your answer.

Problem AP–15. The BBB Company leased property from the CCC Company. The lease contract provides that annual rentals shall be paid in advance in January of each year. The lease runs for 10 years with payments according to the following schedule:

Years 1 through 2—$2,000 per year.
Years 3 through 4—$4,000 per year.
Years 5 through 10—$5,000 per year.

(1) What single immediate sum will pay all of these annual rentals if they are discounted at 5%?

(2) Assuming the amount computed above were set up to be used as a fund to pay the annual rentals, what amount would be in the fund after the payment on the first day of the fourth year?

Problem AP–16. Company Q purchased a 10-year, $1,000 bond on the date it was issued at a price which yielded 2% on a semiannual basis. At the end of the fourth year the following entry was made to record the receipt of 6 months' interest:

Cash	$18.75	
Bond investments	.97	
Interest income		$19.72

What price did the company pay for the bond?

Problem AP–17. A six-year $1,000, 6% bond with interest payable annually is bought to net 5%. What is the price of the bond?

Problem AP–18. A ten-year $1,000, 5% bond with interest payable semi-annually is bought to yield 6%. What is the price of the bond?

Problem AP–19. A 10-year $20,000, $4\frac{1}{2}$% bond with interest payable annually is bought to yield $3\frac{1}{2}$%. What is the price of the bond?

Problem AP–20. A 10-year $10,000, $2\frac{1}{2}$% bond with interest payable annually is bought to yield $3\frac{1}{2}$%. What is the price of the bond?

Problem AP–21. A 3-year $5,000, 6% bond with interest payable semiannually is bought to yield 4%. (a) What is the price of the bond? (b) Prepare the amortization schedule.

Problem AP–22. A 3-year $5,000, 4% bond with interest payable semiannually is bought to yield 6%. (a) What is the price of the bond? (b) Prepare the amortization schedule.

Problem AP–23. How much should be deposited now at $2\frac{1}{2}$% semiannual interest to provide an annuity of $8,000 a year for 20 years, if the start of the annuity is deferred 10 years? If the start of the annuity is deferred 15 years?

Problem AP–24. How much must be deposited now at 4% annual interest to provide an annuity of $5,000 a year for 4 years, if the start of the annuity is deferred 17 years? If the start of the annuity is deferred 12 years?

Problem AP–25. Your client has agreed to sell a property for $60,000. He is to receive $20,000 cash at date of sale and 20 notes of equal amount which will not bear interest. The notes are due serially, one each 6 months starting six months from date of sale. It is agreed that the notes will include in their face an amount which will equal 5% interest to be compounded semiannually.

Compute to the nearest dollar the amount of each note. Show your computations in good form, with each part explained or labeled. (AICPA adapted)

Problem AP–26. Jones, an employee of the Union Company, asks your advice on the following matter:

He is eligible to participate in a company insurance and retirement plan. His payment into the company plan would amount to $500 each 6 months for the next 10 years, and starting with the eleventh year he would receive an annual payment of $1,080 for life. He does not need insurance protection and states that he can save and invest each 6 months the amounts to be paid into the company plan so that he will earn 6% compounded semiannually. Also, he can continue to earn the same rate on his capital after retirement. He would like to have an equal amount per year of funds for 15 years after retirement

Assuming that he can carry out his personal saving and investing plan, how much can he expect to have available each 6 months for the 15 years following his retirement? Compute to the nearest dollar and show your computations in good form.   (AICPA adapted)

Problem AP–27. Reproduced below are the first three lines from the 25 columns of each of several tables of mathematical values. For each of the following items you are to select from among these fragmentary tables the one from which the amount required can be obtained *most directly* (assuming that the complete table was available in each instance):
(1) The amount to which a single sum would accumulate at compound interest by the end of a specified period (interest compounded annually).
(2) The amount which must be appropriated at the end of each of a specific number of years in order to provide for the accumulation, at annually compounded interest, of a certain sum of money.
(3) The amount which must be deposited in a fund which will earn interest at a specified rate, compounded annually, in order to make possible the withdrawal of certain equal sums annually over a specified period starting 1 year from date of deposit.
(4) The amount of interest which will accumulate on a single deposit by the end of a specified period (interest compounded semiannually).
(5) The amount, net of compound discount, which if paid now would settle a debt of larger amount due at a specified future date.

Periods	Table A	Table B	Table C	Table D	Table E	Table F
0	1.0000		1.0000			
1	0.9804	1.0200	1.0200	1.0000	0.9804	1.0200
2	0.9612	2.0604	1.0404	0.4950	1.9416	0.5150
3		3.1216		0.3268	2.8839	0.3468

(AICPA adapted)

Problem AP–28. A loan is made with the proviso that on each interest date a payment shall be made on account of principal equal to the amount of interest then paid, this arrangement to continue until the principal is reduced to approximately one half of the original loan, when a new arrangement will be made.
(1) Show by formula the number of payments required under the first arrangement.
(2) How many payments would be required to pay off the entire loan under the first arrangement? Give formula.   (AICPA adapted)

Problem AP–29. The C Company is planning a pension system for certain of its employees. It wishes to provide funds for meeting the payments under the pension plan and asks your assistance.

The company does not contemplate making any pension payments under the plan until January, 1978. Payments in 1978 and thereafter to the present group of covered employees are expected to be as follows:

January 1, 1978	$ 5,000
January 1, 1979	7,000
January 1, 1980	10,000
January 1, 1981	14,000
January 1, 1982	16,000
January 1, 1983	20,000
January 1, 1984	25,000
January 1, 1985	22,000
January 1, 1986	17,000
January 1, 1987	12,000
January 1, 1988	8,000
January 1, 1989	5,000
January 1, 1990	2,000
January 1, 1991	2,000

Starting on January 1, 1968 and continuing for 10 years, the company will deposit $10,000 a year in a special fund. On January 1, 1967 the company wishes to make a lump sum deposit of an amount sufficient to provide the remaining funds needed for meeting the pensions. It is expected that all the above funds will earn $3\frac{1}{2}\%$ interest compounded annually during the entire life of the fund.

Required:

You are to compute the amount of payment which should be made on January 1, 1967. Show all supporting computations in good form.

(AICPA adapted)

Problem AP–30. In 1967 J-P Bowling Company entered into an agreement with a bank for an unsecured long-term loan of $2,000,000. The loan agreement provides for interest at 5% and lump-sum repayment in 1977. Certain terms of the loan agreement placing restrictions on incurring additional long-term debt and on payment of dividends are here presented in summary:

(A) Additional long-term debt shall not be incurred unless the net tangible assets (investments, plant, and equipment), adjusted to include the proceeds of such long-term debt, will be at least 225% of the total long-term debt after incurring such additional debt.

(B) Long-term debt shall mean the total of all debt outstanding for a period of one year or longer plus an amount equal to the "Capitalized Rent" on unexpired long-term leases of real property. "Capitalized Rent" shall be computed by discounting the aggregate rental obligations under the long-term lease, by years, to the date of the computation at the rate of 5% per annum.

(C) Payment of cash dividends during the period of the loan shall be subject to the following limitations:

(1) Working capital of at least $6,500,000 shall be maintained.
(2) Cash dividends shall not exceed earnings subsequent to December 31, 1966, except that the payment of cash dividends in 1967 may exceed 1967 net income by an amount which is not more than 50% of the net income for 1966.
(3) In 1968 and subsequent years, cash dividends shall be limited to 25% of the prior year's net income.

(4) The total annual cash dividends shall not exceed $2 per share of stock outstanding at the end of any year.

(5) Should cash dividends be paid in excess of restrictions, such excess shall be applied in determining the amounts of dividends which may be paid in subsequent years.

The condensed balance sheet of J-P Bowling Company at December 31, 1968 follows:

Assets

Current assets	$16,787,000
Investments	300,000
Plant and equipment	5,000,000
Goodwill and patents	400,000
	$22,487,000

Liabilities and Owners' Equity

Current liabilities	$ 8,290,000
Note payable to bank	2,000,000
Capital stock (par value, $50)	3,131,000
Contributed capital in excess of par value	2,485,000
Retained earnings	6,581,000
	$22,487,000

An analysis of the Company's retained earnings for 1966, 1967, and 1968 discloses the following:

Balance, December 31, 1965	$5,445,000
Net income for 1966	422,100
Balance, December 31, 1966	5,867,000
Net income for 1967	507,000
Cash dividends paid in 1967	(98,000)
Balance, December 31, 1967	6,276,000
Net income for 1968	522,000
Cash dividends paid in 1968	(124,000)
1% stock dividend—at market value of shares issued	(93,000)
Balance, December 31, 1968	$6,581,000

The Company has a 10-year lease for a warehouse on which the last annual rental payment is due December 31, 1972. The annual rental is $40,000 until December 31, 1969, and $50,000 thereafter. Under an option, the lease may be extended for another 10 years, or portion thereof, at an annual rental of $60,000.

Required:

(1) The amount of cash dividends which may be paid under the loan agreement in 1969, including an indication of the application of each of the limitations contained in the loan agreement.

(2) The amount of additional long-term debt which may be incurred under the loan agreement as of December 31, 1968.   (AICPA adapted)

Tables of amounts
and present values

Amount of I

$$s = (1 + i)^n$$

Periods	1%	1¼%	1½%	1¾%	2%	2¼%	2½%
0	1.	1.	1.	1.	1.	1.	1.
1	1.01	1.0125	1.015	1.0175	1.02	1.0225	1.025
2	1.0201	1.02515625	1.030225	1.03530625	1.0404	1.04550625	1.050625
3	1.030301	1.03797070	1.04567838	1.05342411	1.061208	1.06903014	1.07689063
4	1.04060401	1.05094534	1.06136355	1.07185903	1.08243216	1.09308332	1.10381289
5	1.05101005	1.06408215	1.07728400	1.09061656	1.10408080	1.11767769	1.13140821
6	1.06152015	1.07738318	1.09344326	1.10970235	1.12616242	1.14282544	1.15969342
7	1.07213535	1.09085047	1.10984491	1.12912215	1.14868567	1.16853901	1.18868575
8	1.08285671	1.10448610	1.12649259	1.14888178	1.17165938	1.19483114	1.21840290
9	1.09368527	1.11829218	1.14338998	1.16898721	1.19509257	1.22171484	1.24886297
10	1.10462213	1.13227083	1.16054083	1.18944449	1.21899442	1.24920343	1.28008454
11	1.11566835	1.14642422	1.17794894	1 21025977	1.24337431	1.27731050	1.31208666
12	1.12682503	1.16075452	1.19561817	1.23143931	1.26824179	1.30604999	1.34488882
13	1.13809328	1.17526395	1.21355244	1.25298950	1.29360663	1.33543611	1.37851104
14	1.14947421	1.18995475	1.23175573	1.27491682	1.31947876	1.36548343	1.41297382
15	1.16096896	1.20482918	1.25023207	1.29722786	1.34586834	1.39620680	1.44829817
16	1.17257864	1.21988955	1.26898555	1.31992935	1.37278571	1.42762146	1.48450562
17	1.18430443	1.23513817	1.28802033	1.34302811	1.40024142	1.45974294	1.52161826
18	1.19614748	1.25057739	1.30734064	1.36653111	1.42824625	1.49258716	1.55965872
19	1.2081C895	1.26620961	1.32695075	1.39044540	1.45681117	1.52617037	1.59865019
20	1.22019004	1.28203723	1.34685501	1.41477820	1.48594740	1.56050920	1.63861644
21	1.23239194	1.29806270	1.36705783	1.43953681	1.51566634	1.59562066	1.67958185
22	1.24471586	1.31428848	1.38756370	1.46472871	1.54597967	1.63152212	1.72157140
23	1.25716302	1.33071709	1.40837715	1.49036146	1.57689926	1.66823137	1.76461068
24	1.26973465	1.34735105	1.42950281	1.51644279	1.60843725	1.70576658	1.80872595
25	1.28243200	1.36419294	1.45094535	1.54298054	1.64060599	1.74414632	1.85394410
26	1.29525631	1.38124555	1.47270953	1.56998269	1.67341811	1.78338962	1.90029270
27	1.30820888	1.39851092	1.49480018	1.59745739	1.70688648	1.82351588	1.94780002
28	1.32129097	1.41599230	1.51722218	1.62541290	1.74102421	1.86454499	1.99649502
29	1.33450388	1.43369221	1.53998051	1.65385762	1.77584469	1.90649725	2.04640739
30	1.34784892	1.45161336	1.56308022	1.68280013	1.81136158	1.94939344	2.09756758
31	1.36132740	1.46975853	1.58652642	1.71224913	1.84758882	1.99325479	2.15000677
32	1.37494068	1.48813051	1.61032432	1.74221349	1.88454059	2.03810303	2.20375694
33	1.38869009	1.50673214	1.63447918	1.77270223	1.92223140	2.08396034	2.25885086
34	1.40257699	1.52556629	1.65899637	1.80372452	1.96067603	2.13084945	2.31532213
35	1.41660276	1.54463587	1.68388132	1.83528970	1.99988955	2.17879356	2.37320519
36	1.43076878	1.56394382	1.70913954	1.86740727	2.03988734	2.22781642	2.43253532
37	1.44507647	1.58349312	1.73477663	1.90008689	2.08068509	2.27794229	2.49334870
38	1.45952724	1.60328678	1.76079828	1.93333841	2.12229879	2.32919599	2.55568242
39	1.47412251	1.62332787	1.78721025	1.96717184	2.16474477	2.38160290	2.61957448
40	1.48886373	1.64361946	1.81401841	2.00159734	2.20803966	2.43518897	2.68506384
41	1.50375237	1.66416471	1.84122868	2.03662530	2.25220046	2.48998072	2.75219043
42	1.51878989	1.68496677	1.86884712	2.07226624	2.29724447	2.54600528	2.82099520
43	1.53397779	1.70602885	1.89687982	2.10853090	2.34318936	2.60329040	2.89152008
44	1.54931757	1.72735421	1.92533302	2.14543019	2.39005314	2.66186444	2.96380808
45	1.56481075	1.74894614	1.95421301	2.18297522	2.43785421	2.72175639	3.03790328
46	1.58045885	1.77080797	1.98352621	2.22117728	2.48661129	2.78299590	3.11385086
47	1.59626344	1.79294306	2.01327910	2.26004789	2.53634351	2.84561331	3.19169713
48	1.61222608	1.81535485	2.04347829	2.29959872	2.58707039	2.90963961	3.27148956
49	1.62834834	1.83804679	2.07413046	2.33984170	2.63881179	2.97510650	3.35327680
50	1.64463182	1.86102237	2.10524242	2.38078893	2.69158803	3.04204640	3.43710872
55	1.72852457	1.98028070	2.26794398	2.59652785	2.97173067	3.40002740	3.88877303
60	1.81669670	2.10718135	2.44321978	2.83181628	3.28103079	3.80013479	4.39978975
65	1.90936649	2.24221407	2.63204158	3.08842574	3.62252311	4.24732588	4.97795826
70	2.00676337	2.38589997	2.83545629	3.36828827	3.99955822	4.74714140	5.63210286
75	2.10912847	2.53879358	3.05459171	3.67351098	4.41583546	5.30577405	6.37220743
80	2.21671522	2.70148494	3.29066279	4.00639192	4.87543916	5.93014530	7.20956782
85	2.32978997	2.87460191	3.54497838	4.36943740	5.38287878	6.62799112	8.15696424
90	2.44863267	3.05881260	3.81894851	4.76538080	5.94313313	7.40795782	9.22885633
95	2.57353755	3.25482789	4.11409214	5.19720324	6.56169920	8.27970921	10.44160385
100	2.70481383	3.46340427	4.43204565	5.66815594	7.24464612	9.25404630	11.81371635

Amount of 1

$$s = (1 + i)^n$$

Periods	2¾%	3%	3½%	4%	4½%	5%	6%
0	1.	1.	1.	1.	1.	1.	1.
1	1.0275	1.03	1.035	1.04	1.045	1.05	1.06
2	1.05575625	1.0609	1.071225	1.0816	1.092025	1.1025	1.1236
3	1.08478955	1.092727	1.10871788	1.124864	1.14116613	1.157625	1.191016
4	1.11462126	1.12550881	1.14752300	1.16985856	1.19251860	1.21550625	1.26247696
5	1.14527334	1.15927407	1.18768631	1.21665290	1.24618194	1.27628156	1.33822558
6	1.17676836	1.19405230	1.22925533	1.26531902	1.30226012	1.34009564	1.41851911
7	1.20912949	1.22987387	1.27227926	1.31593178	1.36086183	1.40710042	1.50363026
8	1.24238055	1.26677008	1.31680904	1.36856905	1.42210061	1.47745544	1.59384807
9	1.27654602	1.30477318	1.36289735	1.42331181	1.48609514	1.55132822	1.68947896
10	1.31165103	1.34391638	1.41059876	1.48024428	1.55296942	1.62889463	1.79084770
11	1.34772144	1.38423387	1.45996972	1.53945406	1.62283305	1.71033036	1.89829856
12	1.38478378	1.42576089	1.51106866	1.60103222	1.69588143	1.79585633	2.01219647
13	1.42286533	1.46853371	1.56395606	1.66507551	1.77219610	1.88564914	2.13292826
14	1.46199413	1.51258972	1.61869452	1.73167645	1.85194492	1.97993160	2.26090896
15	1.50219896	1.55796742	1.67534883	1.80094351	1.93528244	2.07892818	2.39655819
16	1.54350944	1.60470644	1.73398604	1.87298125	2.02237015	2.18287459	2.54035168
17	1.58595595	1.65284763	1.79467555	1.94790050	2.11337681	2.29201832	2.69277279
18	1.62956973	1.70243306	1.85748920	2.02581652	2.20847877	2.40661923	2.85433915
19	1.67438290	1.75350605	1.92250132	2.10684918	2.30786031	2.52695020	3.02559950
20	1.72042843	1.80611123	1.98978886	2.19112314	2.41171402	2.65329771	3.20713547
21	1.76774021	1.86029457	2.05943147	2.27876807	2.52024116	2.78596259	3.39956360
22	1.81635307	1.91610341	2.13151158	2.36991879	2.63365201	2.92526072	3.60353742
23	1.86630278	1.97358651	2.20611448	2.46471554	2.75216635	3.07152376	3.81974966
24	1.91762610	2.03279411	2.28332849	2.56330416	2.87601383	3.22509994	4.04893464
25	1.97036082	2.09377793	2.36324498	2.66583633	3.00543446	3.38635494	4.29187072
26	2.02454575	2.15659127	2.44595856	2.77246978	3.14067901	3.55567269	4.54938296
27	2.08022075	2.22128901	2.53156711	2.88336858	3.28200956	3.73345632	4.82234594
28	2.13742682	2.28792768	2.62017196	2.99870332	3.42969999	3.92012914	5.11168670
29	2.19620606	2.35656551	2.71187798	3.11865145	3.58403649	4.11613560	5.41838790
30	2.25660173	2.42726247	2.80679370	3.24339751	3.74531813	4.32194208	5.74349117
31	2.31865828	2.50008035	2.90503148	3.37313341	3.91385745	4.53803949	6.08810064
32	2.38942138	2.57508276	3.00670760	3.50205875	4.08998104	4.76494147	6.45338668
33	2.44793797	2.65233524	3.11194235	3.64830110	4.27402018	5.00318854	6.84058938
34	2.51525626	2.73190530	3.22086033	3.79431634	4.46636154	5.25334797	7.25102528
35	2.58442581	2.81386245	3.33359045	3.94608899	4.66734781	5.51601537	7.68608679
36	2.65549752	2.89827833	3.45026611	4.10393255	4.87737846	5.79181614	8.14725200
37	2.72852370	2.98522668	3.57102543	4.26808986	5.09686049	6.08140694	8.63008712
38	2.80355810	3.07478348	3.69601132	4.43881345	5.32621921	6.38547729	9.15425235
39	2.88065595	3.16702698	3.82537171	4.61636599	5.56589908	6.70475115	9.70350749
40	2.95987399	3.26203779	3.95952942	4.80102063	5.81636454	7.03998871	10.28571794
41	3.04127052	3.35989893	4.09783381	4.99306145	6.07810094	7.39198815	10.90286101
42	3.12490546	3.46069589	4.24125799	5.19278391	6.35161548	7.76158756	11.55703267
43	3.21084036	3.56451677	4.38970202	5.40049527	6.63743818	8.14966693	12.25045463
44	3.29913847	3.67145227	4.54334160	5.61651508	6.93612290	8.55715028	12.98548191
45	3.38986478	3.78159584	4.70235855	5.84117568	7.24824843	8.98500779	13.76461083
46	3.48308606	3.89504372	4.86694110	6.07482271	7.57441961	9.43425818	14.59048748
47	3.57887093	4.01189503	5.03728404	6.31781562	7.91526849	9.90597109	15.46591673
48	3.67728988	4.13225188	5.21358898	6.57052824	8.27145557	10.40126965	16.39387173
49	3.77841535	4.25621944	5.39606459	6.83334937	8.64367107	10.92133313	17.37750403
50	3.88232177	4.38390602	5.58492686	7.10668335	9.03263472	11.46739979	18.42015427
55	4.44631964	5.08214859	6.63314114	8.64636692	11.25630817	14.63563092	24.65032159
60	5.09225136	5.89160310	7.87809090	10.51962741	14.02740793	18.67918589	32.98760085
65	5.83201974	6.82998273	9.35670068	12.79873522	17.48070239	23.83990056	44.14497165
70	6.67925676	7.91782191	11.11282526	15.57161835	21.78413558	30.42642554	59.07593018
75	7.64957472	9.17892567	13.19855038	18.94525466	27.14699629	38.83268592	79.05692079
80	8.76085402	10.64089056	15.67573754	23.04979907	33.83009643	49.56144107	105.79599348
85	10.03357258	12.33570855	18.61785881	28.04360494	42.15845513	63.25435344	141.57890449
90	11.49118322	14.30046711	22.11217595	34.11933334	52.53710530	80.73036505	189.46451123
95	13.16054584	16.57816077	26.26232856	41.51130504	65.47070169	103.03467645	253.54625498
100	15.07242234	19.21863198	31.19140798	50.50494818	81.58851803	131.50125785	339.30208351

Present Value of I

$$v^n = \frac{1}{(1+i)^n} = (1+i)^{-n}$$

Periods	1%	1¼%	1½%	1¾%	2%	2¼%	2½%
0	1.	1.	1.	1.	1.	1.	1.
1	0.99009901	0.98765432	0.98522167	0.98280098	0.98039216	0.97799511	0.97560976
2	0.98029605	0.97546106	0.97066175	0.96589777	0.96116878	0.95647444	0.95181440
3	0.97059015	0.96341833	0.95631699	0.94928528	0.94232233	0.93542732	0.92859941
4	0.96098034	0.95152428	0.94218423	0.93295851	0.92384543	0.91484335	0.90595064
5	0.95146569	0.93977706	0.92826033	0.91691254	0.90573081	0.89471232	0.88385429
6	0.94204524	0.92817488	0.91454219	0.90114254	С.88797138	0.87502427	0.86229687
7	0.93271805	0.91671593	0.90102679	0.88564378	0.87056018	0.85576946	0.84126524
8	0.92348322	0.90539845	0.88771112	0.87041157	С.85349037	0.83693835	0.82074657
9	0.91433982	0.89422069	0.87459224	0.85544135	0.83675527	0.81852161	0.80072836
10	0.90528695	0.88318093	0.86166723	0.84072860	0.82034830	0.80051013	0.78119840
11	0.89632372	0.87227746	0.84893323	0.82626889	0.80426304	0.78289499	0.76214478
12	0.88744923	0.86150860	0.83638742	0.81205788	0.78849318	0.76566748	0.74355589
13	0.87866260	0.85087269	0.82402702	0.79809128	0.77303253	0.74881905	0.72542038
14	0.86996297	0.84036809	0.81184928	0.78436490	0.75787502	0.73234137	0.70772720
15	0.86134947	0.82999318	0.79985150	0.77087459	0.74301473	0.71622628	0.69046556
16	0.85282126	0.81974635	0.78803104	0.75761631	0.72844581	0.70046580	0.67362493
17	0.84437749	0.80962602	0.77638526	0.74458605	0.71416256	0.68505212	0.65719506
18	0.83601731	0.79963064	0.76491159	0.73177990	0.70015937	0.66997763	0.64116591
19	0.82773992	0.78975866	0.75360747	0.71919401	0.68643076	0.65523484	0.62552772
20	0.81954447	0.78000855	0.74247042	0.70682458	0.67297133	0.64081647	0.61027094
21	0.81143017	0.77037881	0.73149795	0.69466789	0.65977582	0.62671538	0.59536629
22	0.80339621	0.76086796	0.72068763	0.68272028	0.64683904	Э.61292457	0.58086467
23	0.79544179	0.75147453	0.71003708	0.67097817	0.63415592	0.59943724	0.56669724
24	0.78756613	0.74219707	0.69954392	0.65943800	0.62172149	0.58624668	0.55287535
25	0.77976844	0.73303414	0.68920583	0.64809632	0.60953087	0.57334639	0.53939059
26	0.77204796	0.72398434	0.67902052	0.63694970	0.59757928	0.56072997	0.52623472
27	0.76440392	0.71504626	0.66898574	0.62599479	0.58586204	0.54839117	0.51339973
28	0.75683557	0.70621853	0.65909925	0.61522829	0.57437455	0.53623388	0.50087778
29	0.74934215	0.69749978	0.64935887	0.60464697	0.56311231	0.52452213	0.48866125
30	0.74192292	0.68888867	0.63976243	0.59424764	0.55207089	0.51298008	0.47674269
31	0.73457715	0.68038387	0.63030781	0.58402716	0.54124597	0.50169201	0.46511481
32	0.72730411	0.67198407	0.62099292	0.57398247	0.53063330	0.49065233	0.45377055
33	0.72010307	0.66368797	0.61181568	0.56411053	0.52022873	0.47985558	0.44270298
34	0.71297334	0.65549429	0.60277407	0.55440839	0.51002817	0.46929641	0.43190534
35	0.70591420	0.64740177	0.59386608	0.54487311	0.50002761	0.45896960	0.42137107
36	0.69892495	0.63940916	0.58508974	0.53550183	0.49022315	0.44887002	0.41109372
37	0.69200490	0.63151522	0.57644309	0.52629172	0.48061093	0.43899268	0.40106705
38	0.68515337	0.62371873	0.56792423	0.51724002	0.47118719	0.42933270	0.39128492
39	0.67836967	0.61601850	0.55953126	0.50834400	0.46194822	0.41988528	0.38174139
40	0.67165314	0.60841334	0.55126232	0.49960098	0.45289042	0.41064575	0.37243062
41	0.66500311	0.60090206	0.54311559	0.49100834	0.44401021	0.40160954	0.36334695
42	0.65841892	0.59348352	0.53508925	0.48256348	0.43530413	0.39277216	0.35448483
43	0.65189992	0.58615656	0.52718153	0.47426386	0.42676875	0.38412925	0.34583886
44	0.64544546	0.57892006	0.51939067	0.46610699	0.41840074	0.37567653	0.33740376
45	0.63905492	0.57177290	0.51171494	0.45809040	0.41019680	0.36740981	0.32917440
46	0.63272764	0.56471397	0.50415265	0.45021170	0.40215373	0.35932500	0.32114576
47	0.62646301	0.55774219	0.49670212	0.44246850	0.39426836	0.35141809	0.31331294
48	0.62026041	0.55085649	0.48936170	0.43485848	0.38653761	0.34368518	0.30567116
49	0.61411921	0.54405579	0.48212975	0.42737934	0.37895844	0.33612242	0.29821579
50	0.60803882	0.53733905	0.47500468	0.42002883	0.37152788	0.32872608	0.29094221
55	0.57852808	0.50497892	0.44092800	0.38512970	0.33650425	0.29411528	0.25715052
60	0.55044962	0.47456760	0.40929597	0.35313025	0.30478227	0.26314856	0.22728359
65	0.52373392	0.44598775	0.37993321	0.32378956	0.27605069	0.23544226	0.20088557
70	0.49831486	0.41912905	0.35267692	0.29688670	0.25002761	0.21065309	0.17755358
75	0.47412949	0.39388787	0.32737599	0.27221914	0.22645771	0.18847391	0.15693149
80	0.45111794	0.37016679	0.30389015	0.24960114	0.20510973	0.16862993	0.13870457
85	0.42922324	0.34787426	0.28208917	0.22886242	0.18577420	0.15087528	0.12259463
90	0.40839119	0.32692425	0.26185218	0.20984682	0.16826142	0.13498997	0.10835579
95	0.38857020	0.30723591	0.24306699	0.19241118	0.15239955	0.12077719	0.09577073
100	0.36971121	0.28873326	0.22562944	0.17642422	0.13803297	0.10806084	0.08464737

Present Value of 1

$$v^n = \frac{1}{(1 + i)^n} = (1 + i)^{-n}$$

Periods	2¾%	3%	3½%	4%	4½%	5%	6%
0	1.	1.	1.	1.	1.	1.	1.
1	0.97323601	0.97087379	0.96618357	0.96153846	0.95693780	0.95238095	0.94339623
2	0.94718833	0.94259591	0.93351070	0.92455621	0.91572995	0.90702948	0.88999644
3	0.92183779	0.91514166	0.90194271	0.88899636	0.87629660	0.86383760	0.83961928
4	0.89716573	0.88848705	0.87144223	0.85480419	0.83856134	0.82270247	0.79209366
5	0.87315400	0.86260878	0.84197317	0.82192711	0.80245105	0.78352617	0.74725817
6	0.84978491	0.83748426	0.81350064	0.79031453	0.76789574	0.74621540	0.70496054
7	0.82704128	0.81309151	0.78599096	0.75991781	0.73482846	0.71068133	0.66505711
8	0.80490635	0.78940923	0.75941156	0.73069021	0.70318513	0.67683936	0.62741237
9	0.78336385	0.76641673	0.73373097	0.70258674	0.67290443	0.64460892	0.59189846
10	0.76239791	0.74409391	0.70891881	0.67556417	0.64392768	0.61391325	0.55839478
11	0.74199310	0.72242128	0.68494571	0.64958093	0.61619874	0.58467929	0.52678753
12	0.72213440	0.70137988	0.66178330	0.62459705	0.58966386	0.55683742	0.49696936
13	0.70280720	0.68095134	0.63940415	0.60057409	0.56427164	0.53032135	0.46883902
14	0.68399728	0.66111781	0.61778179	0.57747508	0.53997286	0.50506795	0.44230096
15	0.66569078	0.64186195	0.59689062	0.55526450	0.51672044	0.48101710	0.41726506
16	0.64787424	0.62316694	0.57670591	0.53390818	0.49446932	0.45811152	0.39364628
17	0.63053454	0.60501645	0.55720378	0.51337325	0.47317639	0.43629660	0.37136442
18	0.61365892	0.58739461	0.53836114	0.49362812	0.45280037	0.41552065	0.35034379
19	0.59723496	0.57028603	0.52015569	0.47464242	0.43330179	0.39573396	0.33051301
20	0.58125057	0.55367575	0.50256588	0.45638695	0.41464286	0.37688948	0.31180473
21	0.56569398	0.53754928	0.48557090	0.43883360	0.39678743	0.35894236	0.29415540
22	0.55055375	0.52189250	0.46915063	0.42195539	0.37970089	0.34184987	0.27750510
23	0.53581874	0.50669175	0.45328563	0.40572633	0.36335013	0.32557131	0.26179726
24	0.52147809	0.49193374	0.43795713	0.39012147	0.34770347	0.31006791	0.24697855
25	0.50752126	0.47760557	0.42314699	0.37511680	0.33273060	0.29530277	0.23299863
26	0.49393796	0.46369473	0.40883767	0.36068923	0.31840248	0.28124073	0.21981003
27	0.48071821	0.45018906	0.39501224	0.34681657	0.30469137	0.26784832	0.20736795
28	0.46785227	0.43707675	0.38165434	0.33347747	0.29157069	0.25509364	0.19563014
29	0.45533068	0.42434636	0.36874815	0.32065141	0.27901502	0.24294632	0.18455674
30	0.44314421	0.41198676	0.35627841	0.30831867	0.26700002	0.23137745	0.17411013
31	0.43128391	0.39998715	0.34423035	0.29640026	0.25550241	0.22035947	0.16425484
32	0.41974103	0.38833703	0.33258971	0.28505794	0.24449991	0.20986617	0.15495740
33	0.40850708	0.37702625	0.32134271	0.27409417	0.23397121	0.19987254	0.14618622
34	0.39757380	0.36604490	0.31047005	0.26355209	0.22389590	0.19035480	0.13791153
35	0.38693314	0.35538340	0.29997686	0.25341547	0.21425444	0.18129029	0.13010522
36	0.37657727	0.34503243	0.28983272	0.24366872	0.20502817	0.17265741	0.12274077
37	0.36649856	0.33498294	0.28003161	0.23429685	0.19619921	0.16443563	0.11579318
38	0.35668959	0.32522615	0.27056194	0.22528543	0.18775044	0.15660536	0.10923885
39	0.34714316	0.31575355	0.26141250	0.21662061	0.17966549	0.14914797	0.10305552
40	0.33785222	0.30655684	0.25257247	0.20828904	0.17192870	0.14204568	0.09722219
41	0.32880995	0.29762800	0.24403137	0.20027793	0.16452507	0.13528160	0.09171905
42	0.32000968	0.28895922	0.23577910	0.19257493	0.15744026	0.12883962	0.08652740
43	0.31144495	0.28054294	0.22780590	0.18516820	0.15066054	0.12270440	0.08162962
44	0.30310944	0.27237178	0.22010231	0.17804635	0.14417276	0.11686133	0.07700908
45	0.29499702	0.26443862	0.21265924	0.17119841	0.13796437	0.11129651	0.07265007
46	0.28710172	0.25673653	0.20546787	0.16461386	0.13202332	0.10599668	0.06853781
47	0.27941773	0.24925876	0.19851968	0.15828256	0.12633810	0.10094921	0.06465831
48	0.27193940	0.24199880	0.19180645	0.15219476	0.12089771	0.09614211	0.06099840
49	0.26466122	0.23495029	0.18532024	0.14634112	0.11569158	0.09156391	0.05754566
50	0.25757783	0.22810708	0.17905337	0.14071262	0.11070965	0.08720373	0.05428836
55	0.22490511	0.19676717	0.15075814	0.11565551	0.08883907	0.06832640	0.04056742
60	0.19637679	0.16973309	0.12693431	0.09506040	0.07128901	0.05353552	0.03031434
65	0.17146718	0.14641325	0.10687528	0.07813272	0.05720594	0.04194648	0.02265264
70	0.14971726	0.12629736	0.08998612	0.06421940	0.04590497	0.03286617	0.01692737
75	0.13072622	0.10894521	0.07576590	0.05278367	0.03683649	0.02575150	0.01264911
80	0.11414412	0.09397710	0.06379285	0.04338433	0.02955948	0.02017698	0.00945215
85	0.09966540	0.08106547	0.05371187	0.03565875	0.02372003	0.01580919	0.00706320
90	0.08702324	0.06992779	0.04522395	0.02930890	0.01903417	0.01238691	0.00527803
95	0.07598469	0.06032032	0.03807735	0.02408978	0.01527399	0.00970547	0.00394405
100	0.06634634	0.05203284	0.03206011	0.01980004	0.01225663	0.00760449	0.00294723

Amount of an Ordinary Annuity of 1

$$s_{\overline{n}|i} = \frac{(1 + i)^n - 1}{i}$$

Periods	1%	1¼%	1½%	1¾%	2%	2¼%	2½%
1	1.	1.	1.	1.	1.	1.	1.
2	2.01	2.0125	2.015	2.0175	2.02	2.0225	2.025
3	3.0301	3.03765625	3.045225	3.05280625	3.0604	3.06800625	3.075625
4	4.060401	4.07562695	4.09090338	4.10623036	4.121608	4.13703639	4.15251563
5	5.10100501	5.12657229	5.15226693	5.17808939	5.20404016	5.23011971	5.25632852
6	6.15201506	6.19065444	6.22955093	6.26870596	6.30812096	6.34779740	6.38773673
7	7.21353521	7.26803762	7.32299419	7.37840831	7.43428338	7.49062284	7.54743015
8	8.28567056	8.35888809	8.43283911	8.50753045	8.58296905	8.65916186	8.73611590
9	9.36852727	9.46337420	9.55933169	9.65641224	9.75462843	9.85399300	9.95451880
10	10.46221254	10.58166637	10.70272167	10.82539945	10.94972100	11.07570784	11.20338177
11	11.56683467	11.71393720	11.86326249	12.01484394	12.16871542	12.32491127	12.48346631
12	12.68250301	12.86036142	13.04121143	13.22510371	13.41208973	13.60222177	13.79555297
13	13.80932804	14.02111594	14.23682960	14.45654303	14.68033152	14.90827176	15.14044179
14	14.94742132	15.19637988	15.45038205	15.70953253	15.97393815	16.24370788	16.51895284
15	16.09689554	16.38633463	16.68213778	16.98444935	17.29341692	17.60919130	17.93192666
16	17.25786449	17.59116382	17.93236984	18.28167721	18.63928525	19.00539811	19.38022483
17	18.43044314	18.81105336	19.20135539	19.60160656	20.01207096	20.43301957	20.86473045
18	19.61474757	20.04619153	20.48937572	20.94463468	21.41231238	21.89276251	22.38634871
19	20.81089504	21.29676893	21.79671636	22.31116578	22.84055863	23.38534966	23.94600743
20	22.01900399	22.56297854	23.12366710	23.70161119	24.29736980	24.91152003	25.54465761
21	23.23919403	23.84501577	24.47052211	25.11638938	25.78331719	26.47202923	27.18327405
22	24.47158598	25.14307847	25.83757994	26.55592620	27.29898354	28.06764989	28.86285590
23	25.71630183	26.45736695	27.22514364	28.02065490	28.84496321	29.69917201	30.58442730
24	26.97346485	27.78808403	28.63352080	29.51101637	30.42186247	31.36740338	32.34903798
25	28.24319950	29.13543508	30.06302361	31.02745915	32.03029972	33.07316996	34.15776393
26	29.52563150	30.49962802	31.51396896	32.57043969	33.67090572	34.81731628	36.01170803
27	30.82088781	31.88087337	32.98667850	34.14042238	35.34432383	36.60070599	37.91200073
28	32.12909669	33.27938429	34.48147867	35.73787977	37.05121031	38.42422178	39.85980075
29	33.45038766	34.69537659	35.99870085	37.36329267	38.79223451	40.28876677	41.85629577
30	34.78489153	36.12906880	37.53868137	39.01715029	40.56807921	42.19526402	43.90270316
31	36.13274045	37.58068216	39.10176159	40.69995042	42.37944079	44.14465746	46.00027074
32	37.49406785	39.05044069	40.68828801	42.41219955	44.22702961	46.13791226	48.15027751
33	38.86900853	40.53857120	42.29861233	44.15441305	46.11157020	48.17601528	50.35403445
34	40.25769862	42.04530334	43.93309152	45.92711527	48.03380160	50.25997563	52.61288531
35	41.66027560	43.57086963	45.59208789	47.73083979	49.99447763	52.39082508	54.92820744
36	43.07687836	45.11550550	47.27596921	49.56612949	51.99436719	54.56961864	57.30141263
37	44.50764714	46.67944932	48.98510874	51.43353675	54.03425453	56.79743506	59.73394794
38	45.95272361	48.26294243	50.71988538	53.33362365	56.11493962	59.07537735	62.22729664
39	47.41225085	49.86622921	52.48068366	55.26696206	58.23723841	61.40457334	64.78297906
40	48.88637336	51.48955708	54.26789391	57.23413390	60.40198318	63.78617624	67.40255354
41	50.37523709	53.13317654	56.08191232	59.23573124	62.61002284	66.22136521	70.08761737
42	51.87898946	54.79734125	57.92314100	61.27235654	64.86222330	68.71134592	72.83980781
43	53.39777936	56.48230801	59.79198812	63.34462278	67.15946777	71.25735121	75.66080300
44	54.93175715	58.18833687	61.68886794	65.45315367	69.50265712	73.86064161	78.55232308
45	56.48107472	59.91569108	63.61420096	67.59858386	71.89271027	76.52250605	81.51613116
46	58.04588547	61.66463721	65.56841398	69.78155908	74.33056447	79.24426243	84.55403443
47	59.62634432	63.43544518	67.55194018	72.00273637	76.81717576	82.02725834	87.66788530
48	61.22260777	65.22838824	69.56521929	74.26278425	79.35351927	84.87287165	90.85958243
49	62.83483385	67.04374310	71.60869758	76.56238298	81.94058966	87.78251126	94.13107199
50	64.46318218	68.88178989	73.68282804	78.90222468	84.57940145	90.75761776	97.48434879
55	72.85245735	78.42245562	84.52959893	91.23016259	98.58653365	106.66788460	115.55092136
60	81.66966986	88.57450776	96.21465171	104.67521588	114.05152942	124.45043493	135.99158995
65	90.93664882	99.37712526	108.80277215	119.33861370	131.12615541	144.32559477	159.11833027
70	100.67633684	110.87199776	122.36375295	135.33075826	149.97791114	166.53961758	185.28411421

Amount of an Ordinary Annuity of 1

$$s_{\overline{n}|i} = \frac{(1 + i)^n - 1}{i}$$

Periods	2¾%	3%	3½%	4%	4½%	5%	6%
1	1.	1.	1.	1.	1.	1.	1.
2	2.0275	2.03	2.035	2.04	2.045	2.05	2.06
3	3.08325625	3.0909	3.106225	3.1216	3.137025	3.1525	3.1836
4	4.16804580	4.183627	4.21494238	4.246464	4.27819113	4.310125	4.374616
5	5.28266706	5.30913581	5.36246588	5.41632256	5.47070973	5.52563125	5.63709296
6	6.42794040	6.46840988	6.55015218	6.63297546	6.71689166	6.80191281	6.97531854
7	7.60470876	7.66246218	7.77940751	7.89829448	8.01915179	8.14200845	8.39388765
8	8.81383825	8.89233605	9.05168677	9.21422626	9.38001362	9.54910888	9.89746791
9	10.05621880	10.15910613	10.36849581	10.58279531	10.80211423	11.02656432	11.49131598
10	11.33276482	11.46387931	11.73139316	12.00610712	12.28820937	12.57789254	13.18079494
11	12.64441585	12.80779569	13.14199192	13.48635141	13.84117879	14.20678716	14.97164264
12	13.99213729	14.19202956	14.60196164	15.02580543	15.46403184	15.91712652	16.86994120
13	15.37692107	15.61779045	16.11303030	16.62683768	17.15991327	17.71298285	18.88213767
14	16.79978639	17.08632416	17.67698636	18.29191119	18.93210937	19.59863199	21.01506593
15	18.26178052	18.59891389	19.29568088	20.02358764	20.78405429	21.57856359	23.27596988
16	19.76397948	20.15688130	20.97102971	21.82453114	22.71933673	23.65749177	25.67252808
17	21.30748892	21.76158774	22.70501575	23.69751239	24.74170689	25.84036636	28.21287976
18	22.89344487	23.41443537	24.49969130	25.64541288	26.85508370	28.13238467	30.90565255
19	24.52301460	25.11686844	26.35718050	27.67122940	29.06356246	30.53900391	33.75999170
20	26.19739750	26.87037449	28.27968181	29.77807858	31.37142277	33.06595410	36.78559120
21	27.91782593	28.67648572	30.26947068	31.96920172	33.78313680	35.71925181	39.99272668
22	29.68556615	30.53678030	32.32890215	34.24796979	36.30337795	38.50521440	43.39229028
23	31.50191921	32.45288370	34.46041373	36.61788858	38.93702996	41.43047512	46.99582769
24	33.36822199	34.42647022	36.66652821	39.08260412	41.68919631	44.50199887	50.81557735
25	35.28584810	36.45926432	38.94985669	41.64590829	44.56521015	47.72709882	54.86451200
26	37.25620892	38.55304225	41.31310168	44.31174462	47.57064460	51.11345376	59.15638272
27	39.28075467	40.70963352	43.75906024	47.08421440	50.71132361	54.66912645	63.70576568
28	41.36097542	42.93092252	46.29062734	49.96758298	53.99333317	58.40258277	68.52811162
29	43.49840224	45.21885020	48.91079930	52.96628630	57.42303316	62.32271191	73.63979832
30	45.69460830	47.57541571	51.62267728	56.08493775	61.00706966	66.43884750	79.05818622
31	47.95121003	50.00267818	54.42947098	59.32833526	64.75238779	70.76078988	84.80167739
32	50.26986831	52.50275852	57.33450247	62.70146867	68.66624524	75.29882937	90.88977803
33	52.65228969	55.07784128	60.34121005	66.20952742	72.75622628	80.06377084	97.34316471
34	55.10022765	57.73017652	63.45315240	69.85790851	77.03025646	85.06695938	104.18375460
35	57.61548391	60.46208181	66.67401274	73.65222486	81.49661800	90.32030735	111.43477987
36	60.19990972	63.27594427	70.00760318	77.59831385	86.16396581	95.83632272	119.12086666
37	62.85540724	66.17422259	73.45786930	81.70224640	91.04134427	101.62813886	127.26811866
38	65.58393094	69.15944927	77.02889472	85.97033626	96.13820476	107.70954580	135.90420578
39	68.38748904	72.23423275	80.72490604	90.40914971	101.46442398	114.09502309	145.05845813
40	71.26814499	75.40125973	84.55027775	95.02551570	107.03032306	120.79977424	154.76196562
41	74.22801898	78.66329753	88.50953747	99.82653633	112.84668760	127.83976295	165.04768356
42	77.26928950	82.02319645	92.60737128	104.81959778	118.92478854	135.23175110	175.95054457
43	80.39419496	85.48389234	96.84862928	110.01238169	125.27640402	142.99333866	187.50757724
44	83.60503532	89.04840911	101.23833130	115.41287696	131.91384220	151.14300559	199.75803188
45	86.90417379	92.71986139	105.78167290	121.02939204	138.84996510	159.70015587	212.74351379
46	90.29403857	96.50145723	110.48403145	126.87056772	146.09821353	168.68516366	226.50812462
47	93.77712463	100.39650095	115.35097255	132.94539043	153.67263314	178.11942185	241.09861210
48	97.35599556	104.40839598	120.38825659	139.26320604	161.58790163	188.02539294	256.56452882
49	101.03328544	108.54064785	125.60184557	145.83373429	169.85935720	198.42666259	272.95840055
50	104.81170079	112.79686729	130.99791016	152.66708366	178.50302828	209.34799572	290.33590458
55	125.32071411	136.07161972	160.94688984	191.15917299	227.91795938	272.71261833	394.17202657
60	148.80914038	163.05343680	196.51688288	237.99068520	289.49795398	353.58371788	533.12818089
65	175.70980889	194.33275782	238.76287650	294.96838045	366.23783096	456.79801118	719.08286076
70	206.51842740	230.59406374	288.93786459	364.29045876	461.86967955	588.52851071	967.93216905

Present Value of an Ordinary Annuity of I

$$a_{\overline{n}|i} = \frac{1 - \dfrac{1}{(1+i)^n}}{i} = \frac{1 - v^n}{i}$$

Periods	1%	1 1/4%	1 1/2%	1 3/4%	2%	2 1/4%	2 1/2%
1	0.99009901	0.98765432	0.98522167	0.98280098	0.98039216	0.97799511	0.97560976
2	1.97039506	1.96311538	1.95588342	1.94869875	1.94156094	1.93446955	1.92742415
3	2.94098521	2.92653371	2.91220042	2.89798403	2.88388327	2.86989687	2.85602356
4	3.90196555	3.87805798	3.85438465	3.83094254	3.80772870	3.78474021	3.76197421
5	4.85343124	4.81783504	4.78264497	4.74785508	4.71345951	4.67945253	4.64582850
6	5.79547647	5.74600992	5.69718717	5.64899762	5.60143089	5.55447680	5.50812536
7	6.72819453	6.66272585	6.59821396	6.53464139	6.47199107	6.41024626	6.34939060
8	7.65167775	7.56812429	7.48592508	7.40505297	7.32548144	7.24718461	7.17013717
9	8.56601758	8.46234498	8.36051732	8.26049432	8.16223671	8.06570622	7.97086553
10	9.47130453	9.34552591	9.22218455	9.10122291	8.98258501	8.86621635	8.75206393
11	10.36762825	10.21780337	10.07111779	9.92749181	9.78684805	9.64911134	9.51420871
12	11.25507747	11.07931197	10.90750521	10.73954969	10.57534122	10.41477882	10.25776460
13	12.13374007	11.93018466	11.73153222	11.53764097	11.34837375	11.16359787	10.98318497
14	13.00370304	12.77055275	12.54338150	12.32200587	12.10624877	11.89593924	11.69091217
15	13.86505252	13.60054592	13.34323301	13.09288046	12.84926350	12.61216551	12.38137773
16	14.71787378	14.42029227	14.13126405	13.85049677	13.57770931	13.31263131	13.05500266
17	15.56225127	15.22991829	14.90764931	14.59508282	14.29187188	13.99768343	13.71219772
18	16.39826858	16.02954893	15.67256089	15.32686272	14.99203125	14.66766106	14.35336363
19	17.22600850	16.81930759	16.42616837	16.04605673	15.67846201	15.32289590	14.97889134
20	18.04555297	17.59931613	17.16863879	16.75288130	16.35143334	15.96371237	15.58916229
21	18.85698313	18.36969495	17.90013673	17.44754919	17.01120916	16.59042775	16.18454857
22	19.66037934	19.13056291	18.62082437	18.13026948	17.65804820	17.20335232	16.76541324
23	20.45582113	19.88203744	19.33086145	18.80124764	18.29220412	17.80278955	17.33211048
24	21.24338726	20.62423451	20.03040537	19.46068565	18.91392560	18.38903624	17.88498583
25	22.02315570	21.35726865	20.71961120	20.10878196	19.52345647	18.96238263	18.42437642
26	22.79520366	22.08125299	21.39863172	20.74573166	20.12103576	19.52311260	18.95061114
27	23.55960759	22.79629925	22.06761746	21.37172644	20.70689780	20.07150376	19.46401087
28	24.31644316	23.50251778	22.72671671	21.98695474	21.28127236	20.60782764	19.96488866
29	25.06578530	24.20001756	23.37607558	22.59160171	21.84438466	21.13234977	20.45354991
30	25.80770822	24.88890623	24.01583801	23.18584934	22.39645555	21.64532985	20.93029259
31	26.54228537	25.56929010	24.64614582	23.76987650	22.93770152	22.14702186	21.39540741
32	27.26958947	26.24127418	25.26713874	24.34385897	23.46833482	22.63767419	21.84917796
33	27.98969255	26.90496215	25.87895442	24.90796951	23.98856355	23.11752977	22.29188094
34	28.70266589	27.56045644	26.48172849	25.46237789	24.49859172	23.58682618	22.72378628
35	29.40858009	28.20785822	27.07559458	26.00725100	24.99861933	24.04579577	23.14515734
36	30.10750504	28.84726737	27.66068431	26.54275283	25.48884248	24.49466579	23.55625107
37	30.79950994	29.47878259	28.23712740	27.06904455	25.96945341	24.93365848	23.95731812
38	31.48466330	30.10250133	28.80505163	27.58628457	26.44064060	25.36299118	24.34860304
39	32.16303298	30.71851983	29.36458288	28.09462857	26.90258883	25.78287646	24.73034443
40	32.83468611	31.32693316	29.91584520	28.59422955	27.35547924	26.19352221	25.10277505
41	33.49968922	31.92783522	30.45896079	29.08523789	27.79948945	26.59513174	25.46612200
42	34.15810814	32.52131874	30.99405004	29.56780136	28.23479358	26.98790390	25.82060683
43	34.81000806	33.10747530	31.52123157	30.04206522	28.66156233	27.37203316	26.16644569
44	35.45545352	33.68639536	32.04062223	30.50817221	29.07996307	27.74770969	26.50384945
45	36.09450844	34.25816825	32.55233718	30.96626261	29.49015987	28.11511950	26.83302386
46	36.72723608	34.82288222	33.05648983	31.41647431	29.89231360	28.47444450	27.15416962
47	37.35369909	35.38062442	33.55319195	31.85894281	30.28658196	28.82586259	27.46748255
48	37.97395949	35.93148091	34.04255365	32.29380129	30.67311957	29.16954777	27.77315371
49	38.58807871	36.47553670	34.52468339	32.72118063	31.05207801	29.50567019	28.07136947
50	39.19611753	37.01287574	34.99968807	33.14120946	31.42360589	29.83439627	28.36231168
55	42.14719216	39.60168667	37.27146681	35.13544550	33.17478752	31.37265438	29.71397928
60	44.95503841	42.03459179	39.38026889	36.96398552	34.76088668	32.74895285	30.90865649
65	47.62660777	44.32098022	41.33778618	38.64059678	36.19746555	33.98034405	31.96457705
70	50.16851435	46.46967562	43.15487183	40.17790267	37.49861929	35.08208492	32.89785698
75	52.58705124	48.48897027	44.84160034	41.58747771	38.67711433	36.06782605	33.72274044
80	54.88820611	50.38665706	46.40732349	42.87993474	39.74451359	36.94978079	34.45181722
85	57.07767600	52.17005958	47.86072218	44.06500479	40.71128999	37.73887655	35.09621486
90	59.16088148	53.84606035	49.20985452	45.15161037	41.58692916	38.44489025	35.66576848
95	61.14298002	55.42112744	50.46220054	46.14793265	42.38002254	39.07656940	36.16917089
100	63.02887877	56.90133936	51.62470367	47.06147304	43.09835164	39.64174052	36.61410526

Present Value of an Ordinary Annuity of I

$$a_{\overline{n}|i} = \frac{1 - \dfrac{1}{(1+i)^n}}{i} = \frac{1 - v^n}{i}$$

Periods	2 3/4%	3%	3 1/2%	4%	4 1/2%	5%	6%
1	0.97323601	0.97087379	0.96618357	0.96153846	0.95693780	0.95238095	0.94339623
2	1.92042434	1.91346970	1.89969428	1.88609467	1.87266775	1.85941043	1.83339267
3	2.84226213	2.82861135	2.80163698	2.77509103	2.74896435	2.72324803	2.67301195
4	3.73942787	3.71709840	3.67307921	3.62989522	3.58752570	3.54595050	3.46510561
5	4.61258186	4.57970719	4.51505238	4.45182233	4.38997674	4.32947667	4.21236379
6	5.46236678	5.41719144	5.32855302	5.24213686	5.15787248	5.07569206	4.91732433
7	6.28940806	6.23028296	6.11454398	6.00205467	5.89270094	5.78637340	5.58238144
8	7.09431441	7.01969219	6.87395554	6.73274487	6.59588607	6.46321276	6.20979381
9	7.87767826	7.78610892	7.60768651	7.43533161	7.26879050	7.10782168	6.80169227
10	8.64007616	8.53020284	8.31660532	8.11089578	7.91271818	7.72173493	7.36008705
11	9.38206926	9.25262411	9.00155104	8.76047671	8.52891692	8.30641422	7.88687458
12	10.10420366	9.95400399	9.66333433	9.38507376	9.11858076	8.86325164	8.38384394
13	10.80701086	10.63495533	10.30273849	9.98564785	9.68285242	9.39357299	8.85268296
14	11.49100014	11.29607314	10.92052028	10.56312293	10.22282528	9.89864094	9.29498393
15	12.15669892	11.93793509	11.51741090	11.11838743	10.73954573	10.37965804	9.71224899
16	12.80457315	12.56110203	12.09411681	11.65229561	11.23401505	10.83776956	10.10589527
17	13.43510769	13.16611847	12.65132059	12.16566885	11.70719143	11.27406625	10.47725969
18	14.04876661	13.75351308	13.18968173	12.65929697	12.15999180	11.68958690	10.82760848
19	14.64600157	14.32379911	13.70983742	13.13393940	12.59329359	12.08532086	11.15811649
20	15.22725213	14.87747486	14.21240330	13.59032634	13.00793645	12.46221034	11.46992122
21	15.79294612	15.41502414	14.69797420	14.02915995	13.40472388	12.82115271	11.76407662
22	16.34349987	15.93691664	15.16712484	14.45111533	13.78442476	13.16300258	12.04158172
23	16.87931861	16.44360839	15.62041047	14.85684167	14.14777489	13.48857388	12.30337898
24	17.40079670	16.93554212	16.05836760	15.24696314	14.49547837	13.79864179	12.55035753
25	17.90831795	17.41314769	16.48151459	15.62207994	14.82820896	14.09394457	12.78335616
26	18.40225592	17.87684242	16.89035226	15.98276918	15.14661145	14.37518530	13.00316619
27	18.88297413	18.32703147	17.28536451	16.32958575	15.45130282	14.64303362	13.21053414
28	19.35002640	18.76410823	17.66701885	16.66306322	15.74287351	14.89812726	13.40616428
29	19.80615708	19.18845459	18.03576700	16.98371463	16.02188053	15.14107358	13.59072102
30	20.24930130	19.60044135	18.39204541	17.29203330	16.28888854	15.37245103	13.76483115
31	20.68058520	20.00042849	18.73627576	17.58849356	16.54439095	15.59281050	13.92908599
32	21.10032623	20.38876553	19.06886547	17.87355150	16.78889086	15.80267667	14.08404339
33	21.50883332	20.76579178	19.39020818	18.14764567	17.02286207	16.00254921	14.23022961
34	21.90640712	21.13183668	19.70068423	18.41119776	17.24675796	16.19290401	14.36814114
35	22.29334026	21.48722007	20.00066110	18.66461323	17.46101240	16.37419429	14.49824636
36	22.66991753	21.83225250	20.29049381	18.90828195	17.66604058	16.54685171	14.62098713
37	23.03641609	22.16723544	20.57052542	19.14257880	17.86223979	16.71128734	14.73678031
38	23.39310568	22.49246159	20.84108736	19.36786423	18.04999023	16.86789271	14.84601916
39	23.74024884	22.80821513	21.10249987	19.58448484	18.22965572	17.01704067	14.94907468
40	24.07810106	23.11477197	21.35507234	19.79277388	18.40158442	17.15908635	15.04629687
41	24.40691101	23.41239997	21.59910371	19.99305181	18.56610949	17.29436796	15.13801592
42	24.72692069	23.70135920	21.83488281	20.18562674	18.72354975	17.42320758	15.22454332
43	25.03836563	23.98190213	22.06268870	20.37079494	18.87421029	17.54591198	15.30617294
44	25.34147507	24.25427392	22.28279102	20.54884129	19.01838305	17.66277331	15.38318202
45	25.63647209	24.51871254	22.49545026	20.72003970	19.15634742	17.77406982	15.45583209
46	25.92357381	24.77544907	22.70091813	20.88465356	19.28837074	17.88006650	15.52436990
47	26.20299154	25.02470783	22.89943780	21.04293612	19.41470884	17.98101571	15.58902821
48	26.47493094	25.26670664	23.09124425	21.19513088	19.53560654	18.07715782	15.65002661
49	26.73959215	25.50165693	23.27656450	21.34147200	19.65129813	18.16872173	15.70757227
50	26.99716998	25.72976401	23.45561787	21.48218462	19.76200778	18.25592546	15.76186064
55	28.18526879	26.77442764	24.26405323	22.10861218	20.24802057	18.63347196	15.99054297
60	29.22266201	27.67556367	24.94473412	22.62348997	20.63802204	18.92928952	16.16142771
65	30.12840005	28.45289152	25.51784916	23.04668199	20.95097913	19.16107033	16.28912272
70	30.91937247	29.12342135	26.00039664	23.39451498	21.20211187	19.34267665	16.38454387
75	31.60995558	29.70182628	26.40668868	23.68040834	21.40363360	19.48496995	16.45584810
80	32.21294098	30.20076345	26.74877567	23.91539185	21.56534493	19.59646048	16.50913077
85	32.73944009	30.63115103	27.03680373	24.10853116	21.69511035	19.68381623	16.54894668
90	33.19915489	31.00240714	27.27931564	24.26727759	21.79924075	19.75226174	16.57869944
95	33.60055671	31.32265592	27.48350415	24.39775559	21.88280030	19.80589059	16.60093244
100	33.95104232	31.59890534	27.65542540	24.50499900	21.94985274	19.84791020	16.61754623

Index

Abatement, 650
Account, difficiency, 733
   realization and liquidation, 739
Accountability, 651
Accountability records, 651–652
Accounting, entities, 3–29
   nature of, 4
   postulates, 6–9
   principles, 9–10
   role of, 4–5
      in investment decisions, 188 189
   social significance of, 10–11
Accounting data for expansion plans, 189–197
Accounting environment, 5–6
Accounting information, uses of, 4
Accounting Principles Board Opinion 6, 152, 548
Accounting Research Bulletin 46, 617
Accounting Research Bulletin 47, 109–110
Accounting Research Bulletin 48, 548–549
Accounting Research Bulletin 51, 248, 251, 255, 270, 352, 353, 385, 410, 441, 459, 491, 509
Accounts payable, amount of, 69
Accounts receivable, new, 748–749
   valuation of, 44–45
Acquisition cost, 36–37

Acquisition of control, 385–388, 392–394
Acts of bankruptcy, 646
Actuarial science, 769–797
Adjunct account, 76
Administration of income, 120–140
Affiliated companies, 303
Allocation of income, capital ratio, 123–125
   corporations, 130–131
   estates and trusts, 131 134
   interest allowance, 127–129
   partnerships, 123–129
   salary allowance, 125–127
   specified ratios, 125
Amount of an annuity, 777
Amount of annuity of 1 tables, 810–811
Amount of 1, 773–775
Amount of 1 tables, 806–807
Annuities, 776–787
   amount of, 77
   deferred, 787–788
   number of periods, 797
   present value of, 782
   relation to compound interest, 779
   tables of, 778, 780, 810–813
Annuity due, 780–782
   present value of, 785–786
Annuity method of depreciation, 174–175, 792–794

JEAN BOYER